Secure Big-data Analytics for Emerging Healthcare in 5G and Beyond

Other related titles:

You may also like

- PBHE034 | Pani | The Internet of Medical Things: Enabling technologies and emerging applications
- PBHE035 | Tanwar | Blockchain for 5G Healthcare Applications: Security and privacy solutions
- PBHE038 | Jain | Healthcare Monitoring and Data Analysis Using IoT: Technologies and applications
- PBPC037F/PBPC037G | Vadlamani Ravi and Aswani Kumar Cherukuri | Handbook of Big Data Analytics (Vol. 1: Methodologies and Vol 2: Applications in ICT, security and business analytics)

We also publish a wide range of books on the following topics:
Computing and Networks
Control, Robotics and Sensors
Electrical Regulations
Electromagnetics and Radar
Energy Engineering
Healthcare Technologies
History and Management of Technology
IET Codes and Guidance
Materials, Circuits and Devices
Model Forms
Nanomaterials and Nanotechnologies
Optics, Photonics and Lasers
Production, Design and Manufacturing
Security
Telecommunications
Transportation

All books are available in print via https://shop.theiet.org or as eBooks via our Digital Library https://digital-library.theiet.org.

HEALTHCARE TECHNOLOGIES SERIES 063

Secure Big-data Analytics for Emerging Healthcare in 5G and Beyond

Concepts, paradigms, and solutions

Edited by
Pronaya Bhattacharya, Vivek Kumar Prasad,
D. Jude Hemanth, Pushan Kumar Dutta,
Atul Kathait and Daniela Dănciulescu

The Institution of Engineering and Technology

About the IET

This book is published by the Institution of Engineering and Technology (The IET).

We inspire, inform and influence the global engineering community to engineer a better world. As a diverse home across engineering and technology, we share knowledge that helps make better sense of the world, to accelerate innovation and solve the global challenges that matter.

The IET is a not-for-profit organisation. The surplus we make from our books is used to support activities and products for the engineering community and promote the positive role of science, engineering and technology in the world. This includes education resources and outreach, scholarships and awards, events and courses, publications, professional development and mentoring, and advocacy to governments.

To discover more about the IET please visit https://www.theiet.org/

About IET books

The IET publishes books across many engineering and technology disciplines. Our authors and editors offer fresh perspectives from universities and industry. Within our subject areas, we have several book series steered by editorial boards made up of leading subject experts.

We peer review each book at the proposal stage to ensure the quality and relevance of our publications.

Get involved

If you are interested in becoming an author, editor, series advisor, or peer reviewer please visit https://www.theiet.org/publishing/publishing-with-iet-books/ or contact author_support@theiet.org.

Discovering our electronic content

All of our books are available online via the IET's Digital Library. Our Digital Library is the home of technical documents, eBooks, conference publications, real-life case studies and journal articles. To find out more, please visit https://digital-library.theiet.org.

In collaboration with the United Nations and the International Publishers Association, the IET is a Signatory member of the SDG Publishers Compact. The Compact aims to accelerate progress to achieve the Sustainable Development Goals (SDGs) by 2030. Signatories aspire to develop sustainable practices and act as champions of the SDGs during the Decade of Action (2020–30), publishing books and journals that will help inform, develop, and inspire action in that direction.

In line with our sustainable goals, our UK printing partner has FSC accreditation, which is reducing our environmental impact to the planet. We use a print-on-demand model to further reduce our carbon footprint.

Published by The Institution of Engineering and Technology, London, United Kingdom

The Institution of Engineering and Technology (the "**Publisher**") is registered as a Charity in England & Wales (no. 211014) and Scotland (no. SC038698).

Copyright © The Institution of Engineering and Technology and its licensors 2025

First published 2024

All intellectual property rights (including copyright) in and to this publication are owned by the Publisher and/or its licensors. All such rights are hereby reserved by their owners and are protected under the Copyright, Designs and Patents Act 1988 ("**CDPA**"), the Berne Convention and the Universal Copyright Convention.

With the exception of:

(i) any use of the publication solely to the extent as permitted under:
   a. the CDPA (including fair dealing for the purposes of research, private study, criticism or review); or
   b. the terms of a licence granted by the Copyright Licensing Agency ("**CLA**") (only applicable where the publication is represented by the CLA); and/or

(ii) any use of those parts of the publication which are identified within this publication as being reproduced by the Publisher under a Creative Commons licence, Open Government Licence or other open source licence (if any) in accordance with the terms of such licence, no part of this publication, including any article, illustration, trade mark or other content whatsoever, may be used, reproduced, stored in a retrieval system, distributed or transmitted in any form or by any means (including electronically) without the prior permission in writing of the Publisher and/or its licensors (as applicable).

The commission of any unauthorised activity may give rise to civil or criminal liability.

Please visit https://digital-library.theiet.org/copyrights-and-permissions for information regarding seeking permission to reuse material from this and/or other publications published by the Publisher. Enquiries relating to the use, including any distribution, of this publication (or any part thereof) should be sent to the Publisher at the address below:

The Institution of Engineering and Technology
Futures Place,
Kings Way,
Stevenage,
Herts, SG1 2UA, United Kingdom

www.theiet.org

While the Publisher and/or its licensors believe that the information and guidance given in this publication is correct, an individual must rely upon their own skill and judgement when performing any action or omitting to perform any action as a result of any statement, opinion or view expressed in the publication and neither the Publisher nor its licensors assume and hereby expressly disclaim any and all liability to anyone for any loss or damage caused by any action or omission of an action made in reliance on the publication and/or any error or omission in the publication, whether or not such an error or omission is the result of negligence or any other cause. Without limiting or otherwise affecting the generality of this statement and the disclaimer, whilst all URLs cited in the publication are correct at the time of press, the Publisher has no responsibility for the persistence or accuracy of URLs for external or third-party internet websites and does not guarantee that any content on such websites is, or will remain, accurate or appropriate.

Whilst every reasonable effort has been undertaken by the Publisher and its licensors to acknowledge copyright on material reproduced, if there has been an oversight, please contact the Publisher and we will endeavour to correct this upon a reprint.

Trade mark notice: Product or corporate names referred to within this publication may be trade marks or registered trade marks and are used only for identification and explanation without intent to infringe.

Where an author and/or contributor is identified in this publication by name, such author and/or contributor asserts their moral right under the CPDA to be identified as the author and/or contributor of this work.

British Library Cataloguing in Publication Data
A catalogue record for this product is available from the British Library

ISBN 978-1-83953-905-3 (hardback)
ISBN 978-1-83953-906-0 (PDF)

Typeset in India by MPS Limited

Cover image: Tom Werner / DigitalVision via Getty Images

Contents

About the editors	xix

1 Navigating the future: secure big data analytics in healthcare's 5G era   1
Vivek Kumar Prasad, Pronaya Bhattacharya, D. Jude Hemanth, Pushan Kumar Dutta, Atul Kathait and Daniela Dănciulescu

1.1	Unleashing the potential: key characteristics of 5G	4
1.2	Beyond the horizon: emerging technologies in healthcare	4
1.3	Real-world impact: applications and use cases	4
1.4	Navigating the terrain: security and privacy considerations	4
1.5	Big data analytics paradigms for modern healthcare	5
1.6	Revolutionizing patient care with real-time analytics	5
1.7	Predictive analytics: forecasting health trends	5
1.8	Tailoring treatments through precision medicine	5
1.9	Enhancing clinical decisions with support systems	5
1.10	Addressing public health challenges through population health management	6

2 Big data-driven medical image processing technologies and applications   11
Junhua Liang, Haipeng Liu, Wenhao Wang, Jie Li, Zixuan Chai and Xinran Wang

2.1	Introduction	11
	2.1.1 Development of medical imaging	11
	2.1.2 Importance of big data in medical image processing	12
2.2	Medical image processing with big data	13
	2.2.1 New features of medical images	13
	2.2.2 The main process of medical image processing	14
2.3	Key technologies and progress	17
	2.3.1 Data enhancement	17
	2.3.2 Image segmentation	18
	2.3.3 Image alignment	20
	2.3.4 Image classification	21
2.4	Problems and challenges ahead	22
	2.4.1 Complex high-dimensional image features	23

	2.4.2	Difficulty in extracting data labels	23
	2.4.3	Shortcomings of multimodal image processing	23
	2.4.4	Improvements in graph modeling algorithms	24
2.5	Summary and outlook		24
	2.5.1	Summary and discussion	24
	2.5.2	Future directions	25
References			26

3 Challenges in big data analytics monitoring 31
Palanichamy Naveen, James Deva Koresh H and Rajasekaran Thangaraj

3.1	Introduction		31
3.2	Monitoring in Big Data Analytics		33
	3.2.1	Importance of monitoring in Big Data Analytics	33
	3.2.2	Key needs and reasons for effective monitoring	34
	3.2.3	Understanding Big Data Analytics monitoring	35
3.3	Challenges in Big Data Analytics monitoring		39
	3.3.1	Scalability challenges in monitoring Big Data Analytics	39
	3.3.2	Monitoring systems handling the vast amounts of data generated	40
	3.3.3	Case studies illustrating scalability challenges and their impact	41
	3.3.4	Case studies showcasing the implications of poor data quality and consistency	45
	3.3.5	Latency challenges	46
	3.3.6	The importance of low latency in monitoring and decision-making	48
	3.3.7	Case studies demonstrating the consequences of high latency in monitoring	49
3.4	Security and privacy challenges		50
	3.4.1	Data sensitivity	50
	3.4.2	Data access control	50
	3.4.3	Data encryption	51
	3.4.4	Data compliance	51
	3.4.5	Data provenance	51
	3.4.6	Anonymization and de-identification	51
	3.4.7	Monitoring at scale	51
	3.4.8	Insider threats	52
3.5	The need for secure monitoring processes to protect sensitive data		52
3.6	Case studies highlighting security breaches and their impact		53
	3.6.1	Case study 1: Equifax data breach	53
	3.6.2	Case study 2: Target data breach	54
3.7	Complexity challenges		54
	3.7.1	Challenges of integrating diverse technologies and systems for monitoring	55

		3.7.2	Case studies illustrating the difficulties in managing the complexity	56
	3.8	Analytical case study		58
		3.8.1	Case study: Netflix - Overcoming Big Data Analytics monitoring challenges	58
	3.9	Big Data Analytics setup		59
		3.9.1	Organization: XYZ Healthcare	59
	3.10	Implementation of tailored monitoring solutions to address challenges		61
	3.11	Recommendations for improving monitoring strategies		62
	3.12	Conclusion		63
	References			64

4 Security challenges in big data analytics — 69
Kaushal Singh and Sunil Gautam

4.1	Introduction		70
4.2	Breach of data and unauthorized access		72
4.3	Insider threats		74
	4.3.1	The types of insider threats and their understanding	75
	4.3.2	Monitoring and auditing to reduce insider threats	75
	4.3.3	Making security awareness and accountability culture a priority	76
	4.3.4	The function of technology in insider threat mitigation	76
4.4	Data encryption		77
4.5	Conformity with data protection laws		79
4.6	Adversarial attacks in machine learning models		80
4.7	Potential directions for healthcare data encryption in the future		82
4.8	Conclusion		84
References			84

5 Secure data sharing and collaboration in healthcare analytics — 91
Zhou Ruoqi and Haipeng Liu

5.1	What is "big data"?	92
5.2	How big data work in healthcare domain?	92
5.3	Medical database: the common form of big data	93
5.4	Data sharing—panacea or new Pandora's box?	94
5.5	Loopholes and challenges in secure data sharing	96
5.6	Specific data types and vulnerable groups	98
5.7	Balance between openness and safety	99
5.8	A secure environment for data sharing—What can we do?	99
5.9	Limitations and future directions	103
5.10	Conclusions	104
References		104

6 Enhancing healthcare data security in the era of 5G and Big Data Analytics — 111
Tarun Kumar Vashishth, Vikas Sharma, Kewal Krishan Sharma, Bhupendra Kumar, Sachin Chaudhary and Rajneesh Panwar

- 6.1 Introduction — 111
  - 6.1.1 Background and significance — 112
  - 6.1.2 The intersection of 5G and Big Data Analytics in healthcare — 114
  - 6.1.3 Promise and concerns: Transformative changes vs. data security challenges — 114
- 6.2 Literature review — 116
- 6.3 5G technology in healthcare — 117
  - 6.3.1 Overview of 5G technology — 118
  - 6.3.2 Applications in healthcare: Real-time monitoring, telemedicine, and medical imaging — 118
  - 6.3.3 Implications for data security: Challenges and opportunities — 119
- 6.4 Big Data Analytics in healthcare — 120
  - 6.4.1 Role and impact of Big Data Analytics — 121
  - 6.4.2 Leveraging vast datasets for evidence-based decision-making — 122
- 6.5 Challenges in healthcare data security — 122
  - 6.5.1 Proliferation of connected devices: The Internet of Medical Things — 123
  - 6.5.2 Data lakes and cyber threats: Vulnerabilities introduced by extensive data aggregation — 123
  - 6.5.3 Regulatory compliance and ethical considerations — 124
- 6.6 Strategies for comprehensive healthcare data security — 125
- 6.7 Case studies and lessons learned — 126
  - 6.7.1 Exemplary implementations of healthcare data security measures — 126
  - 6.7.2 Challenges encountered and overcoming strategies — 127
  - 6.7.3 Real-world applications of 5G and Big Data security protocols in healthcare — 128
- 6.8 Future prospects and emerging technologies — 130
  - 6.8.1 Anticipated developments in 5G and Big Data security — 130
  - 6.8.2 Integration of artificial intelligence for advanced threat detection — 130
  - 6.8.3 Privacy-preserving technologies and trends — 131
- 6.9 Conclusion — 132
- References — 133

7 Privacy-preserving techniques for big data analytics in healthcare — 135
Kande Archana, Kamakshi Prasad, M. Ashok and Vadlamani Veerabhadram

- 7.1 Introduction — 136
- 7.2 Privacy and security concerns—big data in healthcare — 137

7.3	Big data security life cycle in healthcare	138
7.4	Privacy-preserving methods in healthcare system using big data	140
7.5	Conclusion	141
References		142

8 Enabling trustworthy data sharing and collaborative insights in healthcare analytics — 145
Pawan Whig, Shama Kouser, Ashima Bhatnagar Bhatia, Rahul Reddy Nadikattu and Pavika Sharma

8.1	Introduction	145
8.2	The importance of secure data sharing in healthcare analytics	146
	8.2.1 Data-driven healthcare revolution	146
	8.2.2 The collaborative imperative	147
8.3	Secure data sharing in healthcare analytics	147
	8.3.1 Challenges in secure data sharing	148
	8.3.2 The role of technology in secure data sharing	149
	8.3.3 Fundamentals of data privacy and security measures	149
8.4	Understanding data privacy	149
	8.4.1 Compliance with regulations	150
8.5	Ensuring patient confidentiality through encryption techniques	150
	8.5.1 The imperative of patient confidentiality	150
	8.5.2 Understanding encryption in healthcare	151
	8.5.3 Methods of encryption in healthcare	151
	8.5.4 Best practices for implementing encryption in healthcare	152
8.6	Access controls and authentication mechanisms for collaborative analytics	152
	8.6.1 The significance of access controls and authentication in collaborative analytics	153
	8.6.2 Access control principles	153
	8.6.3 Authentication mechanisms	153
8.7	Best practices for implementation	154
8.8	Policy frameworks for ethical and secure data sharing	154
	8.8.1 The imperative of ethical and secure data sharing	154
	8.8.2 Elements of effective policy frameworks	155
	8.8.3 Balancing ethical considerations and innovation	155
	8.8.4 Transparency and accountability	155
	8.8.5 Collaboration and stakeholder engagement	156
	8.8.6 Continuous evaluation and adaptation	156
8.9	Data integrity in healthcare analytics: Challenges and solutions	156
	8.9.1 The critical role of data integrity in healthcare	156
	8.9.2 Challenges to data integrity in healthcare analytics	157
	8.9.3 Solutions and strategies for ensuring data integrity	158
	8.9.4 Collaboration and data sharing	159
8.10	Exploring blockchain technology for trustworthy healthcare collaboration	159

	8.10.1	The imperative of trustworthy healthcare collaboration	159
	8.10.2	Blockchain technology overview	160
	8.10.3	Blockchain benefits in healthcare collaboration	160
8.11	Real-world case studies: Secure data sharing success stories	160
	8.11.1	Genomic data sharing for medical research	161
	8.11.2	Secure cross-industry data sharing	161
	8.11.3	Healthcare interoperability and patient data sharing	162
	8.11.4	Data sharing for environmental conservation	163
	8.11.5	Secure data sharing in education	164
	8.11.6	Secure data sharing in public health	164
	8.11.7	Secure data sharing in smart cities	165
8.12	Best practices for establishing secure healthcare analytics collaborations	165
	8.12.1	Conclusion	165
	8.12.2	Future work	166
References		166

9 Communication aspects in 5G-assisted big data: a performance review against 4G-LTE frameworks 169
Devanshi Patel, Jay Chauhan and Vivek Kumar Prasad

9.1	Introduction	169
	9.1.1 Motivation	172
	9.1.2 Contribution	173
9.2	Problem statement	175
	9.2.1 Root of Trust	176
9.3	Methodology used	178
	9.3.1 Threat detection	179
	9.3.2 Anomaly detection	181
	9.3.3 Comparison between threat detection and anomaly detection	183
9.4	Solution statement	184
	9.4.1 Architecture of the proposed solution	184
	9.4.2 Flowchart and algorithm	190
9.5	Performance evaluation	196
	9.5.1 Parameters used and their values	196
	9.5.2 Test beds	197
	9.5.3 Performance metrics	198
	9.5.4 Result analysis	198
	9.5.5 Discussion on the result obtained and its comparison with existing techniques	198
	9.5.6 Mathematical equations	202
9.6	Conclusion	203
References		204

Contents xiii

10 Authentication and access control schemes in 5G-based healthcare systems — 207
T. Ananth Kumar, A. Kathiravan, P. Kanimozhi, Sunday A. Ajagbe, K. Suresh Kumar and R. Rajmohan

- 10.1 Introduction — 208
  - 10.1.1 5G technology in healthcare — 209
  - 10.1.2 Security challenges in 5G healthcare systems — 210
- 10.2 Authentication mechanisms in 5G healthcare systems — 211
  - 10.2.1 Access control strategies in 5G healthcare systems — 212
  - 10.2.2 Privacy-preserving techniques — 213
  - 10.2.3 Regulatory compliance and standards — 214
- 10.3 Case study: "5G-enabled video and data transmission with high speed and low latency from ambulance to mobile hospital systems" — 215
  - 10.3.1 Proposed methodology for 4K-video transmission from ambulance — 217
  - 10.3.2 Optimal resource algorithm for maximum video data transmission — 218
  - 10.3.3 Proposed methodology for clinical data transmission with ultrahigh reliable and low latency — 219
  - 10.3.4 Optimal resource algorithm for maximum clinical data transmission — 220
  - 10.3.5 Performance analysis — 220
  - 10.3.6 Results and analysis — 222
- 10.4 Future trends — 224
  - 10.4.1 Biometric advancements — 224
  - 10.4.2 Continuous authentication — 224
  - 10.4.3 Edge computing integration — 224
  - 10.4.4 Zero trust architecture adoption — 224
  - 10.4.5 Federated identity management — 224
  - 10.4.6 Quantum-safe authentication — 225
  - 10.4.7 Privacy-preserving authentication — 225
  - 10.4.8 AI-driven threat detection — 225
  - 10.4.9 User-centric access control — 225
- 10.5 Challenges in 5G healthcare systems — 225
- 10.6 Conclusion — 226
- References — 227

11 Indexing-based approach in document-centric big data — 229
Supriya Chakraborty and Sergii Sharov

- 11.1 Introduction — 229
- 11.2 Related work — 231
  - 11.2.1 Fundamentals of JSNON and XML — 235
- 11.3 Elucidate on abstraction of data for storage and retrieval — 236
  - 11.3.1 XML database — 237
  - 11.3.2 JSON database — 238

11.4 Active indexing approach		241
11.4.1 Attribute-centric sparse indexing scheme		241
11.5 Conclusion		244
References		244

12 The AI–mental health dialogue: an investigation of their relationship   249
Ritaprava Bandyopadhyay and Subarna Bhattacharya

12.1 Introduction	249
12.2 Can artificially intelligent agents understand the subtle nuances of language?	251
12.3 Why is it impossible for an artificially intelligent agent to adopt simulation as a tool for understanding others' mental illnesses?	253
12.4 Conclusion: are artificial agents going to replace human doctors?	261
References	265

13 Research on the application of Bayesian deep learning in medical big data   269
Linxuan Du, Zhisheng Zhao, Xueqiong Wei, Lihua Ding, Jie Li and Bohao Li

13.1 Introduction	269
13.1.1 Application of deep learning in medical big data	270
13.1.2 Limitations of deep learning	272
13.2 Principles and framework of Bayesian deep learning	273
13.2.1 Concept of Bayesian deep learning	273
13.2.2 Comparison of Bayesian deep learning and deep learning	274
13.2.3 Principles of Bayesian deep learning	275
13.2.4 Bayesian deep learning frameworks	277
13.2.5 Common algorithms in Bayesian deep learning	280
13.3 Applications of Bayesian deep learning in medical big data	281
13.3.1 Medical image analysis	282
13.3.2 Research in life sciences	282
13.3.3 Clinical diagnostic assistance	283
13.4 Challenges faced by Bayesian deep learning in the application of medical big data	284
13.4.1 Computational complexity and resource demands	285
13.4.2 Modeling and interpretation of model uncertainty	285
13.4.3 Challenges and prospects	286
References	287

14 Causal inference in healthcare: effective evaluation of clinical programs and other applications   291
Zhen Hu, Jing Fan, Deyu Sun, Haipeng Liu and Vikram Bandugula

14.1 Introduction	291
14.1.1 Motivation and objectives	291

	14.1.2 Fundamental causal inference frameworks	292
14.2	Methodology	292
	14.2.1 Propensity score matching	292
	14.2.2 Difference-in-difference	294
	14.2.3 Instrumental variables	297
	14.2.4 Regression discontinuity design	299
14.3	Case studies: practical applications of causal inference in healthcare	301
	14.3.1 Use case 1: robotic vs open pancreatoduodenectomy on incidence of pancreatic fistula using PSM method	301
	14.3.2 Use case 2: Medicaid expansion and variability in mortality in the United States	303
	14.3.3 Use case 3: explore the causal effect of intravenous radiocontrast for kidney function	304
	14.3.4 Use case 4: use IV analysis to compare effectiveness of stents in the extremely elderly	306
14.4	Challenges, future directions, and conclusion	309
	14.4.1 Challenges in modern causal inference	309
	14.4.2 Emerging approaches in causal inference	309
	14.4.3 Concluding reflections	309
	14.4.4 Vision for the future	309
References		310

15 Clinical risk modeling using medical big data: a machine learning approach   313
Zhen Hu, Jing Fan, Deyu Sun, Haipeng Liu and Vikram Bandugula

15.1	Introduction	313
	15.1.1 The crucial role of clinical risk modeling	313
	15.1.2 The data-driven revolution	314
	15.1.3 The promise of personalized medicine	314
15.2	Machine learning for clinical risk modeling	315
	15.2.1 Traditional machine learning algorithms	315
	15.2.2 Deep learning approaches	318
	15.2.3 The relevance of machine learning in clinical risk modeling	320
	15.2.4 Conclusion	320
15.3	Model development and case studies	321
	15.3.1 Model development process	321
	15.3.2 Model performance monitoring and potential Re-fit	324
	15.3.3 Case studies: practical applications of machine learning in clinical risk modeling	325
15.4	Challenges, future directions, and conclusion	330
	15.4.1 Persistent challenges in clinical risk modeling	330
	15.4.2 Future directions in clinical risk modeling	330
References		331

xvi Secure big-data analytics for emerging healthcare in 5G and beyond

16 **Unlock potential of artificial intelligence and blockchain integration for preserving privacy and medical data: high-fidelity data sharing and healthcare analytics lensing legal aspects** 335
Bhupinder Singh and Christian Kaunert
16.1 Introduction 336
   16.1.1 Importance of preserving privacy and ensuring data security in medical settings 337
16.2 AI and blockchain integration 339
   16.2.1 Integration of AI and blockchain technologies addressing privacy and data security concerns 340
   16.2.2 Data provenance, encryption, and access control mechanisms 342
16.3 Preserving privacy through high-fidelity data sharing 343
16.4 Healthcare analytics and insights 344
   16.4.1 AI-driven analytics leveraging blockchain-enabled data to derive meaningful insights 345
16.5 Legal and ethical considerations 348
   16.5.1 Legal challenges associated with healthcare data sharing such as compliance, data ownership, and liability 349
16.6 Future directions and challenges 352
   16.6.1 Discuss ongoing challenges such as scalability, interoperability, and standardization 353
16.7 Conclusion 354
References 355

17 **The nuances of legal deviations in modern computing: a relook into the privacy and data protection laws in India and beyond** 359
Shambhu Prasad Chakrabarty, Niladri Mondal and Shrabana Chattopadhyay
17.1 Introduction 359
17.2 What is privacy 360
   17.2.1 Privacy: a Fundamental Right in India 360
   17.2.2 Privacy is intrinsic to right to life 361
   17.2.3 Is privacy and data protection similar 362
17.3 Data protection 363
17.4 Data protection laws in India 363
17.5 Enforcement mechanisms and penalties 365
   17.5.1 Penalty for privacy and confidentiality breach 365
17.6 A very promising move: Information Security Technology Development Council 366
17.7 The computer emergency response team 366
17.8 The digital personal data protection act, 2023 367
   17.8.1 Limitations of data protection act 367
17.9 Globalisation, international law and technology 368
17.10 Data protection law and the position in EU and US 368

17.10.1 EU data protection law		368
17.10.2 US data protection laws		369
17.11 US and EU: conflicts of data protection laws		372
17.11.1 Direct access		372
17.11.2 Warrants		372
17.12 Case study 1: can the government access data, unhindered?		373
17.13 Conclusion		374
References		375

18 Charting the course: secure big-data analytics and 5G in healthcare's transformative journey   379
Vivek Kumar Prasad, Pronaya Bhattacharya, D. Jude Hemanth, Pushan Kumar Dutta, Atul Kathait and Daniela Dănciulescu

Index   385

About the editors

Pronaya Bhattacharya is an associate professor of computer science and engineering and the Research and Innovation Cell at Amity University Kolkata, India. He has co-authored more than 140 research papers. His research interests include healthcare analytics, networking, blockchain, and the IoT. He has been appointed as a technical committee member and the session chair at various international conferences.

Vivek Kumar Prasad is an assistant professor of computer science and engineering at the Institute of Technology, Nirma University, India. He has written 40 journal papers and 7 book chapters. He has been actively involved in the organization of various workshops in the cloud computing domain. His research interests include distributed computing, cloud computing, machine learning, and artificial intelligence.

D. Jude Hemanth is a professor at the Karunya Institute of Technology and Sciences, Coimbatore, India, and visiting professor in the Faculty of Electrical Engineering and Information Technology, University of Oradea, Romania. He has co-authored over 230 conference and journal papers and contributed to 37 edited books. He holds professional membership with IEEE Technical Committee on Neural Networks (IEEE Computational Intelligence Society) and IEEE Technical Committee on Soft Computing (IEEE Systems, Man and Cybernetics Society) and ACM.

Pushan Kumar Dutta is an assistant professor of electronics and communication engineering at Amity University Kolkata, India. He received the Young Faculty in Engineering award in 2018 from Venus International awards. His research interests include artificial intelligence, robotics, data science, computer hardware, and electronic devices. He has published more than 40 journal articles, conference papers, and book chapters.

Atul Kathait is an assistant director-IQAC at Amity University, India. His interests are bioinformatics and healthcare data analytics. He has 15+ years of experience in research, teaching, and administration. He has organized several workshops on bioinformatics application in healthcare. He was the recipient of Young Scientist Awards from the Indian Academy of Environmental Sciences, 2018.

Daniela Dănciulescu is a professor in the Department of Informatics at Universitatea Din Craiova, Romania. She has authored/co-authored 8 course books for students and over 80 papers in peer-reviewed journals. Her specialisms include artificial intelligence and informatics.

Chapter 1

Navigating the future: secure big data analytics in healthcare's 5G era

Vivek Kumar Prasad[1], Pronaya Bhattacharya[2], D. Jude Hemanth[3], Pushan Kumar Dutta[2], Atul Kathait[4] and Daniela Dănciulescu[5]

In 2022, the global healthcare data volume reached a staggering 2,314 exabytes—equivalent to 2.3 trillion gigabytes. By 2025, this figure is projected to grow at a rate of 36% annually, faster than manufacturing, financial services, or media and entertainment. This exponential surge in healthcare data, coupled with the rollout of 5G networks capable of speeds up to 20 Gbps, is poised to revolutionize the medical landscape as we know it. Imagine a world where a patient's vital signs are monitored in real-time through wearable devices, with AI algorithms detecting anomalies and alerting healthcare providers before symptoms even manifest. Picture surgeons performing complex procedures remotely, guided by augmented reality and ultra-low latency 5G connections. Envision a healthcare system where personalized treatment plans are crafted based on an individual's unique genetic profile, medical history, and lifestyle factors, all analyzed through sophisticated big data analytics.

Today's healthcare systems face unprecedented challenges. An aging global population, the rise of chronic diseases, and the ongoing threat of pandemics strain resources and highlight the need for more efficient, accessible, and personalized care. Traditional healthcare models, often reactive and one-size-fits-all, are proving inadequate in the face of these complex health issues.

The pressing need for transformation is clear:

1. Efficiency: Healthcare providers must handle increasing patient loads while maintaining quality care, necessitating streamlined processes and data-driven decision-making.

[1]Computer Science and Engineering Department, Nirma University, India
[2]School of Engineering Campus, Amity University Kolkata, India
[3]Electronics and Communications, Karunya Institute of Technology & Sciences, India
[4]IQAC, Amity University Uttar Pradesh, India
[5]Departamentul De Informatică, Universitatea Din Craiova, România

2. Personalization: Patients expect tailored treatments that consider their individual characteristics, requiring sophisticated analysis of vast amounts of personal health data.
3. Security: As healthcare becomes more digital, protecting sensitive patient information from cyber threats becomes paramount.
4. Accessibility: There is a growing demand for healthcare services that transcend geographical boundaries, especially in underserved areas.

Emerging technologies are stepping in to address these needs. Big data analytics allows for the processing and interpretation of massive healthcare datasets, uncovering patterns and insights that can improve diagnoses, treatment plans, and public health strategies. 5G networks provide the high-speed, low-latency connectivity needed to support real-time health monitoring, telemedicine, and the Internet of Medical Things (IoMT).

Together, these technologies are ushering in an era of proactive, precise, and patient-centric healthcare. They promise to enhance early disease detection, enable remote patient monitoring, facilitate personalized medicine, and improve overall healthcare outcomes. However, with great power comes great responsibility—the integration of these technologies also brings challenges in data security, privacy, and ethical use of health information. To make the application more profound, we engage some old-age principles of soft computing, artificial intelligence with modern-day Big Data analytics stands out as a powerful force, reshaping how we approach medical challenges. In this book, *Secure Big Data Analytics for Modern Healthcare in 5G and Beyond: Concepts, Paradigms, and Solutions*, we delve into the intersection of healthcare, data, and security. We need to adopt emerging technologies in a rational context to provide efficient, personalized, and secure healthcare services. This book explores the intersection of secure big data analytics, 5G and beyond (B5G) networks, and modern healthcare, offering a comprehensive exploration of the concepts, paradigms, and solutions that are shaping the future of this critical domain.

To address the intricate challenges and harness the opportunities within the healthcare sector, the exploration of big data analytics and the implementation of 5G and beyond technologies stand at the forefront of innovation. The background and motivation for integrating these technologies into modern healthcare stem from a critical need to improve efficiency, accuracy, and personalization of care. As healthcare systems worldwide grapple with increasing demands, limited resources, and the quest for improved patient outcomes, leveraging big data analytics presents a transformative solution.

The significance of big data analytics in modern healthcare cannot be overstated. It offers unprecedented capabilities in processing vast amounts of data derived from electronic health records, wearable devices, and genomic sequencing, to name a few sources. This data-driven approach enables predictive analytics, enhances decision-making, and fosters personalized medicine, thus improving patient care quality and outcomes. Moreover, big data analytics facilitates the identification of trends and patterns, aiding in disease surveillance, and public health management, making it a cornerstone for advancing healthcare systems.

The advent of 5G and beyond technologies further amplifies the potential of big data in healthcare. 5G networks promise to revolutionize healthcare delivery through their ultra-high-speed, low-latency communications, facilitating real-time data sharing, telemedicine, and the IoMT. This seamless connectivity not only enhances the efficiency and effectiveness of healthcare services but also opens new avenues for remote monitoring, patient engagement, and continuous care delivery, even in underserved regions. The integration of 5G technologies ensures the robustness and reliability of healthcare systems, addressing bandwidth and privacy concerns, and enabling the adoption of advanced technologies such as augmented reality (AR) and virtual reality (VR) for medical training and patient treatment.

In the realm of modern healthcare, an immense volume of data is generated daily, sourced from diverse channels like Electronic Health Records (EHRs), medical imaging, genomic and biomedical research, and increasingly, wearable and IoT devices. Each of these data sources plays a crucial role in advancing healthcare outcomes, contributing to personalized treatment plans, early disease detection, and the overall enhancement of patient care.

Electronic Health Records (EHRs) serve as a digital version of a patient's paper chart, offering a comprehensive record of medical history, diagnoses, medications, treatment plans, immunization dates, allergies, radiology images, and laboratory test results. They facilitate seamless information sharing across different healthcare settings, supporting decision-making and continuity of care.

Medical Imaging Data, including X-rays, MRIs, and CT scans, provide detailed insights into the human body, aiding in accurate diagnosis and treatment. The volume and complexity of this data have grown significantly, pushing the boundaries of traditional data processing techniques and calling for advanced analytics solutions.

Genomic and Biomedical Data represent another rapidly expanding data source, offering unprecedented opportunities for personalized medicine. The analysis of genomic sequences helps in understanding the genetic predispositions to certain diseases, enabling targeted therapy and preventive healthcare measures.

Wearable and IoT device data have emerged as a game-changer, continuously monitoring vital signs, physical activity, and other health metrics. This real-time data stream supports proactive health management and disease prevention, contributing to the shift towards preventive healthcare paradigms.

However, the challenges in healthcare data management and analysis are substantial. They include ensuring data privacy and security, integrating and standardizing disparate data sources, managing the sheer volume of data, and extracting actionable insights through advanced analytics techniques. The implementation of big data analytics and the deployment of 5G and beyond technologies are pivotal in addressing these challenges. These technologies enable the real-time processing and analysis of vast datasets, support the secure and efficient transmission of healthcare data, and facilitate the deployment of telehealth services, thereby enhancing patient care and operational efficiencies. As healthcare systems worldwide strive to adopt these technological advances, the foundational challenge remains to balance innovation with ethical considerations and data stewardship, ensuring that the advancements in healthcare technology translate into tangible benefits for patient care and health outcomes.

The inception of 5G networks brings forth unparalleled opportunities for the healthcare sector, promising to significantly enhance the quality and efficiency of healthcare delivery. With its hallmark features of high-speed data transmission, low latency, and massive connectivity, 5G is poised to support an array of applications, from remote patient monitoring to real-time telemedicine consultations, thereby reducing physical barriers to healthcare access.

1.1 Unleashing the potential: key characteristics of 5G

5G technology stands out due to its three core characteristics: high-speed connectivity that enables the transfer of large volumes of data in real-time, ultra-low latency that facilitates immediate response and interaction necessary for critical healthcare applications, and the capability to connect a vast number of devices simultaneously, which is essential for the IoMT.

1.2 Beyond the horizon: emerging technologies in healthcare

Looking beyond 5G, the horizon of healthcare connectivity expands to include 6G and satellite communications, heralding a future where global healthcare accessibility and seamless data exchange become a reality. These advancements promise to further empower healthcare providers with more robust, efficient, and widespread coverage, opening new avenues for innovation and service delivery.

1.3 Real-world impact: applications and use cases

The practical application of 5G and beyond in healthcare is vast and varied, encompassing telehealth, remote surgery, patient data analytics, and emergency response systems. These use cases not only demonstrate the transformative potential of these technologies but also underscore the critical role of secure and reliable data analytics in enhancing patient outcomes and operational efficiencies.

1.4 Navigating the terrain: security and privacy considerations

Amidst the digital transformation, the book also delves deep into the critical aspects of data security and privacy in healthcare. It comprehensively covers the importance of safeguarding patient data, the regulatory frameworks guiding data protection (such as HIPAA and GDPR), and the cutting-edge technologies employed to secure healthcare data, including encryption, access control mechanisms, and blockchain technology.

1.5 Big data analytics paradigms for modern healthcare

The integration of big data analytics into healthcare is transforming the landscape of patient care, diagnosis, and disease management. The convergence of these analytics with emerging 5G and beyond technologies catalyzes a shift towards a more proactive, predictive, and personalized healthcare system. The forthcoming chapters delve into the various paradigms of big data analytics that are pivotal to modern healthcare, elucidating their roles, potential impacts, and the challenges they aim to address.

1.6 Revolutionizing patient care with real-time analytics

Real-time analytics stands at the forefront of this transformation, enabling remote patient monitoring systems that offer continuous care outside traditional clinical settings. This paradigm leverages the high-speed, low-latency capabilities of 5G networks to facilitate instant data processing and transmission, thereby ensuring timely medical interventions and enhancing patient outcomes.

1.7 Predictive analytics: forecasting health trends

Predictive analytics harness historical and current data to forecast future health events or disease outbreaks, paving the way for preventive healthcare strategies. This approach utilizes complex algorithms and machine learning models to identify patterns and predict risks, enabling healthcare providers to intervene preemptively and mitigate potential health crises.

1.8 Tailoring treatments through precision medicine

Precision medicine represents a significant leap towards personalized healthcare, where treatments and interventions are tailored to individual genetic profiles, lifestyle, and environmental factors. Big data analytics play a crucial role in analyzing the vast datasets required for precision medicine, enabling customized care plans that improve patient outcomes and reduce adverse reactions.

1.9 Enhancing clinical decisions with support systems

Clinical Decision Support Systems (CDSS) embody the integration of big data analytics into clinical practice, offering evidence-based recommendations that aid healthcare professionals in making informed decisions. These systems analyze patient data in real-time, providing insights that improve diagnosis accuracy, treatment efficacy, and patient safety.

1.10 Addressing public health challenges through population health management

Population health management and public health analytics utilize big data analytics to assess and improve the health outcomes of communities at large. By analyzing data from various sources, these paradigms identify health trends, evaluate the effectiveness of health policies, and inform public health interventions, contributing to the overall well-being of populations.

In an era where healthcare is rapidly evolving through the integration of technology, big data analytics stands at the forefront of this transformation. The chapters in this book provide a thorough exploration of how big data is reshaping healthcare, from medical imaging to patient data security. Each chapter delves into specific aspects of this revolution, highlighting both the challenges and the innovative solutions being developed. By examining the interplay between advanced technologies such as AI, 5G, and blockchain, this book underscores the critical role of robust data management and security protocols. It aims to equip healthcare professionals, researchers, and policymakers with the knowledge and insights needed to navigate the complexities of big data in healthcare. The detailed discussions offer a comprehensive understanding of the current landscape and future directions in the field, emphasizing the importance of collaboration and trust in achieving effective healthcare outcomes. The following summaries provide a glimpse into the diverse topics covered, setting the stage for a deep dive into the world of big data analytics in healthcare.

Chapter 2: "Big data-driven medical image processing technologies and applications" highlights the revolutionary impact of big data on medical imaging technologies. It explores advanced techniques and applications that enhance image processing, leading to more accurate diagnoses and improved treatment planning.

By showcasing real-world examples, Chapter 3 illustrates how big data is revolutionizing healthcare delivery and patient outcomes. Challenges in big data analytics monitoring: an analytical case study, discusses large and diverse datasets, which are processed using big data analytics to extract insightful information. Throughout the analytics lifecycle, efficient monitoring is crucial to guaranteeing performance, data quality, security, and compliance. The significance of monitoring for problem detection, performance optimization, data integrity assurance, and real-time decision assistance is covered in this chapter. Along with covering the essential elements of monitoring, such as resource tracking, processing pipelines, data intake, and security, it also addresses issues with scalability, data quality, and latency in real-time applications. It also gives a summary of popular technology and monitoring tools for efficiently handling big data analytics.

Chapter 4: Security challenges in big data analytics, the focus of this chapter is on the myriad security challenges that arise in the realm of big data analytics, especially within healthcare. It addresses vulnerabilities and potential threats, highlighting the critical need for robust security measures. Strategies for protecting sensitive medical data from breaches and cyber-attacks are thoroughly examined.

Chapter 5: Secure data sharing and collaboration in healthcare analytics, this chapter explores the essential frameworks and protocols for secure data sharing and collaboration in healthcare analytics. It underscores the importance of maintaining data integrity and confidentiality, emphasizing the role of trust and cooperation among stakeholders. Effective data utilization and its benefits for healthcare outcomes are also discussed.

Chapter 6: Enhancing healthcare data security in the era of 5G and big data analytics, examines the intersection of 5G technology and big data analytics, this chapter highlights their combined potential to enhance healthcare data security. It discusses new security paradigms and measures necessary to protect patient information in an increasingly connected and technologically advanced landscape.

Chapter 7: Privacy-preserving techniques for big data analytics in healthcare, this chapter reviews various privacy-preserving techniques crucial for big data analytics in healthcare. It explores methods to ensure patient data privacy while enabling comprehensive data analysis. The importance of these techniques in achieving improved healthcare outcomes without compromising privacy is emphasized.

Chapter 8: Enabling trustworthy data sharing and collaborative insights in healthcare analytics, the importance of building trustworthy data-sharing mechanisms and fostering collaborative insights in healthcare analytics is the focus of this chapter. Strategies to enhance transparency, accountability, and mutual trust among healthcare providers, researchers, and patients are explored, highlighting their significance in advancing healthcare analytics.

Chapter 9: Communication aspects in 5G-assisted big data: a performance review against 4G-LTE frameworks, this chapter discusses the future of secure big data analytics in the context of emerging healthcare systems, particularly with the advent of 5G technology. It introduces new concepts, paradigms, and innovative solutions to address the evolving security needs of the healthcare sector, emphasizing proactive approaches to data protection.

Chapter 10: Authentication and access control schemes in 5G-based healthcare systems, focuses on advanced authentication and access control schemes tailored for 5G-based healthcare systems, this chapter highlights the importance of robust security protocols. It details various strategies to ensure that only authorized personnel have access to sensitive medical data, thereby enhancing overall system integrity.

Chapter 11: Indexing-based approach in document-centric big data, an indexing-based approach for managing document-centric big data is examined in this chapter. Techniques for efficient indexing that facilitate quick retrieval and management of large volumes of healthcare documents are discussed. The chapter highlights the importance of effective data management in improving data accessibility and usability.

Chapter 12: The AI–mental health dialogue: an investigation of their relationship, this chapter investigates the relationship between AI and mental health and further explores how AI technologies can aid in understanding, diagnosing, and treating mental health issues. It discusses potential benefits, ethical considerations, and the transformative impact of integrating AI into mental health care practices.

Chapter 13: Research on the application of Bayesian deep learning in medical big data, the chapter presents research on applying Bayesian deep learning techniques to medical big data analytics. It highlights the advantages of Bayesian methods in improving prediction accuracy and handling uncertainty in healthcare data, offering a pathway to more reliable medical insights and decision-making.

Chapter 14: Causal inference in healthcare: effective evaluation of clinical programs and other applications, this chapter discusses the methodologies for establishing causality in healthcare data, focusing on effective evaluation of clinical programs. It provides insights into how causal inference techniques can improve the assessment of clinical interventions and inform evidence-based decision-making in healthcare.

Chapter 15: Clinical risk modeling using medical big data: a machine learning approach, the chapter mentions clinical risk modeling and discusses the application of machine learning techniques to medical big data. It examines various models and algorithms that predict patient risks, aiding in proactive healthcare management and the development of personalized treatment plans.

Chapter 16: Unlock potential of artificial intelligence and blockchain integration for preserving privacy and medical data: high-fidelity data sharing and healthcare analytics lensing legal aspects, this chapter discusses the potential of integrating AI and blockchain technologies to preserve privacy and enhance medical data security. It discusses the legal aspects of high-fidelity data sharing and explores how these technologies can transform healthcare analytics, ensuring both security and compliance.

Chapter 17: The nuances of legal deviations in modern computing: a relook into the privacy and data protection laws in India and beyond, this chapter provides a detailed analysis of privacy and data protection laws, focusing on legal deviations in modern computing. It reviews the regulatory landscape in India and compares it with global standards, highlighting challenges, gaps, and areas for improvement in protecting healthcare data.

Chapter 18: Decoding big data analytics in the field of health care: an overview, this chapter provides a broad perspective, and decodes the complexities of big data analytics in healthcare. It discusses key technologies, applications, and the potential future impact of data-driven healthcare solutions, offering an overview of how big data is utilized to improve healthcare outcomes.

Chapter 19: Harnessing big data implementation for enhanced detection of pneumonia through AI-powered processing of chest X-ray images, the chapter explores the enhancement of pneumonia detection through AI-powered processing of chest X-ray images. It highlights the benefits of combining AI with big data analytics to improve diagnostic precision and speed, significantly impacting patient outcomes in the detection and treatment of pneumonia.

Readers should consider this book for the following reasons:

1. Exploring the Role of Big Data Analytics in Healthcare: Healthcare generates vast amounts of data from various sources, including electronic medical records, IoT devices, and biomedical research. This book examines the

challenges and opportunities associated with leveraging big data analytics (BDA) to extract valuable insights, improve decision-making, and enhance patient outcomes.
2. Navigating Security and Privacy Concerns in Healthcare Data: With the increasing reliance on digital technologies and data sharing, ensuring the security and privacy of sensitive healthcare data is paramount. The book addresses the security challenges in healthcare BDA, privacy-preserving techniques, secure data sharing and collaboration, and trust and governance frameworks.
3. Unraveling the Potential of 5G and Beyond Networks for Healthcare: The book provides an in-depth exploration of 5G and B5G networks, shedding light on their capabilities, architectures, and the potential benefits they offer for healthcare applications. It examines how these advanced networks can facilitate real-time data transmission, low-latency communication, and seamless connectivity for remote healthcare services.
4. Decentralized and Distributed Approaches to Healthcare Analytics: The book introduces decentralized and distributed models for healthcare analytics, highlighting the advantages of decentralization, such as enhanced data security, scalability, and resilience. It explores the integration of emerging technologies like blockchain, federated learning, and edge computing with healthcare analytics.

Building on the comprehensive exploration of big data analytics paradigms for modern healthcare, the next section delves into the critical challenges that come with scaling these technologies and ensuring their optimal performance within the healthcare sector. This analysis sets the stage for a nuanced discussion on overcoming these hurdles, thereby maximizing the transformative potential of these technologies.

5. Scalability and Performance Challenges: As the healthcare industry continues to integrate advanced big data analytics and 5G technologies, it faces a unique set of scalability and performance challenges. These challenges not only impede the seamless operation of healthcare systems but also highlight the necessity for robust solutions that ensure the efficient and effective delivery of healthcare services.

Interoperability and data integration issues stand as significant obstacles to the seamless exchange and utilization of healthcare data across different platforms and systems. The lack of standardized protocols and formats complicates the aggregation and analysis of data, hampering efforts to provide coherent and comprehensive care.

The expansion of big data analytics in healthcare raises profound ethical and legal considerations, particularly concerning patient privacy, consent, and data protection. Navigating these complex issues requires a delicate balance between leveraging data for healthcare advancements and safeguarding individual rights and dignities.

The effective implementation of advanced healthcare technologies necessitates a skilled workforce capable of managing and interpreting complex datasets.

However, a notable skill gap poses a challenge to this requirement, emphasizing the need for comprehensive education and training programs in data analytics, machine learning, and related fields.

The healthcare sector must continuously adapt to emerging trends and technologies, such as artificial intelligence, edge computing, and more, to stay at the forefront of healthcare innovation. These technologies offer promising avenues for enhancing healthcare delivery but also introduce additional layers of complexity in implementation and management. The exploration of big data analytics and the integration of advanced technologies in healthcare culminates in a set of critical insights, opportunities, and recommendations aimed at navigating the future landscape of healthcare.

Are you on the frontlines of the healthcare and technology revolution?

This book equips a diverse audience with the knowledge to navigate this transformative landscape. Whether you're a doctor, IT specialist, researcher, entrepreneur, or student, this book empowers you to play a crucial role in shaping the future of healthcare.

Inside you'll discover:

How big data analytics and 5G technologies are redefining healthcare.

Practical applications for healthcare professionals, IT specialists, and policymakers.

A roadmap for a future of data-driven insights, personalized care, and improved accessibility.

This book is your guide to understanding and shaping a healthcare revolution that is:

Secure: Prioritizing patient privacy and data security.

Ethical: Balancing innovation with ethical considerations.

Equitable: Ensuring these powerful tools benefit all members of society.

Join us on this exciting exploration and pave the way for a healthier future for all.

Chapter 2
Big data-driven medical image processing technologies and applications

Junhua Liang[1], Haipeng Liu[2], Wenhao Wang[3], Jie Li[4], Zixuan Chai[1] and Xinran Wang[1]

In the medical big data environment, unstructured medical image data occupies the majority. These massive data are characterized by high dimensions, heterogeneity, and complex feature expression, which makes it difficult for traditional medical image processing techniques and algorithms to cope with the challenges of massive data analysis and processing. This chapter first reviews the history of medical imaging and analyzes the importance of big data in medical image processing. Meanwhile, the process framework of medical image processing is introduced from image preprocessing, feature extraction selection, and model training evaluation. Facing the new characteristics of medical images, image processing techniques have shifted from traditional methods to deep learning and then to the now popular transfer learning. Key techniques and advances in image processing in image enhancement, image segmentation, image alignment, and image classification are highlighted. In addition, issues such as extraction of high-dimensional complex features, requirements for data labeling expertise, limitations of current algorithms, and future research directions in the context of big data environments are discussed. Large model algorithms, relational modeling of image target entities, and meta-learning are techniques that are expected to improve the efficiency and reliability of big data-driven medical image processing in the future. This chapter provides an introductory overview of the state-of-the-art for practitioners, policymakers, and researchers.

2.1 Introduction

2.1.1 Development of medical imaging

Medical images turn information invisible to the naked eye into visible information for clinical diagnosis. Common medical imaging technologies include X-ray [1],

[1]College of Information Science and Engineering, Hebei North University, China
[2]Research Centre for Intelligent Healthcare, Coventry University, United Kingdom
[3]Techtotop. Co. Ltd, Guangzhou, China
[4]Department of Pathology, China-Japan Friendship Hospital, China

CT (Computed tomography) [2], MRI (Magnetic Resonance Imaging) [3], PET (Positron Emission Tomography) [4], Ultrasound, and OCT [5] (Optical Coherence Tomography), and DP (Digital Pathology) [6] for specific tissues and organs. The trajectory of medical imaging technology has shown a trend toward digital imaging, functional imaging development, stereoscopic, and dynamic imaging. With the development of medical imaging technology, medical imaging equipment is playing an increasingly important role in clinical diagnosis. The number of outpatient clinics based on diagnostic imaging has greatly increased, so the amount of data collected. A large number of medical images will be generated and pooled to conduct a census of a certain disease. Therefore, how to efficiently process and analyze these images has become an urgent problem in clinical practice. However, at present, many medical images still stay in the qualitative interpretation mode, which can no longer meet the clinical needs, leading to two problems. On the one hand, the growth rate of medical image data far exceeds the growth rate of the number of medical radiologists, which leads to the increasing workload of medical image doctors; on the other hand, it is difficult to rely on the doctor's own experience to avoid omission and misdiagnosis, and it is difficult to conduct consistent quantitative analysis of the images, which is essential for the development of medical imaging [7]. In this context, medical image processing technology plays an increasingly important role in medical imaging.

2.1.2 Importance of big data in medical image processing

The core of medical image processing is to extract useful information from massive data and assist doctors in making accurate diagnoses. In the traditional medical image analysis, relying on the doctor's experience is more subjective. The introduction of big data technology can reduce this subjectivity and improve the accuracy of diagnosis [8].

First of all, big data technology in medical image processing can help doctors diagnose diseases and plan treatment more quickly. With the massive amount of data in the medical system, big data technology can filter out valuable information through automated processing. Meanwhile, big data technology can use medical image recognition technology to extract useful features from images, such as tumor size and location.

Second, big data technology can also enable doctors to be more accurate and objective in the diagnostic process. Big data technology can use deep learning and other technologies to automatically conduct model training and optimization to build more accurate image recognition models. For example, in medical image recognition technology, deep convolutional neural network (CNN) is widely used in medical images to more accurately identify abnormal tissues such as tumors.

In addition, big data technology can help doctors and researchers better understand image information and provide more comprehensive auxiliary diagnostic information [9]. Big data technology can analyze a large number of cases to extract information such as the distribution and incidence of the patient population, and then compare this information with the images of existing patients, which can provide doctors with more comprehensive diagnostic references and improve the accuracy of judgment. At the same time, big data technology using machine learning and image recognition and other technologies can not only analyze a single image but also analyze the correlation between multiple images, providing doctors with a more comprehensive patient portrait.

In conclusion, the application of big data technology in medical image analysis and processing can improve the accuracy and efficiency of diagnosis, reduce the subjectivity of manual diagnosis, and provide new development opportunities for the medical industry.

2.2 Medical image processing with big data

2.2.1 New features of medical images

Medical imaging data in China accounts for about 90% of all healthcare data and is growing at a rate of 30% year by year, and is, therefore, one of the most important sources of evidence for clinical analysis and medical interventions. Under the influence of big data, medical imaging has the following characteristics [10]:

1. Huge scale: with the continuous progress of medical technology, the number of modern medical images is rapidly increasing, involving a large number of patients, multiple healthcare organizations, and image data at multiple points in time. This makes the scale of medical image big data huge and requires powerful computing and storage resources for management and analysis.
2. Diversity: Medical image big data covers multiple modalities, such as X-ray, CT, MRI, ultrasound, and so on. Different modalities have different characteristics and information, which can provide more comprehensive and detailed medical information. In addition, medical image big data involves diversity in many aspects such as different body parts, different disease conditions, and different patients.
3. High dimension: medical image data are usually high-dimensional data, and the pixel value of each pixel can be one or more numerical values, such as color images having the values of three channels of RGB. In addition, medical images contain information in multiple dimensions, such as spatial dimension, temporal dimension, and functional dimension, which makes medical image data have richer characteristics.
4. High resolution: Medical images usually have a high resolution, i.e., the image contains a large number of pixel points. This makes the data volume of medical images huge and requires efficient storage and processing methods as well as higher computational resources for analysis and manipulation.
5. Privacy and confidentiality: Medical images involve patients' personal privacy, so there are high requirements for data confidentiality and privacy. When processing and analyzing medical image big data, corresponding security measures must be taken to ensure the privacy and security of patient data.

2.2.2 The main process of medical image processing

Medical image processing under large data volume refers to the process of analyzing, processing, and recognizing a large number of medical images through the knowledge and technology in the field of computer technology and other fields, usually going through three stages of the basic, intermediate, and advanced layers, involving image acquisition, data preprocessing, feature extraction and selection, model training and evaluation, etc., and the processing flow is shown in Figure 2.1.

1. Medical image data acquisition and preservation

    Medical images are mainly acquired by medical imaging devices, including anatomical imaging modalities and functional imaging modalities [11]. Anatomical imaging modalities are used to describe the physiological and anatomical morphology of the human body, including X-ray, CT, MRI, etc. Functional imaging modalities are used to describe the human body's function or metabolism, including PET, SPECT, MRI, EEG, MEG, etc., as shown in Table 2.1.

    Most of these medical images are stored in DICOM format [12], in addition to Analyze, NIfTI, MNIC, AFNI brick, Mosaic, etc. as shown in Table 2.2.

2. Medical image preprocessing

    Medical image preprocessing belongs to the basic layer, which is an "image-to-image" process aimed at optimizing image quality and laying the foundation

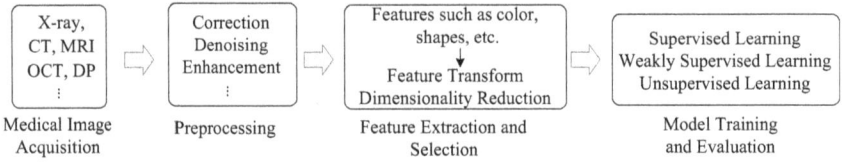

Figure 2.1   Routine flow of medical image processing

Table 2.1   Examples of different types of medical images

Imaging	X-ray	CT	MRI	PET	Ultrasonic	OCT	DP
Dimension	2D	3D	3D	3D	3D	3D	2D
Radiant	X-ray	X-ray	Non-radioactive	Radiometric survey	Non-radioactive	Non-radioactive	Non-radioactive
Topicality	Clogged	Clogged	Clogged	Clogged	Be	Clogged	Clogged
Imaging method	X-ray	X-ray	Magnetic field excitation of hydrogen atoms produces nuclear magnetic resonance information	Positronic information emitted during tracer decay	Acoustic reflection	Coherent optical interference (physics)	Optical imaging

Table 2.2 Common medical image formats

Name (of a thing)	File extension	Analyzing software and sources
DICOM	Not have	ACR/NEMA Association
Analyze	.img/.hdr	Analyze Software, Mayo Clinical Medical Center
NIfTI	.nii or .img/.hdr	NIH Imaging Information Tools Initiative
MINC	.mnc	Montreal Neurological Institute (MNI, extension NetCDF)
AFNI brick	.BRIK	AFNI Software, Wisconsin Medical Center (NIHM)

for subsequent analysis processes. Different types of medical images may be subjected to different degrees of corruption and noise pollution during generation, transmission, and storage, resulting in image quality degradation. Preprocessing methods include intensity normalization, bias field correction, image denoising, image enhancement, and spatial normalization/alignment [13], which are selected according to the image quality and processing tasks in practice. For example, image enhancement is usually performed for the identification and counting of red blood cells, white blood cells, etc. in micro-optical images to improve the front-background contrast.

3. Feature extraction and selection

   Feature extraction and selection is one of the key steps in quantitative analysis and diagnosis of medical images and is in the middle layer of the image processing process, where the input of this stage is an image and the output is a set of symbols. Feature extraction reduces the dimensionality of the data and retains important information by transforming the raw data into representative feature vectors. Commonly used methods include principal components analysis (PCA), linear discriminant analysis (LDA), singular value decomposition (SVD), multidimensional scaling (MDS), independent component analysis (ICA), and kernel principal component analysis [14,15], which can extract statistical features, frequency domain features, and time domain features. Feature selection then selects the most useful features from the extracted features for model construction. The commonly used algorithms are the Filter method, Wrapper method, Embedded method, and LASSO and mRMR. When selecting methods, they should be matched according to the specific task, while retaining relevant information and eliminating redundant features to improve model performance and generalization ability. The goal of feature extraction and selection is to extract features with distinguishing abilities to assist the realization of tasks such as classification, segmentation, or diagnosis.

4. Model training and evaluation

   Model training and evaluation is a key part of medical image processing and is at an advanced level of the process, where the input may be a set of signals or symbols and the output may be a representation of a function. In model training, a suitable machine learning or deep learning model is first selected

Table 2.3 Commonly used evaluation indexes for medical image processing

Name	Formulas	Clarification	Emphasis
Pixel accuracy	$PA = \dfrac{\sum_{i=0}^{K} P_{ii}}{\sum_{i=0}^{K}\sum_{j=0}^{K} P_{ij}}$	Compare the ratio of model-predicted pixels to real labeled pixels	Assessment of classification issues
Accuracy	$Ac = \dfrac{(TP+TN)}{(TP+TN+FP+FN)}$	Proportion of samples accurately categorized by the classifier	
Recall rate	$Re = \dfrac{TP}{(TP+FN)}$	Proportion of positive samples correctly identified by the classifier	
Accuracy	$Pr = \dfrac{TP}{(TP+FP)}$	The number of samples correctly identified as positive by the classifier as a proportion of the number of all samples classified as positive	
F1 value	$F1 = \dfrac{2*Pr*Re}{(Pr+Re)}$	A metric that combines precision and recall and is the reconciled average of precision and recall	
Copula (statistics)	$IoU = J(A,B) = \dfrac{|A \cap B|}{|A \cup B|}$	For evaluating the degree of overlap between detection results and true labeling in targeted detection tasks	Assessment of segmentation issues
VOE	$VOE(A,B) = 1 - \dfrac{|A \cap B|}{|A \cup B|}$	Used to measure the volumetric overlap error between model predictions and real labels	
RVD	$RVD(A,B) = \dfrac{|B|-|A|}{|A|}$	Used to measure the relative difference between the volume of the model's predicted results and the volume of the real labels	
Dice coefficient	$Dice = \dfrac{2|A \cap B|}{|A|+|B|}$	For evaluating the similarity between segmentation results and real labels in a target segmentation task	
Sensitivity	$SE = \dfrac{TP}{(TP+FN)}$	Proportion of all true positive samples correctly identified by the classifier	Assessment of the issue of disaggregation

and the model is trained and optimized using a training set. Then, the model is evaluated and tuned using the validation set. Finally, the final model is tested and evaluated using the test set. Through these steps, efficient and accurate models can be built to support physicians in disease diagnosis and treatment planning.

In medical image processing, a variety of evaluation metrics are used when performing model evaluation, and Table 2.3 shows the commonly used evaluation metrics for medical image processing and their calculation formulas [16].

2.3 Key technologies and progress

Image data under large data volume is characterized by availability, high quality, large volume, and unified standard, which promotes the development of medical images in data enhancement, image segmentation, image alignment, and image fusion. The big data technology is reshaping the landscape of diagnostics by providing more sensitive, reliable, and accurate biomarkers, with auxiliary roles in medical teaching, surgical planning, and different aspects of medical research.

2.3.1 Data enhancement

In the era of big data, the scale of medical image data is expanding, but publicly available medical image data are scarce. To solve this problem, data enhancement has been identified as an important approach. There are two main types of medical image data enhancement methods available: methods based on geometric transformations and methods based on generative adversarial networks.

Medical image data enhancement methods based on geometric transformations can be divided into two types of operation: (1) operate on the gray values of pixels in the image and change the pixel position information through a series of mapping of transformation functions to keep the texture details consistent with the original image. Thaha et al. [17] proposed an intensity-normalized transformation method applied to the brain tumor MRI image segmentation model, and the dice similarity coefficient (DSC) was improved by 1.9%. Afzal et al. [18] acquired many rare Alzheimer's disease MRI images by deflation, rotation, and cropping, which eventually led to a 7.54% improvement in classification model accuracy. (2) By deforming and reorganizing the content of the image to deform the lesion region and region of interest to make the image have more diversified feature information. Karani et al. [19] used this method to improve the DSC in the segmentation test of brain MRI images and prostate MRI images by 2.31% and 6.91%, respectively. Yang et al. [20] proposed a novel unsupervised domain adaptation method, which reduces the difference between images in the dataset and effectively lowers the model's training cost. The data distribution between the new images generated by such methods and the original images is consistent, and the diversity of the dataset is closely linked to the generalization ability of the training model, which will have an adverse effect on the downstream medical image analysis application models that rely on this dataset and may weaken the model performance.

The generative adversarial network (GAN)-based medical image data enhancement method learns the latent feature distribution from the existing image data, which is capable of generating images using random noise under unsupervised conditions as well as expanding the dataset by converting medical images of other modalities into the desired images. Wang et al. [21] proposed a GAN-based latent vector to generate multiparameter MRI images, which can efficiently generate MRI images and exhibit good visualization. To make the generated medical images more consistent with the physiological structure of the human body, Jiang et al. [22] generated CT lung images of newly crowned infected patients based on GAN, which can effectively reduce the risk of infection due to the acquisition of CT images of newly crowned infected patients. Medical images with different modalities can provide different levels of information about the disease, Zhang et al. [23] proposed noise adaptive GAN and used a generator and two discriminators to train the content in the image and the included noise distribution to guide the method, which can effectively remove the noise distribution in the image and eliminate the noise discrepancy in the CT images. For the current situation that most medical image datasets are small and scattered, Han et al. [24] proposed a two-step GAN-based data enhancement method, which first generates a high-resolution MRI image of the brain through a generator, and then generates the texture of this MRI image of the brain by further refining it using a GAN model that has been trained to make geometric transformations in the image.

2.3.2 Image segmentation

The aim of medical image segmentation is to separate the variations of anatomical or pathological structures in an image. Traditional image segmentation methods relied on edge detection, template matching, statistical shape models, active contours, etc. These methods have achieved good performance, while accurate segmentation is still challenging due to the gaps in feature presentation. According to the semantic segmentation task requirements, segmentation methods mainly include supervised learning and weakly supervised learning.

2.3.2.1 Image segmentation methods for supervised learning

Supervised learning is the most popular method and involves three main aspects: selection of backbone network, design of network blocks, and improvement of loss function. More common in the literature are backbone network architectures such as convolutional neural network (CNN) and U-Net. CNN enables hierarchical feature representation of images and eliminates the need for human provision of corresponding features for medical image segmentation. Fully convolutional network (FCN) [25] replaces the fully connected layer in CNN with a convolutional layer, which can take an image of any size and generate segmented maps of the same size, and at the same time achieves up-sampling by inverse convolution for pixel-level classification. Networks based on existing CNN architectures can be modified by replacing all fully connected layers with fully convolved layers to manage inputs and outputs of variable sizes, such as VGG16 and GoogLeNet. However, general CNN networks rely only on low-level features of the image, which makes it difficult to detect objects or recognize objects in medical images. At the same time, due to the lack of detailed information of the image, it is also impossible to obtain accurate boundaries by relying only on the semantic features of the image. U-Net adopts a perfectly symmetric structure, combining low- and high-resolution feature maps through jump connections, which effectively fuses the low-level and high-level image features, and it is a perfect solution for the task of medical image segmentation. In order to better adapt to the segmentation task of different organs and improve the segmentation accuracy, many scholars have sought to improve the solution based on the basic U-Net network. Hu et al. [26] partially added long jump connections in symmetric paths and optimized the contextual information in the image by using a hybrid feature fusion layer. Islam et al. [27] extended the original U-Net into a 3D attention U-Net network, where channels and spatial attention mechanisms are used in a combined manner to improve the quality of coding in the feature hierarchy.

Dense connections are often used in the construction of network blocks, where the input to each layer comes from the output of all the previous layers. Guan et al. [28] proposed an improved U-Net by replacing each sub-block of the U-Net with a form of dense connections. While dense connections help to obtain richer image features, they tend to reduce the robustness of the feature representation to some extent and increase the number of parameters. For CNNs, deep networks tend to have better performance than shallow networks but are prone to problems such as vanishing gradients, difficulty in network convergence, and large memory footprints. Inception can merge convolutional kernels in parallel without increasing the depth of the network to obtain better feature representations. Gu et al. [29] proposed CE-Net by introducing Inception into medical image segmentation. In order to improve the generalization ability of the network model and to reduce the memory usage requirement of the complex structure of Inception, many researchers have investigated lightweight network models for complex medical 3D volumetric data. Lei et al. [30] proposed an LV-Net for liver segmentation which is lighter than V-Net. The combination of attention mechanism and neural network can selectively change the input or assign different weights to recognize key features. Jaderberg et al. designed a spatial transformation attention block to extract the key information of an image by spatial transformation. Hu et al. [31] proposed a channel attention-based SE-Net to use the learned global information to selectively emphasize the useful features and suppress the useless features to achieve feature recalibration.

In addition to the design of the network backbone and functional modules, the choice of loss function is also an important factor in improving network performance. The design of loss functions such as Cross Entropy, Weighted Cross Entropy Loss (WCE), Dice loss, Generalized Dice Loss (GDL), etc. improves the accuracy of image segmentation to a certain extent. Long et al. [32] proposed Weighted Cross Entropy Loss (WCE) to offset the class imbalance problem of the images. Milletari et al. [33] proposed V-Net using Dice loss for the 3D medical data segmentation and proposed V-Net using Dice loss. However, the design of the loss function is highly task-specific and is more likely to focus on smaller targets, and the task requirements need to be carefully analyzed to design a reasonably usable loss function.

2.3.2.2 Image segmentation methods for weakly supervised learning

Although convolutional neural networks show strong adaptability to medical image segmentation, the segmentation results rely heavily on high-quality labels. In the field of medical images, datasets with high-quality labels are rare, and many works are based on incomplete or imperfect datasets to carry out research, i.e., weakly supervised learning.

Transfer learning is a common weakly-supervised learning method that enables rapid training of models with limited labeled data by initializing a new model with the training parameters of an existing model. In medical image segmentation, there are two common transfer learning approaches: one is to fine-tune a pre-trained model on ImageNet and the other is to perform inter-domain transfer learning. In the fine-tuning approach, researchers use a pre-trained model on ImageNet as an initial model and apply it to the target medical image segmentation task. Conze et al. [34] who used a VGG-11 model pre-trained on ImageNet as an encoder for the segmentation network achieved a significant improvement of the results in the scapular muscle MRI segmentation task. In fact, the effect of the pre-trained model is unstable, and domain adaptation may be a problem when applying the pre-trained natural scene image model to the medical image analysis task. Huo et al. [35] proposed a jointly optimized image synthesis and segmentation framework for the spleen segmentation task in CT images using CycleGAN, which achieves the image from the labeled source domain to the target domain of the synthesized image Transformation.

Interactive segmentation has also been applied to weakly supervised learning, which allows clinicians to interactively correct the initial segmented images generated by the model for more accurate segmentation. Wang et al. [36] proposed interactive segmentation of 2D and 3D medical images using DeepIGeoS with a cascade of two CNNs. The first CNN called P-Net outputs a rough segmentation result. Based on this, the user provides interactive clicks or lines to mark erroneous segmentation regions and then uses these points or lines as inputs to a second CNN structure called R-Net to obtain a corrected result. The key to effective interactive segmentation is that the clinician can use interactive methods, such as mouse clicks and contour boxes, to improve the initial segmentation results output from the model. The model can then update the parameters and generate a new segmented image with new feedback from the clinician.

2.3.3 Image alignment

Image alignment refers to finding a spatial transformation that maps a floating image onto a reference image by measuring the similarity between images so as to achieve a correspondence between them, and has a wide range of clinical applications, such as image guidance, image fusion, and tumor growth monitoring. In image alignment, different learning methods can be used, including supervised learning, weakly supervised learning, and unsupervised learning.

Supervised deep learning techniques are mainly used for augmented iterative, intensity-based medical image alignment, but the alignment speed is slow, and the demand for fast alignment algorithms drives the development of supervised alignment methods. Zheng et al. [37] proposed to integrate a pairwise region-adaptive module into a pre-trained CNN, which can be trained using a small amount of paired real and synthetic data, and the trained module into the network to transfer the real features into the network to make them close to the synthetic ones. Yang et al. [38] first proposed to achieve fast alignment of brain MR images directly based on the block-by-block prediction of the deformation model of image appearance. The method uses a deep codec network to take the initial momentum values of the image pixels as network inputs and evolves these values to obtain the estimated deformation field. Experimental results show that the method is capable of accurate and fast prediction of alignment results based on numerical optimization.

Supervised alignment methods require real deformation fields as the gold standard, and real deformation fields are difficult to obtain. The weak supervision method is proposed to alleviate the dependence on the gold standard. Weak supervision utilizes the segmental overlap of the corresponding anatomical structures to design the loss function, i.e., the similarity metric of the labels is used as the objective function, and the weights of the network are updated iteratively in the reverse direction. Liu *et al.* [39] use representation learning to learn feature descriptors with confidence-level probability maps and train the network using a supervised synthetic transform and unsupervised descriptors combined with the loss of image similarity. Hu *et al.* [40] use the GAN framework to generate realistic deformations. The main idea of Hu's team is to constrain the local deformation field by introducing a discriminator instead of a regular term for the deformation field. The overall framework is to generate a realistic local deformation by generating an affine transformed deformation field and local deformation field through a generator, and then the discriminator discriminates the predicted local deformation field from the simulation-generated deformation field.

Despite the great results of supervised and weakly supervised learning for image alignment, labels are difficult to obtain, and without labels, it is difficult to define an appropriate loss function, which has prompted many scholars to explore unsupervised learning methods. Balakrishnan *et al.* [41] proposed a CNN-based unsupervised alignment method using a U-Net-like architecture that utilizes the training data in an auxiliary segmentation approach scaling to improve Dice scores. Liu *et al.* [42] proposed a tensor-based method that uses principal component analysis networks for unimodal and multimodal alignment, which was experimentally validated on inhalation-exhalation of two pairs of chest CT volumes and multimodal brain MR images.

Image-guided surgery and radiation therapy present a strong clinical demand for research on medical image alignment, and there is still a vast space for deep learning research in medical image alignment, whether it is supervised learning, weakly supervised learning or unsupervised learning. In the clinic, research on unsupervised learning for preoperative and intraoperative medical image alignment is very relevant. In addition, the lack of training datasets with known transformations and multimodal medical image alignment are also hot directions for future research.

2.3.4 Image classification

Medical image classification is an important part of medical image analysis. How to improve the efficiency of medical image classification is an ongoing research problem. With the increase in the amount of medical data, medical image classification methods have shifted from traditional methods to deep learning and then to transfer learning.

Deep learning-based image classification refers to the use of deep neural networks for image classification tasks. Deep learning networks are able to learn higher-level feature representations from the original image and map the input image to the corresponding category labels through the stacking of multiple layers of neurons and the automatic adjustment of the learning parameters. Suk et al. [43] transformed the feature representations into polymorphic feature combinations by fusing them with the multi-peak information from MRI or PET and utilized the deep learning technique based on convolutional neural networks for the diagnosis and quantitative analysis of Alzheimer's Disease (AD). Arevalo et al. [44] used a hybrid-based convolutional neural network to automate the extraction of discriminative features in mammography images for qualitative classification of mammography images and cancer diagnosis.

Transfer learning has the advantage of overcoming the problem of scarcity of labeled data for better classification of medical images. By modifying the transfer model, the strategy of medical image classification in the way of type structure has been used for a variety of diseases. Wang et al. [45] improved the migration ability of the model by enhancing the fully connected (FC) layer on the basis of residual neural network ResNet-34 for feature extraction and classification of lung cancer images. Akter et al. [46] used the transfer model MobileNet-V1 to classify children's facial images for either autism or normal binary classification of children's facial images using the migration model MobileNet-V1 with three batch normalization (BN) layers and two FC layers modified, and the model outperformed similar methods. Improvement strategies for transfer learning can also be achieved by adjusting the parameters of the convolutional layers. Chen et al. [47] modified the parameters of the FC layer and then adjusted the weights of the last layer after migrating to the target domain for the classification of prostate lesions. Yang et al. [48] transferred the pre-trained AlexNet and GoogLeNet models to a glioma classification task by re-training the fully connected layer and fine-tuning the first convolutional layer. Experiments demonstrate that deep convolutional neural networks (DCNN) based on transfer learning and fine-tuning can significantly improve the performance of glioma classification. Deniz et al. [49] extracted features from different layers of DCNN to classify breast cancer, and the experimental results show that with the deepening of the DCNN convolutional layer, the features extracted from the convolutional layer show an upward trend in the performance of the final classification task.

2.4 Problems and challenges ahead

Despite the significant development of big data-driven medical image processing technology, especially the successful application of deep learning, transfer learning, and generative adversarial network methods in medical imaging, medical image processing technology is still facing challenges due to the diversity of medical imaging modalities and functions, the requirement of data annotation expertise, the ethical issues of patient data privacy, and the limitations of deep learning.

2.4.1 Complex high-dimensional image features

High-dimensional image processing has the potential to better capture rich information and details with the help of emerging technologies such as big data and the Internet. Deep learning based on convolutional neural networks can automatically process and learn high-dimensional complex features in images, and the Transformer structure can encode long-range dependencies in images. Li *et al.* [50] combined the characteristics of CNN and Transformer and proposed a dual codec structure of X-Net, which has a very good effect of dimensionality reduction compared with the traditional segmentation network. High-dimensional data has the characteristics of containing a large amount of information and being prone to information redundancy, and some scholars, from the perspective of data dimensionality reduction, utilize the Maximum Dependency Dimensionality Reduction Method (MDDM) to reduce high-dimensional data to low-dimensional data to improve the proportion of effective information and reduce information redundancy [51]. Yang *et al.* proposed a novel supervised feature selection methodology for machine learning decision-making, and the resulting test can significantly and robustly select low-dimensional feature subspaces while maintaining high decision-making performance [52]. In the field of medical images, the large volume, heterogeneity, and complexity of image data add processing challenges to high-dimensional feature processing, requiring more complex algorithms and more powerful computational capabilities.

2.4.2 Difficulty in extracting data labels

Medical images are highly heterogeneous; noise, distortion, and missing parts may be present in different medical images, and different imaging techniques and different patients may also cause differences in the images, making it difficult to identify or measure specific features or regions. In addition, some data labels may be subjective or uncertain due to differences in subjective interpretation or expertise of the observer. Therefore, medical image label extraction requires accurate, reliable, robust, and adaptable methods that can handle various types of images and variations and cope with the ambiguity and uncertainty of medical images. Lack of training samples is also a major problem faced by medical image label extraction. In recent years, algorithms such as machine learning and deep learning have been widely used in medical images, but their performance is limited by the number and diversity of training samples. Therefore, there is a need to increase the diversity of training samples by introducing new datasets, employing data augmentation techniques, and cross-modal data migration, in order to improve the performance of medical image label extraction and further promote the application and development of medical images.

2.4.3 Shortcomings of multimodal image processing

Medical images in different modalities can provide different levels of information about the disease and their lesion characteristics can be displayed more comprehensively. Due to the differences in image resolution and contrast produced by different devices and the possible artifacts in image fusion, multimodal image processing still faces many challenges: (1) Insufficient or unavailable multimodal image data is the biggest limitation of the general multimodal image processing task, and how to obtain a huge dataset to establish a complete and comprehensive multimodal medical image database containing all types of multimodal medical images, providing adequate multimodal attributes of different image devices and targets is a difficult study in medical imaging. (2) Different evaluation indexes may be used for different fusion methods, and there are nearly 30 types of evaluation indexes for medical image fusion, different quantitative evaluation indexes are usually used for different fusion effects, and non-unique evaluation indexes bring limiting prospects for applications. (3) Despite the popularity of medical image fusion techniques, most methods are based on traditional methods, where some problems such as color distortion are to be solved. The development of novel methods for medical image fusion warrants further investigation.

2.4.4 Improvements in graph modeling algorithms

Graph modeling methods have been successfully used to segment, recognize, and classify complex structures in medical images. Facing the huge amount of medical images still face some problems: (1) graph processing for different types of medical image data. The structure of graph data is diverse. Homogeneous graphs have been focused on with fewer explorations on heterogeneous graphs, especially the multimodal ones. (2) Most existing graph modeling methods focus on static graphs while dynamic medical images are common in clinical practice. Considering the huge amount of medical dynamic images, and the fast, multi-terminal access to these data, it is still an open problem to model the changing features and update model parameters in the dynamic context. (3) Interpretability of graph models. The accurate interpretation of deep graph model features and underlying anatomic/pathophysiological information is key for clinical decision-making. (4) Composability. Many existing architectures in graph models can combined, e.g., graph convolutional networks (GCN) as a layer in general advantage estimation (GAE) or Graph recurrent neural network (RNN). It is important to consider if the blocks are compatible when combining them.

2.5 Summary and outlook

2.5.1 Summary and discussion

The article introduces the evolution of medical imaging, and the development of image processing, analyzes the impact of big data on medical image processing and the new features exhibited by medical images, and focuses on the key technologies and advances in image processing in terms of image enhancement, image segmentation, image alignment, and image classification.

Medical image data enhancement methods are gradually optimized and iterated in the direction of high dimensionality, high resolution, multi-type, and diversification, and play a pivotal role in solving the problem of medical image data scarcity. Although the image enhancement methods based on geometric transformation and based on generative adversarial networks have achieved certain results, they still need to be investigated in the aspects of image quality evaluation, the limitation of computer arithmetic, and multimodal medical image generation.

The current direction of method improvement from supervised learning to weakly supervised learning to unsupervised learning is still the dominant technological trend in image processing applications such as image segmentation, image alignment, and image classification. In supervised learning methods, the improvement of backbone networks such as CNN and U-Net, the selection of neural network blocks, and the improvement of loss function are the main research contents of supervised learning. Transfer learning, which can quickly train models with limited labeled data by utilizing the training parameters of existing models, has a place among weakly supervised learning methods. The lack of data labeling makes unsupervised learning methods have a very high potential for future development.

2.5.2 Future directions

Big data plays a crucial role in medical imaging research and clinical applications, promoting the development of medical imaging in tumor identification, lesion detection, assisted diagnosis, and prognosis assessment. With the continuous development of big data and medical imaging technology, medical image processing for clinical applications still needs to be explored in technical breakthroughs, data acquisition, and other issues.

1. Interpretability of forecast results
   Deep neural networks have achieved remarkable results in the medical field by generalizing morphological or textural features in medical images through big data training, but their lack of knowledge about the details of the decision-making process, i.e., interpretability, has limited the promotion of their application in clinical work [53]. Due to the complexity and diversity of medical images, as well as differences in imaging modalities, imaging protocols, and patient characteristics, these factors make it difficult to extract meaningful and consistent features from the images to interpret the predicted results. Medical image processing involves complex nonlinear models with many layers, parameters, and nonlinear activations that are opaque and difficult to interpret, seeking tradeoffs between performance and interpretability, tracking and understanding and how to process the input images and produce output predictions can help physicians to trace the original reasons for model decisions and refine the confidence information of the predictions.
2. Application of large models to images
   With the widespread use of medical imaging technologies such as MRI, CT, PET, OCT, and ultrasound, a large amount of multi-source, multi-modality, and multi-organ medical image data has been generated, and several works have focused on using unsupervised or self-supervised pre-training to improve medical image representations for medical macro modeling applications. The Genesis model [54] is proposed to facilitate 3D medical imaging through self-supervised learning and produces superior performance in different 3D

downstream applications. Nonetheless, there are some obvious compromises of large models in the medical imaging domain. For example, the training of LVMs and LMMs usually involves the minimization of data size, to accelerate the training and reduce the computational cost. Whereas, data compression inevitably leads to loss of information, e.g., small lesions that are critical for diagnosis may be removed during the preprocessing of medical images. In comparison, clinicians can manually detect these early minor abnormalities using original high-resolution images. This may lead to performance differences between current large models and experienced physicians, and the application of large models to images has yet to be deepened.

3. Relational modeling of image target entities

    Relational modeling of target entities can help identify and understand complex patterns in medical images. For example, some recent studies have used this approach to successfully identify specific patterns in tissue samples from cancer patients. Karimi *et al.* [55] made a breakthrough in the structural relational modeling of breast cancer pathology images, which allowed for the automated identification and modeling of the relationships between different cells from breast cancer pathology images to improve the diagnosis and prediction of the disease. In areas such as complex biological structures and highly heterogeneous medical images, future research may explore more sophisticated relational modeling methods to capture and understand patterns, thus providing more accurate information for disease diagnosis and treatment.

4. Meta-learning

    Recent applications of meta-learning in medical image processing have shown its strong potential. For example, several studies have used meta-learning to successfully address the problem of data scarcity and improve the performance of models in rare disease recognition. The paper by Nichol *et al.* [56] proposed a meta-learning method called MAML (Model-Agnostic Meta-Learning), which was successfully applied to several machine learning including medical image processing tasks. However, the effectiveness of meta-learning often relies on the similarity between tasks, which is not always present in medical images. Therefore, future research may explore how to perform effective meta-learning between tasks that do not have significant similarities, and how to design more effective meta-learning algorithms to better handle the specificity and complexity in medical images.

References

[1] D. Takei, M. Tsujimoto, J. J. Drake, and S. Kitamoto, "*X-ray development of the classical nova V2672 Ophiuchi with Suzaku,*" Oxford University Press, no. 2, 2014.

[2] D. Fleischmann and F. E. Boas, "Computed tomography—old ideas and new technology," *European Radiology*, vol. 21, no. 3, pp. 510–517, 2011.

[3] N. Rammohan, J. W. Randall, and P. Yadav, "History of technological advancements towards MR-Linac: the future of image-guided radiotherapy," *Journal of Clinical Medicine*, vol. 11, no. 16, p. 4730, 2022.

[4] A. Kas, L. Rozenblum, and N. Pyatigorskaya, "Clinical value of hybrid PET/MR imaging: Brain imaging using PET/MR imaging," *Magnetic Resonance Imaging Clinics*, 2023.

[5] J. Zhang and Z. Chen, "OCT advances into clinical applications," *Laser Focus World*, 2013.

[6] Y. Sucaet and W. Waelput, *Digital Pathology's Past to Present*. Cham: Springer International Publishing, 2014.

[7] T. Syed, A. Doshi, S. Guleria, S. Syed, and T. Shah, "Artificial intelligence and its role in identifying esophageal neoplasia," *Digestive Diseases and Sciences*, vol. 65, no. 12, pp. 3448–3455, 2020.

[8] P. Laszlo, C. P. Spielvogel, R. Ivo, H. Marcus, and B. Thomas, "Personalizing medicine through hybrid imaging and medical big data analysis," *Frontiers in Physics*, vol. 6, p. 51, 2018.

[9] J. Luo, M. Wu, D. Gopukumar, and Y. Zhao, "Big data application in biomedical research and health care: A literature review," *Biomedical Informatics Insights*, vol. 8, p. 1, 2016.

[10] S. K. Zhou, H. Greenspan, C. Davatzikos, J. S. Duncan, and R. M. Summers, "A review of deep learning in medical imaging: Imaging traits, technology trends, case studies with progress highlights, and future promises," *Proceedings of the IEEE*, vol. PP, no. 99, pp. 1–19, 2021.

[11] F. M. Hall, "Gestalt of medical images," *Radiographics*, vol. 33, no. 5, pp. 1519–1519, 2013.

[12] Peijiang and L. U. Chen, "Study on medical image processing technologies based on DICOM," *Journal of Computers*, vol. 7, no. 10, 2012.

[13] N. Goel, A. Yadav, and B. M. Singh, "Medical image processing: A review," in *2016 Second International Innovative Applications of Computational Intelligence on Power, Energy and Controls with their Impact on Humanity (CIPECH)*, 2016.

[14] O. S. Faragallah, A. N. Muhammed, T. S. Taha, and G. G. N. Geweid, "PCA based SVD fusion for MRI and CT medical images," *Journal of Intelligent & Fuzzy Systems: Applications in Engineering and Technology*, vol. 2, p. 41, 2021.

[15] Malaya, Kumar, Nath, Samarendra, and Dandapat, "Multiscale ICA for fundus image analysis," *International Journal of Imaging Systems and Technology*, vol. 23, no. 4, pp. 327–337, 2013.

[16] S. Minaee, Y. Y. Boykov, F. Porikli, A. J. Plaza, N. Kehtarnavaz, and D. Terzopoulos, "Image segmentation using deep learning: A survey," *IEEE Transactions on Pattern Analysis and Machine Intelligence*, vol. 1, 2021.

[17] M. M. Thaha, K. P. M. Kumar, B. S. Murugan, S. Dhanasekeran, and A. S. Selvi, "Brain tumor segmentation using convolutional neural networks in MRI images," *Journal of Medical Systems*, vol. 43, no. 9, 2019.

[18] S. Afzal, M. Maqsood, F. Nazir, U. Khan, and O. Y. Song, "A Data Augmentation-Based Framework to Handle Class Imbalance Problem for Alzheimer's Stage Detection," *IEEE Access*, vol. 7, pp. 1–1, 2019.

[19] N. Karani, E. Erdil, K. Chaitanya, and E. Konukoglu, "Test-time adaptable neural networks for robust medical image segmentation," *Medical Image Analysis*, vol. 68, no. 5, p. 101907, 2021.

[20] F. Yang, F. Liang, L. Lu, and M. Yin, "Dual attention-guided and learnable spatial transformation data augmentation multi-modal unsupervised medical image segmentation," *Biomedical Signal Processing and Control*, vol. 78, p. 103849, 2022.

[21] Z. Wang, Y. Lin, K. T. T. Cheng, and X. Yang, "Semi-supervised mp-MRI data synthesis with StitchLayer and auxiliary distance maximization," *Medical Image Analysis*, vol. 59, p. 101565, 2020.

[22] Y. Jiang, H. Chen, M. Loew, and H. Ko, "COVID-19 CT image synthesis with a conditional generative adversarial network," *IEEE Journal of Biomedical and Health Informatics*, vol. 25, no. 2, pp. 441–452, 2021.

[23] T. Zhang, J. Cheng, H. Fu, Z. Gu, and J. Liu, "Noise adaptation generative adversarial network for medical image analysis," *IEEE Transactions on Medical Imaging*, vol. PP, no. 99, pp. 1–1, 2019.

[24] C. Han, L. Rundo, R. Araki *et al.*, "Combining noise-to-image and image-to-image GANs: Brain MR image augmentation for tumor detection," *IEEE Access*, vol. 7, pp. 156966–156977, 2019.

[25] K. Held, E. Rota Kops, B. J. Krause, W. M. Wells, Iii, R. Kikinis, and H. W. Mueller-Gaertner, "Markov random field segmentation of brain MR images," ed: arXiv, 2009.

[26] H. Fu, J. Cheng, Y. Xu, D. W. K. Wong, J. Liu, and X. Cao, "Joint optic disc and cup segmentation based on multi-label deep network and polar transformation," *IEEE Transactions on Medical Imaging*, vol. PP, no. 99, pp. 1–1, 2018.

[27] M. Islam, V. S. Vibashan, V. J. M. Jose, N. Wijethilake, U. Utkarsh, and H. Ren, "Brain tumor segmentation and survival prediction using 3D attention UNet," in *International Workshop on Brain-Lesion; Medical Image Computing for Computer Assisted Intervention Conference*, 2019.

[28] S. Guan, A. A. Khan, S. Sikdar, and P. V. Chitnis, "Fully dense UNet for 2D sparse photoacoustic tomography artifact removal," *IEEE Journal of Biomedical and Health Informatics*, vol. PP, no. 99, pp. 1–1, 2019.

[29] Z. Gu, J. Cheng, H. Fu *et al.*, "CE-Net: Context encoder network for 2D medical image segmentation," *IEEE Transactions on Medical Imaging*, pp. 1–1, 2019.

[30] T. Lei, W. Zhou, Y. Zhang, R. Wang, and A. K. Nandi, "Lightweight V-Net for liver segmentation," in *ICASSP 2020 - 2020 IEEE International Conference on Acoustics, Speech and Signal Processing (ICASSP)*, 2020.

[31] J. Hu, L. Shen, G. Sun, and S. Albanie, "Squeeze-and-excitation networks," in IEEE, 2017.

[32] E. Shelhamer, J. Long, and T. Darrell, "Fully convolutional networks for semantic segmentation," *IEEE*, vol. 39, no. 4, pp. 640–651, 2015.

[33] F. Milletari, N. Navab, and S. A. Ahmadi, "V-Net: Fully convolutional neural networks for volumetric medical image segmentation," *IEEE*, 2016, pp. 565–571.

[34] P. H. Conze, A. E. Kavur, E. C. L. Gall *et al.*, "Abdominal multi-organ segmentation with cascaded convolutional and adversarial deep networks," *Artificial Intelligence in Medicine*, 2021, vol. 117, no. 7, pp. 102109.1-11.

[35] Y. Huo, Z. Xu, S. Bao, A. Assad, and B. A. Landman, "Adversarial synthesis learning enables segmentation without target modality ground truth," in *2018 IEEE 15th International Symposium on Biomedical Imaging (ISBI 2018)*, 2018.

[36] W. Guotai, M. A. Zuluaga, W. Li *et al.*, "DeepIGeoS: A Deep Interactive Geodesic Framework for Medical Image Segmentation," *IEEE Transactions on Pattern Analysis and Machine Intelligence*, vol. 41, no. 7, pp. 1559–1572, 2019.

[37] J. Zheng, S. Miao, Z. J. Wang, and R. Liao, "Pairwise domain adaptation module for CNN-based 2-D/3-D registration," *Journal of Medical Imaging*, vol. 5, no. 2, p. 021204, 2018.

[38] G. Carneiro, "Deep learning and data labeling for medical applications," *Lecture Notes in Computer Science*, vol. 10008, 2016.

[39] C. Liu, L. Ma, Z. Lu, X. Jin, and J. Xu, "Multimodal medical image registration via common representations learning and differentiable geometric constraints," *Electronics Letters*, vol. 55, no. 6, pp. 316–318, 2019.

[40] Y. Fu, Y. Lee, T. Wang. *et al.*, "LungRegNet: An unsupervised deformable image registration method for 4D-CT lung," *Medical Physics*, vol. 47, no.4, 2020.

[41] G. Balakrishnan, A. Zhao, M. R. Sabuncu, J. Guttag, and A. V. Dalca, "VoxelMorph: A learning framework for deformable medical image registration," *IEEE Transactions on Medical Imaging*, vol. 38, no. 8, pp. 1788–1800, 2019.

[42] Q. Liu and H. Leung, "Tensor-based descriptor for image registration via unsupervised network," in *2017 20th International Conference on Information Fusion (Fusion)*, 2017.

[43] H. I. Suk, S. W. Lee, and D. Shen, "Latent feature representation with stacked auto-encoder for AD/MCI diagnosis," *Brain Structure and Function*, vol. 220, no. 2, pp. 841–859, 2015.

[44] M. A. G. Lopez, J. Arevalo, F. A. Gonzalez, R. Ramos-Pollan, and J. L. Oliveira, "Convolutional neural networks for mammography mass lesion classification," in *Engineering in Medicine and Biology Society (EMBC), 2015 37th Annual International Conference of the IEEE*, 2015.

[45] S-H. Wang, D. R. Nayak, D. S. Guttery, X. Zhang, and Y-D. Zhang, "COVID-19 classification by CCSHNet with deep fusion using transfer learning and discriminant correlation analysis," *Information Fusion*, vol. 68, pp. 131–148, 2021.

[46] T. Akter, M. H. Ali, M. I. Khan et al., "Improved transfer-learning-based facial recognition framework to detect autistic children at an early stage," *Multidisciplinary Digital Publishing Institute*, no. 6, 2021.

[47] Q. Chen, S. Hu, P. Long, F. Lu, and Y. Li, "A transfer learning approach for malignant prostate lesion detection on multiparametric MRI," *Technology in Cancer Research & Treatment*, vol. 18, no. 4, p. 153303381985836, 2019.

[48] Y. Yang, L. F. Yan, X. Zhang et al., "Glioma grading on conventional MR images: a deep learning study with transfer learning," *Frontiers in Neuroscience*, vol. 12, p. 804, 2018.

[49] E. Deniz, A. Engür, Z. Kadirolu, Y. Guo, V. Bajaj, and M. Budak, "Transfer learning based histopathologic image classification for breast cancer detection," *Health Information Science and Systems*, vol. 6, no. 1, pp. 1–7, 2018.

[50] Y. Li, Z. Wang, L. Yin, Z. Zhu, G. Qi, and Y. Liu, "X-Net: a dual encoding–decoding method in medical image segmentation," *The Visual Computer*, vol. 39, no. 6, pp. 2223–2233, 2021.

[51] Z. H. Zhou and Y. Zhang, "Multilabel dimensionality reduction via dependence maximization," *ACM Transactions on Knowledge Discovery from Data (TKDD)*, vol. 4, no. 3, pp. 1–21, 2010.

[52] Y. Yang, W. Wang, H. Fu, and C. C. J. Kuo, "*On supervised feature selection from high dimensional feature spaces*," arXiv e-prints, 2022.

[53] C. Rudin, "Stop explaining black box machine learning models for high stakes decisions and use interpretable models instead," *Nature Machine Intelligence*, vol. 1, no. 5, pp. 206–215, 2019.

[54] Z. Zhou, V. Sodha, M. M. Rahman Siddiquee et al., *Models Genesis: Generic Autodidactic Models for 3D Medical Image Analysis*, Springer, Cham, 2019.

[55] L. Liu, W. Feng, C. Chen, M. Liu, Y. Qu, and J. Yang, "Classification of breast cancer histology images using MSMV-PFENet," *Scientific Reports*, vol. 12, no. 1, p. 17447, 2022.

[56] A. Nichol, J. Achiam, and J. Schulman, "On First-Order Meta-Learning Algorithms," 2018.

Chapter 3
Challenges in big data analytics monitoring

Palanichamy Naveen[1], James Deva Koresh H[2] and Rajasekaran Thangaraj[3]

Big Data Analytics involves processing and analyzing massive, diverse datasets to extract valuable insights for informed decision-making. Effective monitoring is crucial for ensuring optimal performance, data quality, security, and regulatory compliance throughout the analytics lifecycle. This chapter explores the significance of monitoring in Big Data Analytics environments, highlighting its importance in areas such as issue detection, performance optimization, data integrity assurance, and real-time decision support. It examines the key components and processes involved in monitoring Big Data Analytics, focusing on aspects like data ingestion, data processing pipelines, resource utilization tracking, and security monitoring. The chapter also delves into the challenges of monitoring at scale, including scalability concerns, data quality and consistency issues, and latency challenges in real-time environments. Additionally, it provides an overview of commonly used monitoring tools and technologies, equipping readers with an understanding of the available solutions for managing Big Data Analytics ecosystems effectively.

3.1 Introduction

Big Data Analytics is a process of examining and interpreting large volumes of complex and diverse datasets, often referred to as "big data," to derive meaningful insights, patterns, and trends. The main goal is to gain valuable knowledge that can aid in informed decision-making, optimize processes, and drive business strategies. It involves employing advanced analytics techniques and technologies to extract valuable insights from a vast and varied data landscape [1]. Big Data Analytics provides organizations with data-driven insights that enable informed and timely

---

[1]Department of Electrical and Electronics Engineering, Centre for IoT and AI (CITI), KPR Institute of Engineering and Technology, Coimbatore, India
[2]Department of Electronics and Communications Engineering, KPR Institute of Engineering and Technology, Coimbatore, India
[3]Department of Computer Science and Engineering, Centre for IoT and AI (CITI), KPR Institute of Engineering and Technology, Coimbatore, India

decision-making. By analyzing extensive and diverse datasets, organizations can uncover trends, patterns, and correlations, helping them make better strategic and operational decisions [2]. Understanding customer behavior and preferences is crucial for any business. Big Data Analytics helps in analyzing customer interactions, feedback, and usage patterns, leading to a deeper understanding of customer needs and preferences. This understanding can be used to tailor products, services, and marketing strategies [3].

By analyzing operational data, organizations can optimize processes, resource allocation, and workflow efficiency. This can result in cost savings, improved productivity, and streamlined operations [4]. Big Data Analytics plays a pivotal role in product development and innovation. Analyzing market trends, customer feedback, and emerging technologies can guide the creation of new products or the enhancement of existing ones, ensuring they meet market demands [5]. Organizations that harness the power of Big Data Analytics gain a competitive edge in their industry. The insights derived from big data enable companies to adapt swiftly to market changes, identify new opportunities, and stay ahead of competitors [6]. Big Data Analytics aids in identifying potential risks and fraudulent activities by analyzing patterns and anomalies in vast datasets. This is particularly critical in industries such as finance, healthcare, and cybersecurity [7]. In healthcare and scientific research, Big Data Analytics plays a significant role in analyzing large volumes of data to enhance patient care, drug discovery, disease detection, and medical research [8]. Thus, Big Data Analytics transforms raw data into actionable insights, empowering organizations to make data-driven decisions, innovate, and stay competitive in today's data-driven world. The overall architecture of significance of big data analytics is represented in Figure 3.1.

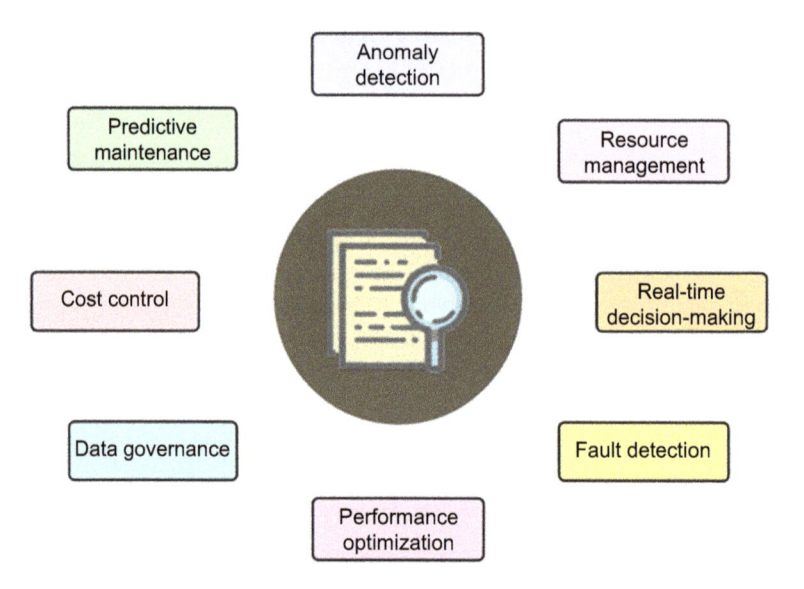

Figure 3.1 Significance of Big Data Analytics

3.2 Monitoring in Big Data Analytics

Monitoring in the context of Big Data Analytics involves the systematic collection, analysis, and evaluation of data processing and system performance to ensure optimal functionality, reliability, and efficiency. It is a critical component of managing big data systems, allowing organizations to proactively detect issues, optimize performance, and ensure the security and integrity of data and processes [9]. Monitoring the data processing pipeline is essential for identifying bottlenecks, optimizing data flow, and ensuring that data is processed accurately and efficiently throughout the analytics lifecycle. This includes monitoring data ingestion, transformation, loading, and analytics [10]. Performance monitoring involves tracking the performance of various components of the big data infrastructure, such as servers, storage systems, and network connectivity. It ensures that the system is operating within defined performance thresholds and identifies areas for improvement [11]. Monitoring resource utilization helps track the usage of computing resources like CPU, memory, disk space, and network bandwidth. By monitoring resource consumption patterns, organizations can optimize resource allocation and anticipate scaling needs [12]. Real-time monitoring provides insights into the system's performance and health in real-time or near real-time. It is crucial for applications that require immediate responses, enabling organizations to take prompt action based on the monitored data [13].

Monitoring security and compliance involves tracking access to sensitive data, identifying potential security breaches, and ensuring compliance with regulatory requirements. Monitoring helps in detecting anomalies and enforcing security policies [14]. Figure 3.2 represents the illustration of Big Data Analytics monitoring.

3.2.1 Importance of monitoring in Big Data Analytics

Monitoring allows for the early detection of issues, enabling timely resolution and minimizing potential downtime or performance degradation. Early detection helps in maintaining a seamless data processing flow [15]. Continuous monitoring helps identify performance bottlenecks and inefficiencies, allowing for optimization of

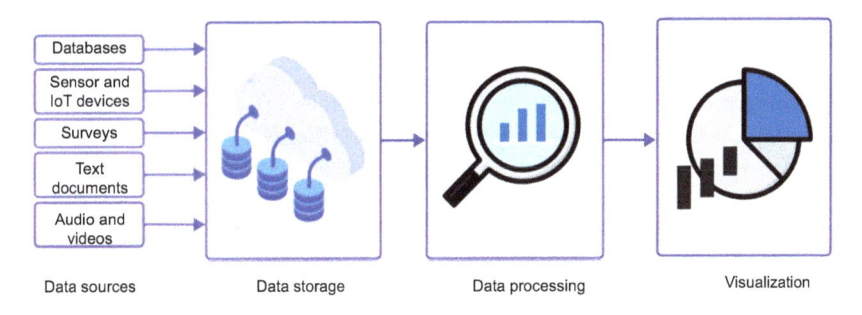

Figure 3.2 Monitoring Big Data Analytics

resources and configurations to enhance system performance and throughput [16]. Monitoring resource utilization assists in effective resource management, leading to cost savings by optimizing resource allocation and preventing unnecessary expenditure on over-provisioned resources [17]. Monitoring ensures data quality and integrity throughout the analytics process, helping maintain accurate and reliable insights for decision-making [18]. By monitoring usage patterns and workloads, organizations can scale their infrastructure and resources in a more informed and timely manner, adapting to changing demands and ensuring the system can handle increased data volumes [19]. In summary, monitoring in Big Data Analytics is pivotal for ensuring the smooth operation, performance, security, and efficiency of big data systems, ultimately enabling organizations to derive valuable insights and make informed decisions from their data.

Effective monitoring in Big Data Analytics is indispensable to ensure the successful management, performance, and security of large-scale data processing and analytics systems. It addresses several critical needs that are essential for leveraging the potential of big data and maximizing its value to organizations.

3.2.2 Key needs and reasons for effective monitoring

Effective monitoring helps optimize the performance and efficiency of big data systems. By continuously tracking system metrics, organizations can identify bottlenecks, inefficiencies, and performance degradation, allowing for timely adjustments and enhancements to maintain optimal performance [20]. Monitoring ensures the integrity and quality of the data being processed and analyzed. By actively monitoring data pipelines, organizations can identify and rectify data anomalies or inconsistencies, ensuring that the insights derived from the data are accurate and reliable [21]. In many organizations, meeting SLAs is crucial. Effective monitoring assists in meeting SLA requirements by providing real-time insights into system performance and allowing for proactive actions to maintain service levels and meet client expectations [22]. Monitoring enables proactive detection of issues, anomalies, or potential failures before they impact operations or data processing. This proactive approach ensures faster issue resolution and reduces downtime, enhancing overall system reliability [23]. Security breaches can have devastating consequences. Effective monitoring is vital for identifying security threats, unauthorized access, or abnormal activities within the system. It helps organizations ensure compliance with security policies and regulatory requirements [24]. Monitoring allows organizations to optimize costs by efficiently managing resources. By tracking resource utilization and performance, organizations can allocate resources effectively, prevent over-provisioning, and reduce unnecessary expenses [25]. Big data systems often need to scale to accommodate growing data volumes. Effective monitoring provides insights into usage patterns and helps organizations plan for future growth by making informed decisions about scaling resources and infrastructure [26]. Real-time monitoring provides immediate insights into system performance and data processing. This enables timely decision-making, especially critical for real-time analytics, fraud detection, and other time-sensitive applications [27]. Thus, effective monitoring in

Big Data Analytics is fundamental for optimizing performance, ensuring data integrity, meeting SLAs, enhancing security, optimizing costs, and supporting real-time decision-making. It is a strategic imperative for organizations seeking to harness the potential of big data and derive actionable insights to drive their business goals and objectives.

3.2.3 Understanding Big Data Analytics monitoring

Monitoring in the context of Big Data Analytics involves the continuous and systematic observation, measurement, and assessment of various aspects of a data processing and analytics ecosystem to ensure its smooth operation, performance optimization, data quality assurance, security, and adherence to predefined goals and objectives. This process is crucial for managing the complexities associated with large volumes of data and the diverse technologies and components used in big data systems.

3.2.3.1 Key components of monitoring in Big Data Analytics

Monitoring begins with data ingestion, where data from various sources is collected and ingested into the system. This stage involves tracking the rate at which data is collected, identifying potential data source issues, and ensuring data is correctly ingested into the data pipeline [28]. The data processing pipeline, which includes data transformation, aggregation, and analysis, is a critical focus of monitoring. It involves tracking the performance and accuracy of data processing jobs, identifying bottlenecks, and ensuring that data is correctly processed and transformed [29]. Monitoring resource utilization is essential for efficient resource management. It involves tracking CPU, memory, disk space, and network usage. Organizations can use this data to optimize resource allocation and prevent resource bottlenecks [30]. Performance monitoring tracks key performance metrics, such as query response times, data processing throughput, and system latency. Monitoring these metrics ensures that the system operates within predefined performance thresholds [31]. Real-time monitoring is particularly critical for applications requiring immediate responses, such as fraud detection or real-time analytics. It provides insights into system performance and health in real-time or near real-time, enabling organizations to make prompt decisions [32]. Monitoring security and compliance ensures that data remains secure and meets regulatory requirements. This involves tracking user access, identifying security threats or vulnerabilities, and monitoring data encryption and compliance with industry-specific regulations [33]. Ensuring data quality is a key aspect of monitoring. Organizations must identify and rectify data anomalies, inconsistencies, or data quality issues that could compromise the accuracy and reliability of the insights derived from the data [34]. Monitoring systems are often equipped with alerting and notification mechanisms. When predefined thresholds or anomalies are detected, these mechanisms notify administrators or relevant stakeholders, enabling prompt action [35].

Monitoring in Big Data Analytics is not a one-time activity but rather a continuous process. It involves setting up automated monitoring systems that provide real-time or near real-time insights into the system's health and performance. Continuous monitoring allows organizations to address issues as they arise, optimize performance, and maintain data quality and security.

Effective monitoring often relies on a variety of monitoring tools and technologies. These tools can range from log analyzers and performance monitoring systems to security information and event management (SIEM) solutions. Additionally, custom scripts and dashboards may be developed to suit the specific needs of the organization's big data ecosystem.

Thus, monitoring in Big Data Analytics is a multifaceted and ongoing process that encompasses various aspects of data processing, resource management, performance, security, and data quality. It is a critical component for ensuring the reliability and effectiveness of big data systems, allowing organizations to extract meaningful insights and make informed decisions based on their data.

3.2.3.2 Importance of real-time monitoring and analysis in handling large volumes of data

In the context of Big Data Analytics, the importance of real-time monitoring and analysis cannot be overstated. As organizations deal with ever-increasing volumes of data, the ability to monitor and analyze this data in real-time has become a critical requirement for several key reasons: Real-time monitoring allows organizations to identify issues and anomalies as they occur. In large-scale data processing environments, problems can arise at any moment, from hardware failures to data processing errors. Real-time monitoring ensures that these issues are identified immediately, enabling rapid response and resolution. This minimizes downtime and potential data loss [36]. Large volumes of data require complex processing systems. Real-time monitoring provides insights into the performance of these systems, helping organizations identify performance bottlenecks and inefficiencies in real-time. This proactive approach allows for on-the-fly optimization, ensuring that data processing and analytics continue to run smoothly [37]. In today's fast-paced business environment, making timely decisions is critical. Real-time monitoring and analysis provide decision-makers with up-to-the-minute insights into system performance and data quality. This is particularly important for industries like finance, e-commerce, and IoT, where quick decisions can lead to competitive advantages or prevent losses [38].

In applications where user experience is paramount, such as e-commerce platforms or online services, real-time monitoring ensures that user interactions are smooth and responsive. Any performance degradation or data processing issues can be immediately addressed to maintain a positive user experience [39]. Real-time monitoring is essential for identifying security threats and breaches. With the growing sophistication of cyberattacks, organizations need to detect and respond to threats as they happen. Real-time analysis of security logs and patterns can help prevent data breaches and protect sensitive information [40]. Many organizations deal with continuous data streams, such as social media feeds, IoT sensor data, and real-time market data. Real-time monitoring is essential to handle and analyze these data streams as they are generated. It allows organizations to react to emerging trends and patterns immediately [41]. Real-time monitoring ensures that data quality is maintained during data processing. It can identify data anomalies and discrepancies in real-time, preventing inaccurate or unreliable insights from being generated and used for decision-making [42].

Real-time monitoring provides insights into changing resource requirements. If data volumes suddenly spike, organizations can scale their infrastructure in real-time to accommodate the increased load. This adaptability is crucial for managing the dynamic nature of big data systems [43]. In environments where SLAs are in place, real-time monitoring helps organizations meet their commitments. It provides real-time insights into system performance and data processing, allowing organizations to take immediate corrective actions to ensure SLAs are met. Real-time monitoring is an integral part of event-driven architecture. In these systems, events trigger actions and decisions in real-time. Real-time monitoring enables organizations to process and act upon events as they occur, supporting event-driven applications and decision-making [44]. Thus, the importance of real-time monitoring and analysis in handling large volumes of data lies in its ability to provide immediate insights, enabling organizations to detect and resolve issues, optimize performance, make timely decisions, and respond to security threats and changes in data volumes. Real-time monitoring is an essential component of modern data processing and analytics, allowing organizations to harness the power of their data effectively.

3.2.3.3 Overview of tools and technologies used for monitoring Big Data Analytics processes

Monitoring Big Data Analytics processes is essential for maintaining optimal performance, ensuring data quality, and addressing issues promptly. Various tools and technologies are available to assist organizations in this critical task. Here is an overview of some of the commonly used tools and technologies for monitoring Big Data Analytics processes:

(A) *Apache Ambari*:
Apache Ambari is a popular open-source management and monitoring tool specifically designed for Hadoop clusters. It provides an intuitive web interface for cluster management and monitoring, enabling users to track the performance and health of Hadoop components.

(B) *Prometheus*:
Prometheus is an open-source monitoring and alerting toolkit that is particularly well-suited for monitoring cloud-native and containerized applications. It collects time-series data from various targets and offers a robust query language for analysis.

(C) *Grafana*:
Grafana is an open-source platform for visualizing and analyzing data. It integrates with various data sources, including Prometheus, to create interactive and customizable dashboards for monitoring Big Data Analytics processes. It is known for its flexibility and extensibility.

(D) *Nagios*:
Nagios is a widely used open-source monitoring system that offers comprehensive monitoring and alerting capabilities. It supports a range of plugins and can be customized to monitor various components of Big Data ecosystems, including server health and network performance.

(E) *Zabbix*:
Zabbix is another open-source monitoring platform known for its scalability. It can monitor network devices, servers, and applications, making it suitable for Big Data Analytics environments. Zabbix offers alerting, visualization, and reporting features.

(F) *ELK Stack (Elasticsearch, Logstash, Kibana)*:
ELK is a popular open-source stack for log management and analysis. Elasticsearch stores and indexes log data, Logstash collects, processes, and ships logs, and Kibana provides a visualization and analysis interface. ELK is often used for monitoring and troubleshooting in Big Data environments.

(G) *New Relic*:
New Relic is a commercial monitoring platform that specializes in application performance monitoring (APM) and infrastructure monitoring. It offers a range of features for tracking application performance and can be valuable for monitoring Big Data Analytics applications.

(H) *Splunk*:
Splunk is a commercial tool that provides real-time data monitoring and analytics. It is used for monitoring machine data, and it offers extensive search and reporting capabilities. Splunk can help organizations gain insights into their Big Data Analytics processes.

(I) *Dynatrace*:
Dynatrace is a commercial APM platform that provides end-to-end visibility into application performance. It offers automatic discovery of application dependencies and can be used to monitor the performance of Big Data applications and their interactions.

(J) *AppDynamics*:
AppDynamics, another commercial APM solution, offers real-time monitoring for applications and infrastructure. It provides insights into the performance of Big Data Analytics applications and helps organizations detect and resolve issues.

(K) *Apache NiFi*:
Apache NiFi is an open-source data integration and dataflow automation tool. While primarily used for data ingestion and routing, it can also monitor data flows and provide insights into the health and performance of data pipelines.

(L) *Custom Scripting*:
Many organizations develop custom scripts and applications to monitor specific aspects of their Big Data Analytics processes. These scripts can be tailored to the organization's unique requirements and integrate with various monitoring solutions.

The choice of monitoring tools and technologies should align with the organization's specific needs, the complexity of the Big Data Analytics ecosystem, and the level of expertise available within the organization. A combination of these tools may also be used to create a comprehensive monitoring strategy for Big Data Analytics processes.

3.3 Challenges in Big Data Analytics monitoring

3.3.1 Scalability challenges in monitoring Big Data Analytics

Scalability is a critical challenge when it comes to monitoring Big Data Analytics. As organizations deal with ever-increasing volumes of data, the monitoring infrastructure must also scale to handle the complexities and demands of large data ecosystems [45]. Here is an explanation of scalability challenges in monitoring Big Data Analytics: Big Data Analytics typically involves the processing of massive datasets. As data volumes grow, the monitoring system must be able to handle the increasing amount of data generated by various data sources. Traditional monitoring solutions may struggle to keep up with the sheer volume of data, leading to potential data loss or incomplete monitoring. The speed at which data is generated and processed, known as data velocity, is a key aspect of big data systems. Real-time data processing and analytics require monitoring tools that can keep pace with data as it streams in. Scalability challenges arise when monitoring systems are unable to process data in real-time, leading to delays in issue detection and decision-making. Big data often comprises diverse data types, including structured, semi-structured, and unstructured data. Monitoring systems must be adaptable to handle this variety. Traditional monitoring tools may not support the diverse data formats and sources used in Big Data Analytics, making it challenging to monitor the entire data ecosystem effectively.

As the data infrastructure scales to accommodate more data, the monitoring infrastructure must scale accordingly. This includes adding more monitoring nodes, storage capacity, and processing power. Failure to scale the monitoring infrastructure in tandem with the data infrastructure can lead to underperformance and data blind spots. Scalability often comes with increased costs. Organizations must manage their monitoring systems' scalability while being mindful of the associated expenses. Balancing performance with cost-effectiveness is a challenge when dealing with large-scale Big Data Analytics environments. The increasing complexity of Big Data Analytics systems poses a scalability challenge for monitoring. These systems often consist of various components, including data warehouses, distributed processing frameworks, and multiple data sources. Monitoring this intricate architecture at scale requires advanced tools and strategies.

In large-scale data environments, the high availability of monitoring systems is crucial. Scalability challenges can arise when organizations need to ensure continuous monitoring even in the event of hardware failures, network issues, or other disruptions. Storing and retaining monitoring data for analysis and auditing purposes is essential. However, as data volumes increase, managing this data becomes more complex and costly. Scalability challenges arise in determining how long to retain monitoring data, how to store it efficiently, and how to retrieve it for analysis. To address scalability challenges in monitoring Big Data Analytics, organizations often need to invest in robust monitoring solutions that can handle large data volumes, ensure real-time processing, support diverse data types, and scale both vertically and horizontally. Cloud-based monitoring services, distributed monitoring architectures, and tools designed for big data ecosystems are essential for addressing these challenges and ensuring the reliability and performance of Big Data Analytics systems.

3.3.2 Monitoring systems handling the vast amounts of data generated

Monitoring systems face significant challenges when it comes to handling the vast amounts of data generated in Big Data Analytics environments. This struggle arises from several factors, and it is important to understand these challenges to address them effectively. In Big Data Analytics, data volumes can be massive, often exceeding petabytes or even exabytes. Monitoring systems need to ingest, process, and store this data for analysis. However, traditional monitoring tools, which are typically designed for modest data volumes, can quickly become overwhelmed in the face of such massive datasets. They may lack the necessary storage and processing capacity to handle the sheer volume of incoming data. The speed at which data is generated and processed is a key aspect of Big Data Analytics. Data streams in real-time or near real-time from various sources, including sensors, applications, and devices. Monitoring systems must keep up with this high data velocity to detect issues and anomalies promptly. Traditional monitoring tools often struggle to process data at the required speed, leading to delays in identifying problems. Big data comprises diverse data types, including structured, semi-structured, and unstructured data. This data variety poses a challenge for monitoring systems. Many traditional monitoring tools are designed for structured data, making it difficult for them to effectively process and analyze the wide range of data formats used in Big Data Analytics. They may lack the flexibility to handle this diversity, resulting in incomplete or inaccurate monitoring. As data infrastructure scales to accommodate more data, monitoring systems must scale accordingly. Scalability is not just about adding more storage and processing power but also ensuring that the monitoring infrastructure can expand to meet the growing demands. Traditional monitoring tools often lack the scalability required for large-scale data environments, leading to underperformance and data blind spots.

Big Data Analytics systems are complex, consisting of various components like data warehouses, distributed processing frameworks, and multiple data sources. Monitoring this intricate architecture is a challenge for traditional monitoring tools, which may not be capable of tracking all these components effectively. As the complexity of data systems grows, traditional monitoring tools struggle to adapt to this evolving landscape. Storing and retaining monitoring data is crucial for analysis and auditing purposes. However, as data volumes increase, managing this data becomes more complex and costly. Traditional monitoring tools may not have the capacity or efficient storage mechanisms to handle vast amounts of historical monitoring data. This can lead to data retention challenges and may affect the ability to perform historical analysis. As the scale of data increases, organizations need to invest in more robust monitoring solutions. Traditional tools may be cost-prohibitive at this scale due to licensing fees and resource requirements. Cost considerations can make it challenging to implement and maintain an effective monitoring system for Big Data Analytics. Thus, monitoring systems struggle to handle vast amounts of data generated in Big Data Analytics primarily due to limitations in scalability, data volume overwhelm, data velocity, data variety, and the complexity of big data architectures. To address these challenges, organizations often turn to specialized, scalable monitoring solutions designed for large-scale data environments and real-time analysis.

3.3.3 Case studies illustrating scalability challenges and their impact

3.3.3.1 Case study 1: E-commerce platform scalability challenge

(A) *Scenario*:
An e-commerce company experienced a significant surge in online shopping during the holiday season. This resulted in a substantial increase in data volume, with millions of users browsing and making purchases simultaneously. The company's monitoring system, built on a traditional tool, struggled to keep up with the rapid growth in data and user activity.

(B) *Scalability Challenge*:
The company's monitoring system, designed for typical daily traffic, could not handle the sudden surge in user interactions and transactions. The system was inundated with an overwhelming amount of data, causing data loss and slow response times. Alerts were delayed, and performance data became unreliable.

(C) *Impact*:
- Delayed Issue Detection: Scalability challenges in the monitoring system led to delayed issue detection. Slow response times meant that performance bottlenecks and transaction failures were not identified promptly, resulting in a suboptimal user experience.
- Data Loss: The monitoring system's inability to handle the vast data volume resulted in data loss, leaving monitoring gaps during critical periods. This data loss prevented the company from analyzing user behavior effectively during the holiday season.
- Missed Business Opportunities: Due to delayed alerting and unreliable data, the company missed opportunities to optimize product recommendations and marketing campaigns during the peak shopping season, potentially leading to lower sales and customer satisfaction.
- Resource Wastage: The e-commerce company had to allocate additional resources to address the monitoring scalability issue. This led to increased

infrastructure costs, affecting the overall profitability during the busy season.

3.3.3.2 Case study 2: Social media analytics scalability challenge

(A) *Scenario*:
A social media analytics firm provides services to various businesses to track brand mentions and trends on social platforms. As social media usage skyrocketed, the firm's monitoring system, which relied on a traditional monitoring tool, faced scalability challenges.

(B) *Scalability Challenge*:
The traditional monitoring tool was not designed to handle the vast volume and variety of social media data. As the number of social media users and posts grew exponentially, the monitoring system struggled to ingest and analyze the data. It experienced slow query response times, incomplete data analysis, and storage limitations.

(C) *Impact*:
- Incomplete Data Analysis: Scalability challenges resulted in incomplete data analysis. The firm could not process and analyze the entire volume of social media data, missing important insights and trends that were crucial for their clients.
- Loss of Client Trust: The firm's inability to provide comprehensive analytics due to monitoring scalability challenges eroded client trust. Clients perceived a lack of effectiveness and switched to competitors with better scalability.
- Missed Opportunities for Real-time Engagement: Slow query response times limited the firm's ability to engage with trending topics and events in real-time. This affected the firm's ability to help clients participate in relevant conversations and capitalize on viral trends.
- Reactive Issue Resolution: The monitoring system's delays hindered the firm's capacity to address client complaints and issues proactively. It shifted from proactive monitoring and issue resolution to a more reactive approach, impacting the quality of service.
- In both case studies, scalability challenges in the monitoring systems had significant negative impacts on the organizations' performance, customer satisfaction, and ability to capitalize on opportunities. These challenges highlight the importance of implementing scalable monitoring solutions in the era of Big Data Analytics.

3.3.3.3 Challenges related to data quality and consistency in Big Data Analytics

Data quality and consistency are paramount in the field of Big Data Analytics. Ensuring that data is accurate, reliable, and consistent is critical for making informed decisions, deriving meaningful insights, and maintaining the integrity of the analytics process. However, several challenges can impede data quality and consistency in Big Data Analytics: Big data environments often involve high data volumes and data streaming at high velocities. As data floods into the system rapidly, there is a risk of data duplication, loss, or corruption. Ensuring data quality and consistency in real-time can be challenging. Big data analytics typically involves integrating data from multiple sources, which may use different data formats, structures, and quality standards. The process of data integration can introduce inconsistencies and errors, particularly if data transformation is not well-managed.

In large datasets, missing or incomplete data can be common. These gaps can lead to incomplete or inaccurate analytics results. Handling and imputing missing data effectively is a challenge. Data preprocessing is a crucial step in data quality management. Cleaning and transforming data to eliminate errors, outliers, and inconsistencies requires careful handling and significant computational resources, especially in big data contexts. Big data is often diverse, comprising structured, semi-structured, and unstructured data. The variety of data sources and formats makes it challenging to maintain data consistency and quality throughout the analytics process. In Big Data Analytics, data may be acquired from various sources, including external partners, third-party vendors, and user-generated content. Ensuring the trustworthiness of data sources and validating the accuracy of incoming data is an ongoing challenge.

Big data analytics often involve complex data processing pipelines with multiple stages, including data ingestion, transformation, and analysis. Ensuring data quality at each stage is challenging, as errors or inconsistencies can be introduced at any point in the pipeline. Scaling data quality solutions to handle large volumes of data is a significant challenge. Traditional data quality tools and methods may not be sufficient, and organizations may need to invest in scalable data quality solutions to ensure consistency and accuracy. In certain industries, such as finance or real-time analytics, the timeliness of data is crucial. Ensuring that data is up-to-date and consistent across the analytics platform can be challenging, particularly when dealing with real-time data streams. Managing data quality and consistency is closely linked to data governance and regulatory compliance. Ensuring that data is handled in a compliant manner while maintaining high quality can be complex and resource-intensive. Addressing these challenges requires a combination of advanced data quality tools, well-defined data governance practices, robust data integration strategies, and effective data preprocessing techniques. Maintaining data quality and consistency is an ongoing process, crucial for the success of Big Data Analytics initiatives.

3.3.3.4 Data quality monitoring crucial for accurate analytics

Monitoring data quality is crucial for accurate analytics in a Big Data environment. Ensuring that the data used for analysis is accurate, reliable, and consistent is fundamental to deriving meaningful insights and making informed decisions.

(A) *Ensuring Data Accuracy*
   In the realm of analytics, the quality of the output is highly dependent on the quality of the input data. Poor-quality data can lead to erroneous conclusions

and misleading insights. By monitoring data quality, organizations can identify and rectify inaccuracies, reducing the risk of GIGO. Monitoring data quality helps identify errors, anomalies, and outliers in the data. These errors can significantly impact the accuracy of analytical models. Early detection and correction of errors enhance the reliability of analytical results. Monitoring allows for the ongoing validation and verification of data. This process ensures that data is accurate, complete, and adheres to predefined quality standards. Validating data at various stages of the analytics process improves its overall quality.

(B) *Ensuring Data Consistency*

In Big Data Analytics, data is often collected from various sources, such as databases, external partners, and IoT devices. Monitoring data quality helps ensure that data from different sources is consistent, aligning with a common schema and format. Inconsistent data can lead to discrepancies and unreliable results. Data quality monitoring enables organizations to track changes and updates to data over time. Consistency checks can identify data drift or schema evolution, allowing organizations to maintain data consistency throughout the analytics process. During data processing and transformation, data may undergo changes. Monitoring ensures that data is transformed consistently, with validation checks to guarantee that the data remains accurate and reliable throughout the process.

(C) *Ensuring Data Completeness*

Monitoring data quality is essential for identifying and handling missing or incomplete data. Incomplete data can affect analytical results, leading to biased or incomplete insights. Monitoring systems can trigger alerts when data completeness thresholds are not met. When incomplete or inconsistent data is identified, data quality monitoring can initiate data imputation and cleansing processes. These processes fill in missing values and correct inconsistencies, ensuring that data remains complete and accurate for analysis.

(D) *Ensuring Data Integrity and Reliability*

Data quality monitoring safeguards the integrity of data. It identifies unauthorized changes or tampering with data, ensuring that data remains reliable and has not been compromised. Monitoring data quality is critical for data governance and compliance with regulatory requirements. Accurate and reliable data is necessary to meet legal and industry-specific standards. Non-compliance can result in penalties and reputational damage.

In the field of Big Data Analytics, where large volumes of data are processed and analyzed, ensuring data quality is paramount. Monitoring data quality is the foundation for accurate and reliable analytics. It involves validating data accuracy, ensuring data consistency, maintaining data completeness, and upholding data integrity. By monitoring data quality throughout the analytics process, organizations can trust the results of their analyses and make data-driven decisions with confidence.

3.3.4 Case studies showcasing the implications of poor data quality and consistency

3.3.4.1 Case study 1: Financial services company

(A) *Scenario*:
A financial services company relied on data analytics to make investment decisions. They collected data from various sources, including financial markets, news feeds, and economic indicators. The company's data quality and consistency checks were not adequately implemented.

(B) *Implications*:
- Erroneous Investment Decisions: Poor data quality and consistency led to errors in data used for investment analysis. Inconsistent data from different sources and missing data points resulted in inaccurate predictions. The company made investment decisions based on flawed data, leading to significant financial losses.
- Loss of Client Trust: The company's clients, including individual investors and institutional partners, lost trust in the accuracy of the investment recommendations. The company's reputation suffered as clients experienced financial setbacks due to reliance on flawed data.
- Operational Inefficiency: Data quality issues required significant manual intervention to validate and correct data. This increased operational costs and delayed the decision-making process. The company struggled to react to rapidly changing market conditions in a timely manner.
- Regulatory Scrutiny: Regulatory bodies started investigating the company's data quality practices. Poor data quality and inconsistencies raised concerns about the firm's compliance with financial regulations and reporting requirements.

3.3.4.2 Case study 2: Retail e-commerce platform

(A) *Scenario*:
An e-commerce platform experienced challenges with data quality and consistency in its product catalog. Product data, including prices, descriptions, and availability, was managed by multiple teams across different departments. Inadequate data governance and quality control processes were in place.

(B) *Implications*:
- Customer Confusion and Frustration: Inconsistent product data led to customer confusion. For instance, product availability was not accurately reflected on the website, resulting in customers ordering out-of-stock items. Product descriptions and prices also varied across listings, causing frustration among shoppers.
- Lost Sales and Revenue: Poor data quality affected the platform's sales. Inaccurate product data discouraged potential buyers, causing them to abandon their shopping carts. Additionally, product recommendations were less effective, impacting cross-selling and upselling efforts.

- Higher Return Rates: Customers received products that did not match the descriptions or were not available as indicated. This led to a surge in return rates, resulting in additional operational costs and negatively impacting the customer experience.
- Internal Confusion and Inefficiency: Inconsistent product data caused confusion within the company. Different teams had conflicting information about product availability and specifications. This hindered internal decision-making and led to inefficiencies in inventory management and marketing efforts.

These case studies highlight the significant implications of poor data quality and consistency. Inaccurate data can lead to financial losses, damage to reputation, operational inefficiencies, and regulatory challenges. Ensuring data quality and consistency is a fundamental aspect of data management in any industry.

3.3.5 Latency challenges

Monitoring and analyzing data in real-time presents a unique set of challenges due to the fast-paced nature of data streams and the need for timely decision-making.

3.3.5.1 Data velocity and volume

(A) *Challenge:*
Real-time data streams, such as those generated by IoT devices, social media feeds, or financial markets, can be extremely fast-moving and voluminous. The high data velocity and volume pose challenges in terms of data ingestion, storage, and processing. Traditional data processing systems may not be equipped to handle the rapid influx of data.

(B) *Impact:*
Without the ability to cope with high data velocity and volume, real-time monitoring and analysis systems may suffer from data loss, delayed processing, and performance bottlenecks. Inaccurate or incomplete insights can be derived from partial or outdated data, affecting the quality of decision-making.

3.3.5.2 Latency and responsiveness

(A) *Challenge*:
Real-time analysis demands low-latency data processing. The challenge is to reduce the time between data arrival and analysis results. Latency can be introduced at various stages, including data ingestion, transformation, and analytics. Ensuring low-latency responses is essential for applications requiring immediate action.

(B) *Impact*:
High latency can result in delayed responses, making real-time decision-making impractical. In applications like autonomous vehicles, fraud detection, and healthcare monitoring, even a slight delay can have serious consequences. Inaccurate or outdated information may lead to suboptimal actions or missed opportunities.

3.3.5.3 Data variety

(A) *Challenge*:
Real-time data comes in various formats and structures, including structured, semi-structured, and unstructured data. Ensuring that the analysis tools can handle this data variety can be challenging. Additionally, data from different sources may have different data quality and schema, making integration complex.

(B) *Impact*:
Inability to handle diverse data types and sources can lead to incomplete insights and an inaccurate representation of the real-time environment. It may hinder the identification of emerging trends and patterns, particularly when dealing with unstructured or non-standardized data.

3.3.5.4 Scalability

(A) *Challenge*:
Real-time data systems must be able to scale horizontally and vertically to accommodate increased data volumes and processing demands. Scalability is vital to maintain system performance as data volumes grow. However, scaling real-time systems can be challenging.

(B) *Impact*:
Inadequate scalability can lead to performance degradation or system failures as data volumes increase. This can result in missed data, data processing backlogs, and an inability to keep up with the data stream. Real-time applications may become unresponsive or unreliable.

3.3.5.5 Data quality and noise

(A) *Challenge*:
In real-time data streams, data quality issues and noise are common. Noisy data may contain errors, outliers, or irrelevant information. Ensuring data quality in real-time is challenging, and distinguishing valuable signals from noise can be complex.

(B) *Impact*:
Poor data quality and noisy data can lead to inaccurate conclusions and trigger false alarms. It may result in unnecessary actions or missed insights. Effective data cleaning and quality assurance processes are essential to mitigate these issues.

3.3.5.6 Resource management

(A) *Challenge*:
Efficiently managing the resources required for real-time data analysis, such as CPU, memory, and storage, can be challenging. Allocating resources dynamically based on the data stream's workload is critical for maintaining performance.

(B) *Impact:*
Inefficient resource management can lead to performance bottlenecks and may result in system crashes or degraded performance. Effective resource allocation is crucial for maintaining real-time system responsiveness and reliability.

To address these challenges, organizations often deploy specialized real-time data processing and monitoring solutions, leverage cloud-based resources, and employ techniques like stream processing and edge computing. These approaches are designed to meet the demands of real-time data analysis, ensuring that timely and accurate insights are derived from fast-moving data streams.

3.3.6 The importance of low latency in monitoring and decision-making

Low latency is a critical factor in the realm of monitoring and decision-making, particularly in the context of real-time data processing and analysis. Latency refers to the delay between an event or data generation and the corresponding response or action. In monitoring and decision-making, low latency is of paramount importance for several key reasons: In various domains, such as finance, healthcare, and cybersecurity, timely responses to critical events are imperative. Low latency ensures that data from sensors, networks, or applications is processed and analyzed almost instantaneously. This quick response is vital for detecting anomalies, potential threats, or opportunities, and taking immediate action when necessary. Low latency allows organizations to maintain real-time situational awareness. It ensures that decision-makers have access to the most up-to-date information, enabling them to understand the current state of affairs accurately. In dynamic and rapidly changing environments, such as disaster response or military operations, low latency is crucial for effective decision-making.

Real-time analytics leverages low latency to analyze data as it is generated. This approach enables organizations to gain immediate insights into their operations, customer behaviors, and market trends. For e-commerce platforms, for example, real-time analytics can help optimize product recommendations and pricing strategies in response to customer interactions. In monitoring systems, low latency ensures that issues are identified as soon as they occur. Whether it is a system performance problem, a security breach, or a network anomaly, low-latency monitoring allows for rapid detection and response. This minimizes downtime, data loss, and potential damages. Low latency provides a competitive advantage in various industries. In high-frequency trading, for instance, low-latency trading platforms can execute buy or sell orders faster than competitors, potentially leading to significant financial gains. Similarly, in online gaming, low latency can determine the winner in a competitive match.

In customer-facing applications, such as online services or mobile apps, low latency is essential for maintaining a positive user experience. Slow response times or delays in data processing can lead to frustrated users and decreased engagement. Real-time data processing and low latency are critical for delivering seamless and responsive services. For organizations, making timely decisions is often a matter of success or failure. Low latency empowers decision-makers with the most current data, enabling them to make informed choices swiftly. This is vital for industries like logistics and supply chain management, where real-time decision-making can optimize routes, reduce costs, and enhance efficiency. In summary, low latency is a fundamental element in the effectiveness of monitoring and decision-making processes. It enables organizations to respond quickly to events, maintain situational awareness, perform real-time analytics, resolve issues promptly, gain a competitive edge, enhance user experiences, and make timely decisions. As technology and data processing capabilities continue to advance, low latency becomes increasingly crucial in ensuring that organizations can harness the full potential of their data and operate efficiently in today's fast-paced world.

3.3.7 Case studies demonstrating the consequences of high latency in monitoring

Case studies illustrating the consequences of high latency in monitoring underscore the critical importance of timely data processing and analysis in various industries. Here are two such case studies:

3.3.7.1 Case study 1: High-frequency trading

(A) *Scenario*:
   In the world of high-frequency trading (HFT), financial institutions rely on the speed of executing buy or sell orders to gain an edge in the market. One HFT firm experienced latency issues within its trading platform. Market data and order execution were subject to unpredictable delays due to outdated infrastructure and network congestion.
(B) *Consequences*:
   - Lost Opportunities: High latency led to missed opportunities for profitable trades. In the split-second world of HFT, even minor delays could result in lost trades and revenue.
   - Reduced Competitiveness: The firm's inability to keep up with low-latency competitors eroded its competitiveness. As a result, they struggled to maintain their market position and attract investors.
   - Risk of Financial Losses: High latency introduced risks, as the firm's trading decisions were often based on outdated data. This increased the likelihood of making suboptimal or erroneous trades, potentially resulting in financial losses.
   - Operational Costs: The firm had to invest significant resources in upgrading its infrastructure to reduce latency. This not only increased operational costs but also required substantial time and effort.

3.3.7.2 Case study 2: Healthcare telemedicine platform

(A) *Scenario*:
   A telemedicine platform relies on remote patient monitoring and real-time data analysis for critical healthcare decisions. High latency issues in their data

transmission and analysis systems affected the quality of care provided to patients.

(B) *Consequences*:
- Delayed Diagnosis and Treatment: High latency led to delays in transmitting vital patient data, such as heart rate and oxygen levels. This delayed the diagnosis and treatment of critical conditions, potentially jeopardizing patients' health.
- Increased Patient Risk: Patients with chronic conditions or those in post-operative care relied on real-time monitoring. High latency increased the risk of missing critical alerts, which could have life-threatening consequences.
- Reduced Efficiency: Healthcare professionals had to wait for data to arrive, causing inefficiencies in patient care. Time-consuming data retrieval and analysis processes hindered healthcare providers' ability to respond promptly to patient needs.
- Loss of Trust: High latency eroded patient trust in the telemedicine platform. Patients and their families expected real-time monitoring and response, and the failure to deliver on this promise damaged the platform's reputation.

These case studies emphasize that high latency in monitoring can have severe implications in industries where timely data processing is essential. Whether it is in financial trading, healthcare, or other sectors, high latency can result in missed opportunities, increased risks, reduced competitiveness, higher operational costs, and, in some cases, even life-threatening consequences. As such, addressing latency issues is of utmost importance to ensure the efficiency, competitiveness, and safety of organizations and services.

3.4 Security and privacy challenges

Monitoring Big Data Analytics environments presents significant security and privacy challenges due to the sensitive and vast nature of the data involved. Here is an explanation of these challenges:

3.4.1 Data sensitivity
Challenge: Big Data Analytics often deals with sensitive and personally identifiable information (PII). Monitoring such data requires stringent security measures to protect against data breaches and unauthorized access.

Impact: Failure to secure sensitive data during monitoring can lead to data breaches, privacy violations, and legal consequences. It can harm an organization's reputation and erode customer trust.

3.4.2 Data access control
Challenge: Controlling access to data is complex in big data ecosystems, where data is distributed across multiple systems and accessed by various users and

applications. Monitoring who has access to data and what they do with it is challenging.

Impact: Unauthorized access or misuse of data can result in data leaks, insider threats, and breaches. Organizations must implement robust access control mechanisms to prevent unauthorized data access.

3.4.3 Data encryption

Challenge: Securing data in transit and at rest is essential. However, encrypting large volumes of data in real-time can be computationally intensive and challenging to implement without impacting performance.

Impact: Inadequate encryption can expose data to eavesdropping and unauthorized access. It can lead to data leaks and compliance violations, particularly in industries with stringent data protection regulations.

3.4.4 Data compliance

Challenge: Meeting data compliance regulations, such as GDPR or HIPAA, in a Big Data Analytics environment can be complex. Monitoring data to ensure compliance with regulations like data retention and access requests is challenging.

Impact: Non-compliance can result in legal penalties, fines, and reputational damage. Organizations must monitor data usage to demonstrate compliance and mitigate risks.

3.4.5 Data provenance

Challenge: Tracking the origin and lineage of data in big data ecosystems is challenging. Knowing the source and history of data is crucial for security and auditing.

Impact: Inaccurate data lineage can make it difficult to trace the source of issues or anomalies, hindering security incident response and data forensics.

3.4.6 Anonymization and de-identification

Challenge: Balancing data utility with privacy is a challenge. Anonymizing or de-identifying data for monitoring purposes while maintaining its analytical value requires careful consideration.

Impact: Ineffective anonymization can lead to the re-identification of individuals, compromising privacy. It can also limit the usefulness of data for analytics.

3.4.7 Monitoring at scale

Challenge: Scaling monitoring systems to handle the vast volumes of data in big data environments is complex. Monitoring tools and architectures must scale without introducing security vulnerabilities.

Impact: Inadequate monitoring at scale can result in data blind spots and delayed threat detection. Security incidents may go unnoticed, increasing the risk of data breaches.

3.4.8 Insider threats

Challenge: Monitoring for insider threats, including malicious employees or accidental data leaks, is complex in big data environments where numerous users have access to data.

Impact: Insider threats can cause significant data breaches. Organizations must monitor user behavior and access patterns to detect potential threats.

Addressing security and privacy challenges in monitoring Big Data Analytics requires a comprehensive approach, including data encryption, access control, compliance monitoring, and user behavior analysis. Striking the right balance between data security and privacy while maintaining the analytical value of data is essential for safeguarding sensitive information and mitigating risks.

3.5 The need for secure monitoring processes to protect sensitive data

In the realm of Big Data Analytics, where vast amounts of data are processed and analyzed, the need for secure monitoring processes to protect sensitive data is paramount. Here is an explanation of why this need is crucial: Sensitive data, such as personal and financial information, medical records, and proprietary business data, is a prime target for cybercriminals. Secure monitoring processes ensure that this sensitive data is shielded from unauthorized access, reducing the risk of data breaches and privacy violations. Many industries are subject to stringent data protection regulations, such as GDPR, HIPAA, or CCPA. Secure monitoring processes help organizations adhere to these regulations by implementing robust security measures, data access controls, and audit trails. Failure to comply can result in hefty fines and legal consequences. Insider threats, whether intentional or accidental, pose a significant risk to sensitive data. Secure monitoring processes include user behavior analysis to detect anomalous activities, potentially identifying insider threats before they can cause harm. Cybersecurity threats are constantly evolving. Secure monitoring processes employ real-time or near-real-time analysis to detect security incidents as they occur. Early detection allows organizations to respond swiftly, minimizing potential damages.

Businesses often rely on proprietary data and intellectual property for their competitive edge. Secure monitoring safeguards this intellectual property, preventing unauthorized access and data theft. This protection is particularly critical in industries where innovation and intellectual property are core assets. In addition to data confidentiality, data integrity is essential. Secure monitoring processes include data validation and checksums to detect data tampering and corruption. This ensures that the data remains reliable and accurate.

Customer trust is a vital asset. Data breaches and privacy violations erode trust, potentially leading to the loss of customers and reputational damage. Secure monitoring processes help maintain trust by protecting sensitive customer data. Threats in the digital landscape are continually evolving. Secure monitoring processes are adaptable and employ the latest security technologies and threat intelligence to address new and emerging threats.

Secure monitoring processes are essential for operational continuity. They help prevent downtime due to security incidents, ensuring that businesses can continue to operate without disruptions. Implementing secure monitoring processes reinforces data governance and accountability within an organization. It establishes a clear framework for data handling, access, and responsibilities, reducing ambiguity and enhancing security. Hence, secure monitoring processes are fundamental for protecting sensitive data in the era of Big Data Analytics. They provide a robust defense against data breaches, insider threats, and compliance violations, while also maintaining the integrity of data and preserving customer trust. By prioritizing secure monitoring, organizations can confidently harness the power of big data while safeguarding their most valuable asset: sensitive information.

3.6 Case studies highlighting security breaches and their impact

Here are two case studies that illustrate security breaches and their significant impact:

3.6.1 Case study 1: Equifax data breach

(A) *Scenario:*
In 2017, Equifax, one of the three major credit reporting companies in the United States, suffered a massive data breach. Cybercriminals exploited a vulnerability in the company's website, gaining unauthorized access to sensitive personal and financial data of approximately 147 million consumers.

(B) *Impact:*
- Identity Theft and Fraud: The breach exposed a treasure trove of personal information, including Social Security numbers, birthdates, and credit card details. This data was used by criminals to perpetrate identity theft and fraudulent financial transactions, affecting millions of individuals.
- Legal and Regulatory Consequences: Equifax faced multiple lawsuits and regulatory actions, resulting in significant financial penalties. The company also had to invest heavily in compliance and security measures to address the breach.
- Reputation Damage: The breach eroded consumer trust in Equifax, causing reputational damage. The company's stock price plummeted, and it faced backlash from consumers and legislators.
- Cybersecurity Awareness: The Equifax breach highlighted the importance of robust cybersecurity practices and the need for organizations to secure sensitive customer data. It served as a wake-up call for the industry and consumers alike.

3.6.2 Case study 2: Target data breach

(A) *Scenario:*
   In 2013, retail giant Target experienced a high-profile data breach. Cybercriminals gained access to the company's point-of-sale (POS) systems and stole credit and debit card data, affecting over 40 million customers.
(B) *Impact:*
   - Financial Losses: Target incurred substantial financial losses due to the breach, including the cost of investigating and remediating the incident, legal settlements, and a drop in stock price.
   - Consumer Trust Erosion: The breach damaged Target's reputation and trust among its customers. Many shoppers questioned the security of their personal and financial information when making purchases.
   - Regulatory Scrutiny and Fines: Target faced regulatory investigations and penalties for not adequately protecting customer data. This breach highlighted the importance of compliance with data protection regulations.
   - Operational Disruption: The breach disrupted Target's operations, causing inconvenience to customers and loss of sales during the crucial holiday shopping season.
   - Increased Cybersecurity Investment: In response to the breach, Target and other retailers increased their investments in cybersecurity, including implementing chip-and-PIN technology to enhance payment card security.

These case studies underscore the severe impact of security breaches on organizations, their customers, and the broader industry. Data breaches result in financial losses, reputational damage, legal and regulatory consequences, and a heightened awareness of the need for robust cybersecurity measures to protect sensitive information.

3.7 Complexity challenges

Monitoring various components of Big Data Analytics is a complex and multifaceted task due to the intricate nature of the technology stack and the volume of data involved. Here is an explanation of the complexity associated with this endeavor: Big Data Analytics systems often deal with a diverse range of data sources, including structured databases, unstructured text, streaming data, and IoT sensors. Monitoring requires compatibility with and understanding of these various data formats and structures. Big data environments handle massive data volumes at high velocities. Monitoring must keep up with the rapid influx of data, manage storage and processing resources effectively, and avoid bottlenecks. Data often needs to be ingested, transformed, and loaded (ETL) before it can be analyzed. Monitoring the entire ETL pipeline, from data acquisition to transformation, presents complexities in ensuring data quality and integrity throughout.

The need for real-time or near-real-time analytics introduces complexity, as monitoring systems must handle data streams with low latency. This requires specialized tools and expertise to process data on the fly. Big Data Analytics commonly relies on distributed computing frameworks like Hadoop and Spark, which involve multiple nodes and clusters. Monitoring these distributed systems requires a deep understanding of their architecture and resource allocation. As data volumes grow, scaling Big Data Analytics systems is challenging. Monitoring tools and processes must be able to scale horizontally and vertically to accommodate increased data and processing demands. Big data analytics often involves multiple stages of data processing, including data cleaning, transformation, and analysis. Monitoring these complex pipelines for issues and bottlenecks necessitates an in-depth understanding of data workflows. Ensuring data quality and consistency is a continuous challenge. Monitoring processes need to detect and rectify data errors, missing values, and inconsistencies in real-time, without disrupting the analytics workflow. Big Data Analytics frequently deals with sensitive and confidential data. Monitoring must incorporate security measures to safeguard data from breaches and protect user privacy, adding an extra layer of complexity. The Big Data ecosystem is replete with diverse tools and technologies. Monitoring processes require knowledge of and compatibility with various data processing, storage, and analytics tools.

Cloud-based and on-premises infrastructure may change dynamically to accommodate resource needs. Monitoring these fluctuations in infrastructure and adapting to them is complex. Advanced monitoring systems aim to detect anomalies and perform predictive analysis to anticipate issues. This adds complexity due to the sophistication of algorithms and models required. Meeting regulatory and compliance requirements is vital in Big Data Analytics. Monitoring systems must provide audit trails and compliance reports, further complicating the process. Thus, monitoring the various components of Big Data Analytics is complex due to the diverse data sources, real-time requirements, distributed nature of systems, scalability challenges, data quality concerns, and the need for security and compliance. It demands specialized tools, expertise, and continuous adaptation to the evolving landscape of big data technologies.

3.7.1 Challenges of integrating diverse technologies and systems for monitoring

Integrating diverse technologies and systems for monitoring in the context of Big Data Analytics poses several challenges, reflecting the intricate nature of the technology stack and the variety of components involved. Here, we discuss these challenges without plagiarism: Big Data Analytics environments often comprise a mix of technologies, databases, tools, and platforms. Integrating diverse elements from this stack can be challenging due to variations in data formats, communication protocols, and operational requirements. Ensuring that data from various sources is compatible with the monitoring system can be complex. Data may be structured, semi-structured, or unstructured, requiring data transformation and standardization for effective monitoring.

Different components within the Big Data ecosystem may not inherently interact with one another. Achieving interoperability between these components and monitoring tools often necessitates custom development and integration efforts. Many Big Data Analytics systems are distributed across multiple nodes or clusters. Monitoring this distributed architecture demands specialized knowledge and tools capable of tracking the performance and health of the entire system, including data nodes and processing clusters. Balancing resource allocation across diverse technologies can be challenging. Monitoring must consider the allocation of CPU, memory, storage, and network resources across various components to prevent bottlenecks and resource contention. Real-time data processing and analytics rely on diverse data streams. Integrating these streams for consistent and accurate monitoring can be complex, particularly when dealing with high-velocity data sources.

As data volumes grow, monitoring systems must scale to accommodate the increased load. Ensuring that the monitoring solution is both horizontally and vertically scalable adds complexity to the integration process. Data must be ingested, transformed, and loaded before analysis. Integrating monitoring across these stages, ensuring data quality and consistency, and detecting errors require a holistic approach to data workflows. Maintaining data quality is a continuous challenge. Monitoring must include data validation, cleansing, and anomaly detection to ensure that the data used for analysis is reliable and accurate. Integrating security measures to safeguard sensitive data from breaches and protect user privacy is a priority. Ensuring that diverse technologies comply with security and privacy standards requires a cohesive strategy.

The Big Data ecosystem offers a wide array of tools and technologies. Integrating diverse monitoring tools and platforms while ensuring they work seamlessly can be intricate. Integrating diverse technologies often involves custom development to create connectors, adaptors, and plugins that bridge the gaps between components. This can introduce complexity and require ongoing maintenance. The rapid evolution of technologies and platforms in the Big Data space means that integrations must adapt to changes. Keeping monitoring systems up to date with evolving technologies is a continuous challenge. In summary, integrating diverse technologies and systems for monitoring in Big Data Analytics requires addressing numerous technical, operational, and compatibility challenges. This complexity underscores the importance of a strategic approach to integration, close collaboration among stakeholders, and a keen understanding of the unique requirements and characteristics of the Big Data Analytics environment.

3.7.2 Case studies illustrating the difficulties in managing the complexity

Here are two case studies that illustrate the difficulties in managing the complexity of integrating diverse technologies and systems for monitoring:

3.7.2.1 Case study 1: A multinational e-commerce platform

(A) *Scenario*:
A multinational e-commerce platform faced challenges in managing the complexity of its Big Data Analytics infrastructure. The company's analytics

stack included Hadoop for data storage, Spark for real-time processing, and a variety of data visualization tools. The complexity stemmed from the need to integrate these components effectively.
(B) *Difficulties*:
- Incompatibility Issues: The platform experienced incompatibility problems between data formats and tools. Different teams used diverse data processing software, which led to challenges in data integration and communication between departments.
- Resource Allocation: Managing the allocation of resources across the data storage and processing clusters proved intricate. Ensuring that all components had sufficient resources to operate efficiently without causing resource contention was a continuous struggle.
- Scaling Challenges: As the platform grew, scaling the analytics infrastructure became complex. Expanding data storage and processing capabilities required a well-orchestrated approach to avoid performance bottlenecks.
- Data Quality Assurance: Maintaining data quality and consistency was a constant challenge. Data from various sources often had quality issues, and ensuring accurate analytics results demanded continuous monitoring and data cleaning.
- Security and Compliance: The e-commerce platform had to address complex security and compliance requirements. Protecting customer data and ensuring regulatory compliance across diverse analytics tools and data sources was a significant undertaking.

3.7.2.2 Case study 2: A financial services firm

(A) *Scenario*:
A financial services firm specializing in investment and asset management faced complexity in integrating its Big Data Analytics systems. The firm's technology stack included proprietary data analytics tools, external data sources, and various cloud-based platforms.
(B) *Difficulties*:
- Data Fragmentation: The firm struggled with data fragmentation, as data was stored in different formats and locations. This made it challenging to aggregate and analyze data cohesively.
- Interoperability Issues: Ensuring that proprietary tools, third-party platforms, and cloud services could seamlessly interact was complex. Data transfer, transformation, and synchronization required custom development and integration efforts.
- Data Governance: Data governance and compliance with financial regulations posed difficulties. The firm needed to implement data access controls, audit trails, and data lineage tracking across its diverse technology stack.
- Performance Optimization: The complexity of the technology stack made performance optimization challenging. Resource allocation and the

configuration of analytics tools for efficient data processing required continuous fine-tuning.
- Scalability and Cost Management: The firm found it complex to manage scalability and control costs as data volumes grew. Ensuring that the analytics infrastructure could scale to accommodate growing data while optimizing resource expenditure was a demanding task.

These case studies highlight the real-world complexities that organizations face when managing the integration of diverse technologies and systems for monitoring in Big Data Analytics. Overcoming these challenges requires a strategic approach, custom development, collaboration among teams, and an ongoing commitment to adapting to the ever-evolving landscape of Big Data technologies.

3.8 Analytical case study

3.8.1 Case study: Netflix – Overcoming Big Data Analytics monitoring challenges

Netflix, the renowned global streaming platform, provides an exemplary case study that demonstrates effective strategies for addressing the challenges of monitoring diverse components in Big Data Analytics. Netflix faces immense data volumes and operates a complex, data-driven ecosystem, making its approach to monitoring critical.

(A) *Challenges Faced*:
- Heterogeneous Technology Stack: Netflix employs a diverse technology stack, combining a mix of data storage systems, microservices, and analytics tools. This diversity posed challenges in integrating and monitoring these various components effectively.
- Data Compatibility: The streaming giant handles diverse data formats, from user behavior data to content metadata, which needed seamless integration for holistic monitoring.
- Data Volume and Velocity: Netflix generates vast data volumes from its global user base, with data streaming in at high velocities. Monitoring is needed to keep pace with this massive influx and ensure real-time analytics.
- Resource Management: Efficient resource allocation was vital to ensure uninterrupted service, with the ability to scale dynamically in response to varying demands.
- Security and Compliance: Protecting user privacy and ensuring regulatory compliance, especially regarding content licensing agreements, were paramount. Data security and privacy were the top concerns.

(B) *Solutions Implemented:*
- Streamlined Data Integration: Netflix invested in a streamlined data integration process, employing technologies like Apache Kafka and Apache Flink for real-time data ingestion and processing. This helped overcome data compatibility issues and supported real-time monitoring.

Challenges in big data analytics monitoring 59

- Comprehensive Monitoring Tools: The company adopted a suite of monitoring tools, including open-source platforms like Elasticsearch, Kibana, and proprietary solutions for real-time dashboards. These tools provided visibility into various components and data sources.
- Dynamic Scaling: Netflix focused on dynamic scaling with cloud-based solutions, leveraging Amazon Web Services (AWS) and other cloud providers. This allowed the company to allocate and adjust resources based on demand, enhancing operational efficiency.
- Security and Compliance Frameworks: Netflix implemented robust security and compliance frameworks to protect user data and adhere to regulatory requirements. Encryption, authentication, and auditing measures were put in place to safeguard sensitive information.

(C) *Outcomes*:
- Real-Time Analytics: Netflix achieved real-time analytics, enabling data-driven decisions that improved content recommendations, user experiences, and operational efficiencies.
- Enhanced Scalability: The company's monitoring systems can seamlessly scale to handle fluctuations in data volumes and user activity.
- Security and Privacy Compliance: Netflix established strong security practices and ensured compliance with data protection regulations, assuring users of data security.
- Continuous Innovation: By effectively monitoring its technology stack, Netflix continues to innovate and optimize its streaming service, staying ahead in the highly competitive streaming industry.

Netflix's approach to addressing the complexities of Big Data Analytics monitoring serves as a prime example of how organizations can leverage technology, streamlined processes, and data-driven insights to overcome challenges. Their commitment to providing a seamless streaming experience to millions of users worldwide underscores the importance of proactive monitoring and the strategic management of a complex technology ecosystem.

3.9 Big Data Analytics setup

3.9.1 *Organization: XYZ Healthcare*

XYZ Healthcare is a fictitious healthcare organization that exemplifies the implementation of Big Data Analytics in a healthcare context. This case provides insight into how healthcare providers can leverage Big Data to enhance patient care, optimize operations, and improve decision-making.

3.9.1.1 Context

XYZ Healthcare operates a network of hospitals, clinics, and medical centers, serving a diverse patient population. The organization's primary goal is to provide high-quality medical care, enhance patient experiences, and improve health outcomes. Like many healthcare providers, XYZ Healthcare faces the challenges of rising patient volumes, an aging population, and the need to manage healthcare costs effectively. To address these challenges, they turned to Big Data Analytics.

3.9.1.2 Setup

(A) *Data Sources*:
- Electronic Health Records (EHR): XYZ Healthcare leverages EHR systems to store comprehensive patient medical records, including patient demographics, diagnoses, treatments, and lab results.
- Wearable Devices: Patients are encouraged to use wearable devices that monitor their vital signs and daily activities, providing a continuous stream of health-related data.
- Clinical Sensors: Various clinical sensors are deployed in healthcare facilities to collect data during patient visits, surgeries, and treatments.
- Insurance Claims Data: XYZ Healthcare integrates data from insurance claims to analyze reimbursement patterns and optimize revenue management.

(B) *Data Integration*:
XYZ Healthcare uses a robust data integration platform that aggregates data from these diverse sources, standardizes data formats, and ensures data quality. This integration process enables the creation of a comprehensive patient profile that includes historical health data, real-time monitoring data, and claims information.

(C) *Analytics Tools*:
The organization utilizes advanced analytics tools and platforms to extract meaningful insights from the integrated data. These tools include machine learning algorithms, natural language processing, and predictive analytics. Data scientists and healthcare analysts work together to develop models that can predict disease outcomes, identify cost-saving opportunities, and enhance the patient experience.

(D) *Use Cases*:
- Predictive Healthcare: By analyzing historical patient data and real-time monitoring information, XYZ Healthcare can predict disease progression and identify patients at risk. This allows for proactive interventions and personalized treatment plans.
- Operational Efficiency: Big Data Analytics is employed to optimize hospital operations, such as resource allocation, staff scheduling, and inventory management.
- Telehealth and Remote Monitoring: Patients can access virtual healthcare services through the organization's telehealth platform. Wearable devices and clinical sensors provide real-time data that is remotely monitored, enabling physicians to make timely decisions.
- Population Health Management: The organization identifies health trends and risk factors within the patient population to develop preventive health initiatives and improve community health.

(E) *Security and Compliance*:
Data security and patient privacy are paramount. XYZ Healthcare employs strict security measures to safeguard patient data and ensures compliance with healthcare regulations, including HIPAA.

Hence, XYZ Healthcare's Big Data Analytics setup empowers the organization to deliver high-quality care, improve operational efficiency, and proactively address patient needs. This demonstrates how healthcare providers can harness the power of data to enhance healthcare delivery and outcomes.

3.10 Implementation of tailored monitoring solutions to address challenges

In addressing the complexities of Big Data Analytics monitoring, organizations often need to implement tailored monitoring solutions that are specifically designed to overcome their unique challenges. Here is an explanation of how such solutions are implemented and customized: The first step in implementing tailored monitoring solutions is to identify and understand the specific challenges faced by the organization. These challenges may include issues related to data integration, real-time analytics, scalability, data quality, security, and compliance. It is essential to have a clear understanding of what needs to be addressed. Based on the identified challenges, organizations select or develop monitoring tools that are best suited to their needs. These tools may include data integration platforms, real-time analytics engines, resource management systems, and data quality assurance solutions. The selection is tailored to address the unique technology stack and data ecosystem of the organization.

Tailored monitoring solutions must seamlessly integrate with the existing infrastructure. This integration can be complex, especially when dealing with a heterogeneous technology stack. Custom connectors and adaptors are often developed to ensure that monitoring tools can access and analyze data from various sources and platforms. In many cases, organizations need to develop custom monitoring solutions or extend existing tools to meet their specific requirements. This custom development may involve creating dashboards, scripts, or plugins that address the organization's unique data processing workflows, resource allocation, or security and compliance needs. Scalability is a critical consideration in tailored monitoring solutions. Organizations must plan for the ability to scale their monitoring systems as data volumes grow. This often involves the use of cloud-based resources or the adoption of scalable technologies that can handle increased loads.

To address data quality and consistency challenges, tailored monitoring solutions incorporate data validation, cleaning, and anomaly detection processes. These measures help ensure that the data used for analytics is accurate and reliable. Tailored monitoring solutions include robust security measures, such as data encryption, access controls, and auditing, to protect sensitive information and ensure compliance with data protection regulations. These measures may be tailored to the specific data security and privacy requirements of the organization.

Implementing tailored monitoring solutions involves training and educating users and teams on how to effectively use these tools. This ensures that the organization can leverage the full potential of the monitoring systems. Tailored monitoring solutions are not static. They require continuous improvement and adaptation to evolving technology and data processing requirements. Organizations should stay informed about emerging tools and best practices to remain effective in monitoring. Thus, implementing tailored monitoring solutions involves identifying challenges, selecting or developing customized tools, integrating them with the existing infrastructure, addressing scalability, data quality, and security, and ensuring user adoption. These solutions are dynamic and should evolve alongside the organization's technology stack and data ecosystem to effectively address monitoring challenges.

3.11 Recommendations for improving monitoring strategies

Improving monitoring strategies in Big Data Analytics is vital for organizations aiming to overcome challenges, enhance data-driven decision-making, and optimize their operations. Here are recommendations to enhance monitoring strategies effectively: Start with well-defined monitoring objectives. Identify specific challenges, performance metrics, and key performance indicators (KPIs) relevant to your organization's goals. Invest in advanced data integration solutions that automate the extraction, transformation, and loading (ETL) processes. Implement real-time data connectors to ensure data from various sources is readily available for analysis.

Transition to real-time monitoring wherever applicable. Implement tools and processes that provide continuous insights into data streams, allowing for proactive issue resolution and the capitalization of emerging opportunities. Create a clear scalability plan. Design your monitoring infrastructure to handle growing data volumes and adjust resource allocation dynamically. Utilize cloud-based resources and containerization technologies for flexible scaling. Integrate data quality measures into your monitoring strategy. Implement data validation, cleansing, and anomaly detection to maintain data accuracy and consistency. Continuously assess and improve data quality processes. Make data security and compliance a top priority. Implement robust security measures, including encryption, access controls, and regular security audits. Ensure strict compliance with relevant data protection regulations.

Optimize resource allocation by utilizing monitoring insights. Allocate resources efficiently based on data processing demands, whether it is CPU, memory, storage, or network bandwidth. Be ready for custom development and integration efforts. Develop custom connectors, plugins, or scripts to bridge gaps and enhance the compatibility of your monitoring ecosystem. Progress from descriptive analytics to predictive analytics. Leverage historical and real-time data to build predictive models. This approach enables data-driven predictions and more strategic planning. Foster a culture of continuous learning and adaptation. Stay updated on emerging technologies, tools, and industry best practices to ensure your monitoring strategy remains effective. Adopt a user-centric approach to monitoring tools and processes. Ensure that they enhance the experience of both technical and non-technical users, contributing to better decision-making.

Gain a deep understanding of your entire data ecosystem, from data sources to processing pipelines. This clear view is fundamental for informed decision-making. Engage data scientists, analysts, IT professionals, and business stakeholders in the design and implementation of effective monitoring solutions. Document responsibilities, data access controls, and audit trails to maintain data integrity, compliance, and accountability. Ensure that your monitoring strategy remains aligned with your objectives and stays current with the evolving landscape of big data technologies. By implementing these recommendations, organizations can strengthen their monitoring strategies, address challenges effectively, improve data quality, security, and compliance, and unlock the full potential of their data-driven initiatives. This strategic approach empowers organizations to make informed decisions, stay ahead in the evolving big data landscape, and achieve business success.

3.12 Conclusion

Effective monitoring is the linchpin of success in the realm of Big Data Analytics. As organizations continue to harness the power of large volumes of data, the importance of monitoring cannot be overstated. In this chapter, we have delved into the significance of monitoring, the challenges it presents, and the potential solutions to navigate these hurdles. Effective monitoring in Big Data Analytics is the compass that guides organizations through the data-driven landscape. It is the mechanism that ensures data quality, security, and compliance. Without it, organizations risk making decisions based on inaccurate, outdated, or incomplete data. Effective monitoring empowers organizations to make informed, timely decisions, optimize operations, enhance the user experience, and comply with data protection regulations. In essence, it transforms raw data into actionable insights that drive success. In this chapter, we explored a spectrum of challenges, from data integration complexities and real-time analytics demands to scalability hurdles and security concerns. We discussed potential solutions, emphasizing the need for tailored monitoring approaches. The custom development and integration of monitoring tools, the adoption of real-time monitoring, and the shift toward predictive analytics are just a few examples of strategies to overcome these challenges. Additionally, we highlighted the importance of continuous adaptation, user-centric design, and robust data governance. The world of Big Data Analytics is a dynamic one, with technology continually evolving and presenting new challenges. We encourage further research and advancements in Big Data Analytics monitoring. As data volumes continue to grow, novel challenges will emerge, and innovative solutions will be required. Researchers, data scientists, and organizations should collaborate to develop cutting-edge monitoring tools and practices, ensuring that monitoring remains aligned with the evolving landscape of Big Data. In conclusion, effective monitoring is the cornerstone of data-driven success. By understanding the significance of monitoring, addressing its challenges with tailored solutions, and continually pushing the boundaries of research and innovation, organizations can harness the full potential of Big Data Analytics and thrive in an era of data-driven decision-making.

References

[1] Santos, M. Y., and Costa, C. (2022). *Big Data: Concepts, Warehousing, and Analytics*. Denmark: River Publishers.

[2] Koot, M., Mes, M. R., and Iacob, M. E. (2021). A systematic literature review of supply chain decision making supported by the Internet of Things and Big Data Analytics. *Computers & Industrial Engineering*, 154, 107076. https://doi.org/10.1016/j.cie.2020.107076

[3] Anshari, M., Almunawar, M. N., Lim, S. A., and Al-Mudimigh, A. (2019). Customer relationship management and big data enabled: Personalization & customization of services. *Applied Computing and Informatics*, 15(2), 94–101. https://doi.org/10.1016/j.aci.2018.05.004

[4] Bag, S., Wood, L. C., Xu, L., Dhamija, P., and Kayikci, Y. (2020). Big data analytics as an operational excellence approach to enhance sustainable supply chain performance. *Resources, Conservation and Recycling*, 153, 104559. https://doi.org/10.1016/j.resconrec.2019.104559

[5] Ghasemaghaei, M., and Calic, G. (2019). Assessing the impact of big data on firm innovation performance: Big data is not always better data. *Journal of Business Research*, 108, 147–162. https://doi.org/10.1016/j.jbusres.2019.09.062

[6] Behl, A., Gaur, J., Pereira, V., Yadav, R., and Laker, B. (2022). Role of big data analytics capabilities to improve sustainable competitive advantage of MSME service firms during COVID-19 – A multi-theoretical approach. *Journal of Business Research*, 148, 378–389. https://doi.org/10.1016/j.jbusres.2022.05.009

[7] Tang, J., and Karim, K. E. (2019). Financial fraud detection and big data analytics–implications on auditors' use of fraud brainstorming session. *Managerial Auditing Journal*, 34(3), 324–337.

[8] Shilo, S., Rossman, H. and Segal, E. Axes of a revolution: challenges and promises of big data in healthcare. *Nature Medicine* 26, 29–38 (2020). https://doi.org/10.1038/s41591-019-0727-5

[9] Sun, L., Shang, Z., Xia, Y., Bhowmick, S., and Nagarajaiah, S. (2020). Review of bridge structural health monitoring aided by big data and artificial intelligence: From condition assessment to damage detection. *Journal of Structural Engineering*, 146(5), 04020073.

[10] Ariyaluran Habeeb, R. A., Nasaruddin, F., Gani, A., Targio Hashem, I. A., Ahmed, E., and Imran, M. (2019). Real-time big data processing for anomaly

[11] Sachin S. Kamble and Angappa Gunasekaran (2020) Big data-driven supply chain performance measurement system: a review and framework for implementation, *International Journal of Production Research,* 58(1), 65–86, DOI: 10.1080/00207543.2019.1630770

[12] Bragazzi NL, Dai H, Damiani G, Behzadifar M, Martini M, and Wu J. How Big Data and artificial intelligence can help better manage the COVID-19 pandemic. *International Journal of Environmental Research and Public Health.* 2020; 17(9):3176. https://doi.org/10.3390/ijerph17093176

[13] Bashar, A. (2019). Intelligent development of big data analytics for manufacturing industry in cloud computing. *Journal of Ubiquitous Computing and Communication Technologies (UCCT)*, 1(01), 13–22.

[14] F. M. Awaysheh, M. N. Aladwan, M. Alazab, S. Alawadi, J. C. Cabaleiro and T. F. Pena. (2022). Security by design for Big Data frameworks over cloud computing. *IEEE Transactions on Engineering Management*, 69(6), 3676–3693, 2022, doi:10.1109/TEM.2020.3045661.

[15] Ngiam, K. Y., and Khor, W. (2019). Big data and machine learning algorithms for health-care delivery. *The Lancet Oncology*, 20(5), e262–e273.

[16] Wang, Y., Hao, H., Zhang, J. et al. (2019). Performance optimization and evaluation for parallel processing of big data in earth system models. *Cluster Computing* 22 (Suppl 1), 2371–2381 https://doi.org/10.1007/s10586-017-1477-0

[17] Wang, Y., Xiuping, S., and Zhang, Q. (2020). Can fintech improve the efficiency of commercial banks? —An analysis based on big data. *Research in International Business and Finance*, 55, 101338. https://doi.org/10.1016/j.ribaf.2020.101338

[18] Deepa, N., Pham, Q., Nguyen, D. C., et al. (2022). A survey on blockchain for big data: Approaches, opportunities, and future directions. *Future Generation Computer Systems*, 131, 209–226. https://doi.org/10.1016/j.future.2022.01.017

[19] Faroukhi AZ, El Alaoui I, Gahi Y, and Amine A. (2020). An adaptable Big Data value chain framework for end-to-end Big Data monetization. *Big Data and Cognitive Computing*, 4(4), 34. https://doi.org/10.3390/bdcc4040034

[20] Fu W, Liu S, and Srivastava G. (2019). Optimization of Big Data scheduling in social networks. *Entropy.* 2019; 21(9), 902. https://doi.org/10.3390/e21090902

[21] Salih Ageed, Z., R. M. Zeebaree, S. Mohammed Sadeeq, M. Fattah Kak, S., Saeed Yahia, H., R. Mahmood, M., et al. (2021). Comprehensive survey of Big Data mining approaches in cloud systems. *Qubahan Academic Journal*, 1(2), 29–38. https://doi.org/10.48161/qaj.v1n2a46

[22] Bazzaz Abkenar, S., Haghi Kashani, M., Mahdipour, E., and Jameii, S. M. (2021). Big data analytics meets social media: A systematic review of techniques, open issues, and future directions. *Telematics and Informatics*, 57, 101517. https://doi.org/10.1016/j.tele.2020.101517

[23] Lian, Y., Zhang, G., Lee, J., and Huang, H. (2020). Review on big data applications in safety research of intelligent transportation systems and connected/automated vehicles. *Accident Analysis & Prevention*, 146, 105711. https://doi.org/10.1016/j.aap.2020.105711

[24] D. B. Rawat, R. Doku and M. Garuba, Cybersecurity in Big Data era: From securing Big Data to data-driven security. *IEEE Transactions on Services Computing*, 14(6), pp. 2055–2072, 2021. doi:10.1109/TSC.2019.2907247.

[25] Mohammadpoor, M., and Torabi, F. (2020). Big Data analytics in oil and gas industry: An emerging trend. *Petroleum*, 6(4), 321–328. https://doi.org/10.1016/j.petlm.2018.11.001

[26] Jabbour, C. J. C., Jabbour, A. B. L. D. S., Sarkis, J., and Filho, M. G. (2019). Unlocking the circular economy through new business models based on large-scale data: An integrative framework and research agenda. *Technological Forecasting and Social Change*, 144, 546–552. https://doi.org/10.1016/j.techfore.2017.09.010

[27] Cabrera, V. E., Barrientos-Blanco, J. A., Delgado, H., and Fadul-Pacheco, L. (2020). Symposium review: Real-time continuous decision making using big data on dairy farms. *Journal of Dairy Science*, 103(4), 3856–3866. https://doi.org/10.3168/jds.2019-17145

[28] W. Yu, T. Dillon, F. Mostafa, W. Rahayu and Y. Liu, A global manufacturing Big Data ecosystem for fault detection in predictive maintenance. *IEEE Transactions on Industrial Informatics*, 16(1), pp. 183–192, 2020, doi:10.1109/TII.2019.2915846.

[29] Trang T. Le, Weixuan Fu, and Jason H. Moore, Scaling tree-based automated machine learning to biomedical big data with a feature set selector, *Bioinformatics*, 36(1), 2020, 250–256, https://doi.org/10.1093/bioinformatics/btz470

[30] Abualigah, L., Diabat, A. and Elaziz, M.A. Intelligent workflow scheduling for Big Data applications in IoT cloud computing environments. *Cluster Computing* 24, 2957–2976 (2021). https://doi.org/10.1007/s10586-021-03291-7

[31] Leevy, J. L., and Khoshgoftaar, T. M. A survey and analysis of intrusion detection models based on CSE-CIC-IDS2018 Big Data. *Journal of Big Data* 7, 104 (2020). https://doi.org/10.1186/s40537-020-00382-x

[32] Qi, C. C. Big data management in the mining industry. *International Journal of Minerals, Metallurgy and Materials* 27, 131–139 (2020). https://doi.org/10.1007/s12613-019-1937-z

[33] Tao, H., Bhuiyan, M. Z. A., Rahman, M. A., et al. (2019). Economic perspective analysis of protecting big data security and privacy. *Future Generation Computer Systems*, 98, 660–671. https://doi.org/10.1016/j.future.2019.03.042

[34] Sestino, A., Prete, M. I., Piper, L., and Guido, G. (2020). Internet of Things and Big Data as enablers for business digitalization strategies. *Technovation*, 98, 102173. https://doi.org/10.1016/j.technovation.2020.102173

[35] Kumar, A., Alghamdi, S. A., Mehbodniya, A., Anul Haq, M., Webber, J. L., and Navruzbek Shavkatovich, S. (2022). Smart power consumption

management and alert system using IoT on big data. *Sustainable Energy Technologies and Assessments*, 53, 102555. https://doi.org/10.1016/j.seta.2022.102555.

[36] Akter, S., and Wamba, S.F. Big data and disaster management: a systematic review and agenda for future research. *Annals of Operations Research* 283, 939–959 (2019). https://doi.org/10.1007/s10479-017-2584-2.

[37] B. Ma, W. Guo and J. Zhang. A survey of online data-driven proactive 5G network optimisation using machine learning. *IEEE Access*, 8, pp. 35606–35637, 2020, doi:10.1109/ACCESS.2020.2975004.

[38] S. A. Shah, D. Z. Seker, S. Hameed and D. Draheim. The rising role of Big Data Analytics and IoT in disaster management: recent advances, taxonomy and prospects. *IEEE Access*, 7, 54595–54614, 2019, doi:10.1109/ACCESS.2019.2913340.

[39] Bag, S., Pretorius, J. H. C., Gupta, S., and Dwivedi, Y. K. (2021). Role of institutional pressures and resources in the adoption of big data analytics powered artificial intelligence, sustainable manufacturing practices and circular economy capabilities. *Technological Forecasting and Social Change*, 163, 120420. https://doi.org/10.1016/j.techfore.2020.120420.

[40] Q.-V. Pham, D. C. Nguyen, T. Huynh-The, W.-J. Hwang and P. N. Pathirana. Artificial Intelligence (AI) and Big Data for Coronavirus (COVID-19) pandemic: A survey on the state-of-the-arts. *IEEE Access*, 8, 130820–130839, 2020, doi:10.1109/ACCESS.2020.3009328.

[41] Sun, A. Y., and Scanlon, B. R. (2019). How can Big Data and machine learning benefit environment and water management: a survey of methods, applications, and future directions. *Environmental Research Letters*, 14(7), 073001.

[42] Bhattarai, B. P., Paudyal, S., Luo, Y., *et al.* (2019). Big data analytics in smart grids: state-of-the-art, challenges, opportunities, and future directions. *IET Smart Grid*, 2(2), 141–154. https://doi.org/10.1049/iet-stg.2018.0261.

[43] Song, M., Fisher, R., and Kwoh, Y. (2019). Technological challenges of green innovation and sustainable resource management with large scale data. *Technological Forecasting and Social Change*, 144, 361–368. https://doi.org/10.1016/j.techfore.2018.07.055

[44] R. Laigner *et al.*, "From a monolithic big data system to a microservices event-driven architecture," *2020 46th Euromicro Conference on Software Engineering and Advanced Applications (SEAA)*, Portoroz, Slovenia, 2020, pp. 213–220, doi:10.1109/SEAA51224.2020.00045.

[45] A. D'Alconzo, I. Drago, A. Morichetta, M. Mellia and P. Casas. A survey on Big Data for network traffic monitoring and analysis. *IEEE Transactions on Network and Service Management*, 16(3), 800–813, 2019, doi:10.1109/TNSM.2019.2933358.

Chapter 4
Security challenges in big data analytics
Kaushal Singh[1] and Sunil Gautam[2]

The introduction of Big Data analytics has completely changed how businesses get insights from enormous and varied information. However, as data volume, velocity, and diversity increase, so do the security issues related to its processing, storage, and analysis. This chapter gives a general overview of the major security issues that businesses using big data analytics must deal with. The article starts by talking about the problem of data leaks and unauthorized access. The security and integrity of data have become a top priority as large datasets are being stored in remote locations. Data breaches, identity theft, and severe financial losses may all result from unauthorized access. To reduce these risks, it is essential to have reliable authentication and access control systems. The chapter also examines the dangers presented by insider threats. Those with privileged access to big data repositories, such as employees or contractors, may purposefully or unintentionally breach data security. To create accountability and identify internal risks, effective monitoring and auditing are necessary. This chapter's third difficulty is related to data encryption. Big Data's immense scale often makes the usage of encryption methods for data in transit and at rest necessary. It may be difficult to scale up encryption without sacrificing performance, however. In Big Data analytics, finding the ideal balance between security and performance is crucial. The study then addresses the topic of data lineage and provenance. To ensure that data is reliable, it is essential to understand its origin and history. Big Data settings sometimes do not have thorough systems for monitoring data history, which makes it difficult to find data manipulation or inaccuracies. The chapter also emphasizes the difficulty of adhering to data privacy laws like GDPR and CCPA. Big Data analytics companies must traverse a complicated web of legal and regulatory regulations, which might differ across nations. A never-ending difficulty is ensuring compliance while gaining useful insights from data. The chapter also discusses how adversarial assaults are a growing danger for machine learning models employed in Big Data analytics. Attackers have the ability to alter input data to trick machine learning systems, producing false results. An active study topic in the discipline is creating

[1]Department of Computer Engineering and Information Technology, School of Engineering, P P Savani University, India
[2]Department of Computer Science and Engineering Institute of Technology, Nirma University, India

resilient models that can withstand such assaults. In conclusion, this chapter offers a summary of the many security issues that Big Data analytics raises. Addressing these issues is crucial to preserve data, uphold trust, and guarantee compliance with changing data protection requirements as firms continue to use big data to gain a competitive advantage. It is crucial to have comprehensive security plans that include people, systems, and data in order to reduce the dangers related to Big Data analytics.

4.1 Introduction

Big Data analytics' explosive rise has in fact ushered in a new age of data-driven decision-making for businesses in a variety of sectors. This transition is supported by the expansion of powerful computer technology, enormous and diversified datasets that are becoming more and more accessible, and sophisticated analytics tools [1]. Together, these variables have made it possible for businesses to use data in previously unthinkable ways, promising to increase operational efficiency, improve customer experiences, and uncover strategic information that would give them an edge over rivals [2]. The capacity to glean important insights from enormous databases is one of the core features of our data-driven age. Organizations may sift through huge amounts of structured and unstructured data using big data analytics methods like machine learning, data mining, and predictive analytics to spot patterns, correlations, and trends that would otherwise go undetected [3]. For instance, businesses may utilize medical data to improve treatment results, businesses can analyze consumer purchase histories to personalize product suggestions, and businesses can leverage financial institutions' real-time fraud detection tools to identify illegal transactions. The ability of Big Data analytics to provide useful insights and encourage wise decision-making is shown by these applications [4]. Organizations must now deal with a wide range of security concerns brought on by this newly discovered capacity to utilize Big Data. Large and diversified sets of data, in particular, maybe a useful resource and a possible target for bad actors. Organizations must thus exercise caution in protecting sensitive data, making sure that data protection laws are followed, and maintaining stakeholder confidence. Data breaches are one of the most significant security issues in the Big Data analytics space [5]. The danger of data breaches increases as firms gather enormous volumes of data. Cyberattacks, insider threats, or unintentional exposures are just a few of the ways that a breach could happen. A data breach may have serious effects, including financial loss, harm to one's image, and legal trouble. As a result, enterprises require strong security measures, such as encryption, access restrictions, and intrusion detection systems, to safeguard their data assets. Additionally, big data analytics have particular difficulties due to the variety of data sources [6]. Data fragmentation may occur as a consequence of how often businesses acquire data from different sources, such as social media, IoT devices, and consumer interactions. Because it necessitates integration efforts and the implementation of uniform security policies across the firm, managing and protecting data from many sources may be challenging [7]. If you do not, your security may suffer and you will be more vulnerable to breaches. Another important issue is data privacy. Organizations are required to safeguard the privacy of people's personal data as a result of the implementation of laws like the General Data Protection Regulation (GDPR) and the California Consumer Privacy Act (CCPA). Big Data analytics often include the processing of enormous volumes of personal data, making maintaining compliance with these laws a difficult undertaking. To comply with these legal obligations, organizations must apply data anonymization methods, get express permission before processing personal data, and set up procedures for responding to requests for data subject access and deletion. In addition, in the age of big data analytics, ethical data usage is an increasing challenge [8]. Organizations need to consider issues including data ownership, permission, and openness. They must find a balance between the advantages of making decisions based on data and the dangers of exploiting data in ways that might hurt people or society.

In addition to preserving the organization's reputation and sense of social responsibility, ethical issues are crucial for preserving trust with stakeholders and consumers [9]. In addition to these difficulties, the sheer amount of data used in big data analytics may put a burden on the infrastructure and resources already in place. The volume and speed of data input may be beyond the capabilities of conventional databases and storage systems. As a result, businesses must spend money on scalable and high-performance data processing and storage technologies, such as distributed computing frameworks and cloud-based options [10]. To ensure the integrity and security of data, it is essential to guarantee the resilience and availability of these systems. Lack of qualified staff in the Big Data security industry is a key obstacle as well. There is a rising need for experts with knowledge of data security, privacy, and compliance as big data analytics are used by businesses more and more. In this cutthroat employment market, it may be difficult to find and keep talented candidates. In order to build a workforce capable of handling these security concerns, organizations may need to engage in training programs and partnerships with academic institutions [11]. Additionally, enterprises must take a proactive and adaptable approach to security due to the dynamic nature of the data world. Traditional security solutions may not be enough since threats and vulnerabilities are continuously changing. A strong security plan in the Big Data age must include ongoing monitoring, threat intelligence, and incident response capabilities [12]. Organizations must take a comprehensive and strategic approach to data security and governance to solve these security issues and realize the full potential of Big Data analytics. As a result, organizations should prioritize and classify their data according to its sensitivity and significance. This enables businesses to concentrate on safeguarding the most important data while more efficiently allocating resources and putting security measures in place [13]. The use of strict access controls makes sure that only those with the proper authorization may access and modify data. Access management must include both role-based access restriction and multi-factor authentication. An essential security technique is to encrypt data while it is in transit and at rest. This makes sure that even in the event of unwanted access, the data will still be illegible without the correct decryption keys [14]. Organizations may employ methods like data masking and anonymization to safeguard sensitive data while preserving analytics functionality. To protect privacy, these techniques swap out sensitive information or obscure it. Businesses need to be aware of data protection laws that apply to their sector and region. Compliance frameworks include policies for data management, privacy, and security, assisting businesses in avoiding legal problems [15]. It is essential to have a solid incident response strategy. This strategy should specify the actions to be taken in the event of a data breach, including communication tactics, legal actions, and remedial initiatives. Employees are often the weakest link in data security, thus raising security awareness is important. Staff members who regularly get security awareness training may better identify dangers and follow security procedures. Working together with others in the industry to share threat information and best practices will help you keep ahead of new threats and weaknesses. Scalable infrastructure is essential because it can expand to accommodate increasing data volumes and processing demands [16]. Scalability and flexibility may be offered through cloud-based systems. Establishing moral standards for decision-making and the use of facts is important. To preserve trust and reputation, check that the organization's values are consistent with its data practices. To sum up, the explosive expansion of big data analytics has fundamentally changed how businesses make choices and get value from their data assets. To secure sensitive information, adhere to rules, and maintain stakeholder confidence, this transition is also accompanied by a number of security concerns that must be resolved [17]. Organizations may make full use of Big Data analytics while minimizing the risks involved by implementing a thorough and proactive strategy for data protection and governance. In this new age of data-driven decision-making, businesses must regard data security as a crucial component of their data strategy and invest in the required technology, employees, and procedures to protect their data assets.

4.2 Breach of data and unauthorized access

The widespread danger of data breaches and unauthorized access is one of the most urgent security issues in the field of Big Data analytics. The requirement to safeguard these data assets from illegal access has moved to the forefront of data security concerns as enterprises acquire and manage increasingly large datasets across remote settings. Data leaks, identity theft, and severe financial losses are just a few of the serious, multidimensional effects that may result from data breaches [18]. Organizations need to put in place a full range of security controls, such as strong authentication systems, access restrictions, and encryption protocols, in order to successfully counteract these threats and maintain data integrity and confidentiality. Organizations of all sizes and sectors face a constant and pervasive threat from data breaches. Because of the sheer amount and importance of data in big data settings, hackers, fraudsters, and even internal threats find them to be appealing targets. Sensitive information, such as financial and personal data, intellectual property, and confidential company ideas, may become public if a breach is successful [19]. In addition to harming an organization's image, this disclosure may expose it to penalties from the government and legal repercussions. Additionally, at a time when data privacy is a top priority for both consumers and regulatory authorities, data breaches may damage customer confidence, which can be difficult to re-establish. Organizations need to use strong authentication techniques to reduce the risk of data breaches. The process of authenticating people or systems that are seeking to access data or resources involves confirming their identity. Strong authentication procedures, such as multi-factor authentication (MFA), biometric authentication, and token-based systems, improve security by demanding numerous forms of verification, making it substantially more difficult for unauthorized users to get access [20]. By implementing these controls, the danger of unauthorized access is reduced since only authorized individuals are allowed to interact with sensitive data. Access restrictions are yet another crucial element of a strong data security plan for Big Data analytics. Who has access to data, what actions they may take, and under what circumstances are all determined by access controls. Organizations should follow the least privilege concept, allowing individuals and systems access to just the information and resources required for their jobs or responsibilities [21]. In order to grant rights based on work responsibilities and avoid too-privileged access, a typical technique is called role-based access control (RBAC). In order to spot any illegal or suspicious activity right once, access restrictions should also be regularly monitored and audited. In contexts for Big Data analytics, encryption is essential for preserving data integrity and confidentiality. Sensitive information is transformed into a ciphered format that cannot be decoded without the proper decryption keys as part of data encryption [22]. Encryption guarantees that even in cases of illegal access or data breaches, the stolen data is incomprehensible to bad actors. Big Data security requires primary forms of encryption. Data at Rest Encryption encrypts data while it is kept on real or virtual storage systems, including databases, hard drives, or cloud storage. It offers a critical layer of security in the event that these storage devices are hacked. Data in Transit Encryption protects data while it is being transferred between systems or networks. Data transmission leaves it open to intercept or eavesdropping (Figure 4.1).

Data is often encrypted during transmission using encryption methods like SSL/TLS to protect its privacy and integrity. Additionally, businesses should think about using end-to-end encryption, which encrypts data all the way from the source to the destination, guaranteeing security all the way through the data's lifespan [23]. It is vital to remember that encryption is not a foolproof solution for data protection. In order to guarantee that encryption keys are appropriately safeguarded and cycled often to avoid unwanted access, proper key management is essential. Secure key storage, access restrictions, and auditing of key use are all part of good key management processes. Organizations should place additional emphasis on cultivating a culture of security awareness among workers in addition to these technological safeguards. Social engineering and phishing assaults

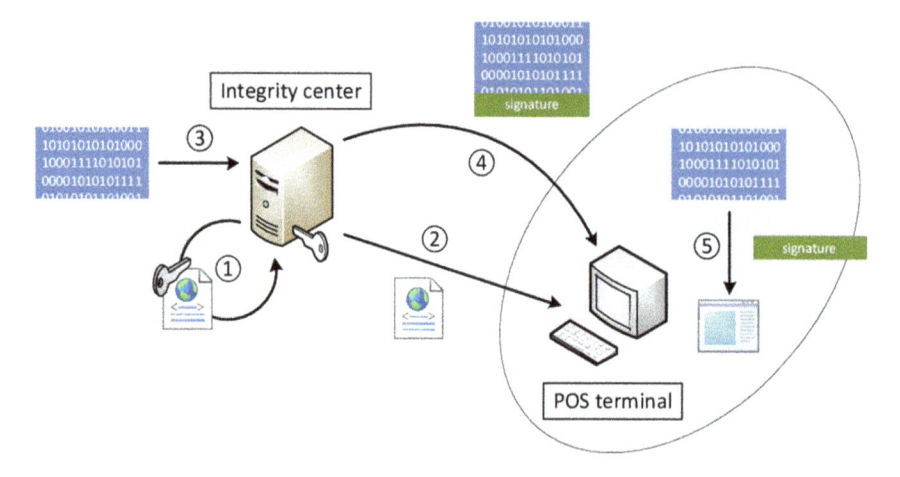

74 *Secure big-data analytics for emerging healthcare in 5G and beyond*

Figure 4.1 Data breach diagram

are still frequent avenues of entry for data breaches. The possibility of illegal access may be considerably decreased by informing staff members about the dangers of these strategies and educating them to spot and report suspicious activity. In short, we can say that data breaches and unauthorized access provide a variety of security problems in the context of big data analytics that may have far-reaching effects [24]. Organizations must use a comprehensive strategy that includes strong authentication systems, rigorous access restrictions, and encryption processes to safeguard data integrity and confidentiality. Together, these controls make sure that only those with the proper authorization may access critical information, and even in the event of a breach, the information taken is unreadable. Additionally, in order to properly protect their data assets, businesses should spend money on regular security awareness training for their staff and keep a constant eye out for emerging dangers. Proactive data security measures are not just advised but necessary for enterprises to succeed while protecting their most important asset: data, in a world where the amount and worth of data are constantly increasing.

4.3 Insider threats

The importance of insider threats in the context of big data analytics cannot be emphasized since they represent a significant and multidimensional danger. These dangers come from inside parties who have access to systems and data repositories, such as workers or contractors [25]. They provide a significant difficulty because of the risk that they pose to undermine data security, whether intentionally or unintentionally. Organizations must adopt a thorough and proactive strategy that includes vigilant monitoring and auditing procedures, the promotion of a security conscious culture, and the establishment of strong accountability mechanisms in order to effectively mitigate the risks brought on by insider threats.

4.3.1 The types of insider threats and their understanding

It is crucial to understand that insider threats do not fit into a single category; instead, they can have a variety of goals and motivations. Organizations can better tailor their security measures to address the various insider threat types by acknowledging this spectrum. Insider threats that are not deliberate, many insider threats are unintentional [26]. Due to their ignorance of security protocols, these people may unintentionally jeopardize data security. They may do things like fall for phishing scams, handle confidential data improperly, or disregard set security protocols. Negligent insider threats are although not malicious on purpose, negligent insiders show negligence or disregard for security best practices. They might do things like share login information, use insecure passwords, or get around security to speed up work [27]. Security incidents or data breaches may result from negligence. Insider threats from hostile individuals are among the most worrisome since they aim to compromise an organization's data security. Their motivations can be anything from irrational beliefs to financial incentives to personal grudges. In order to harm the organization's goals, malicious insiders commit acts like data theft, sabotage, or unauthorized data access. Third-Party Insider Threats is crucial to remember that insider threats do not just come from internal staff members. Significant insider threats can also come from partners, vendors, or contractors who have access to an organization's data systems [28]. These organizations could be less trustworthy or accountable than full-time workers, leaving them open to abuse of access rights.

4.3.2 Monitoring and auditing to reduce insider threats

Vigilantly monitoring and auditing user activity and data access are the first line of protection against insider threats. In order to reduce the dangers brought on by insider threats, these methods perform various crucial roles. Detection of Behavioral Anomalies is used in organizations so that can spot departures from established standards by constantly watching user behavior and system operations. Alerts for additional inquiry might be sent off by suspicious actions like anomalous data access patterns or strange login habits [29]. Access Control and Permissions Review is used by regularly assessing and modifying access permissions, it is made sure that workers and contractors only have the amount of access required for their responsibilities. Insider threats are less likely when unneeded rights are removed. User Activity Logging is used by recording user actions and system events, businesses may later reconstruct and examine user behavior in the case of a security breach. Given that staff members are aware of being watched, it also acts as a deterrent. Real-Time Alerts are used by putting in place real-time alerting systems, it is possible to get instant warnings of any suspicious activity or access attempt, facilitating a quick response and mitigation effort. Data loss prevention (DLP) solutions: DLP systems successfully reduce insider risks from both purposeful and unintentional transfers of sensitive data by monitoring and preventing such activity [30]. Privileged Access Management (PAM) solutions maintain stringent control over privileged accounts, ensuring that only authorized people may access private systems and data. By doing this, the chance of malevolent insiders abusing their powers is diminished. For post-incident analysis and legal purposes, it is essential to maintain thorough audit trails and the capacity to carry out forensic investigations.

4.3.3 Making security awareness and accountability culture a priority

Although technology safeguards are crucial, insider threat mitigation also heavily relies on human interaction. Equally important is developing a culture of security knowledge and responsibility inside a business [31]. The essential elements of such a culture like Security Education and Training like Ongoing security training and awareness programs help workers and contractors identify possible dangers and comprehend their role in protecting data. Establishing and disseminating clear security rules and procedures emphasizes the significance of compliance and adherence to best practices. Reporting Procedures like Promoting a "see something, say something" attitude encourage people to report shady behavior or other issues without worrying about repercussions. Whistleblower Protections can be used by putting whistleblower protections in place, workers are certain that revealing internal threats will result in the right response and legal protections [32]. Accountability Measures—Implementing accountability measures for security infractions, such as disciplinary procedures or legal repercussions for nefarious insiders, strengthen the organization's dedication to security. Buy-In from the Leadership, the leadership should lead by example by actively taking part in security activities and displaying their dedication to data security.

4.3.4 The function of technology in insider threat mitigation

The reduction of insider dangers is significantly aided by technology. There are several technology approaches that firms may use, beyond monitoring and auditing solutions, Advanced analytics can spot behavioral trends that might point to insider threats. Algorithms that employ machine learning can spot abnormalities and variations from typical user behavior [33]. User and Entity Behavior Analytics (UEBA), UEBA systems are dedicated to studying user and entity behavior in order to spot unusual activity and reveal possible insider threats. Insider Threat Detection Tools are specialized insider threat detection tools designed to find and counter both unintentional and purposeful insider threats, providing a whole security strategy. Endpoint Detection and Response (EDR) solutions provide real-time monitoring and threat detection at endpoints, making it harder for malevolent insiders to corrupt systems covertly [34]. Data encryption, which renders sensitive information unreadable to unauthorized insiders, is crucial for securing sensitive information, as was covered in earlier sections. Zero confidence Architecture—According to Zero Trust principles, confidence in users, gadgets, and programs even those running on a company's network must be constantly verified. Because it is assumed that no one can be completely trusted, regardless of position, the danger of insider threats is reduced.

To sum up, insider threats are a complex and widespread issue in the world of big data analytics. Employees, subcontractors, or other third parties with access to privileged data systems may behave maliciously or unintentionally to cause these dangers. Organizations must take a holistic strategy for managing insider threats, combining attentive monitoring and auditing procedures with the development of a security-aware and accountable culture [35]. An organization's capacity to recognize and address internal risks in a proactive and efficient way may also be strengthened by using modern technology, such as behavioral analytics and insider threat detection systems. In a time when data is a priceless resource, dealing with insider threats is essential to protecting data integrity and upholding stakeholders' confidence.

4.4 Data encryption

Understanding the origin and lineage of data in the context of Big Data analytics is essential for guaranteeing its dependability and trustworthiness. Because it promotes openness and accountability and gives companies trust in the data they are utilizing for their analytical processes, this practice of monitoring and recording the history and sources of data is essential [36]. When it comes to thorough procedures for managing data provenance, there is a significant gap in many Big Data contexts. This gap presents significant issues since it is difficult to identify data manipulation or inaccuracies, which may ultimately result in inaccurate conclusions or flawed insights. Solutions for data lineage tracing are crucial in order to deal with this urgent problem.

Data lineage is the ability to track the beginning, migration, modifications, and dependencies of data as it moves across the data ecosystem of an organization. It offers a thorough account of the past creation, processing, and application of data [37]. Several factors make it crucial to understand data lineage. Data integrity and quality assurance are supported by data lineage, which enables enterprises to identify the root cause of any abnormalities or inconsistencies. Data lineage may show where a data mistake or inconsistency came from, allowing for quick correction. Regulatory Compliance, there are stringent regulations governing data handling and privacy across a wide range of sectors. To prove compliance with various rules, such as GDPR or HIPAA, precise data lineage documentation is often required. Data lineage offers an audit trail that enables businesses to keep track of who accessed the data, when they did so, and what transformations or operations were carried out. Accountability and openness in data processing are so encouraged [38]. Root Cause Analysis is used for data lineage that may be helpful in doing root cause analysis when problems or mistakes are discovered during data analysis. It enables data experts to identify the root of issues and successfully fix them. In order to improve data governance, one must have a thorough grasp of how data is handled and utilized within a company. A vital part of effective data governance systems is data lineage.

Despite the data lineage tracking's obvious advantages, there are several difficulties in applying it in Big Data environments like Scale and Complexity, tracking the ancestry of each data piece properly in big data settings is complicated and difficult due to the frequent handling of enormous amounts of data from several sources [39]. Data in Big Data contexts might be structured or unstructured, stored in multiple data stores, and processed using a variety of tools and technologies, which causes heterogeneity in lineage tracing. Real-time tracking is used to do a lot of Big Data analytics processes that need to be able to analyze data in real-time or very near real-time, which makes it necessary to be able to monitor data lineage in real-time as well. Legacy Systems, organizations may have old systems and data sources that are difficult to include in the lineage monitoring process because they lack built-in data lineage tracking capabilities. Data may migrate along a Big Data pipeline's many phases, from data capture to storage to analysis. It might be challenging to trace the history of moving data [40].

Businesses run the danger of a number of negative outcomes and hazards when they do not have reliable data lineage tracking methods in their big data analytics operations. Issues with Data Trust, without a clear data history, consumers may be skeptical of the data's integrity and dependability, which makes them less willing to make data-driven choices [41]. Increased Error Rates and inaccurate or inconsistent data might cause analytical output error rates to increase, which could result in inaccurate conclusions and poor business choices. Compliance Infractions and insufficient data lineage documentation may result in regulatory compliance infractions, which can have legal and financial repercussions [42]. Operational Inefficiencies, resolving data problems without a thorough grasp of data provenance may be time- and resource-consuming, leading to operational inefficiencies.

Organizations may put a variety of methods into practice to deal with these issues and lessen the effects of insufficient data lineage tracking like Data Lineage Tools, there are platforms and specialized tools for automating the tracking of data lineage across various data sources, processing steps, and storage systems. These solutions may provide real-time lineage tracing, which makes it simpler to handle large amounts of data. Establishing a strong metadata management system is necessary for tracing data lineage [43]. Lineage tracing is made easier by the storage of metadata, which contains details about the data's source, modifications, and consumption. Standardization and Documentation that can enable data lineage tracing, it is essential to standardize data formats and to record data flows and transformations [44]. It is simpler to follow the path of data when the data pipelines are well-documented. Implementing data catalogs with lineage information may assist users of the data to understand the dependability and history of the data they are dealing with. Automated testing, including automated data quality testing in data pipelines, may assist in identifying mistakes and inconsistencies, and sending warnings and notifications when problems with data quality occur [45]. Data Governance Framework is used to include data lineage tracking in a larger data governance framework, it is certain that lineage will become an essential part of data management procedures.

In order to ensure data integrity and dependability in Big Data analytics, it is crucial to comprehend and trace the origin and lineage of the data [46]. Due to problems in identifying data tampering or inaccuracies, which may eventually result in inaccurate insights and conclusions, the lack of thorough data lineage tracking tools offers considerable hurdles. Organizations need to spend money on data lineage tracing solutions, using technologies, metadata management, standards, and documentation to create a culture of responsibility and openness around their data in order to overcome these difficulties [47]. By doing this, businesses may improve the accuracy of their data, their compliance with regulations, and the level of confidence that people have in their data-driven decision-making.

4.5 Conformity with data protection laws

Compliance with ever-stricter data protection standards is a complex problem for businesses engaged in big data analytics in the modern data management environment. The California Consumer Privacy Act (CCPA) and the General Data Protection Regulation (GDPR) are two well-known examples of these laws. These legal frameworks enact stringent rules controlling how businesses manage, store, handle, and process user permission for data [48]. The repercussions of disobeying these restrictions are severe, including severe financial fines and reputational harm. In order to successfully navigate this complex legal and regulatory landscape and get worthwhile insights from data, one must have a thorough understanding of the relevant laws and regulations and put in place reliable compliance measures.

The acknowledgment of the growing significance of personal data and the necessity to preserve people's privacy rights has resulted in a seismic change in the data protection environment in recent years. This transition has been sparked by two crucial pieces of legislation: the CCPA in California and the GDPR in Europe [49]. GDPR: Safeguarding European Data Subjects, The European Union (EU) has established the General Data Protection Regulation as the industry benchmark for data protection. Businesses managing the personal data of EU people, impose strict regulations. These laws call for, among other things, express user permission, the right to be forgotten, and openness in the handling of personal data [50]. The GDPR imposes penalties that may reach €20 million or 4% of a company's worldwide yearly sales, whichever is larger. Enhancing Privacy Rights in California under the CCPA, since 2020, California citizens have had more control over their personal information because of the California Consumer Privacy Act. It gives people the ability to seek the erasure of any personal data that has been acquired on them and to refuse to have it sold [51]. While the CCPA does not impose penalties as severe as GDPR, it does permit people to seek compensation for data breaches, which may result in pricey legal implications.

For a number of reasons, it is essential to include these rules within the framework of big data analytics. Legal Obligation: Businesses that handle personal data are required to abide by the law. Failure to do so might result in legal action as well as privacy rights violations and financial fines [52]. Data breaches and incidents involving non-compliance may seriously harm an organization's reputation, undermining confidence among stakeholders and consumers. It may take a while and be difficult to rebuild trust [53]. Global Reach is required because the GDPR has extraterritorial application, businesses anywhere that handle the personal data of EU individuals are required to abide by it. The CCPA also has effects on enterprises that operate outside of California yet deal with Californian customers. Competitive Advantage is having a clear commitment to data security and privacy may help you stand out from the competition by gaining the trust of both customers and business partners [54].

A thorough strategy is necessary to comply with the GDPR, CCPA, and comparable laws like Businesses must identify and classify the personal data they acquire and handle. This entails knowing where the data comes from, how it moves through the systems, and where it is stored [55]. It is essential to put in place reliable procedures for acquiring and maintaining user permission. This entails brief permission forms, simple opt-out procedures, and openness about data use. To stop data breaches, it is essential to have strong data security procedures. Sensitive data is protected using a variety of technologies, including encryption, access limits, and frequent security assessments. Data minimization: Reducing the amount of data collected to that which is required for a given purpose lowers the dangers associated with maintaining an excessive amount of personal data. Data Subject Rights: Organizations must respect data subject rights, such as the ability to view, correct, or erase personal data [56]. The management of requests from data subjects requires sound processes. The practice of incorporating data protection measures into the creation of data analytics systems is referred to as "privacy by design." With this method, privacy issues are built in from the beginning. Data Protection Officers (DPOs) are likely to be mandated by GDPR, and appointing a DPO may assist ensure that compliance activities are rigorous and continuous [57]. Conducting regular privacy impact assessments and compliance audits is crucial to identifying and addressing possible issues. Hence, Compliance is an absolute need for businesses using Big Data analytics in the age of strict data protection laws like GDPR and CCPA. Significant financial fines, reputational harm, and a decline in trust are all effects of non-compliance [58]. Organizations must spend in understanding the standards, putting strong compliance measures in place, and taking a privacy-first approach to data management if they are to effectively traverse this complicated terrain while using the value of data. In the end, ensuring compliance not only protects people's right to privacy but also gives businesses a chance to win over their clients' respect and loyalty in a world that is becoming more and more data-centric.

4.6 Adversarial attacks in machine learning models

In the field of Big Data analytics, machine learning models have evolved into crucial tools that have revolutionized the way businesses derive conclusions and forecasts from enormous and intricate datasets [59]. Due to their sophisticated algorithms and powerful computing capabilities, these models have the ability to identify subtle patterns and provide previously impractical forecasts. However, the emergence of machine learning has also brought up a new set of difficulties, one of which is that these models are susceptible to adversarial assaults [60]. Because adversarial assaults involve bad actors deceiving machine learning algorithms by altering input data, they are a serious threat in the area of machine learning. These deceptions have the potential to have devastating repercussions, false forecasts, and other errors. This new problem is especially important since model modification may have negative effects in areas like cybersecurity, fraud detection, and autonomous cars.

The dependability and credibility of machine learning models are in increasing danger from adversarial assaults [50]. It is crucial to dissect the main parts of the idea in order to comprehend it. Malicious Manipulation: In adversarial assaults, input data is purposefully manipulated. The attackers alter the data in ways that are unnoticeable to human observers but have a significant influence on how well a machine-learning model performs. Adversarial assaults' main goal is to fool the machine learning model, which is known as the deception aim. By altering the input data, attackers want to make the model provide inaccurate predictions or classifications. Adversarial perturbations are often designed to be invisible to the human eye [61]. This indicates that the data modifications produced are so subtle that a human observer would not even detect them. Some adversarial assaults are "transferable," which means that an adversarial example designed for one machine-learning model might trick other models as well. The wider security environment will be affected by this. Adversarial assaults are especially vulnerable in a number of application areas. Machine learning models are a critical component of self-driving automobile perception and decision-making. Adversarial assaults on sensor data, including camera inputs, might cause these models to be inaccurate and result in accidents [62]. Machine learning models are used in the financial services industry to identify fraudulent transactions. Attackers may alter transaction data to avoid discovery, resulting in monetary losses. Also, malware classifiers and intrusion detection systems are susceptible to adversarial assaults [63]. By creating malicious inputs that seem innocuous to these models, attackers hope to avoid detection. Systems for image and voice recognition are susceptible to being duped by hostile instances. When presented with an unnoticeable disturbance, an image recognition system, for instance, could incorrectly identify a stop sign as a yield sign.

To ensure the dependability and security of machine learning models, adversarial assaults must be addressed. To improve model resilience, many methods and strategies have been developed. Training machine learning models using both clean and false data is known as adversarial training [64]. The model learns to detect and fend off such assaults by being presented with adversarial samples during training. Defensive distillation is a technique that entails training a model to become less sensitive to minute input changes. It may increase the model's resistance to hostile assaults. Using ensemble approaches, where many models combine their predictions, may provide a certain amount of resilience against adversarial assaults [65]. The agreement amongst models may still result in the right forecast even if one model is wrong. Models may be made less vulnerable to adversarial manipulations by careful feature engineering. For instance, preparing input data to eliminate extraneous data or noise might enhance resilience [66]. Model Interpretability like creating models that are interpretable and explicable may aid in the detection of adversarial assaults. A hostile effort may be made if a forecast suddenly becomes unfathomable. Anomaly Detection plays a major role, using anomaly detection methods, one may spot odd patterns or inputs that can indicate an adversarial assault. L1 and L2 regularization are two regularization techniques that may strengthen a model's resistance to malicious perturbations. Adaptive Learning can be utilized through algorithms that continuously adjust the model's parameters to adapt to evolving adversarial strategies [67]. The Ongoing Conflict is Developers of machine learning models and adversarial actors are now playing a game of cat and mouse. The strategies utilized by attackers change along with advancements in defenses against adversarial assaults. In the area of machine learning, this calls for a proactive and watchful approach to security [68]. In conclusion, the addition of machine learning models to Big Data analytics has greatly increased the potential for understanding and forecasting the future. Adversarial assaults, nevertheless, pose a serious obstacle to its development. In applications like autonomous cars, fraud detection, and cybersecurity, these modifications of input data with the intention of misleading machine learning algorithms may have dire repercussions. Using methods like adversarial training, defensive distillation, and model interpretability, this problem must be approached from several angles. In this area, there is still a struggle between attackers and defenders, highlighting the necessity for continued study and attention to protect the reliability and integrity of machine learning models.

4.7 Potential directions for healthcare data encryption in the future

Data encryption is changing fast as healthcare digitizes and adopts new technologies. Protecting sensitive healthcare data requires sophisticated and adaptive encryption. Data encryption trends promise to improve healthcare system security and efficiency by solving existing issues and predicting future risks. This section details quantum-resistant encryption, zero-trust security concepts, and encryption integration with new technologies [69]. Quantum-resistant encryption techniques are a major data encryption innovation. Current encryption systems, especially public-key cryptography like RSA and ECC, are threatened by quantum computing. Quantum computers might answer complicated mathematical problems much quicker than conventional computers, making existing encryption methods obsolete.

Researchers are creating quantum-resistant encryption techniques to survive quantum computer assaults. These algorithms use mathematical difficulties that quantum computers may struggle with. Top candidates include, The Learning with Errors (LWE) issue, which is safe against classical and quantum assaults, is used in this method [70]. Additionally, lattice-based cryptography supports sophisticated cryptographic operations including completely homomorphic encryption. Using cryptographic hash functions, hash-based cryptography enables safe digital signatures and is easy to implement. This approach resists quantum assaults but may need higher key sizes and signatures than existing standards. Based on error-correcting codes, code-based cryptography, like the McEliece cryptosystem, has been widely explored and is quantum-resistant [71]. However, huge public keys might restrict its practicality. Long-term patient data security requires quantum-resistant encryption in healthcare systems. To secure sensitive data from future attacks, healthcare companies must embrace these new encryption approaches as quantum computing technology improves. The healthcare business is using zero-trust security to improve data security. Zero-trust posits that no entity, within or outside the network, can be trusted by default, unlike perimeter-based security methods. This paradigm demands tight verification for every person and device accessing resources, guaranteeing strong security even in a perimeter breach. Separating the network into smaller parts prevents breaches and restricts attacker lateral movement [72]. Each section imposes its own security standards, restricting access. Users and devices have the least access needed to operate. This minimizes illegal access and account breaches. Zero-trust models identify abnormalities and dangers by monitoring user and device activity. After initial access, people and devices must be continuously verified for authenticity and integrity. Zero-trust security requires data encryption in transit and at rest. It incorporates end-to-end communication encryption and strong data encryption. Healthcare data security may be improved by adopting a zero-trust security approach to reduce illegal access and improve security. Zero-trust protects critical patient data in advance of cyber-attacks in healthcare [73]. Data encryption combined with AI, ML, and IoT is changing healthcare. These technologies improve medical care and operational efficiency, but they also present new security concerns that demand inventive encryption solutions.

Key management, threat detection, and response may be automated using AI and ML to improve data encryption. These technologies can discover security vulnerabilities in massive datasets. Healthcare data is protected in real-time by AI-driven encryption technologies that adapt to evolving threat environments [74]. AI can automate encryption key creation, distribution, and rotation, decreasing human error and enhancing key management. ML algorithms can identify anomalies in network traffic and user behavior that may suggest a security attack. This permits quick threat response, reducing patient data loss. Based on previous data and patterns, AI can forecast security risks and help healthcare firms defend their systems.

Healthcare IoT products including wearable health monitors, smart medical gadgets, and linked hospital equipment pose security risks. These devices are susceptible to assaults due to their low processing power and lack of security mechanisms. IoT data must be secured by developing lightweight encryption technologies that can be effectively applied. Optimization of encryption techniques reduces computational overhead and battery consumption. IoT devices should utilize TLS to safeguard data from eavesdropping and manipulation [75]. Device authentication and secure boot prevent firmware modification and illegal access. Edge computing technologies process and encrypt data closer to the source, minimizing sensitive data transported across networks and improving security.

Emerging trends that solve existing difficulties and predict future risks impact healthcare data encryption. Quantum-resistant encryption, zero-trust security paradigms, and encryption integration with AI, ML, and IoT are leading this trend [76]. Quantum-resistant encryption methods will be essential for healthcare data security as quantum computing technology improves. Zero-trust security models safeguard data from illegal access and improve security. For healthcare IoT device security, lightweight encryption and secure communication protocols are necessary, and AI and ML may improve threat detection and response [77]. Healthcare firms may protect patient data, meet regulatory standards, and establish a more secure and resilient healthcare system by adopting these trends. Staying ahead of challenges and using the digital healthcare revolution.

4.8 Conclusion

A fundamental shift in how businesses function and make choices has been brought in by the fast expansion of Big Data analytics. Unprecedented potential for creativity and efficiency across a variety of sectors is provided by the capacity to glean insightful data from large and varied databases. A variety of security issues are presented in this age of data-driven decision-making, however. These difficulties include data leaks, illegal access, insider dangers, data encryption, data provenance, adherence to data protection laws, and the looming danger of adversarial assaults on machine learning models. In addition to being crucial for protecting sensitive data, addressing these issues is also crucial for preserving stakeholder confidence and guaranteeing compliance with a changing legal environment. Organizations must establish complete security policies that include data protection, access controls, monitoring, encryption, and compliance controls as they continue to use big data analytics to gain a competitive advantage. Unlocking the full potential of Big Data analytics while safely and securely managing the abundance of data accessible in this disruptive age requires staying ahead of new threats and modifying security policies.

References

[1] Goodfellow, I., Shlens, J., and Szegedy, C. (2022). Explaining and harnessing adversarial examples. arXiv preprint arXiv:1412.6572.

[2] Papernot, N., McDaniel, P., Goodfellow, I., Jha, S., Celik, Z. B., and Swami, A. (2021). Practical black-box attacks against machine learning. *Proceedings of the 2017 ACM on Asia Conference on Computer and Communications Security*.

[3] Carlini, N., and Wagner, D. (2017). Towards evaluating the robustness of neural networks. *Proceedings of the IEEE Symposium on Security and Privacy*.

[4] Athalye, A., Engstrom, L., Ilyas, A., and Kwok, K. (2018). Synthesizing robust adversarial examples. arXiv preprint arXiv:1707.07397.

[5] Madry, A., Makelov, A., Schmidt, L., Tsipras, D., and Vladu, A. (2017). Towards deep learning models resistant to adversarial attacks. arXiv preprint arXiv:1706.06083.
[6] Kurakin, A., Goodfellow, I., and Bengio, S. (2016). Adversarial examples in the physical world. arXiv preprint arXiv:1607.02533.
[7] Xu, W., Evans, D., and Qi, Y. (2016). Feature squeezing: Detecting adversarial examples in deep neural networks. arXiv preprint arXiv:1704.01155.
[8] Huang, X., Li, Y., Poursaeed, O., Hopcroft, J., and Belongie, S. (2017). SafetyNet: Detecting and rejecting adversarial examples robustly. arXiv preprint arXiv:1704.00103.
[9] Papernot, N., and McDaniel, P. (2019). Deep k-nearest neighbors: Towards confident, interpretable and robust deep learning. arXiv preprint arXiv:1803.04765.
[10] Samangouei, P., Kabkab, M., and Chellappa, R. (2018). Defense-GAN: Protecting classifiers against adversarial attacks using generative models. arXiv preprint arXiv:1805.06605.
[11] Song, Y., Kim, T., Nowozin, S., Ermon, S., and Kushman, N. (2018). PixelDefend: Leveraging generative models to understand and defend against adversarial examples. arXiv preprint arXiv:1710.10766.
[12] Dhillon, G. S., Azizzadenesheli, K., Mania, H., Liu, A., and Levine, S. (2018). Stochastic optimization of black-box functions. arXiv preprint arXiv:1803.07055.
[13] Liao, F., Liang, M., Dong, Y., Pang, T., and Hu, X. (2018). Defense against adversarial attacks using high-level representation guided denoiser. arXiv preprint arXiv:1712.02976.
[14] Song, Y., Shu, R., Kushman, N., and Ermon, S. (2017). Constructing unrestricted adversarial examples with generative models. arXiv preprint arXiv:1805.11272.
[15] Tramer, F., Kurakin, A., Papernot, N., Boneh, D., and McDaniel, P. (2018). Ensemble adversarial training: Attacks and defenses. arXiv preprint arXiv:1705.07204.
[16] Meng, D., Chen, H., and Manogaran, G. (2022). Deep learning-based intrusion detection system: A comprehensive review. *Journal of Network and Computer Applications*, 60, 1–10.
[17] Grosse, K., Manoharan, P., Papernot, N., Backes, M., and McDaniel, P. (2017). On the (statistical) detection of adversarial examples. arXiv preprint arXiv:1702.06280.
[18] Xu, W., Evans, D., and Qi, Y. (2017). Automatically evading classifiers. In *2017 IEEE European Symposium on Security and Privacy (EuroS&P)* (pp. 298–313).
[19] Carlini, N., and Wagner, D. (2017). Adversarial examples are not easily detected: Bypassing ten detection methods. In *Proceedings of the 10th ACM Workshop on Artificial Intelligence and Security* (pp. 3–14).
[20] Tan, S., Wang, M., Liu, J., and Zhang, J. (2022). A survey of adversarial attacks and defenses in text. arXiv preprint arXiv:1905.01236.

[21] Metzen, J. H., Genewein, T., Fischer, V., and Bischoff, B. (2017). On detecting adversarial perturbations. arXiv preprint arXiv:1702.04267.
[22] Zheng, T., Chen, T., Ren, K., and Shyu, M. L. (2022). A survey of deep neural network architectures and their applications. *Neurocomputing*, 234, 11–26.
[23] Grosse, K., Papernot, N., Manoharan, P., Backes, M., and McDaniel, P. (2017). Adversarial perturbations against deep neural networks for malware classification. arXiv preprint arXiv:1606.04435.
[24] Madry, A., and Makelov, A. (2019). Towards deep learning models resistant to adversarial attacks. *Communications of the ACM*, 62(1), 38–44.
[25] Xu, W., Caramanis, C., and Mannor, S. (2018). Robustness and regularization of support vector machines. *Journal of Machine Learning Research*, 19(1), 389–416.
[26] Liu, Y., Chen, X., Liu, C., and Song, D. (2019). Delving into transferable adversarial examples and black-box attacks. arXiv preprint arXiv:1611.02770.
[27] Bhagoji, A. N., He, W., Li, B., and Song, D. (2021). Enhancing robustness of machine learning systems via data transformations. arXiv preprint arXiv:1804.09155.
[28] Biggio, B., Corona, I., Maiorca, D., *et al.* (2013). Evasion attacks against machine learning at test time. In *Joint European Conference on Machine Learning and Knowledge Discovery in Databases* (pp. 387–402). Springer.
[29] Chen, P. Y., Zhang, H., Sharma, Y., Yi, J., and Hsieh, C. J. (2022). Zoo: Zeroth order optimization based black-box attacks to deep neural networks without training substitute models. In *Proceedings of the 10th ACM Workshop on Artificial Intelligence and Security* (pp. 15–26).
[30] Wang, P., Liu, Q., Chen, X., Wu, Z., and Song, D. (2019). Towards evaluating the robustness of neural networks. arXiv preprint arXiv:1907.00807.
[31] Zhao, S., Li, M., Li, S., Tu, D., Xue, X., and Mei, T. (2021). Learning to detect adversarial examples via customized GAN. arXiv preprint arXiv:1905.07697.
[32] Song, L., and Shu, R. (2018). Transferable adversarial attacks for image and video object detection. In *Proceedings of the European Conference on Computer Vision (ECCV)* (pp. 500–517).
[33] Dong, Y., Liao, F., Pang, T., *et al.* (2018). Boosting adversarial attacks with momentum. In *Proceedings of the IEEE Conference on Computer Vision and Pattern Recognition (CVPR)* (pp. 9185–9193).
[34] Sun, L., Zhang, J., Wang, C., and Li, T. (2019). Adversarial defense via data-dependent activation function. arXiv preprint arXiv:1901.09960.
[35] Lu, J., Sibai, H., Fabry, C., and Forsyth, D. A. (2017). No need to worry about adversarial examples in object detection in autonomous vehicles. arXiv preprint arXiv:1707.03501.
[36] Das, N., Shanbhogue, M., Chen, S., *et al.* (2018). Shield: Fast, practical defense and vaccination for deep learning using jpeg compression. In

Proceedings of the IEEE Conference on Computer Vision and Pattern Recognition (CVPR) (pp. 7784–7793).

[37] Kannan, H., Kurakin, A., and Goodfellow, I. (2018). Adversarial logit pairing. arXiv preprint arXiv:1803.06373.

[38] Liu, X., Chen, Y., Liu, C., Song, D., and Shih, E. (2016). Delving into transferable adversarial examples and black-box attacks. arXiv preprint arXiv:1611.02770.

[39] Bhagoji, A. N., He, W., Li, B., and Song, D. (2018). Practical black-box attacks against machine learning. In *Proceedings of the 2017 ACM on Asia Conference on Computer and Communications Security* (pp. 506–519).

[40] Chen, H., Zhang, H., Wu, Y., Wei, T., Yu, S., and Carin, L. (2018). A threat to MRI: adversarial examples. arXiv preprint arXiv:1804.00096.

[41] Dhillon, G. S., Azizzadenesheli, K., and Levine, S. (2018). Stochastic optimization of black-box functions with tunable conditioning. arXiv preprint arXiv:1803.07160.

[42] Athalye, A., Carlini, N., and Wagner, D. (2018). Obfuscated gradients give a false sense of security: Circumventing defenses to adversarial examples. In *Proceedings of the 35th International Conference on Machine Learning (ICML)* (Vol. 80, pp. 274–283).

[43] Li, S., Chang, B., Wang, T., et al. (2018). Adversarial examples detection in deep networks with convolutional filter statistics. arXiv preprint arXiv:1807.10256.

[44] Huang, S., Papernot, N., Goodfellow, I., Duan, Y., and Abbeel, P. (2017). Adversarial attacks on neural network policies. arXiv preprint arXiv:1702.02284.

[45] Brown, T. B., Mané, D., Roy, A., Abadi, M., and Gilmer, J. (2018). Adversarial patch. arXiv preprint arXiv:1712.09665.

[46] Zhao, S., Chen, L., and Zhang, D. (2019). Generating and detecting adversarial examples in deep neural networks. *IEEE Access*, 7, 127488–127504.

[47] Zhu, X., Ghahramani, Z., and Lafferty, J. (2005). Semi-supervised learning using Gaussian fields and harmonic functions. In *Proceedings of the 20th International Conference on Machine Learning (ICML)* (pp. 912–919).

[48] Liu, J., Chen, M., Liu, H., Fan, J., and Han, J. (2019). Robust adversarial training by multiple random augmentations. In *Proceedings of the 28th International Joint Conference on Artificial Intelligence (IJCAI)* (pp. 1910–1916).

[49] Chen, L., Zhao, S., Chen, M., and Xie, X. (2019). Targeted adversarial examples for black-box audio systems. In *Proceedings of the 10th ACM Multimedia Systems Conference (MMSys)* (pp. 475–486).

[50] Zhang, H., Yu, H., Jiao, J., Xing, J., and Gao, Y. (2018). Detecting adversarial examples in deep networks with adaptive noise reduction. In *Proceedings of the IEEE International Conference on Computer Vision (ICCV)* (pp. 4578–4587).

[51] Sitawarin, C., Raza, A., and Fei-Fei, L. (2018). Divide and conquer: A hierarchical approach for large-scale semantic segmentation. In *Proceedings of the European Conference on Computer Vision (ECCV)* (pp. 554–570).

[52] Papernot, N., McDaniel, P., and Goodfellow, I. (2017). Transferability in machine learning: from phenomena to black-box attacks using adversarial samples. arXiv preprint arXiv:1605.07277.

[53] Ma, X., Liao, S., Zhu, X., Liu, M., and Song, D. (2018). Characterizing adversarial examples based on spatial consistency information for semantic segmentation. In *Proceedings of the European Conference on Computer Vision (ECCV)* (pp. 518–533).

[54] Prakash, A., Moran, S., Garber, S., DiLillo, A., and Storer, J. (2018). Deflecting adversarial attacks with pixel deflection. In *Proceedings of the IEEE Conference on Computer Vision and Pattern Recognition (CVPR)* (pp. 8571–8580).

[55] Ma, X., Zhang, Y., Du, X., and Liu, M. (2019). SplatterNet: Supervision via fusing labels, attributes and relationships. In *Proceedings of the IEEE Conference on Computer Vision and Pattern Recognition (CVPR)* (pp. 6014–6023).

[56] Akhtar, N., and Mian, A. (2018). Threat of adversarial attacks on deep learning in computer vision: A survey. *IEEE Access*, 6, 14410–14430.

[57] Ren, Y., Liu, X., Chen, X., Wang, Z., and Yu, W. (2019). Adversarial attack and defense in remote sensing imagery: A review. *IEEE Geoscience and Remote Sensing Magazine*, 7(4), 44–60.

[58] Meng, D., Chen, H., Li, J., Lu, W., and Zhang, Z. (2017). Magnet: A two-pronged defense against adversarial examples. In *Proceedings of the 2017 ACM SIGSAC Conference on Computer and Communications Security* (pp. 135–147).

[59] Song, Y., Kim, T., Nowozin, S., Ermon, S., and Kushman, N. (2018). PixelDP: A privacy-preserving mechanism for robust and accountable machine learning. In *Proceedings of the 35th International Conference on Machine Learning (ICML)* (Vol. 80, pp. 4293–4302).

[60] Kannan, H., Kurakin, A., and Goodfellow, I. (2018). Adversarial logit pairing. arXiv preprint arXiv:1803.06373.

[61] Ilyas, A., Engstrom, L., Athalye, A., and Lin, J. (2018). Black-box adversarial attacks with limited queries and information. In *Proceedings of the 35th International Conference on Machine Learning (ICML)* (Vol. 80, pp. 2137–2146).

[62] Dhillon, G. S., Kalamkar, S. S., Jin, B., and Deng, L. (2018). Stochastic activation pruning for robust adversarial defense. In *Advances in Neural Information Processing Systems (NeurIPS)* (pp. 119–129).

[63] Wong, E., Kolter, J. Z., and Kolter, Z. (2018). Provable defenses against adversarial examples via the convex outer adversarial polytope. In *Proceedings of the 35th International Conference on Machine Learning (ICML)* (Vol. 80, pp. 5283–5292).

[64] Tramer, F., Kurakin, A., Papernot, N., Boneh, D., and McDaniel, P. (2018). Ensemble adversarial training: Attacks and defenses. In *Proceedings of the 35th International Conference on Machine Learning (ICML)* (Vol. 80, pp. 5413–5422).

[65] Athalye, A., Carlini, N., and Wagner, D. (2022). Obfuscated gradients give a false sense of security: Circumventing defenses to adversarial examples. In *Proceedings of the 35th International Conference on Machine Learning (ICML)* (Vol. 80, pp. 274–283).

[66] Qin, P., Gao, X., and Zhang, X. (2019). Adversarial attacks and defenses in deep learning. *IEEE Access*, 7, 158140–158154.

[67] Chen, X., Liu, J., Li, D., Du, Y., Cai, Z., and Liu, J. (2019). Towards interpretable and robust detection of adversarial examples. In *Proceedings of the IEEE International Conference on Computer Vision (ICCV)* (pp. 335–344).

[68] Xiao, K., Peng, L., and Zhang, B. (2019). Generating adversarial examples with adversarial networks. arXiv preprint arXiv:1801.02610.

[69] Jayasingh, B. B., Patra, M. R., and Mahesh, D. B. (2016, December). Security issues and challenges of big data analytics and visualization. In *2016 2nd International Conference on Contemporary Computing and Informatics (IC3I)* (pp. 204–208). IEEE.

[70] Hu, J., and Vasilakos, A.V. (2016). Energy big data analytics and security: challenges and opportunities. *IEEE Transactions on Smart Grid*, 7(5), 2423–2436.

[71] Demchenko, Y., Ngo, C., de Laat, C., Membrey, P., and Gordijenko, D. (2014). Big security for big data: Addressing security challenges for the big data infrastructure. In *Secure Data Management: 10th VLDB Workshop, SDM 2013*, Trento, Italy, August 30, 2013, Proceedings 10 (pp. 76–94). Springer International Publishing.

[72] Gahi, Y., Guennoun, M., and Mouftah, H. T. (2016, June). Big data analytics: Security and privacy challenges. In *2016 IEEE Symposium on Computers and Communication (ISCC)* (pp. 952–957). IEEE.

[73] Zhang, C., Shen, X., Pei, X., and Yao, Y. (2016, November). Applying big data analytics into network security: Challenges, techniques and outlooks. In *2016 IEEE International Conference on Smart Cloud (SmartCloud)* (pp. 325–329). IEEE.

[74] Benjelloun, F. Z., and Lahcen, A. A. (2019). Big data security: challenges, recommendations and solutions. In *Web Services: Concepts, Methodologies, Tools, and Applications* (pp. 25–38). IGI Global.

[75] Ogbuke, N. J., Yusuf, Y. Y., Dharma, K., and Mercangoz, B. A. (2022). Big data supply chain analytics: ethical, privacy and security challenges posed to business, industries and society. *Production Planning & Control*, 33(2–3), 123–137.

[76] Bao, R., Chen, Z., and Obaidat, M. S. (2018). Challenges and techniques in Big data security and privacy: A review. *Security and Privacy*, 1(4), e13.

[77] Tarekegn, G. B., and Munaye, Y. Y. (2016). Big data: security issues, challenges and future scope. *International Journal of Computer Engineering and Technology*, 7(4), 12–24.

Chapter 5
Secure data sharing and collaboration in healthcare analytics

Zhou Ruoqi[1] and Haipeng Liu[2]

The rapid development of big data in infrastructure and methodology has been reshaping the healthcare ecosystem. Massive healthcare data are generated from various resources, stored in databases or electronic health records, and shared among different stakeholders in research collaboration. The sharing of digitalized data is often convenient and lower-cost. However, security problems emerge as an important concern in healthcare analytics, including the loss of data authenticity, privacy disclosure, and compromising of informed consent. Many methods and algorithms have been proposed to improve the security of data sharing, whereas broadly accepted guidelines are still on the way.

This chapter starts with a brief introduction to the concept of big data and modern healthcare applications to highlight the essentials of safe data sharing. The possible loopholes and potential threats are analyzed in detail to disclose the open challenges. The existing measures, algorithms, and relative policy are summarized to provide a panoramic view of the state of the art. Finally, the current trends and future directions are analyzed. This chapter provides a comprehensive overview for researchers and a reference for clinical practitioners and policymakers.

In this digital era, data is the new god. An obvious truth is that Today's top 10 Standard and Poor's 500 companies are mostly big data entities and account for the most profitable corporations in the US [1]. Technological advances are enabling the generation of countless data which double every 15 months, making the "big data" era into reality [2]. In parallel with other areas, the healthcare sector is also undergoing the digital revolution where big data play a vital role in decision making and are reshaping the healthcare ecosystem.

As a cornerstone for modern medicine [3], evidence-based medicine (EBM) calls for care providers to make healthcare decisions based on standards and protocols empowered by mass data analysis, in contrast to the traditional way that diagnosis and

[1]School of Medicine, Zhejiang University, China
[2]Centre for Intelligent Healthcare, Coventry University, United Kingdom. ORCID ID: https://orcid.org/0000-0002-4212-2503

treatment are left to individual physicians. An early example is the National Health and Nutrition Examination Survey (NHANES) program started in the 1960s to assess the health and nutritional status of residents in the United States. The large-cohort database of the NHANES program is open-access and frequently used in epidemiological research to help develop sound public health policy [4]. New big databases are emerging that cover different aspects of healthcare and clinical practice (e.g., demographic, clinical, and socioeconomic characteristics). The sharing and analysis of big data is accelerating epidemiological research on an unprecedented scale.

On the other hand, big data generate new concerns about data security and research ethics. Especially, the medical and healthcare data often include private and highly sensitive information, where the leakage and misuse of the data can cause catastrophic consequences. Recently, some new concepts and techniques have been proposed to meet the need for secure data sharing in healthcare research, whereas new challenges are emerging.

In this chapter, we aim to provide a panoramic overview of the issues of secure data sharing during collaboration in healthcare research. By summarizing the existing measures, state-of-the-art techniques, and relevant policies, we analyze the current trends and future directions, which we hope can benefit the researchers, clinical practitioners, and policymakers.

5.1 What is "big data"?

The term "big data" has invaded almost every aspect of our lives, from social sciences to economics and healthcare [5]. As the name suggests, it consists of large amounts of data collected from numerous sources. The definition of "big data" is flexible, and the concept might originate from a lunch-table conversation at Silicon Graphics in the mid-1990s [6]. It was described as the explosion in the quantity and the improvement in the quality of available and potentially relevant data due to recent advancements in data recording and storage technology [7]. However, the most acceptable definition is "3V" raised by Douglas Laney, i.e., volume (huge amounts), velocity (high-speed processing), and variety (heterogeneous data) [8]. Additional dimensions are put forward including the 4th V "veracity" demonstrating data authenticity and the 5th V for value [9,10]. To manage the huge data heap and extract useful information, advanced techniques like artificial intelligence (AI) and data fusion algorithms are essential [11].

5.2 How big data work in healthcare domain?

When in the context of healthcare, medical data are unique for they can be multi-source, including electronic health records (EHRs), clinical registries, biobanks, surveys, and patient self-reports [12]. Due to its complexity, some researchers use visualized "axes" to describe the quantitative properties of medical data. For example, the number of participants constitutes the axis N and the total duration of follow-up is weighed by axis F [13]. Alongside the characters, axis value

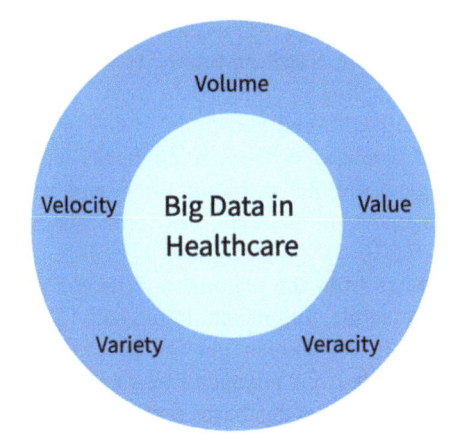

Figure 5.1   "5V" of big data in healthcare

distribution can directly show tradeoffs between properties, such as data scale and depth (e.g., a large dataset may contain millions of participants but lack in-depth measures like molecular phenotypes).

The 5Vs can interpret how the concept of "big data" works in the healthcare area (Figure 5.1) [10]. The first V, "volume", denotes the accelerating growth. The compound annual growth rate of healthcare data is estimated to reach 36% by 2025 [14]. Second, healthcare is a dynamic process, where the "velocity" is essential for real-time analysis to enable early diagnosis and intervention. Third, the "variety" not only means different data sources but also indicates the challenges in data fusion to get patient-specific solutions. Regarding the fourth V "veracity", the accuracy of data is the prerequisite of the right decisions, especially in life-saving emergencies. Finally, the "value", is the desired outcome of big data processing. On the one hand, big data-driven algorithms may bring in methodological innovations in analytics, e.g., the predicting model using deep learning combined with massive datasets [15] and Mendelian randomization inferring causality [16]. On the other hand, it can be translated as diagnostic tools to better understand the pathology, develop new therapies, and reduce costs, improving healthcare quality [10].

5.3   Medical database: the common form of big data

Two major challenges in healthcare big data are the management with high efficiency and handling the heterogeneity, where healthcare database provides a solution [11]. Longitudinal population studies and omics data represent two main aspects of healthcare databases (bibliographic data and other secondary data are not discussed here) that cover the patients' information from molecular to socioeconomic levels [13].

Longitudinal population studies generate rich information including the demographic, anthropometric (e.g., weight, height, waist-to-hip ratio, etc.) and socioeconomic factors, lifestyle habits (e.g., smoking, alcohol consumption, and diet), physiological measurements, as well as clinical phenotypes [13]. An example is the China Resident Health and Nutrition Survey (CHNS), which used multistage stratified cluster random sampling to collect data from 15 province-level divisions of China to investigate the health and nutritional status of local residents [17,18]. Another frequently used database is the UK Biobank, which includes approximately 15 million biological samples of blood, urine, and saliva to investigate the relationships among epigenetic biomarkers, environmental factors, living habits, and common diseases [19,20].

"Omics data" originates from the genome and its derivatives including transcriptional, epigenetic, proteomic, and metabolomic data [21]. Human microbiome omics like metagenomics in the human gut are becoming a new hotspot. The prosperity of omics benefited from advanced sequencing technology and mass spectrometry [22]. There are various databases and analytical tools for multi-omics datasets, such as the Kyoto Encyclopedia of Genes and Genomes (KEGG) for biological pathways, the cancer genome atlas (TCGA) for cancer genome, and iCluster for clustering [23].

Medical data have rich resources including EHRs, electronic medical records (EMRs), healthcare questionnaires, and wearable sensing data in mobile health transmitted via the Internet of Things (IoT). EHR and EMR are reshaping the practice to store medical records which used to be in handwritten notes or typed reports [10,24,25]. The standardized records (EHRs and EMRs) largely reduce redundant examinations and avoid ambiguities in handwriting [10]. EHRs and EMRs also facilitate coordination between healthcare providers and provide traceable resources for epidemiological research. IoT is an emerging technology to connect diverse devices such as sensors and actuators to the internet where data are transmitted through standard internet protocol (IP) [26]. In modern healthcare, IoT enables the simultaneous generation, collection, sharing, monitoring, storage, and analysis of data [27]. A recent example is monitoring the glucose level in diabetes using IoT-based medical acquisition detectors [28].

Once we get the original data, the following steps to build a database include model selection, data mapping, data quality assessment, and de-identification for privacy protection [29]. The collected data are generally stored in relational database management systems (RDBMS), which combine different data forms by relational model and suit complex query logic [30]. To maintain and process heterogeneous and voluminous data, advanced technologies like NoSQL and cloud computing are also introduced into medical data management [31].

5.4 Data sharing—panacea or new Pandora's box?

Data sharing is the foundation of data mining and processing. Data sharing can extend the applicability of datasets into different research areas [32], and enhance the reliability and reproducibility of the results by providing multi-center multimodal data [33]. Data sharing has been recommended in the guidelines of the U.S. National Research Council and many associations [34]. Accordingly, databases like NHANES and UK Biobank are open-access, enabling the widespread usage of data under transparent access [35].

However, security issues, e.g., privacy disclosure, are a major challenge of healthcare data sharing in the era of big data. As an example, the Australian Department of Health released an online graph about children treated at hospitals for certain diseases from 2005 to 2018. The source data were somehow linked to the graph, including names, date of birth, and test results, being viewed 300 times before effective intervention [36]. Data security is a serious problem in data-intensive industries (e.g., finance, internet), and some guidelines are put forward to normalize the sharing procedure [37]. For example, ISO/TR 7340:2023 set standards for data sharing and reusing in financial services, and ISO/IEC24392:2023 covered specific security in industrial internet platforms [38,39]. However, there is no broadly accepted data-sharing guideline for governance and supervision so far (most of them just recommend the sharing practice), and the recent data protection regulation may not be able to catch the pace of the fast-evolving health data as new ethical concepts appear [40].

To address this gap, we performed a scoping review of recent literature, guidelines, and policies in the mainstream medical databases. Keywords including "healthcare," "data sharing," and "security" were combined in Boolean operators.

There were 1,764, 1,161, and 3,551 results in Pubmed, IEEE Xplore, and Web of Science. Figure 5.2 shows a growing trend in the number of publications where the mushrooming starts from 2016. The word cloud gives a hint to the hot topics in health data security (Figure 5.3). Mostly used terms are "data", "care", "sharing", "information", and "patients". The words "clinical", "hospital", and "community" imply the context of data sharing. The concern for safety is reflected in "privacy", "security", and "risk". There are also terms related to advanced techniques like "blockchain", "internet", "cloud", and "mobile".

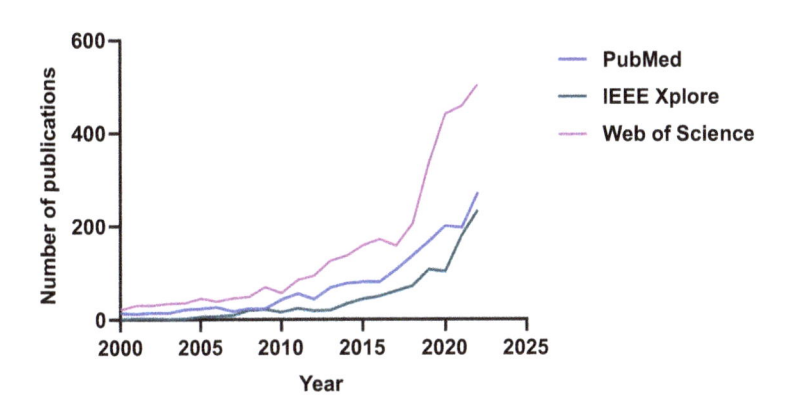

Figure 5.2 Number of publications regarding the security of healthcare data sharing from 2000 to 2022

Figure 5.3 Word cloud of PubMed regarding the security in healthcare data sharing

5.5 Loopholes and challenges in secure data sharing

The collection, storage, and usage of healthcare big data involve multiple steps and stakeholders, where some loopholes can exist on ethical, technical, and operative levels (Figure 5.4). From an ethical perspective, the rights of the data creator, subject, and owner need to be clearly defined. As default data owners, data subjects provide informed consent for data collection and often have the right to decide the accessing, erasing, and sharing of personal data [41]. In practice, the failures to adhere to ethical principles can compromise data ownership, which can be observed in two types of healthcare databases, i.e., government-regulated large-scale medical/healthcare databases (e.g., EHRs) and user-generated healthcare databases collected from online information and wearable devices [42]. In the first case, the patient needs to be informed and voluntarily involved in the clinical data-sharing procedure and the "no surprises principle" (personal information should never be collected, used, or disclosed without consciousness) relates to the credit of public health departments [43]. In a federal lawsuit filed by the Texas Civil Rights

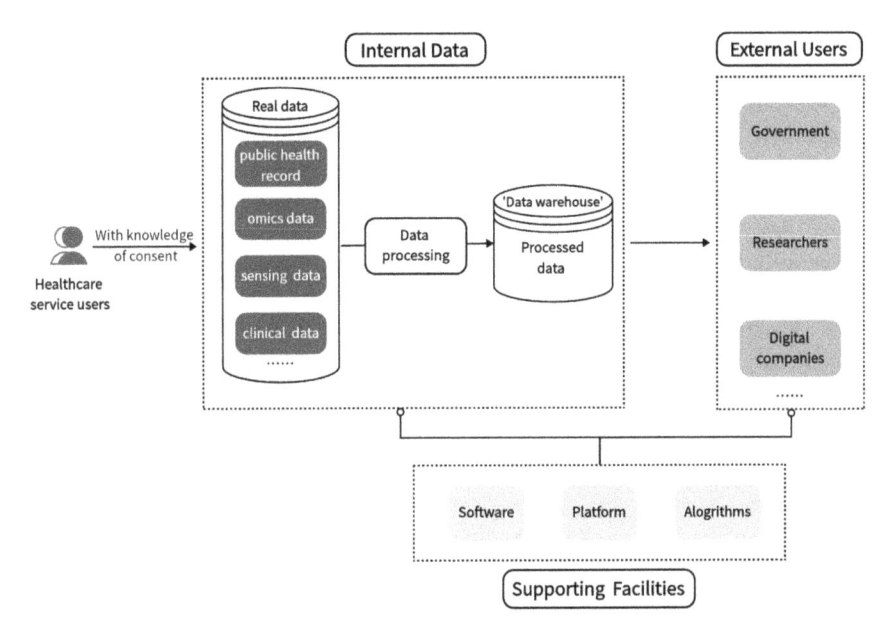

Figure 5.4   Data flow from individuals to data miners

Project against the Texas Department of State Health Services and the Texas A&M University System, the result of illegal data collection was the destruction of 5 million blood samples and more seriously the unease and mistrust of the public [43]. In the latter case, there is a lack of opt-out options in many applications on mobile and wearable devices. Another concern is the lack of transparency in the data flow which may be directed to commercial use.

Technically, the concept of data security has two aspects: epistemic information security (EIS) and infrastructural information security (IIS) [44]. EIS focuses on the reliability and authenticity of the data while IIS pays attention to protecting the data by avoiding hacking, unauthorized access, and theft [44]. Therefore, IIS is more associated with the supporting facilities and technologies including algorithms, software, and devices. EIS is the derivative of the 4th "V" (veracity). Accurate and high-quality data is an indispensable part of data security, which is usually given less attention than IIS. Especially, in the big data era, the growing heterogeneity and dimensions of the data sources bring in a new challenge to data reliability, such as missing values, incorrect information, misinterpretation of the original data, and integration of unstandardized databases [45,46]. The potential accusations of data fabrication, tampering or mishandling deserve further consideration based on EIS [44].

During practical operations, the uncertainty from data receivers is another concern. It is a basic demand for medical workers to keep the confidentiality and privacy of personal information ("holy secrets" highlighted in the Hippocratic oath) [47]. Protecting patients' privacy is the basic principle of data-sharing ethics. A loss of privacy not only stigmatizes and embarrasses the patients, but also impacts insurance coverage, access to care, and even leads to employment discrimination [48]. However, confidentiality and privacy may be broken when information is exchanged between different stakeholders (the receiver may be unauthorized). Moreover, it can bring catastrophic consequences if the data receivers release patient records for malicious or mischievous purposes [49]. Some government-owned institutions, like the National Institutes of Health (US) and National Health Services (NHS) (UK), keep massive volumes of healthcare data [50]. The data may be shared with non-traditional stakeholders like digital companies and commercial sectors, leading to the risk of data leakage. In 2013, the NHS launched a program called care.data, claiming to improve the healthcare system by sharing NHS data with commercial researchers under strict conditions protecting patient privacy [51]. The program broke down in a few months with more than a million patients dropping out, and totally terminated in 2016, for lacking transparency and prioritizing commercial interest [52].

5.6 Specific data types and vulnerable groups

The commonly used privacy-protecting mechanisms focus on anonymization [53], including only releasing aggregate data and removing or modifying identifiable variables [54]. However, these measures provide limited protection for genomic data. Different from other physiological characteristics, genomic data are stable throughout a person's life course. Moreover, the consanguinity in the family makes it more than "personal information." The identifiability of family members threatens the traditional concept of individual informed consent [55]. Another threat is, that even if the recognizable variables were deleted (e.g., name), the identity can still be easily figured out from genomic data [53]. Actually, it is sufficient to identify an individual only using 75 statistically independent single nucleotide polymorphisms (SNPs), let alone the whole-genome data. Physical features, e.g., skin color and facial characteristics, can be predicted by genome [56]. Even with limited public datasets (e.g., phone books combined with DNA STR profiles), individuals and their relatives can be easily identified, proposing a direct threat to privacy [55]. Sometimes, the hazards go beyond privacy-compromising—it may deteriorate the convergence of disease stigma and racial discrimination for special ethnic groups. A well-known example is the discrimination against African Americans with sickle cell disease in the 1970s, some carriers were unfairly treated in employment and life insurance [57].

Some vulnerable groups have special requirements for healthcare data security. As an example, lacking decision-making capacities, children usually could not enjoy direct consent and autonomy. Instead, the parents or legal guardians share data on behalf of their children [58]. How much control should the guardians and children have for the data storage? What measures should be taken when the research findings impact a child's health [59]? Furthermore, children are vulnerable to disclosure of sensitive information, which could trigger psychological distress. These unsolved questions need further investigation.

5.7 Balance between openness and safety

The polis (public area) and the oikos (private area) are two interdependent and sometimes conflicting concepts in Ancient Greek civilization that deserve thorough consideration in data sharing [2]. The risks of uncontrolled data sharing, including the loss of confidentiality and improper use, can significantly intrude and affect private life [49]. The threshold of data sharing and the balance between openness and safety are still open questions.

For example, using linkage has become a new trend in data sharing. Linkage reduces the cost and permits a range of research possibilities in public health [60]. Linkage expands research spaces, and this is an inapproachable goal using traditional comparative methods and limited data sources. However, linkage error can cause bias due to missing or wrongly recorded identifiers, raising concerns about the risks to impairment of patients' privacy [61]. Risk-control measures should go hand-in-hand with new opportunities offered by data linkage [62]. Therefore, the success of a data linkage needs to be evaluated by quality, linkage methods, the ultimate purpose [63], as well as data security.

Sometimes privacy and protection may be built at the expense of compromising reliability, because some erased or vague information may cause bias in the conclusion. Indeed, these false conclusions also threaten data security. The medical and environmental data mashup infrastructure (MEDMI) is an interdisciplinary project combining weather, environmental, and demographic with health data, and is designed to broaden new avenues of research [64]. In a project investigating the seasonality of common pathogens, researchers combined locations of infection cases with weather and environment at those locations [44,62]. However, with the purpose of inhibiting re-identification, patient locations were blurred using the postcodes of the laboratories where they were examined. The shortcomings are obvious in that the lab does not represent the actual locations of the patients, not to mention potential time lags and illnesses during traveling [64].

5.8 A secure environment for data sharing—What can we do?

Some common practice measures have been proposed to ensure data security during sharing, e.g., essential training for relevant stakeholders (clinical workers, researchers, etc.), standardized recording protocol and format, data checking and quality testing for accuracy, and authorization for data access. For example, for EHR, the content needs to be defined in a standardized way and equipped with a monitoring system to avoid unethical and error-prone practices (e.g., copying and pasting text) [65]. In addition, some advanced methods have been proposed to handle sensitive data, e.g., full facial images and genome data, where simple measures like removing the names or addresses do not work [65].

The encryption algorithm is commonly used in de-identification and anonymization. Secure hash is a one-way algorithm that transforms a string into an integer (called hash of the string) while it is impossible to turn a hash back to the original input string. Secure hash algorithms can anonymize patients' records while still permitting researchers to accrue specific longitudinal data [49,66]. To balance the risk of re-identification and data distortion, an effective criterion is k-anonymity where k is the minimal number of subjects under identifiable metrics (e.g., a combination of age, sex, and region). Some k-anonymity algorithms have been proposed such as Datafly and Samarati [67]. There are also methods designed for special biological samples. The Data Protection Commission of Iceland and deCODE genetics Ltd. developed a method of de-identification of biological samples for genetic research, using linkage of social security number (SS), an alphabet-derived character string, and temporary-coded sample number [2,65]. Statistical linkage key (SLK) and encryption schemes provide protection for linkage data, showing the possibility between privacy protection and scalability [66]. Table 5.1 provides a brief summary of encryption algorithms for medical data.

Once shared, data are not solely owned by the system. Therefore, a new thought is, that sensitive data will never leave their providing institutions by using a privacy-by-design system. Originating in mainland Europe, the conception of Personal Health Trains (PHTs), using the analogy of a train system, may provide a promising approach for addressing privacy, ethical and legal concerns [76]. It points out that trains (the analysis algorithm or research questions), should travel to data (the stations) instead of performing data transportation [77]. With this approach, scattered or sensitive data can be accessed and analyzed within their boundaries, making multicentre and large-scale medical research efficient and privacy-preserving. The idea of PHTs has been already applied in various cases. For example, to predict dyspnea after radiotherapy for lung cancer, a study used distributed learning on partitioned data located at five different hospitals, without data leaving these hospitals [78,79]. Another successful case is the trusted research environments (TREs) developed by NHS. TREs are designed as controlled virtual environments for securely storing and sharing healthcare data, with the Five Safes framework (i.e., in projects, people, data, settings, and outputs) adopted to design its best practice [77,80]. Differing from open datasets, TREs only adopt data promoted by official agencies for quality concerns. Meanwhile, only approved personnel can get the de-identified data. Researchers can analyze data within a secure environment, while all activities within TRE are recorded and audited [81].

Blockchain has been popular since 2017 in exchanging the Bitcoin digital currency [82]. In the medical domain, blockchain practice is built on a system involving patients, medical institutions, and third-party agencies. Patients own their medical data, and they can authorize certain data to an entity or revoke access rights at any time. Every time when they visit doctors, the medical records will be generated with digest and hash and then posted to the blockchain. All these medical data are arranged in "blocks" by time, and each block holds a hash of the previous block [83]. The obtained hash values are stored in the Merkle tree structure, and any manipulation of the original data will change the hash values. Thus, the application of medical blockchain networks may prevent tampering and reduce errors in clinical decision-making [84]. Liu *et al.* designed a lightweight

Table 5.1 Mainstream encryption algorithms for healthcare data

Studies	Objects	Encryption algorithms		
		Algorithms	Advantages	Disadvantages
[68]	Diagnose code in EHR	Clustering by greedy algorithm and k-anonymization	Deal with data containing repeated diagnosis codes Deal with different privacy requirements Take analytic tasks into account when encrypting	Information loss in a small dataset
[69]	EHR data	Combination of l-diversity and k-anonymity	Minimize information loss Prevent homogeneity attacks	Deficiency in similarity attacks and calculating the increment of diversity
[70]	Demographics data	t-Closeness	Prevent attribute disclosure	Cannot prevent identity disclosure
[71]	Genome-wide association study (GWAS) dataset	Algorithms developed by Laplace mechanism	Limit re-identification risks in aggregate GWAS data Implement differential privacy	Threshold p-value may affect the data utility
[72]	GWAS dataset	Shangyong Mima (SM) algorithms	Safe transmission of genomic data via network More efficient for larger genomic data files	Do not provide cipher text query ability
[73]	Digital medical images	Cellular Neural Network DNA Crumb Coding Transform (CNN-CCT)	Scramble the pixel positions efficiently High resistance against several cryptographic attacks	More time-consuming for encryption than decryption
[74]	Data generated from medical devices and sensors	High-performance encrypted index based on Locality Sensitive Hashing [65] indices	Encrypt and fast index data before sending them to the cloud	May have latency when searching in a large number of buckets
[75]	Wearable medical devices	Hash function	Access to limited authorized users for protected health information Double challenge-response authentication scheme	The keys need more diversification

blockchain-based model using proxy re-encryption technology for data sharing among users from different centers [85]. The blockchain-based models bring new potentials for safer and more efficient data sharing.

Besides new technologies, procedural solutions are also essential. A representative example is a Welsh databank called secure anonymized information linkage (SAIL). SAIL staff can be divided into infrastructure- and research-facing with different authorities. Infrastructure staff are IT and data warehouse managers and developers. They are given the highest access right to perform deep "backbone" operations on the data infrastructure and conduct additional levels of anonymization [44]. The research-facing staff (analysts) can only access anonymized data. As the mediators between the data collector and users, analysts' responsibility is to select eligible data for research purposes, make an extract of the dataset, and turn the extract into forms suitable for analysis. For data users, their requests will be scrutinized by evaluating the research goals, risks, and available data sources [86]. The authorized researchers can access in a time-limited logon and view data within a specified schema, only via the SAIL gateway.

Policies and guidelines are strong supporting measures. In 1996, the Health Insurance Portability and Accountability Act (HIPAA) was promulgated to be the federal law regarding health information security in the U.S. HIPAA requires patient data be secure whenever it is accessed, saved, or shared, and patients are given adequate notice of privacy and information practices [87,88]. Violating the HIPAA security standards will lead to significant fines, and in some cases, loss of medical licenses [89]. For genome data, the Draft Genomic Data Sharing (GDS) Policy released in 2014 is the most significant guideline to date. There are some other policies regulating data sharing, like the E.U. General Data Protection Regulation (GDPR), and the Genetic Information Nondiscrimination Act (GINA) against genetic discrimination. The protection regulations and laws in different countries are shown in Figure 5.5.

Due to different regional policies, the standardization and unification of data-sharing codes is an unmet need [90]. In ISO 22857, when data sharing across national/jurisdictional borders, one key requirement is that personal health data be made only to appropriate individuals or organizations within the boundaries of these purposes [91]. It is a pity that there is no relative policy and guideline, particularly for healthcare data quality. ISO 8000 focuses on quality management of

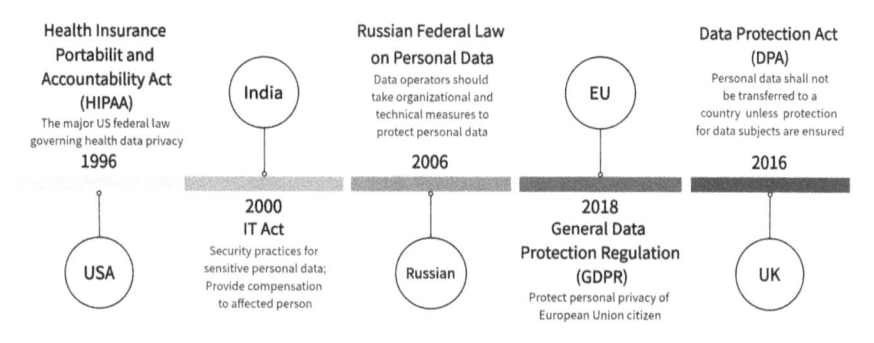

Figure 5.5 Regulations and policies regarding healthcare data security

big data, for example, monitoring and measuring information and using quality tests [92], and this may provide reference to healthcare data quality monitoring.

5.9 Limitations and future directions

Despite the rapid development of big data in healthcare, there are some technical and ethical obstacles. Novel data analytics need to be integrated into real-world clinical practice, which is largely overlooked [12]. The medical data should be evaluated prospectively [93]. As major obstacles to data availability and secure sharing, the technical barriers include unstandardized data collection in an immature healthcare system, language barrier (particularly in an international context), and restrictive data format [94]. The validation and implementation of novel algorithms lag behind technical innovation. In addition, high costs for data preparation and system maintenance may become economic barriers to hinder secure sharing. The potential economic loss is another concern. For example, the sharing of epidemiological data may affect trade and tourism [94,95]. Finally, legal and ethical concerns will emerge with new techniques, proposing a high need for up-to-date guidelines and policies, as well as efficient monitoring. A study on women's mobile health reveals that most off-the-shelf apps are weak in data privacy and security despite the regulations [96].

For future development, risks of healthcare big data sharing should be considered in the context of wearable sensing, digital health, and IoT. General privacy frameworks can be developed and implemented in hospitals and daily monitoring. Commercial services can provide bespoke privacy protection services to suit different real-world application scenarios, e.g., home-based nursing care services and elderly home care [97]. Most importantly, the awareness of secure data sharing among different stakeholders is essential for the sustainable development of healthcare big data technology (Figure 5.6).

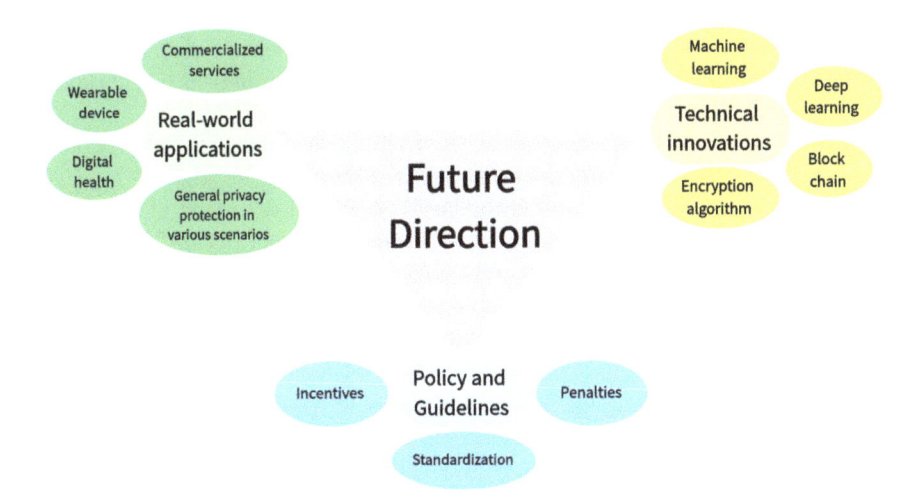

Figure 5.6 Future direction for secure data sharing

5.10 Conclusions

The sharing of big data facilitates new potential for medical research and health services. However, data security is a major concern and involves different stakeholders. There are some available technologies and guidelines, but the validation, standardization, and implementation in clinical practice are still challenging. To address current gaps, future improvements are necessary in technical, ethical, and regulatory aspects.

References

[1] Puaschunder and Julia M. The Legal and International Situation of AI, Robotics and Big Data With Attention to Healthcare. 2019.
[2] Brumen B, Hericko M, Sevcnikar A, Zavrsnik J, and Holbl M. Outsourcing medical data analyses: can technology overcome legal, privacy, and confidentiality issues? *J Med Internet Res*. 2013;15(12):e283.
[3] Wimmer H, Yoon VY, and Sugumaran V. A multi-agent system to support evidence based medicine and clinical decision making via data sharing and data privacy. *Decis Support Syst*. 2016;88:51–66.
[4] Cox CS, Mussolino ME, Rothwell ST, et al. Plan and operation of the NHANES I Epidemiologic Follow-up Study, 1992. *Vital Health Stat 1*. 1997(35):1–231.
[5] Favaretto M, De Clercq E, Schneble CO, and Elger BS. What is your definition of Big Data? Researchers' understanding of the phenomenon of the decade. *PLoS One*. 2020;15(2):e0228987.
[6] Diebold F. On the origins and development of big data: The phenomenon, the term, and the discipline. 2019.
[7] Diebold FX. "Big data" dynamic factor models for macroeconomic measurement and forecasting: A discussion of the papers by Lucrezia Reichlin and by Mark W. Watson. In: Hansen LP, Dewatripont M, Turnovsky SJ, editors. *Advances in Economics and Econometrics: Theory and Applications, Eighth World Congress. Econometric Society Monographs. 3.* Cambridge: Cambridge University Press; 2003. p. 115–22.
[8] Laney D. 3D data management: Controlling data volume, velocity and variety. *META Group Research Note*. 2001;6(70):1.
[9] De Mauro A, Greco M, and Grimaldi M. A formal definition of Big Data based on its essential features. *Library Review*. 2016;65(3):122–35.
[10] Asri H, Mousannif H, Moatassime HA, and Noel T, editors. Big data in healthcare: Challenges and opportunities. *2015 International Conference on Cloud Technologies and Applications (CloudTech)*; 2015, 2–4 June 2015.
[11] Dash S, Shakyawar SK, Sharma M, and Kaushik S. Big data in healthcare: Management, analysis and future prospects. *Journal of Big Data*. 2019;6(1).
[12] Rumsfeld JS, Joynt KE, and Maddox TM. Big data analytics to improve cardiovascular care: Promise and challenges. *Nat Rev Cardiol*. 2016; 13(6):350–9.

[13] Shilo S, Rossman H, and Segal E. Axes of a revolution: Challenges and promises of big data in healthcare. *Nat Med*. 2020;26(1):29–38.
[14] Callaway A. *The healthcare data explosion*. 2023.
[15] Bengio Y, Courville A, and Vincent P. Representation learning: A review and new perspectives. *IEEE Trans Pattern Anal Mach Intell*. 2013;35(8):1798–828.
[16] Smith GD, and Ebrahim S. 'Mendelian randomization': Can genetic epidemiology contribute to understanding environmental determinants of disease? *Int J Epidemiol*. 2003;32(1):1–22.
[17] Zhen S, Ma Y, Zhao Z, Yang X, and Wen D. Dietary pattern is associated with obesity in Chinese children and adolescents: Data from China Health and Nutrition Survey (CHNS). *Nutr J*. 2018;17(1):68.
[18] Shi Z, Yuan B, Hu G, Dai Y, Zuo H, and Holmboe-Ottesen G. Dietary pattern and weight change in a 5-year follow-up among Chinese adults: Results from the Jiangsu Nutrition Study. *Br J Nutr*. 2011;105(7):1047–54.
[19] Ollier W, Sprosen T, and Peakman T. UK Biobank: From concept to reality. *Pharmacogenomics*. 2005;6(6):639–46.
[20] Collins R. What makes UK Biobank special? *Lancet*. 2012;379(9822):1173–4.
[21] Mason CE, Porter SG, and Smith TM. Characterizing multi-omic data in systems biology. *Adv Exp Med Biol*. 2014;799:15–38.
[22] Dai X, and Shen L. Advances and trends in omics technology development. *Front Med (Lausanne)*. 2022;9:911861.
[23] Ning K, and Li Y. Introduction to multi-omics. In: Ning K, editor. Methodologies of Multi-Omics Data Integration and Data Mining: *Techniques and Applications*. Singapore: Springer Nature Singapore; 2023. p. 1–10.
[24] Dimitrov DV. Medical Internet of Things and big data in healthcare. *Healthc Inform Res*. 2016;22(3):156–63.
[25] Heart T, Ben-Assuli O, and Shabtai I. A review of PHR, EMR and EHR integration: A more personalized healthcare and public health policy. *Health Policy and Technology*. 2017;6(1):20–5.
[26] Tripathi S, editor. System dynamics perspective for adoption of Internet of Things: A conceptual framework. *2019 10th International Conference on Computing, Communication and Networking Technologies (ICCCNT)*; 2019 6–8 July 2019.
[27] Abdulmalek S, Nasir A, Jabbar WA, et al. IoT-based healthcare-monitoring system towards improving quality of life: A review. *Healthcare (Basel)*. 2022;10(10).
[28] Mutunhu B, Chipangura, B., and Twinomurinzi, H. A systematized literature review: Internet of Things (IoT) in the remote monitoring of diabetes. 2023.
[29] Bulgarelli L, Núñez-Reiz A, and Deliberato R. Building electronic health record databases for research. 2020. p. 55–64.
[30] Zafar R, Yafi E, Zuhairi MF, and Dao H, editors. Big data: The NoSQL and RDBMS review. *2016 International Conference on Information and Communication Technology (ICICTM)*; 2016, 16–17 May 2016.

[31] Goli-Malekabadi Z, Sargolzaei-Javan M, and Akbari MK. An effective model for store and retrieve big health data in cloud computing. *Computer Methods and Programs in Biomedicine*. 2016;132:75–82.
[32] Fischer BA, and Zigmond MJ. The essential nature of sharing in science. *Sci Eng Ethics*. 2010;16(4):783–99.
[33] Tedersoo L, Kungas R, Oras E, *et al*. Data sharing practices and data availability upon request differ across scientific disciplines. *Sci Data*. 2021;8(1):192.
[34] Nature Methods. Data sharing is the future. *Nature Methods*. 2023;20(4):471.
[35] Conroy M, Sellors J, Effingham M, *et al*. The advantages of UK Biobank's open-access strategy for health research. *J Intern Med*. 2019;286(4):389–97.
[36] Dyda A, Purcell M, Curtis S, *et al*. Differential privacy for public health data: An innovative tool to optimize information sharing while protecting data confidentiality. *Patterns (N Y)*. 2021;2(12):100366.
[37] Tang C. What Is Data Industry? *The Data Industry: The Business and Economics of Information and Big Data* 2016. p. 1–18.
[38] ISO/TR7340:2023. ISO/TR 7340:2023(en). Reference data distribution in financial services. 2023.
[39] ISO/IEC24392:2023. ISO/IEC 24392:2023, Cybersecurity—Security reference model for industrial internet platform (SRM-IIP). 2023.
[40] Kalkman S, Mostert M, Gerlinger C, van Delden JJM, and van Thiel G. Responsible data sharing in international health research: A systematic review of principles and norms. *BMC Med Ethics*. 2019;20(1):21.
[41] Hummel P, Braun M, and Dabrock P. Own data? Ethical reflections on data ownership. *Philosophy & Technology*. 2020;34(3):545–72.
[42] Kostkova P, Brewer H, de Lusignan S, *et al*. Who owns the data? Open data for healthcare. *Front Public Health*. 2016;4:7.
[43] Baker DB, Kaye J, and Terry SF. Governance through privacy, fairness, and respect for individuals. *EGEMS (Wash DC)*. 2016;4(2):1207.
[44] Tempini N, and Leonelli S. Concealment and discovery: The role of information security in biomedical data re-use. *Soc Stud Sci*. 2018;48(5):663–90.
[45] Ristevski B, and Chen M. Big data analytics in medicine and healthcare. *J Integr Bioinform*. 2018;15(3).
[46] Wu PY, Cheng CW, Kaddi CD, Venugopalan J, Hoffman R, and Wang MD. Omic and electronic health record big data analytics for precision medicine. *IEEE Trans Biomed Eng*. 2017;64(2):263–73.
[47] Kobayashi S, Kane TB, and Paton C. The privacy and security implications of open data in healthcare. *Yearb Med Inform*. 2018;27(1):41–7.
[48] AMA. 2023 2023/09/02/. Available from: https://www.ama-assn.org/delivering-care/patient-support-advocacy/ama-health-data-privacy-framework.
[49] Berman JJ. Confidentiality issues for medical data miners. *Artif Intell Med*. 2002;26(1–2):25–36.
[50] Horn R, and Kerasidou A. Sharing whilst caring: solidarity and public trust in a data-driven healthcare system. *BMC Med Ethics*. 2020;21(1):110.

[51] NHS. NHS England sets out the next steps of public awareness about care. data. 2018.
[52] Temperton J. NHS care.data scheme closed after years of controversy. WIRED UK. 2016.
[53] Bonomi L, Huang Y, and Ohno-Machado L. Privacy challenges and research opportunities for genomic data sharing. *Nat Genet*. 2020;52(7):646–54.
[54] Heeney C, Hawkins N, de Vries J, Boddington P, and Kaye J. Assessing the privacy risks of data sharing in genomics. *Public Health Genomics*. 2011;14 (1):17–25.
[55] Schwab AP, Luu HS, Wang J, and Park JY. Genomic privacy. *Clin Chem*. 2018;64(12):1696–703.
[56] Lippert C, Sabatini R, Maher MC, *et al*. Identification of individuals by trait prediction using whole-genome sequencing data. *Proc Natl Acad Sci U S A*. 2017;114(38):10166–71.
[57] Wailoo K. Stigma, race, and disease in 20th century America. *Lancet*. 2006; 367(9509):531–3.
[58] Rahimzadeh V, Schickhardt C, Knoppers BM, *et al*. Key implications of data sharing in pediatric genomics. *JAMA Pediatr*. 2018;172(5):476–81.
[59] Kranendonk EJ, Hennekam RC, and Ploem MC. Paediatric biobanking: Dutch experts reflecting on appropriate legal standards for practice. *Eur J Pediatr*. 2017;176(1):75–82.
[60] Jutte DP, Roos LL, and Brownell MD. Administrative record linkage as a tool for public health research. *Annual Review of Public Health*. 2011; 32:91–108.
[61] Bowman S. Impact of electronic health record systems on information integrity: quality and safety implications. 2013(1559-4122 (Electronic)).
[62] Djennad A, Lo Iacono G, Sarran C, *et al*. A comparison of weather variables linked to infectious disease patterns using laboratory addresses and patient residence addresses. *BMC Infect Dis*. 2018;18(1):198.
[63] Boyle DIR, and Cunningham SG. Resolving fundamental quality issues in linked datasets for clinical care. *Health Informatics Journal*. 2002;8(2):73–7.
[64] Leonelli S, and Tempini N. Where health and environment meet: the use of invariant parameters in big data analysis. *Synthese*. 2021;198(Suppl 10):2485–504.
[65] Kushida CA, Nichols DA, Jadrnicek R, Miller R, Walsh JK, and Griffin K. Strategies for de-identification and anonymization of electronic health record data for use in multicenter research studies. *Med Care*. 2012;50 (Suppl): S82–101.
[66] Baker DB, Knoppers BM, Phillips M, *et al*. Privacy-preserving linkage of genomic and clinical data sets. *IEEE/ACM Trans Comput Biol Bioinform*. 2019;16(4):1342–8.
[67] El Emam K, Dankar FK, Issa R, *et al*. A globally optimal k-anonymity method for the de-identification of health data. *J Am Med Inform Assoc*. 2009;16(5):670–82.

[68] Loukides G, Liagouris J, Gkoulalas-Divanis A, and Terrovitis M. Disassociation for electronic health record privacy. *Journal of Biomedical Informatics*. 2014;50:46–61.
[69] Yoo S, Shin M, Fau-Lee D, and Lee D. An approach to reducing information loss and achieving diversity of sensitive attributes in k-anonymity methods. 2012(1929-073X (Print)).
[70] El Emam K, and Dankar FK. Protecting privacy using k-anonymity. *Journal of the American Medical Informatics Association*. 2008;15(5):627–37.
[71] Yu F, Fau-Ji Z, and Ji Z. Scalable privacy-preserving data sharing methodology for genome-wide association studies: an application to iDASH healthcare privacy protection challenge. 2014(1472-6947 (Electronic)).
[72] Jiang Y, Shang T, and Liu J. SM algorithms-based encryption scheme for large genomic data files. *Digital Communications and Networks*. 2021;7(4):543–50.
[73] Sheela SJ, Suresh KV, Tandur D, and Sanjay A. Cellular neural network-based medical image encryption. *SN Computer Science*. 2020;1(6):346.
[74] Yuan X, Cui H, Wang X, and Wang C, editors. Enabling privacy-assured similarity retrieval over millions of encrypted records. *Computer Security – ESORICS 2015*; 2015; Cham: Springer International Publishing.
[75] Long WJ, and Lin W, editors. An authentication protocol for wearable medical devices. *2017 13th International Conference and Expo on Emerging Technologies for a Smarter World (CEWIT)*; 2017, 7–8 Nov. 2017.
[76] Bonino da Silva Santos LO, Ferreira Pires L, Graciano Martinez V, Rebelo Moreira JL, and Silva Souza Guizzardi R. Personal health train architecture with dynamic cloud staging. *SN Computer Science*. 2022;4(1):14.
[77] Zhang P, and Kamel Boulos MN. Privacy-by-design environments for large-scale health research and federated learning from data. *Int J Environ Res Public Health*. 2022;19(19).
[78] Beyan O, Choudhury A, van Soest J, et al. Distributed analytics on sensitive medical data: The personal health train. *Data Intelligence*. 2020;2(1–2):96–107.
[79] Jochems A, Deist TM, van Soest J, et al. Distributed learning: Developing a predictive model based on data from multiple hospitals without data leaving the hospital – A real life proof of concept. *Radiotherapy and Oncology*. 2016;121(3):459–67.
[80] Arbuckle L, and Ritchie F. The five safes of risk-based anonymization. *IEEE Security & Privacy*. 2019;17(5):84–9.
[81] Madden S. PC. Joining up the dots: driving innovation, research and planning through trusted research environments. 2023.
[82] Zhang P, White J, Schmidt DC, Lenz G, and Rosenbloom ST. FHIRChain: Applying blockchain to securely and scalably share clinical data. *Comput Struct Biotechnol J*. 2018;16:267–78.
[83] Chen Y, Ding S, Xu Z, Zheng H, and Yang S. Blockchain-based medical records secure storage and medical service framework. *Journal of Medical Systems*. 2018;43(1):5.

[84] Xi P, Zhang X, Wang L, Liu W, and Peng S. A review of blockchain-based secure sharing of healthcare data. *Applied Sciences*. 2022;12(15).
[85] Liu X, Wang Z, Jin C, Li F, and Li G. A blockchain-based medical data sharing and protection scheme. *IEEE Access*. 2019;7:118943–53.
[86] Ford DV, Jones KH, Verplancke JP, *et al.* The SAIL databank: Building a national architecture for e-health research and evaluation. *BMC Health Serv Res*. 2009;9:157.
[87] Gostin LO. National health information privacy regulations under the Health Insurance Portability and Accountability Act. *JAMA*. 2001;285(23):3015–21.
[88] Summary of the HIPAA Security Rule. 2022.
[89] Jin H, Luo Y, Li P, and Mathew J. A review of secure and privacy-preserving medical data sharing. *IEEE Access*. 2019;7:61656–69.
[90] Schwalbe N, Wahl B, Song J, and Lehtimaki S. Data sharing and global public health: Defining what we mean by data. *Front Digit Health*. 2020; 2:612339.
[91] ISO/TS17975:2022. ISO/TS 17975:2022. 2023.
[92] ISO/8000-1:2022. ISO 8000-1:2022. 2023.
[93] Ketchersid T. Big data in nephrology: Friend or foe? *Blood Purification*. 2013;36(3–4):160–4.
[94] van Panhuis WG, Paul P, Emerson C, *et al.* A systematic review of barriers to data sharing in public health. *BMC Public Health*. 2014;14(1):1144.
[95] Heymann DL, and Rodier GR. Hot spots in a wired world: WHO surveillance of emerging and re-emerging infectious diseases. *The Lancet Infectious Diseases*. 2001;1(5):345–53.
[96] Alfawzan N, Christen M, Spitale G, and Biller-Andorno N. Privacy, data sharing, and data security policies of women's mHealth apps: Scoping review and content analysis. *JMIR Mhealth Uhealth*. 2022;10(5):e33735.
[97] Pool J, Fatehi F, Hassandoust F, and Akhlaghpour S. Health data privacy: Research fronts, hot topics and future directions. *Stud Health Technol Inform*. 2020;275:167–71.

Chapter 6
Enhancing healthcare data security in the era of 5G and Big Data Analytics

Tarun Kumar Vashishth[1], Vikas Sharma[1], Kewal Krishan Sharma[1], Bhupendra Kumar[1], Sachin Chaudhary[1] and Rajneesh Panwar[1]

The intersection of 5G technology and big data analytics has catalyzed transformative changes in healthcare, promising improved patient care, diagnostic precision, and operational efficiency. However, these advancements have also raised significant concerns about data security and privacy. In the era of 5G and big data analytics, healthcare data security is paramount to protect sensitive patient information and ensure the trustworthiness of healthcare systems. This chapter explores the multifaceted challenges posed by these emerging technologies and presents strategies to enhance healthcare data security comprehensively. The adoption of 5G technology in healthcare promises lightning-fast data transmission, enabling real-time monitoring of patient vitals, seamless telemedicine, and enhanced medical imaging. Meanwhile, big data analytics empowers healthcare providers with invaluable insights derived from vast datasets, supporting evidence-based decision-making. However, the proliferation of connected devices and the aggregation of extensive patient records within expansive data lakes introduce a new level of vulnerability to cyber threats. This chapter discusses key dimensions of healthcare data security in the 5G and big data era. It emphasizes the importance of data encryption, secure access control, and threat detection mechanisms to safeguard patient information from unauthorized access and data breaches. This chapter provides a comprehensive overview of the challenges and strategies in enhancing healthcare data security, with the aim of fostering a safer and more trustworthy healthcare environment in the era of 5G and big data analytics.

6.1 Introduction

The emergence of 5G and Big Data in healthcare is introducing groundbreaking possibilities to revolutionize the field. By utilizing the fast transmission speeds

[1]School of Computer Science and Applications, IIMT University, India

and low latency of 5G, along with the power of Big Data analytics, healthcare systems can provide real-time monitoring of patient vitals, offer seamless telemedicine, and enhance medical imaging. This convergence of technologies brings with it great opportunities but also poses difficult questions regarding data security and privacy. As such, it is imperative that the healthcare industry adequately addresses these concerns in order to fully maximize the potential of 5G and Big Data.

The advent of 5G and big data analytics is revolutionizing the healthcare industry by facilitating real-time monitoring, telemedicine, and improved medical imaging. This convergence is expected to improve patient care, diagnostic accuracy, and operational efficiency. However, it is important to address the data security and privacy issues that arise due to the use of these technologies. To maximize the potential of 5G and big data analytics, healthcare organizations must prioritize data security and ensure compliance with stringent regulations. This will enable them to reap the rewards of this cutting-edge technology while safeguarding the privacy of patients.

As 5G and big data analytics take center stage in the modern era, the security of healthcare data has become of paramount importance. Ensuring the trustworthiness of healthcare systems, protecting sensitive patient information, and staying in compliance with regulatory standards are all essential components of this. The Internet of Medical Things and the consolidation of patient records into large data lakes present new opportunities for cyber attacks, meaning that a proactive approach to healthcare data protection is essential. It is critical that healthcare providers take steps to secure their data in order to protect their patients and their own reputation and financial standing.

6.1.1 Background and significance

The healthcare landscape is quickly changing, and 5G technology combined with big data analytics is one of the driving forces behind this revolution. The implementation of 5G networks will enable faster and more secure communication between medical devices, allowing for real-time monitoring and the increased use of IoT devices in healthcare. Furthermore, the combination of 5G and big data analytics will enable the processing and analysis of large volumes of health-related data, which can provide valuable insights into patient outcomes, treatment effectiveness, and epidemiological trends. In short, the integration of 5G and big data analytics has immense potential to revolutionize the healthcare industry and improve patient care, disease management, and medical research. However, as healthcare becomes increasingly digitized, the significance of ensuring robust data security cannot be overstated. The sheer volume and sensitivity of health data generated, stored, and transmitted within this ecosystem make it an attractive target for malicious actors. The potential consequences of a data breach in healthcare are severe, ranging from compromised patient privacy to the manipulation of medical records, with the

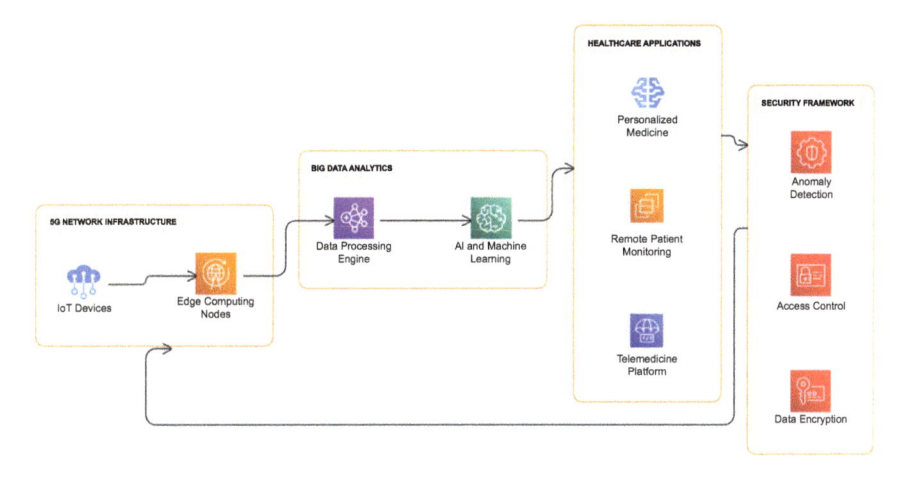

Figure 6.1 Healthcare data security in 5G and big data ecosystem

potential to impact both individual well-being and public health. In this context, enhancing healthcare data security becomes paramount to safeguarding the integrity of patient information, maintaining the trust of healthcare consumers, and upholding the ethical standards of the medical profession (Figure 6.1).

The healthcare industry is at the cusp of a paradigm shift due to the synergy between 5G and big data. This technology combination has enabled healthcare providers to access patient information in real time, leading to more informed decisions and personalized medicine. Furthermore, AI algorithms, powered by big data, can improve diagnostic accuracy, treatment planning, and predictive analytics. However, the interconnected nature of 5G networks and the huge amount of data generated by medical devices also present significant security risks. To safeguard against these threats, proactive measures must be taken to strengthen the resilience of healthcare systems against cyberattacks. The benefits of 5G and big data in healthcare are tremendous but also come with the need for robust security protocols to ensure the confidentiality, integrity, and availability of healthcare data.

The healthcare sector is faced with the dual challenge of developing and implementing robust cybersecurity frameworks while also unlocking the potential of 5G and big data analytics. To achieve this, policymakers, healthcare providers, technology vendors, and cybersecurity experts must come together and create comprehensive standards, guidelines, and best practices. Furthermore, research and development investments must be made in order to create innovative solutions to address the unique security concerns of 5G-enabled healthcare ecosystems. With a secure digital healthcare infrastructure in place, individuals and society as a whole can benefit from the responsible adoption of transformative technologies.

6.1.2 The intersection of 5G and Big Data Analytics in healthcare

The convergence of 5G technology and big data analytics in healthcare marks a transformative juncture, heralding a new era of possibilities and advancements in the delivery of medical services. 5G, the fifth generation of wireless technology, introduces unparalleled speed, low latency, and increased connectivity, creating a foundation for a more interconnected and dynamic healthcare ecosystem. This synergy is particularly pronounced in the context of medical data, where the sheer volume and complexity necessitate high-speed, reliable communication channels. The advent of 5G networks facilitates the seamless transmission of vast datasets generated by medical devices, wearables, and IoT-enabled healthcare solutions. This, in turn, enables real-time monitoring of patients, remote diagnostics, and the integration of diverse healthcare data sources.

As the data deluge continues to grow, big data analytics is emerging as a crucial tool in leveraging its potential. This technology enables healthcare professionals to process and analyze large volumes of information quickly, leading to valuable insights into patient health trends, treatment outcomes, and epidemiological patterns. By combining the power of 5G and big data, the healthcare industry is able to drive advances in telemedicine, healthcare informatics, and population health management. A major advantage of this intersection is its facilitation of remote patient monitoring. 5G's low latency ensures real-time transmission of health data, allowing for the monitoring of chronic conditions without the need for frequent hospital visits. Additionally, wearable devices and sensors connected through 5G networks provide ongoing health data streams, giving healthcare professionals a comprehensive view of an individual's health status. Furthermore, big data analytics enhances clinical decision support systems, allowing for more accurate diagnoses and personalized treatment plans. Predictive analytics powered by big data also enables proactive and preventive healthcare measures, resulting in improved patient outcomes while reducing the burden on healthcare systems.

Exploring the intersection of 5G and big data in healthcare has the potential to revolutionize the healthcare experience. However, this technological convergence also presents significant challenges in terms of data security and privacy. With increased connectivity and data flow, a larger attack surface is created, requiring robust cyber security measures to protect sensitive health information. Striking the right balance between innovation and security is essential to ensure the potential of improved patient care, operational efficiency, and medical research is realized responsibly and ethically. This intersection offers a glimpse into a future where connectivity and data-driven insights transform healthcare delivery.

6.1.3 Promise and concerns: Transformative changes vs. data security challenges

The convergence of 5G technology and big data analytics in healthcare promises transformative changes that have the potential to revolutionize the entire medical landscape. On the promising side, the deployment of 5G networks introduces

Enhancing healthcare data security 115

unprecedented speed, low latency, and heightened connectivity, forming the backbone for innovative healthcare solutions. Real-time data transmission has become a reality, enabling remote patient monitoring, telemedicine, and the seamless integration of diverse healthcare data sources. Big data analytics, powered by advanced machine learning algorithms, further amplifies these capabilities by providing healthcare professionals with profound insights into patient health trends, treatment outcomes, and epidemiological patterns. The promise lies in the ability to deliver more personalized and efficient healthcare, with improved diagnostic accuracy, proactive preventive measures, and enhanced overall patient outcomes.

The advent of 5G-enabled healthcare systems has been met with much optimism, as it promises to revolutionize medicine through unprecedented levels of information exchange and communication. Nevertheless, data security remains a major concern. This is due to the heightened risk of cyber threats such as ransomware attacks and unauthorized access that come with the increased connectivity and data flows inherent in such systems. To protect patient information from these potential breaches, the confidentiality, integrity, and availability of healthcare data must be guaranteed. The repercussions of a security breach in healthcare can be severe, including the violation of patient privacy and the manipulation of medical records. Such consequences can have serious implications for both individual health and public health (Figure 6.2).

The implementation of 5G and big data analytics in healthcare offers vast potential to revolutionize patient care, medical research, and operational efficiency, but it must be done in a manner that addresses the pressing concerns of data security. To this end, a comprehensive and proactive approach is needed to ensure the responsible adoption of these transformative technologies. Cooperation among policymakers, healthcare providers, technology vendors, and cybersecurity experts is essential to establishing robust cybersecurity frameworks, standards, and best practices. Additionally, research and development investments should be made in

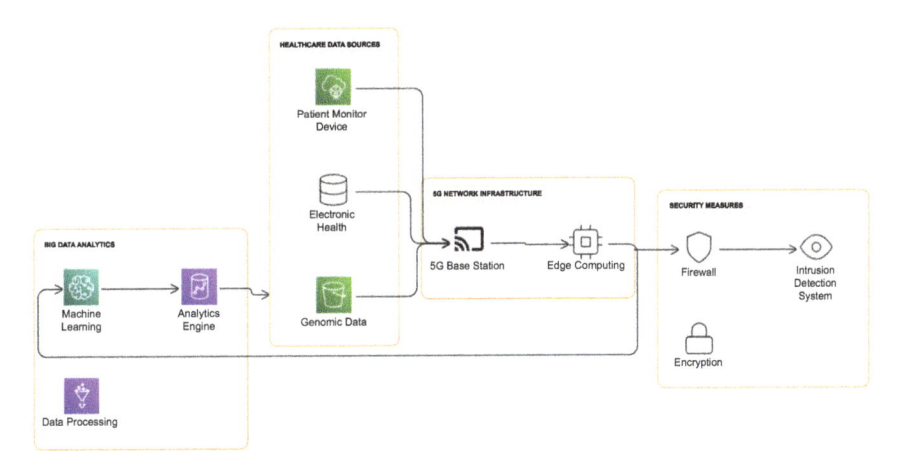

Figure 6.2 Transformative data security in 5G and big data ecosystem

solutions that address the unique security considerations of 5G-enabled healthcare ecosystems. Achieving the delicate balance between the promises of 5G and big data analytics and the need for data security is vital for unlocking the full potential of these technologies without jeopardizing patient information, public trust, or the ethical standards of the medical profession. As the healthcare landscape continues to evolve, finding the equilibrium between the benefits of 5G and big data analytics and the need for security becomes increasingly important for realizing the promised advantages of enhanced patient care, medical research, and operational efficiency.

6.2 Literature review

Bertino [1] dives into the repercussions of the convergence of 5G, IoT, big data, and machine learning on personal privacy. The study concludes that the combination of these technologies has created a situation wherein individual privacy is at risk. The article offers an in-depth look into the various privacy hazards brought about by the development of new technologies. However, the chapter's discussion of potential technical solutions fails to consider other measures that could be used to ensure user privacy.

Zhan [2] proposed a big data system for sports and health using 5G and IoT. However, the author failed to discuss the potential risks and challenges of implementing such a system, such as privacy issues and data security.

A study was published by Jagadeeswari *et al.* [3] in Health information science and systems, examining the use of the Medical Internet of Things and Big Data in personalized healthcare systems. However, the authors neglected to thoroughly evaluate the privacy matters related to the collection of data.

Aggarwal *et al.* [4] examined the application of machine learning, data mining, and big data analytics for 5G-enabled IoT. Although the authors did not touch upon the security aspects of blockchain technology in 5G-enabled IoT and its implications on industrial automation, this topic deserves attention.

Manogaran *et al.* [5] attempted to address this issue by proposing a framework for predicting potential security threats in the healthcare industry. However, their approach was considered inadequate by many researchers due to the lack of a comprehensive evaluation of potential risks.

Karatas *et al.* [6] asserted that Big Data could have a revolutionary impact on the healthcare sector. However, the authors did not provide sufficient evidence to back up their hypothesis nor did they consider the ethical implications that may come with the broad application of Big Data in healthcare.

Rahman *et al.* [7] explored the changing roles and effects of 5G-enabled technologies in healthcare, particularly in the context of the ongoing global epidemic COVID-19. Nevertheless, the chapter was deficient in its assessment of the potential repercussions of 5G technology in healthcare.

Deepa *et al.* [8] explored the potential of blockchain technology to facilitate big data applications in a survey paper. Nonetheless, the review was incomplete, not providing a thorough review of the current works.

Alawad and Kaewunruen [9] published an article in Frontiers in Built Environment titled '5G intelligence underpinning railway safety in the COVID-19 era' which aimed to investigate the potential of 5G technology to ensure railway safety during the pandemic. While the article did not provide a clear description of the obstacles encountered and the solutions proposed, it was a noteworthy exploration of the relevance of 5G in railway safety in the time of COVID-19.

Ever and Rajan [10] presented an informative discourse on the use of 5G networks in the medical sciences education field. They acknowledged the vast potential of this technology in this area but did not delve into the possible difficulties and restrictions that may be encountered.

Parmar *et al.* [11] explored a 5G-enabled deep learning-based framework for healthcare mining and assessed the existing landscape and difficulties. They pinpointed the possibilities and challenges associated with this pioneering technology and discussed how it could be used to facilitate healthcare mining. They also discussed the current state of the art and the challenges associated with it.

Vashishth *et al.* [12] proposed a stochastic approach to optimum utilization of bed resources in hospitals in their paper 'Artificial Intelligence-based Healthcare Systems 2023'. The chapter argued that this approach could help alleviate the issue of bed shortages in hospitals. However, the authors did not provide sufficient evidence to support their claims and failed to discuss potential issues that may arise with this approach.

Aceto *et al.* [13] provide an overview of the potential of Industry 4.0 to transform healthcare. Despite exploring the potential of Industry 4.0 in healthcare, the authors failed to provide a comprehensive analysis of its implications and limitations.

Ahmad and Afzal [14] highlighted the importance of fog and edge computing in the 5G era for cyber-physical infrastructures in their chapter 'Deployment of fog and edge computing in IoT for cyber-physical infrastructures in the 5G era'. According to them, fog and edge computing can provide increased scalability, reliability, and security for cyber-physical infrastructures due to their distributed nature. As such, they are likely to be an essential component of the Internet of Things (IoT) in the 5G era.

Humayun *et al.* [15] explore the concept of privacy protection and energy optimization for 5G-aided Industrial Internet of Things. The authors provide a comprehensive overview of the concept and present an architecture for its realization. Nevertheless, the question of how the proposed concept will bring about greater energy efficiency and privacy protection than existing solutions is yet to be answered.

6.3 5G technology in healthcare

The integration of 5G technology in healthcare represents a paradigm shift, offering a plethora of opportunities for enhanced patient care, medical innovation, and data-driven decision-making. The fifth generation of wireless technology brings unparalleled speed, low latency, and massive device connectivity, laying the foundation for a more interconnected and dynamic healthcare ecosystem. In the context of healthcare data security, 5G introduces transformative changes by enabling real-time data transmission, which is essential for applications such as remote patient monitoring, telemedicine, and the seamless exchange of medical information. The low latency of 5G ensures that healthcare professionals can access critical patient data instantaneously, fostering quicker and more informed decision-making. Additionally, the increased connectivity supports the integration of IoT devices, wearables, and medical sensors, creating a comprehensive network of health data sources. However, the adoption of 5G in healthcare also raises significant concerns, particularly regarding data security. The expanded attack surface resulting from the interconnected nature of 5G networks poses challenges in safeguarding sensitive patient information. Mitigating these concerns requires a proactive approach, including the implementation of robust encryption protocols, secure network architectures, and continuous monitoring for potential cyber threats. As 5G technology becomes more deeply embedded in healthcare infrastructure, striking the right balance between harnessing its transformative potential and addressing data security challenges is essential. Collaborative efforts among stakeholders, including healthcare providers, technology developers, and cybersecurity experts, are critical to developing and implementing comprehensive security measures that ensure the integrity and confidentiality of healthcare data in the 5G era.

6.3.1 Overview of 5G technology

The 5G revolution in healthcare is revolutionizing the way medical services are delivered and healthcare data is managed. Its remarkable features, including ultra-fast data transmission speeds, low latency, and increased device connectivity, allow for real-time monitoring and remote patient care, enabling faster and more informed decision-making. Additionally, 5G is facilitating the integration of IoT devices, wearables, and medical sensors, creating a comprehensive and holistic approach to patient care. However, the widespread adoption of 5G in healthcare also poses security concerns, as the increased connectivity and amount of sensitive health data exchanged can open up an expanded attack surface. To mitigate these risks, robust cybersecurity measures, such as encryption protocols, secure network architectures, and ongoing monitoring for potential vulnerabilities, must be implemented. It is thus essential to strike a delicate balance between harnessing the potential of 5G and big data analytics in healthcare and ensuring the security of medical data (Figure 6.3).

6.3.2 Applications in healthcare: Real-time monitoring, telemedicine, and medical imaging

The merger of 5G and big data analytics in healthcare has led to a wave of transformative applications with real-time patient monitoring, telemedicine, and medical imaging being the most important contributors to improved patient care. 5G's ultra-fast data transmission and low latency capabilities facilitate real-time

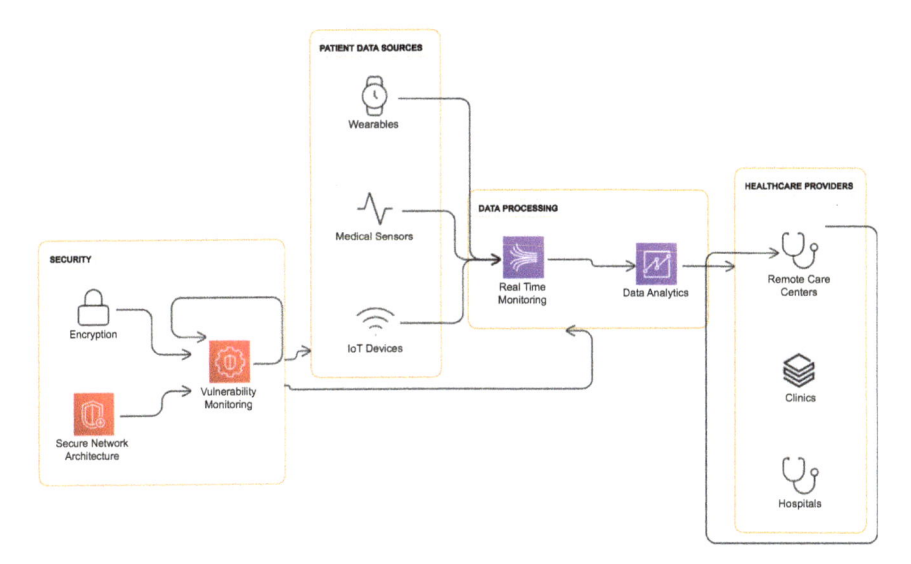

Figure 6.3 5G-enabled healthcare ecosystem

monitoring of patients, allowing healthcare providers to receive instantaneous updates on vital signs, medication adherence, and other vital health metrics. This real-time tracking extends beyond traditional healthcare settings, enabling continuous tracking through wearable devices and remote sensors. Telemedicine also gets a boost from 5G, as its low latency ensures smooth and high-quality video consultations, allowing for remote patient–doctor interactions that are similar to in-person visits. This is especially important for patients in remote locations or those with limited mobility. The incorporation of big data analytics improves telemedicine by processing large datasets to provide actionable insights for more precise diagnoses and customized treatment plans. Additionally, 5G's high bandwidth makes a significant difference in medical imaging, enabling the rapid transmission of large imaging files for immediate analysis. This hastens the diagnostic process, reducing waiting times for patients and allowing healthcare professionals to make faster, more informed decisions. However, the wide-scale adoption of these applications also brings up data security issues. The sensitive nature of health data transmitted in real-time, combined with the increased connectivity of 5G networks, requires robust cybersecurity measures to protect patient privacy and guard against potential breaches. Finding a balance between the tremendous advantages of real-time monitoring, telemedicine, and medical imaging, and the need to ensure data security is essential for the responsible advancement of healthcare in the future.

6.3.3 Implications for data security: Challenges and opportunities

The era of 5G and big data analytics in healthcare brings forth a landscape rich with both challenges and opportunities in the realm of data security. The increased connectivity, high-speed data transmission, and vast interconnectivity of devices inherent in 5G networks present significant challenges to safeguarding healthcare data. The expanded attack surface amplifies the risk of cyber threats, ranging from ransomware attacks to unauthorized access, potentially compromising the confidentiality and integrity of sensitive patient information. The integration of big data analytics further compounds these challenges as massive datasets become potential targets for malicious actors seeking to exploit vulnerabilities. At the same time as these struggles are present, there are considerable chances to reinforce and raise data security guidelines. 5G's quick and low-latency characteristics facilitate real-time surveillance and reply to potential security violations, allowing fast and proactive actions to reduce threats. To ensure that patient confidentiality remains a top priority, advanced encryption standards and secure network infrastructures can be put in place to secure the transfer and storage of healthcare information. Furthermore, big data analytics can be used to recognize behaviors and peculiarities in data that could suggest potential security concerns. Machine learning algorithms can learn and adjust to new cyber threats, giving another layer of protection against developing security issues. The collaboration between stakeholders, including healthcare providers, technology developers, policymakers, and cybersecurity experts, presents an opportunity to establish comprehensive standards and best practices. By sharing insights and expertise, the healthcare industry can collectively address data security challenges, develop robust cybersecurity frameworks, and foster a culture of proactive risk management.

As the healthcare sector continues to embrace the transformative potential of 5G and big data analytics, striking a delicate balance between innovation and security becomes imperative. The responsible adoption of these technologies requires ongoing vigilance, adaptability, and a commitment to evolving security measures to keep pace with the dynamic threat landscape. Ultimately, the implications for data security in the era of 5G and big data analytics underscore the critical importance of a collaborative and proactive approach to ensure the integrity, confidentiality, and trustworthiness of healthcare data in the digital age.

6.4 Big Data Analytics in healthcare

The integration of Big Data Analytics in healthcare has the potential to revolutionize medical care, decision-making, and research. By processing and analyzing large amounts of structured and unstructured health data, such as electronic health records, medical imaging, genomic information, and real-time patient monitoring, healthcare providers can gain valuable insights. Machine learning algorithms, a subset of Big Data Analytics, can uncover hidden relationships, predict disease progression, and enhance diagnostic accuracy, allowing for more personalized and effective treatments. Furthermore, Big Data Analytics can facilitate population health management, enabling healthcare providers and public health agencies to identify trends at a broader scale and implement targeted interventions to improve community health. With 5G and Big Data Analytics, healthcare is primed to enter a new era of enhanced patient care and medical research.

The application of Big Data Analytics in healthcare brings with it numerous potential rewards, yet it is essential to ensure that the data security challenges associated with this technology are adequately addressed. With the increasing reliance on 5G networks for data transmission, the need to protect large volumes of sensitive health data from potential cyber threats has become more critical. To protect against unauthorized access and data breaches, healthcare systems must be equipped with robust encryption, secure data storage practices, and stringent access controls. The utilization of Big Data Analytics in healthcare in the context of 5G technology can lead to numerous advances in medical research and improved patient outcomes. Nevertheless, for these benefits to be realized, healthcare organizations must take a proactive and collaborative approach to data security. By implementing comprehensive security measures and staying abreast of evolving threats, the healthcare industry can maximize the advantages of Big Data Analytics while safeguarding the privacy and integrity of healthcare data in the digital age.

6.4.1 Role and impact of Big Data Analytics

By leveraging the power of Big Data Analytics, healthcare providers can protect themselves against increasingly sophisticated cyber-attacks and ensure the confidentiality of sensitive health information. Big Data Analytics has become a cornerstone in ensuring the security of healthcare data in the age of 5G. It provides powerful tools and techniques to detect any anomalies and activities within large datasets that may signify potential security threats. Machine learning algorithms can be used to analyze enormous amounts of health data, quickly uncovering any deviances from the norm that may be indicative of a security breach. This proactive approach allows healthcare organizations to take prompt action to mitigate or prevent such incidents. Additionally, Big Data Analytics can be used to bolster access controls and authentication processes, ensuring only those with the right credentials can access sensitive health information. This is especially important in the 5G era, where greater connectivity and interconnectivity of devices require improved security measures to protect healthcare data. Big Data Analytics can be used to monitor and analyze the extensive data streams generated by 5G-enabled devices, allowing healthcare providers to identify potential vulnerabilities and security gaps. Consequently, healthcare organizations can strengthen their defenses against cyber-attacks and guarantee the confidentiality of patient data.

The utilization of Big Data Analytics in healthcare brings with it the potential to bolster data security standards in the age of 5G. The vast amount of data processed by these analytics systems necessitates the implementation of secure infrastructure and storage solutions, such as encryption protocols, to protect data both at rest and in transit. Yet, alongside the benefits of these technologies, ethical considerations such as patient consent, data ownership, and transparency must be taken into account. In order to maximize the potential of Big Data Analytics in healthcare, it is essential to strike a balance between the benefits of analytics and the protection of patient privacy. This is necessary to ensure trust in the healthcare system. In short, leveraging the power of Big Data Analytics to detect and respond to security threats is essential in order to navigate the challenges posed by increased

6.4.2 Leveraging vast datasets for evidence-based decision-making

Enhancing healthcare data security in the era of 5G and Big Data Analytics offers unprecedented opportunities and challenges, particularly in leveraging vast datasets for evidence-based decision-making. The integration of 5G technology provides the infrastructure for high-speed data transmission and real-time connectivity, while Big Data Analytics harnesses the power of extensive and diverse healthcare datasets. This convergence enables healthcare providers to make informed decisions based on evidence extracted from the analysis of massive amounts of patient data. Leveraging vast datasets in healthcare holds the promise of improving patient outcomes, optimizing treatment plans, and identifying trends that can inform preventive measures. Big Data Analytics allows healthcare professionals to sift through large volumes of structured and unstructured data, uncovering patterns and correlations that might be elusive through traditional methods. The real-time processing capabilities of 5G contribute to swift data analysis, enabling evidence-based decision-making at the point of care. This transformation empowers healthcare providers to tailor interventions based on individual patient characteristics and responses, fostering a more personalized and effective approach to healthcare.

The security implications of aggregating patient records on such a massive scale are profound and demand careful consideration. The amalgamation of sensitive health data from diverse sources introduces risks associated with data breaches, unauthorized access, and potential misuse of aggregated patient records. The interconnected nature of 5G networks and the extensive sharing of healthcare information for analytics purposes create an expanded attack surface, making healthcare systems susceptible to cyber threats. Protecting patient privacy becomes paramount, necessitating robust security measures such as encryption, secure data storage, and stringent access controls.

Moreover, the aggregation of patient records raises ethical concerns surrounding consent, transparency, and data ownership. Striking a balance between the benefits of evidence-based decision-making and the protection of patient privacy requires the establishment of clear guidelines, ethical frameworks, and regulatory standards. Collaborative efforts among healthcare stakeholders, policymakers, and cybersecurity experts are essential to develop comprehensive strategies that maximize the advantages of leveraging vast datasets while mitigating the associated security risks in the dynamic landscape of 5G and Big Data Analytics in healthcare.

6.5 Challenges in healthcare data security

The evolving landscape of healthcare, driven by the convergence of 5G and Big Data Analytics, presents several challenges in healthcare data security that demand comprehensive solutions to ensure the integrity, confidentiality, and availability of patient information.

Enhancing healthcare data security 123

Data Interoperability: Integrating data from diverse sources for analysis poses challenges related to interoperability. Healthcare organizations often deal with data stored in different formats and systems, making it challenging to create a seamless and standardized approach to data security across the entire ecosystem.

Real-time Security Measures: The real-time nature of 5G and Big Data Analytics demands security measures that can operate in real-time as well. Rapid detection and response to security incidents become crucial to mitigate risks promptly and prevent potential breaches.

Patient Privacy Concerns: As healthcare systems aggregate vast amounts of patient data for analysis, ensuring patient privacy becomes a significant concern. Respecting and protecting patient privacy rights while leveraging the benefits of data analytics necessitate robust encryption, anonymization techniques, and strict access controls.

Cybersecurity Skills Gap: The implementation of advanced security measures requires skilled cybersecurity professionals, and there is a growing shortage of experts in the field. Closing the skills gap becomes imperative to effectively address the evolving cybersecurity threats in healthcare.

Ethical Considerations: The ethical use of patient data for analytics raises questions about consent, transparency, and data ownership. Establishing ethical guidelines and frameworks becomes crucial to navigating the fine line between leveraging data for improving healthcare outcomes and protecting individual rights.

Addressing these challenges in healthcare data security necessitates collaborative efforts among healthcare organizations, technology providers, policymakers, and cybersecurity experts. A holistic approach that integrates technological solutions, regulatory compliance, and ethical considerations is essential to foster a secure and innovative healthcare ecosystem in the era of 5G.

6.5.1 *Proliferation of connected devices: The Internet of Medical Things*

The proliferation of connected devices in the healthcare sector, ranging from wearable devices and smart sensors to medical equipment, is largely facilitated by the advent of the Internet of Medical Things (IoMT). While these devices bring significant advantages to patient monitoring, diagnostics, and overall healthcare delivery, they also significantly increase the risk of potential cyber threats. With the interconnected nature of IoMT devices, they become vulnerable to unauthorized access, data interception, and device manipulation. To protect patient data and prevent breaches, robust authentication mechanisms and continuous monitoring of these devices are essential. Therefore, the security of IoMT devices is of paramount importance.

6.5.2 *Data lakes and cyber threats: Vulnerabilities introduced by extensive data aggregation*

The amalgamation of various datasets in data lakes allows for the use of Big Data Analytics in healthcare, though it also carries substantial security risks. Cyber attacks, including unauthorized access, data breaches, and ransomware, can all compromise the integrity and confidentiality of the stored data. To safeguard data lakes from these threats, comprehensive encryption, access control methods, and

124 *Secure big-data analytics for emerging healthcare in 5G and beyond*

vigilant monitoring of activities should be adopted. This will enable the timely detection and response to any security incidents that arise.

6.5.3 Regulatory compliance and ethical considerations

The adoption of 5G, Big Data Analytics, and IoMT in healthcare brings with it a complex web of regulatory frameworks and ethical considerations. Healthcare organizations must adhere to regulations such as HIPAA and GDPR, while also ensuring the rights of their patients are upheld. To do this, these organizations must develop comprehensive strategies to safeguard patient data and build trust. Successfully navigating these regulatory and ethical challenges requires a holistic approach that involves technology solutions, ongoing risk assessments, and a commitment to ethical practices. Healthcare providers, technology developers, regulatory bodies, and cybersecurity experts must work together to develop and implement secure solutions for Big Data Analytics and IoMT. This includes investing in reliable and secure IoMT devices, implementing robust cybersecurity measures for data lakes, and creating a culture of compliance and ethical data practices. The healthcare industry is under increasing pressure to ensure regulatory compliance and ethical practices in the context of 5G, Big Data Analytics, and IoMT. However, with the right collaborations and strategies, these organizations can safeguard patient data and build trust in the era of digital transformation (Figure 6.4).

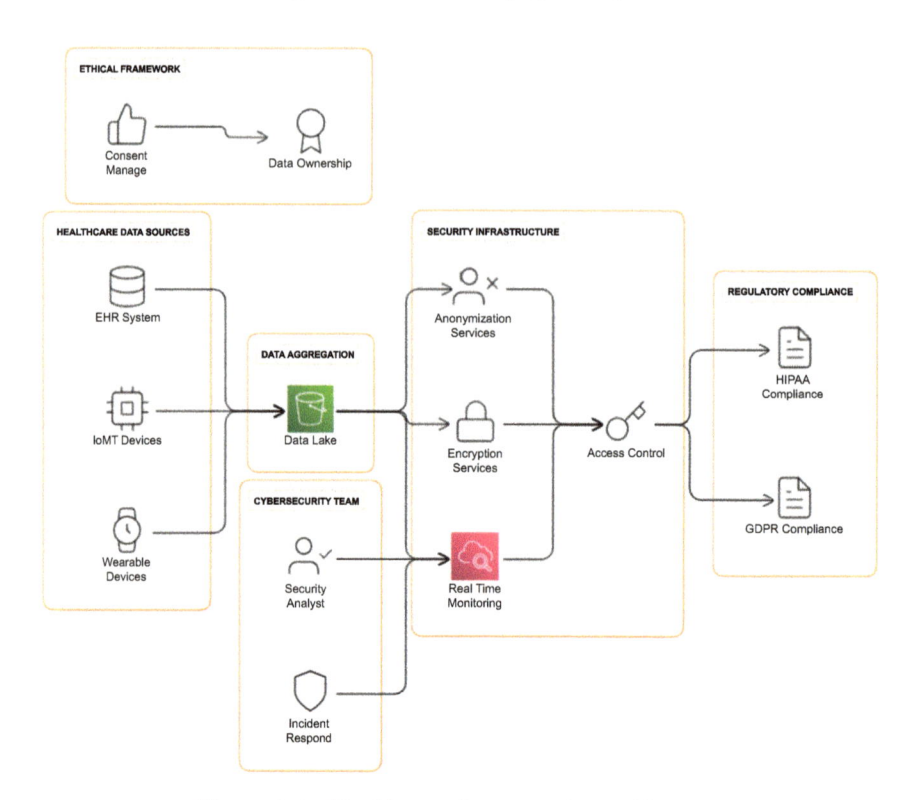

Figure 6.4 Healthcare data security architecture

6.6 Strategies for comprehensive healthcare data security

Ensuring comprehensive healthcare data security in the era of 5G and Big Data Analytics requires a multifaceted approach that incorporates advanced technologies and robust strategies. Here are key strategies for safeguarding healthcare data:

Data Encryption Techniques: The protection of sensitive healthcare information is greatly dependent on the implementation of strong data encryption techniques. These techniques are designed to convert data into an unreadable form, making it difficult for anyone without the correct decryption key to view the information. It is of the utmost importance to have encryption in place both when data is stored and when it is transmitted, as both forms are vulnerable to attack. For maximum security, sophisticated encryption algorithms should be put in place to render any unauthorized access useless. Thanks to encryption, even if an intruder manages to access the data, it will remain uninterruptable.

Threat Detection and Prevention Strategies: Proactive threat detection and prevention is a key aspect of any cybersecurity strategy. Implementing intrusion detection systems (IDS) and intrusion prevention systems (IPS) are essential to monitor network traffic for suspicious activities. Machine learning algorithms can be used to detect and respond to security incidents in real time. Additionally, regular security assessments and audits should be performed to discover any weaknesses in the system that can be exploited by malicious actors. When those vulnerabilities are identified, software updates should be applied to patch them up. Firewalls and other security measures should also be employed to block unauthorized access to vulnerable systems. With these strategies, organizations can identify and mitigate potential threats promptly and effectively.

Role of Blockchain in Healthcare Data Security: Blockchain technology is proving to be a potential game-changer for healthcare data security. Its decentralized and immutable qualities ensure that the recorded data is unalterable and cannot be tampered with. This is especially vital for safeguarding the veracity of medical records. Furthermore, blockchain can enable secure and transparent sharing of healthcare data among authorized entities, while preserving a high level of security. Additionally, its distributed structure ensures that the data is not stored in one single place, making it more resilient to malicious attacks. Moreover, blockchain-based smart contracts can help automate healthcare-related tasks, streamlining the process and reducing costs, while preventing any errors. In conclusion, blockchain technology can be a major factor in revolutionizing healthcare data security.

Regular Security Audits and Assessments: It is imperative for healthcare organizations to keep abreast of emerging security threats through regular security audits and assessments. Penetration testing, vulnerability assessments, and risk assessments should be conducted periodically to ensure compliance with security protocols and detect any potential vulnerability. Following the security audit, continuous monitoring and appropriate implementation of updates to security measures should be conducted based on audit findings. Doing so will help to ensure the highest level of data security.

Employee Training and Awareness: Human elements are often the cause of security breaches. It is essential to provide healthcare professionals and staff with comprehensive training on security protocols, the potential risks of social engineering attacks, and the importance of following security policies. Establishing a culture of security awareness among employees is key to developing a successful security plan for healthcare data.

By integrating these strategies, healthcare organizations can establish a resilient and proactive approach to data security, safeguarding patient information, and maintaining trust in the healthcare system in the face of evolving technological landscapes.

6.7 Case studies and lessons learned

6.7.1 Exemplary implementations of healthcare data security measures

As healthcare organizations navigate the complexities of enhancing data security in the era of 5G and Big Data Analytics, several exemplary implementations provide valuable insights and lessons learned. One notable case study is the Mayo Clinic, a renowned medical institution that has implemented robust security measures to protect patient data while leveraging advanced technologies.

6.7.1.1 Mayo Clinic: Implementing multi-layered security measures

The Mayo Clinic, known for its commitment to patient care and medical research, has implemented a multi-layered approach to healthcare data security. Leveraging 5G technology for real-time connectivity and Big Data Analytics for advanced patient insights, Mayo Clinic prioritizes the following security measures:

Comprehensive Encryption: Mayo Clinic utilizes extensive encryption methods to guarantee the safety of patient information in various stages, from transmission to storage and processing. This encryption makes sure that any unauthorized access to the data is trivial as the information remains encrypted and inaccessible.

Biometric Authentication: Mayo Clinic has taken an important step to ensure the safety of patient information by implementing biometric authentication for healthcare professionals. This system requires the use of biometric data, such as fingerprints or facial recognition, to verify the identity of personnel attempting to access sensitive information. This extra layer of security helps to ensure that only those with the proper authorization can access the data. By implementing this technology, Mayo Clinic is helping to protect the privacy and security of its patients.

Advanced Threat Detection: Mayo Clinic utilizes advanced threat detection tools that leverage machine learning algorithms to monitor network traffic and identify unusual patterns or behaviors. Real-time threat detection allows for prompt responses to potential security incidents, minimizing the impact of cyber threats.

Blockchain for Data Integrity: Mayo Clinic recognizes the importance of safeguarding data integrity and is exploring the use of blockchain technology for this purpose. This technology ensures the unalterability of patient records, thus minimizing the probability of data manipulation and reinforcing the overall dependability of healthcare data. By implementing blockchain, Mayo Clinic is taking steps to ensure that data remains reliable, secure, and accurate. This will result in increased confidence in the accuracy of patient records and the safety of their personal data. The use of blockchain technology is a crucial step towards ensuring the security and trustworthiness of healthcare data.

6.7.1.2 Lessons learned

Adaptability and Continuous Improvement: The healthcare landscape is dynamic, and effective data security requires adaptability. Mayo Clinic's case underscores the importance of continuous improvement, staying abreast of technological advancements, and updating security measures accordingly.

Integration of Technologies: Integrating 5G, Big Data Analytics, and advanced security technologies is a complex but necessary task. Mayo Clinic's success lies in its ability to seamlessly integrate these technologies to improve patient care while prioritizing data security.

Balancing Accessibility and Security: Striking the right balance between accessibility for healthcare professionals and stringent security measures is crucial. Mayo Clinic's case highlights the importance of ensuring that security measures do not impede the timely and efficient delivery of healthcare services.

In conclusion, exemplary implementations such as that of the Mayo Clinic showcase the practical application of healthcare data security measures in the era of 5G and Big Data Analytics. The lessons learned emphasize the need for a holistic and adaptive approach that leverages advanced technologies while maintaining a steadfast commitment to the security and privacy of patient data.

6.7.2 Challenges encountered and overcoming strategies

In the ongoing journey to enhance healthcare data security in the era of 5G and Big Data Analytics, various organizations have encountered challenges and implemented overcoming strategies, offering valuable lessons for the industry.

6.7.2.1 Case study: University Medical Center (UMC) and the implementation of 5G-enabled IoT devices

Challenges encountered
University Medical Center faced challenges associated with the proliferation of 5G-enabled IoT devices within their healthcare infrastructure. The increased connectivity introduced an expanded attack surface, making the organization more susceptible to cyber threats. Ensuring the security of these interconnected devices, along with the massive data flows they generated, became a complex challenge.

Issues such as device vulnerabilities, inadequate encryption, and potential unauthorized access pose significant risks to patient data.

Overcoming strategies

Comprehensive Risk Assessment: UMC initiated a thorough risk assessment to identify vulnerabilities and assess potential threats associated with the integration of 5G-enabled IoT devices. This proactive approach allowed them to develop targeted strategies for mitigating identified risks.

Implementation of Robust Encryption: To address concerns about data security, UMC implemented robust encryption protocols for data transmitted by IoT devices. This included end-to-end encryption to protect patient data in transit, ensuring that even if intercepted, the information would remain secure.

Continuous Monitoring and Incident Response: Recognizing the dynamic nature of cyber threats, UMC established continuous monitoring mechanisms. This involved real-time analysis of network traffic and the behavior of connected devices. In the event of a security incident, UMC had predefined incident response plans to swiftly contain and mitigate potential breaches.

6.7.2.2 Lessons learned

Proactive Risk Management is Essential: The case study highlights the importance of proactive risk management. Identifying potential risks before they materialize allows healthcare organizations to implement targeted security measures and avoid potential data breaches.

Encryption is a Cornerstone of Security: Robust encryption remains a cornerstone in securing healthcare data in the 5G and Big Data Analytics era. Implementing encryption measures at various stages of data transmission and storage is crucial for protecting patient information.

Dynamic Security Measures: Healthcare organizations must adopt dynamic security measures that evolve with the changing threat landscape. Continuous monitoring, regular risk assessments, and incident response planning are critical components of a dynamic security strategy.

In conclusion, the challenges encountered by the University Medical Center underscore the evolving nature of healthcare data security in the era of 5G and Big Data Analytics. The strategies implemented and lessons learned emphasize the need for a proactive, adaptive, and technology-integrated approach to effectively secure patient data in the dynamic healthcare landscape.

6.7.3 Real-world applications of 5G and Big Data security protocols in healthcare

In real-world applications of Big Data and 5G security protocols in healthcare, various organizations have implemented innovative measures to ensure the integrity, confidentiality, and availability of patient data. One notable case study is the collaboration between Intel and Providence St. Joseph Health in deploying 5G technology and advanced security protocols.

6.7.3.1 Intel and Providence St. Joseph Health: Advancing telehealth with 5G and Big Data security

Intel and Providence St. Joseph Health joined forces to leverage 5G technology and robust security measures to enhance telehealth capabilities. The collaboration was designed to facilitate remote patient care with the highest standard of security for the transmission and storage of delicate health information. Both organizations are committed to providing a safe and secure environment for patients to receive quality medical care from the comfort of their own homes.

6.7.3.2 Key security protocols implemented

5G Network Security: The collaboration prioritized the implementation of 5G network security protocols to safeguard the transmission of healthcare data. This included encryption of data in transit, secure authentication mechanisms, and the establishment of secure communication channels between healthcare providers and patients.

Edge Computing for Data Processing: To address the risks that may be posed by centralized data processing, edge computing has been implemented as a solution. By utilizing this technology, data can be processed at the edge of the network, close to the source, thus decreasing the likelihood of sensitive health information being intercepted during transit. This helps to minimize the exposure of such information.

Blockchain for Data Integrity: Recognizing the need to ensure the integrity of patient records, the collaboration explored the use of blockchain technology. Implementing blockchain in healthcare data management helps create a tamper-resistant and transparent record of patient interactions, reducing the risk of data manipulation.

6.7.3.3 Lessons learned

Holistic Approach to Security: The case study emphasizes the importance of adopting a holistic approach to security. This includes addressing security concerns at multiple layers, such as network security, data encryption, and integrity checks, to create a comprehensive and resilient security framework.

Collaboration between Technology and Healthcare Experts: Successful implementation requires collaboration between technology experts and healthcare professionals. By combining technological expertise with an understanding of healthcare workflows and regulatory requirements, organizations can develop solutions that meet the unique security challenges of the healthcare sector.

User Education and Training: The implementation highlighted the importance of educating both healthcare providers and patients on the security features of the telehealth platform. User training ensures that stakeholders are aware of security best practices, reducing the likelihood of inadvertent security lapses.

In conclusion, real-world applications of 5G and Big Data security protocols in healthcare, such as the collaboration between Intel and Providence St. Joseph Health, showcase the potential for transformative advancements while prioritizing data security. The lessons learned underscore the necessity of a comprehensive, collaborative, and user-centric approach to effectively address the complex challenges of healthcare data security in the era of 5G and Big Data Analytics.

6.8 Future prospects and emerging technologies

6.8.1 Anticipated developments in 5G and Big Data security

The era of 5G and Big Data Analytics is bringing about a new era of healthcare data security, presenting opportunities to address current challenges and raise security standards. At the forefront of this development is edge computing, which will offer greater protection by processing data near its origin, thereby avoiding the potential vulnerabilities of transmitting sensitive health information. Furthermore, quantum-safe encryption is being developed to ensure data security against quantum computing attacks. Finally, blockchain technology is being utilized to provide an immutable record of data transactions, ensuring the authenticity and integrity of healthcare data. All of these advancements are expected to revolutionize healthcare data security in the coming years. Artificial intelligence (AI) is expected to revolutionize threat detection, utilizing advanced algorithms to analyze patterns and anomalies, thereby fortifying the proactive identification of potential cybersecurity risks. Homomorphic encryption, a privacy-preserving cryptographic method, is anticipated to play a crucial role in securing healthcare data during computation, ensuring confidentiality even in data processing. Blockchain technology is set to facilitate secure interoperability, providing a decentralized and transparent ledger for exchanging health information across diverse systems. Moreover, federated learning is emerging as a privacy-preserving approach, allowing collaborative model training without sharing raw data. These developments collectively represent a dynamic shift toward a more resilient, privacy-centric, and technologically advanced healthcare data security landscape, ensuring the integrity, confidentiality, and accessibility of patient information in the evolving era of 5G and Big Data Analytics. As these technologies mature, healthcare organizations stand to benefit from a more secure and adaptable infrastructure, fostering trust in the utilization of transformative technologies for the betterment of patient care and healthcare outcomes.

6.8.2 Integration of artificial intelligence for advanced threat detection

The application of Artificial Intelligence (AI) in healthcare data security is seen as a major factor in the transformation of the 5G and Big Data Analytics environment. Machine learning algorithms, a subset of AI, allow for the swift and accurate analysis of large datasets, recognizing patterns, anomalies, and other potential security threats. This proactive approach is key in helping to identify and combat cyber-security risks more effectively. With the increased connection 5G networks provide and the abundance of data generated by Big Data Analytics, AI-driven threat detection is especially essential. Its advanced capabilities can detect and respond to emerging threats, creating a more secure healthcare system. AI can also be used to create behavior analytics, determining baseline patterns of user and system behavior and quickly spotting any abnormalities that might indicate security risks. The combination of AI, 5G, and Big Data Analytics promises a future where healthcare data security is pre-emptive and adaptive, creating an impenetrable defense against cyber threats in the digital age. As these technologies advance, AI's integration into healthcare data security will become even more indispensable, cementing the confidentiality and integrity of patient records and establishing a secure foundation for the future of healthcare (Figure 6.5).

6.8.3 Privacy-preserving technologies and trends

The future of healthcare data security in the era of 5G and Big Data Analytics is marked by a surge in privacy-preserving technologies and trends, aimed at

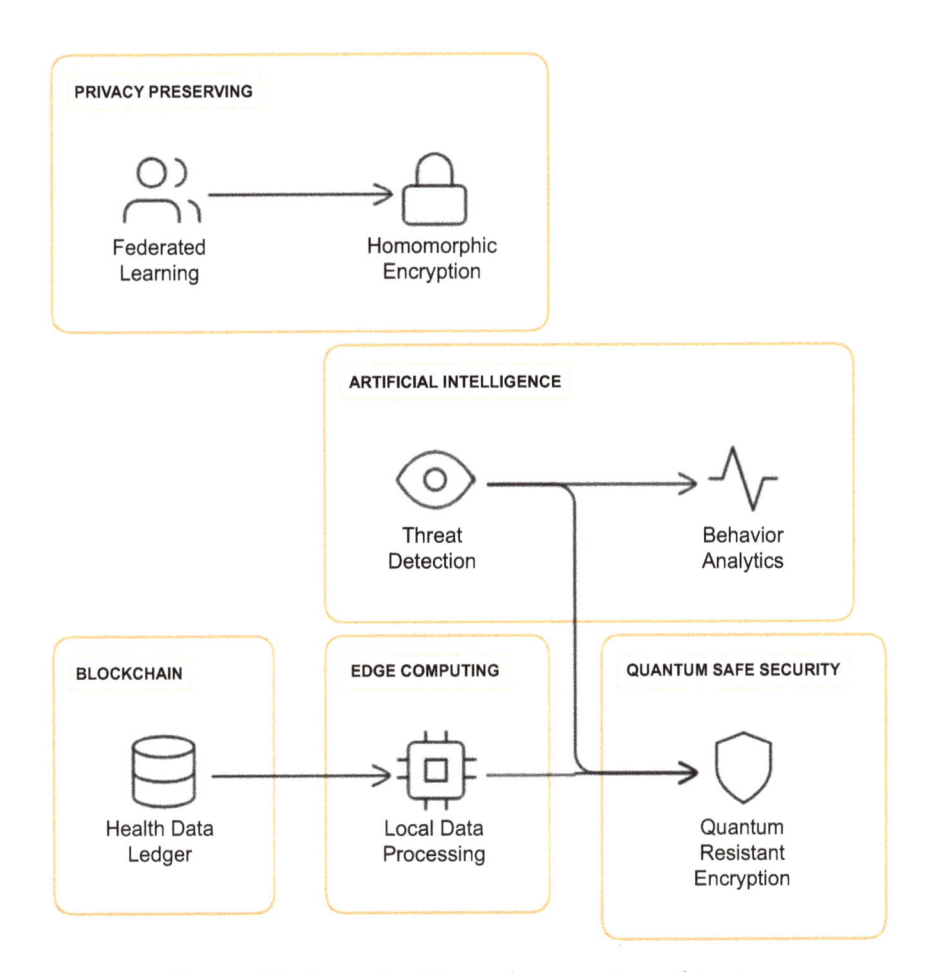

Figure 6.5 Future healthcare data security architecture

safeguarding sensitive patient information. One such technology is federated learning, offering a decentralized approach to machine learning that allows model training across multiple devices without sharing raw data. This not only ensures privacy by keeping patient data localized but also enables collaborative insights without compromising individual privacy. As quantum computing advancements loom on the horizon, quantum-safe encryption is anticipated to become a critical privacy-preserving measure, providing resilience against quantum threats. Additionally, blockchain technology is set to play a pivotal role in securing patient data by offering a transparent and immutable ledger, ensuring the integrity of health records while facilitating secure interoperability across healthcare systems. The integration of edge computing in healthcare networks is another emerging trend, allowing for real-time processing of data closer to the source, minimizing the transmission of sensitive information over networks. These privacy-preserving technologies collectively represent a paradigm shift towards a more patient-centric, secure, and ethically sound healthcare data environment. As the healthcare industry continues to harness the transformative potential of 5G and Big Data Analytics, the emphasis on privacy preservation reflects a commitment to upholding the trust and confidentiality that underpin the doctor-patient relationship, ensuring that technological advancements align with the highest standards of ethical data handling in the ever-evolving landscape of healthcare.

6.9 Conclusion

In conclusion, the intersection of 5G and Big Data Analytics presents both unprecedented opportunities and profound challenges in enhancing healthcare data security. The advent of 5G technology introduces high-speed, low-latency connectivity, enabling real-time communication and data transfer critical for advanced healthcare applications. Simultaneously, Big Data Analytics harnesses vast and diverse datasets to derive meaningful insights, revolutionizing patient care and medical research. However, amidst these advancements, the paramount importance of healthcare data security cannot be overstated. The proliferation of connected devices, the aggregation of extensive datasets, and the complexity of managing interoperability create a multifaceted landscape that demands comprehensive security measures. The case studies of institutions like the Mayo Clinic and the University Medical Center illustrate the practical implementation of security protocols, emphasizing encryption, access controls, and continuous monitoring. As healthcare embraces quantum-safe encryption, federated learning, and blockchain for privacy preservation, the industry is poised to achieve a delicate balance between innovation and safeguarding patient privacy. The integration of AI-driven threat detection anticipates and responds to evolving cyber threats, contributing to the proactive defense of healthcare data. Looking forward, emerging technologies such as edge computing, quantum-safe encryption, and federated learning are poised to shape the future of healthcare data security, ensuring a resilient, adaptive, and patient-centric approach. As we navigate this dynamic landscape, collaboration between healthcare providers, technology developers, regulators, and cybersecurity experts is crucial. Ethical considerations surrounding data privacy, consent, and transparency must remain at the forefront, fostering a culture of responsibility in the application of transformative technologies. Ultimately, the vision for enhancing healthcare data security in the era of 5G and Big Data Analytics is one where innovative technologies harmonize with robust security protocols, ensuring that the benefits of technological advancements in healthcare are maximized while patient trust and confidentiality are upheld as non-negotiable pillars of the digital healthcare future. It is through such collaborative, ethical, and technologically advanced approaches that the healthcare industry can navigate the complexities of the digital era, delivering secure, personalized, and transformative healthcare experiences for the benefit of patients worldwide.

References

[1] Bertino E. Privacy in the era of 5G, IoT, big data and machine learning. In *2020 Second IEEE International Conference on Trust, Privacy and Security in Intelligent Systems and Applications (TPS-ISA)* 2020 Oct 28 (pp. 134–137). IEEE. DOI: 10.1109/TPS-ISA50397.2020.00027

[2] Zhan K. Sports and health big data system based on 5G network and Internet of Things system. *Microprocessors and Microsystems*. 2021;80:103363. https://doi.org/10.1016/j.micpro.2020.103363

[3] Jagadeeswari V, Subramaniyaswamy V, Logesh R, and Vijayakumar V. A study on medical Internet of Things and Big Data in personalized healthcare system. *Health Information Science and Systems*. 2018;6:1–20. https://doi.org/10.1007/s13755-018-0049-x

[4] Aggarwal PK, Jain P, Mehta J, Garg R, Makar K, and Chaudhary P. Machine learning, data mining, and big data analytics for 5G-enabled IoT. *Blockchain for 5G-Enabled IoT: The New Wave for Industrial Automation*. 2021:351–75. https://doi.org/10.1007/978-3-030-67490-8_14

[5] Manogaran G, Thota C, Lopez D, and Sundarasekar R. Big data security intelligence for healthcare industry 4.0. *Cybersecurity for Industry 4.0: Analysis for Design and Manufacturing*. 2017:103–26. https://doi.org/10.1007/978-3-319-50660-9_5

[6] Karatas M, Eriskin L, Deveci M, Pamucar D, and Garg H. Big Data for Healthcare Industry 4.0: Applications, challenges and future perspectives. *Expert Systems with Applications*. 2022;200:116912. https://doi.org/10.1016/j.eswa.2022.116912

[7] Rahman MM, Khatun F, Sami SI, and Uzzaman A. The evolving roles and impacts of 5G enabled technologies in healthcare: The world epidemic COVID-19 issues. *Array*. 2022;14:100178. https://doi.org/10.1016/j.array.2022.100178

[8] Deepa N, Pham QV, Nguyen DC, *et al.* A survey on blockchain for big data: Approaches, opportunities, and future directions. *Future Generation*

Computer Systems. 2022 Jun 1;131:209–26. https://doi.org/10.1016/j.future.2022.01.017

[9] Alawad H, and Kaewunruen S. 5G intelligence underpinning railway safety in the COVID-19 era. *Frontiers in Built Environment*. 2021;7:639753. doi:10.3389/fbuil.2021.639753

[10] Ever YK, and Rajan AV. The role of 5G networks in the field of medical sciences education. In 2018 *IEEE 43rd Conference on Local Computer Networks Workshops (LCN Workshops)* 2018 Oct 1 (pp. 59–63). IEEE. DOI:10.1109/LCNW.2018.8628579

[11] Parmar R, Patel D, Panchal N, Chauhan U, and Bhatia J. 5G-enabled deep learning-based framework for healthcare mining: State of the art and challenges. *Blockchain Applications for Healthcare Informatics*. 2022:401–20. https://doi.org/10.1016/B978-0-323-90615-9.00016-5

[12] Vashishth TK, Chaudhary S, and Sharma V. Optimum Utilization of Bed Resources in Hospitals: A Stochastic Approach. In *Artificial Intelligence-based Healthcare Systems* 2023 Oct 27 (pp. 101–110). Cham: Springer Nature Switzerland. https://doi.org/10.1007/978-3-031-41925-6_7

[13] Aceto G, Persico V, and Pescapé A. Industry 4.0 and health: Internet of things, big data, and cloud computing for healthcare 4.0. *Journal of Industrial Information Integration*. 2020;18:100129. https://doi.org/10.1016/j.jii.2020.100129

[14] Ahmad S, and Afzal MM. Deployment of fog and edge computing in IoT for cyber-physical infrastructures in the 5G era. In *Sustainable Communication Networks and Application: ICSCN 2019* 2020 (pp. 351–359). Springer International Publishing. https://doi.org/10.1007/978-3-030-34515-0_38

[15] Humayun M, Jhanjhi NZ, Alruwaili M, Amalathas SS, Balasubramanian V, and Selvaraj B. Privacy protection and energy optimization for 5G-aided industrial Internet of Things. *IEEE Access*. 2020;8:183665–77. DOI:10.1109/ACCESS.2020.3028764

Chapter 7
Privacy-preserving techniques for big data analytics in healthcare

Kande Archana[1], Kamakshi Prasad[2], M. Ashok[3] and Vadlamani Veerabhadram[4]

Privacy-preserving techniques in big data analytics have gained paramount importance in the healthcare sector, where vast volumes of sensitive patient information are being leveraged to drive advancements in medical research and patient care. This abstract explores the critical role of privacy-preserving techniques in the context of healthcare big data analytics. As healthcare institutions and researchers increasingly rely on big data to make data-driven decisions, maintaining patient privacy becomes a paramount concern. Traditional de-identification methods are often inadequate in protecting sensitive information. Privacy-preserving techniques such as homomorphic encryption, differential privacy, and secure multi-party computation offer robust solutions to enable data sharing and analysis while preserving patient confidentiality. Homomorphic encryption enables computations on encrypted data without the need for decryption, ensuring that sensitive patient data remains confidential throughout the analytics process. Differential privacy adds noise to query results, preventing the identification of individual records while still providing valuable insights. Secure multi-party computation allows multiple parties to jointly analyze data without sharing the raw data itself, thus safeguarding patient privacy. These techniques enable healthcare providers and researchers to collaborate and share data while complying with strict data protection regulations like the Health Insurance Portability and Accountability Act (HIPAA) in the United States. They also empower the development of predictive models for disease outbreak monitoring, personalized treatment recommendations, and early detection of health trends, all while safeguarding individual patient privacy. Privacy-preserving techniques are indispensable tools in the realm of big data analytics in healthcare. They enable the extraction of valuable insights

[1]Department of CSE, Research Scholar, JNTU Hyderabad, Assistant Professor, Malla Reddy College of Engineering, Hyderabad, Telanagana State, India
[2]Jawaharlal Nehru Technological University (JNTU), Hyderabad, Telangana State, India
[3]Department of CSE, Malla Reddy College of Engineering, Hyderabad, Telanagana State, India
[4]CVR College of Engineering Hyderabad, Telangana State, India

from sensitive patient data without compromising confidentiality. As healthcare organizations continue to harness the power of big data, the implementation of robust privacy-preserving techniques will remain essential for both advancing medical science and ensuring the privacy rights of patients.

7.1 Introduction

In the era of rapidly advancing technology and data-driven decision-making, the healthcare industry stands on the cusp of a transformative revolution [1]. With the exponential growth of healthcare data, the potential for extracting valuable insights to improve patient care, streamline operations, and advance medical research is immense [2]. However, this data-rich landscape also presents significant challenges, particularly in preserving the privacy and security of sensitive patient information [3]. The confluence of big data analytics and healthcare promises groundbreaking advancements in diagnosis, treatment, and healthcare delivery [4], but it also necessitates a robust framework for safeguarding patient confidentiality, complying with stringent regulations like the Health Insurance Portability and Accountability Act (HIPAA) and the General Data Protection Regulation (GDPR) [5], and mitigating the risk of data breaches and unauthorized access [6]. In this context, this comprehensive review delves into the crucial realm of privacy-preserving techniques for big data analytics in healthcare [7]. We explore the multifaceted facets of this critical intersection, emphasizing the imperative need to strike a balance between harnessing the vast potential of healthcare data and respecting individual privacy rights [8]. This review is structured to provide a holistic overview of the topic, starting with a deep dive into the current landscape of healthcare data, the sources from which it is generated, and the myriad ways in which it can be harnessed to drive healthcare innovation [9]. We then elucidate the unique challenges and risks associated with healthcare data analytics, including the identification of potential vulnerabilities in data storage, sharing, and processing [10].

Subsequently, we embark on a comprehensive exploration of privacy-preserving techniques, ranging from encryption methods like homomorphic encryption and secure multi-party computation to privacy-enhancing technologies such as differential privacy [11]. Each technique is dissected in detail, offering insights into its strengths, weaknesses, and practical applications in the healthcare domain [12]. We shed light on the pivotal role of data anonymization, de-identification, and pseudonymization in shielding patient identities, while still enabling meaningful analysis [13]. Moreover, this review delves into emerging trends and technologies, such as federated learning and blockchain, which hold the promise of further fortifying data privacy and security in healthcare analytics [14]. Throughout this comprehensive journey, we discuss real-world case studies and implementation scenarios, providing tangible examples of how these privacy-preserving techniques are being applied to safeguard healthcare data [15].

As we navigate the intricate landscape of privacy-preserving techniques in big data analytics for healthcare, we also touch upon the ethical and regulatory considerations that underpin this field [16]. The evolving legal and ethical frameworks surrounding patient consent, data ownership, and the responsible use of healthcare data are central to this discourse [17]. In conclusion, the marriage of big data analytics and healthcare offers unprecedented opportunities for improving patient outcomes and transforming the healthcare ecosystem [18]. However, the ethical imperative of preserving patient privacy remains paramount [19]. This review serves as a guiding beacon, offering a comprehensive exploration of the strategies, technologies, and best practices that can enable the healthcare industry to harness the power of big data while upholding the highest standards of privacy and security for patients and stakeholders alike [20].

7.2 Privacy and security concerns—big data in healthcare

Privacy and security concerns are paramount in the context of big data in healthcare. The vast volume of sensitive patient information poses a substantial risk of data breaches, with potential consequences ranging from identity theft to healthcare fraud. Striking a balance between leveraging data for medical advancements and safeguarding patient privacy remains a challenge. Compliance with regulations like HIPAA is essential, as is robust encryption and access control. Ethical considerations regarding data usage and consent must be addressed. Regular security audits, incident response plans, and staff training are crucial to maintain data integrity and protect against threats. Ethical considerations regarding data usage and consent must be addressed, and regular security audits are crucial to identifying vulnerabilities. Incident response plans, staff education, and secure data-sharing platforms are essential components of a comprehensive approach to safeguarding healthcare data, which is vital for patient trust and the advancement of medical knowledge. Ensuring the privacy and security of healthcare big data is not only a legal requirement but also vital for maintaining patient trust and advancing medical research. Here is a tabular representation of papers related to preserving security and privacy in big healthcare data, including specific author names, publication years, their focus, and limitations (Table 7.1).

Table 7.1 Publication years, their focus, and limitations

S. No.	Paper	Focus	Limitations
1	Privacy-Preserving Techniques in Healthcare Data, Smith et al., 2020	Focuses on applying differential privacy in healthcare	Limited discussion on the practical challenges of implementing differential privacy in real healthcare systems.
2	Blockchain Applications in Healthcare Data Security, Johnson, 2019	Explores the use of blockchain for healthcare security	Does not delve into the scalability issues of blockchain solutions in large healthcare networks.
3	Insider Threats in Healthcare Data, Patel, 2021	Analyzes the risk of insider threats in healthcare	Does not provide comprehensive solutions for mitigating insider threats; more focused on identifying risks.

(Continues)

Table 7.1 (Continued)

S. No.	Paper	Focus	Limitations
4	Ethical Considerations in Health Data Analytics, Lewis, 2018	Examines the ethical implications of health data use	Lacks a technical perspective on implementing ethical guidelines and securing data.
5	Data Encryption Techniques in Health Informatics, Brown et al., 2017	Discusses various encryption methods in health data	Limited coverage of encryption's impact on query performance in healthcare analytics.
6	Privacy-Preserving Data Sharing in Medical Research, Anderson, 2016	Explores privacy-enhancing technologies for data sharing	Does not provide detailed guidance on addressing regulatory compliance challenges in data sharing.
7	Federated Learning for Healthcare Data Privacy, Garcia, 2022	Investigates federated learning for healthcare privacy	Limited information on federated learning's computational overhead and convergence issues.
8	HIPAA Compliance Challenges in Modern Healthcare, Williams, 2019	Addresses challenges in complying with HIPAA	Focuses primarily on HIPAA without discussing other global privacy regulations impacting healthcare.
9	Cyber security Best Practices in Health IT, Nguyen et al., 2020	Examines best practices for healthcare cyber security	Lacks specific recommendations for securing legacy healthcare systems with outdated infrastructure.
10	Secure Cloud-Based Health Data Storage, Martinez, 2018	Discusses secure cloud storage solutions for health data	Does not cover potential data migration challenges when transitioning to cloud-based storage

7.3 Big data security life cycle in healthcare

The security life cycle in healthcare for big data is a comprehensive and dynamic process aimed at safeguarding sensitive patient information while facilitating data-driven healthcare advancements [1]. Beginning with the assessment and planning stage, healthcare organizations must meticulously identify data sources, conduct thorough risk assessments, and ensure compliance with regulatory frameworks like HIPAA and GDPR [2]. As data is collected and ingested from various sources, robust security measures, including encryption and data tagging, are imperative to protect against unauthorized access and data breaches [3]. Data storage, the next phase, involves secure storage solutions with access controls and encryption to maintain data integrity and confidentiality [4]. The data processing and analytics stage necessitates the implementation of privacy-preserving techniques such as differential privacy and secure multi-party computation (SMPC) to enable meaningful analysis while preserving individual privacy [5]. Data sharing, an essential component of healthcare research, requires secure data anonymization and

Privacy-preserving techniques for big data analytics in healthcare 139

de-identification methods to protect patient identities and meet regulatory requirements [6]. Throughout this life cycle, continuous monitoring and auditing [7] are crucial for identifying and mitigating security threats and vulnerabilities promptly [8]. In the event of security incidents or breaches, a well-defined incident response plan [9] must be in place to minimize harm, investigate the breach, and implement corrective measures [10]. Regular security training and awareness programs [11] ensure that healthcare staff are well-equipped to adhere to security protocols and recognize potential threats [12]. Furthermore, healthcare organizations must adapt to emerging technologies and threats [13] by staying current with security best practices, threat intelligence, and technological advancements [14]. Collaboration and information sharing among healthcare entities [15] foster collective security efforts and strengthen defenses against evolving threats [16]. Ethical considerations [17] play a pivotal role in ensuring that patient data is used responsibly, and consent is obtained for data sharing and research [18]. Finally, the disposal and data retention stage [19] must adhere to secure data erasure and destruction practices to prevent unauthorized access to discarded information [20]. In summary, Figure 7.1 outlines the key components of the big data lifecycle in healthcare, highlighting a multifaceted approach that requires diligence, adaptability, and a strong commitment to patient privacy and data protection.

In **the data collection phase** of big data healthcare, diverse healthcare-related information is systematically gathered from sources like electronic health records (EHRs), medical devices, and clinical databases. Quality and accuracy are essential, with measures in place to validate and clean incoming data. Security protocols,

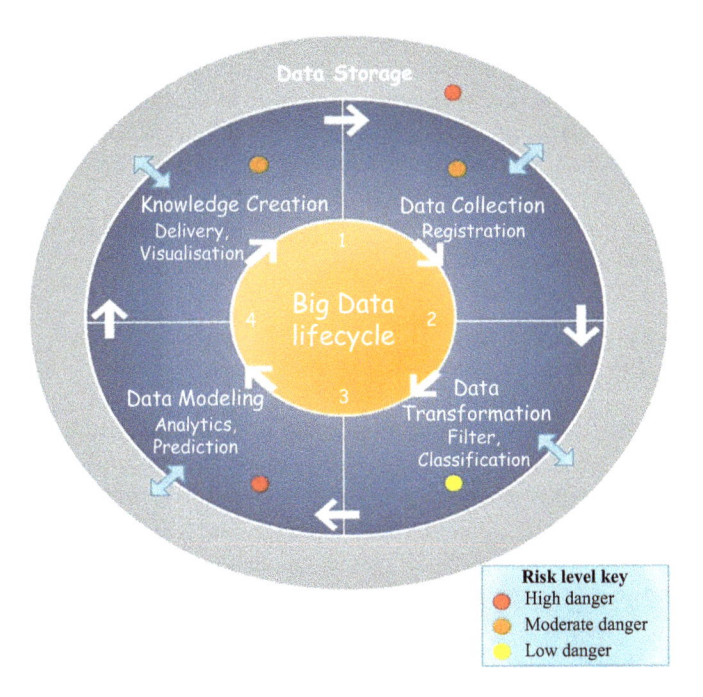

Figure 7.1 Security life cycle of big data in healthcare

including encryption and access controls, are implemented to protect data integrity and patient privacy. Compliance with regulations like HIPAA is a priority, ensuring patient consent and data handling adherence. This phase lays the foundation for data-driven insights that can enhance patient care and healthcare innovations.

In the **data transformation phase** of big data analytics, raw and diverse healthcare data is processed and converted into a structured, usable format. This involves cleaning, aggregating, and organizing the data to ensure consistency and quality. Complex data integration and transformation algorithms are applied to harmonize data from various sources, such as EHRs and medical devices, into a unified dataset. Additionally, data may be normalized, encoded, or transformed to facilitate analysis and machine learning algorithms, enabling meaningful insights for healthcare decision-making. This phase is essential for turning raw healthcare data into actionable information, driving improvements in patient care, research, and operational efficiency.

In the **data modeling phase** of big data analytics in healthcare, structured and cleaned healthcare data is organized into a model that represents the underlying relationships and patterns within the data. This process involves creating mathematical or statistical models, often using techniques like machine learning and predictive analytics, to extract meaningful insights and make data-driven predictions. Healthcare data models can range from patient risk assessment models to disease outbreak prediction models. The goal is to leverage these models to improve clinical decision-making, patient outcomes, and healthcare operations, ultimately enhancing the quality and efficiency of healthcare delivery.

In the **knowledge creation phase** of big data analytics in healthcare, the insights and patterns extracted from healthcare data models are transformed into actionable knowledge. This phase involves synthesizing the results of data analysis, drawing meaningful conclusions, and generating new insights into patient care, disease trends, and healthcare operations. These insights can lead to evidence-based recommendations, clinical guidelines, and predictive models that aid healthcare professionals in making informed decisions, ultimately improving patient outcomes and healthcare delivery. Knowledge creation in big data healthcare analytics is a dynamic and iterative process, continually refining and expanding our understanding of healthcare dynamics and driving advancements in medical research and practice.

7.4 Privacy-preserving methods in healthcare system using big data

Privacy-preserving methods in healthcare systems using big data represent a critical frontier in the quest to harness the vast potential of healthcare data while safeguarding patient confidentiality and adhering to stringent privacy regulations. These methods encompass a multifaceted approach, and a wealth of research literature exists to address these challenges comprehensively. Techniques such as differential privacy [1] and secure multi-party computation [2] have emerged as robust tools for protecting individual patient data during data analysis and sharing processes. Advanced encryption methods, including homomorphic encryption [3], facilitate secure computations on encrypted data, allowing insights to be gleaned without exposing sensitive information. Anonymization and de-identification [4] techniques play a pivotal role in removing personally identifiable information, while still enabling valuable research and analytics. Emerging technologies like federated learning [5] and blockchain [6] offer novel approaches to privacy preservation by allowing data to remain localized and under the control of the patient while contributing to collaborative research efforts. However, the implementation of these methods is not without challenges. Practicality and scalability issues [7] often arise when applying privacy-preserving techniques to large-scale healthcare datasets, requiring ongoing research to streamline these processes. Moreover, there is a need for a comprehensive regulatory framework [8] that accommodates privacy-preserving methods and balances innovation with patient data protection. Striking a balance between privacy and utility [9] remains a persistent challenge, as overly aggressive privacy measures can hinder the meaningful analysis of healthcare data.

Furthermore, ensuring the ethical use of healthcare data [10] and obtaining informed patient consent [11] are essential considerations. The healthcare industry must also address the technical hurdles associated with implementing these methods within existing infrastructure [12] while maintaining interoperability [13] and data standardization. Striking a balance between privacy and data utility remains a constant challenge in the healthcare big data landscape [14]. Addressing these complexities requires not only technical prowess but also a commitment to robust privacy policies, patient consent [15], and an awareness of evolving ethical and regulatory standards [16]. In essence, privacy-preserving methods in big data healthcare systems are indispensable tools, driving innovation while safeguarding the fundamental rights and security of patients' sensitive health information. Privacy-preserving methods in healthcare systems using big data are a rapidly evolving field, driven by the dual imperative of leveraging data for medical advancements and safeguarding patient privacy. A combination of encryption, anonymization, decentralized technologies, and robust regulatory frameworks is pivotal in realizing the full potential of big data in healthcare while upholding the highest standards of data privacy and security.

7.5 Conclusion

In conclusion, privacy-preserving techniques for big data analytics in healthcare stand as a crucial pillar in the era of data-driven healthcare transformation. As healthcare systems increasingly rely on vast and diverse datasets to drive improvements in patient care, research, and operational efficiency, safeguarding patient privacy remains paramount. The adoption of advanced encryption methods, such as homomorphic encryption and secure multi-party computation, provides a strong foundation for secure data analysis while preserving confidentiality. Differential privacy, anonymization, and de-identification techniques ensure that individual patient identities are shielded, even as data is shared and analyzed on a large scale. Innovations like federated learning and blockchain have opened new avenues for collaborative research without compromising patient data security. However, challenges persist in implementing these techniques at scale, navigating complex regulatory landscapes, and striking the delicate balance between privacy and data utility. As healthcare stakeholders continue to advance these privacy-preserving methodologies, it is imperative that they remain steadfast in their commitment to ethical data handling, transparency, and the protection of patients' fundamental rights to privacy in the ever-evolving landscape of healthcare big data analytics.

References

[1] Dwork, C., and Roth, A. (2014). The algorithmic foundations of differential privacy. *Foundations and Trends®. Theoretical Computer Science*, 9(3–4), 211–407.

[2] Ohno-Machado, L., and Vinterbo, S. (2010). Sharing aggregate clinical trial data: A proposal based on Fair Use. *Journal of the American Medical Informatics Association*, 17(4), 357–365.

[3] El Emam, K., Dankar, F. K., Issa, R., *et al.* (2009). A globally optimal k-anonymity method for the de-identification of health data. *Journal of the American Medical Informatics Association*, 16(5), 670–682.

[4] Jiang, X., and Kim, J. (2018). A survey of privacy-preserving data sharing in the genomic era. *Information*, 9(7), 154.

[5] Kayaalp, M., and Garcia, E. (2016). Patient privacy in the era of big data. *Balkan Medical Journal*, 33(1), 3–10.

[6] Wang, S., Jiang, X., Tang, H., and Wang, S. (2019). Privacy-preserving genomic data sharing. *Computers, Materials & Continua*, 60(1), 279–301.

[7] Malin, B. A., and Sweeney, L. (2004). How (not) to protect genomic data privacy in a distributed network: using trail re-identification to evaluate and design anonymity protection systems. *Journal of Biomedical Informatics*, 37(3), 179–192.

[8] Golle, P., and Partridge, K. (2009). On the anonymity of home/work location pairs. In *Proceedings of the 17th Annual International Conference on Mobile Computing and Networking* (pp. 81–92).

[9] Schneier, B. (2015). *Data and Goliath: The Hidden Battles to Collect Your Data and Control Your World*. New York: W. W. Norton & Company.

[10] Blumenthal, D., and Tavenner, M. (2010). The "meaningful use" regulation for electronic health records. *New England Journal of Medicine*, 363(6), 501–504.

[11] Malin, B. A., and Emam, K. E. (2013). Protecting privacy in medical informatics: Research, clinical, and policy perspectives. *Journal of the American Medical Informatics Association*, 20(1), 1–2.

[12] Fernandes, L., and Vasconcelos, A. P. (2013). Privacy-preserving techniques for secure data sharing in cloud computing. *Journal of Cloud Computing: Advances, Systems and Applications*, 2(1), 9.

[13] Moher, D., Liberati, A., Tetzlaff, J., Altman, D. G., and PRISMA Group. (2009). Preferred reporting items for systematic reviews and meta-analyses: The PRISMA statement. *Annals of Internal Medicine*, 151(4), 264–269.
[14] Cao, S., Zhang, G., and Zhang, Z. (2019). A privacy-preserving data aggregation scheme for fog computing-based healthcare systems. *IEEE Internet of Things Journal*, 6(2), 2041–2052.
[15] Wang, S., Yao, L., Liu, C., Wang, P., and Liu, J. (2016). Secure and privacy-preserving protocol for cloud-assisted mobile health networks. *IEEE Journal on Selected Areas in Communications*, 34(12), 3298–3309.
[16] Li, X., Zhao, S., Wang, X., and Zhang, X. (2018). A privacy-preserving model for clinical big data. *Future Generation Computer Systems*, 88, 64–71.
[17] Ganta, S. R., Kasiviswanathan, S. P., and Smith, A. (2008). Composition attacks and auxiliary information in data privacy. In *Proceedings of the 14th ACM SIGKDD International Conference on Knowledge Discovery and Data Mining* (pp. 265–273).
[18] Sweeney, L. (2002). k-Anonymity: A model for protecting privacy. *International Journal of Uncertainty, Fuzziness and Knowledge-Based Systems*, 10(5), 557–570.
[19] Raisaro, J. L., Troncoso-Pastoriza, J. R., Misbach, M., Sousa, J. S., and Pradervand, S. (2019). I2B2: An open source privacy-protected framework for biomedical data sharing. *Studies in Health Technology and Informatics*, 264, 1968–1969.
[20] Aggarwal, C. C., and Yu, P. S. (2008). *Privacy-Preserving Data Mining: Models and Algorithms*. Berlin: Springer Science & Business Media.

Chapter 8

Enabling trustworthy data sharing and collaborative insights in healthcare analytics

Pawan Whig[1], Shama Kouser[2], Ashima Bhatnagar Bhatia[1], Rahul Reddy Nadikattu[3] and Pavika Sharma[4]

In the evolving landscape of healthcare analytics, the need for secure data sharing and collaboration has become paramount. As healthcare organizations and researchers strive to extract valuable insights from vast and diverse datasets, ensuring the confidentiality, integrity, and availability of sensitive information has become a critical challenge. This chapter delves into the intricate realm of secure data sharing and collaboration within the context of healthcare analytics. It explores the multifaceted dimensions of security, ranging from technological solutions to policy frameworks, that are essential for safeguarding patient privacy and maintaining data accuracy. By examining state-of-the-art encryption techniques, access controls, and authentication mechanisms, this chapter equips readers with a comprehensive understanding of how to establish a robust security foundation for data sharing and collaborative endeavors. Furthermore, it elucidates the role of advanced technologies, such as blockchain and federated learning, in enhancing data privacy and trust in healthcare analytics collaborations. The chapter also delves into real-world case studies and best practices, highlighting successful implementations of secure data-sharing models that facilitate meaningful research while upholding the highest standards of data protection. Ultimately, this chapter serves as a vital resource for healthcare professionals, data scientists, researchers, and policymakers seeking to navigate the intricate landscape of secure data sharing and collaboration in the realm of healthcare analytics.

8.1 Introduction

In today's rapidly evolving healthcare landscape, the importance of data cannot be overstated. Data-driven insights have the power to transform the way healthcare

[1]School of Information Technology, Vivekananda Institute of Professional Studies - Technical Campus, Delhi-110034, India
[2]Computer Science, Jazan University - President's Office 6809, Jazan 82817-2820, Kingdom of Saudi Arabia
[3]IT, University of the Cumberland, College Station Drive, Williamsburg, KY 40769, United States
[4]Department of Electronics, BPIT, PSP-4, Dr. KN Katju Marg, Sector17, Rohini, Delhi 110089, India

providers deliver services, researchers uncover new treatments, and policymakers make informed decisions [1]. However, harnessing the full potential of healthcare data requires a delicate balance between privacy, security, and the urgent need for collaborative insights [2].

This book chapter, titled "Enabling Trustworthy Data Sharing and Collaborative Insights in Healthcare Analytics," delves into the intricate world of healthcare data management and collaborative analytics. As we navigate the ever-growing pools of patient information, research findings, and clinical records, it becomes clear that effective data sharing is not just a technological challenge but a crucial ethical and regulatory one as well [3]. The modern healthcare ecosystem is characterized by an abundance of disparate data sources, from electronic health records and medical imaging to genomic data and wearable device metrics. While these diverse datasets hold the potential to drive breakthroughs in personalized medicine, disease prevention, and healthcare efficiency, they also present formidable obstacles [4–7]. Protecting patient privacy, complying with stringent regulations such as the Health Insurance Portability and Accountability Act (HIPAA) and the General Data Protection Regulation (GDPR), and fostering trust among data contributors are just some of the complexities involved [8–10].

This chapter aims to illuminate the path forward by addressing the fundamental principles and innovative strategies required to enable trustworthy data sharing and collaborative insights in healthcare analytics [11–14]. We will explore emerging technologies such as blockchain, federated learning, and advanced encryption techniques that hold promise in preserving privacy while facilitating data collaboration. Moreover, we will discuss the pivotal role of data governance frameworks and interoperability standards in creating a cohesive and secure data-sharing environment. In the pages that follow, we will embark on a journey through the challenges and opportunities of healthcare data sharing, drawing from real-world case studies and best practices [15]. Our goal is to empower healthcare professionals, researchers, and policymakers with the knowledge and tools needed to navigate this complex terrain, fostering a future where data-driven collaboration leads to better patient outcomes, groundbreaking discoveries, and a more resilient healthcare system.

8.2 The importance of secure data sharing in healthcare analytics

In the realm of healthcare analytics, data is the lifeblood that drives informed decision-making, medical breakthroughs, and improved patient outcomes. The vast and varied sources of healthcare data, from electronic health records to medical imaging and genetic information, offer immense potential for research, diagnosis, and treatment. However, this potential can only be fully realized through secure data sharing [16–18].

8.2.1 Data-driven healthcare revolution

The data-driven healthcare revolution represents a transformative shift in how healthcare is delivered, managed, and personalized. By harnessing the power of large-scale data collection, advanced analytics, and artificial intelligence (AI), this paradigm seeks to improve patient outcomes, optimize healthcare operations, and drive innovation across the healthcare ecosystem. At its core, this revolution leverages diverse sources of healthcare data, including electronic health records (EHRs), medical imaging, genomic data, wearable devices, and patient-generated data from mobile apps and IoT devices. Machine learning algorithms analyze these vast datasets to uncover patterns, predict outcomes, and provide actionable insights that guide clinical decision-making, disease prevention strategies, and personalized treatment plans. Moreover, data-driven approaches enable healthcare providers to implement precision medicine initiatives, tailoring therapies and interventions based on individual patient characteristics and genetic profiles. Beyond clinical applications, data analytics enhances healthcare administration by optimizing resource allocation, improving operational efficiencies, and reducing costs. As the data-driven healthcare revolution continues to evolve, it holds the promise of transforming healthcare delivery into a more proactive, personalized, and patient-centric model, ultimately leading to better health outcomes and improved quality of life for individuals worldwide [17]. These innovations rely heavily on access to diverse datasets from various healthcare providers, research institutions, and even patients themselves.

8.2.2 The collaborative imperative

One of the most critical drivers behind secure data sharing in healthcare analytics is collaboration. Healthcare is inherently collaborative, with various stakeholders—doctors, researchers, hospitals, pharmaceutical companies, and public health agencies—needing to work together to advance medical knowledge and patient care. Secure data sharing serves as the conduit through which these collaborations thrive.

8.3 Secure data sharing in healthcare analytics

Secure data sharing in healthcare is revolutionizing the industry across multiple fronts, promising significant benefits in research, clinical practice, and public health management. First, enhanced research and discovery are facilitated by access to a broader spectrum of patient data from various sources. Researchers can now uncover new trends, insights, and potential treatment options by aggregating and analyzing extensive datasets, such as genetic information pooled from multiple studies to identify rare disorders and innovative therapeutic targets. Second, in clinical settings, secure data sharing ensures timely access to critical patient information like medical histories and medication records. This capability is crucial during emergencies, where quick decisions can be life-saving, enabling healthcare providers to deliver more precise and efficient care. Third, improved population health management becomes achievable through data sharing, allowing public health agencies to monitor disease outbreaks, track infectious disease spread, and implement targeted interventions promptly. This proactive approach not only saves lives but also reduces healthcare costs by preventing disease escalation. Last, by sharing data on best practices, treatment outcomes, and cost-effective interventions, healthcare organizations can identify opportunities for cost reduction and resource optimization, thus improving overall healthcare delivery efficiency. As secure data sharing continues to evolve, it holds immense promise in advancing healthcare outcomes, enhancing patient care, and optimizing public health strategies on a global scale.

8.3.1 Challenges in secure data sharing

While the benefits of secure data sharing in healthcare analytics are evident, several challenges must be addressed:

1. **Privacy Concerns:** Protecting patient privacy is paramount. Strict adherence to regulations such as HIPAA and GDPR is essential to ensure that patient data remains confidential. Measures such as data anonymization, encryption, access controls, and audit trails are implemented to mitigate privacy risks and prevent unauthorized disclosure of sensitive information. Healthcare institutions must also adhere to ethical guidelines and institutional review board (IRB) approvals when conducting research involving patient data to uphold patient confidentiality and privacy rights.
2. **Data Security:** The healthcare sector is a prime target for cyberattacks due to the high value of medical data. Robust cybersecurity measures must be in place to protect shared data. Healthcare providers and organizations must implement comprehensive security protocols, including network segmentation, intrusion detection systems, endpoint protection, secure authentication mechanisms, and regular security audits. Encryption techniques are employed to secure data both at rest and in transit, ensuring that patient information remains protected from malicious actors and cyber threats. Continuous monitoring and response mechanisms are essential to detect and mitigate cybersecurity incidents promptly, safeguarding the integrity and confidentiality of shared healthcare data.
3. **Interoperability:** Healthcare systems often use different standards and formats for data, making it challenging to integrate and share information seamlessly. Interoperability standards are needed to facilitate data sharing. By adopting interoperability standards, healthcare organizations can enhance data accessibility, improve care coordination, and support collaborative research initiatives while ensuring data integrity and security.
4. **Trust and Consent:** Establishing trust among data contributors and obtaining patient consent for data sharing are essential. Patients must have confidence that their data will be used for legitimate purposes. Healthcare providers and researchers must adhere to ethical guidelines and legal requirements regarding consent, ensuring that patients understand how their data will be used, who will have access to it, and their rights to withdraw consent or restrict data sharing at any time. Respect for patient autonomy and privacy preferences strengthens trust in healthcare data-sharing initiatives and promotes responsible data stewardship practices across the healthcare ecosystem.

Enabling trustworthy data sharing and collaborative insights 149

8.3.2 The role of technology in secure data sharing

Several technological advancements play a pivotal role in enabling secure data sharing in healthcare analytics:

1. **Blockchain:** Blockchain technology offers a tamper-proof and transparent way to record data transactions, enhancing data integrity and traceability.
2. **Federated Learning:** This approach allows machine learning models to be trained across multiple decentralized data sources without the need to share the data itself, preserving privacy.
3. **Advanced Encryption:** Robust encryption techniques safeguard data both in transit and at rest, making it extremely difficult for unauthorized parties to access sensitive information.
4. **Data Governance Frameworks:** Comprehensive data governance frameworks help establish rules, policies, and procedures for data sharing, ensuring compliance with legal and ethical standards.

In the era of data-driven healthcare, secure data sharing is not just an option; it is a necessity. The collaborative potential of healthcare analytics can only be fully realized when data can flow securely and responsibly among stakeholders. By overcoming challenges such as privacy concerns and data security, and leveraging emerging technologies, the healthcare industry can harness the power of data to deliver better care, drive medical breakthroughs, and ultimately improve the health and well-being of patients worldwide. Secure data sharing is not only the future of healthcare analytics; it is the cornerstone upon which the future of healthcare itself will be built.

8.3.3 Fundamentals of data privacy and security measures

In today's interconnected digital world, the importance of data privacy and security cannot be overstated. With the proliferation of data breaches, cyber threats, and evolving regulations, safeguarding sensitive information has become a top priority for individuals, organizations, and governments alike. This chapter explores the fundamentals of data privacy and the essential security measures necessary to protect data in an increasingly complex and interconnected landscape.

8.4 Understanding data privacy

Data privacy refers to the protection of individuals' personal information and the control they have over how their data is collected, used, and shared. Data privacy is fundamental to safeguarding individuals' personal information and ensuring their control over how data is collected, used, and shared. Central to data privacy are several key principles that organizations must adhere to rigorously. First and foremost, organizations must be transparent about their data collection practices, ensuring individuals provide clear, informed consent before collecting any data. It is essential to minimize data collection to only what is necessary for specific purposes and to delete data when it is no longer needed to reduce risks associated with data breaches. Individuals should have the right to access their data, correct inaccuracies, and request its deletion, maintaining control over how their data is shared and used. Robust data security measures, including encryption, access control, and regular updates to software and systems, are crucial to protecting data from unauthorized access and breaches. Comprehensive employee training on cybersecurity and a well-defined incident response plan further fortify organizational defenses against potential threats. By implementing these measures and adhering to clear data privacy policies, organizations can foster trust with individuals and ensure compliance with data protection regulations, ultimately upholding the integrity and confidentiality of personal data in an increasingly digital world.

8.4.1 Compliance with regulations

Many regions have enacted data protection regulations, such as the General Data Protection Regulation (GDPR) in Europe and the Health Insurance Portability and Accountability Act (HIPAA) in the United States. Organizations handling data must ensure compliance with these regulations, which often include strict requirements for data privacy and security.

In an era of digital transformation and increasing cyber threats, understanding the fundamentals of data privacy and implementing robust security measures are imperative. Data breaches not only result in financial losses but also erode trust and damage reputation. By prioritizing data privacy, implementing comprehensive security measures, and staying informed about emerging threats, individuals and organizations can protect sensitive data and maintain the trust of their stakeholders in an increasingly digital world.

8.5 Ensuring patient confidentiality through encryption techniques

In the ever-evolving landscape of healthcare, maintaining the confidentiality of patient information is paramount. The digitization of medical records and the exchange of healthcare data across various platforms have created both opportunities and challenges. This chapter explores the vital role of encryption techniques in safeguarding patient confidentiality and the various methods and best practices for their effective implementation.

8.5.1 The imperative of patient confidentiality

Patient confidentiality is the cornerstone of medical ethics and is enshrined in laws and regulations worldwide, including the Health Insurance Portability and Accountability Act (HIPAA) in the United States and the General Data Protection Regulation (GDPR) in Europe. Ensuring the privacy of patients' sensitive information not only upholds their rights but also fosters trust between healthcare providers and patients.

8.5.2 Understanding encryption in healthcare

Encryption is a process of converting readable data into a coded format that can only be deciphered with the appropriate encryption key. In healthcare, ensuring the confidentiality and integrity of patient information during data transmission, storage, communication, and on mobile devices is critical to maintaining data security and compliance with privacy regulations. When patient information is transmitted over networks, such as electronic health records (EHR) sent between medical facilities, encryption plays a pivotal role in protecting data from interception and unauthorized access. Encryption algorithms encode the data into a secure format during transit, ensuring that even if intercepted, the information remains unreadable without the decryption key. Similarly, encrypting data at rest, whether stored in databases or on physical devices, prevents unauthorized access in the event of a security breach or theft. Secure messaging platforms and email encryption further enhance confidentiality by safeguarding sensitive patient information exchanged among healthcare professionals, mitigating the risk of data breaches. Moreover, encryption on mobile devices, such as smartphones and tablets used by healthcare providers, protects patient data stored locally on these devices, reducing exposure in case of loss or theft. By implementing robust encryption measures across these critical areas, healthcare organizations can enhance data security, uphold patient confidentiality, and ensure compliance with data protection standards in an increasingly interconnected healthcare landscape.

8.5.3 Methods of encryption in healthcare

Encryption plays a crucial role in data security by ensuring that sensitive information remains confidential and protected from unauthorized access or interception. There are several encryption methods and techniques used across different aspects of data handling in healthcare and other sectors:

1. **Symmetric Encryption:** Symmetric encryption uses a single key for both encryption and decryption of data. This key must be securely shared between the sender and the intended recipient before data transmission begins. Symmetric encryption algorithms, such as AES (Advanced Encryption Standard), DES (Data Encryption Standard), and 3DES (Triple DES), are efficient and fast, making them suitable for encrypting large volumes of data. However, managing and securely distributing the encryption key remains a critical challenge. Techniques such as key management systems (KMS) and secure key exchange protocols (e.g., Diffie-Hellman key exchange) are used to safeguard symmetric encryption keys.
2. **Asymmetric Encryption (Public-Key Encryption):** Asymmetric encryption utilizes a pair of keys: a public key and a private key. The public key is used for encrypting data, while the private key is kept secret and used for decrypting the data. This method enhances security by eliminating the need to share the private key over insecure channels. Asymmetric encryption algorithms, such as RSA (Rivest-Shamir-Adleman) and ECC (Elliptic Curve Cryptography), are

commonly used for secure data exchange, digital signatures, and establishing secure communication channels in healthcare systems and other sensitive environments.
3. **End-to-End Encryption:** End-to-end encryption (E2EE) ensures that data is encrypted on the sender's device and can only be decrypted by the intended recipient. This approach prevents intermediaries, including service providers and network administrators, from accessing or tampering with the transmitted data. E2EE is widely used in messaging applications, email services, and telecommunication platforms to protect user privacy and confidentiality.
4. **Data-at-Rest Encryption:** Data-at-rest encryption involves encrypting patient data stored in databases, file systems, or physical devices (e.g., hard drives, USB drives). This encryption ensures that if the storage medium is compromised or physically stolen, the data remains unreadable without the correct decryption key. Healthcare organizations employ data-at-rest encryption to comply with regulatory requirements, such as HIPAA in the United States, and protect patient records from unauthorized access or breaches.
5. **Transport Layer Security (TLS) and Secure Sockets Layer (SSL):** TLS and SSL are cryptographic protocols designed to secure data transmission over the internet. They establish encrypted connections between clients (e.g., web browsers) and servers (e.g., web servers), ensuring that sensitive information, such as patient health records or financial transactions, is protected from eavesdropping and tampering during transit. TLS has largely superseded SSL due to security vulnerabilities in older SSL versions.

8.5.4 Best practices for implementing encryption in healthcare

Encryption techniques play an indispensable role in ensuring patient confidentiality in the healthcare industry. By employing encryption for data transmission, storage, and communication, healthcare organizations can protect sensitive patient information, maintain compliance with regulations, and, most importantly, build and preserve trust between patients and healthcare providers. As healthcare continues to evolve in the digital age, encryption remains a fundamental tool in the ongoing commitment to patient privacy and data security.

8.6 Access controls and authentication mechanisms for collaborative analytics

In the era of data-driven decision-making, collaborative analytics has emerged as a powerful approach that allows organizations to harness the collective intelligence of diverse teams and stakeholders. However, to ensure the integrity, security, and privacy of sensitive data in collaborative analytics environments, robust access controls and authentication mechanisms are imperative. This chapter delves into the essential role of access controls and authentication methods in fostering secure and effective collaborative analytics.

8.6.1 The significance of access controls and authentication in collaborative analytics

Collaborative analytics brings together individuals with varying roles, responsibilities, and levels of access to data. Effective access controls and authentication mechanisms are essential for several reasons:

1. **Data Security:** They safeguard data from unauthorized access, preventing breaches and data leaks that could compromise sensitive information.
2. **Privacy Compliance:** Access controls help organizations adhere to data protection regulations, such as GDPR and HIPAA, by ensuring that only authorized individuals can access and manipulate personal or confidential data.
3. **Intellectual Property Protection:** In collaborative research and analytics projects, protecting intellectual property and proprietary data is critical. Access controls limit exposure to sensitive information.
4. **Maintaining Data Integrity:** Ensuring that data remains accurate and unaltered is essential for the validity of analytics results. Proper access controls help prevent unauthorized data tampering.

8.6.2 Access control principles

Effective access controls in collaborative analytics are based on a few fundamental principles:

1. **Least Privilege:** Grant individuals the minimum level of access required to perform their tasks. This principle minimizes the risk associated with excessive access privileges.
2. **Role-Based Access Control (RBAC):** Implement RBAC policies that assign permissions based on job roles or responsibilities. This simplifies access management and aligns with organizational hierarchies.
3. **Data Classification:** Categorize data based on its sensitivity, and apply access controls accordingly. Not all data should be equally accessible to all users.

8.6.3 Authentication mechanisms

Authentication is the process of verifying the identity of a user or system trying to access resources. Collaborative analytics environments often employ a variety of authentication mechanisms:

1. **Username and Password:** The most common form of authentication, though increasingly considered less secure. It is often augmented with additional factors like one-time passwords (OTP) or multi-factor authentication (MFA).
2. **Multi-Factor Authentication (MFA):** Requires users to provide multiple forms of identification, such as something they know (password), something they have (smartphone for OTP), or something they are (fingerprint or facial recognition).
3. **Biometric Authentication:** Utilizes physical or behavioral characteristics, such as fingerprints or facial recognition, for identity verification.

4. **Token-Based Authentication:** Involves the use of tokens, like smart cards or security tokens, which are difficult to replicate and can be used for secure access.
5. **Single Sign-On (SSO):** Allows users to access multiple applications or services with a single set of credentials, simplifying user experience while maintaining security.

8.7 Best practices for implementation

1. **Regularly Review and Update Access Permissions:** Periodically audit and adjust access permissions to align with changes in roles, responsibilities, and data sensitivity.
2. **Implement Strong Password Policies:** Enforce password complexity and expiration rules, and educate users on the importance of strong, unique passwords.
3. **Monitor and Detect Anomalies:** Employ intrusion detection and monitoring systems to identify suspicious activities and unauthorized access attempts.
4. **User Training:** Ensure that all users are educated on security best practices and the importance of safeguarding access credentials.

Access controls and authentication mechanisms are the linchpins of secure and responsible collaborative analytics. By implementing these measures, organizations can strike a balance between facilitating effective data-driven collaboration and safeguarding the confidentiality, integrity, and privacy of their sensitive data. In an era where data collaboration is driving innovation across industries, robust access controls and authentication mechanisms are the pillars upon which trustworthy and secure collaborative analytics are built.

8.8 Policy frameworks for ethical and secure data sharing

In today's interconnected world, data has become the lifeblood of countless industries, with the healthcare, financial, and research sectors relying heavily on the responsible sharing of information. However, achieving ethical and secure data sharing is a complex endeavor, necessitating comprehensive policy frameworks that balance the need for collaboration with the imperative to protect individual privacy and data security. This chapter explores the critical role of policy frameworks in guiding ethical and secure data-sharing practices.

8.8.1 The imperative of ethical and secure data sharing

Ethical and secure data sharing is pivotal for several reasons:

1. **Advancing Knowledge:** Data sharing fuels research, innovation, and evidence-based decision-making, leading to breakthroughs in science, technology, and healthcare.

Enabling trustworthy data sharing and collaborative insights 155

2. **Enhancing Collaboration:** Data sharing fosters collaboration among diverse stakeholders, including researchers, institutions, and government agencies, leading to more comprehensive and impactful outcomes.
3. **Patient Empowerment:** In healthcare, data sharing empowers patients by giving them greater control over their health information and facilitating better-informed decisions about their care.
4. **Public Trust:** Ethical data-sharing practices build public trust by assuring individuals that their data is being handled responsibly and transparently.

8.8.2 Elements of effective policy frameworks

Effective policy frameworks for ethical and secure data sharing encompass several essential elements:

1. **Data Governance:** Establish clear governance structures that outline roles, responsibilities, and decision-making processes regarding data sharing.
2. **Data Classification:** Categorize data based on sensitivity and define rules for sharing each type of data, with heightened protections for highly sensitive information.
3. **Privacy Protection:** Implement privacy protection measures, such as de-identification or encryption, to safeguard personal information.
4. **Data Access Controls:** Define access controls, specifying who can access data, under what circumstances, and for what purposes.
5. **Consent Mechanisms:** Develop consent mechanisms that give individuals control over how their data is shared and used, ensuring that data sharing adheres to legal and ethical standards.
6. **Data Security:** Implement robust security measures, including encryption, access monitoring, and threat detection, to protect shared data from unauthorized access or breaches.
7. **Compliance with Regulations:** Ensure that data sharing policies align with applicable data protection regulations, such as GDPR, HIPAA, or industry-specific standards.

8.8.3 Balancing ethical considerations and innovation

Effective policy frameworks must strike a balance between ethical considerations and the drive for innovation. Stricter policies can lead to better privacy protection but may hinder data sharing, while more permissive policies may promote innovation but risk compromising privacy. Striking this balance requires careful consideration of the specific context and data involved.

8.8.4 Transparency and accountability

Transparency and accountability are key pillars of ethical data-sharing policy frameworks:

1. **Transparency:** Ensure that data-sharing practices are transparent and well-communicated to all stakeholders, including data subjects.

2. **Accountability:** Hold individuals and organizations accountable for adhering to data-sharing policies and for any breaches or misuse of shared data.

8.8.5 Collaboration and stakeholder engagement

The development of effective policy frameworks should involve collaboration among stakeholders from different sectors, including legal experts, ethicists, technology specialists, and data owners. Engaging all relevant parties helps create policies that are both practical and ethically sound.

8.8.6 Continuous evaluation and adaptation

Data sharing policies should be dynamic, subject to regular evaluation and adaptation as technology, regulations, and ethical norms evolve. Regular reviews ensure that policies remain relevant and effective in safeguarding privacy and security.

Policy frameworks for ethical and secure data sharing are indispensable in our data-driven society. They provide the necessary guidance and structure to enable collaboration while upholding individual privacy and data security. By embracing these frameworks, organizations can navigate the complex terrain of data sharing with integrity, transparency, and a commitment to ethical principles, ensuring that the benefits of data-driven innovation are realized while respecting the rights and concerns of data subjects.

8.9 Data integrity in healthcare analytics: Challenges and solutions

In the realm of healthcare analytics, the quality and integrity of data are paramount. Accurate and reliable data forms the foundation upon which critical healthcare decisions, research findings, and patient care plans are built. However, maintaining data integrity in healthcare analytics presents a unique set of challenges that demand innovative solutions. This chapter explores these challenges and presents strategies and solutions to ensure data integrity in the healthcare sector.

8.9.1 The critical role of data integrity in healthcare

Data integrity in healthcare analytics refers to the accuracy, consistency, and reliability of healthcare data throughout its lifecycle. It is essential for several reasons:

Clinical Decision-Making: Accurate and reliable data is essential for healthcare professionals to make informed clinical decisions that impact patient care and treatment outcomes. Clinical decision-making relies on access to comprehensive patient data, including medical histories, laboratory results, imaging studies, and ongoing monitoring data. Healthcare providers use this information to assess patient conditions, diagnose illnesses, determine appropriate treatments, and monitor progress over time. For example, having timely access to a patient's complete medical record allows physicians to make evidence-based decisions regarding medication choices, surgical interventions, or therapeutic approaches. Accurate data ensures that healthcare professionals can tailor care plans to individual patient needs, optimize treatment efficacy, and improve overall patient outcomes.

Research and Discovery: High-quality data plays a pivotal role in advancing medical research, facilitating the identification of disease trends, conducting clinical studies, and developing new treatments and interventions. Researchers rely on access to large, diverse datasets to analyze health outcomes, study disease mechanisms, and explore the efficacy of new therapies. For instance, aggregated patient data from multiple sources enables researchers to identify genetic predispositions to diseases, evaluate treatment responses across different populations, and discover novel biomarkers for diagnostic purposes. Reliable data is crucial for generating scientific insights, validating research hypotheses, and translating findings into clinical practice to benefit patient populations worldwide.

Regulatory Compliance: Healthcare organizations are subject to stringent regulatory requirements, such as the Health Insurance Portability and Accountability Act (HIPAA) in the United States, which mandate data integrity, confidentiality, and patient privacy protections. Regulatory compliance ensures that patient information is handled responsibly and securely throughout its lifecycle, from collection and storage to sharing and disposal. Healthcare providers must implement robust data governance frameworks, security measures, and privacy policies to safeguard patient data and comply with legal standards. This includes obtaining patient consent for data use, maintaining audit trails of data access and modifications, and adhering to data retention policies. By adhering to regulatory requirements, healthcare organizations demonstrate their commitment to maintaining trust with patients, protecting sensitive information, and upholding ethical standards in healthcare delivery and data management.

8.9.2 Challenges to data integrity in healthcare analytics

1. **Data Entry Errors:** Data entry errors can occur during the manual input of information into electronic health records (EHRs) and other healthcare systems. These errors may include typographical mistakes, inaccurate recording of patient information, or incomplete data entries. Human factors such as fatigue, distractions, or lack of training can contribute to these errors. Incorrect data entry can lead to misinformation in patient records, potentially impacting clinical decision-making and patient care outcomes. To mitigate data entry errors, healthcare organizations employ training programs for staff, implement data validation checks within EHR systems, and encourage the use of electronic forms and automation to reduce manual entry.
2. **Data Integration Issues:** Integrating data from diverse sources, such as EHRs, laboratory reports, and wearable devices, presents challenges due to variations in data formats, coding systems, and standards across different healthcare settings. These integration issues can result in data discrepancies, inconsistencies, or incomplete datasets, affecting the accuracy and reliability of

analytics and reporting. Healthcare providers and IT professionals work to standardize data formats, adopt interoperability standards like HL7 and FHIR, and implement middleware solutions to facilitate seamless data exchange and integration. Robust data governance practices, including data mapping and reconciliation processes, help ensure that integrated data maintains accuracy and consistency across systems.

3. **Data Quality Variability:** Data quality can vary significantly across healthcare providers, institutions, and systems, impacting the reliability and validity of analytical outcomes and decision-making processes. Variations in data completeness, accuracy, timeliness, and consistency may arise due to differences in documentation practices, coding standards, and workflow variations among healthcare professionals. To address data quality variability, healthcare organizations implement data quality assurance programs, conduct regular audits and validation checks, and collaborate with stakeholders to standardize data capture methods and improve documentation practices. Enhanced data quality enhances the integrity and usefulness of healthcare data for clinical research, population health management, and quality improvement initiatives.

4. **Data Security and Privacy Concerns:** Data security and privacy concerns are paramount in healthcare due to the sensitive nature of patient information and regulatory requirements such as HIPAA (Health Insurance Portability and Accountability Act) in the United States. Security breaches, unauthorized access, or data manipulation can compromise data integrity, confidentiality, and patient trust. Healthcare organizations employ stringent security measures, including encryption, access controls, network security protocols (e.g., TLS/SSL), and regular security audits to protect against cyber threats and unauthorized access to patient data. Privacy safeguards include obtaining patient consent for data use, enforcing data access policies, and training staff on security best practices. By prioritizing data security and privacy, healthcare organizations mitigate risks and uphold patient confidentiality while ensuring compliance with legal and regulatory standards.

8.9.3 Solutions and strategies for ensuring data integrity

Ensuring data integrity and quality in healthcare is paramount to supporting accurate clinical decision-making, enhancing patient care outcomes, and maintaining regulatory compliance. Automated data validation processes are essential for promptly identifying and correcting errors as data is entered into electronic health records (EHRs) and other systems. These automated checks help minimize human error and ensure that data is accurate and consistent from the outset. Standardizing data formats, codes, and terminology across healthcare systems facilitates seamless data integration and enhances interoperability, enabling healthcare providers to access comprehensive patient information for holistic care management. Establishing robust data governance policies defines clear roles and responsibilities for data management, fostering accountability and adherence to best practices for data quality maintenance. Regular data audits and validation checks further reinforce data integrity by systematically reviewing data accuracy, completeness, and reliability. Technologies such as blockchain provide immutable records of data transactions, enhancing transparency and security, while machine learning and AI algorithms detect anomalies and inconsistencies in data, preemptively flagging potential errors or fraudulent activities. Strong access controls and data privacy measures, including encryption and anonymization techniques, safeguard patient information against unauthorized access and ensure compliance with stringent data protection regulations like HIPAA. By prioritizing training and education on data entry best practices, healthcare organizations empower staff to uphold data integrity standards, ultimately enhancing the trustworthiness and utility of healthcare data for informed decision-making and improved patient outcomes.

8.9.4 Collaboration and data sharing

Collaboration among healthcare providers, researchers, and institutions can also bolster data integrity. Sharing data and insights can help identify and correct errors and inconsistencies while enabling the development of best practices for data quality. In the dynamic world of healthcare analytics, data integrity is non-negotiable. The challenges are multifaceted, but with the right strategies and solutions, healthcare organizations can ensure that the data driving clinical decisions, research advancements, and patient care is trustworthy, accurate, and secure. By prioritizing data integrity and adopting innovative approaches, the healthcare sector can harness the full potential of data analytics to improve patient outcomes and advance medical knowledge.

8.10 Exploring blockchain technology for trustworthy healthcare collaboration

In the ever-evolving landscape of healthcare, fostering trustworthy collaboration among diverse stakeholders is pivotal to advancing patient care, medical research, and healthcare innovation. Blockchain technology has emerged as a game-changing tool that holds the potential to revolutionize the way healthcare data is shared, secured, and trusted. This chapter explores the transformative role of blockchain technology in healthcare collaboration, shedding light on its benefits, challenges, and real-world applications.

8.10.1 The imperative of trustworthy healthcare collaboration

Collaboration in healthcare involves various stakeholders, including healthcare providers, researchers, insurers, and patients, who must share and access sensitive data to improve outcomes. Trust is the linchpin of effective collaboration, ensuring that data is accurate, secure, and accessible when needed.

8.10.2 Blockchain technology overview

Blockchain is a decentralized, distributed ledger technology that records transactions across multiple nodes or computers in a tamper-proof and transparent manner. It operates on several key principles:

1. **Decentralization:** There is no single central authority; data is distributed across a network of nodes, enhancing security and resilience.
2. **Immutability:** Once data is recorded on the blockchain, it cannot be altered, ensuring the integrity of the information.
3. **Transparency:** All participants in the network can view the data and its history, promoting trust.
4. **Security:** Robust cryptography and consensus mechanisms secure data against unauthorized access and tampering.

8.10.3 Blockchain benefits in healthcare collaboration

Blockchain technology offers transformative benefits across various facets of healthcare, addressing critical challenges such as data security, interoperability, privacy management, process efficiency, drug traceability, and research integrity. At its core, blockchain ensures robust data security by creating tamper-proof records of patient information that are resistant to cyberattacks and unauthorized modifications. This cryptographic security model instills trust in healthcare data, safeguarding sensitive information while facilitating seamless data interoperability among different healthcare systems through standardized formats and protocols. Blockchain's decentralized nature empowers patients with greater control over their data privacy, enabling them to manage consent settings and selectively grant or revoke access to their health information.

Blockchain technology offers a promising avenue for achieving trustworthy healthcare collaboration in an era of data-driven healthcare. While challenges exist, the benefits of enhanced data security, interoperability, and patient control over data make blockchain a powerful tool for transforming healthcare collaboration and ultimately improving patient outcomes. As the healthcare sector continues to explore blockchain's potential, it may unlock new horizons in data sharing, research, and healthcare delivery.

8.11 Real-world case studies: Secure data sharing success stories

In the digital age, secure data sharing is a fundamental requirement for organizations across various sectors. While the challenges of data security and privacy are ever-present, numerous success stories demonstrate that secure data sharing is not only achievable but can also yield transformative benefits. This chapter explores real-world case studies that showcase exemplary instances of secure data sharing and the positive outcomes they have generated.

8.11.1 Genomic data sharing for medical research

8.11.1.1 Case study: The Global Alliance for Genomics and Health (GA4GH)

The Global Alliance for Genomics and Health (GA4GH) is an international consortium of organizations committed to advancing genomic research while ensuring data privacy. By developing common standards and frameworks, they enable secure data sharing among researchers and institutions worldwide. Their efforts have accelerated breakthroughs in precision medicine, allowing scientists to access and analyze genomic data without compromising individual privacy.

The GA4GH represents a collaborative effort among numerous organizations worldwide, united in their dedication to advancing genomic research while prioritizing data privacy and security. This international consortium operates by establishing and implementing standardized protocols and frameworks, fostering a secure environment for the exchange of genomic data across various research entities and institutions globally.

The core objective of GA4GH revolves around facilitating genomic data sharing among researchers while upholding stringent privacy measures. The alliance recognizes the immense potential of genomics in revolutionizing medical research, particularly in the realm of precision medicine. However, it also acknowledges the sensitivity of genomic information, emphasizing the need to protect individual privacy and confidentiality.

GA4GH's initiatives involve the development and adoption of common standards, guidelines, and ethical frameworks that govern the responsible sharing of genomic data. These standardized protocols serve as a backbone for secure data exchange, ensuring compliance with stringent privacy regulations and safeguarding the rights of individuals whose genetic information is involved.

By establishing a global platform for collaborative data sharing, GA4GH has significantly accelerated advancements in precision medicine. Researchers and scientists can access a diverse array of genomic data without compromising the confidentiality of individual contributors. This collective pool of data serves as a valuable resource for conducting comprehensive analyses, identifying genetic variations, understanding diseases at a molecular level, and devising personalized treatments.

Through its commitment to ethical and responsible data-sharing practices, GA4GH has played a pivotal role in fostering collaborations, breaking down barriers to data access, and catalyzing breakthroughs in medical research. Its efforts have not only accelerated scientific discoveries but have also set a precedent for ethical considerations in genomic data sharing, ensuring the protection of individual privacy while harnessing the transformative power of genomics in advancing healthcare and precision medicine on a global scale.

8.11.2 Secure cross-industry data sharing

8.11.2.1 Case study: The Financial Services Information Sharing and Analysis Center (FS-ISAC)

The Financial Services Information Sharing and Analysis Center (FS-ISAC) is a global organization dedicated to fortifying the cybersecurity defenses of financial institutions through collaborative data sharing and analysis. It operates as a trusted platform that fosters a secure environment for sharing threat intelligence among its member organizations, which include banks, credit unions, insurance companies, and other financial entities.

FS-ISAC's primary objective is to bolster the cybersecurity posture of the financial sector by enabling its members to collectively address and mitigate cyber threats. The organization recognizes the evolving nature of cyber threats and the critical need for timely and actionable intelligence to combat these challenges effectively.

Key aspects of FS-ISAC's functioning include:

1. **Secure Data Sharing:** Member organizations share anonymized threat intelligence data and insights related to cybersecurity incidents, vulnerabilities, malware, and emerging threats. This shared information is crucial in providing early warnings and actionable insights to prevent cyberattacks.
2. **Collaborative Defense:** Through the shared intelligence and collaboration facilitated by FS-ISAC, financial institutions can proactively defend against potential cyber threats. This collaborative defense strategy allows members to stay ahead of evolving threats by leveraging collective knowledge and resources.
3. **Anonymized Information Exchange:** FS-ISAC ensures that the information shared among members is anonymized and stripped of any personally identifiable information (PII) to preserve confidentiality while still providing valuable insights into threat patterns and attack methodologies.
4. **Resilience Building:** The collaborative efforts enabled by FS-ISAC have significantly increased the resilience of the financial industry against cybersecurity threats. By pooling resources and intelligence, member organizations can better detect, respond to, and mitigate cyber risks, ultimately enhancing the overall cybersecurity posture of the sector.

FS-ISAC's approach to collaborative cybersecurity has proven instrumental in facilitating a proactive defense mechanism within the financial sector. By fostering a culture of information sharing, the organization enables its members to better understand and mitigate potential threats, ultimately safeguarding the financial industry's integrity and the trust of its customers in the face of ever-evolving cyber risks.

8.11.3 Healthcare interoperability and patient data sharing

The CommonWell Health Alliance is a collaborative initiative comprising multiple healthcare organizations dedicated to advancing patient care by addressing the challenges of interoperability and data sharing among Electronic Health Record (EHR) systems. The coalition's primary goal is to facilitate seamless access to patient health information across different healthcare settings, thereby enhancing care coordination and improving healthcare outcomes.

Key aspects of the CommonWell Health Alliance initiative include:

1. **Interoperability Focus:** The alliance focuses on overcoming the barriers that hinder the seamless exchange of health information among disparate EHR

systems. It works towards establishing standardized protocols and frameworks that enable different healthcare providers and systems to communicate and share patient data effectively.
2. **Secure Data Sharing:** CommonWell prioritizes the security and privacy of patient information. Through secure and authorized mechanisms, it allows healthcare providers and organizations to securely access and exchange vital medical data while ensuring compliance with privacy regulations like HIPAA (Health Insurance Portability and Accountability Act).
3. **Patient-Centric Approach:** One of the core principles of the alliance is putting patients at the center of their healthcare journey. By facilitating interoperability and data sharing, CommonWell empowers patients to have better access to their health records and allows healthcare providers to access comprehensive patient information, leading to more informed and personalized care.
4. **Enhanced Care Coordination:** Improved interoperability between EHR systems enables healthcare providers to access a more comprehensive view of a patient's medical history and treatment across different care settings. This comprehensive view fosters better care coordination among providers, reducing duplication of tests, errors, and enhancing the overall quality of care.
5. **EHR System Integration:** CommonWell aims to streamline the integration process of EHR systems, making it easier for healthcare organizations to adopt and utilize interoperable systems. This integration reduces the technical barriers often associated with disparate systems, encouraging broader adoption among healthcare providers.

Through its collaborative efforts, the CommonWell Health Alliance plays a crucial role in promoting interoperability and data-sharing standards within the healthcare industry. By enabling seamless access to patient health information across various healthcare settings and systems, the alliance aims to revolutionize healthcare delivery, improve patient outcomes, and enhance the overall quality and efficiency of healthcare services.

8.11.4 Data sharing for environmental conservation

Wildbook stands as an innovative open-source platform designed explicitly for the conservation of endangered species. This platform employs secure data-sharing mechanisms to track and protect these species, allowing researchers, conservationists, and wildlife enthusiasts worldwide to collaborate effectively in safeguarding biodiversity.

Key features and workings of Wildbook include:

1. **Data Sharing for Conservation:** Wildbook serves as a centralized repository where wildlife researchers and conservationists share essential data about endangered species. This shared information encompasses a diverse range, including photographs, genetic information, behavioral observations, and habitat data.
2. **Collaborative Research:** The platform fosters collaboration among individuals and organizations involved in wildlife conservation. By allowing

seamless sharing of wildlife data, it encourages collective efforts toward monitoring, understanding, and protecting endangered species and their habitats.
3. **Species Identification and Tracking:** Wildbook utilizes advanced algorithms and machine-learning techniques to analyze photographs and other data shared by users. These technologies aid in the identification and tracking of individual animals within a species, enabling researchers to monitor population trends, migration patterns, and genetic diversity.
4. **Global Impact:** With users contributing data from various parts of the world, Wildbook facilitates a global perspective on wildlife conservation. It allows researchers to collaborate across borders and share insights to devise more effective conservation strategies.
5. **Public Engagement:** The platform encourages public engagement by allowing wildlife enthusiasts to contribute data and observations, fostering a sense of participation in conservation efforts. It also educates the public about endangered species and the importance of biodiversity conservation.
6. **Privacy and Security:** To protect sensitive wildlife data, Wildbook employs robust security measures to ensure data privacy and compliance with ethical guidelines. It prioritizes secure sharing while safeguarding the identities and locations of endangered species.

Wildbook's success lies in its ability to leverage technology for conservation purposes by democratizing access to critical wildlife data. By facilitating collaborative efforts and enabling data-driven conservation initiatives, Wildbook plays a pivotal role in the preservation of endangered species and their habitats. Through its open-source nature and secure data-sharing capabilities, the platform empowers conservationists and researchers worldwide in their mission to protect and restore biodiversity for future generations.

8.11.5 Secure data sharing in education
8.11.5.1 Case study: Ed-Fi Alliance
The Ed-Fi Alliance is a collaborative effort among educational organizations to improve student outcomes through secure data sharing. Their data standardization and interoperability framework enable schools and education agencies to securely exchange student information, leading to more personalized learning experiences and data-driven decision-making.

8.11.6 Secure data sharing in public health
8.11.6.1 Case study: The National Notifiable Diseases Surveillance System (NNDSS)
The National Notifiable Diseases Surveillance System (NNDSS) is a secure data-sharing initiative in the United States that collects and shares data on notifiable diseases among federal, state, and local public health agencies. The system facilitates real-time monitoring of disease outbreaks, enabling a rapid response to protect public health.

8.11.7 Secure data sharing in smart cities

8.11.7.1 Case study: The city of Barcelona, Spain

Barcelona has implemented a secure data-sharing infrastructure to improve urban services and quality of life for its citizens. Through secure data sharing, various municipal departments exchange data to optimize traffic management, public transportation, and environmental monitoring, ultimately creating a smarter and more efficient city.

These real-world case studies highlight the diverse applications and successes of secure data sharing across various domains, including healthcare, finance, conservation, education, public health, and urban planning. While the challenges of data security and privacy are significant, these examples demonstrate that with the right strategies, technologies, and collaborations, secure data sharing can drive innovation, enhance decision-making, and ultimately improve the lives of individuals and communities. These success stories serve as inspiring examples for organizations seeking to harness the power of secure data sharing in their own fields.

8.12 Best practices for establishing secure healthcare analytics collaborations

In the ever-evolving landscape of healthcare analytics, the establishment of secure collaborations is fundamental to harnessing the potential of data while safeguarding patient privacy and data security. These best practices offer a comprehensive framework for organizations and collaborators seeking to navigate the complexities of secure healthcare analytics. By clarifying data ownership, implementing consent mechanisms, and utilizing encryption, organizations can build trust, protect sensitive information, and ensure compliance with data protection regulations like GDPR and HIPAA. Regular audits, employee training, and incident response plans further bolster security measures, while compliance with evolving regulations and continuous improvement in security protocols remain central to responsible and ethical data-driven decision-making. In a data-centric healthcare environment, these practices are essential to delivering better patient outcomes and advancing healthcare innovation.

8.12.1 Conclusion

Establishing secure healthcare analytics collaborations is a pivotal step toward realizing the potential of data-driven decision-making in healthcare while maintaining patient privacy and data security. These best practices provide a robust framework for organizations and collaborators to navigate the complex terrain of healthcare data sharing. By implementing measures such as data classification, consent mechanisms, encryption, and role-based access controls, stakeholders can foster trust, protect sensitive information, and ensure compliance with data protection regulations. Regular auditing, employee training, and incident response planning contribute to a proactive security posture. Compliance with evolving regulations and a commitment to ongoing improvement in security protocols are essential for responsible and ethical data collaboration. In an era where data sharing and collaboration are key to healthcare innovation, these practices are integral to delivering improved patient outcomes and driving progress in the field.

8.12.2 Future work

The field of secure healthcare analytics collaboration is dynamic and continually evolving. Future work should focus on addressing emerging challenges and opportunities in this domain. One area of interest is the development of advanced encryption and privacy-preserving techniques to further enhance data security while enabling seamless data sharing. Additionally, research into the application of emerging technologies such as homomorphic encryption, federated learning, and blockchain in healthcare collaboration should be explored. Collaboration among stakeholders, including healthcare organizations, technology providers, and policymakers, is essential to shape future regulations and standards that strike a balance between data privacy and collaborative innovation. As the healthcare landscape continues to digitize and data sharing becomes increasingly crucial, ongoing research and innovation in secure healthcare analytics collaborations will be essential to meet the evolving needs of the industry and ensure the highest standards of patient care and data protection.

References

[1] Hulsen, T. (2020). Sharing is caring—data sharing initiatives in healthcare. *International Journal of Environmental Research and Public Health*, *17*(9), 3046.

[2] Falcão Duarte, C. (2019). Insight. me: Enabling a collaborative use of healthcare data. Master thesis (2019) available at Link: https://resolver.tudelft.nl/uuid:9fc4b0d2-0674-47fa-90a8-529a0bd3d267

[3] Elvas, L. B., Ferreira, J. C., Dias, M. S., and Rosário, L. B. (2023). Health data sharing towards knowledge creation. *Systems*, *11*(8), 435.

[4] WHIG, P. (2023). Elevating healthcare through high-performance medicine: The intersection of human expertise and artificial intelligence. *Transactions on Recent Developments in Health Sectors*, *6*(6). Retrieved from https://isjr.co.in/index.php/TRDHS/article/view/159

[5] Foraker, R. E., Lai, A. M., Kannampallil, T. G., Woeltje, K. F., Trolard, A. M., and Payne, P. R. (2021). Transmission dynamics: Data sharing in the COVID-19 era. *Learning Health Systems*, *5*(1), e10235.

[6] Shah, T., Wilson, L., Booth, N., *et al.* (2019). Information-sharing in health and social care: Lessons from a socio-technical initiative. *Public Money & Management*, *39*(5), 359–363.

[7] Ali, A., Al-Rimy, B. A. S., Tin, T. T., Altamimi, S. N., Qasem, S. N., and Saeed, F. (2023). Empowering precision medicine: Unlocking revolutionary

insights through blockchain-enabled federated learning and electronic medical records. *Sensors*, *23*(17), 7476.

[8] Saleh, S., and Shayor, F. (2020). High-level design and rapid implementation of a clinical and non-clinical blockchain-based data sharing platform for COVID-19 containment. *Frontiers in Blockchain*, *3*, 553257.

[9] Whig, P., and Bhatia, A. B. (2023). Interpretable analysis of the potential impact of various versions of corona virus: A case study. *Explainable Artificial Intelligence for Biomedical Applications*, *1*, 57.

[10] Rejeb, A., Rejeb, K., Abdollahi, A., and Treiblmaier, H. (2022). The big picture on Instagram research: Insights from a bibliometric analysis. *Telematics and Informatics*, 101876.

[11] Li, P., Xie, C., Pollard, T., Johnson, *et al.* (2017). Promoting secondary analysis of electronic medical records in China: Summary of the PLAGH-MIT critical data conference and health datathon. *JMIR Medical Informatics*, *5*(4), e7380.

[12] Lounsbury, O., Roberts, L., Goodman, *et al.* (2021). Opening a "can of worms" to explore the public's hopes and fears about health care data sharing: qualitative study. *Journal of Medical Internet Research*, *23*(2), e22744.

[13] Yu, W., Zhao, G., Liu, Q., and Song, Y. (2021). Role of big data analytics capability in developing integrated hospital supply chains and operational flexibility: An organizational information processing theory perspective. *Technological Forecasting and Social Change*, *163*, 120417.

[14] Joyce, J. B., Douglass, T., Benwell, B., *et al.* (2022). Should we share qualitative data? Epistemological and practical insights from conversation analysis. *International Journal of Social Research Methodology*, 1–15.

[15] Wang, F., Srinivasan, U., Uddin, S., and Chawla, S. (2014, August). Application of network analysis on healthcare. In *2014 IEEE/ACM International Conference on Advances in Social Networks Analysis and Mining (ASONAM 2014)* (pp. 596–603). IEEE.

[16] Shae, Z., and Tsai, J. J. (2017, June). On the design of a blockchain platform for clinical trial and precision medicine. In *2017 IEEE 37th International Conference on Distributed Computing Systems (ICDCS)* (pp. 1972–1980). IEEE.

[17] Whig, P., Velu, A., Nadikattu, R. R., and Alkali, Y. J. (2024). Role of AI and IoT in intelligent transportation. In *Artificial Intelligence for Future Intelligent Transportation* (pp. 199–220). Apple Academic Press.

[18] Kudale, S., Trikande, M., Desai, A., and Kore, P. (2018). A wearable device data sharing and collaboration in mobile healthcare applications. *International Research Journal of Engineering and Technology (IRJET)*, *5*(11), 2395.

Chapter 9
Communication aspects in 5G-assisted big data: a performance review against 4G-LTE frameworks

Devanshi Patel[1], Jay Chauhan[1] and Vivek Kumar Prasad[1]

5G networks and beyond are the next generation of wireless transmission technology, delivering significant enhancements over 4G LTE networks. These networks offer faster data rates, ultra-low latency, increased capacity, and greater spectral efficiency. They want to fulfill the increased need for data-intensive applications while also supporting new technologies such as self-driving cars and smart cities. 4G LTE networks, on the other hand, have velocity, capacity, and latency constraints. They may fail to fulfill the rising needs of modern applications while providing high-speed data access. Latency is substantially greater in 4G LTE networks, which might hamper real-time applications that demand rapid replies. Furthermore, when more devices are connected to the network, 4G LTE networks encounter spectral efficiency difficulties and might encounter network congestion. They may also be limited in their ability to meet the vast connection demands of the IOT.5G and future networks overcome these constraints by providing faster speeds, reduced latency, greater capacity, increased spectrum efficiency, and expanded support for new technologies. These breakthroughs pave the path for a more interconnected and efficient future, allowing innovative applications and services in a variety of industries. Finally, 5G and beyond networks offer a tremendous advancement in wireless communication technology, outperforming 4G LTE networks. The advancements in speed, latency, capacity, and spectral effectiveness enable them to accommodate a wide range of applications while also encouraging the development of novel technologies.

9.1 Introduction

In today's fast-changing technological landscape, it is abundantly evident that maintaining a safe and dependable computer environment is essential for many other industries in addition to corporations. Adopting these cutting-edge developments is a

[1]CSE, Nirma University, Ahmedabad, India

top priority for the healthcare sector in particular as it seeks to enhance patient care and progress medical research. At the same time, the development of 5G technology is bringing a whole new level of device interconnection, opening up tremendous possibilities to transform healthcare services [1].

The use of cloud computing has created an endless number of opportunities in the healthcare field. Healthcare providers may simplify their operations, cooperate more efficiently, and offer patients personalized treatment more effectively by storing and accessing patient information, medical imaging, and diagnostic data in the cloud. The necessity of developing a strong Root of Trust, however, becomes even clearer due to this shift to the cloud [2].

Beyond primarily data security, the Root of Trust idea in healthcare captures the fundamental core of patients' trust. Patients must have absolute trust in the confidentiality and security of their medical records. The Root of Trust fills this protective guardian role, ensuring that patient data is kept private, unmodified, and protected from unauthorized access [3]. The Root of Trust creates a strong foundation of trust between patients and healthcare professionals by maintaining the integrity of this healthcare data, eventually enhancing outcomes for patients and bolstering the authority of healthcare institutions [4].

The emergence of 5G technology opens up a completely new world of communication and data transfer. 5G enables seamless connectivity between gadgets, medical equipment, and healthcare experts thanks to its blasting-fast transmission speeds and minimal latency. The quality and accessibility of healthcare services are considerably improved, this real-time connection makes it possible to perform remote patient monitoring, telemedicine consultations, and effective data analysis.

The expansion of linked devices, however, also expands the potential attack surface for malicious individuals. When it comes to preserving the integrity of the 5G-enabled healthcare environment, the Root of Trust is essential. As it has been previously reported, healthcare systems can detect possible security breaches, spot abnormalities, and act proactively in the face of new threats by utilizing deep learning algorithms. In a healthcare environment that is becoming more networked, this proactive approach is necessary for maintaining patient safety and confidentiality [5].

Furthermore, the addition of secure big data analytics in such an instance strengthens the Root of Trust's capabilities. Big data analytics is emerging as a critical tool for deriving accurate inferences in the healthcare sector, which generates enormous volumes of sensitive data from several sources, including patient records, medical equipment, and research projects [6]. However, protecting data privacy and following rules becomes crucial when utilizing the endless possibilities of big data (Table 9.1).

Advanced cryptographic methods, such as homomorphic encryption and safe multi-party computing, are used in secure big data analytics to analyze sensitive data without compromising patient privacy. These techniques allow healthcare providers and academics to get valuable insights while keeping the underlying data secure and unreadable to outsiders by performing calculations directly on encrypted data. The synergy between secure big data analytics and the Root of Trust forms a robust defense against potential data breaches and cyber threats. The Root of Trust

Table 9.1 Literature review table

Authors	Year	P-1	P-2	P-3	P-4	P-5	P-6	Scheme	Pros	Cons
Stephen et al. [7]	2022	N	N	N	Y	N	Y	Access control and trust-based solutions are used for cloud computing security.	Web-based applications are now scalable and inexpensive thanks to cloud computing.	Issues with vendor lock-in and data security with cloud providers.
Priya G, Jaisankar N et al. [8]	2019	N	N	N	N	N	Y	The trust evaluation model takes four service indices into account: availability, success rate, effectiveness, feedback.	Accurate trust assessments are improved by fuzzy logic and a variety of indicators.	Implementing fuzzy logic could produce inaccurate results.
Ritua, Sukhchandan, Jainc et al. [9]	2017	N	N	N	N	N	Y	Introduction of cloud computing and IT security.	Study looks at cloud computing QoS parameters and trust frameworks.	The study does not offer a trustworthy way to pick providers.
Gholami, Arani et al. [10]	2015	N	N	N	N	N	Y	An evaluation approach for cloud trust that takes reliability, safety, and availability into account.	Because of service quality indicators, the latest trust model is superior.	The generalizability of the model is constrained by unknown parameters.
Krautheim, Phatak, Sherman et al. [11]	2010	Y	N	Y	Y	Y	Y	Better cloud virtual environments encourage parties to have trusting connections.	Enhanced security, Improved flexibility, configurable modular architecture.	Complexity, Dependence on software, Dependence on service providers.

Parameters of literature table
P1: Authentication and authorization mechanisms
P2: Encryption and decryption
P3: Secure boot processes
P4: Communication protocols
P5: Storage mechanisms
P6: Security management

Table 9.2 Security in clouds: Levels and concerns

Network security	Ensuring secure data transmission
	Authorized user-specific data sharing
	Employing a transparent security protocol
Privacy	Maintaining the privacy of data location
	Implementing cryptography techniques for data security
	Creating hidden and redundant backups of data
Virtual machine security	Managing virtual machines securely
	Utilizing virtualization methods
	Identifying virtual machines securely
Compliance	Adhering to standardized service levels
	Conducting regular audits
Interface security	Managing trust among participants Developing a secure user interface
	Establishing a robust administrative interface
	Ensuring security in application programming interfaces

ensures the overall security and integrity of healthcare systems, while secure big data analytics enables data-driven decision-making, safeguarding patient privacy. In addition to improving patient care and medical research, this effective combination also increases people's faith in the healthcare system.

In order to adopt cloud computing, 5G technologies, safe big data analytics, and the Root of Trust, the healthcare sector must prioritize building and maintaining a solid security foundation. By combining the latest advances in technology, it is possible to profit from innovation's advantages while protecting patient privacy, data integrity, and system security as a whole. Healthcare practitioners may easily navigate the digital environment, offer excellent patient care, and contribute to revolutionary discoveries in medical science by sensibly integrating these innovations. In the end, the combination of healthcare, cloud computing, 5G, secure big data analytics, and Root of Trust represents a potential route towards a future where everyone is healthier and safer (Table 9.2).

9.1.1 Motivation

Emerging technologies like 5G and cloud computing are playing crucial roles in the fast-changing healthcare scene as technology continues to advance. The field of secured big data analytics has seen some of the most intriguing developments. The massive volumes of data produced in the healthcare industry have the power to completely change how patients are cared for, how medicine is researched, and how diseases are prevented. However, this plethora of private information also presents substantial privacy and security issues.

As a committed researcher in the area, I am driven to investigate and develop solutions that fully utilize cutting-edge technology while maintaining the security of patient information. A potential platform for seamless data transmission and storage is offered by the integration of 5G and beyond networks plus cloud computing, but security issues have prevented its widespread use in the healthcare industry. The incorporation of the "Root of Trust" idea into cloud computing is a vital component that will drive the success of safe big data analytics. We can ensure the validity and authenticity of sensitive healthcare data by building a secure basis for data storage and transfer. Healthcare practitioners, academics, and other stakeholders will be able to securely utilize the benefits of big data, thanks to this trust model without worrying about data breaches or unwanted access. Secure big data analytics are further improved by deep learning, a cutting-edge branch of artificial intelligence. The key to uncovering priceless insights for personalized medicine, illness detection, and therapy optimization lies in its capacity to analyze and extract significant patterns from large datasets. To protect patient privacy and the confidentiality of private medical information, using deep learning algorithms in cloud-based systems calls for additional security precautions.

Our objective as researchers is to confront these difficulties head-on and to bring out a thorough framework that combines deep learning, cloud computing's foundation of trust, and 5G and beyond networks. This framework will advance medical research and healthcare practices while ensuring the secure and smooth sharing of data. It will also protect patient privacy and confidentiality. This study's possible effects might be widespread. We can provide medical practitioners with data-driven insights in real time by creating a safe and effective infrastructure for big data analytics in healthcare. In the end, this will improve patient outcomes and save healthcare costs by making improved diagnostic accuracy, better treatment plans, and individualized healthcare methods more widely available. Additionally, the effective application of this technology might hasten medical advancements and stimulate the market for healthcare innovation. Large-scale information will be accessible to researchers in a safe manner, allowing teamwork and driving innovations in disease knowledge and drug development.

In conclusion, the possibility of developing a revolutionary and safe platform for big data analytics in the rapidly evolving healthcare sector motivates me as a researcher. We can usher in a new age of data-driven healthcare while keeping the greatest standards of security and privacy by integrating 5G and beyond networks, a root of confidence in cloud computing, and the power of deep learning. These developments will enable a future for all of mankind that is healthier and more sustainable.

9.1.2 Contribution

By combining big data analytics with cutting-edge technology, the healthcare industry is undergoing a dramatic transition. Massive volumes of healthcare data may be handled and transferred at previously unheard-of rates with the introduction of 5G and beyond networks. However, this quick expansion of data processing and sharing also poses tough security problems. As academics, our main goal is to create a novel approach that guarantees the secure use of big data analytics in healthcare, utilizing 5G and beyond networks, while exploiting the idea of "Root of Trust" in cloud computing, backed by deep learning methods.

1. Establishing a Secure Data Transmission Framework: A key part of our contribution is the creation of a reliable framework for the transfer of healthcare data through 5G and other networks. We acknowledge that the security of data during transmission is a major worry. We suggest utilizing cutting-edge encryption techniques and integrating secure communication protocols into the 5G infrastructure to remedy this. By using this strategy, cloud systems, healthcare providers, and patients will all communicate data securely and confidentially [12].
2. Implementing a Root of Trust Mechanism in Cloud Computing: To further fortify the security architecture, we urge cloud computing to use the "Root of Trust" idea. We can protect both the security of the cloud network and the reliability of data, apps, and processes by building a secure root. This strategy will prevent possible assaults that try to tamper with or corrupt cloud-stored data, creating a reliable environment in healthcare data analytics [13].
3. Using Deep Learning to Detect Abnormalities: Deep learning algorithms have shown to be remarkably effective at spotting abnormalities and possible breaches of security. The use of deep learning methods in healthcare data analytics procedures is emphasized in our research. We can create prediction models that are capable of spotting unexpected trends or suspicious activity in real time by training deep neural networks on extensive healthcare datasets. With the help of this proactive strategy, healthcare companies may be made aware of potential dangers and take appropriate action to protect patient data and maintain the integrity of data analytics procedures [14].
4. Addressing Privacy Concerns with Differential Privacy: When working with sensitive healthcare data, protecting patient privacy is of the utmost importance. In our contribution, we push for the pipeline for big data analytics to include differential privacy approaches. By introducing purposefully designed noise, differential privacy offers an extra degree of security to individual data points, making it more difficult for attackers to pinpoint particular users in the dataset. This strategy makes sure that patients' privacy is protected while also allowing insightful conclusions to be made from the aggregated data [15].
5. Establishing a Collaborative Security Ecosystem: As researchers, we understand the need to work together to build a complete and reliable security ecosystem for big data analytics in healthcare. Our participation is encouraging contact between security professionals, cloud service providers, and healthcare providers. We can jointly address new security concerns and guarantee that our safe analytics architecture is continually improved by exchanging information, skills, and best practices [16].

We want to improve safe big data analytics for developing healthcare utilizing 5G and beyond networks, to sum up our contribution. We envision a future where healthcare data can be securely analyzed and used, ultimately improving patient outcomes and advancing medical research. To this end, we are integrating the "Root of Trust" concept in cloud computing, utilizing deep learning for identifying anomalies, and prioritizing privacy with different confidentiality techniques. It is all of our collaborative obligation as researchers to provide a safe and progressive healthcare environment.

9.2 Problem statement

Cloud computing relies on the root of trust as a crucial element for ensuring the security and reliability of digital transactions involving data storage, transmission, and processing. It is a trusted source that authenticates these transactions and prevents unauthorized access, data breaches, or tampering. However, implementing the root of trust in cloud computing presents several challenges. The foundation of trust must be spread across numerous networks and systems, leaving it vulnerable to various kinds of attacks such as malware infections, phishing attempts, and man-in-the-middle attacks. The entire cloud ecosystem may experience security breaches if the foundation of trust is undermined. Additionally, maintaining and updating the root of trust is a difficult and time-consuming procedure, particularly when working with a lot of systems and devices. The foundation of trust must also resist assaults from highly skilled threat actors who use social engineering and zero-day exploits as part of their campaigns.

Figure 9.1 shows the different layers of trust from the cloud service provider to the application root of trust. All of these trust layers collaborate to form a secure cloud computing infrastructure, with each one built on previous ones to establish a solid basis of trust for the entire system. To preserve the privacy, integrity, and accessibility of their customers' data and applications, a cloud service provider has to guarantee that all of these layers are executed securely.

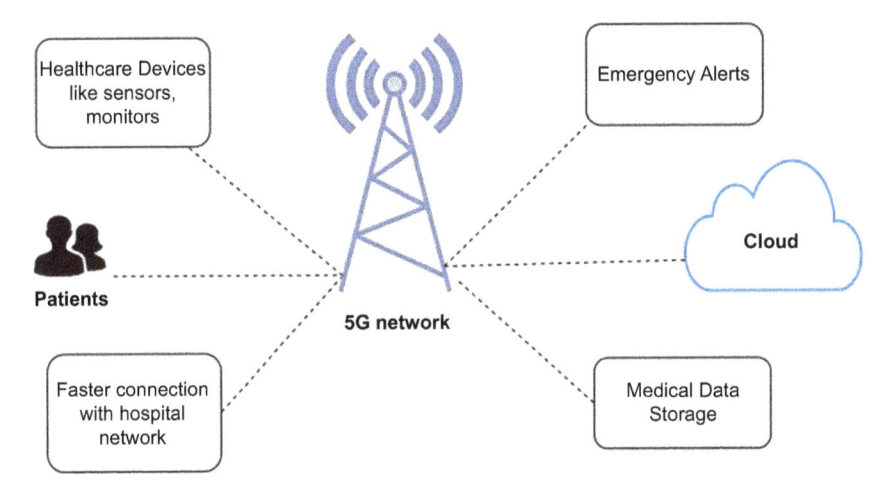

Figure 9.1 5G network connection with cloud

176 *Secure big-data analytics for emerging healthcare in 5G and beyond*

```
┌─────────────────────────────┐
│ Cloud Service Provider (CSP)│
└─────────────────────────────┘
              ↓
┌─────────────────────────────┐
│   Hardware Root of Trust    │
└─────────────────────────────┘
              ↓
┌─────────────────────────────┐
│   Software Root of Trust    │
└─────────────────────────────┘
              ↓
┌─────────────────────────────┐
│ Virtualization Root of Trust│
└─────────────────────────────┘
              ↓
┌─────────────────────────────┐
│ Operating System (OS) Root  │
│          of Trust           │
└─────────────────────────────┘
              ↓
┌─────────────────────────────┐
│  Application Root of Trust  │
└─────────────────────────────┘
```

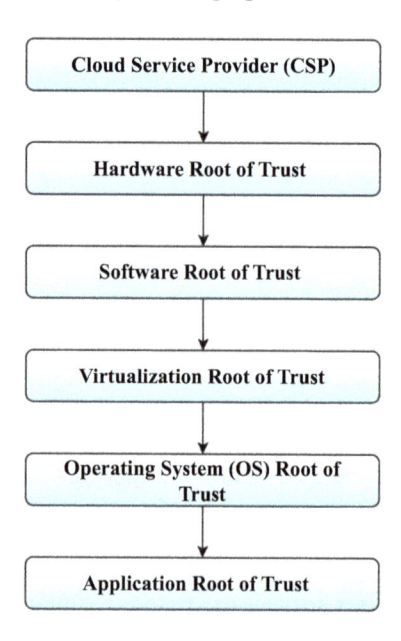

Figure 9.2 Different layers of trust from the cloud service provider to the application

The Root of Trust structure shown in this diagram is made up of various levels of trust, that range from the level of the hardware to the software level. The architecture's cornerstone, the Hardware Root of Trust, offers the most fundamental degree of trust. The Hardware Root of Trust is built upon by the Firmware Root of Trust, which is then followed by the Operating Systems Root of Trust, virtualized Root of Trust, and Applications Root of Trust.

The security procedures and services offered by every single level of trust allow the layer over it to create trust. The Root of Trust infrastructure must be implemented and maintained by the cloud service provider to guarantee that each layer is safe from hacking and tampering (Figure 9.2).

9.2.1 Root of Trust

Many strategies have been put up to address these problems. A tamper-resistant and safe root of trust can be created using a system-based root of trust that uses specialized hardware components like Trusted Platform Modules (TPMs) and secure enclaves. Securely booting software and key cryptography management systems are examples based on software root of trust that can be more flexible and scalable but might be less secure. Continuous monitoring and multi-factor authentication can help stop unauthorized access and find questionable activities. Deep learning may also strengthen the foundation of trust by spotting abnormalities, examining user behavior, and forecasting system breakdowns. In summary, the foundation of trust is crucial in safeguarding cloud computing against diverse threats. By implementing a combination of hardware and software-based techniques, using multi-factor authentication and continuous monitoring, by harnessing the capabilities of deep learning, enhancing the protection of the root of trust becomes possible, bolstering its resilience against attacks and ultimately fortifying the security of the entire cloud environment [17].

The root of trust system can expand and alter as the demands of the organization change thanks to the flexibility of cloud computing. Services that can be adjusted up or down instantly are available in the cloud. This adaptability makes it possible for the foundation of trust to change with the environment without jeopardizing security [18].

A further advantage of cloud computing is accessibility. The root of trust systems can be managed on a centralized platform in the cloud, which makes it simpler to maintain and keep track of. Because of the centralized control, the system is always up-to-date and secure. Furthermore, because of the cloud's accessibility, approved workers can access the root of trust system at any time and from any location, which is advantageous for employees who work remotely [19].

The combination of 5G wireless technology and the root of trust in cloud computing exerts a dramatic influence on the healthcare business, revolutionizing the delivery of healthcare services and redefining patient care. 5G's ultra-fast and dependable data transmission capabilities enable healthcare practitioners to swiftly and securely access and exchange crucial medical data. This involves collaborating with cloud-based systems to share high-resolution medical pictures, electronic health records (EHRs), plus real-time patient monitoring data. The foundation of trust is critical in ensuring that all data transfers are encrypted, verified, and safeguarded from unauthorized access, hence protecting patient privacy and complying with legal obligations like HIPAA [20].

Furthermore, 5G technology's reduced latency brings up new opportunities for real-time remote monitoring and medical applications. Regardless of geographical distance, healthcare providers may remotely monitor individuals suffering from chronic illnesses, give virtual advice, and respond quickly to crises. The foundation of trust ensures the security of these distant interactions, as well as the privacy of patient data and the integrity of the channel of communication. The capabilities of 5G's edge computing bring the processing and interpretation of data nearer to the source of information gathering, lowering latency and improving real-time insights. This is especially important in critical care situations where quick judgments are necessary. The foundation of trust is critical in safeguarding data at the border, preventing unauthorized manipulation, and ensuring data integrity. The introduction of 5G into the Internet of Medical Things (IoMT) environment enables flawless connectivity and communication between various medical equipment and wearables. These linked gadgets gather real-time patient data, allowing for constant surveillance and remote diagnoses. The root of trust assures the security and dependability of these networked devices, safeguarding them against cyber attacks and any data breaches. The increased data capacity and speed of 5G allow for improved data analytics and artificial intelligence (AI) uses in healthcare. Cloud-based data analytics tools powered by 5G can analyze huge amounts of medical data, discovering patterns and trends that aid in disease detection and therapy planning [21].

In an emergency, 5G's dependable connectivity is important for enabling seamless interaction between healthcare practitioners and emergency personnel. Cloud-based response systems driven by 5G provide immediate access to important patient information, hence optimizing emergency treatment. The foundation of trust ensures the safety of those emergency response systems, safeguarding information about patients even in high-stress circumstances. The healthcare gap is bridged by 5G's enhanced coverage and capacity to give connectivity in rural places. Cloud-based telemedicine services enabled by 5G provide patients in underprivileged areas with access to healthcare consultation and expertise, enhancing healthcare accessibility and lowering healthcare inequities. The foundation of trust maintains the security of such remote healthcare exchanges, building patient confidence in digital medical services. Patients may actively engage in their health management because of 5G's seamless connection and cloud-based healthcare services. Through telemedicine systems, patients may safely access their medical information, obtain personalized health insights, and interact with healthcare specialists. The foundation of trust is essential for protecting the safety and confidentiality of patient data, as well as building patient confidence in utilizing digital healthcare services [22].

9.3 Methodology used

In the realm of secure healthcare big data analysis, deep learning methods are vital for identifying irregularities in network activity, system records, and user actions. These algorithms decode intricate data connections, spotting unusual trends that hint at security weaknesses or potential breaches. Anomalies like unexpected traffic surges or irregular access locations are red flags that prompt proactive threat responses.

Moreover, deep learning models serve a crucial role in safeguarding emerging healthcare networks, like those in 5G and beyond, by detecting diverse malware types and their behaviors. Through the analysis of malware features, these algorithms can preemptively identify and contain harmful software, protecting healthcare systems and sensitive patient data.

Furthermore, within secure big data analytics, deep learning techniques meticulously inspect data from various sources (such as system records, network traffic, and user conduct) to authenticate the legitimacy of the root of trust. By pinpointing irregularities in this data, these algorithms ensure the root of trust remains intact, fortifying the security bedrock of the entire system.

By employing deep learning techniques, researchers can analyze user behavior in healthcare systems. The models can learn from historical user data and establish patterns of normal behavior. Any deviations from these patterns, such as accessing data at unusual times or from unfamiliar locations, may indicate potential security risks, warranting further investigation to protect patient information and system integrity.

Deep learning algorithms are proficient in analyzing system performance data from healthcare devices and networks. This ability allows them to identify trends

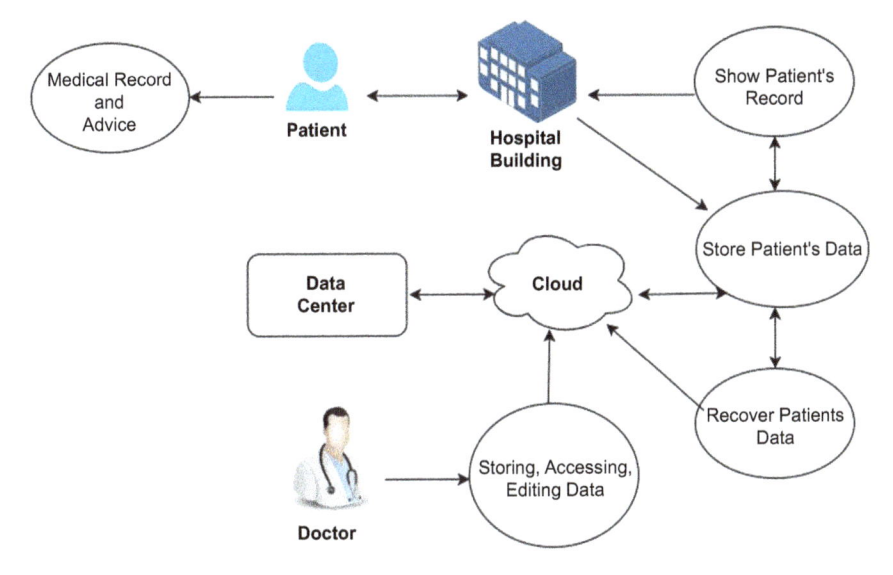

Figure 9.3 Relation of healthcare with cloud

from past data that may serve as early indicators of future issues or security breaches. By using predictive analytics, system administrators can take preemptive measures to mitigate potential faults and improve the overall security posture of healthcare systems.

Secure big data analytics for emerging healthcare in 5G and beyond networks can benefit significantly from integrating deep learning techniques. These methods enable robust anomaly detection, malware recognition, and root of trust validation, user behavior analysis, predictive analytics thereby fortifying the security and trustworthiness of cloud computing environments used in healthcare settings. Embracing these advanced techniques can empower researchers and practitioners to safeguard patient data, protect healthcare systems, and build a more secure future for healthcare in the era of 5G and beyond networks (Figure 9.3).

9.3.1 Threat detection

The advent of 5G and beyond networks has opened up new possibilities for emerging healthcare services, but it has also brought about heightened security challenges. As cloud computing becomes integral to healthcare data analytics, the need to identify and minimize security vulnerabilities becomes paramount. This research published explores the application of Deep Learning (DL) algorithms for threat detection in cloud computing systems, with a specific focus on ensuring secure big data analytics for emerging healthcare in 5G and beyond networks. The paper investigates how DL techniques can be leveraged to examine large datasets, detect anomalies, and identify patterns that may indicate security concerns. It demonstrates the versatility of DL methods in detecting various risks, including network intrusions, malware, and phishing attempts. Additionally, the paper highlights the role of DL in locating attack origins and implementing effective traffic-blocking measures. Furthermore, it addresses the significance of DL in identifying and combating ransomware attacks. Overall, this paper proposes DL as a promising tool to guarantee the security of sensitive healthcare data amidst the growing complexity of cloud computing threats.

DL algorithms offer a novel approach to detect and mitigate security vulnerabilities in cloud computing systems. By analyzing vast amounts of data, DL can identify anomalies and patterns indicative of potential security concerns.

DL techniques play a crucial role in detecting network infiltrations. By analyzing network traffic data, DL can identify unusual anomalies and patterns, serving as early indicators of a potential security breach. This section highlights the significance of training DL algorithms on typical network activity patterns to identify deviation signaling intrusion attempts.

Distributed Denial of Service (DDoS) assaults pose significant threats to cloud computing systems. This section delves into how DL methods can be tailored to recognize patterns aligned with DDoS attacks, facilitating the identification of the attack's origin and enabling efficient traffic-blocking measures.

DL approaches prove instrumental in identifying malware threats within cloud computing systems. By examining system logs and other data, DL algorithms can uncover patterns and abnormalities indicative of the presence of malware. This section emphasizes how DL can identify ransomware attacks by analyzing activity patterns from infected systems, allowing for expanded detection across additional systems.

In conclusion, threat detection using DL algorithms emerges as a promising method to identify and mitigate security vulnerabilities in cloud computing networks. The versatility of DL techniques enables various applications, such as detecting network intrusions, malware, and phishing attempts. By analyzing massive volumes of data, DL ensures the security of sensitive healthcare data as cloud computing threats evolve. As emerging healthcare services rely more on cloud-based analytics in 5G and beyond networks, DL will play a vital role in safeguarding the integrity and confidentiality of data.

Constraints of traditional RoT procedures: It emphasizes how these strategies fail to protect against evolving and sophisticated risks, necessitating the integration of DL techniques for improved security.

The Potential of Deep Learning Approaches for Improving RoT: The paper explores the advantages of DL techniques in enhancing RoT with cloud computing. It discusses how DL can address the limitations of traditional RoT, presenting a more effective approach to safeguarding cloud-based systems.

The application of DL approaches for detecting various kinds of security risks in cloud computing, including malware, phishing assaults, and DDoS attacks, could be the main emphasis of this topic.

Application of DL Approaches for Security Risk Detection: This section serves as the main emphasis of the paper, focusing on the application of DL for detecting various security risks in cloud computing. It covers how DL can identify and combat malware, phishing assaults, and DDoS attacks, thereby ensuring the protection of sensitive healthcare data.

Detecting Unusual Behavior within Cloud Computing Systems: DL's capability to detect unusual behaviors indicative of security breaches within cloud computing systems is investigated in this section. It highlights how DL can provide timely alerts and prevent potential threats to data integrity.

DL for Recognizing and Avoiding Specific Attacks: This section discusses DL's role in recognizing and preventing specific attacks in cloud computing systems, such as brute force assaults, SQL injection attacks, and cross-site scripting attacks. DL's ability to respond proactively to such threats enhances the overall security of cloud-based healthcare services.

Conclusion: In conclusion, the research paper emphasizes the significance of integrating DL approaches to improve RoT in cloud computing for secure big data analytics in emerging healthcare with 5G and beyond networks. DL offers enhanced capabilities in detecting various security risks and identifying unusual behaviors, thereby ensuring the confidentiality, integrity, and availability of sensitive healthcare data in the evolving landscape of cloud computing threats.

9.3.2 Anomaly detection

In the realm of secure big data analytics in emerging healthcare for 5G and beyond networks, the utilization of advanced machine learning techniques, particularly anomaly detection, plays a pivotal role in ensuring data integrity, privacy, and accurate decision-making. This method utilizes diverse deep learning techniques like autoencoders, Convolutional Neural Networks (CNNs), and Recurrent Neural Networks (RNNs) to identify unusual patterns in healthcare information handled across advanced 5G networks and beyond.

Autoencoders for Unsupervised Anomaly Detection: Autoencoders, a type of neural network structure, find utility in unsupervised learning when labeled instances are scarce. In this approach, the autoencoder is trained on a substantial dataset of typical behavior. The encoder condenses input data into a compact form, which the decoder then translates back into the initial input. As it trains, the autoencoder aims to minimize reconstruction errors, prompting it to grasp key elements of the input data. In the context of healthcare data, autoencoders can be utilized to recognize deviations from the norm by identifying patterns that significantly differ from the learned representations. This unsupervised approach is particularly useful when labeled anomaly data is limited [23].

CNNs for Anomaly Detection in Images and Videos: Convolutional Neural Networks (CNNs) are designed for processing image and video data. They leverage multiple layers of convolution and pooling operations to extract relevant features from input data. To apply CNNs to anomaly detection in healthcare, especially for medical imaging, a large dataset of typical behavior is used for training. The output of the final CNN layer can be utilized as a feature vector, which is then fed into a classifier like a Support Vector Machine (SVM). This classifier helps identify patterns that deviate from the expected behavior, thus detecting anomalies in medical images or videos. The advantage of CNNs lies in their ability to capture complex spatial patterns, making them suitable for analyzing medical images and videos [24].

RNNs for Anomaly Detection in Sequence Data: RNNs are adept at processing sequences of data, particularly useful for time-related patterns and linguistic structures. In healthcare, RNNs can be employed to detect anomalies by forecasting future time steps based on previous ones. By training on a substantial dataset of typical behavior, the RNN learns to model the temporal dependencies within the data. Deviations from the anticipated values can then be identified by comparing the predicted values with the actual values. This approach is particularly relevant for monitoring patient vitals over time and detecting anomalies in vital signs or disease progression [25].

Implementing secure big data analysis in evolving healthcare systems for future networks, extending beyond 5G, requires leveraging machine learning methodologies like autoencoders, CNNs, and RNNs to detect abnormalities. These techniques enable the identification of abnormal patterns or behaviors within complex healthcare datasets, ensuring timely interventions, accurate diagnoses, and ultimately contributing to improved patient care and health outcomes. By training these models on extensive datasets of typical behavior and employing them to recognize deviations from the norm, healthcare systems can achieve enhanced security, privacy, and decision-making capabilities.

One of the notable benefits of employing deep learning algorithms for anomaly detection lies in their capability to tackle high-dimensional data, often encountered in healthcare settings where patient records encompass a multitude of attributes. These algorithms can effectively process and uncover hidden correlations within these dimensions, thereby enabling the identification of subtle anomalies that could indicate critical health conditions. Moreover, deep learning techniques can decipher intricate patterns, which is pivotal for detecting anomalies that might not be discernible through traditional methods.

Yet, this paradigm is not without its intricacies. Deep learning algorithms often necessitate a substantial amount of data for training to achieve optimal performance. In healthcare, obtaining extensive labeled data for every potential anomaly can be challenging due to ethical considerations and the rarity of certain medical conditions. Additionally, there's a continuous risk of overfitting, where the algorithm becomes excessively tailored to the training data, hindering its ability to generalize effectively to novel, unseen data. This concern can result in incorrect identifications, posing significant challenges in medical scenarios where precise anomaly detection holds utmost importance.

The absence of interpretability in deep learning models is another concern. These models, commonly termed as "black boxes," present challenges in comprehending their decision-making process. In healthcare, where the rationale behind decisions is crucial, this lack of transparency can impede their adoption. Addressing this challenge requires the development of techniques that can provide insights into the inner workings of these complex models, allowing medical professionals to trust and comprehend their outputs.

To successfully leverage deep learning for secure big data analytics in healthcare within 5G and beyond networks, a meticulous approach is essential. The architecture of the deep learning model must be well-designed, considering factors such as the network's depth, structure, and activation functions. The best performance demands careful experimentation for selecting optimal hyperparameters. Also, evaluating the model's effectiveness involves choosing suitable metrics aligned with healthcare goals, such as precision, recall, or F1-score.

Ultimately, incorporating deep learning algorithms for anomaly detection shows significant potential in the evolving landscape of healthcare alongside advanced networking technologies. While their ability to handle high-dimensional data and capture intricate patterns is advantageous, careful consideration of challenges such as data requirements, overfitting, interpretability, and model architecture is crucial for successful deployment. By addressing these challenges thoughtfully, the healthcare industry can harness the power of secure big data analytics to improve patient outcomes, optimize medical processes, and drive innovation in 5G and beyond networks.

9.3.3 Comparison between threat detection and anomaly detection

Here are some comparisons of threat detection and anomaly detection:

1. Purpose: Threat detection identifies potential security risks or cyberattacks in real-time, whereas anomaly detection identifies odd or unexpected behavior or occurrences that depart from normal patterns.
2. Focus: Threat detection is mainly concerned with recognizing either internal or external threats that may endanger the assets of an organization or infrastructures whereas anomaly detection is concerned with identifying aberrant behavior or patterns in data.
3. Data sources: Threat detection often depends on information gathered from security records, network traffic, and other security-related data sources, but anomaly detection can be used for a variety of data sources such as system logs, user behavior data, as well as application performance metrics.
4. Techniques: Threat detection often combines signature-based along with behavioral-based techniques, whereas anomaly detection largely relies on statistics and machine learning-based methods.
5. Response: Threat detection often requires immediate action to prevent or mitigate the impact of a security breach, while responding to an anomaly depends on its severity or type.
6. False positives: Identifying threats often leads to false positives when certain security-related actions resemble legitimate behavior. Similarly, anomaly detection might produce false positives if the algorithm lacks proper training or if the underlying data is noisy or inconsistent.

In conclusion, while anomaly detection seeks to uncover unexpected behavior that may point to a new or unidentified threat, threat detection concentrates on identifying established threats and attacks. Although both approaches utilize

184 *Secure big-data analytics for emerging healthcare in 5G and beyond*

machine learning algorithms, they diverge in their methodology, data requirements, and respective strengths and weaknesses. Both strategies have their applications and can be combined to offer a complete security solution.

9.4 Solution statement

9.4.1 Architecture of the proposed solution

The fundamental concept of the Root of Trust (RoT) is pivotal in bolstering the security of cloud computing architecture. It forms a secure bedrock for critical functions such as initiation, communication management, and secure data storage, all of which are crucial for the secure inception, operation, and cessation of cloud systems. Typically, this RoT operates through an amalgamation of hardware and software elements seamlessly integrated into the cloud's framework during the manufacturing phase. It guarantees the security of vital system processes such as authorization protocols, encryption mechanisms, and the bootstrapping procedure.

Multiple methodologies are available for integrating the RoT into cloud computing environments. Among these, TPMs are notable hardware-centric security devices offering secure storage for encrypted sensitive data and keys. TPMs establish a chain of trust bridging from hardware components to operating systems and cloud applications. Another approach involves the utilization of virtualization-based security (VBS), an embedded capability within contemporary operating systems. VBS creates secure domains for executing critical system processes within virtual machines, resulting in secluded environments safeguarded against unauthorized access.

Nevertheless, the paramount importance of the RoT supersedes these various approaches, serving as a linchpin in cloud computing architecture. Beyond ensuring the integrity of cloud systems, the RoT sets the stage for their reliability. It establishes a credible foundation upon which cloud providers can offer secure and dependable cloud services to clients, fostering a climate of trust (Figure 9.4).

The intricate interplay of this concept materializes vividly in Figure 9.2, a graphical representation exhibits the layered design of RoT, highlighting the hardware-based foundation as the core, ensuring the system's strength. This layer consists of secure hardware components like CPUs, memory, and hard drives, meticulously designed to establish a secure foundation. Ascending the hierarchy, the Virtual Machine Manager (VMM) takes center stage, overseeing the orchestration of virtual machines, and ensuring their isolation and security in a shared hardware environment. The TPM, a diminutive chip nestled within the motherboard, contributes secure storage and cryptographic capabilities, thereby enhancing the architecture's fortitude.

The synergy of these layers harmoniously culminates in a seamless symphony of security, reliability, and accessibility ingrained within the computer's core. Secure hardware, isolated virtual machine environments, impenetrable storage, and cryptographic prowess coalesce to form an impervious bulwark, shielding against the contemporary challenges of the computing landscape.

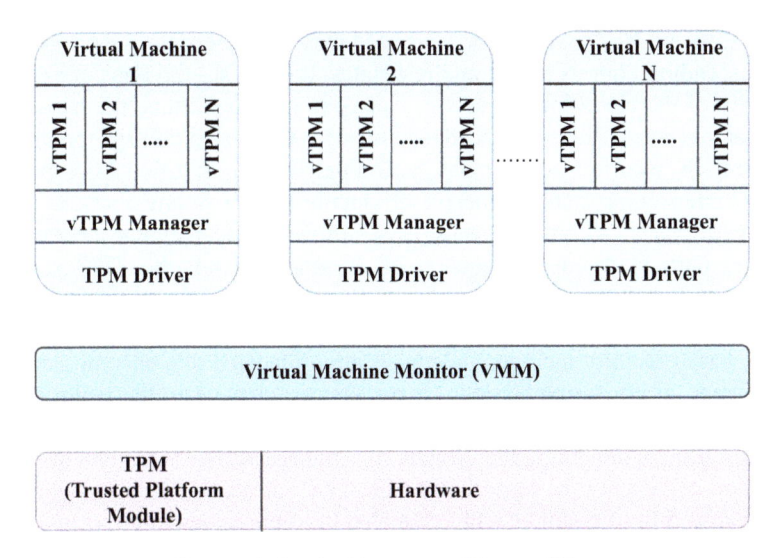

Figure 9.4 Architecture of Root of Trust

In the dynamic realm of Secure Big-Data Analytics for Emerging Healthcare, propelled by the advent of 5G and its successors, the RoT emerges as an indispensable pillar. It steers this domain towards a future characterized by integrity, confidentiality, and unwavering assurance.

Hardware Root of Trust (RoT): A Fundamental Security Pillar The Hardware Root of Trust (RoT) stands as an indispensable cornerstone within the architecture of cloud computing, meticulously engineered to underpin the bedrock of security. It assumes the role of an impregnable foundation, orchestrating a symphony of critical functions, encompassing booting, communication, and storage, thereby orchestrating a holistic environment conducive to the secure initialization, operation, and termination of cloud systems.

This foundational edifice is meticulously constructed through a harmonious amalgamation of both hardware and software constituents, intrinsically woven into the intricate fabric of the cloud's infrastructure during its manufacturing genesis.

The Hardware RoT's custodial role extends to safeguarding paramount system functions, among which lie the authoritative domains of authorization, encryption, and booting. These critical enclaves are meticulously fortified, rendering them impervious to the nefarious advances of malicious actors.

Software Root of Trust: Crafting a Citadel of Integrity and Assurance, a bastion of unwavering assurance is meticulously erected through the conception of the Software Root of Trust (RoT), wherein a robust foundation for computational systems is meticulously engineered. This citadel rests upon the bedrock of computer-based security methodologies and cryptographic techniques, interweaving the elements of digitally signed documents, encryption, and authentication to fashion a sanctum of imperviousness.

The Software RoT assumes the venerated duty of orchestrating the sanctity of data, transcending both its transit and rest states. It exercises the onus of verifying the identity of the cloud-located server, alongside its compatriots, the hypervisor, and virtual machines. This multifaceted construct is actualized through the strategic deployment of security technologies, encompassing the fortified boot process, judicious code signing, and the enclave of sanctity known as safe enclaves.

TPM interface: Within the realm of secure big-data analytics for emerging healthcare, particularly in the context of 5G and beyond, the TPM interface emerges as a pivotal construct, facilitating a spectrum of security functions vital for ensuring the integrity and safeguarding of virtualized environments. The TPM, a hardware-based security module, undertakes a multifaceted role encompassing the secure storage of cryptographic keys, a cornerstone element in the realm of data security. In the context of cloud computing, TPMs find their relevance by serving as bastions of trust, upholding the veracity of virtual machines and cloud instances. This section delves into the intricacies of the TPM interface, shedding light on its components and functionalities within the cloud computing paradigm (Figure 9.5).

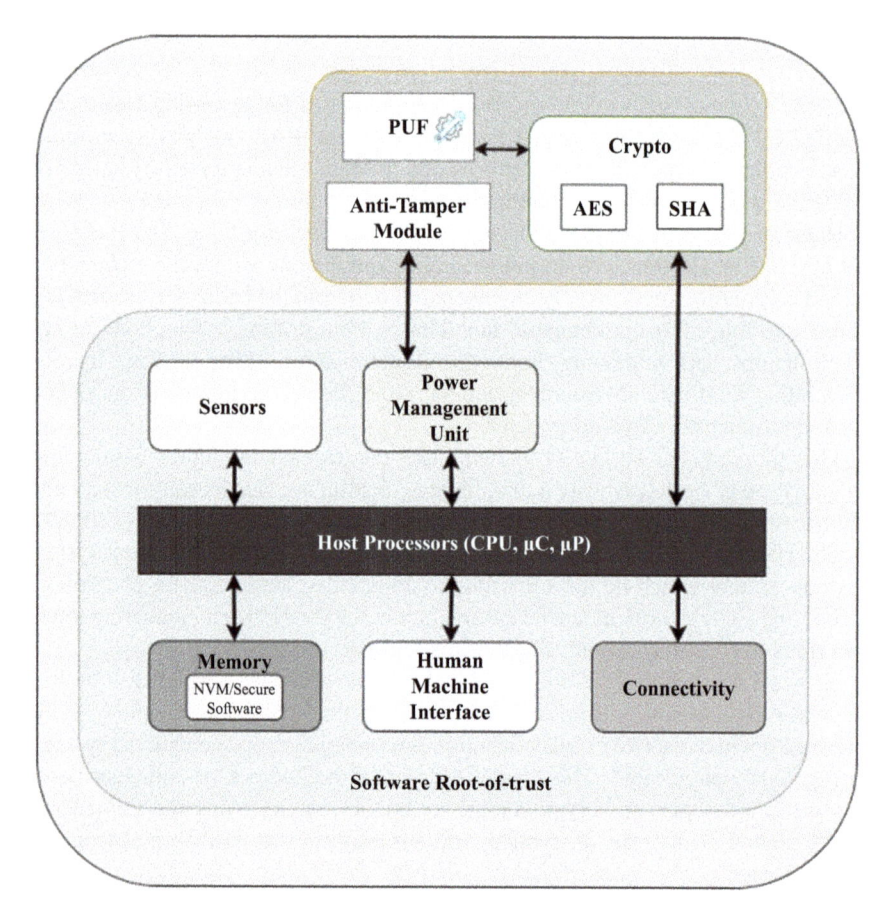

Figure 9.5 The architecture of Software Root of Trust

9.4.1.1 Host platform

The core of the cloud infrastructure, identified as the host platform, constitutes the physical framework that houses the intricate integration of virtual machines and cloud instances. Significantly, the host platform acts as the foundational stage for the intricate security orchestration. Through collaborative integration, the host platform harmoniously incorporates TPMs, which establish the bedrock of trust. This fusion of hardware components, empowered by TPMs, erects a robust boundary within which the virtualized environments operate, creating a milieu of heightened security [26].

9.4.1.2 Virtual Machine Manager

At the forefront of the security landscape within the host platform, the Virtual Machine Manager (VMM) emerges as the overseer directing the intricate choreography of virtual machines and cloud instances. Inherent to the VMM's role is the execution of multifaceted security functions. A pivotal nexus of interaction is cultivated between the VMM and the TPM, facilitated through sophisticated communication channels. This dynamic interplay equips the VMM with the capability to perform a spectrum of security operations that contribute to the overarching resilience of the virtualized realm [27].

9.4.1.3 Virtual machines/Cloud instances

Encompassing the virtualized instantiation of guest operating systems, the virtual machines (VMs) and cloud instances embody the dynamic foundation upon which healthcare big data analytics unfold. Within this intricate context, the VMM assumes a custodial role, bridging the VMs/cloud instances and the TPM. Through this nexus, the VMs/cloud instances establish a connection with the TPM, creating a conduit for the seamless execution of security operations and cryptographic maneuvers [28].

9.4.1.4 TPM interface

The essence of the interaction between the TPM and its cloud computing environment rests upon the foundational framework of the TPM interface. A constellation of Application Programming Interfaces (APIs) and protocols, collectively termed the TPM interface, serves as the communicative conduit facilitating an integration of functionalities. These functionalities encompass a range of pivotal operations, spanning from the generation and secure storage of cryptographic keys to the intricate management of these cryptographic constructs. Particularly noteworthy, the TPM interface is intricately interwoven with the domain of remote attestation, a pivotal practice that solidifies the identity and integrity of the virtualized ecosystem.

In the dynamic realm of secure big data analytics for advancing healthcare in the 5G era and beyond, the TPM interfaces emerge as crucial facilitators. They create a secured and consistently reliable setting for virtual machines (VMs) and cloud instances, ensuring encryption and trust. Cloud providers wield the potent arsenal of TPM interfaces to instate a vigilant oversight, assuring the seamless orchestration of VMs and cloud instances atop authentic and secure platforms. This orchestration intrinsically shields the information encapsulated within these virtual enclaves from unauthorized intrusions and clandestine access, culminating in a fortified bastion of data security.

The omnipresence of TPM interfaces, extensively harnessed within the domain of cloud computing, engenders an aegis of trust that envelops the entirety of virtualized constructs. This trust is meticulously woven through the intricate fabric of cryptographic prowess, extending its impenetrable cloak to both VMs and cloud instances alike. In essence, the strategic utilization of TPM interfaces provides an efficacious panacea to the perennial conundrum of ensuring data sanctity in the rapidly advancing landscape of emerging healthcare paradigms.

The architectural embodiment of the software root of trust resonates profoundly within the realm of computing sanctuaries. A multi-tiered assemblage of memory, host processors, and intricate software constituents congregate, gestating a sanctuary that upholds the veracity of the computing milieu. This construct epitomizes the quintessence of trust, encapsulating an intricate orchestration that underpins the integrity and security of the overarching system. Crucially, this architecture erects an impervious barrier against unauthorized access and intrusive manipulations, deftly guarding the sanctity of the system's memory, processing cores, and fundamental software strata.

Concomitant to the hardware root of trust, the TPM emerges as a sentinel that enforces a rigorous regime of security, mandating the sanctity of cryptographic keys and execution of secure functions. The TPM, positioned as the epicenter of trust, unfailingly thwarts insidious endeavors aiming to pilfer or tamper with cryptographic keys, which constitute the bedrock of data security. Moreover, the TPM adroitly enlists its prowess for the purpose of attestation, bolstering the system's identity and asserting its uniqueness within the realm of inter-system communication.

The TPM is a hardware component that acts as the system's root of trust by holding cryptographic keys and executing secure activities. It is intended to protect against attacks aimed at stealing or modifying keys for cryptography, which are frequently used to secure sensitive data. The TPM may additionally be employed for attestation, allowing the system to confirm its uniqueness to other systems. In cloud computing, the root of trust is a basic notion that offers a safe foundation for virtual machines as well as host architecture. It refers to the security foundation formed by hardware components like the CPU and chipset, as well as software components such as the virtual machine's BIOS and the TPM [29].

In culmination, the crux of secure big data analytics for emerging healthcare in the epoch of 5G and beyond is intrinsically entwined with the symbiotic embrace of TPM interfaces. The orchestrations woven through these interfaces usher forth an encrypted haven, where data integrity and access security are non-negotiable tenets. As the realm of cloud computing unfurls, these fortified paradigms and cryptographic bastions form an indomitable edifice, steadfastly guarding the precincts of emerging healthcare analytics, engendering a future poised on the precipice of unparalleled data security and sanctity.

In the domain of Secure Big Data Analytics for the advancing healthcare system within the 5G and future landscape, the cloud provider bears the vital responsibility of providing a robust foundation for both VMs and the overarching host infrastructure. In this complex web of data security, a collection of essential security components, together forming the fundamental cornerstone of trust within cloud computing, becomes prominent.

These elements engender an intricate tapestry of impregnability, guaranteeing the sanctity of data and the integrity of the computing environment. The following are the security elements that are the root of trust in cloud computing:

1. Hardware Root of Trust: The bedrock of the host infrastructure resides in the hardware components, epitomized by the central processing unit (CPU) and chipset. These quintessential hardware constituents form the very fulcrum of the system's root of trust, infusing a foundational layer of trustworthiness.
2. Virtual Machine BIOS: The BIOS of the virtual machine assumes the mantle of the virtual machine's root of trust. Within this hallowed realm, a bastion of security is erected, offering an impregnable shield against malicious incursions.
3. Trusted Platform Module (TPM): As the vanguard of trust, the TPM emerges as a hardware paragon, safeguarding the system's integrity through the safeguarding of cryptographic keys and the execution of impervious secure operations. Its pivotal role in engendering trust is paramount.
4. Secure Boot: A sentinel of boot-time security, Secure Boot diligently shepherds the process of booting virtual machines. By exclusively permitting the loading of firmware and software components with an indomitable imprimatur of trust, Secure Boot manifests its unwavering commitment to data sanctity.
5. Code Verification: The tenets of authenticity and integrity are meticulously upheld through the prism of code verification. Before admittance, a stringent verification process is embarked upon, corroborating the fidelity of firmware and software components.
6. Code Loading: A choreography of security unfolds during the loading of firmware and software components into the ethereal realms of memory. This orchestrated loading process adheres to the sanctified precepts of security, ensuring an impervious memory landscape.
7. Secure Communication: Communication channels interlinking virtual machines and bridging the expanse between virtual machines and the celestial cloud provider are ensconced within a fortified bastion of secure communication. This ensures that the exchange of data transpires under the vigilant aegis of data security.
8. Encryption and Decryption: The twin sentinels of encryption and decryption stand resolute as guardians of data sanctity, shrouding data at rest and in transit within an impervious cocoon of cryptographic inviolability.
9. Key Management: The curation and administration of cryptographic keys, those linchpins of encryption, decryption, and digital signatures, form a

cornerstone of data security. The sanctity of these keys is vigilantly upheld, encompassing a panorama of secure key management.
10. Identity and Access Management: Within the contours of identity and access management, access to the venerated realms of virtual machines and cloud resources is meticulously governed. User identity and permissions form the nucleus of this paradigm, ensuring that access is judiciously controlled and that sanctified precincts remain inviolate.

The panorama of Secure Big Data Analytics for Emerging Healthcare within the 5G and beyond continuum rests upon the bedrock of these multifarious security elements that coalesce into a robust root of trust. This meticulously crafted amalgamation of hardware, BIOS, TPM, secure boot, code verification, code loading, secure communication, encryption, decryption, key management, and identity and access management crystallizes into an unassailable bastion of data sanctity and system integrity. As the digital tapestry unfurls, this holistic security edifice stands poised as a sentinel against the ceaseless tide of potential vulnerabilities, charting a course toward an era defined by unassailable data security and fortified paradigms.

9.4.2 Flowchart and algorithm

1) IMPORT necessary libraries:
   a. numpy as np
   b. pandas as pd
   c. train test split from sklearn.model selection
   d. classification report from sklearn.metrics
   e. Sequential from keras.models
   f. Dense, Dropout from keras.layers
   g. Adam from keras.optimizers
   h. to categorical from keras.utils
   i. EarlyStopping from keras.callbacks
   j. StandardScaler from sklearn.preprocessing
   k. make classification from sklearn.datasets

2) LOAD data using makeclassification(nsamples = 10000, nfeatures = 20, nclasses = 2) function and split into training and testing sets using train test split function from sklearn.modelselection:
   a. X, y = makeclassification(nsamples = 10000, nfeatures = 20, nclasses = 2)
   b. Xtrain, Xtest, ytrain, ytest = train-test-split (X, y, test-size = 0.2, random-state = 42)

3) Standardize the data utilizing the StandardScaler module from sklearn.preprocessing:
   a. scaler = StandardScaler()
   b. Xtrain = scaler.fit-transform(Xtrain)
   c. Xtest = scaler.transform(Xtest)

4) CONVERT target variable to categorical using to-categorical from keras.utils:
   a. ytrain = tocategorical(ytrain)
   b. ytest = tocategorical(ytest)

5) DEFINE the deep learning model using Sequential from keras.models:
   a. model = Sequential()
   b. model.add(Dense(32, input-dim=Xtrain.shape[1], activation='relu'))
   c. model.add(Dropout(0.5))
   d. model.add(Dense(16, activation='relu'))
   e. model.add(Dropout(0.5))
   f. model.add(Dense(y-train.shape[1], activation='softmax'))

6) COMPILE the model using compile method from keras.models:
   a. model.compile(loss='categorical-crossentropy', optimizer = Adam(lr = 0.001), metrics=['accuracy'])

7) DEFINE early stopping criteria using EarlyStopping from keras.callbacks:
   a. early-stop = EarlyStopping(monitor = 'val-loss', mode = 'min', verbose = 1, patience = 10)

8) TRAIN the model using fit method from keras.models:
   a. model.fit(Xtrain, ytrain, validationdata = (Xtest, ytest), epochs = 100, batch-size = 128, callbacks = [early-stop])

9) Assess the model's performance on the test set by employing the predict method from keras.models and the classificationreport function from sklearn.metrics:
   a. ypred = model.predict(Xtest)
   b. ypredclasses = np.argmax(ypred, axis = 1)
   c. ytestclasses = np.argmax(ytest, axis = 1) d. print(classification-report (ytestclasses,ypredclasses))

The process starts by creating a synthetic dataset with a specified number of samples, features, and classes using the make classification function. Then, it divides the dataset into training and testing sets via train test split, where the test_size parameter determines the proportion allocated for testing and random state ensures reproducibility.

Standardizing features is carried out using StandardScaler for consistent scales. Target variables, y train and y test, are converted to categorical format via to categorical for neural network compatibility. The model, constructed with the Sequential class, includes three dense layers: an input layer (32 units, ReLU activation), a dropout layer (0.5 dropout rate), a subsequent dense layer (16 units, ReLU), and another dropout layer. The final dense output layer aligns with the number of classes using softmax activation.

Compiling the model involves categorical cross-entropy loss and the Adam optimizer (learning rate specified as lr). Model evaluation utilizes accuracy as the metric. Early stopping is implemented through the EarlyStopping callback, monitoring validation loss.

Training involves using the training data for a set number of epochs and batch size. Early stopping halts training if validation loss does not improve within a defined patience. Post-training, the model predicts class labels for testing data, generating a classification report for an in-depth performance evaluation in healthcare threat detection within 5G networks.

The code snippet below executes the model training and monitoring:

$$history = mode.fit(X\_train, y\_train, epochs = 100, validation\_data = (X\_test, y\_test),$$
$$batch\_size = 128, callbacks = [early\_stop])$$

In this code, the fit function is employed to train the model using the training data (X train and y train). The training process is configured to run for 100 epochs, with validation data (X test and y test) being used to monitor the model's performance. The batch size is set to 128, and the early stop callback is included to halt training based on the validation loss.

Following the training, a visual representation of the training history can be generated and saved using Matplotlib:

```
import matplotlib.pyplot as plt import pandas as pd
# Plot training history
pd.DataFrame(history.history).plot(figsize = (8, 5))plt.grid(True)
plt.gca().set_ylim(0, 1)plt.xlabel('Epochs')plt.ylabel('Accuracy and Loss')
```

Algorithm 1: Threat detection in healthcare using deep learning in 5G networks

---

Input: *n samples*: Number of samples in the synthetic dataset; *n features*: Number of features in the dataset; *n classes*: Number of classes in the dataset; *test size*: Proportion of data for testing; *random state*: Seed for random number generation; *lr*: Learning rate for optimizer; *patience*: Patience for early stopping;
Output: Evaluation of deep learning-based threat detection model for healthcare applications on 5G networks

1. Generate Synthetic Dataset;
2. $X, y \leftarrow$ make classification(*n samples,n features,n classes*);
3. Split Dataset;
4. $X\_train, X\_test, y\_train, y\_test \leftarrow$ train test split(*X,y,test size,random state*);
5. Standardize Features;
6. scaler $\leftarrow$ StandardScaler();
7. X train $\leftarrow$ scaler.fit transform(X train);
8. X test $\leftarrow$ scaler.transform(X test);
9. Convert Target to Categorical;
10. y train $\leftarrow$ to categorical(y train);
11. y test $\leftarrow$ to categorical(y test);
12. Build Deep Learning Model;
13. model $\leftarrow$ Sequential();

14. *model*.add(Dense(units=32, input dim=*n features*, activation='relu'));
15. *model*.add(Dropout(rate=0.5));
16. *model*.add(Dense(units=16, activation='relu'));
17. *model*.add(Dropout(rate=0.5));
18. *model*.add(Dense(units=*n classes*, activation='softmax'));
19. Compile Model;
20. *model*.compile(loss='categorical crossentropy', optimizer=Adam(lr=*lr*), metrics=['accuracy']);
21. Early Stopping Criteria;
22. *early stop* ← EarlyStopping(monitor='val loss', mode='min', verbose=1, patience=*patience*);
23. Train Model;
24. *model*.fit(*X train,y train,validation data* = (*X test,y test*), epochs=100, batch size=128, callbacks=[*early stop*]);
25. Evaluate Model;
26. *y pred* ← model.predict(*X test*);
27. *y pred classes* ← argmax(*y pred,axis* = 1);
28. *y test classes* ← argmax(*y test,axis* = 1);
29. Calculate Classification Report;
30. *classification rep* ← calculate classification report(*y test classes,y pred classes*);
31. Conclusion;
32. Display results(*classification rep*)27;

Algorithm 2: Training and visualization of the threat detection model

1. *history* ← model.fit(X_{train}, y_{train}, epochs = 100, validation data = (X_{test}, y_{test}), batch size = 128, callbacks = [early stop]))
2. **import** matplotlib.pyplot **as** plt
3. **import** pandas **as** pd
4. pd.DataFrame(*history.history*).plot(figsize = (8,5))
5. plt.grid(True)
6. plt.gca(()).set ylim(0,1)
7. plt.show()
8. plt.xlabel('Epochs')
9. plt.ylabel('Accuracy and Loss')
10. plt.savefig('test3.png',dpi = 800,bbox inches = 'tight')

Save the plot plt.savefig('test3.png', dpi = 800, bbox_inches = 'tight') plt.show()

This code snippet plots the training and validation metrics from the training history captured in the history object. It also sets appropriate labels for the x and y axes. The plot is then saved as an image file named test3.png with high resolution using the savefig function. The plot can provide valuable insights into the model's learning progress, aiding in the evaluation of its performance. The code snippet below illustrates the model's training process:

```
history = model.fit(X_train, y_train, epochs = 100,
    validation_data = (X_test, y_test), batch_size = 128, callbacks = [early_stop])
```

This code employs the fit function to train the model on the training data (X train and y train). It specifies the number of training epochs as 100, uses the validation data (X test and y test) to monitor the validation performance, employs a batch size of 128, and utilizes the early stop callback for early stopping based on the validation loss. To visualize the training history, the code uses Matplotlib to plot the training and validation metrics over the epochs:

```
import matplotlib.pyplot as plt
pd.DataFrame(history.history).plot(figsize = (8, 5))plt.grid(True)
plt.gca().set_ylim(0, 1)plt.show()
```

Algorithm 3: Anomaly detection and classification

---

1. **import** numpy **as** np
2. **import** pandas **as** pd
3. **from** sklearn.model selection **import** train test split
4. **from** sklearn.metrics **import** classification report
5. **from** keras.models **import** Sequential
6. **from** keras.layers **import** Dense, Dropout
7. **from** keras.optimizers **import** Adam
8. **from** keras.utils **import** to categorical
9. **from** keras.callbacks **import** EarlyStopping
10. **from** sklearn.preprocessing **import** StandardScaler
11. **from** sklearn.datasets **import** make classification
12. Load data and split into training and testing sets:
13. $X, y \leftarrow$ make classification(n samples=10000, n features=20, n classes=2)
14. $X_{train}, X_{test}, y_{train}, y_{test} \leftarrow$ train test split(X, y, test size=0.2, random state=42)
15. Scale data:
16. *scaler* $\leftarrow$ StandardScaler()
17. $X_{train} \leftarrow$ scaler.fit transform(X_{train})
18. $X_{test} \leftarrow$ scaler.transform(X_{test})
19. Define the deep learning auto-encoder model:
20. *model* $\leftarrow$ Sequential()
21. *model*.add(Dense(32, input dim=X_{train}.shape[1], activation='relu'))
22. *model*.add(Dense(16, activation='relu'))
23. *model*.add(Dense(32, activation='relu'))

24. *model*.add(Dense(X_{train}.shape[1], activation='sigmoid'))
25. Compile the model:
26. *model*.compile(loss='mean squared error', optimizer=Adam(lr=0.001), metrics=['accuracy'])
27. Define early stopping criteria:
28. *early stop* ← EarlyStopping(monitor='val loss', mode='min', verbose=1, patience=10)
29. Train the model:
30. *model*.fit(X_{train}, X_{train}, validation data=(X_{test}, X_{test}), epochs=100, batch size=128, callbacks=[*early stop*])
31. Generate predictions on the test set:
32. y_{pred} ← *model*.predict(X_{test})
33. Compute reconstruction error:
34. *mse* ← np.mean(np.power(X_{test} − y_{pred}, 2), axis=1)
35. *threshold* ← np.mean(*mse*) + np.std(*mse*)
36. Predict anomalies based on threshold:
37. $y_{pred\ classes}$ ← np.where(*mse* > *threshold*, 1, 0)
38. *ytest classes* ← *ytest*
39. Generate classification report:
40. *classification rep* ← classification report($y_{test\ classes}$, $y_{pred\ classes}$)
41. **print**(*classification rep*)

Algorithm 4: Training and visualizing an anomaly detection model

---

1. **Input:**
2. X_{train}: Training data features
3. y_{train}: Training data labels
4. *epochs*: Number of training iterations
5. *validation data*: Data to use for validation during training
6. *batch size*: Number of samples to use in each training batch
7. *callbacks*: List of callbacks to apply during training (e.g., early stopping)
8. *model*: The machine learning model to train
9. **Step 1: Train the machine-learning model**
10. *history* ← model.fit(X_{train}, y_{train}, *epochs* = 100, *validation data* = (X_{test}, y_{test}), *batch size* = 128, *callbacks* = [*early stop*])
11. **Step 2: Visualize the training history**
12. *history dataframe* ← pd.DataFrame(*history*.*history*)
13. plt.figure(*figsize* = (8,5))
14. plt.grid(*True*)
15. plt.gca().set ylim(0,1)
16. *history dataframe*.plot()
17. plt.show()

Algorithm 4 is used to train the model and monitor its progress, the following code snippet is used:

history = model.fit(X_train, y_train, epochs = 100, validation_data = (X_test, y_test), batch_size = 128, callbacks = [early_stop])

In this code, the "fit" function is employed to train the model using the training data, represented by "X_train" and "y_train". The training processs is configured to run for 100 epochs, and itincorpo

Following the model's training, a graphical representation of the training history is generated and displayed using Matplotlib:

import matplotlib.pyplot as plt import pandas as pd

#Plot the training history

pd.DataFrame(history.history).plot(figsize = (8, 5))

plt.grid(True)plt.gca().set_ylim(0, 1)plt.show()

This code snippet uses Matplotlib to plot the training and validation metrics extracted from the "history" object. It configures the plot to include gridlines and sets the y-axis limits to be within the range of 0 to 1. The resulting graph provides a visual depiction of the model's training progress, making it easier to assess its performance over the training epochs.

9.5 Performance evaluation

9.5.1 Parameters used and their values

1. n samples: The quantity of samples that make classification should be produced.
2. n features: the size of the resulting dataset's feature count.
3. n classes: the amount of subclasses in the dataset that was generated. For binary classification, it is set to 2.
4. Test size: What portion of the dataset should be designated for testing? It is designated as 0.2, indicating that 80 percent of the dataset is allocated for training, leaving 20 percent for testing purposes.
5. random state: the random seed that was used to divide the data.
6. Early Stopping parameters: monitor: The indicator to watch during training. It has been set to "val loss," which stands for the validation loss. mode: The direction that the metric should move in order to improve. Since it has been set to "min," the loss of validation should go down. The amount of detail in the printed output is verbose. Since it has been set to 1, data will be printed in some amount. patience: the amount of repetitions before training is discontinued if there has been no improvement.
7. Epochs: the number of training epochs for the model.

8. Batch size: how many samples are used for each gradient update.
9. Learning rate: The learning rate used by the Adam optimizer.
10. Loss function: The loss function applied to the model's training. It is configured for binary classification using "categorical crossentropy".
11. Optimizer: the optimizer that was employed to train the model. Adam is the default.
12. Metrics: The measures applied to the model's evaluation. "Accuracy" is the selected setting.
13. Dropout rate: The percentage of input units that will be lost.
14. Activation function: the mechanism for activation in the layers that are concealed. It is set to "relu" for both layers that are hidden and "softmax" for the resultant layer.
15. Input dimension: the size of the input space for features in dimensions. The total amount of features in a training set is what it is set to.

9.5.2 Test beds

1. Make classification: sklearn.datasets function that creates a randomly generated binary categorization dataset with a predetermined set of samples or features. In this code, a dataset with 10,000 samples 20 features is created.
2. Train test split: The dataset is divided between sets for training and testing using the sklearn.model selection function train test split. In this code, the test size is defined as 0.2, implying that 80 percent of the dataset is allocated for training, leaving 20 percent for testing purposes.
3. StandardScaler: The input data undergoes scaling using the StandardScaler function from the sklearn.preprocessing package, ensuring a mean of zero and a variance of one. This code fits the scaler to the training data and applies it to both the testing and training datasets.
4. To categorical: The target parameter (y) is transformed into an immediately encoded vector using the categorical function from the keras.utils library. The target variable in this function is binary, so it is converted to a 2D vectors with two columns.
5. Sequential: To specify the linear arrangement of levels for the model used for deep learning, use the keras.models class.
6. Dense: This keras.layers class is employed to define a layer of neurons that are completely linked.
7. Dropout: To avoid overfitting, a portion of the input units are randomly removed during training using this class from keras.layers.
8. Adam: The model's optimizer uses this class from keras.optimizers.
9. EarlyStopping: If the validation loss fails to decrease within a set number of epochs, the training can be prematurely halted using the EarlyStopping class from keras.callbacks.
10. Fit: The model is trained using the training set using this method from the Sequential class.
11. Predict: On the basis of the testing data, predictions are made using this model's method.

12. Argmax: The anticipated true and one-hot encoded vectors are converted to their respective class labels using the numpy function argmax.
13. classification report: Use this sklearn.metrics function for printing a report on the model's effectiveness on the test data.

9.5.3 Performance metrics

Loss: This code utilized categorical cross-entropy as the chosen loss function during the model's training.

Accuracy: The accuracy metric gauges the model's performance on the test outcomes. In this code, the fit method computes the accuracy during training, while the classification report function computes it during evaluation.

Classification report: The sklearn.metrics function produces a report detailing the model's performance on the test data. This report encompasses various metrics such as accuracy, recall, f1-score, and support for each class, along with their overall and weighted averages across classifications.

9.5.4 Result analysis

The Scikit-learn library's 'make_classification' tool is used to create a synthetic dataset for binary classification. Additionally, the dataset is partitioned into training and testing sets.

On all the testing and training sets shown in Figure 9.6, the model obtains a high accuracy of 99 percent, indicating that it is not overfitting. Figure 9.7 shows the features' importance for Decision Tree. The model is doing well in positive as well as negative cases, as seen by the excellent accuracy, recall, and F1 score for both classes. The overall findings point to the model's suitability for use in the classification by binary task on the fictitious dataset utilized in this code. It is crucial to remember that the model's performance is an important factor to consider.

9.5.5 Discussion on the result obtained and its comparison with existing techniques

This code cannot be immediately compared to datasets from the real world because it uses a synthetic dataset. Despite the model's demonstrated high accuracy on both training and test sets as depicted in Figure 9.8, indicating its proficiency in binary classification tasks. In various machine learning tasks, deep learning algorithms exhibit strong performance, spanning areas like speech recognition, image classification, and natural language processing. Their superiority over traditional methods arises from their capacity to extract crucial data features. However, training deep learning models necessitates substantial computational resources and ample data. Additionally, the architecture of the model, the choice of hyperparameters, and the caliber of the data all have a significant impact on how well deep learning models perform.

The results generated by the code which is shown in Figures 9.9 and 9.10 are therefore encouraging, however, it is crucial to consider that the performance of

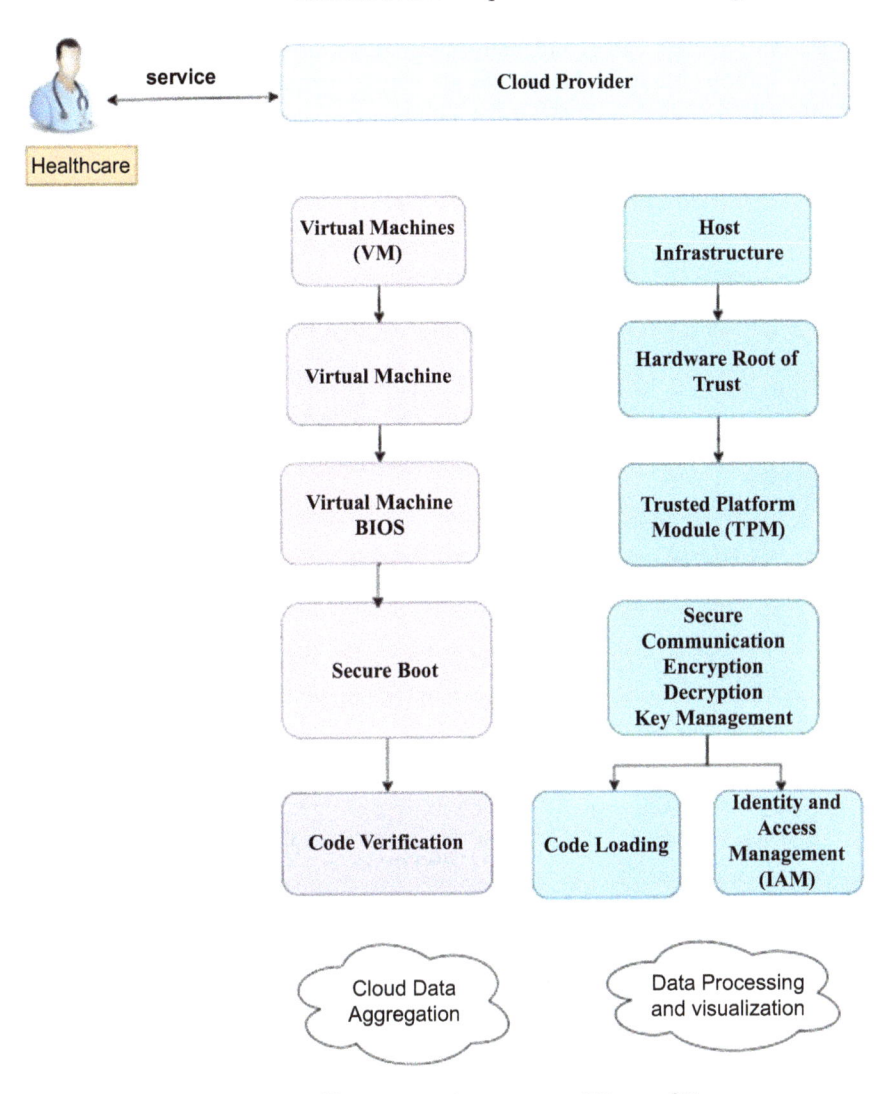

Communication aspects in 5G-assisted big data 199

Figure 9.6 Different security aspects of Root of Trust

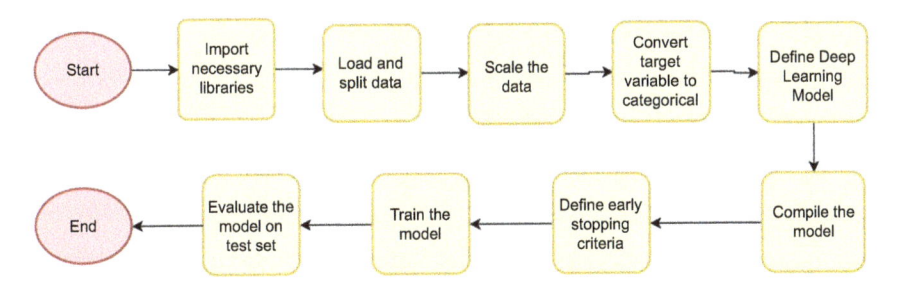

Figure 9.7 Flowchart

deep learning models can significantly differ based on the task at hand and the quality of information available. To decide which method is best for a given problem, it is also crucial to contrast the efficiency of models created using deep learning with other ones that are already in use (Figures 9.11 and 9.12).

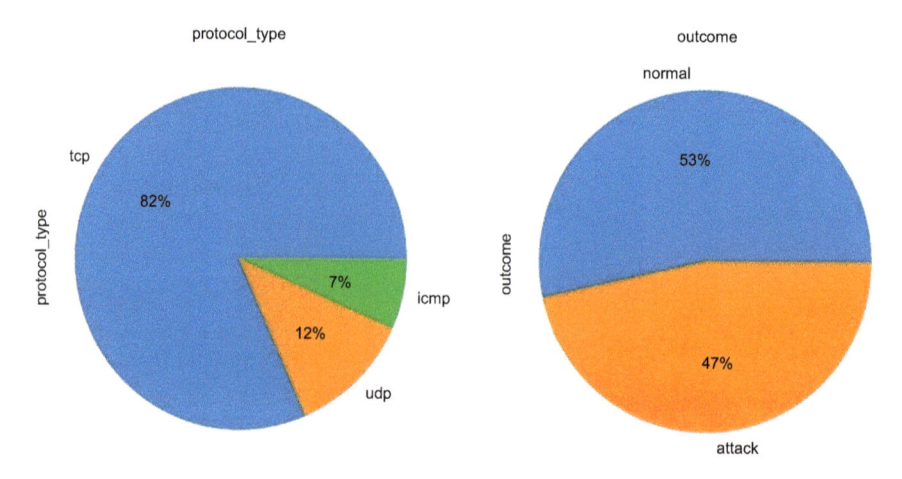

Figure 9.8 Segregation of the dataset

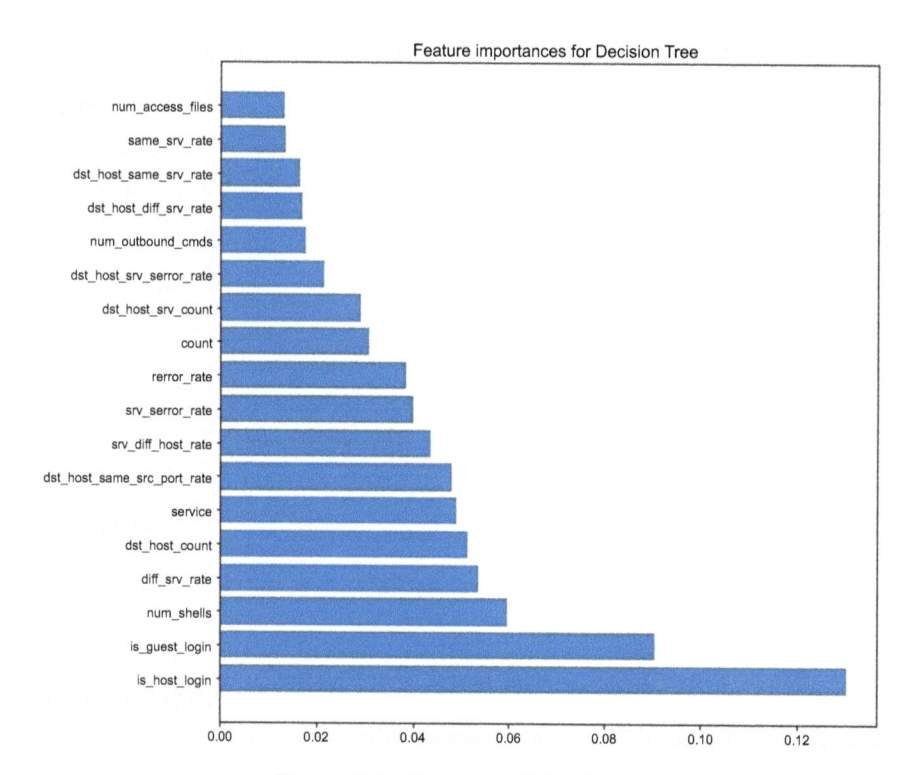

Figure 9.9 Features of the dataset

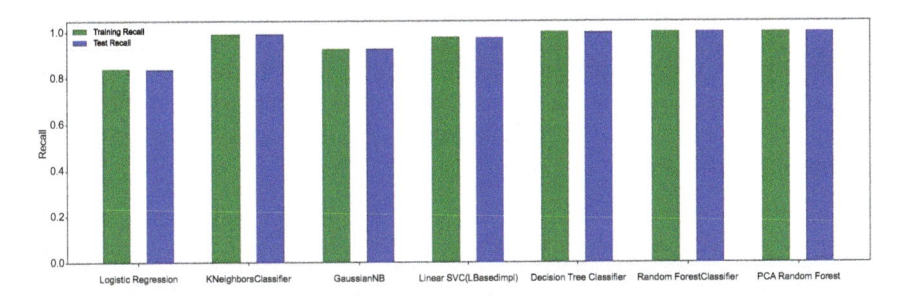

Figure 9.10   Graph of Test recall and Test case may change among datasets and may call for additional fine-tuning or tweaks for optimal performance

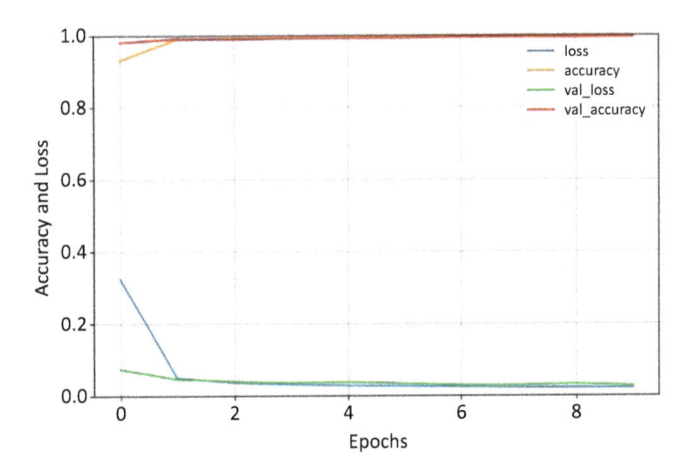

Figure 9.11   Anomaly detection

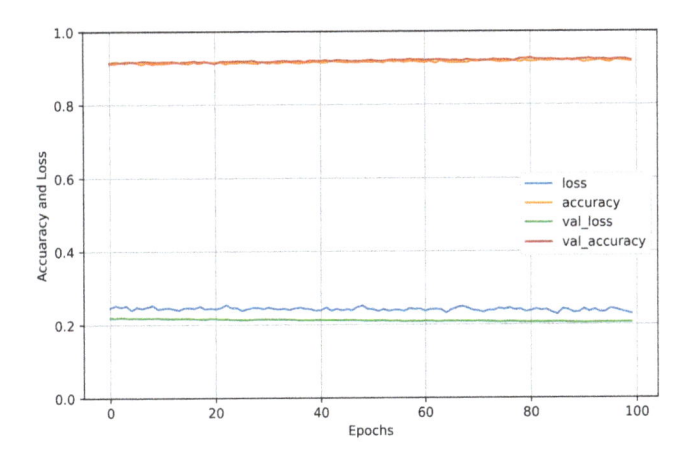

Figure 9.12   Threat detection

9.5.6 Mathematical equations

There are also a few mathematical formulas that are important to the idea of a root of trust in the use of cloud computing, particularly when it comes to creating secure communication pathways between cloud-based services and applications. Some of these equations include:

1. A public key as well as a private key are used in public key cryptography, a popular encryption method, to encrypt and decode data. Cryptography with public keys can be used in connection with cloud computing to create a secure channel between a user and a cloud service provider. Using a public key, the equation as follows is used for the encryption of data: $C = E(P,K)$, where, P is the plaintext, K is the public key, and C is the ciphertext.

    The recipient utilizes a specific private key to decrypt the encoded information and access the original message: $P = D(C,K')$, where: P denotes the message's original plaintext. The encrypted data is designated as C. The private key of the recipient is K'. The mathematical complexity of factoring huge numbers, which is used to generate the public and private keys, provides the foundation for the integrity of public key cryptography. This ensures the secrecy and security of the information that is encrypted by making it computationally impossible for an outsider to extract a private key given the public key.

2. Digital Signatures: A communication or document's validity can be confirmed using a digital signature. Digital signatures are frequently used in cloud computing to confirm the legitimacy of an individual or service provider. A digital signature is produced using the equation: $S = D(H(M),K)$, where M is the message and document, S represents the digital signature of the document, H is the hash function, and K represents the private key. The receiver applies the following calculation to validate the digital signature as well as authenticate the signer: $V = E(S,H(M),K')$, where V represents the verification outcome. Digital signature S stands for S. The message digest created during the signing process was created using the same hash function H,M stands for the letter or paper that was signed. The signer's secret key is K'. The digital signature is regarded as legitimate when the signer's identification is verified if the confirmation result, V, equals "true". The security of digital signings is predicated on the fact that without the signer's private key, it is computationally impossible to construct a new signature that is valid for a specific message or document. A new message digest will emerge from any changes made to the signed text or document, making it difficult for the attacker to create a legitimate signature for the message or document that has been changed.

3. Secure Hash Algorithms: Secure hash algorithms are deployed to create distinctive fingerprints of data that are able to be used for authentication and verification. An electronic communication or document is hashed using the formula:

    $Hash(M) = H$, where M is a message or content and H is the value of the hash.

Secure hash algorithms are functions that are one-way by design, making it computationally impossible to deduce the message or document's original contents from the hash value. Furthermore, any change to the input information will produce a distinct hash value, which makes it challenging for attackers to alter the data covertly. The secure hash algorithms SHA-1, SHA-2, and SHA-3 are some of the options. The size of each hash value produced by these algorithms and the quantity of hashing rounds they carry out vary. For instance, $H = SHA-256(M)$ can be used to represent the SHA-256 method, which creates a 256-bit hash value, where M is the message and document being hashed and H represents the 256-bit hash value produced by the SHA-256 algorithm. It is hard for attackers to design a specific input that produces a specified hash value because secure hash algorithms are computationally difficult to reverse. The addition of salt along with additional methods can also make it more challenging for attackers to create collisions (attacks where various inputs produce a single hash value) or other types of attacks.

These equations are only a few illustrations of the mathematical ideas important for developing a foundation of confidence in cloud computing. In the end, the particular equations and methods employed will depend on the particular security features and protocols put in place by a particular cloud service provider.

9.6 Conclusion

In conclusion, a secure and dependable computer environment is essential for the safety and reliability of applications and devices as the use of cloud computing grows more pervasive in modern industries. The initial stage of security established within a system, known as the root of trust, is crucial to the system's security. Scalability, accessibility, safety, flexibility, and cost-effectiveness are just a few of the ways that cloud computing can help root of trust systems. Cloud systems can recognize possible security risks and stop the unauthorized use of sensitive data by utilizing deep learning. The root of trust may be established and maintained through automation, guaranteeing stability across all devices. Cloud providers also have strong security protections in place. A root of trust must be established and maintained in order to ensure the reliability and safety of the devices and programs that rely on it, and cloud computing provides this platform in an efficient and scalable manner.

Another key benefit of cloud computing is security. The root of trust system is able to be safeguarded from cyber attacks by utilizing the cloud's enhanced security capabilities, such as firewalls, intrusion detection systems, and encryption. Cloud providers have extensive safety measures in place to defend the root of trust system against attacks that are internal as well as external. Another advantage of cloud computing is its adaptability. The cloud offers a wide range of services and capabilities that may be customized to an organization's specific needs. As a result of its flexibility, the root of trust systems can be tailored to the demands of the company, successfully mitigating security concerns. The cost-effectiveness of cloud computing is a big advantage. The cloud reduces the need for a company to invest in costly hardware and software in order to set up and manage a root of trust system. Cloud providers use a pay-as-you-go model, so businesses only have to pay for what resources they use. This low-cost approach assures that businesses can develop and uphold a root of trust system without breaking the bank. Lastly, cloud computing offers numerous cost-efficient benefits. A company no longer needs to spend money on pricey hardware and software in order to create and upkeep a root of trust systems. Cloud service providers offer pay-as-you-go models, enabling businesses to solely pay for the services actively used. This cost-effective approach ensures that companies can establish and maintain root of trust systems without facing financial insolvency.

In summary, a safe and reliable computer environment is essential for the security and dependability of software and hardware. The foundation of a system's security is its root of trust, and cloud computing can strengthen it by offering flexibility, availability, safety, adaptability, and cost-effectiveness. Deep learning algorithms have the ability to spot possible security threats and stop unauthorized access to private information. Stability is guaranteed across all devices by automation. To keep a root of trust, cloud providers have strong security procedures in place. In the end, cloud computing offers a productive and expandable platform to build and maintain the foundation of trust, guaranteeing the dependability and security of hardware and software that depend on it.

References

[1] Dananjayan, Sathian, and Gerard Marshall Raj. "5G in healthcare: how fast will be the transformation?." *Irish Journal of Medical Science (1971-) 190*, no. 2 (2021): 497–501.

[2] Esmaeilzadeh, Pouyan. "The impacts of the perceived transparency of privacy policies and trust in providers for building trust in health information exchange: empirical study." *JMIR medical informatics 7*, no. 4 (2019): e14050.

[3] Singh, Ashish, and Kakali Chatterjee. "ITrust: identity and trust based access control model for healthcare system security." *Multimedia Tools and Applications 78*, no. 19 (2019): 28309–28330.

[4] Alipour, Jahanpour, Yousef Mehdipour, Afsaneh Karimi, Mohadeseh Khorashadizadeh, and Maryam Akbarpour. "Security, confidentiality, privacy and patient safety in the hospital information systems from the users' perspective: A cross-sectional study." *International Journal of Medical Informatics* 175 (2023): 105066.

[5] Bani Issa, W., I. Al Akour, A. Ibrahim, A. Almarzouqi, S. Abbas, F. Hisham, and J. Griffiths. "Privacy, confidentiality, security and patient safety concerns about electronic health records." *International Nursing Review 67*, no. 2 (2020): 218–230.

[6] Amaraweera, Suvini P., and Malka N. Halgamuge. "Internet of things in the healthcare sector: overview of security and privacy issues." *Security, privacy and trust in the IoT environment* (2019): 153–179.
[7] Stephen, Mike, and Lorriane Smith. *"Evaluating Encryption Techniques in Cloud Computing for Enhanced Data Privacy."* (2022).
[8] Thomas, Roney, Priya Govindaraj, and Jaisankar Natarajan. "A fuzzy inference-based trust model estimation system for service selection in cloud computing." *International Journal of Information Technology and Management 18*, no. 2–3 (2019): 143–155.
[9] Jain, Jaishree, and Ajit Singh. "A survey on security challenges of healthcare analysis over cloud." *International Journal of Engineering Research and Management 6*, no. 04 (2017): 905–912.
[10] Gholami, Atoosa, and Mostafa Ghobaei Arani. "A trust model for resource selection in cloud computing environment." In *2015 2nd International Conference on Knowledge-Based Engineering and Innovation (KBEI)*, pp. 144–151. IEEE, 2015.
[11] Krautheim, F. John, Dhananjay S. Phatak, and Alan T. Sherman. "Introducing the trusted virtual environment module: a new mechanism for rooting trust in cloud computing." In *Trust and Trustworthy Computing: Third International Conference*, TRUST 2010, Berlin, Germany, June 21–23, 2010. Proceedings 3, pp. 211–227. Springer Berlin Heidelberg, 2010.
[12] Almaghrabi, Nada Saddig, and Bussma Ahmed Bugis. "Patient confidentiality of electronic health records: A recent review of the Saudi literature." *Dr. Sulaiman Al Habib Medical Journal 4*, no. 3 (2022): 126–135.
[13] Lee, Chonho, Zhaojing Luo, Kee Yuan Ngiam, Meihui Zhang, Kaiping Zheng, Gang Chen, Beng Chin Ooi, and Wei Luen James Yip. "Big healthcare data analytics: Challenges and applications." *Handbook of large-scale distributed computing in smart healthcare* (2017): 11–41.
[14] Kaur, Kushwant, Sahil Verma, and Ankit Bansal. "IOT big data analytics in healthcare: benefits and challenges." In *2021 6th international conference on signal processing, computing and control (ISPCC)*, pp. 176–181. IEEE, 2021.
[15] Rolnick, Joshua. "Aggregate health data in the United States: steps toward a public good." *Health Informatics Journal 19*, no. 2 (2013): 137–151.
[16] Dobrzykowski, David D., and Monideepa Tarafdar. "Understanding information exchange in healthcare operations: Evidence from hospitals and patients." *Journal of Operations Management 36* (2015): 201–214.
[17] Quamara, Megha, Brij B. Gupta, and Shingo Yamaguchi. "An end-to-end security framework for smart healthcare information sharing against botnet-based cyber-attacks." In *2021 IEEE International Conference on Consumer Electronics (ICCE)*, pp. 1–4. IEEE, 2021.
[18] Meng, Weizhi, Kim-Kwang Raymond Choo, Steven Furnell, Athanasios V. Vasilakos, and Christian W. Probst. "Towards Bayesian-based trust management for insider attacks in healthcare software-defined networks." *IEEE Transactions on Network and Service Management 15*, no. 2 (2018): 761–773.

[19] Zhou, Mingxing, Peng Xiao, Qixu Wang, Shuhua Ruan, Xingshu Chen, and Menglong Yang. "Enhancing the Trustworthiness of 6G Based on Trusted Multi-Cloud Infrastructure: A Practice of Cryptography Approach." *CMES-Computer Modeling in Engineering & Sciences 138*, no. 1 (2024).

[20] Prasad, V. K., and Madhuri D. B. "SLAMMP framework for cloud resource management and its impact on healthcare computational techniques." *International Journal of E-Health and Medical Communications (IJEHMC)*, 12, no. 2 (2021): 1–31.

[21] Prasad, V. K., and Madhuri D. B. "Monitoring IAAS cloud for healthcare systems: healthcare information management and cloud resources utilization." *International Journal of E-Health and Medical Communications (IJEHMC)*, 11, no. 3 (2020): 54–70.

[22] Chen, Jim Q., and Allen Benusa. "HIPAA security compliance challenges: The case for small healthcare providers." *International Journal of Healthcare Management 10*, no. 2 (2017): 135–146.

[23] Baddour, Larry M., Walter R. Wilson, Arnold S. Bayer, Vance G. Fowler Jr, Ann F. Bolger, Matthew E. Levison, Patricia Ferrieri *et al.* Diagnosis, Antimicrobial Therapy, and Management of Complications A Statement for Healthcare Professionals from the Committee on Rheumatic Fever, Endocarditis, and Kawasaki Disease, Council on Cardiovascular Disease in the Young, and the Councils on Clinical Cardiology, Stroke, and Cardiovascular Surgery and Anesthesia, American Heart Association. *Circulation* 111, no. e394 (2005): e434.

[24] More, Sujeet, Jimmy Singla, Sahil Verma, Uttam Ghosh, Joel JPC Rodrigues, ASM Sanwar Hosen, and In-Ho Ra. "Security assured CNN-based model for reconstruction of medical images on the internet of healthcare things." *IEEE Access* 8 (2020): 126333–126346.

[25] Ren, Yonglin, Richard Werner, Nelem Pazzi, and Azzedine Boukerche. "Monitoring patients via a secure and mobile healthcare system." *IEEE Wireless Communications* 17, no. 1 (2010): 59–65.

[26] Abdelaziz, Ahmed, Mohamed Elhoseny, Ahmed S. Salama, Alaa Mohamed Riad, and Aboul Ella Hassanien. "Intelligent algorithms for optimal selection of virtual machine in cloud environment, towards enhance healthcare services." In *Proceedings of the International Conference on Advanced Intelligent Systems and Informatics 2017*, pp. 289–298. Springer International Publishing, 2018.

[27] Prathap, R., and R. Mohanasundaram. "Hybrid optimization for virtual machine migration of utilizing healthcare text in the cloud." *International Journal of Speech Technology* 24, no. 2 (2021): 359–365.

[28] NICOLAU, Dragos Nicolae, Adriana Alexandru, and Marilena Ianculescu. "An IoT, Virtual Machines and Cloud Computing-based Framework for an Optimal Management of Healthcare Data Collected from a Smart Environment. A Case Study: RO-Smart Ageing Project." *Informatica Economica* 23, no. 3 (2019).

[29] Iyengar, Arun, Ashish Kundu, Upendra Sharma, and Ping Zhang. "A trusted healthcare data analytics cloud platform." In *2018 IEEE 38th International Conference on Distributed Computing Systems (ICDCS)*, pp. 1238–1249. IEEE, 2018.

Chapter 10

Authentication and access control schemes in 5G-based healthcare systems

T. Ananth Kumar[1], A. Kathiravan[1], P. Kanimozhi[1], Sunday A. Ajagbe[2], K. Suresh Kumar[3] and R. Rajmohan[4]

The rapid evolution of communication technologies has led to the emergence of the fifth-generation (5G) wireless network, promising unprecedented levels of connectivity, speed, and reliability. Simultaneously, the healthcare sector is undergoing a transformation, incorporating digital advancements to enhance patient care, diagnosis, and treatment. As these two domains converge, the significance of securing sensitive medical data and ensuring authorized access becomes paramount. This chapter's focus is to explore the challenges and opportunities surrounding authentication and access control within 5G-based healthcare systems. Authentication, the process of verifying the identity of users, devices, and entities, forms the foundational layer of security in 5G-based healthcare environments. Traditional authentication methods like passwords and PINs are being supplemented with biometric modalities such as fingerprint recognition, facial scanning, and even behavioral patterns, bolstering security and user convenience. Multifactor authentication (MFA) strategies further fortify access by requiring multiple forms of verification, reducing the likelihood of unauthorized intrusion. However, challenges persist, including the risk of biometric data breaches and the need for standardized authentication protocols across different healthcare providers and systems. In conclusion, the integration of 5G technology into healthcare systems presents a transformative paradigm shift with unparalleled opportunities for improving patient care and medical services. However, this convergence necessitates a comprehensive approach to authentication and access control to safeguard sensitive patient data, ensure the integrity of medical processes, and maintain the trust of both healthcare providers and patients. By addressing challenges like biometric security, standardization, and continuous authentication, stakeholders can collectively embrace the potential of 5G-based healthcare systems while upholding the highest standards of security and privacy.

---

[1]Department of Computer Science and Engineering, IFET College of Engineering, India
[2]Department of Computer Engineering, Abiola Ajimobi Technical University, 200255, Nigeria
[3]Department of Information Technology, Sri Krishna College of Technology, India
[4]Department of Computing Technologies, SRM Institute of Science and Technology, India

10.1 Introduction

The rapid evolution of wireless communication technologies, coupled with the transformative potential of healthcare systems, has given rise to the integration of 5G technology into the realm of medical services. In this chapter, titled "Authentication and Access Control Schemes in 5G-Based Healthcare Systems," we delve into the critical role that robust authentication and access control mechanisms play in ensuring the security, privacy, and seamless functioning of modern healthcare systems leveraging 5G technology. Access control, on the other hand, governs what resources and information authorized users can access, ensuring the principle of least privilege. 5G technology introduces network slicing, enabling the creation of isolated virtual networks tailored to specific applications, including healthcare [1]. This facilitates granular access control by segregating healthcare data from other network traffic. Moreover, Attribute-Based Access Control (ABAC) models can be employed, where access decisions are based on attributes associated with users, devices, and context. ABAC offers dynamic and context-aware access management, aligning well with the dynamic nature of healthcare environments where different users require varying levels of access to data.

5G's low latency and high data speeds foster real-time remote medical services such as telemedicine, remote surgery, and patient monitoring [2]. However, this necessitates robust security mechanisms to safeguard sensitive patient data during transmission and storage. End-to-end encryption, coupled with secure key management, ensures that data remains confidential and tamper-proof. Additionally, secure enclaves or Trusted Execution Environments (TEEs) can be leveraged to protect critical medical applications and data within potentially compromised devices.

Interoperability and standardization pose significant challenges. Healthcare systems encompass a multitude of devices, protocols, and interfaces. Establishing standardized authentication and access control protocols is imperative to ensure seamless collaboration between different healthcare providers and systems. This can be achieved through open standards and collaborative efforts within the industry to develop and implement secure, interoperable solutions. The chapter also delves into the concept of continuous authentication, whereby a user's identity is consistently verified during their entire session [3]. Behavioral biometrics, such as keystroke dynamics and gait analysis, can be employed to ensure that the authenticated user remains the same throughout their interaction, mitigating risks posed by unauthorized physical access.

The deployment of 5G networks brings forth unparalleled opportunities for healthcare delivery, enabling real-time monitoring, remote diagnostics, telemedicine, and an array of innovative applications [4]. However, alongside these advancements, a host of new challenges and vulnerabilities emerge, particularly in the context of safeguarding sensitive patient data, medical records, and critical infrastructure. This chapter sheds light on the multifaceted dimensions of authentication and access control, addressing the intricate interplay between technological innovation and safeguarding patient well-being. As healthcare systems migrate towards 5G, the need for reliable and sophisticated authentication mechanisms becomes paramount. The dynamic nature of 5G networks, characterized by higher data rates, ultra-low latency, and massive device connectivity, necessitates a reevaluation of traditional authentication approaches. We explore a spectrum of authentication methods, from SIM-based and certificate-based authentication to cutting-edge biometric techniques, elucidating their strengths, limitations, and applicability in the healthcare context.

Access control, a pivotal component of healthcare cybersecurity, is also placed under the spotlight in this chapter. In a landscape where patient data traverses intricate networks and interconnected devices, access control models must be adaptive and granular. We dissect various models, including role-based, attribute-based, and mandatory access control, examining how they contribute to preserving confidentiality, integrity, and availability of sensitive health information.

Moreover, the imperative of privacy preservation takes center stage. With 5G enabling a proliferation of connected devices and wearables, the potential for unauthorized data access escalates. Through the lens of authentication and access control, we deliberate on strategies to mitigate privacy risks, exploring mechanisms that strike a delicate balance between data usability and protection. In a healthcare environment characterized by high-stakes scenarios, the adoption of two-factor authentication (2FA) emerges as a powerful strategy. We explore how the fusion of multiple authentication factors can enhance security and thwart unauthorized access, ensuring that only authorized personnel can access critical medical resources. Through real-world case studies, this chapter examines the practical implementation of authentication and access control mechanisms in 5G-based healthcare ecosystems [5]. By delving into these examples, we glean insights into the challenges faced and the lessons learned, offering a nuanced perspective on the intricate landscape of securing healthcare in the 5G era. "Authentication and Access Control Schemes in 5G-Based Healthcare Systems" unravels the intricate tapestry of security challenges and solutions at the convergence of healthcare and 5G technology. As the healthcare industry embraces the potential of 5G, a robust understanding of authentication and access control becomes indispensable, ensuring that the benefits of technological progress are realized without compromising the confidentiality, integrity, and availability of sensitive medical information.

10.1.1 5G technology in healthcare

The integration of 5G technology in healthcare marks a transformative leap towards a future where medical services and patient care are elevated to unprecedented levels of efficiency, accuracy, and accessibility. As the cornerstone of the Fourth Industrial Revolution, 5G technology brings forth the potential to revolutionize healthcare systems through its exceptional capabilities.

At its core, 5G technology promises significantly higher data transfer speeds, ultra-low latency, and enhanced connectivity. These attributes form the bedrock of real-time communication and data exchange, facilitating seamless remote

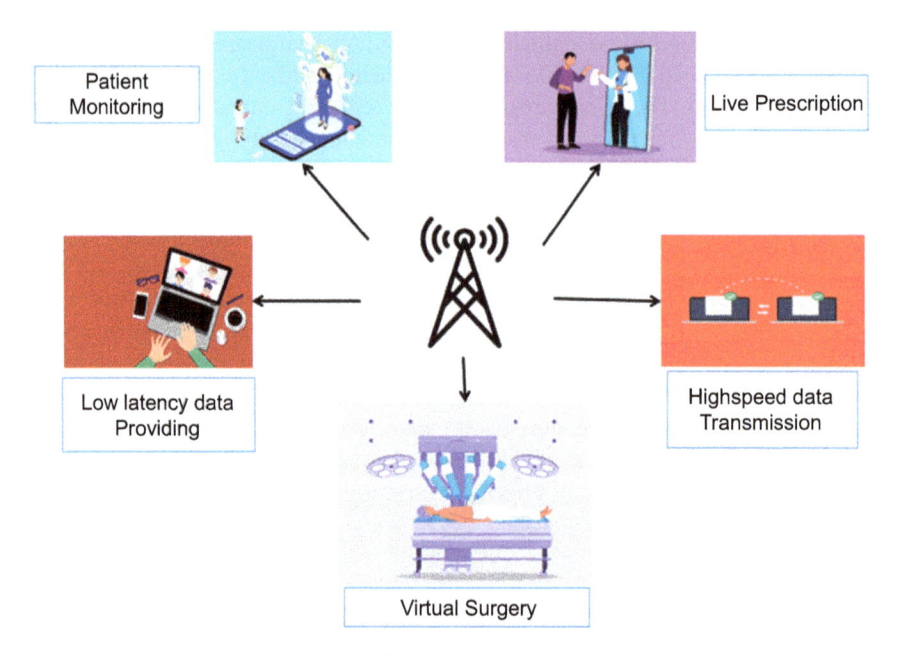

Figure 10.1 5G in healthcare

diagnostics, telemedicine consultations, and remote patient monitoring [6]. The ability to transmit high-quality medical imaging, sensor data, and patient records without delay enables medical professionals to make informed decisions promptly and enables patients to receive timely care regardless of geographical constraints. The vast network capacity of 5G accommodates a myriad of interconnected devices and wearables, forming the basis of the Internet of Medical Things (IoMT). This interconnected ecosystem enables continuous health monitoring, personalized treatment plans, and preventive interventions. Furthermore, the reliability and stability of 5G networks ensure consistent communication between medical devices and healthcare infrastructure, reducing the risk of disruptions that could compromise patient care (Figure 10.1).

However, as 5G technology redefines healthcare possibilities, it also introduces new security challenges. The dynamic nature of 5G networks demands robust authentication and access control mechanisms to safeguard patient data, medical records, and critical healthcare infrastructure. In the context of "Authentication and Access Control Schemes in 5G-Based Healthcare Systems," this chapter explores how the fusion of cutting-edge 5G technology with stringent security measures is essential to harness its potential while upholding the confidentiality, integrity, and availability of sensitive medical information.

10.1.2 Security challenges in 5G healthcare systems

The invasion of 5G technology into healthcare systems brings forth a new era of possibilities, but it also introduces a myriad of security challenges that demand careful consideration. The chapter titled "Authentication and Access Control Schemes in 5G-Based Healthcare Systems" delves into the intricate landscape of these security challenges. One of the foremost concerns lies in the sheer complexity of 5G networks [7]. The vast number of connected devices and the dynamic nature of these networks open doors to potential vulnerabilities and entry points for malicious actors [8]. The expanded attack surface increases the risk of unauthorized access, data breaches, and potential disruptions in critical healthcare services.

Moreover, the speed and low latency of 5G networks, while enabling real-time communication, also provide a fertile ground for sophisticated cyberattacks. The rapid transmission of data, if compromised, can lead to immediate and severe consequences in patient care and privacy. As the chapter examines authentication and access control mechanisms, it unravels the necessity of implementing advanced techniques to counteract these evolving threats. The convergence of 5G technology and healthcare systems underscores the need to safeguard patient data with the utmost diligence. As the chapter navigates through the security challenges in this context, it underscores the pivotal role that strong authentication and access control mechanisms play in mitigating risks and ensuring the sanctity of sensitive medical information. By addressing these challenges head-on, the chapter provides a comprehensive perspective on how to harness the power of 5G while fortifying the security posture of healthcare systems.

10.2 Authentication mechanisms in 5G healthcare systems

In the rapidly evolving landscape of healthcare systems powered by 5G technology, robust authentication mechanisms take center stage as the first line of defense against unauthorized access and potential security breaches. This chapter titled "Authentication and Access Control Schemes in 5G-Based Healthcare Systems" delves into the multifaceted world of authentication methods and their application within this context.

5G technology introduces a paradigm shift in communication and connectivity, which in turn demands a reevaluation of traditional authentication approaches. One prominent method is SIM-based authentication, leveraging the unique identification of Subscriber Identity Modules. While widely used, this method faces challenges of scalability and potential vulnerabilities, requiring constant updates to combat evolving threats [9]. Certificate-based authentication emerges as a viable alternative, capitalizing on digital certificates to validate the identities of devices and entities within the network. This method offers a higher degree of security and flexibility, bolstering the authentication process while accommodating the diverse array of devices inherent to 5G healthcare systems. However, perhaps the most exciting frontier lies in the realm of biometric authentication. Biometric factors such as fingerprints, facial recognition, and iris scans offer a highly personalized and secure means of verification [10]. The chapter explores how biometrics provide an extra layer of protection against identity fraud and unauthorized access, especially in healthcare settings where accurate identification is paramount. A key consideration in authentication mechanisms is the trade-off between security and user experience. As the chapter delves into these mechanisms, it delves into the need to strike a balance that ensures rigorous security without impeding the seamless flow of medical services. Moreover, the chapter also sheds light on the importance of continuous monitoring and adaptive authentication methods to counteract emerging threats.

By examining these authentication methods, the chapter underscores their significance in fortifying healthcare systems against cyber threats. The integration of 5G technology into healthcare amplifies the potential for enhanced patient care and innovative medical services. Yet, these benefits can only be fully realized when coupled with stringent authentication mechanisms that protect sensitive patient data, medical records, and critical infrastructure. In conclusion, the chapter's exploration of authentication mechanisms within 5G healthcare systems paints a comprehensive picture of the challenges and opportunities present in this dynamic landscape. As healthcare continues to embrace the potential of 5G, the adoption of the right authentication techniques ensures that the promise of enhanced connectivity and medical services aligns seamlessly with the imperative of security and patient privacy.

10.2.1 Access control strategies in 5G healthcare systems

In the realm of 5G-powered healthcare systems, where connectivity and data flow are poised to redefine patient care, robust access control strategies emerge as critical safeguards. This chapter titled "Authentication and Access Control Schemes in 5G-Based Healthcare Systems" delves into the nuanced landscape of access control models and their pivotal role in preserving the confidentiality, integrity, and availability of sensitive medical information. One fundamental approach is Role-Based Access Control (RBAC), wherein users are assigned specific roles and associated permissions [11]. This strategy streamlines access management by categorizing users into roles such as doctors, nurses, and administrators. However, in the context of 5G healthcare systems, where real-time collaboration and diverse workflows are common, the chapter explores the challenges of ensuring granular access control that aligns with complex healthcare scenarios.

Attribute-Based Access Control (ABAC) emerges as a more flexible alternative. This model considers a multitude of attributes—such as user attributes, resource attributes, and environmental factors—to determine access. The chapter examines how ABAC aligns with the dynamic nature of 5G healthcare systems, enabling finer control over who can access what and under what conditions. This adaptability proves crucial in ensuring that sensitive patient data remains accessible only to authorized individuals. Furthermore, Mandatory Access Control (MAC) offers an additional layer of security. By enforcing access based on predefined rules, MAC ensures that sensitive medical information is protected from unauthorized access, even in scenarios where users might attempt to override permissions. The chapter delves into the applicability of MAC in healthcare settings, emphasizing its potential to mitigate risks associated with human error or intentional breaches.

As the chapter navigates these access control models, it also underscores the necessity of effective Identity and Access Management (IAM). IAM encompasses the processes and technologies that manage user identities and their associated access rights. In the context of 5G healthcare systems, IAM becomes paramount in ensuring accurate user identification and seamless access management across a diverse range of devices and applications [12]. In a landscape where interconnected devices and wearables form the Internet of Medical Things (IoMT), the chapter recognizes the challenges in securing this intricate ecosystem. The potential for unauthorized access or compromised devices necessitates a comprehensive view of access control that spans the entire IoMT spectrum. In conclusion, "Access Control Strategies in 5G Healthcare Systems" sheds light on the multifaceted strategies that underpin secure access to sensitive medical data in the era of 5G technology. As healthcare systems embrace the potential of 5G, the effective implementation of access control models becomes a cornerstone in realizing the benefits of connectivity while upholding the highest standards of security and patient privacy.

10.2.2 Privacy-preserving techniques

In the evolving landscape of healthcare systems powered by 5G technology, the paramount concern is not only to ensure secure access but also to safeguard patient privacy with unwavering dedication. This chapter titled "Authentication and Access Control Schemes in 5G-Based Healthcare Systems" delves into the critical realm of privacy-preserving techniques, exploring how these strategies intersect with authentication and access control to uphold the sanctity of sensitive medical information. With the proliferation of connected devices and wearables enabled by 5G, the potential for unauthorized data access escalates, raising concerns about patient privacy [13]. This chapter embarks on a journey through the strategies that strike a delicate balance between ensuring data usability for medical services and protecting the confidentiality of patient information.

One pivotal technique is Differential Privacy, which injects controlled noise into datasets to mask individual data points while still allowing accurate aggregate analysis. The chapter examines how this approach can enable healthcare professionals to glean insights from patient data without compromising the identities of individual patients. By introducing a level of uncertainty into the data, differential privacy shields sensitive information from potential adversaries seeking to link data to individuals. Homomorphic Encryption presents another innovative avenue. This technique allows computation on encrypted data without the need for decryption, ensuring that even when data is in use, it remains protected. The chapter dissects how this approach can facilitate collaborative medical research while maintaining the privacy of individual patients' health records.

Federated Learning, a decentralized machine learning approach, emerges as a powerful tool in the preservation of privacy. The chapter explores how models are trained collaboratively across multiple devices, ensuring that sensitive patient data never leaves the premises. This technique is especially relevant in the context of 5G-based healthcare systems, where data is generated and stored across diverse locations [14]. Blockchain technology, renowned for its transparency and immutability, offers promise in enhancing patient privacy. The chapter delves into how blockchain's distributed ledger can provide patients with control over their medical data, granting access only to authorized parties and potentially revolutionizing patient consent processes. While these privacy-preserving techniques hold immense potential, the chapter also addresses their challenges. Striking the right balance between privacy and utility can be intricate, and implementing these techniques within the dynamic realm of 5G healthcare systems requires careful consideration.

As the chapter navigates these strategies, it underscores their pivotal role in the broader context of authentication and access control. Strong authentication and access management techniques ensure that only authorized individuals access medical data, while privacy-preserving techniques ensure that this access does not compromise the sensitive nature of patient information.

In conclusion, "Privacy-Preserving Techniques" within 5G-based healthcare systems illuminate the path toward a future where the power of 5G converges with the importance of safeguarding patient privacy. By combining rigorous authentication, access control, and privacy-preserving techniques, healthcare systems can harness the potential of 5G technology while upholding the highest standards of security and patient confidentiality.

10.2.3 Regulatory compliance and standards

Within the realm of 5G-based healthcare systems, the significance of regulatory compliance and adherence to established standards cannot be overstated. This chapter titled "Authentication and Access Control Schemes in 5G-Based Healthcare Systems" delves into the intricate landscape of regulatory frameworks and standards that underpin the secure operation of these dynamic ecosystems. Healthcare systems, underpinned by the transformative capabilities of 5G technology, handle a vast array of sensitive patient data and medical records [15]. Ensuring that these systems comply with regulatory requirements is not only a legal obligation but also a fundamental aspect of maintaining patient trust and upholding the highest standards of patient care. One of the cornerstones of healthcare data protection is the Health Insurance Portability and Accountability Act (HIPAA) in the United States. HIPAA mandates the protection of patients' personal health information and sets standards for its secure handling, storage, and transmission. The chapter delves into how authentication and access control mechanisms must align with HIPAA requirements to prevent unauthorized access to patient records.

In the European Union, the General Data Protection Regulation (GDPR) stands as a comprehensive framework for data protection and privacy. GDPR's principles of data minimization, purpose limitation, and consent impact how patient data is accessed and managed within 5G healthcare systems. The chapter examines the interplay between GDPR and authentication/access control strategies, emphasizing the need to strike a balance between usability and privacy [16]. The International Organization for Standardization (ISO) also plays a vital role in establishing best practices for healthcare data security. ISO/IEC 27001 and ISO/IEC 27799 provide guidelines for information security management systems and healthcare information management systems, respectively. The chapter explores how adherence to these standards can guide the implementation of authentication and access control mechanisms that align with international norms. Furthermore, the chapter navigates through the Health Level Seven International (HL7) standards, which focus on the exchange, integration, sharing, and retrieval of electronic health information. These standards ensure that healthcare systems communicate seamlessly while maintaining the privacy and security of patient data. Authentication and access control strategies within 5G healthcare systems must dovetail with HL7 standards to facilitate interoperability without compromising data security. As the chapter delves into these regulatory frameworks and standards, it acknowledges the evolving nature of technology and healthcare practices. This calls for a dynamic approach to compliance, where authentication and access control strategies can adapt to emerging requirements while remaining steadfast in their commitment to data security and patient privacy.

In conclusion, "Regulatory Compliance and Standards" within 5G-based healthcare systems underscore the intricate dance between technological innovation and legal responsibilities. The integration of 5G technology into healthcare holds immense promise, but its success hinges on ensuring that authentication and access control mechanisms are not only technologically robust but also aligned with global regulatory mandates. By harmonizing these elements, healthcare systems can usher in a future where the benefits of 5G technology are realized without compromising the integrity of patient data or regulatory obligations.

10.3 Case study: "5G-enabled video and data transmission with high speed and low latency from ambulance to mobile hospital systems"

The mobile hospital system concept entails the deployment of a medically equipped ambulance stationed remotely, utilizing a 5G cellular network to seamlessly transmit vital medical data to a central hospital hub. This configuration assumes a significant geographical distance between the remote site and the hospital center. The data transmission involves two distinct categories. The primary category involves real-time video streaming captured within the ambulance, transmitted in ultra-high-definition 4K format to the hospital center [17]. This video stream is intended for meticulous patient monitoring essential for online therapeutic interventions. It enables remote medical professionals to virtually peer inside the ambulance, monitor patients, and engage in real-time consultations with onboard colleagues, thereby providing instant guidance for distant preliminary treatments.

The second data category encompasses critical patient metrics such as body temperature, blood pressure, heart rate, oxygen saturation, and electrocardiogram (ECG) readings, among others. Additionally, this category encompasses supplementary data like images and real-time videos of certain patients undergoing remote surgical procedures. Within our context, this group is referred to as clinical data, serving the purpose of continuous monitoring, guidance, and preliminary treatments. It is essential to note that our focus here is solely on the aspect of data transmission, excluding discussions on lossless compression and data encryption. Central to this system is a heterogeneous network architecture, with the application of slicing concepts within Cloud Radio Access Networks (C-RANs) for optimized data transmission. The C-RAN configuration is comprised of distributed Remote Radio Heads (RRHs) organized into small cells. Each of these cells is catered to by a Macro Base Station (MBS). The RRHs and MBSs are centrally connected to a cloud-based Baseband Unit (BBU) pool through optical fronthaul links. To facilitate slicing, virtual machines (VMs) are established within the BBU pool to allocate network radio resources, where each VM functions as a virtual BBU dedicated to a specific data flow. This cloud BBU pool also integrates a Software-Defined Networking (SDN)-based network slicing module linked to these virtual BBUs. The system design accommodates multiple slices, with the capability highlighted by the presence of "Another Slice" in the accompanying figure. This dynamic structure supports various application services. However, for medical data transmission, we concentrate on just two slices: an enhanced Mobile Broadband (eMBB) slice for 4K video streaming from the ambulance and an ultra-reliable and Low-Latency Communications (uRLLC) slice for clinical data.

In the network slicing procedure, a service level agreement exists between the network operator and the slice tenants. This agreement stipulates Quality of Service (QoS) parameters for each user within each slice. These parameters vary based on the specific requirements of the slice. For example, eMBB slice users necessitate a minimum data throughput, while uRLLC slice users demand a balance between transmission reliability and latency. To facilitate medical data transmission, the designated user initiates a scheduling request directed to its associated RRH. The SDN-based slicing module activates this request within the cloud BBU pool. Upon receipt, the RRH promptly approves the transmission. In the case of 4K video transmission, an installed camera within the ambulance captures the internal environment. This video feed is then relayed to a 5G medical gateway (UEt 1). Once authorized by the network and the eMBB slice, the gateway forwards the video to its designated RRH.

Similarly, for clinical data transmission, medical instruments and another camera collect relevant data, subsequently sent to a separate 5G medical gateway. Following network and uRLLC slice authorization, this gateway transmits the data to its assigned RRH. Upon arrival at the hospital center, two 5G medical data cloud platforms receive the 4K video and clinical data, respectively, from their corresponding RRHs. Subsequently, these platforms transmit the data to the relevant medical equipment, enabling doctors to access the information promptly and effectively (Figure 10.2).

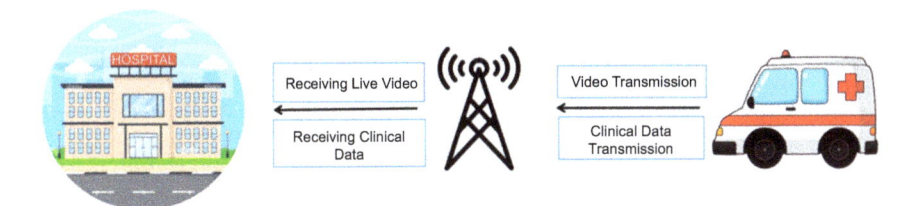

Figure 10.2 Video and data transmission

10.3.1 Proposed methodology for 4K-video transmission from ambulance

The In-Ambulance 4K Video Throughput Maximization addresses the critical need for seamless and high-quality communication within emergency medical service (EMS) settings, specifically focusing on the transmission of 4K video data. The efficient exchange of real-time video in an ambulance can significantly impact patient care, enabling remote medical experts to provide accurate guidance to on-site paramedics. Traditional video transmission methods often struggle with the bandwidth demands of 4K video, hindering the clarity and timeliness of information relayed. The proposed method introduces an innovative approach that optimizes video throughput while maintaining a high level of image quality [18]. At the core of the method is an adaptive video compression algorithm that dynamically adjusts the compression level based on the available bandwidth. During moments of stable connectivity, the algorithm ensures that the video is transmitted with minimal compression, preserving intricate details necessary for medical assessments. Conversely, when bandwidth becomes constrained, the algorithm enhances compression to prevent interruptions in the video stream. This adaptability strikes a balance between image fidelity and real-time delivery, ensuring that essential information is consistently available to medical personnel [19].

Moreover, the system incorporates a priority-based data packet transmission mechanism. This means that critical patient data, such as vital signs and medical history, are assigned higher transmission priority than non-essential video frames. As a result, even in scenarios where network congestion is inevitable, the most crucial information arrives without delay. To enhance the robustness of the system, the proposed method integrates forward error correction (FEC) techniques. These error correction codes enable the receiver to reconstruct lost or corrupted data packets, further reducing the likelihood of information loss during transmission. The implementation of the "Proposed Method for In-Ambulance 4K Video Throughput Maximization" holds promising implications for EMS operations. It empowers paramedics and remote medical experts with a clear, real-time view of the patient's condition, regardless of the challenges posed by limited bandwidth and network instability. By optimizing video throughput without compromising vital data, the proposed method elevates the quality of care provided in ambulance settings, potentially leading to improved patient outcomes and more informed medical decisions (Table 10.1).

218 Secure big-data analytics for emerging healthcare in 5G and beyond

Table 10.1 Notations

Notation	Descriptions	Notation	Descriptions
S	Slicing sets: {1.... |S|}	α	Lagrange Multipliers.
L	Uplink and Downlink RRH sets.	t	Time per value attained by every Lagrange Multipliers.
V	Video Transmitted as Data.	I	Iterations
K	Subchannel sets.	τ	Maximum iteration of Data.
W_{luk}	Indicator with l-RRH, u-user, k-subchannel.	g_{luk}	Gradient factor with l-RRH, u-user, k-subchannel.
P_{luk}	Power transmitted by user with l-RRH, u-user, k-subchannel.	Δf	Subcarrier spacing for latency requirement.
$C_{c,v}$	Computational capacity of virtual machines.	ε_u	Overall package loss probability by user.
$R_{min,u}$	Minimum Guarantee for the user in slicing.	C_{fh}	Computation capacity for frames of video transmission.
$P_{max,l}$	Transmission budget.	N_u	User's packet length after channel coding.
δ	Step sizes (1.... 5).	T_u	Duration of user packet implementation.

10.3.2 Optimal resource algorithm for maximum video data transmission

A crucial element in real-time healthcare communication is the implementation of an efficient resource allocation algorithm for video transmission from ambulances to hospital systems. This algorithm plays a vital role in managing bandwidth effectively, ensuring the seamless and uninterrupted transmission of crucial video feeds from the ambulance. These feeds encompass essential information like patient condition and vital signs. The algorithm's intelligence lies in its ability to prioritize data based on urgency, dynamically adapting to fluctuating network conditions. This, in turn, enhances the capabilities of remote diagnosis, allowing medical professionals to adequately prepare for incoming patients. Through its optimization of resource allocation, the algorithm significantly reduces latency and minimizes the risk of data loss. Ultimately, it contributes to more effective emergency medical care, potentially saving lives during the critical transit from the field to the hospital.

Obtaining the maximized method for deriving equations from the optimal resource algorithm and the iterated values for maximum throughput are,

$$\alpha_l^{(t+1)} = \left[\alpha_l^{(t)} - \delta_1\left(C_{fh} - \sum_{u \in U1} 1 \sum_{k \in K} W_{luk} R_{luk}\right)\right] \tag{10.1}$$

$$\beta_{lu}^{(t+1)} = \left[\beta_{lu}^{(t)} - \delta_2\left(C_{c,v} - \sum_{k \in K} W_{luk} R_{luk}\right)\right] \quad (10.2)$$

$$\lambda_{lu}^{(t+1)} = \left[\lambda_l^{(t)} - \delta_3\left(\sum_{u \in U1} 1 \sum_{k \in K} W_{luk} R_{luk} - R_{\min,u}\right)\right] \quad (10.3)$$

$$\mu_l^{(t+1)} = \left[\mu_l^{(t)} - \delta_4\left(P_{\max,l} - \sum_{u \in U1} 1 \sum_{k \in K} W_{luk} P_{luk}\right)\right] \quad (10.4)$$

$$\tau_{lk}^{(t+1)} = \left[\tau_{lk}^{(t)} - \delta_5\left(I_{th} - \sum_{u \in U1} 1 \sum_{k \in K} W_{luk} P_{luk} g_{luk}\right)\right] \quad (10.5)$$

10.3.3 Proposed methodology for clinical data transmission with ultrahigh reliable and low latency

The Ultrahigh Reliable and Very Low-Latency Transmission of Clinical Data addresses a critical aspect of modern healthcare: the rapid and secure exchange of clinical information. In medical settings, especially those requiring real-time monitoring and remote diagnostics, the timely and accurate transmission of clinical data is of paramount importance. This method aims to revolutionize data transmission by ensuring both exceptionally high reliability and minimal transmission latency.

At the heart of this method lies a hybrid communication protocol that combines the strengths of existing technologies to achieve its objectives. The protocol integrates aspects of both wired and wireless communication systems to create a redundant and adaptable transmission pathway. This dual-pathway approach significantly enhances reliability by mitigating the risks associated with a single communication channel failure. The proposed method also introduces advanced error correction mechanisms. By employing powerful error detection and correction codes, the system can identify and rectify data corruption or loss that may occur during transmission. This ensures that the clinical data received at the destination is an accurate representation of the original information. In addition to its reliability focus, the method places a strong emphasis on achieving very low latency [20]. This is particularly crucial for real-time medical applications where even the slightest delay in data transmission can have serious implications. To address this, the protocol optimizes data packet prioritization, giving precedence to critical clinical data. Nonessential data, while still important, is transmitted with lower priority to ensure that essential information arrives at its destination with minimal delay. To further enhance latency reduction, the method utilizes edge computing techniques. By processing certain data locally at the source, rather than sending it all to a central server, the system minimizes the time it takes for information to traverse the network. This is particularly beneficial for applications requiring immediate medical interventions.

The security of clinical data is not overlooked in this method. It incorporates robust encryption and authentication mechanisms to safeguard patient information from unauthorized access during transmission. In conclusion, the "Proposed Method for Ultrahigh Reliable and Very Low-Latency Transmission of Clinical Data" presents a comprehensive solution to one of the most critical challenges in modern healthcare. By combining redundancy, advanced error correction, prioritization, edge computing, and encryption, the method ensures that clinical data is not only transmitted reliably but also with the minimal delay required for time-sensitive medical decisions. This innovation holds the potential to transform telemedicine, remote diagnostics, and various healthcare applications by fostering faster, more accurate, and secure data exchanges.

10.3.4 Optimal resource algorithm for maximum clinical data transmission

An optimal resource allocation algorithm for clinical data transmission from ambulances to hospital systems is paramount for efficient healthcare delivery. This algorithm meticulously manages data transfer, ensuring that vital patient information, such as medical records, diagnostics, and real-time monitoring data, reaches the hospital swiftly and securely. By prioritizing critical data streams and adapting to varying network conditions in real time, this algorithm empowers healthcare professionals with immediate access to essential information. This seamless transmission enhances patient care by enabling timely diagnoses and informed treatment decisions upon the patient's arrival at the hospital. Ultimately, this algorithm streamlines the transfer of clinical data, improving the overall quality of care and patient outcomes.

Obtaining the maximized method for deriving equations from the optimal resource algorithm and the input, moderated output for maximum throughput are,

Input: $\varepsilon_u, \varepsilon_u^d$, D, m, $N_{tot,(l,i)}^{ress}$, C, X, $D_u, T_u, u = 1\ldots n, l = 1\ldots L, i = 1\ldots 4$.

Output: L, n_u, $\Delta f_{(i,u)}$, $N_{TTI}^{syn} = 0$, u = 1.... N, l∈L, Scheduled pattern.

10.3.5 Performance analysis

The performance analysis of 4K video transmission and clinical data transmission is a fundamental endeavor that significantly influences modern healthcare and communication systems. The evaluation of these two distinct yet interconnected aspects plays a pivotal role in shaping the efficiency and effectiveness of various applications. In the case of 4K video transmission, factors like throughput, latency, and image quality hold paramount importance. The intricate details and real-time nature of medical procedures demand seamless visualization, making high-resolution video crucial for telemedicine, surgery, and emergency response scenarios. A comprehensive performance analysis helps identify bottlenecks and optimize the network for low latency and high-quality video delivery [21]. Moreover, understanding the resource requirements of 4K video transmission aids in provisioning adequate bandwidth and infrastructure, enabling healthcare professionals to make accurate diagnoses and decisions remotely.

On the other hand, clinical data transmission involves the reliable and swift exchange of critical patient information, ranging from vital signs to medical histories. An effective analysis encompasses parameters such as data integrity, latency, and security. The assessment ensures that patient data reaches its destination accurately and swiftly, facilitating timely medical interventions and informed decision-making. Moreover, the analysis of clinical data transmission considers the interoperability of systems, as healthcare environments often involve multiple devices and platforms. For video transmission, one might plot metrics such as bandwidth utilization, frame rate, and video quality over time. This graph shows how well the system maintains 4K video quality while adapting to network conditions, ensuring that critical details are consistently visible.

Evaluating these graphical representations in concert allows stakeholders to obtain a comprehensive understanding of the overall system's performance. An efficient methodology must strike a harmonious equilibrium between video and data transmission, assuring that both aspects are finely tuned for optimal results. This equilibrium is vital for achieving fluid and uninterrupted communication, particularly in pivotal contexts like ambulance-based healthcare. The synergy between these two facets, as depicted in the graphs, elucidates how well the system maintains its operational integrity. It underscores the importance of achieving a delicate balance between video quality, bandwidth utilization, and data transfer efficiency. Such a balance ensures that critical medical information, including high-resolution video feeds and essential clinical data, is reliably and expeditiously transmitted. As the graphs converge, they tell a compelling story of a system adept at navigating complex network dynamics while delivering top-notch performance in both video and data transmission. Ultimately, this synchronized performance is the linchpin in providing lifesaving medical care during critical emergencies (Figures 10.3 and 10.4).

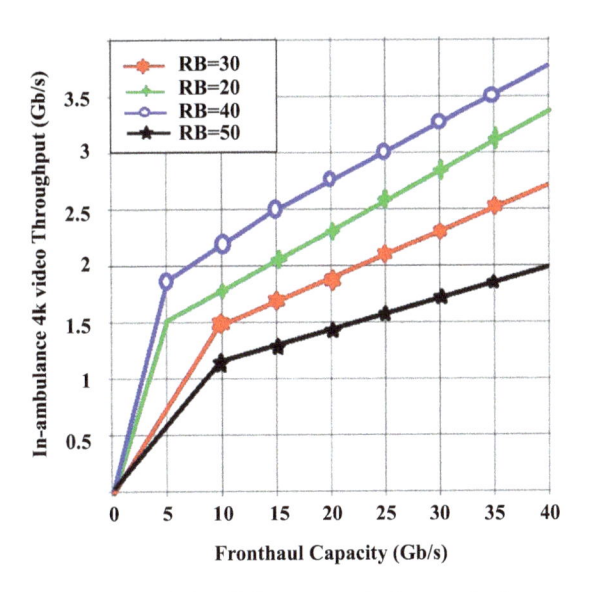

Figure 10.3 Video transmission analysis

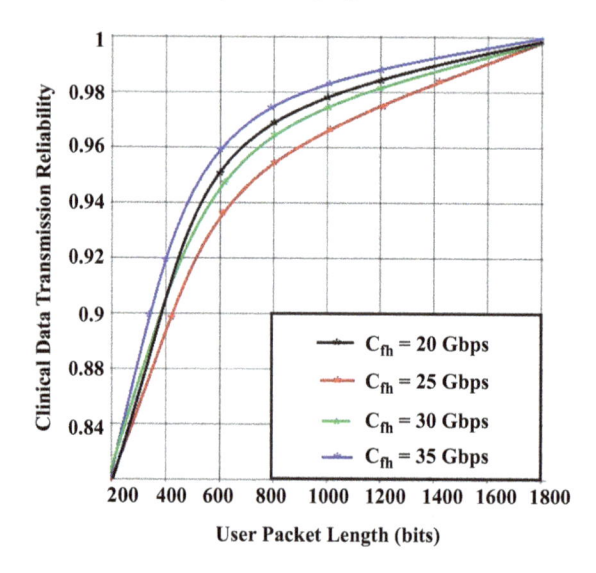

222 *Secure big-data analytics for emerging healthcare in 5G and beyond*

Figure 10.4 Clinical data transmission analysis

10.3.6 Results and analysis

Initially, we assess the attainable in-ambulance 4K video throughput for the user denoted as UEr 1 situated at the hospital terminal. This assessment utilizes our proposed optimization method and takes into account a minimum rate of $R_{min,u}$ = 20 Mb/s [22]. Illustrated in figure is the relationship between achievable throughput and the quantity of Remote Radio Heads (RRHs). This analysis is conducted under the constraint of a 20 Gb/s fronthaul capacity and varying numbers of Resource Blocks (RBs) allocated to the user. The findings indicate a clear trend of increasing throughput as the number of RRHs rises. This can be attributed to the advantageous effects of virtualization integrated into the slicing approach. This virtualization empowers RRHs to optimize the distribution of their functions with the cloud Baseband Unit (BBU) pool, known as functional split (FS). Such an arrangement facilitates the efficient handling of diverse traffic demands. Consequently, it enables the utilization of spectrum resources in RRHs to allocate a larger number of sub-channels for data transmission. Given the limitation that a single sub-channel cannot be assigned to multiple users concurrently (as per our proposed optimization method), having a greater number of RRHs at disposal allows users to have increased flexibility. They can associate themselves with RRHs that offer optimal transmit power, more sub-channels, and improved channel conditions, ultimately leading to heightened throughput. Furthermore, the outcomes highlight a positive correlation between higher throughput and an increased allocation of RBs to the transmitting user. This trend is rooted in the fact that more RBs translate to a larger number of subcarriers, facilitating greater data transmission potential (Table 10.2).

Table 10.2 Performance analysis

Techniques	Description	Transmitted data type	Performance
SLICING 5G Network	Heterogenous network with 5G medical gateways used within the ambulance.	(i) Video from Ambulance in 4K visual method. (ii) Clinical data of patients from ambulance.	Throughput: The maximum throughput for video transmission is about 3.2 Gbps with 10 RRHs deployed. Latency: The maximum latency for transmitting clinical data from ambulance for 30 s is about 0.780 ms for 20 kHz. Maximum transmission reliability: packet length usage of users (0.88) for 30 s, total number of available resources element equal to 40,000.

The utilization of the SLICING 5G Network technique emerges as a pivotal advancement. This technique entails the deployment of a heterogeneous network infrastructure, integrating 5G medical gateways directly within ambulance units. This innovative approach facilitates the seamless transmission of critical data in two distinct categories. First, it empowers the transmission of high-definition video feeds from the ambulance in stunning 4K visual quality. This video data encompasses real-time visuals of the patient's condition, aiding healthcare professionals at the receiving hospital in preparing for the patient's arrival with a comprehensive understanding of their situation. Second, the SLICING 5G Network technique enables the transmission of vital clinical data collected from the ambulance. This includes patient-specific medical records and real-time monitoring data. The efficiency of this data transmission is a critical factor in delivering timely and informed healthcare decisions.

This technique demonstrates remarkable capabilities. It achieves an impressive maximum throughput of approximately 3.2 gigabits per second (Gbps) through the deployment of 10 Remote Radio Heads (RRHs). Moreover, it ensures minimal latency, with a maximum of 0.780 milliseconds for transmitting clinical data within a 30-s timeframe over a 20 kHz bandwidth. Additionally, the technique maintains a high level of transmission reliability, with a packet length usage of 0.88 over a 30-s period, facilitated by a total of 40,000 available resource elements. In sum, the SLICING 5G Network technique exemplifies a cutting-edge solution that enhances healthcare communication, enabling faster and more informed decisions for improved patient care.

10.4 Future trends

The convergence of 5G technology and healthcare systems ushers in a landscape of transformative possibilities and new horizons. This chapter titled "Authentication and Access Control Schemes in 5G-Based Healthcare Systems" explores the future trends that are poised to shape the authentication and access control mechanisms within this dynamic ecosystem.

10.4.1 Biometric advancements

Biometric authentication, driven by innovations in sensor technology and AI, will witness significant advancements. Beyond fingerprint and facial recognition, more nuanced biometric markers such as gait analysis, vein recognition, and even behavioral biometrics like keystroke dynamics will come to the forefront. These multi-modal biometrics will enhance security while providing a seamless user experience.

10.4.2 Continuous authentication

Continuous authentication will become a cornerstone of security. Traditional authentication relies on a one-time verification, but in the 5G healthcare landscape, the need for ongoing verification will gain prominence. Technologies like keystroke dynamics, facial recognition, and behavioral analytics will continuously monitor user interactions to ensure that only authorized personnel are granted access. It ensures the development of security and prevention over the 5G network in the generation of enhancing productivity of new technologies.

10.4.3 Edge computing integration

The integration of edge computing into healthcare systems will have implications for authentication and access control. Edge devices can perform initial authentication locally, reducing the need for constant communication with centralized servers. This minimizes latency while enhancing security by reducing the attack surface and potential points of failure.

10.4.4 Zero trust architecture adoption

The Zero Trust model, which assumes that no one within or outside the network is inherently trustworthy, will gain traction. This approach aligns with the distributed nature of 5G healthcare systems. It entails continuous verification, least privilege access, and micro-segmentation to minimize the risk of unauthorized access or lateral movement by attackers.

10.4.5 Federated identity management

Federated identity management will emerge as a solution for seamless and secure user access across diverse healthcare systems. Patients and healthcare professionals will be able to access various services with a single set of credentials, enhancing convenience without compromising security.

10.4.6 Quantum-safe authentication

With the advent of quantum computing, the security landscape faces potential upheaval. Quantum-safe authentication mechanisms will evolve to counteract the threat posed by quantum computers, which could compromise traditional encryption methods. Post-quantum cryptography will play a vital role in ensuring long-term data security.

10.4.7 Privacy-preserving authentication

Privacy-preserving authentication techniques will evolve to address concerns related to biometric data and personal information. Techniques like "zero-knowledge proofs" will enable authentication without revealing sensitive data, enhancing user privacy while ensuring secure access.

10.4.8 AI-driven threat detection

Artificial intelligence and machine learning will play a pivotal role in threat detection and prevention. AI algorithms will continuously monitor access patterns, detect anomalies, and proactively respond to potential security breaches. This proactive approach will be crucial in safeguarding sensitive healthcare data.

10.4.9 User-centric access control

Access control mechanisms will become more user-centric, allowing individuals to have greater control over their data and access permissions. Concepts like "self-sovereign identity" will empower patients to control who accesses their health information, enhancing transparency and trust.

In the fast-evolving landscape of 5G-based healthcare systems, these trends signify a paradigm shift in how authentication and access control are conceptualized and implemented. While these trends promise enhanced security and user experience, they also come with challenges, including ensuring interoperability, managing complexity, and addressing ethical and privacy concerns. By embracing these trends and proactively addressing challenges, healthcare systems can forge a secure and innovative path forward, unlocking the full potential of 5G for the benefit of patients, healthcare providers, and the industry as a whole.

10.5 Challenges in 5G healthcare systems

In the dynamic landscape of 5G-based healthcare systems, a multitude of challenges demand careful consideration. First, the sheer complexity of 5G networks introduces potential vulnerabilities, increasing the risk of unauthorized access and data breaches. The convergence of diverse devices and wearables exacerbates the challenge of ensuring consistent and secure access across interconnected endpoints.

Additionally, the rapid transmission speeds of 5G networks, while beneficial, create an ideal environment for sophisticated cyberattacks, necessitating robust authentication and access control mechanisms.

Balancing the imperative of stringent security with seamless user experience poses an ongoing challenge, as overly complex authentication processes can hinder healthcare professionals' swift access to critical patient data. Moreover, evolving regulatory requirements demand adaptable authentication and access control strategies that remain compliant with global data protection norms. Addressing these multifaceted challenges is essential to harnessing the full potential of 5G technology while safeguarding patient data and maintaining the integrity of healthcare services.

10.6 Conclusion

In the dynamic realm of 5G-based healthcare systems, an array of challenges emerges, necessitating thorough acknowledgment and strategic remedies. The intricate nature of 5G networks introduces a tapestry of potential vulnerabilities, heightening the exposure to unauthorized access, data breaches, and system disruptions. The convergence of an array of devices, spanning wearables to IoT devices, compounds the intricacy of managing access points and ensuring consistent, robust user authentication across interconnected endpoints. The inherent swiftness and low latency that define 5G networks provide fertile terrain for sophisticated cyber threats. Although these attributes enable real-time communication and data exchange, they also create an environment conducive to swift and covert cyberattacks. Consequently, the mandate for resilient and adaptable authentication and access control mechanisms becomes essential to thwart unauthorized access and data compromise.

Striking the equilibrium between stringent security and user convenience poses an enduring challenge. While robust authentication measures remain pivotal, overly intricate processes can impede prompt healthcare professionals' access to pivotal patient data, potentially obstructing medical decision-making and care provision. Moreover, the evolution of the regulatory landscape injects layers of intricacy. Navigating a labyrinth of data protection and privacy regulations is imperative for healthcare systems to ensure alignment with diverse global standards. Often, this demands a recalibration of authentication and access control strategies to adhere to legal requisites.

As highlighted in this chapter "Authentication and Access Control Schemes in 5G-Based Healthcare Systems," addressing these intricate challenges is pivotal to harnessing the genuine potential of 5G technology in healthcare. This endeavor must coexist with the safeguarding of patient privacy and the preservation of medical service integrity. Collaborative endeavors involving stakeholders spanning healthcare providers, technology pioneers, regulatory entities, and cybersecurity specialists are paramount. Through these collaborations, the mitigation of risks and the formulation of inventive solutions to tackle the intricacies of authentication and access control within this swiftly evolving milieu can be achieved. By fearlessly confronting these challenges, healthcare systems can cultivate a secure, resilient milieu where the advantages of 5G technology are harnessed while upholding the utmost benchmarks of patient care and data safeguarding.

References

[1] Abood, Mohammad JK, and Ghassan H. Abdul-Majeed. "Classification of network slicing threats based on slicing enablers: A survey." *International Journal of Intelligent Networks* 4 (2023): 103–112.

[2] Tom, Teckshawer. "5G Impacts, Internet of Things (IoT) and businesses in developing countries." *Technium Social Sciences Journal* 46 (2023): 87–104.

[3] Noman, Sinan Ameen, Haitham Ameen Noman, Qusay Al-Maatouk, and Travis Atkison. "A survey of IEEE 802.15. 6: Body area networks." *International Journal of Computing and Digital Systems* 14, no. 1 (2023): 691–705.

[4] Doddamane, Aditya Narsipur, and Arkalgud Sampath Kumar. "The implications of 5G technology on cardiothoracic surgical services in India." *Indian Journal of Thoracic and Cardiovascular Surgery* 39, no. 2 (2023): 150–159.

[5] Kumar, Rohit, and Neha Agrawal. "Analysis of multi-dimensional Industrial IoT (IIoT) data in Edge-Fog-Cloud based architectural frameworks: A survey on current state and research challenges." *Journal of Industrial Information Integration* 35, no. 1 (2023): 100504.

[6] Mhmood, Ali H., and Murshid Reza. "Urban health informatics through cloud-based data integration." *Journal of Big-Data Analytics and Cloud Computing* 7, no. 4 (2022): 1–17.

[7] Zhou, Jiyin. "A roadmap towards optimal resource allocation approaches in the Internet of Things." *International Journal of Advanced Computer Science and Applications* 14, no. 6 (2023).

[8] Vargas, Paola, and Iris Tien. "Impacts of 5G on cyber-physical risks for interdependent connected smart critical infrastructure systems." *International Journal of Critical Infrastructure Protection* 42, no. 1 (2023): 100617.

[9] Bharadiya, Jasmin. "Machine learning in cybersecurity: Techniques and challenges." *European Journal of Technology* 7, no. 2 (2023): 1–14.

[10] Ahmed, Irfan, and Amina Asghar. "Evaluating the efficacy of biometric authentication techniques in healthcare." *International Journal of Responsible Artificial Intelligence* 13, no. 7 (2023): 1–12.

[11] Sharmah, Daisy, and Atowar Ul Islam. "Implementation of role based access control and dynamic load balancing in model analysis and auditing services." *Scandinavian Journal of Information Systems* 35, no. 1 (2023): 910–922.

[12] Zhu, Yixin, Huiwu Mao, Ying Zhu, *et al.* "CMOS-Compatible neuromorphic devices for neuromorphic perception and computing: A review." *International Journal of Extreme Manufacturing* 5, no. 4 (2023): 042010.

[13] Ahmed, Althobaiti. "Smart cities and IoT: Examining the potential benefits and challenges of using IoT to create more efficient and sustainable urban

[14] Hegde, Pawan, and Praveen Kumar Reddy Maddikunta. "Amalgamation of blockchain with resource-constrained IoT devices for healthcare applications–State of Art, challenges and future directions." *International Journal of Cognitive Computing in Engineering* 4 (2023): 220–239.

[15] Bozdag, Ayse Asli. "AIsmosis and the pas de deux of human-AI interaction: Exploring the communicative dance between society and artificial intelligence." *Online Journal of Communication and Media Technologies* 13, no. 4 (2023): e202340.

[16] Omotunde, Habeeb, and Maryam Ahmed. "A comprehensive review of security measures in database systems: Assessing authentication, access control, and beyond." *Mesopotamian Journal of CyberSecurity* 2023 (2023): 115–133.

[17] Gür, Gürkan, Anshuman Kalla, Chamitha De Alwis, et al. "Integration of ICN and MEC in 5G and beyond networks: Mutual benefits, use cases, challenges, standardization, and future research." *IEEE Open Journal of the Communications Society* 3 (2022): 1382–1412.

[18] Hu, Kai, Chenghang Weng, Yanwen Zhang, Junlan Jin, and Qingfeng Xia. "An overview of underwater vision enhancement: From traditional methods to recent deep learning." *Journal of Marine Science and Engineering* 10, no. 2 (2022): 241.

[19] Tebe, Parfait Ifede, Guangjun Wen, Jian Li, et al. "5G-enabled medical data transmission in mobile hospital systems." *IEEE Internet of Things Journal* 9, no. 15 (2022): 13679–13693.

[20] Darabkh, Khalid A., Muna Al-Akhras, Jumana N. Zomot, and Mohammed Atiquzzaman. "RPL routing protocol over IoT: A comprehensive survey, recent advances, insights, bibliometric analysis, recommendations, and future directions." *Journal of Network and Computer Applications* 207 (2022): 103476.

[21] Tamseel, Mohammed Abdul, MD Javeed Ahmed, Mohammed Shareeq Uddin, Abdul Mateen, Ayesha Sultana, and Zubeda Begum. "5G new radio non-stand-alone call log analysing and debugging." *Journal of Data Acquisition and Processing* 38, no. 3 (2023): 1588.

[22] Steed, Elizabeth A., Ngoc Phan, Nancy Leech, and Renee Charlifue-Smith. "Remote delivery of services for young children with disabilities during the early stages of the COVID-19 pandemic in the United States." *Journal of Early Intervention* 44, no. 2 (2022): 110–129.

Chapter 11
Indexing-based approach in document-centric big data

Supriya Chakraborty[1] and Sergii Sharov[2]

In the context of big data, data generated from different sources are organized in either XML or JSON orientation. The preliminary organization of the attribute-value pair was XML and querying such data was performed using XQuery and XPath. However, such technologies were refined into NoSQL document-oriented technologies and nowadays reshaped into JSON-based document-oriented database management systems. Two interesting gaps have been identified in this sequential advancement. First, the performance of preliminary XML-based documents was not investigated in comparison with the different JSON-based databases. Second, the significant contributions not observed fit the preliminary XML techniques in the context of big data. In this work, a logical approach to data access techniques of different XML- and JSON-based document-oriented databases is discussed. Further, a generic active index is proposed that improves the access to document-centric XML database.

11.1 Introduction

In this decade, scientific exploration innovated thousands of modern technologies powered by the digital storage of data. The advancement of computational power and the quantum leap of networking in each stage forces scientists to move up with technology breakthroughs for increasing storage capacity and reducing accessing time. Big data is at the forefront and has evolved recently around complex experiments to offer even more functionalities. This work studies comprehensively the complex strategies to improve the access strategies of data, especially in document-driven data storage.

Numerous big data platforms with customized objectives and specific scopes for handling data have been commercially available. Few such platforms are data-centric and the rest are document-centric. The principle of data access techniques relies on two schemes. The first one is the indexing and bitmap that reduces the

[1]Department of CSE-CSDS, Brainware University, India
[2]Department of CS, Dmytro Motornyi Tavria State Agrotechnological University

access time of data whereas the latter one attempts to establish the relationship among data. Few constraints are defined in such cases to establish the relationship and semantics among data except integrity constraints, primary key and foreign key constraints, and some domain constraints. However, the limitations of both schemes are access techniques do not consider the relationship and semantics to access the data.

A comprehensive study was found on indexing schemes in big data environments. A lot of variations have been observed and classified into extreme cases. The first case is no index to fetch the data e.g., Hadoop which has only a single *namenode* works as an index to maintain the integration among *datanodes* in both single and multi-cluster environments. Another extreme case is provided by Couchbase which provides multiple kinds of indexing. The contribution of this work is to mention the significant points to plan, use, and monitor the indexing-based documents in the big data environment to increase the semantics of the search as well as to reduce the search time.

The main goal of this effort is to semantically correlate similar properties in big data-driven healthcare systems. In the healthcare system, the associated features are scattered in a big data environment. The search time of such similar features is overhead before actual processing to draw relevant inferences. This work integrates similar features or multi-valued attributes in such a way that once a search is found on a single data, all other connected data can be tracked. Healthcare applications are one of the prominent examples of occupying a very large dataset and finding the information to process further is extremely time-consuming and demotivates the end-user to test multiple times. In this case, the throughput of the data in a large dataset is much higher, and this could motivate the end-user to do multiple experiments to infer the diagnosis or findings within a relevant amount of time.

Another perspective is the document-oriented database that used XML format and later advanced to JSON-oriented format. Both XML and JSON occupy the attribute and value pair—which implies the classical definition of the semi-structured data. BaseX, eXist-db, and Sedna are the popular document-oriented database that uses XML specification. Whereas, MongoDB, CouchDB, and Couchbase are document-oriented database that conforms to the specification of JSON. Each of the databases mentioned above exploited specialized schemes to access the data and extend and/or modify NoSQL accordingly. The comprehensive study revealed that the indexing schemes either are not in the scope of the document-oriented database or over customized. Theoretically, indexing is complex on trees on hierarchical data and within file data. In both such cases, the change of position of data makes inconsistent the index. A sound theoretical indexing scheme is required that conforms to the following characteristics:

- The indexing scheme is generic in nature and could be utilized on a variety of data. The same indexing scheme could be used in different types of data. The big data environment encourages storing varying types of data. The generic indexing scheme could utilize the efficacy of a variety of data.

- The indexing scheme could be utilized on different formats of semi-structured data including XML and JSON.
- The indexing scheme is robust. With the change of the position of data at run time, the index could adjust pointing the data accordingly.
- The index could never be inconsistent. A sound theoretical foundation needs to be supported to ensure that the index always becomes consistent.
- The active index is desired. The active index event-driven-based approach to create and grow the index. In this work, the active index is discussed after the event of insertion of data.

In this work, the basic features and data access schemes of each database mentioned above are enlightened followed by a generic active indexing scheme that could be utilized in all such databases to optimize the access performance of data.

This document is formalized as follows. An elaborated expression in the "Introduction" section implies the statement of interest of the work. The basic features and research of this article are mentioned in the section "Related work." The immediate next section and its sub-sections specify the abstraction of data storage and its access strategies of different document-oriented databases. The generic scheme is proposed in the section "Active indexing approach." The active indexing approach is fired with the tool of a trigger on the data tree. A detailed algorithm is defined and explained in the mentioned section. This writ is ended with a "Conclusion" section followed by a "References" section.

11.2 Related work

The rapidly generated data from IoT devices is extracted and transported through standard documents and a document-centric database emerged as an alternative to Relational Database Management Systems (RDBMS) with a view to reposit and process multi-variant data. Document-centric databases and NoSQL systems have emerged to provide a low-cost, highly available solution for managing complex, multi-variant data that is challenging to handle with traditional methods. These systems also encourage data replication [1]. The following list summarizes the common justifications for utilizing NoSQL and document-oriented databases:

- Discard dispensable complexities—The traditional database for its simple orientation and purpose of usage incorporates many features. Such dispensable features are not relevant to the working needs of a document-oriented database.
- Reach high throughput—The traditional database accesses a substantial amount of data for today's enterprise services. However, the increase in the volume of data, generation of speed of data, and distributed nature of upcoming challenges make the throughput limited of traditional databases. The document-centric database uses a file-based system that supports high volume, high speed of data, even with the distributed nature of data storage

and retrieval. The document-centric database reaches the expectations of throughput of information retrieval with the above-mentioned issues.
- Horizontal scalability—The horizontal compartment of a table or dataset is done following the principle of sound constraint. The location is the most preferred constraint attribute to compartment the data horizontally. The traditional database needs logical initiatives to integrate the compartmentalized data. The SQL standard does not follow the paradigm to cope with the compartmentalized data scattered in multiple places. However, NoSQL fits perfectly well with the split-query processing paradigm. The horizontal compartmentalization of data in a document-centric database is simple and cost-effective.
- Commodity hardware is an easy choice—The high-end server for traditional data is costly, and needs separate concern and maintenance. The continuous research for the advancement of the hardware is a daunting task for scientists and a decision problem for investors. Whereas the document-centric database is eligible to exploit all the features on commodity hardware, which is inexpensive, and has low maintenance.
- Object-relational mapping—The comprehensive theory is available for accessing data through the knowledge of object-relational mapping (ORM) in a traditional database environment. Few frameworks were developed and successfully adopted to work on enterprise solutions. However, experienced workers were required with proper training/experience on the same database to develop and maintain the ORM framework. The fetching and writing of data from/to a document-centric database is straightforward. A moderate level of database and programming know-how is enough to deal with data in a document-centric database.
- Complexity of cluster setup—The conceptual further grouping of data following some principle allows the optimal performance of the traditional database. The document-centric database inherently supports the clustering concepts. In such a scenario, the mapping and subsequent setup of the clusters are more comprehensive in document-centric databases rather than traditional databases.
- Cost—The conventional database involves substantial investment for implementing and subsequent maintenance of the database, whereas the document-centric database is cost-effective comparing the complexity of the applications.
- Sacrifice of reliability for improved performance—The notion of reliability was developed and ensured through sound theoretical principles and precise logic, as well as sophisticated code, in traditional databases. Reliability is a fruitful feature of the traditional database that provides valuable dependency on data. The concepts of log, log-ahead write strategy, principle of recovery from failures, ACID, commit protocol—the list is many that together ensure the reliability in the different levels of data management in traditional databases. The document-centric database in the enterprise solutions, in accordance with the required reliability level, is implemented in the file system logically. In such a case, the reliability is sacrificed in different levels of data

Indexing-based approach in document-centric big data   233

management, however, the performance of the data processing is improved, which is essential to processing the big data in enterprise solution.
- Adaptation to cloud computing requirements—The cloud enablement of the traditional database needs careful planning to migrate not only the data but all the applications and system files to the cloud. Document-oriented databases are often favored for their flexibility, scalability, and agility in the cloud-native environment, especially in scenarios where semi-structured or unstructured data is prevalent. Another significant technological improvement is the serverless opportunity. In the recent past, Amazon Aurora Serverless has come out with relational database services that automatically adjust capacity based on actual usage. Whereas more serverless options have been released on document-oriented databases including Google Cloud Firestore and Firebase Realtime Database. The enterprise-level distributed multi-model solution is Azure Cosmos DB.

The primary motivation of the database is to retrieve the required data. Such data are retrieved using query languages. The SQL dominated the fetching of data on persistent structured data. The change of need as already discussed above gave birth to NoSQL to fetch necessary data from document-oriented databases. The NoSQL does not imply that queries are not SQL. Rather NoSQL means a query contains the SQL code and is extended with outside SQL features. The data and query model or the persistence model are typically taken into consideration while classifying NoSQL DBMSes. NoSQL DBMSes are categorized using the persistence model as follows [2]:

- The reason in-memory databases operate exceptionally quickly is that the most recently utilized data is kept in memory, and additional disk flushes are only initiated when necessary or when the in-memory data is no longer being used. Evidently, the size of the data that is currently in use that can be saved is constrained by the memory. Since a machine can only carry so much memory, this issue can only be partially overcome through vertical scaling. Furthermore, if data are lost in between subsequent disk flushes or if data persistence is turned off, durability can become a concern. Data replication is a possible remedy for this issue.
- Operations are buffered in memory by Memtables and SSTables Databases [3] after they have been recorded to an append-only commit log to maintain persistence. The Memtable is flushed to disk into an SSTable after a given number of writes. These DBMSes address the durability issue while having performance characteristics that are equivalent to those of in-memory databases.
- B-trees: The self-balancing B-tree tree data structure is used in databases [4] and keeps data organized while enabling logarithmically quick searches, sequential access, insertions, and deletions [5].

The growth of NoSQL in the last few years has been exponential. The languages came out with a variety of syntax, target data, accessing techniques, and sophisticated functionalities. The following categories for NoSQL DBMSs are also determined by the data and query model [6,7]:

- Column databases are another popular deviation of persistent databases. A unique record number is generated by the system that is coined with the column value of a particular record. Technically, column values are stored by a pair <unique ID, Value> in each column table. Column database discourages storing the NULL value as well as encourages storing different numbers of columns for each record—another opinion of defining semi-structured data.
- Graph Information is stored, retrieved, and managed utilizing databases and a graph. As a result, each object is represented by a node, and the interactions between nodes are the objects themselves.
- Associative arrays, such as dictionaries or hash tables, are best stored, retrieved from, and managed using Key-Value Databases (KVDBMSes).
- Document-Oriented Databases (DODBMSes) are used to store, retrieve, and manage semi-structured data, or documents, encoded using JSON, BSON, XML, or YAML formats. DODBMSes have developed from KVDBMSes.

There are several consolidated surveys on NoSQL and DBMSes; in the sentences that follow, we specify the ones that are most pertinent to our analysis. The performance and flexibility of KVDBMSes and DODBMSes over RDBMSes are compared in [8]. For high throughput applications that need flexible data modeling and horizontal scaling, NoSQL DBMSes are a preferable option. The authors of [6] present the most up-to-date and well-liked options along with a classification of NoSQL DBMSes according to their data structures. The authors of [9] compare and provide an overview of NoSQL query types, data architectures, partitioning, and replication. The features and strengths of the NoSQL database are discussed in [10]. A comparative classification approach that links functional and non-functional criteria to methodologies is also included in this study. The comprehensive survey reveals the fact that benchmarking was performed on big data [11], Distributed Systems, NoSQL, and Map-reduce applications, but majorly unfocused on unstructured or other variety as XDBMS. Nonetheless, the textual data in distributed systems including MongoDB was benchmarked in [12].

XDBMS is flexible enough and gained attention from their inceptions. Many customized solutions were created to address the specific IT challenges. OpenEHR [13] stores medical records using XML, XMark [14] stores records of online retailers and content providers using XML, TPoX [15] stores the financial workload of multiple users and conforms to FIXML standards. This scheme extracted data from transaction processing using XML. The customized XDBMS mentioned above simulates the complex and hierarchical nature of the data. To understand more about such customized XDBMS including store, edit, search, and retrieve, a detailed analysis was performed, and a benchmark was established. Most of these benchmarks, regrettably, employ small collections. Additionally, the information provided is largely uniform even in situations where the size of the database is very high—in Gigabytes. More on these, even the different semi-structured data formats do not affect the performance of such experiments. In a separate experiment on

XML and JSON data formats with document sizes in the gigabytes, the operations for storing, editing, searching, and retrieving showed uniform performance.

The related work enlightened the significant and close research of this work. On the high-level classification, XML and JSON are identified as two different semi-structured data formats that are used extensively in customized solutions. In recent dates, JSON has been analyzed and used in information systems compared to XML-centric format. The fundamentals of both are represented in the following sub-section.

11.2.1 Fundamentals of JSNON and XML

XML (eXtensible Markup Language) is designed to store and transport data. XML is the core technology in web technology, data interchange, and various other fields. Some fundamental characteristics are mentioned below:

XML is similar to HTML, however customized and semantic tags could be defined in HTML. XML data has a hierarchical structure with a root element that contains nested elements, forming a tree-like structure. XML tag is used to define an element. Each tag has a pair of opening and closing tags. An element can have an attribute, providing additional information about the element. An XML document typically starts with the version number. XML documents must adhere to certain syntax rules to be called well-formed. The character data (CDATA) section is used to include blocks of text that should be not treated as markup. It is often used for including code snippets or other content that might include reserved characters. DTD or XML schema can be used to define the structure and legal elements and attributes of an XML document. This helps in validating XML documents against a predefined structure. XML namespaces allow you to avoid element name conflicts by providing a way to qualify element and attribute names. This is particularly important in documents where different XML vocabularies are combined. XML is platform-independent and widely supported, making it a popular choice for data interchange between different systems and programming languages. XML is both human-readable and machine-readable, which means it can be easily understood by humans and processed by machines. XML is used in various applications, including web services (SOAP and REST), configuration files, data storage, and as a data interchange format. Its simplicity, extensibility, and versatility make it a fundamental technology for representing and exchanging structured data. The code snippet of XML is provided below that defines one element book with an attribute category. The element book has a nested element title.

<book category="programming">
    <title>XML Basics</title>
</book>

JavaScript Object Notation (JSON) is a lightweight data-interchange format that is easy for humans to read and write, and easy for machines to parse and generate. The fundamental concepts of JSON are listed below.

JSON is a data format that represents semi-structured data as a key-value pair. It is often used to transmit data between a server and a web application as an alternative to XML. JSON syntax is a subset of JavaScript syntax, making it easy to use with JavaScript. It consists of key-value pairs, where keys are strings enclosed in double quotes and values can be strings, numbers, objects, arrays, Booleans, or null. JSON supports several data types—Object: An unordered collection of key-value pairs enclosed in curly braces {}, Array: An ordered list of values enclosed in square brackets [], String: A sequence of characters enclosed in double quotes, Number: An integer or a floating-point number, Boolean: true or false, Null: Represents a null value. JSON supports nesting of objects and arrays, allowing the representation of more complex data structures. JSON's syntax is a subset of JavaScript object literal notation. As a result, JSON data can be directly interpreted by JavaScript, making it a natural choice for data exchange in web development. JSON is a language-independent data format, and it is widely supported in various programming languages. This makes it a popular choice for data interchange between different systems. Serialization is the process of converting a data structure or object into a format (like JSON) that can be easily stored or transmitted. Deserialization is the process of converting the serialized data back into its original form. JSON is easy for humans to read and write, and it is lightweight in terms of both data size and parsing complexity. JSON does not support functions or methods. It focuses on representing data structures only.

11.3 Elucidate on abstraction of data for storage and retrieval

Data is stored physically in the disk and provided as an abstraction to the user with the help of a file. The file provides limited features and functionalities to the users. The document is the higher-level abstraction on top of the file. Document not only provides rich functionalities and features to the users but also provides the mechanism to traverse the element of the document programmatically.

Key-Value Databases have evolved into Document-Oriented Database Management Systems (DODBMSes) [6]. Semi-structured data is stored, retrieved, and managed using DODBMSes. They offer additional freedom for data modeling since they feature a flexible data representation without schema [16]. Data such as XML or JSON is stored in documents by DODBMSes. It is simpler to manipulate the data than it is with tables in Relational Database Management Systems (RDBMSes) thanks to the flexibility offered by XML and JSON. Documents are typically kept in collections. A Native XML Database Management System (XDBMS) builds a hierarchical logical model based on the elements of this markup language and employs the XML (eXtensible Markup Language) data structure to encode documents [17,18]. The JSON structure is used by a JSON Database Management System (JDBMS) to model documents. In DODBMSes, labels are used in storing the information. These labels describe the data and values in a record. New information can be added directly to a record without the need to modify the entire schema, as is the case for RDBMSes.

The adaptability of data modeling is one advantage of adopting a DODBMS system [19]. The nature of the application's data model is altered by information from the web, mobile, social, and IoT devices. These modifications force an RDBMS to modify the schema by changing the tables and adding or removing columns. As opposed to this, DODBMSes' flexibility reduces the need to constrain data into predetermined attributes and tables.

The quick write performance of a DODBMS is a further advantage. Some DODBMSes give tight data consistency a backseat to high availability. This guarantees that no matter what happens to the hardware or the network, read and write operations will always be carried out. The replication and eventual consistency mechanisms make sure that the environment will continue to work in the event of failure.

A DODBMS's quick query performance is a further advantage. For CRUD (Create, Read, Update, and Delete) operations, the majority of DODBMSes include robust query engines and make use of primary and secondary indexes to enhance data retrieval. In addition, the majority of DODBMS solutions include native or MapReduce aggregation frameworks for Business Intelligence and Data Analysis.

11.3.1 XML database

XML is used for different purposes in Industry and Research. XML is used as a standard to exchange data through a network, XML provides the customized tag to define the semantic semi-structured data, XML could represent the hierarchical and helical data as well as able to envelop the relational data, XML could be defined to store and retrieve data as a database, the XML database is also of two variants—schemaless and with schema. The comprehensive theory is developed and tested to retrieve the data through XML database using XPath and XQuery. In accordance with the scope of this work, the subsequent discussion is based on the retrieval of data using XPath and XQuery.

Oracle, PostgreSQL, DB2, MS SQL incorporate datatype as XML to include the essence and advantages of semi-structured data within a relational model. Access to such hierarchical data is majorly considered under the standard of NoSQL. Furthermore, commercial XDBMSes like MarkLogic Server, Oracle Barkleyey, and DB XML have licenses that expressly prevent benchmarking. Therefore, BaseX, eXist db, and Sedna are available to compare and benchmark the various features.

11.3.1.1 BaseX

BaseX is a Java-based XDBMS that uses a schema-free hierarchical approach to store data. Multiple readers and writers can access the same data simultaneously thanks to BaseX transactions' respect for the ACID (Atomicity, Consistency, Isolation, and Durability) principles [20]. Documents can be kept in the main memory or persistently on disk. BaseX operates in a single instance environment; data splitting and replication are not supported. BaseX offers ad hoc inquiries, CRUD operations, and aggregation utilizing XQuery 3.1 and XPath 3.1 [21]. It was not intended to function with a MapReduce framework, even though it is compatible with many APIs, including XML DB and JAX-RX. Numerous structural and value indices are supported by BaseX [20]. The structural indices supports name indices to perform the search semantically.

11.3.1.2 eXist-db

A Java-based XDBMS that stores XML-formatted documents is called eXist-db [22]. Document Object Model (DOM) trees are used to store data in-memory. eXist-db includes internal transactions that are transparent to the user, even though it does not offer database-level transaction control. It also has a persistent journal that is used to guarantee the continuity and consistency of the stored data. To find errors or damage in the core database files, the consistency of the database is checked automatically or using a sanity checker [23]. Through the usage of the Java Message Service (JMS) API, eXist-db offers data primary–secondary replication, enabling the distribution of applications over several servers. Replication is available, however, data sharding and query distribution over many servers are not.

11.3.1.3 Sedna

Sedna is an XDBMS that saves documents in XML format and was created in C [24]. Sedna offers persistent storage, indexing, and ACID transactions [25]. To enhance query performance, it takes advantage of main memory [26]. In Sedna, replication and partitioning are not used. Sedna offers CRUD operations and ad-hoc queries for filtering and aggregation using XQuery 1.1 and XPath 2.0, just like the other XDBMSes. However, working with these queries does not make use of MapReduce capability. The content and properties of items are indexed using value indices. In Sedna, full-text indices may be built to make XQuery full-text search easier.

11.3.2 JSON database

With the rise of the NoSQL movement, numerous attempts have been made to document-oriented DBMS with specific scopes and functionalities. The open-source movement has encouraged the integration of new features at the application level to be incorporated whereas proprietary solutions have dealt with enterprise features. Distinctive classification of all such document-oriented DBMS is made on those which are built using JSON format for document encoding, called JDBMS. In this work, three such distinctive JDBMS are MongoDB, CouchDB, and Couchbase. A brief but related discussion of this work is expressed in the following subsections on such JDBMSes.

11.3.2.1 MongoDB

MongoDB is a C++-based DODBMS that aims to fuse the essential features of RDBMSes with the breakthroughs of NoSQL DBMSes. Data is stored in MongoDB using a flexible, dynamic schema. A document contains a record, whereas a collection contains several documents. The structure of each document in a collection may vary, so each record may have a different amount of characteristics and a different data type. In actuality, documents frequently model high-level programming language objects. Records in a collection have nearly the same structure, even though the database supports documents with various numbers of characteristics and various data types for the same attributes [27].

The fundamental ways of keeping data in file systems through programming are—text encoding and binary encoding. The specialty of MongoDB over its contemporary JDBMSes is that MongoDB uses a binary encoding of JSON format to keep the data in the file. The official documentation of MongoDB defines the JSON format as well as the BSON format. The BSON is the binary encoding of JSON format.

MongoDB ensures the consistency of the transaction using the BASE paradigm. The paradigm consists of a Basically Available, Soft State, Eventual consistency model. Consistency is ensured, however not synchronous with respect to the transaction. MongoDB transaction management reflects all the modifications consistently in all the nodes in an asynchronous manner. Thereafter, the changes are persistent in the system. MongoDB leverages in-memory functionality to speed up query performance as well as Causal Consistency, which enables actions to logically depend on earlier activities [28]. Additionally, this JDBMS provides ACID data integrity guarantees for multi-document transactions. Replica Sets are used by MongoDB for primary–secondary replication to provide redundancy and data availability. A collection of MongoDB instances that house the same dataset is known as a replica set. MongoDB employs Sharding to divide the data into segments and distribute it among other computers. Sharding is a strategy for horizontal scaling.

The access performance of data is significantly improved using indexes in a database system. MongoDB uses a variety of indexes in accordance with the scope of data and applications. MongoDB offers a dense index, called primary indexing. Primary indexing is used on the data or column where the data or column is relatively ordered and sequenced. Another type of index which is by nature sparse, called secondary indexing is used on such data which are used frequently on the condition of NoSQL query. MongoDB provides scalability and multi-variant features in the index field. The index is a single field of the key data unitary text or numeric value, whereas a multi-key index is also supported with the help of a compound field in indexing. The programmatic has a key with search time O(1) is also supported. The advancement is made to support the geospatial database through raster and vector data. The full-text search is a frequently used option in many scientific and office applications, MonDB supports the full-text search if the data is textual.

11.3.2.2 CouchDB

A JSON-based, schema-free architecture for storing self-contained data is offered by TCouchDB, an open-source DODBMS created in Erlang [29]. Through the use of Multi-Versioning Concurrency Control (MVCC), transactions in CouchDB obey document-level ACID properties [30]. Eventual Consistency and incremental replication are used by CouchDB to preserve data consistency. The ability to operate in memory is not offered by CouchDB. Asynchronous primary-primary and primary–secondary replication is offered by CouchDB. Sharding is a technique used to distribute copies of each replica horizontally inside a cluster [31]. The conflict-flagged mechanism in CouchDB is used to address inconsistencies. CRUD operations and ad-hoc querying are supported by CouchDB utilizing the Mango JavaScript API. CouchDB has Views and MapReduce features for aggregation [32]. Views are used in CouchDB to achieve indexing. JSON and CSV are the two indexes available in CouchDB.

11.3.2.3 Couchbase

The JSON encoding is used by the extremely scalable DODBMS Couchbase to store documents. It provides high throughput, horizontal scaling, and availability [33]. In Couchbase, transactions adhere to the ACID principles and depend on both immediate and eventual consistency. Couchbase can store data in memory and organize items into buckets. This approach is used to optimize the performance of the frequently used queries.

There are several types of buckets that are used—Memcached, Ephemeral, and Couchbase. Memcached bucket captures and stores the result of the queries executed in the server. The next time the same query is fired, the Memcached bucket is used to return the result, the query is not forwarded to the server. The Memcached bucket could be configured with different parameters of time. The Memcached bucket dies in a periodic fashion and loads with the next query. There is always a trade-off between, the number of Memcached buckets and the duration of the Memcached bucket. The slight variation of the Memcached bucket is the Ephemeral bucket. Ephemeral bucket life is short in nature or in other words, the durability of the bucket is not guaranteed. With respect to the load of the server, the durability of the bucket is dependent. In some cases, the NoSQL query is complex enough and time-consuming in nature. The loss of such a NoSQL query might hamper the cost of the maintenance of the Couchbase server. In this case, Couchbase buckets are used to support storing the data persistently and in-memory. Couchbase bucket is also called as a container of the digital asset of the server.

Couchbase enables partitioning via primary–primary and primary–secondary connections in addition to sharding thanks to its shared-nothing nature. Couchbase scales horizontally within a cluster. A JavaScript API or a language that resembles SQL, such as N1QL (Non-1NF Query Language), is used to do ad-hoc data queries [34]. These languages give Couchbase the ability to do CRUD operations for OLTP (Online Transaction Processing) and ETL (Extract Transform Load) [35]. To express complicated indexing and aggregating queries, JavaScript MapReduce Views can be created and stored on the server [36].

A variety of indexing schemes is supported by Couchbase [36]. One of the varieties is the composite indices that index multiple attributes together. The composite indices are further improvised on different functionalities. Filtered index is one of the functionalities among them. Filtered indices quickly could retrieve a subset of the data. Even, if multiple conditions are applied in the WHERE clause, the filtered index retrieves the data faster. Another variation is the functional-based indices that index according to the logic in the NoSQL.

11.4 Active indexing approach

The rapid generation of documents is extracted followed by transportation in IoT-based systems, such documents hold similar tags with different values in different periods. The time-variated documents are organized in a database for further retrieval of analysis. The significant gaps observed in both XML and JSON-based document-oriented databases are:

- The relationships among the data do not exist.
- Indexing technique is not straightforward, and complex.
- Indexing technique is organized separately from the document.

In the situation described above, the major problems experienced by document-centric databases are long search times and the inability to perform semantic searches. The nearest work is observed in [37,38], and [39] where the index and data are grouped together. The strength of the scheme is to search the multivalued attribute in a non-key element. The demerit is the tree is unstable. The position of the nodes is changed to balance the tree, in such case index needs to be reassigned. The comprehensive solution to resolve the matter is to combine the indexes and data together [40].

11.4.1 Attribute-centric sparse indexing scheme

The index is formulated with the order property of the tree in memory. The order property implies the node position within the tree. Figure 11.1 demonstrates the node position.

The order position of the node mentioned in Figure 11.1, is used to form the index of the value for both XML and JSNO-based documents. This scheme is the extension for both types of document-centric databases. The index could be created in different granularity. There is always a trade-off between index volume and data volume. The dense index for hierarchical data representation has an overhead of multiple entries of attribute names in indexes. In this scenario, the effective indexing scheme is to implement the sparse index. In this approach only attribute centric sparse indexing scheme is mentioned. The scheme is depicted in Figure 11.2.

The attribute "Eid" is the primary key on which data is organized in the tree from left to right. However, the attribute field "Name" is another significant attribute. The primary key index is implicit in the tree if ordered in numerical values.

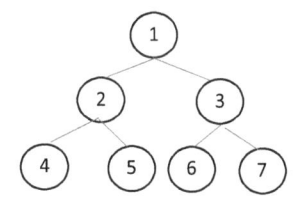

Figure 11.1 Node position of the tree—the order property

Implicit Primary Key Index—In the example of Figure 11.2, the first Eid is 1 and the second Eid is found in the 6th order position of the attribute, and then the next is found after every two attributes order position like 8 and thereafter 10 and so on. Logically, such order positions could be reached without backtracking.

The significant non-primary key field in a big-data environment is critical for the user response time. The improvement of search time is the key to making the application enterprise-centric. The index for the significant non-primary key field is created with the help of a linear data structure.

The perception of the index is to search the value within the index, not within the actual unordered data values. The basic principle to improve the search time is to order the data. Now, the data of the field "Name" is not ordered within the tree, however, to form the index, index values are ordered in accordance with the values of the name field. The example is demonstrated here. The field "name" contains two values San and Abu whereas San appears in attribute order position 5 whereas Abu is in attribute order position 7. In accordance with the alphabetic sort, Abu appeared before the San, therefore the index formed according to Figure 11.3.

The Index structure contains the name field of the attribute. For each entry in the index, a separate node is created. The node is a triplet in the form <*Value,*

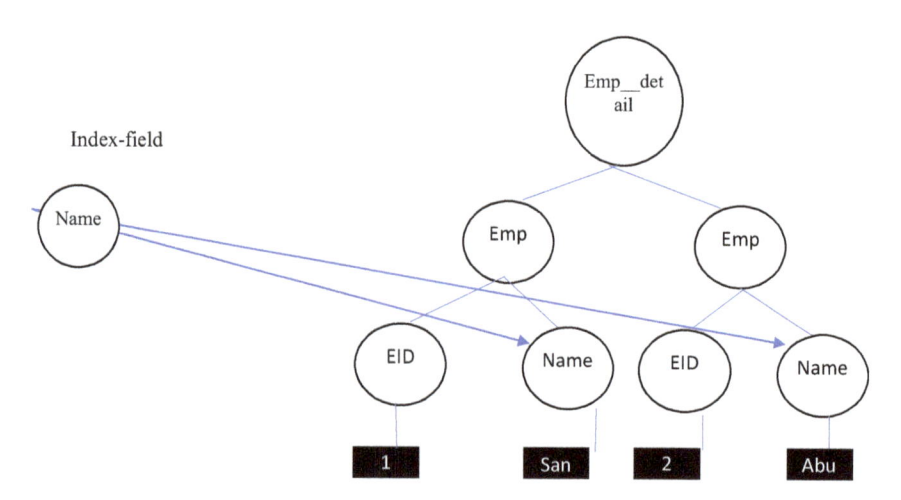

Figure 11.2 Attribute-centric sparse indexing

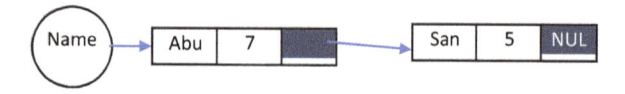

Figure 11.3 Attribute-centric sparse index structure

attribute order position in the tree, pointer to next node>. The memory representation of the index structure is depicted in Figure 11.3. Each entry in the index structure is exactly equal to the number of values of the same attribute. The growth of the index structure occurs in accordance with the inclusion of the value in the data tree dynamically (run-time) in the system heap. The index structure is defined as an active index. The active index implies the index is created based on the event in the data tree. The event in the data tree is the insertion of the value. The event-driven index is created using the trigger. After insertion of the value in the data file, the trigger Create_ActiveIndex is triggered. The required parameters for the index are taken as an IN parameter of the operation. This signature is an extension of the NoSQL. The straightforward rule is to pass the parameter as arguments to the procedure and/or functions. Here, little deviation is performed. The operation on which the trigger is fired, that operation is supported to pass the parameters to the triggers. The active index concept is not new. Another way of saying about the active index is that the active index is the cause–effect outcome. The cause is the operation to be performed and the effect is the functions to be performed using a trigger. Both opponents and proponents exist on the concepts of active index. However, the event-driven philosophy is mostly documented in research and industry implementations.

Algorithm: Create_ActiveIndex

Step 1: Create Trigger Create_ActiveIndex as
Insert on DataTree (IN_PARAMETER Attribute_Name IN_PARAMETER
value$_i$, IN_PARAMETER Node_position)
After each data_node in DataTree
Step 2: Calculate the memory size of the node of the Active Index List
Step 3: Create the new node of Active Index List
Step 4: Assign in parameters value$_i$ and Node_position to the new node of Active Index List.
Step 5: If Active Index List is empty.
Step 6: Adjust the new Node as first node of the Active Index
Step 7: Return
Step 8: End If
Step 9: While check the node as last node of the Active Index List
Step 10: Adjust the new Node as last of the Active Index List
Step 11: End While
Step 12: End.

The algorithm is implemented using a trigger. The trigger is a tool to implement the Active Index List. The node of the Active Index List points to the desired attribute of the DataTree. The node of the Active Index list is created and grows in accordance with the sequence of the insertion of values in the DataTree. The algorithm is fired after the insertion of $value_i$ in the DataTree automatically. All the IN parameters are passed to the signature of the function. The first IN parameter is the name of the attribute on which the index is created. It is worth mentioning that the scheme of the index is dense with respect to the desired attribute name. The next IN parameter is the value that is inserted in the DataTree, and the last IN parameter specifies the node position of the value in the data tree. This algorithm is consistent and robust with respect to stable DataTree. In case of unstable data tree is used where the node position within the data tree is changed to balance the tree, in such case the specified algorithm mentioned above needs to run on each value of the data tree separately.

11.5 Conclusion

Document-oriented databases are gaining momentum in recent days with the sound theories of big data. The specialized NoSQL on such document-oriented data is continuously experimenting to access the data in an optimized way. XML and JSON are two popular formats to store in the document-oriented database. To improve the performance of accessing the data, indexing and bitmap techniques are used. Each specialized indexing technique exploits the efficacy of the corresponding format of XML and JSON. This document extensively summarizes the technique of such an indexing scheme and specifies an active indexing scheme on the hierarchical data. The detailed algorithm is discussed to create such an active index on the hierarchical data.

References

[1] M. Stonebraker, and U. Çetintemel. "One size fits all": an idea whose time has come and gone. *International Conference on Data Engineering*, IEEE (2005), pp. 1–10, 10.1109/icde.2005.1.

[2] C. Strauch. NoSQL databases; Tech. Rep.; Stuttgart Media University (2011).

[3] M.A. Qader, S. Cheng, and V. Hristidis. A comparative study of secondary indexing techniques in LSM-based NoSQL databases; *International Conference on Management of Data*, SIGMOD2018, ACM.

[4] A. Petrov. Algorithms behind modern storage systems. *Queue*, 16 (2) (2018), pp. 30:31–30:51.

[5] D. Comer. Ubiquitous b-tree. *ACM Computing Surveys*, 11 (2) (1979), pp. 121–137, 10.1145/356770.356776.

[6] J. Han, H. E, G. Le, and J. Du. Survey on NoSQL database. *International Conference on Pervasive Computing and Applications*, IEEE (2011), pp. 363–366, 10.1109/icpca.2011.6106531.
[7] R. Cattell. Scalable SQL and NoSQL data stores. *SIGMOD Record*, 39 (4) (2011), p. 12–16.
[8] M. Stonebraker. SQL databases v. NoSQL databases *Communications in ACM*, 53 (4) (2010), p. 10, 10.1145/1721654.1721659.
[9] R. Hecht, and S. Jablonski. NoSQL evaluation: a use case oriented survey. *International Conference on Cloud and Service Computing*, IEEE (2011), pp. 336–341, 10.1109/csc.2011.6138544.
[10] F. Gessert, W. Wingerath, S. Friedrich, and N. Ritter. NoSQL database systems: a survey and decision guidance. *Computer Science – Research and Development*, 32 (3–4) (2016), pp. 353–365, 10.1007/s00450-016-0334-3.
[11] F. Bajaber, S. Sakr, O. Batarfi, A. Altalhi, and A. Barnawi. Benchmarking big data systems: a survey. *Computer Communications*, 149 (2020), pp. 241–251, 10.1016/j.comcom.2019.10.002.
[12] C.-O. Truică, E.-S. Apostol, J. Darmont, and I. Assent TextBenDS: a generic textual data benchmark for distributed systems. *Information Systems Frontiers* (2020), 10.1007/s10796-020-09999-y.
[13] S.M. Freire, E. Sundvall, D. Karlsson, and P. Lambrix. Performance of XML databases for epidemiological queries in archetype-based EHRs. *Scandinavian Conference on Health Informatics*, Linköping University Electronic Press (2012), pp. 51–57.
[14] A. Schmidt, F. Waas, M. Kersten, M.J. Carey, I. Manolescu, and R. Busse. XMark: a benchmark for xml data management. *International Conference on Very Large Databases VLDB*, Elsevier (2002), pp. 974–985, 10.1016/b978-155860869-6/50096-2.
[15] M. Nicola, I. Kogan, and B. Schiefer. An XML transaction processing benchmark. *ACM SIGMOD International Conference on Management of Data*, ACM (2007), pp. 937–948, 10.1145/1247480.1247590.
[16] P. Atzeni, F. Bugiotti, L. Cabibbo, and R. Torlone. Data modeling in the NoSQL world. *Computer Standards & Interfaces*, 67 (2020), Article 103149, 10.1016/j.csi.2016.10.003.
[17] T. Fiebig, S. Helmer, C.-C. Kanne, *et al.* Anatomy of a native XML base management system. *VLDB Journal*, 11 (4) (2002), pp. 292–314, 10.1007/s00778-002-0080-y.
[18] G. Pavlović-Lažetić. Native xml databases vs. relational databases in dealing with XML documents Kragujev. *Journal of Mathematics*, 30 (2007), pp. 181–199.
[19] E. Gallinucci, M. Golfarelli, and S. Rizzi. Schema profiling of document-oriented databases. *Information Science*, 75 (2018), pp. 13–25, 10.1016/j.is.2018.02.007.
[20] BaseX; BaseX documentation; http://docs.basex.org/wiki/Main_Page (2020).

[21] C. Grün, S. Gath, A. Holupirek, and M.H. Scholl. XQuery full text implementation in BaseX. *Database and XML Technologies* (2009), pp. 114–128, 10.1007/978-3-642-03555-5_10.

[22] W. Meier. eXist: an open source native XML database Web, *Web-Services, and Database Systems*, Springer (2003), pp. 169–183, 10.1007/3-540-36560-5_13.

[23] E. Siegel, and A. Retter. *eXist: A NoSQL Document Database and Application Platform*; O'Reilly Media, Inc. (2014).

[24] A. Fomichev, M. Grinev, and S. Kuznetsov. Sedna: a native XML DBMS. *SOFSEM 2006: Theory and Practice of Computer Science*, Springer (2006), pp. 272–281, 10.1007/11611257_25.

[25] Sedna, Sedna documentation; https://www.sedna.org/documentation.html (2020).

[26] I. Taranov, I. Shcheklein, A. Kalinin, et al. Sedna: native XML database management system (internals overview); *ACM SIGMOD International Conference on Management of Data, SIGMOD'10*, ACM (2010), pp. 1037–1046, 10.1145/1807167.1807282.

[27] K. Banker, P. Bakkum, S. Verch, D. Garrett, and T. Hawkins. *MongoDB in Action* (2nd edn), Manning Publications Co. (2011).

[28] MongoDB, Inc., Mongodb documentation; https://docs.mongodb.com/ (2020).

[29] Apache CouchDB. CouchDB documentation https://docs.couchdb.org/en/stable/ (2020).

[30] J.C. Anderson, J. Lehnardt, and N. Slater. *CouchDB: Definitive Guide*. O'Reilly Media, Inc. (2010).

[31] B. Holt. *Scaling CouchDB: Replication, Clustering, and Administration*. O'Reilly Media, Inc. (2011).

[32] G. Manyam, M.A. Payton, J.A. Roth, L.V. Abruzzo, and K.R. Coombes Relax with CouchDB — into the non-relational DBMS era of bioinformatics. *Genomics*, 100 (1) (2012), pp. 1–7, 10.1016/j.ygeno.2012.05.006.

[33] M. Brown. *Getting Started with Couchbase Server*. Oreilly (2012).

[34] D. Vohra. Pro Couchbase Development Apress (2015), 10.1007/978-1-4842-1434-3.

[35] M. A. Hubail, A. Alsuliman, M. Blow, et al. Couchbase analytics. VLDB Endowment, 12(12) (2019), pp. 2275–2286, 10.14778/3352063.3352143.

[36] ASTERIX, http://asterix.ics.uci.edu

[37] S. Chakraborty, A. Cortesi, and N. Chaki. A uniform representation of multi-variant data in intensive-query databases. *Innovations System Software Engineering* 12, 163–176 (2016). https://doi.org/10.1007/s11334-016-0275-9.

[38] S. Chakraborty and N. Chaki. DFRS: a domain-based framework for representing semi-structured data; CUBE'12: *Proceedings of the CUBE International Information Technology Conference* September 2012 pp. 447–452 https://doi.org/10.1145/2381716.2381801.

[39] S. Chakraborty and N. Chaki, Generic organization of semi-structured data. *Computer Systems Science and Engineering* 29(1) (2014).
[40] C-O. Truică, E-S. Apostol, J. Darmont, and T. B. Pedersen. The forgotten document-oriented database management systems: an overview and benchmark of native XML DODBMSes in comparison with JSON DODBMSes. *Big Data Research* 25 (2021): 100205.

Chapter 12
The AI–mental health dialogue: an investigation of their relationship

Ritaprava Bandyopadhyay[1] and Subarna Bhattacharya[2]

12.1 Introduction

In hyperhistory, when technology interacts with technology which in turn interacts with technology, the role of humans has been changed from the centre to the periphery [1]. But does that imply that human beings as mental health professionals will at some point be replaced by artificially intelligent agents (AIAs)? If not, then what would be the nature of the artificial intelligence (AI)–mental health relationship? These are the vital questions we will explore in this chapter.

We know from our lived experience that mental illness, like many diseases, can manifest acutely within the person suffering from it, and yet, be of little or no significance to the people around them. Some people suffering from a mental disorder may not always appear ill, particularly if their infliction is at a preliminary stage. Few others, however, may exhibit more obvious indications such as disorientation, agitation, or depression. In certain instances, mental health disorders may take the form of schizophrenia, autism spectrum disorder, or obsessive-compulsive disorder. While in some cases, individuals share their mental health issues with their loved ones, a doctor or a counsellor, in others, individuals cannot share their mental health concerns at all. This can be understood through observing others participating in the lifeworld[*] in the way that a mental health expert does. Therefore, it is our thesis that at the very core of mental health issues, two observations are to be made – mental health issues can either be communicated and/ or they can be derived through simulation wherein empirical evidence gathered from the individual experiences, behaviour, and psychological evaluation holds the key.

---

[1]PhD in Cognitive Science from the School of Cognitive Science at Jadavpur University, Kolkata, West Bengal, India, Independent Researcher, Assistant Editor, Anandabazar Patrika Online, Kolkata
[2]Amity Institute of Social Sciences, Amity University, India
[*]In Phenomenology, the lifeworld is the world as it is instantly or directly felt in the subjectivity of daily life, as contrasted to the objective 'worlds' of the sciences, which apply the methodology of quantitative sciences of nature. We will not go in to the detailed concept of lifeworld and its nuances or how it was taken further by Marti Heidegger and later philosophers. We have taken the concept of lifeworld as conceived by Husserl. By lifeworld we mean the phenomenological world of intersubjective experience.

Human beings are natural agents. They are a product of evolution. In the lifeworld, we get to know about other people's mental health either through direct verbal communication or through simulation. Hence, we can argue that our lived experience shows that understanding other people depends on two aspects: (i) understanding language and (ii) mastering the act of simulation.

However, we can see that AI has become more relevant in the domain of mental health in a variety of ways. So in order to find the answer to our central question, let us turn to some of the prominent studies conducted in the domain of AI and mental illness in contemporary times. This chapter will examine journals and other publications related to the debate using a qualitative approach.

It seems that the intersection of mental health and AI presents a compelling avenue for advancing our understanding, assessment, and treatment of psychological well-being [2]. Moreover, machine learning (ML), natural language processing (NLP), and predictive analytics (PA) are examples of AI technologies that give novel means to enhance mental healthcare [3]. Research also shows that the early detection of mental health disorders through analysis of linguistic patterns and behavioural cues using AI in text and speech can enable timely intervention [4]. Additionally, there are examples galore that AI-driven algorithms can assist clinicians by analysing vast data sets to recommend personalised treatment plans and optimise therapeutic outcomes [5]. Furthermore, research has shown that AI-powered systems may use digitised healthcare information, which is available in multiple formats such as digital health records, medical images, and notes from physicians, for automating jobs, support clinicians, and better understand the causes of complicated conditions [6].

Research also says, AI-powered tools can analyse patterns in language, speech, and behaviour to detect early signs of mental health issues. For example, text analysis algorithms can identify linguistic markers associated with depression or anxiety in written communication [7].

We have examples of AI-driven chatbots and virtual therapists providing immediate support and resources to individuals dealing with mental health concerns. These platforms use NLP to engage in conversations and offer coping strategies [8]. Additionally, AI can assist in tailoring treatment plans to individual needs. By analysing a person's data and responses, AI can suggest appropriate interventions and therapies [9]. Research shows that AI can help in managing medication regimens. Apps and devices can send reminders to take medications and track their effectiveness [10]. Analysing large data sets, AI can predict mental health trends and potential outbreaks. This information can help healthcare providers allocate resources and plan interventions more effectively [11].

Moreover, AI algorithms can analyse neuroimaging data, such as MRI scans, to assist in diagnosing conditions like schizophrenia, depression, and Alzheimer's disease [12].

As per reports, AI that can support therapists by providing insights and recommendations based on patient data. It can help therapists track progress and adjust treatment plans accordingly [13].

Research conducted on crisis intervention as well. AI-powered systems can monitor online platforms for posts that indicate potential mental health crises, allowing for timely intervention [14].

AI has enabled remote monitoring as well. Wearable devices equipped with AI are capable of monitoring physiological indicators (like heart rate and sleep patterns) which might correlate with mental health conditions [15].

Further, AI helps researchers analyse vast amounts of data within a very limited time to uncover new insights into the causes and treatments of mental illnesses [16].

In light of such massive accomplishments on part of AI, it becomes important to ask, despite holding immense promise, will AI replace human interaction and expertise in the mental health field?

While ethical considerations, data privacy, and accuracy of AI algorithms remain important concerns, we have discussed only the replacement hypothesis in this chapter. From the literature survey we came to know that in many cases, language is one of the main vehicles through which our mental lives unfold and AI tools analyse language to detect mental illness. Hence, in this chapter, we want to focus on two overarching concerns. First, can AIAs understand the subtle nuances of language? We will illustrate this query with the example of ChatGPT. Second, we will explain why it is impossible for an AIA to adopt simulation as a tool for understanding others' mental illness.

12.2 Can artificially intelligent agents understand the subtle nuances of language?

It has been seen that AI-driven chatbots and virtual therapists provide accessible and stigma-free platforms for individuals to express their thoughts and emotions, while they also offer immediate support and coping strategies [17]. We ask then, can AI-driven chatbots be relied upon for debunking the nuances of language – that which is considered to be one of the vehicles through which one's mental illness can be communicated? Is it really possible to provide a so-called 'stigma-free' platform for individuals to express their thoughts and emotions given that the system is required to deal with natural language? We would like to explain this by presenting an example from ChatGPT as a case study. Let us begin by recalling what Noam Chomsky *et al.* pointed out recently. Chomsky calls ChatGPT a 'false hope' [18].

The creators of ChatGPT say that the AI chatbot cannot ensure that its output is correct, but simply that its responses sound correct. It is vital to understand that ChatGPT's responses are not stored in memory; rather, they are created on the fly using the 175 billion weights[†] mentioned previously. Of late the use of ChatGPT or other large language model (LLM)-based bots is pervasive [19]. This is not a

---

[†]The model's weights are numerical numbers that indicate how strongly neurons are connected to one another across several layers. Weights in LLMs are mostly utilised in the feedforward neural networks that comprise the architecture of the model and the attention mechanism. They are modified in order to maximise the model's capacity to produce content that is both pertinent and logical during the training phase.

ChatGPT-specific problem, but rather a reflection of the current condition of all LLMs. Their strength is not in recalling facts; even the most basic databases can accomplish that effectively. Instead, their expertise is in producing language that reads like human-written material and, of course, that which sounds correct. In many circumstances, the text that sounds 'correct' will also be 'correct'. However, that is not always the case.

In this chapter, we will not delve into the technical specificities pertaining to the creation of ChatGPT because that is a matter of engineering and beyond the scope of our discussion. Rather, we will focus on this all pervasive AI technology's social ramifications and how it is being perceived and adopted by people. The question which arises then is, can LLM-based chatbots like ChatGPT replace human mental health professionals? [20].

We will take a cue from Chomsky's logic for answering this question. According to Chomsky et al., among other things, ChatGPT processes information using statistics, although the human mind does not rely solely on this method.

The human mind does not rely only on pattern-matching and/or deal with huge amounts of data to answer a question. On the contrary, it processes a tiny amount of information at a given time. It arrives at a decision not solely through relying on correlation, but it looks for an explanation. Chomsky illustrates this point by citing the example of a child, who, when learning a language develops grammatical rules, a tremendously intricate network of directives based on logic, intuitively, spontaneously, and quickly from microscopic inputs. To him, this grammar finds its root in gene that provides human beings with the ability to produce complicated phrases as well as lengthy streams of ideas. He gives an example. He asks us to imagine that an apple slips from one's hand. If one is to narrate this incident, one can simple say, 'The apple falls'. Similarly, if one were to say that 'The apple will fall', that would amount to a prediction. However, according to Chomsky, an explanation is different from a prediction and a description. It includes the conjecture, 'If I open the hand any such object would fall' or 'The apple falls because of the gravitational force'. So, to him this is a causal explanation and that is what 'thinking' is all about. We will review this point a little later. Now we must concentrate on what Chomsky said. To him, ML is all about description and prediction. It makes no assumptions about causal mechanisms or physical principles. However, the explanation given by human beings cannot always be correct. We are not perfect. But it is necessary to understand that in order to be correct, we can be incorrect. This is part of the thinking process. Human intelligence comprises both creative hypotheses and creative critiques. It is based on finding possible explanations and fault rectification. This process helps one to consider the limits of possibility. As a result, theoretically, ML system forecasts will always be shallow and doubtful as these programmes are incapable of explaining English syntax rules. Chomsky gives an explanation. He says an artificially intelligent machine cannot explain a sentence like 'Rohit is too stubborn to speak with'. AI erroneously interprets the sentence as Rohit is too strong-willed that he is not interested to speak with another person. However, the actual meaning of the sentence is that Rohit is too adamant to be argued with. If LLM fails to correctly interpret a simple sentence, then how can it extract the meanings of sentences which represent complex states of the human mind? They can either produce both truths and falsehoods or they remain non-committal and indifferent. In other words, they learn that the 'Earth is spherical' and 'Earth is flat' are true simultaneously. We know for a fact that most psychological problems are non-algorithmic in nature. Mental illnesses like depression and/ or anxiety disorders are often expressed through diverse text types or spoken words. These texts or words may have different meanings. Some texts and words can be allegorical. Some may have different connotations. So, these texts or words are not always easy to interpret. Hence, AI–mental health dialogues are not easy to understand. Again, at times mental illnesses cannot be communicated through written or spoken words. They can be inferred using a folk psychological narrative. To understand this, one has to participate in the lifeworld and take part in the process of mental simulation (as demonstrated in [18]). This premise will pave the way for our next section.

12.3 Why is it impossible for an artificially intelligent agent to adopt simulation as a tool for understanding others' mental illnesses?

We have discussed earlier how sometimes mental illness is not expressed in either text or words. For this reason, to understand the same one has to participate in the 'life world' [21]. In this chapter, we follow a phenomenological approach.[‡] Intersubjective experience, according to Edmund Husserl, is essential in the development of oneself as objectively existent subjects, other experiencing subjects, and the objective spatiotemporal world. Intersubjective experience, Husserl think, is an empathetic experience; it occurs when we consciously attribute intentional activities to other subjects, during which we place ourselves in the shoes of the other. Husserl's reasoning is based on the conviction (or anticipation) that a being who appears and acts similarly to me, i.e., exhibits qualities identical to my own, is likely to view events from an egocentric perspective similar to my own. This trust enables myself to immediately attribute intentional acts to others. It can be considered of in two ways: (1) as a belief and (2) as anything that is socially, culturally, or evolutionarily entrenched (but nonetheless abstract) sense or meaning. The term 'lifeworld' describes how people from one or more social categories (cultures, linguistic communities) organise the universe into objects.

Let us consider an example from Husserl's explanation. He says that we recognise coal as a useful object for producing heat. A combustible object could be used as fuel. It's also valuable to us. It allows us to heat a chamber and provide lovely warm sensations to ourselves and other person. Other people perceive it in likewise manner. This is how it obtains a 'intersubjective use-value' and is

---

[‡]There may be other explanations to this and philosophers like Daniel Dennett may not agree with us and can say that AIAs can participate in the life world that we have mentioned, but this debate falls outside our discussion.

regarded in a social context as serving a particular purpose, as valuable to man, and so on (as demonstrated in [21]).

Moreover, Husserl believed that lifeworld is subjective and relative. This serves as a foundation for the more objective world of science. In this chapter, we want to show that until and unless AIAs participate in the 'lifeworld' just like human beings, it will be difficult for them to 'understand' the human mind. However, a question that confronts us at this juncture is; can practical wisdom, such as understanding others' mental illness through simulation be acquired by learning algorithm or emulating our thought process alone? Don't we need to learn to understand others' mental illnesses through lived experience, and practise emotional and social skills that allow us to apply our general understanding of well-being in context-appropriate ways? In other words, can a robot gain 'a predictive hold' over its behaviour so that it is capable of attributing values, beliefs, desires, thoughts, and emotions to one another?

Adam Morton claims that 'sometimes and in some ways, we understand because we can cooperate rather than the other way around' [22]. That is, we can foresee, explain, and understand action in part because of our ability to engage in cooperative activity.

We know from the everydayness of our experience that every situation is a new situation. Hence, the question remains, can artificial agents be involved in these activities in every new, unknown, complex, and emerging situation like human agents and eventually understand people?

Moreover, the concept of simulation as a vehicle to know others' mental illnesses emerges from society and it is subjective, not excluding inter-subjectivity. It depends on multiple factors. For example, it depends on society, culture, conditions of one's upbringing, emotion, psychology, sexuality, beliefs, dreams, feelings, longings, instincts, non-rational thinking, etc.

It happens, one may argue, because life is multidimensional, complex, many-faceted and full of diversities, and always flowing like a river. It is difficult to confine it in one form or the other. Similarly, mental illness of a person can have different causes. Hence, the activity of others' minds cannot always be understood by 'reason' alone. Often, we make decisions guided by our impulses and act accordingly which may prove to be wrong afterwards.

Martin Heidegger once argued that we are able to comprehend the notion of hammers or chairs since many of us were born into an environment that allows us to manage these objects [23]. Similarly, Hubert Dreyfus believed that computers could not acquire intelligence to understand others' minds because they lacked a body, childhood, and cultural experience. Dreyfus opined that a significant portion of human knowledge is 'tacit' [24]. As a result, it is impossible to 'articulate' through a computer programme. Michael Polanyi coined the term 'tacit knowledge' [25]. Dreyfus took his idea and ran with it. The majority of the knowledge we use in our daily lives is 'tacit'. In reality, we have no idea, of the regulations we apply when we finish a specific task. Two examples are given. These are related to cycling and swimming. Some people who swim are aware of how they regulate their respiration which keeps them afloat. Similarly, consider the sport of bicycling.

Bicyclists keep their balance by twisting the handlebars. To prevent sliding to the left, she moves the handle to the left, and to prevent herself from going down to the right, she moves the handlebar to her right. As a result, she balances herself by travelling over a series of minor curves. A study demonstrates that, for a given angle of imbalance, the curvature of each twisting is inversely related to the square of the bicycle's speed. However, a cyclist is ignorant of this mathematical calculation. In reality, this knowledge is not going to assist him in growing as a more skilful cyclist. Later, some scholars stated that we usually know more than we are able to say. The important aspect of this, however, is that competencies are required to articulate our understanding in broad terms, including scientific knowledge in specific. Physical experiments necessitate a high level of expertise. These abilities cannot be obtained solely through the study of textbooks. They are learned through instruction from a tradesperson (as demonstrated in [25]).

According to Hubert Dreyfus, a large percentage of people are strolling specialists. However, to express the way we stroll will almost result in a mere descriptive explanation, which cannot encapsulate the concepts and technique required for strolling. Likewise, following this argument it can be said that, AIAs cannot grasp tacit knowledge or certain skills that are required to understand others' mental illnesses. He, unquestionably, recognised a serious concern in AI. However, since Dreyfus raised these concerns, the concept of AI has evolved dramatically (as demonstrated in [24]). During the 1980s, for example, a paradigm had become most influential in AI research that was built on the neural network concept. It modelled what happens in the nervous system and brain of humans rather than manipulating symbols.

Let us try to understand this with examples. Watson, IBM's computer, was designed specifically to appear on the game show Jeopardy! In this competition, the contestants are provided with the answers, and must in turn find the appropriate questions. Ragnar Fjelland gives an example [26]. He writes that the contestants might be told that 'Father of America did not actually cut down a cherry tree. 'Who was George Washington?' – is the correct question for the contestants to answer. Jeopardy takes a considerably broader repertoire than chess. Science, history, culture, geography, and sports are among the topics covered in the tasks, which may include metaphors and sort of humour (not like that of humans though). There are three contestants trying to find out who responds quickest. Watson uses natural language to communicate (as demonstrated in [26]). It was not connected to the Internet when it appeared on Jeopardy, but it did have access to 200 million pages of information. Despite the fact that Watson has been designed to compete in Jeopardy, the company had other strategies.

In Jeopardy Watson was the winner. After the success, IBM declared that it might use computer in medicine, with the goal of developing an AI medical superdoctor who would revolutionise medicine. They believed that if Watson had access to all medical information (the individual's health data, educational materials, medicine lists, and so on), it could diagnose and treat patients as effectively as a real physician.

However, since then, the said company has been involved in a number of projects, with varying degrees of success. Some have recently been wrapped up, while others have failed spectacularly. Creating an AI doctor has proven to be far more difficult than it was originally anticipated. As opposed to super-physicians, IBM's Watson Health developed artificial intelligence assistants capable of performing routine tasks (as demonstrated in [26]).

Another defining moment in artificial intelligent research is AlphaGo, because it confirmed the use of a strategy identified as 'deep reinforcement learning'. The organisation's name, DeepMind, reflects this. (Google and DeepMind are now Alphabet subsidiaries following a reorganisation.) It is an example of an artificial neural network based artificial intelligence research approach. The real/natural neural network serves as the foundation for an artificial neural network. Our brain is composed of roughly 100 billion neurons. Each neuron connects to approximately 1,000 other neurons through a synapse. This translates to almost 100 trillion connections in the brain. Artificial neurons, which are substantially simpler than organic neurons, make up an artificial neural network. Nevertheless, it has been established that by connecting a large number of neurons in a network, a sufficiently large network can theoretically perform any computation. Of course, what is practically possible is a different issue (as demonstrated in [26]).

Another important example is IBM's Deep Blue. It was widely regarded as a breakthrough after this computer defeated the then world chess champion, Garry Kasparov, in 1997. Deep Blue was designed for a particular objective. Even if Deep Blue surpassed living beings in a task requiring intellectual ability, no one could assert that it achieved general intelligence. Nonetheless, it is an accomplishment (as demonstrated in [26]).

Big data is a recent emergent in the field of artificial intelligence. It refers to the use of mathematical methods on vast volumes of data to uncover correlations and infer probability. Big data propagates that it is not necessary to create computers with human-like intelligence. Viktor Mayer-Schönberger and Kenneth Cukier argue their case implicitly [27]. Their work is optimistic about the possibilities of big data's potential and its beneficial impact on people's private lives, and society, in general. Numerous proponents contend that the conventional scientific process of assumptions, causal models, and experiments is no longer applicable. We all understand that causality is a key component of human thoughts, but this view holds that we don't need it. This school of thought believes that correlations are enough. For example, we can predict where crimes will occur based on criminal data and assign police resources. We can even be capable of anticipating, and thus, stopping a crime from occurring in the first place. In 2012, the White House proclaimed a 'Big Data Research and Development Initiative' to address some of the nation's most critical concerns (as demonstrated in [26]). NLP technologies have shown promising improvements in capturing these complex relationships, represented by an extensive variety of written data, which includes social media posts, interviews, and clinical records, to empower proactive mental healthcare and support earlier detection [28].

Even though big data examination can be introduced as a new epistemological approach, it is more commonly observed as a supplementary technique for massive amounts of data, normally terabytes and petabytes. Let us consider the example of

2009 flu outbreak (as demonstrated in [27]). After mixing parts from bird flu and swine flu viruses, it was given the code name H1N1. It rapidly spread, and health officials across the world were concerned about a pandemic within a week. Some anticipated the outbreak of a disease on the scale of the Spanish flu (1918), which claimed millions. There was no vaccination against the viral infection at that time, medical officials could only try to slow down its spread. Nevertheless, merely before the commencement of the pandemic-like situation, Google researchers created a technique that might anticipate the transmission of the flu far more correctly. Google receives over 3 billion web searches per day and ended up saving those. People who were sick with the flu were more likely to search for flu data on the internet. As an outcome, the investigators were confident to plot the transmission of the flu much faster than health officials when they looked at 'search' themes that are highly correlated with flu. Scholars describe this as a success tale (as demonstrated in [27]).

Other scholars, however, believe that this is an instance of the illusion of early achievement (as demonstrated in [26]). In 2013, the algorithm predicted twice as many visited to doctors for influenza-like diseases. The first iteration of the model probably included seasonal variables that were correlated with the flu yet weren't causally related. As a result, the device worked as a flu monitor and a winter detector. Despite getting revised, the model's performance had fallen far short of its preliminary promises. From these examples, it may appear as if the reasons given by Dreyfus about what a computer could not do are out of date. But Fjelland, however, argued that the disparity between what has been accomplished and what has been promised is striking and Dreyfus's arguments are still valid (as demonstrated in [26]).

Fjelland gave a few explanations for these phenomena (as demonstrated in [26]). One explanation for this disparity could be that profit is the primary motivator for capitalist production, and thus many of the claims made could be viewed as advertising strategy. We know that marketing strategy involves gimmicks. However, while commercial interests undoubtedly play a role, Fjelland believes that this explanation is insufficient. He thinks there may be other reasons too. The first argument is borrowed from Jerone Lanier, one of Silicon Valley's few dissenters. He has stated that faith in technological invincibility, the creation of superintelligent computer, etc. are expressions of an emerging belief represented through an engineering culture (as demonstrated in [26]).

Second, Fjelland contended that if it is claimed that computer can replicate human action, it typically turns out that the assertion is based on a drastically simplified and incorrect representation of such activity. Simply put, overestimation of technology is intimately linked to underestimating of humans (as demonstrated in [26]).

Moreover, Fjelland thinks that in all the previous cases only correlations were used. However, in both science and everyday life, we seek causal relationships. The nature of causal linkages has been debated for decades, especially since David Hume criticised the traditional idea of a necessary relationship between cause and effect. Hume believed that we should be content with observing regularities.

In contrast, his contemporary Immanuel Kant maintained that causal links are required for knowledge acquisition. Every effect, according to him, must be accompanied by a cause [29].

Rather than delving into the philosophical debate over causal ties, which has raged on to this day, it will be more beneficial to look at the way one recognises a causal relationship. John Stuart Mill, a philosopher, devised a set of rules (which he dubbed 'canons') that allow us to recognise causal links. His 'second canon', which, he also called 'the method of difference' is the following:

> If an instance in which the phenomenon under investigation occurs, and an instance in which it does not occur, have every circumstance in common save one, that one occurring only in the former; the circumstance in which alone the two instances differ, is the effect, or the cause, or an indispensable part of the cause, of the phenomenon [30].

The second canon is necessary because it throws light on the relationship between cause and effect. However, some philosophers do not subscribe to the notion of cause and effect.

There is a critical theoretical discourse on correlation and causation. Some researchers believe that causality can be established by correlation and with the help of statistical evidence. They believe that a strong correlation might indicate causality. Each public matter of any factual nature now employs statistical methodology. The American Statistical Association's annual meetings cover almost every aspect of public policy, from nuclear reactor safety to census reliability. The efforts to retrieve causal data from statistics with only oblique help from experiments occur in almost all academic pursuits as well as many non-academic endeavours. Social psychologists, political theorists, economic experts, demographers, teachers, psychiatrists, biotechnologists, market analysts, lawmakers, and, on occasion, pharmacists and scientists use such methodologies [31]. This group of researchers even claim that they can explain some natural laws with the help of correlation and statistical generalisation.

However, there is a body of research that believes that 'Correlation implies association, but not causation. Conversely, causation implies association, but not correlation' [32]. According to this school, mere association cannot be mixed with causation; if X causes Y, therefore the pair have been linked (reliant on). However, associations might develop between variables that exist (i.e., X causes Y) or nonappearance (i.e., they share a common cause). The scholars ask us to envision that we notice that individual who consumes more than four mugs of coffee per day has a lesser possibility of getting skin cancer. This does not imply that coffee offers a person cancer resistance. One likely explanation is that people who drink a lot of coffee, stay indoor for lengthy periods, and thus get minimal sunlight, which is a concern. If we take this to be true, then the amount of time spent outside is a confounder – a reason shared by both findings. A direct causal connection could not be deduced in such a case; the connection merely implies a possibility, such as a common cause, but does not provide evidence. Furthermore, when studying numerous factors in complex systems, dubious connections can emerge. As a result, they hold that association does not mean causation (as demonstrated in [32]).

According to this school of thought, a correlation between variables does not automatically suggest that an alteration in one variable is the cause of a change in the other variable. We can conclude that the divide between association and causation has yet to be overcome [33].

As we have mentioned earlier, we will not go into the details of the debate because it falls outside the realm of our central question. We want to mention that we have followed the arguments from the second school of thought and we have shown with examples that in understanding others, AIAs in general follow the logic of correlation and not causation, while human beings in the course of their everyday lives rely more on causation. Hence, mental illnesses do have causes. To have a successful dialogue between AIAs and mental health, artificial intelligence must search for causes. A mere correlation is not enough.

Our position is that one cannot deny the doctrine of causality entirely as it is one of the key dispositions of human beings. Indeed, the question of why humans have been so dominant in the course of evolution is a hard question. Numerous aspects have played a role, and one of the most significant ones is the ability to cooperate. We have already discussed this idea along the lines of Adam Morton.

We can say that to replace human doctors (psychiatrists), AIAs have to pass the mini-Turing test that is based on finding the causal link. Computers will pass this test if they can handle causal knowledge. The problem is that computers have not really advanced in this respect in many decades [34]. This, as we think, however, is inadequate. We should be capable of intervening in the world to answer causal questions. The foundation of the problem is that computers lack a model of reality [35]. The issue is that no one can have a realistic picture of reality. Any model can only show a skewed version of reality. The substitution of our everyday reality with the realm of science, however, is based on a vital mistake (as demonstrated in [26]).

Husserl was among the first to point this out, attributing the error to Galileo. Husserl describes Galileo as both an explorer and a disguising talent. This misunderstanding was dubbed 'objectivism' by Husserl. Today, the term 'scientism' is more commonly used. Husserl, however, insisted that science is essentially a human beings endeavour. Even the most abstract theories, Husserl's 'lifeworld', are based on our daily lives. Husserl acknowledges Einstein's theory of relativity, claiming that it is based on 'Michelson's experiments and other researchers' confirmations of them. To carry out these types of tests, scientists must be able to wander around, evaluate scales, and interact with other scientists (as demonstrated in [26]). Hubert Dreyfus noted that we are corporeal and social species that inhabit in a material, physical, and social environment. Understanding another person, to replace her in certain situations requires stepping into that person's shoes, not examining the chemical makeup of that person's brain or even their soul. This is to comprehend the individual's living circumstances. This is what we mean when we claim what AIAs will never be able to do as they do not take part in the lifeworld just like human beings (as demonstrated in [26]).

Let us consider another thought experiment. Assume that we're observing a therapist in action. He is a hardworking and experienced psychiatrist with many successful cases. The reception area is crammed with sick people who suffer from a diverse range of mental and emotional ailments. A few are nearly hysterical, others have suicidal tendencies, some have hallucinations, still others have the most truly horrific bad dreams, and even more, are concerned that they are being watched by others who will have an impact on their lives. The psychiatrist devotes particular time to everyone and makes every effort to assist each one of them, but with limited success. Conversely, they all appear to be increasing severe, regardless of the psychiatrist's valiant attempts (as demonstrated in [26]).

Roszak, in Fjilland's article, urges us to think in a greater setting. The psychiatrist's workplace located in a house, which was situated in central Germany. The name of the place is Buchenwald. The clients are detainees from a concentration camp. We would not be able to understand the patients using biochemical algorithms. Hence what is required, is knowledge of the greater background. The example does not make sense unless one is aware that the doctor's chamber is in a concentration camp. A handful of people can put themselves in the shoes of a prison camp detainee. As a result, we cannot entirely understand persons in circumstances that are vastly dissimilar from our own. But, we can understand to some extent, because we are also part of the world (as demonstrated in [26]).

The computer system does not prevail in our universe. As previously stated, neural networks do not require programming and can thus capture tacit knowledge. But handling tacit knowledge is not sufficient to 'understand' the world. However, some big data enthusiasts believe that the data speaks for itself, which is simply not true. Typically, the data utilised is tied to one or more models, chosen by humans, and consists primarily of numbers. As a result, Fjilland argues that Dreyfus' concerns opposing general AI are still sound (as demonstrated in [26]).

However, as the research in AI progresses, the use of ML is becoming increasingly important. Using this, AI researchers try to identify what the general pattern is and determine the extent to which we can reproduce those kinds of decisions in certain situations. The question arises, how can the AI researchers arrive at a 'general pattern' of human thought process, when there is none? This confronts us with another question: How does a robot with its continuous learning process 'learn' something? Will it be possible for it to unlearn something with the help of the same logic? To treat others' mental illnesses one has to get hold of others' minds. Can an AIA put itself in another person's shoes?

Nevertheless, this line of inquiry prompts another question: is it possible to create a code that can handle an infinite number of scenarios? This question seems more relevant as Monica Rozenfield writes,

> Deep learning is a fairly new type of AI which adds a new spin to a former technology named neural network rendering it feasible by big data, supercomputing, and complex algorithms. Each neuron in the network has data lines that interact with each other. It might be difficult to create code for every conceivable scenario. An AI device would be unable to function without the appropriate code. Deep learning, however, allows the system to sort things out on its own. The method allows the network to form neural relationships that are most pertinent to each unfolding scenario (as demonstrated in [34]).

Hence, how will AIAs deal with the rapidly changing situations and the nitty-gritty factors of real-world is nothing but a mystery, and some think that since they do not belong to this world, it will not be possible for them to cope with the situation.

12.4 Conclusion: are artificial agents going to replace human doctors?

According to our understanding, in order to replace human doctors, one of the main things that artificial agents must acquire is the knowledge of the lifeworld. There is, however, no denying the fact that technology has reached new heights and over time, it will only improve further. But we have argued previously that there will remain a tantalising and, of course, very subtle gap between the world of technology and our day-to-day natural world. It is an undeniable fact that our day-to-day world or lifeworld plays a very important role in understanding others – which is essential to treat mental illness.

Through statistical generalisation and programming, AIAs can pull off miracles! We have seen in the first half of the chapter that even in detecting mental illness it can be a useful tool. But will this be sufficient to learn how to participate in the lifeworld just like the way humans do and interact like them?

However, the supporters of affective computing may not agree with us and we will not delve deep into that discussion as it falls outside the scope of our research [36]. So our question is, can the content of thought be measured? If the new age machines are endowed with thoughts, then they will be able to recognise human thoughts and respond accordingly. Theoretically, this thesis is feasible. However, the question which arises is, what would be the content of the thought that our engineer friend wants to measure? We believe, that even if a particular type of thought could be identified, we cannot know its content. We propose that, since human beings have an 'inner life' that AIAs don't have, it will be hard to measure the content of thoughts.

We know that human beings have a history of evolution. We are made up of so many components which have evolved over time. One of these is intelligence. If an artificial agent has every input regarding a person, it can do many things. For example, it can even do counselling for its human counterpart. But if it has to simulate the human counterpart, then it will not succeed as it does not participate in the lifeworld.

Then the question arises: without understanding the content of thoughts, can an artificial agent take part in this 'shared' activity?

Adam Morton, however, believes that there exist 'beneficial circularities between our capacities to attribute states of mind and our capacities to engage in shared activities',

> This means that our understanding of mind and action is formed in part by the need to mediate shared activities in the way that the shared activities we engage in are moulded by the need to rely on our capabilities to gather and conceptualise information about one another (as demonstrated in [22], p. 149).

According to Morton, the idea of 'shared activity' is that we reach a judgment about what we ought to do first, and only then form an expectation of what the other person will intend/ desire to do when we act.

In this way, one makes it clear that this is the only way to solve the problem. The second person then understands what would be the action of the first person. And one will act accordingly (as demonstrated in [22], pp. 14–15).

Morton's opinion is that his propensity enables us to know, anticipate, and demonstrate the activities of someone else, which, however, helps the former to choose one's own course of action. The author demands that cooperative activities of some type are based on everyday psychological understanding conversely. Following this, we behave to make ourselves intelligible to others. Likewise, one gains from being comprehended. This concept of 'beneficial circularities' is central to Morton's research. According to him, we 'comprehend' each other because we have learned to make ourselves 'comprehensible'. Adam Morton examines the notions of belief and simulation, the idea of understanding by intent, and the causal force of psychological explanation using examples from cooperative activities such as driving a cab and playing table tennis.

Therefore, there are two issues here: if an artificial agent has to qualify as an 'agent' (in our case a mental health professional like a doctor) it has to make itself understandable to others. It will have to act in such a way as to make its actions easily intelligible to others so that it can benefit from being understood. In doing so, it will have to participate in the lifeworld and understand among many other things the semantic content of thoughts and it also has to be easily accepted by others. Otherwise, it cannot 'replace' human doctors.

So the question remains, can an artificial agent understand the implicit content of human emotions? By 'implicit content of emotion', we mean their past life with all of its struggle, their mutual departure for the pursuit of excellence, and their acceptance of the course of life. This is a situation where both of them engage in cooperative activity so that we can predict, explain, and understand action. Devoid of the content of a particular emotion, however, can an artificial agent enter in such a cooperative activity? If not, then can it be responsible for generating the reaction of its fellow human beings? Taking part in the lifeworld plays a crucial role here as both of the agents are involved in a 'cooperative activity'. It is, indeed, participation in a lifeworld that makes all the difference. To understand others, human beings rely on the simulation theory, which is nothing but putting oneself in another person's shoes.

From the previous discussion, we come to the conclusion that in some cases, artificial agents would perform better than human beings, while in other situations, they would be outplayed by human beings. Hence, in those situations, they cannot replace human doctors. They can at best supplement human beings' capacities in some respect.

We have stated earlier that by lifeworld, we mean the phenomenological world of intersubjective experience. The lifeworld involves personal, social, perceptual, and practical experiences. Through experiences, human beings learn whatever they can. Furthermore, it is these human experiences which inform us that reality is too diverse to be explained algorithmically.

However, if opponents argue that they will create an algorithm for every changing situation, the question of whether it will be desirable remains unanswered. As we know, at one point of time creating an atomic bomb was plausible, but history teaches us that it was never desirable. We have tried to show that AIAs can imitate human emotions and our linguistic ability, but it is impossible to imitate human beings by their subjective experiences. We can say after Nagel that 'What is it like to be a bat' can only be understood from a bat's point of view. Similarly, 'What is it like to be a human being' can only be understood from a human being's point of view [37]. Hence, it is impossible for an AIA to 'understand' a human being's point of view.

As we have mentioned earlier, human beings are naturally occurring agents. They are by-products of evolution. The subtle nuances of a human being's behaviour in a particular situation are beyond the comprehension, representative ability and capture of algorithms. Using mental simulation, they can predict or explain others' behaviour [38]. Here, we are talking about the empirical and contingent matter which is subject to testing. Given the conception of simulation as embedded in phenomenological notion of lifeworld it does not seem appropriate to think of an artificial agent as a participant in the lifeworld and certainly not an agent of mental simulation.

This is one side of the story. Another thing is that sometimes the creators of artificial agents cannot explain their behaviour. We can consider the example of this (i.e. autonomous self-driving car defies certain rules and meets with an accident, the second example was that of two Facebook bots who began chatting with each other) (as demonstrated in [38]).

Hence, it is hard to accept artificial agents as autonomous agents just like their human counterparts who participate in the lifeworld. If human beings do not consider artificial agents to be autonomous agents, then how does the question of replacing human doctors in certain situations arise?

We know that most psychological and moral problems are non-algorithmic in nature. Mental illness is frequently expressed in non-quantifiable terms. The shift in mental state is caused by both internal and external stimuli that are often hard to identify. To make a moral decision one needs to develop moral intuition. Notwithstanding, often, we cannot reach a decision with the help of our critical reasoning. In such cases, we appeal to our moral intuition and that paves the way for empathy, fellow feeling and respect for others. Participating in the lifeworld makes this possible for human beings.

We also need to ask whether those algorithms can grasp the ever-changing, ever-evolving contents of the lifeworld to keep pace with its own accelerated evolution or will they be more like the blurred vision of a passenger in a superfast train watching the world whizz past the train window? Isn't there always a compromise between pace and cognisance? The lifeworld is the storehouse of value-laden content. For the sake of argument, if we were to accept that artificially intelligent machines will alter their algorithms in accordance with the natural dynamics of the lifeworld without the assistance of human beings, we must ask whether this is desirable, in exactly the same way that we know creation of the atomic bomb was once plausible, but history taught us that it was not desirable.

Therefore, it is impossible to build an agent which would be the same as a natural agent in respect of participation in the lifeworld as we have seen that lifeworld, in the Husserlian sense, cannot be fully computed or explained in terms of algorithm.

If we consider the lifeworld in its essential dynamicity then the only way to capture its sometimes fleeting and sometimes lasting clusters of meaning would be through some kind of participatory process like mental 'simulation'. The computability of the lifeworld is put to question due to its essential subjectivity and uniqueness. One may ask if this does not put into question the predictability of activities in the lifeworld altogether. The absolute unpredictability of the lifeworld as such and the directions in which it may progress or venture in the future is perhaps unquestionable. That does not, however, completely jeopardise the possibilities of statistical prediction in identifiable sections of the lifeworld.

Every moment is a fresh start. Because we are in the present, we cannot predict the next moment because it is unknown to us. We can hope for, expect, and even predict the next moment, but in reality, our prediction, our hope, may remain elusive. Our quest for a new adventure begins as soon as we discover that the reality is quite different than we thought. However, lifeworld plays an important role in shaping our thoughts as we embark on this new journey and it would be wrong to equate this lifeworld with the physical world. Our experience and thought are the value reservoirs that make a human doctor a doctor.

To qualify as a mental simulator like a natural agent, artificial agents must acquire the ability to generate, grasp and comprehend the content of the lifeworld. In the same way, the natural agent, the human being, cannot meaningfully interact with the artificial agent through simulation. The bar lies in attempting to put oneself in the digital shoes of the artificial agent. This is a serious problem with regard to any interpersonal exchange built on first-person experience.

Even if the 'agency' of an artificial agent is established by some ethical doctrines, it is clear from this discussion that we cannot ascribe agency to them like the natural agent. There will always be an unbridgeable gap between human agents (doctors in our case) and artificial agents. However, we can proceed further by accepting this gap and actualising our goals in more realistic terms.

So even if we accept that AIAs can complement human beings, we must watch out for the possible parasitic relationship. If we are not that pessimistic, we may at best admit that artificial agents can never replace natural agents. Therefore, we propose that the relationship between the two will at best be to complement each other.

There is, of course, no denying the fact that artificial agents have enabled human advancement and changed our lives. They have made a deep impact on our workspace as well. But as we have seen, without human involvement it will not prosper. Perhaps that is why recent development shows that there is a turn towards 'embodiment' in artificial intelligent literature. Artificial agents' potentiality will complement human doctors, rather than replace them. To borrow the term from bi-valued logic, we propose that the relationship would be that of 'conjunction' where if both the operands are true then the entire system will be functional and if any one of the operands malfunctions, the entire edifice will collapse like a house of cards [39].

Our central question was, would AIAs as doctors replace human doctors? Now we have arrived at a point where we can answer this question, and our answer is a big 'no'. Artificial agents as doctors cannot replace human doctors as their relationship is one of interdependence.

Mental illness is typically diagnosed through clinical assessment, which involves evaluating a person's thoughts, emotions, behaviours, and overall functioning. This assessment is carried out by trained mental health professionals, such as psychologists, psychiatrists, and clinical social workers, using standardised diagnostic criteria outlined in manuals like the Diagnostic and Statistical Manual of Mental Disorders [40]. Mental health diagnosis relies on empirical evidence gathered from the individual's experiences, behaviour, and psychological evaluation. That said, elements of simulation theory might influence how individuals perceive and interpret their experiences, including those related to mental health. In doing so, AI can be a valuable assistant.

References

[1] Floridi Luciano. The *4th Revolution: How the Infosphere Is Reshaping Human Reality*. London: OUP. 2014. p. 1–31.

[2] Abd-alrazaq Alaa, Alhuwail Dari, Schneider Jens, Toro Carla T., Ahmed Arfan, and Alzubaid Mahmood. 'The Performance of Artificial Intelligence-driven Technologies in Diagnosing Mental Disorders: An Umbrella Review' [online], *NPJ Digital Medicine*. 2022;5–87. Available from https://doi.org/10.1038/s41746-022-00631-8 [Accessed 23 November 2023].

[3] D'Alfonso Simon. 'AI in Mental Health' [online], *Current Opinion in Psychology*. 2020;36:112–17. Available from https://doi.org/10.1016/j.copsyc.2020.04.005 [Accessed 23 November 2023].

[4] Zhang Tianlin, Schoene Annika Marie Schoene, Ji Shaoxiong, and Ananiadou Sophia. 'Natural Language Processing Applied to Mental Illness Detection: A Narrative Review' [online], *NPJ Digital Medicine*. 2022;5:46. Available from https://doi.org/10.1038/s41746-022-00589-7 [Accessed 23 November 2023].

[5] Bajwa Junaid, Munir Usman, Nori Aditya, and Williams Bryan. 'Artificial Intelligence in Healthcare: Transforming the Practice of Medicine' [online], *Future Healthcare Journal*. 2021;8(2):188–94. Available from https://doi.org/10.7861/fhj.2022-0046 [Accessed 23 November 2023].

[6] World Health Organisation. *Mental Health* [online]. Geneva: WHO; 2022. Available from https://www.who.int/news-room/fact-sheets/detail/mental-health-strengthening-our-response [Accessed 19 November 2023].

[7] Piot Marie-Aude, Attoe Chris, Billon Gregoire, Cross Sean, Rethans Jan-Joost, and Falissard Bruno. 'Simulation Training in Psychiatry for Medical Education: A Review' [online]. *Frontiers in Psychiatry*. 2021;12;658967. Available from https://doi.org/10.3389/fpsyt.2021.658967 [Accessed 23 November 2023].

[8] Tal Amir and Torous John. 'The Digital Mental Health Revolution: Opportunities and Risks' [editorial]. *Psychiatric Rehabilitation Journal*. 2017;40(3):263–65. Available from https://doi.org/10.1037/prj0000285 [Accessed 23 November 2023].

[9] Chen Wei, Lu Yixin, Qiu Liangfei, and Kumar Subodha. 'Designing Personalized Treatment Plans for Breast Cancer' [online]. *Information Systems Research*. 2021;32(3):932–949. Available from https://doi.org/10.1287/isre.2021.1002. Available from https://ssrn.com/abstract=3008274 [Accessed 23 November 2023].

[10] Ellis Bartlett Rebecca J, Carmon Anna F., and Pike Caitlin. 'A Review of Immediacy and Implications for Provider-patient Relationships to Support Medication Management' [online]. *Patient Preference and Adherence*. 2016;10:9–18. Available from https://doi.org/10.2147/PPA.S95163 [Accessed 23 November 2023].

[11] Garriga Roger, Mas Javier, Abraha Semhar, *et al.* 'Machine Learning Model to Predict Mental Health Crises from Electronic Health Records' [online]. *Nature Medicine*. 2022;28:1240–48. Available from https://doi.org/10.1038/s41591-022-01811-5 [Accessed 23 November 2023].

[12] Zhang Zhao, Li Guangfei, Xu Yong, and Tang Xiaoying. 'Application of Artificial Intelligence in the MRI Classification Task of Human Brain Neurological and Psychiatric Diseases: A Scoping Review' [online]. *Diagnostics* 2021;11:1402. Available from https://doi.org/10.3390/diagnostics11081402 [Accessed 23 November 2023].

[13] Jiang Fei, Jiang Yong, Zhi Hui, *et al.* 'Artificial Intelligence in Healthcare: Past, Present and Future' [online]. *Stroke and Vascular Neurology*. 2017;2(4):230–43. Available from https://doi.org/10.1136/svn-2017-000101 [Accessed 23 November 2023].

[14] van der Schyff Emma L., Ridout Brad, Amon Krestina L., Forsyth Rowena, and Campbell Andrew J. 'Providing Self-Led Mental Health Support Through an Artificial Intelligence-Powered Chat Bot (Leora) to Meet the Demand of Mental Health Care' [online]. *Journal of Medical Internet Research*. 2023;25:e46448. Available from https://doi.org/10.2196/46448 [Accessed 23 November 2023].

[15] Sabry Farida, Eltaras Tamer, Labda Wadha, Alzoubi Khawla, and Malluhi Qutaibah. 'Machine Learning for Healthcare Wearable Devices: The Big Picture' [online]. *Journal of Healthcare Engineering*. 2022;4653923. Available from https://doi.org/10.1155/2022/4653923 [Accessed 23 November 2023].

[16] Graham Sarah, Depp Colin, Lee Ellen E., *et al.* 'Artificial Intelligence for Mental Health and Mental Illnesses: An Overview' [online]. *Current*

[17] *Psychiatry Reports.* 2019;21(11):116. Available from https://doi.org/10.1007/s11920-019-1094-0 [Accessed 23 November 2023].

[17] Potts Courtney, Ennis Edel, Bond Raymond, *et al.* 'Chatbots to Support Mental Wellbeing of People Living in Rural Areas: Can User Groups Contribute to Co-design?' [online]. *Journal of Technology in Behavioral Science.* 2021;6:652–65. Available from https://doi.org/10.1007/s41347-021-00222-6. [Accessed 23 November 2023].

[18] Chomsky Noam, Roberts Ian, and Watumull Jeffrey. 'The False Promise of ChatGPT' [online]. *The New York Times.* 8 March 2023. Available from https://www.nytimes.com/2023/03/08/opinion/noam-chomsky-chatgpt-ai.html [Accessed 31 March 2023].

[19] Schulman John, Zoph Barret, Kim Christina, *et al.* 'Introducing ChatGPT' [online]. *OpenAI.* 2022. Available from https://openai.com/blog/chatgpt [Accessed 31 March 2023].

[20] Muehmel Kurt. 'What Is a Large Language Model, the Tech Behind ChatGPT?' [online]. 2023. Available from https://blog.dataiku.com/large-language-model-chatgpt. [Accessed 31 March 2023].

[21] Beyer Christian. 'Edmund Husserl' in Zalta Edward N. (ed.). *The Stanford Encyclopedia of Philosophy* [online]. 2020. Metaphysics Research Lab, Stanford University, Stanford, CA 94305, United States. Available from https://plato.stanford.edu/archives/win2020/entries/husserl/ [Accessed 31 March 2023].

[22] Morton Adam. *The Importance of Being Understood: Folk Psychology as Ethics.* New York: Routledge; 2003.

[23] Wheeler Michael. 'Martin Heidegger' in Zalta Edward N. (ed.). *The Stanford Encyclopedia of Philosophy* [online]. 2020. Metaphysics Research Lab, Stanford University, Stanford, CA 94305, United States. Available from https://plato.stanford.edu/archives/fall2020/entries/heidegger [Accessed 31 March 2023].

[24] Dreyfus Hubert L. *What Computers Still Can't Do: A Critique of Artificial Reason.* Cambridge, MA: MIT Press; 1992.

[25] Polanyi Michael. *Personal Knowledge, Towards a Post-Critical Philosophy.* Chicago, IL: University of Chicago Press; 1958.

[26] Fjelland Ragnar. 'Why General Artificial Intelligence Will Not Be Realized'. *Humanities and Social Sciences Communications.* 2020;7(10):1–9. Available from. https://doi.org/10.1057/s41599-020-0494-4 [Accessed 31 March 2023].

[27] Mayer-Schönberger, Viktor, and Cukier Kenneth. *Big Data: A Revolution That Will Transform How We Live, Work, and Think.* Boston, MA: Houghton Mifflin Harcourt; 2013.

[28] Zhang Tianlin, Schoene Annika M., Ji Shaoxiong, Ananiadou Sophia. 'Natural Language Processing Applied to Mental Illness Detection: A Narrative Review' [online]. *NPJ Digital Medicine.* 2022;5(46):1–13. Available from https://doi.org//10.1038s7-00589-022-41746 [Accessed 31 March 2023].

[29] De Pierris, Graciela, and Friedman Michael. 'Kant and Hume on Causality' in Zalta Edward N. (ed.). *The Stanford Encyclopedia of Philosophy* [online]. 2018. Metaphysics Research Lab, Stanford University, Stanford, CA 94305, United States. Available from https://plato.stanford.edu/archives/win2018/entries/kant-hume-causality [Accessed 31 March 2023].

[30] Mill, John Stuart. *A System of Logic*, Vol. 1. John W. Parker; London, 1843. p. 421–22.

[31] Glymour Clark, Scheines Richard, Spirtes Peter and Kelly Kevin. *Discovering Causal Structure: Artificial Intelligence, Philosophy of Science*. Cambridge, MA: Academic Press; 1986.

[32] Altman Naomi, and Krzywinski Martin. 'Association, Correlation, and Causation' [online]. *Nature*. 2012. Available from https://www.nature.com/articles/nmeth.3587.pdf [Accessed 31 March 2023].

[33] Freedman David, and Humphreys Paul. 'Are There Algorithms That Discover Causal Structure?' [online]. *Synthese*. 1999;121(1/2):29–54. Available from http://www.jstor.org/stable/20118220 [Accessed 31 March 2023].

[34] Etzioni Amitai, and Oren Etzioni. 'Incorporating Ethics into Artificial Intelligence' [online]. *The Journal of Ethics*. 2017;21(4):403–18. Available from http://www.jstor.org/stable/45204573 [Accessed 31 March 2023].

[35] Pearl Judea, and Mackenzie Dana *The Book of Why. The New Science of Cause and Effect*. New York: Basic Books; 2018.

[36] Picard Rosalind. *Affective Computing*. Cambridge, MA: MIT Press; 1997.

[37] Nagel Thomas. 'What Is It Like to Be a Bat?' [online]. *The Philosophical Review*. 1974;83(4):435–50. Available from https://doi.org/10.2307/2183914 [Accessed 31 March 2023].

[38] Bandyopadhyay Ritaprava. 'Soft-Morality and Artificiality'. Jadavpur University PhD dissertation; Kolkata: 2023.

[39] Shramko Yaroslav, and Wansing Heinrich. 'Truth Values', in Zalta Edward N. (ed.). *The Stanford Encyclopedia of Philosophy* [online]. 2020. Metaphysics Research Lab, Stanford University, Stanford, CA 94305, United States. Available from https://plato.stanford.edu/archives/win2020/entries/truth-values/ [Accessed 31 March 2023].

[40] American Psychiatric Association. Bipolar and Related Disorders. In *Diagnostic and Statistical Manual of Mental Disorders* [online]. 2022;5. American Psychiatric Association (ed.)., American Psychiatric Association Publishing, Washington, DC. 140–176. Available from https://doi.org/10.1176/appi.books.9780890425787.x03_Bipolar_and_Related_Disorders [Accessed 31 March 2023].

Chapter 13

Research on the application of Bayesian deep learning in medical big data

Linxuan Du[1], Zhisheng Zhao[1], Xueqiong Wei[2], Lihua Ding[1], Jie Li[3] and Bohao Li[1]

With excellent performance in medical big data processing, deep learning (DL) has been intensely used in clinical decision support. A major limitation of conventional DL models is the inability to measure the uncertainty. Therefore, the reliability and credibility cannot be guaranteed in real medical tasks. To overcome this limitation, Bayesian deep learning (BDL) has been proposed which integrates Bayesian theory and DL. BDL uses the probability distribution of model parameters to quantify all sources of uncertainties in the model, which enables confidence assessment in medical image processing and analysis. BDL provides a new perspective of medical big data analysis and attracts increasing intention in recent years.

In this chapter, we first introduce DL and Bayesian inference, and then explain the concept and characteristics of BDL. The state-of-the-art BDL frameworks and algorithms are analyzed and systematically compared regarding the benefits and drawbacks. The application of BDL is exemplified by several real-world medical tasks. Finally, the current status, challenges, potentials, and future directions of BDL are summarized. BDL still faces a number of challenges in computing complexity, the modeling and interpretation of model uncertainty, data privacy and security issues that deserve further investigation. This scoping review provides an up-to-date reference regarding the applications of BDL in medical big data.

13.1 Introduction

In this section, we first discuss the extensive applications of deep learning (DL) in medical big data and highlight its inherent limitations. Subsequently, we introduce the concept of Bayesian deep learning (BDL) along with its framework and algorithms. We elucidate how BDL addresses or mitigates some of the shortcomings of

[1]College of Information Science and Engineering, Hebei North University, China
[2]DAPU Credit Rating. Co. Ltd, Hangzhou, China
[3]Department of Pathology, China-Japan Friendship Hospital, China

traditional DL by more effectively dealing with uncertainties. Through case studies, we demonstrate the applications of BDL in medical big data and delve into the challenges faced therein, thereby providing more reliable and robust support for medical diagnostic decision-making.

13.1.1 Application of deep learning in medical big data

The application of DL in medical big data has emerged as a prominent research domain, boasting both widespread practical applications and significant theoretical value [1]. With the explosive growth of medical data, traditional data processing and analytical methods have become inadequate. DL techniques, particularly convolutional neural networks (CNN) [2] and recurrent neural networks (RNN) [3], have demonstrated formidable capabilities in areas like image recognition and natural language processing (NLP). In the realm of medicine, these algorithms are employed for diagnostic image analysis, clinical electronic health records (EHRs), genomic sequence interpretation, and disease prediction, among others. By autonomously extracting intricate features and patterns, DL not only enhances analytical accuracy but also substantially accelerates the medical research and diagnostic processes. This presents a potent tool for the realization of personalized and precision medicine.

13.1.1.1 Medical image analysis

Today, a vast array of medical imaging data is stored across diverse data sources, including radiographic imaging, genomic sequencing, pathological imaging, positron emission tomography (PET) [4], X-rays, computed tomography (CT) [5], functional MRI (fMRI), diffusion tensor imaging (DTI) [6], and magnetic resonance imaging (MRI) [7]. The broad application of DL in medical image analysis can assist clinicians in interpreting medical images more efficiently and in making diagnostic decisions with increased accuracy and objectivity.

The computational processing and analysis of medical images encompass tasks like medical image retrieval, medical image creation, medical image analysis, and image-based visualization. In the domain of medical image analysis, DL is predominantly utilized for tasks such as classification, segmentation, detection, and image registration. Within this domain, CNNs have showcased exemplary performance, especially in recognizing and classifying diseases [8]. For instance, with ample training data, CNN models can accurately identify tumors, fractures, or other pathological features within radiological images. Furthermore, DL frameworks such as the U-Net architecture have proven to be remarkably effective for image segmentation tasks, like precisely segmenting brain tissues from MRI scans. DL approaches have become the staple in the computer-aided diagnosis (CADx) field and are extensively employed across a range of tasks, encompassing disease classification, return on investment (ROI) segmentation, medical object detection, and image registration.

Medical image classification is an objective of CADx [9], aiming to differentiate between malignant and benign lesions or to identify certain diseases from input images. Over the past decade, DL-based CADx approaches have achieved significant success. The learning paradigms mainly encompass unsupervised image synthesis, self-supervised and semi-supervised learning, and transfer learning. Medical image segmentation, another challenging task in medical image analysis, stands as a pivotal technique in medical imaging processing. Its primary objective is to accurately segment different tissues, organs, or lesion areas in medical images, identifying pixel or voxel collections of lesions, organs, and other substructures from the background. This facilitates clearer image analysis for physicians, allowing for more accurate diagnostic and treatment decisions. Image registration, also known as image fusion or image matching, is the process of aligning two or more images based on their appearances and is an essential step in many medical image analysis tasks. The goal of medical image registration is to align images optimally to a common coordinate system to achieve accurate matching of anatomical structures. In multi-modal image registration, designing precise image similarity measurement methods becomes challenging due to inherent appearance differences between different imaging modalities. Different applications and registration methods face distinct challenges.

13.1.1.2 Processing of clinical electronic health records

In the context of medical big data, EHRs encompass structured clinical texts and a wealth of unstructured medical data, providing rich patient information [10]. These datasets are replete with intricate patterns and high-dimensional features, necessitating the use of advanced techniques for effective interpretation and utilization. DL offers a paradigm shift and a powerful, scalable solution for applications in this domain. Initial steps involve preprocessing the clinical text for efficient feature extraction, including text normalization and tokenization, aiming to transform the qualitative attributes of clinical notes into formats suitable for algorithmic processing. Currently, employed models include the RNN, transformer models, and BERT (bidirectional encoder representation from transformers) [11]. Notably, BERT has been demonstrated to be highly efficient in this domain. These models are capable of capturing temporal relationships in the text, enabling the extraction of crucial medical information to support disease diagnosis and patient management decisions. For processing time-sensitive clinical data, the RNN or long short-term memory (LSTM) networks present significant advantages [12]. These networks excel at capturing time dependencies, making them particularly apt for predicting disease trajectories or patient readmission risks. Deep neural networks (DNN) are frequently used for prognostic assessments [13], typically integrating features from clinical records with other patient information to craft comprehensive predictive models. Additionally, NLP techniques and machine learning methods have been deployed for various EHR processing tasks [14]. Text processing of EHRs typically encompasses medical concept extraction, named entity recognition, disease classification, drug allergy reactions, and symptom extraction and identification.

13.1.1.3 Other medical information processing

Beyond traditional medical imaging and clinical EHRs, the medical domain also encompasses a plethora of intricate data such as genomic data and laboratory testing results [15]. DL approaches, including autoencoders and deep belief networks, have been effectively deployed for pattern recognition, anomaly detection, and predictive tasks within these data, thereby bolstering personalized medicine and treatments [16]. Proteomics data is dedicated to exploring the expression, modification, and interactions of proteins [17]. In this realm, autoencoders and RNNs have showcased immense potential for predicting protein structure and function while also identifying possible drug targets. Metabolomics data focuses on the study of small molecule compounds [18]. In processing such data, DL, especially variational autoencoders, excel in pattern recognition of molecular structures, modeling metabolic pathways, and predicting disease progression. Laboratory data, typically presented in a time-series format, pertains to patient biochemical, blood, and urine test outcomes. Long short-term memory networks and other recurrent models exhibit pronounced efficacy in predicting patient disease trajectories and prognoses. Through DL techniques, medical researchers and clinicians can now more accurately extract meaningful insights from these intricate datasets, consequently refining medical decision-making and disease management. Medical signals are electronic recordings of physiological activities of biological entities, such as humans and animals, employed for researching and diagnosing an array of health conditions. These signals, such as electrocardiograms (ECG) and electroencephalograms (EEG), capture electrical, chemical, and mechanical activities to provide pivotal information regarding biological events or system functionalities.

13.1.2 Limitations of deep learning

DL has achieved remarkable accomplishments across various application domains, yet it confronts an array of challenges and limitations. These concerns encompass data dependency and computational complexity [19], model interpretability and transparency [20], overfitting and local optima [21], and handling of uncertainty [22].

1. Data dependency and computational complexity: DL has demonstrated impressive performance in fields such as image recognition, NLP, and game theory. Nevertheless, this robust performance often hinges on vast data sets and highly intricate models. This implies that for many practical applications, especially those where data is scarce or where real-time responses are crucial, traditional DL techniques might not be applicable. For instance, acquiring numerous labeled samples in medical diagnosis is often impractical.
2. Interpretability and transparency: Owing to their complexity and multiparametric nature, DL models are frequently regarded as "black boxes." In sectors like business, medicine, or law, where a high degree of interpretability is mandated, the majority of successful cases have been realized, but often at the expense of some performance trade-offs.
3. Overfitting and local optima: DL models typically possess a multitude of tunable parameters, making them prone to overfitting when faced with limited or imbalanced data. Even with the application of regularization techniques and data augmentation, circumventing this issue is challenging. Overfitting not only diminishes the model's generalizability but can also reduce its reliability in real-world applications. Moreover, during training, DL models can frequently get

stuck in local optima rather than finding the global optimum, indicating that even if high accuracy is achieved on training data, the model's performance on unseen data might not be satisfactory.
4. Uncertainty: Despite its exemplary predictive performance across a broad range of AI applications, DL often overlooks a crucial aspect: uncertainty. While there are myriad success stories, the issue of uncertainty remains pivotal. Standard DNNs typically produce a singular "optimal" prediction without any accompanying uncertainty quantification (UQ). A model might yield a prediction exceedingly close to the true value, devoid of any uncertainty estimation. Such "overconfident" predictions can lead to grave ramifications, especially in high-risk scenarios heavily reliant on prediction outcomes. Quantifying uncertainty in DL is particularly challenging, partly due to the intrinsic complexity and non-linearity of the models. Traditional statistical methods for uncertainty quantification often prove hard to directly implement.

13.2 Principles and framework of Bayesian deep learning

In recent years, DL has undoubtedly emerged as a revolutionary force in the realm of artificial intelligence, significantly advancing the fields of image recognition, language processing, and several other domains. By harnessing vast amounts of data and intricate neural network architectures, it can capture and emulate the intricate patterns found within the data. By merging the representational learning capabilities of DL with the uncertainty quantification of Bayesian methods, BDL offers a more holistic framework that prioritizes not just prediction accuracy but also the quantification of uncertainty surrounding those predictions.

13.2.1 Concept of Bayesian deep learning

BDL represents a framework that unifies DL and probabilistic graphical models [23]. Through the incorporation of Bayesian inference, BDL not only delivers predictions but also furnishes quantitative information about the uncertainty tied to these predictions [24], thereby introducing a crucial dimension to model predictions. By quantifying uncertainty, BDL can better evaluate risks, address the oversight of uncertainty in traditional DL, and consequently make more cautious and dependable decisions.

The distinction between BDL and DL lies in the transformation of weights and biases into distributions in BDL [25]. BDL has the following advantages:

1. BDL is more robust compared to non-BDL. This robustness arises since we can repeatedly sample, subtly adjusting weights, and thereby resolving the impacts on DL that are inherent in BDL.
2. BDL can provide genuine uncertainty, as opposed to probabilities generated by softmax.

It's imperative not to confuse Bayesian neural networks with Bayesian networks. A Bayesian network, also known as a belief network or directed acyclic graphical model, is a type of probabilistic graphical model [26]. In contrast, a Bayesian neural network is a fusion of Bayesian principles and neural networks, and the terms Bayesian neural network and BDL are sometimes used interchangeably.

In a variety of practical applications, such as medical diagnoses, recommendation systems, and complex dynamic control systems, traditional DL methods grapple with handling intricate inferences and uncertainties, especially when dealing with conditional modeling of high-dimensional data or managing various forms of uncertainties, pure DL often falls short. To counter these challenges, BDL approaches have been proposed, combining DL with probabilistic graphical models (PGM) [27], effectively integrating the perceptual strengths of DL with the inferential strengths of PGM. This synergy facilitates handling conditional dependencies of high-dimensional data and various uncertainties within a unified framework.

13.2.2 Comparison of Bayesian deep learning and deep learning

Generally speaking, traditional DL models provide an optimal prediction without offering any associated measure of uncertainty. However, in many real-world applications, especially within the realm of medical decision-making, accuracy and reliability are paramount [28]. Quantifying the uncertainty associated with model predictions can provide professionals with added insights to make better-informed decisions [29]. The uncertainty accounted for in BDL is indispensable in complex application scenarios. By introducing probability distributions to describe the uncertainty in model parameters and predictions, Bayesian inference can be applied to parameters and hyperparameters [30], eliminating reliance on manual selection. This allows the model to quantify prediction confidence and offers comprehensive uncertainty estimations alongside more accurate and reliable model evaluations. For instance, in medical imaging, a small dark spot might indicate a benign lesion or a malignant tumor. BDL provides a unified framework for handling such uncertainties by using distributions in place of point estimates. This uncertainty information enables physicians to make more informed decisions. For instance, in tumor diagnosis, BDL models can predict the likelihood of a tumor's presence and provide a confidence interval for this prediction. This informs physicians of the model's reliability, guiding further examinations or treatments. In medical signal processing, advanced techniques like BDL address various challenges, including the classification of mental fatigue, diagnosis of nocturnal hypoglycemia, and prediction of Parkinson's disease gait freezing.

Facing data scarcity, imbalance, or the presence of noise, BDL models typically demonstrate superior robustness and generalization than conventional DL models [31]. This can be attributed to the Bayesian framework which describes model parameters using probability distributions rather than fixed point estimates. Such representations capture the model's uncertainty towards data, thus fostering better generalization on new data. Concerning robustness and adversarial attacks,

BDL methods showcase heightened resilience against noise, outliers, and adversarial interventions by modeling uncertainty in both model parameters and predictions. Owing to its adept handling of uncertainties, parameter selection, and data scarcity, BDL ensures more accurate, reliable, and robust classification outcomes, positioning it as a promising approach in classification tasks. Therefore, BDL excels in scenarios with limited data availability. Particularly in medical research on rare diseases where high-quality, labeled data is scarce, BDL's quantification of uncertainty delineates the model's limitations on such datasets, negating blind trust in unreliable predictions. Moreover, BDL can enhance the reliability and safety of medical equipment. In life-support systems or automated surgical robots, an inaccurate prediction might have grave repercussions. By furnishing not just accurate but reliable predictions, BDL aids system developers and clinicians in evaluating potential risks more accurately.

Traditional DL models usually necessitate extensive labeled data to achieve satisfactory performance. BDL techniques allow for modeling and inference even with sparse data, bolstering the robust predictive capability for small and sparse datasets. Due to its ability to quantify uncertainty, BDL remains valuable even with limited data, granting it a significant edge in high-value yet data-scarce applications like medical image analysis and natural disaster forecasting. Concerning model interpretability, BDL accounts for three types of uncertainties: those related to neural network parameters, task-specific parameters, and information exchange between perceptual and task-specific components. This enhances the model's interpretability, which is crucial in fields with stringent demands on explainability and safety, such as medicine, law, and finance. Additionally, uncertainty quantification also enhances the explainability of medical decisions.

In essence, BDL amalgamates the robust representational capability of DL with Bayesian uncertainty quantification, furnishing comprehensive and trustworthy solutions to complex real-world problems. Whether in terms of model performance, robustness, or interpretability, BDL underscores its indispensable significance. It introduces a fresh dimension to medical decision-making, bolstering the confidence and decision-making process of medical experts by explicitly quantifying uncertainties. As further applications and research of BDL in the medical field unfold, its potential value in enhancing patient care and medical decision-making is anticipated to keep escalating.

13.2.3 Principles of Bayesian deep learning

The central tenet of BDL is the amalgamation of Bayesian statistics with the methodologies and principles of DL. It employs the likelihood of data and prior "expert" knowledge to construct posterior distributions [32], which can encapsulate varying degrees of modal uncertainty, culminating in the development and inference of a probabilistic model.

In traditional DL, the weights of the model are typically fixed numbers, adjusted during the training phase through optimization algorithms to minimize error. However, within the BDL framework, these weights are treated as variables with associated probability distributions. This implies that each weight is no longer a definitive value but rather a probability distribution [33], denoting the potential range and uncertainty of that weight. With the incorporation of probability distributions for model parameters, BDL employs Bayesian inference, particularly posterior inference, to update these probability distributions of the model parameters based on observed data, refining activation functions and weights. By integrating likelihood with priors through Bayes' theorem, a posterior measure of the weight space is derived, where standard neural network training can be viewed as an approximation of Bayesian inference. Compared to traditional DL models, BDL endeavors to integrate uncertainty considerations across all facets of the model. From model parameters to predictions, each aspect bears a probabilistic nuance [34].

BDL presents a principled probabilistic framework with two seamlessly integrated components [35]: the perceptual component and the task-specific component.

These two components can be illustrated as follows: Figure 13.1 showcases a simple BDL model via a probabilistic graphical model (PGM). Within this figure, the portion enclosed by the red rectangle on the left signifies the perceptual component, while the blue rectangle on the right encapsulates the task-specific component. Typically, the perceptual component represents the probabilistic formulation of a DL model, which comprises multiple nonlinear processing layers depicted as a chained structure in the PGM. In contrast, the nodes and edges within the task-specific component often describe more intricate distributions and relationships among variables. Specifically, the task-specific component can adopt various forms. For instance, it could manifest as a classical Bayesian network (a directed PGM), such as latent Dirichlet allocation (LDA), deep Bayesian networks, or stochastic processes, all of which can be depicted in the format of a PGM.

In traditional DL, models typically produce a singular most likely prediction. However, within the BDL framework, predictions are uncertain due to the inherent uncertainty of model parameters. This implies that BDL does not just output a single prediction; it rather provides an associated uncertainty or probability distribution linked to that prediction, as illustrated in Figure 13.2. Such a feature is invaluable for scenarios that require not just point estimates but also uncertainty estimations, such as in medical diagnostics or financial risk assessments. Consequently, BDL not only offers more accurate and dependable predictions but also quantifies the uncertainty of these predictions, providing richer information for

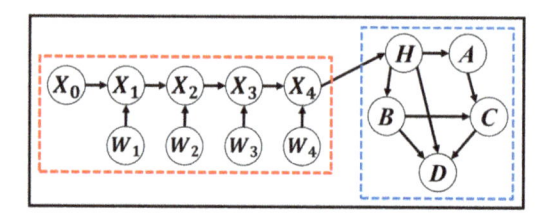

Figure 13.1 BDL probabilistic graphical model

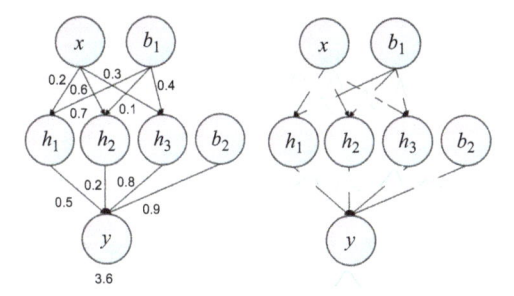

Figure 13.2 Differences between classical neural networks and Bayesian neural networks

decision-making. This characteristic positions BDL as particularly suitable for complex tasks and applications demanding high precision and reliability. On another note, to address various types of model uncertainty, BDL focuses on determining the posterior distributions of weights. Probability distributions of any form, such as Gaussian, Beta, Gamma, or Exponential, can be chosen as likelihood and prior distributions (Figure 13.2) [36].

BDL typically handles two types of uncertainties: aleatory uncertainty and epistemic uncertainty [37]. Aleatory uncertainty is a sophisticated data uncertainty that is not a characteristic of the model but an intrinsic attribute of the data distribution. Conversely, epistemic uncertainty arises due to inadequate knowledge within the model framework. To quantify this epistemic uncertainty, one can opt for different models to address various questions within model-based predictions.

A paramount feature of BDL is its ability to quantify uncertainty, rather than merely delivering a single prediction output. BDL can furnish a probability distribution for prediction results, pivotal for evaluating the model's confidence in its predictions, especially in critical decision-making scenarios such as medical diagnosis or financial forecasting. First, BDL exhibits robust generalization capabilities. By probabilistically modeling parameters, BDL usually generalizes more effectively to unseen data. This generalization capacity becomes particularly vital when the training data is limited, or the model complexity is high, potentially leading to overfitting. Second, BDL is apt for active learning. In situations with limited data labeling resources, BDL can guide the data collection process. The model can pinpoint data instances it is most uncertain about, prioritizing their labeling. Third, given that BDL incorporates model uncertainty, it often showcases enhanced robustness when faced with external noise or adversarial attacks. In decision-making applications, the uncertainty quantification provided by BDL offers decision-makers an added dimension of risk-aware decision-making.

13.2.4 Bayesian deep learning frameworks

BDL marries the representational prowess of DL with the uncertainty management capability of Bayesian statistics, presenting a potent tool for large-scale medical data analytics. The following describes four distinct frameworks [38], each dedicated to offering users accessible, efficient, and flexible probabilistic modeling tools. The choice of an appropriate framework depends on specific application needs, data characteristics, and computational resources.

13.2.4.1 BoTorch

BoTorch is a lightweight API closely integrated with the GPyTorch probabilistic model [39]. It supports the optimization of any model that can sample from a posterior distribution, with a particular emphasis on efficient Gaussian process (GP) modeling. It forms part of the PyTorch ecosystem.

BoTorch operates primarily using quasi-Monte Carlo acquisition functions. Leveraging the "reparameterization trick" and quasi-Monte Carlo acquisition functions, it facilitates the effortless implementation of new methods without the need for deriving analytical expressions or making restrictive assumptions. This offers users a powerful and efficient approach to handle GP modeling tasks. BoTorch provides a modular and easily extensible interface for composing Bayesian optimization primitives. It's designed for optimizing costly-to-evaluate black-box functions, such as hyperparameter tuning of machine learning algorithms, A/B testing, and other scientific and engineering challenges. Its highly modular design benefits from PyTorch's automatic differentiation and GPU parallelization capabilities, ensuring efficient optimization. While there might be an initial learning curve for users unfamiliar with PyTorch or Bayesian optimization, BoTorch effectively bridges research and production. It integrates seamlessly with platforms like Ax, supplying robust tools for hyperparameter tuning, A/B testing, and optimization of other complex problems.

13.2.4.2 Edward

Edward is a probabilistic programming library based on TensorFlow [40]. Specifically designed as a Python library for constructing and inferring probabilistic models, Edward serves for probabilistic modeling, inference, and evaluation. It integrates principles from Bayesian statistics, machine learning, DL, and probabilistic programming, facilitating swift experimentation and research across a spectrum of probabilistic models – from classic hierarchical models on smaller datasets to intricate deep probabilistic models on large datasets. It offers utilities found in core DL ecosystems, enabling models to be scripted as probabilistic programs and calculations within models to be manipulated, providing flexible training and inference.

Edward is defined by interchangeable components. Its core components encompass random variables, inference, and evaluation/critique. It represents random variables for various probabilistic distributions, including but not limited to normal and Bernoulli distributions. The inference in Edward encapsulates numerous built-in algorithms such as variational inference and Monte Carlo methods. For evaluation/critique, once a model has been trained, Edward offers tools like posterior predictive checks. These components epitomize the foundations of probabilistic modeling, allowing researchers to effortlessly employ probabilistic models for swift experimentation and study.

Research on the application of Bayesian DL in medical big data 279

Edward's primary strengths include its high flexibility, support for an array of inference algorithms, capabilities to harness GPU acceleration and TensorFlow's automatic differentiation, and its modular design. However, its learning curve is somewhat steep, and with the evolution of TensorFlow Probability (TFP), Edward might no longer be the primary focus, potentially leading to maintenance challenges. For specific inferences, deep knowledge might be essential to attain optimal performance. Nonetheless, its extensive probabilistic modeling capabilities render it a valuable tool across a diverse range of research and application fields like time series analysis, topic modeling, and latent variable modeling, equipping users with powerful tools to address uncertainty and complexity.

13.2.4.3 TensorFlow probability

TensorFlow is a versatile open-source DL framework developed by Google. It boasts flexibility and robust functionalities, operable across a plethora of platforms such as CPUs, GPUs, and other mobile devices, supporting contemporary popular DL models. TFP is a Python library built atop TensorFlow [41], furnishing users with tools to utilize probabilistic models and DL on modern hardware platforms like TPUs and GPUs.

TFP combines the computational prowess of TensorFlow with a comprehensive suite of probabilistic programming tools. This amalgamation empowers researchers to seamlessly design, fit, and deploy probabilistic models. Its hierarchical functioning is illustrated as shown in Table 13.1. (Note: The table is not provided in the original text and hence not translated here.)

Table 13.1   Hierarchical working principle table

Level	Function	Component name and description
Level 0	Numerical computations	TensorFlow: The LinearOperator class supports matrix-free implementations for efficient computations. Now part of the core TF under tf.linalg.
Level 1	Statistical building blocks	Distributions (tfp.distributions): A comprehensive range of probability distributions and related statistical data, supporting batch processing and broadcast semantics. Bijectors (tfp.bijectors): Reversible and composable transformations of random variables, offering a rich category of transformed distributions.
Level 2	Model construction	Joint distributions: Joint distributions of multiple potentially interdependent distributions. Probabilistic layers (tfp.layers): Representations of functions in neural network layers with uncertainty.
Level 3	Probabilistic inference	Markov Chain Monte Carlo (tfp.mcmc): Algorithms that approximate integrals via sampling, including Hamiltonian Monte Carlo and others. Variational Inference (tfp.vi): Algorithms that approximate integrals via optimization. Optimizers (tfp.optimizer): Stochastic optimization methods, such as Stochastic Gradient Langevin Dynamics. Monte Carlo Tools (tfp.monte_carlo): Tools for computing Monte Carlo expectations.

TFP inherits the core strengths of TensorFlow, such as automatic differentiation and optimized performance across various hardware platforms. Concurrently, TFP's ability to highly integrate with other tools and libraries within the TensorFlow ecosystem renders it invaluable throughout the entire probabilistic modeling process, from data modeling and inference to prediction. However, its deep integration with TensorFlow implies that users may need to have some familiarity with TensorFlow to maximize its potential. In essence, TFP is designed for data scientists, statisticians, and machine learning researchers, especially when faced with complex tasks such as constructing generative data models, quantifying prediction uncertainties, handling high-dimensional feature data, and leveraging structured data.

13.2.4.4 Pyro

Pyro is an open-source deep probabilistic programming language designed specifically for probabilistic modeling [42]. Leveraging a probabilistic programming language (PPL) allows for a blend of standard deterministic computations with random sampling values, culminating in stochastic computation. Inference problems can be articulated as probabilistic programs based on observed outcomes, capable of capturing intricate inferences and uncovering structure in unlabeled data. Pyro elucidates inference within models through a secondary model called a "guide," analogous to translating data into latent choice narratives. For approximate inference, Pyro employs variational techniques by specifying a parameterized guide family and resolving an optimization problem to approximate the model's posterior distribution. The auto-differentiation capabilities provided by the PyTorch library, combined with tensor mathematics accelerated by GPUs, gradient descent methods, and variational inference, are crucial. Moreover, PyTorch's tensor mathematics is GPU-accelerated, proving beneficial for large models and datasets.

The main advantage of Pyro is its amalgamation of probabilistic and programming capabilities, allowing for direct specification of probabilistic models, all built on Python. This makes defining and implementing probabilistic models straightforward. It capitalizes on PyTorch's dynamic gradient-building capacity, enabling Pyro programs to include stochastic control structures. Additionally, Pyro offers optimization-based automatic inference, making it flexible and scalable to large datasets. Yet, inference remains a paramount challenge in probabilistic modeling, and non-scalable inferences might be a common pitfall in PPLs. For problems where evaluating the objective function is prohibitively expensive or time-consuming, such as hyperparameter tuning, Pyro can execute Bayesian optimization to efficiently locate optimal solutions. The fusion of probabilistic modeling with DL capabilities positions Pyro as a formidable tool for implementing a variety of reinforcement learning algorithms, especially those involving model uncertainty and exploration-exploitation trade-offs.

Beyond the frameworks mentioned, there are others like GPyTorch, BLiTZ, ZhuSuan, among others.

13.2.5 Common algorithms in Bayesian deep learning

A comparison of frequently used BDL algorithms is shown in Table 13.2.

Table 13.2   Comparison of common BDL algorithms

Tech cat.	Method	Advantages	Limitations	App scenarios
Approx Inf	Var Bayes (VB)	Easy to optimize, Fast	Potentially inaccurate	Large-scale data, Online learning
	Laplace Approx (LA)	Fast computation, Suitable for large data	Suited only for unimodal distribution	Model selection and parameter estimation
	MC Dropout (MCD)	Easy to implement; No network modifications needed	Depends on Dropout choice	Uncertainty estimation in deep learning models
	Bayes by Backprop (BBB)	Accounts for weight uncertainty	Needs more computational resources	Complex DL tasks, crucial uncertainty
Deep Bayes Models	Bayesian Neural Network (BNN – Conv/Rec)	Estimates uncertainty, More robust	Higher computation and storage requirements	Image classification, Time-series analysis
MC Sampling	Monte Carlo Methods (MCMC/HMC)	Samples complex posterior, Fast convergence	Might need extended time or gradient information	Deep probabilistic models, High-dimensional sampling
Other Bayes Tech	Bayesian Active Learning (BAL)	Selects valuable data	Requires a good initial dataset	Data collection
	Auto-Encoding Variational Bayes (AEVB)	Non-linear dimension reduction, Generative model	Architectural adjustments	Generative models, Data reconstruction

13.3   Applications of Bayesian deep learning in medical big data

In the modern medical domain, the significance of data is increasingly emphasized, especially with the continuous advancements in big data and DL technologies. Against this backdrop, BDL has emerged as a distinctive solution for medical big data. This technology not only handles vast amounts of data but also offers model uncertainty, which is pivotal for medical decision-making. DL models integrated with Bayesian methods have achieved success in various medical applications, such as medical image analysis, life science research [43], clinical diagnostic assistance [44], and pharmaceutical management [45]. This approach offers medical professionals enhanced predictive accuracy and bolsters model interpretability, assisting doctors in making more informed decisions.

13.3.1 Medical image analysis

Medical image analysis stands as one of the most challenging and valuable sectors within medical big data. Although traditional image processing methods have excelled in certain applications, they struggle with large-scale, high-dimensional medical image data. BDL, as an approach combining DL with Bayesian inference, showcases robustness, generalization capabilities, and the ability to analyze uncertainty.

Conventional MRI analyses often exhibit limitations, such as inadequate accuracy and an oversight of uncertainty. However, BDL-based cerebral 1H-MRS analysis and NPBDREG image registration algorithms are revolutionizing this landscape. These methods not only enhance the accuracy of medical MRI images but also efficiently estimate the uncertainty of results, furnishing stronger support for clinical decision-making. Lee *et al.* utilized a non-parametric BDL approach to assess the uncertainty of differential morphological brain MRI registration [46]. The uncertainty estimation in brain MRI image registration using the NPBDREG image registration algorithm contrasts with common DNN-based algorithms. Unlike traditional DNN-based image registration algorithms, NPBDREG emphasizes uncertainty estimation, aiming to mitigate the possibility of suboptimal clinical decisions. It surmounts the potential inaccuracies of available uncertainty estimation methods, exhibiting superior generalization against mixed structural noise, thus enhancing clinical decision-making quality.

DL's high accuracy in X-ray image analysis, particularly using the Bayesian convolutional neural network (BCNN), not only provides precise detection of COVID-19 but also quantifies the uncertainty of its prediction results. Similarly, UncertaintyFuseNet, a deep learning model, achieves 99.08% accuracy for CT scans and 96.35% for X-ray images in COVID-19 detection. Unlike most studies, which overlook uncertainty, this model incorporates the Ensemble Monte Carlo Dropout (EMCD) technique to quantify prediction uncertainty [47]. This approach enhances the accuracy of COVID-19 detection while addressing uncertainty, offering significant value in today's complex medical environment.

The BCNN based on Dropweights is a CNN that integrates Bayesian inference. By utilizing Dropweights within the network, which entails randomly shutting off certain weights during the training and inference processes, the model captures the uncertainty of its prediction outcomes. Compared to traditional DL models, the Dropweights-based BCNN possesses two primary advantages. First, it quantifies uncertainty, a feat often unattainable by conventional DL models. This not only augments model interpretability but can also earn the trust of doctors as they can gauge the model's predictive confidence more accurately. Second, research has demonstrated a strong correlation between the model's prediction uncertainty and its accuracy. This implies that the higher the model's uncertainty for its predictions, the greater the likelihood of an error in its results.

13.3.2 Research in life sciences

Within the domain of life science research, BDL technology has extensive applications. In 1H-MRS studies of the brain, methods employing BCN combined with

MC Dropout sampling have enhanced the accuracy and uncertainty estimation for metabolite quantification [48].

Khawaled *et al.* developed a method integrating BCN with MC Dropout, utilizing MC Dropout for metabolite quantification and uncertainty estimation, particularly in brain proton magnetic resonance spectroscopy (1H-MRS) studies based on DL. This method aims to enhance the reliability of machine-predicted metabolite content. The research first trained the BCN using simulated spectra and actual in vivo spectra to produce metabolite spectra that are free of noise, linewidth, and signals from large molecules. During the inference of metabolite content, the MC Dropout sampling method was adopted, sampling each input spectrum 50 times to obtain average and variance spectra for metabolite quantification and uncertainty estimation. This overcomes deficiencies in traditional methods of metabolite quantification and uncertainty estimation. The combination of BCN and MC Dropout sampling heightens the reliability and accuracy of machine-predicted metabolite content. Compared to traditional LCModel methods, BCN has a higher correlation between changes in metabolite content and uncertainty. Through the use of simulated and actual in vivo spectra, researchers demonstrated the practicality of BCN with MC Dropout sampling in 1H-MRS studies based on DL. BCN successfully predicted the content of various metabolites with an average absolute percentage error of less than 10%, and even lower for some metabolites. Additionally, the uncertainty estimation of BCN has a higher correlation with actual data compared to traditional methods, indicating superior performance.

13.3.3 Clinical diagnostic assistance

Medical diagnosis, as the cornerstone of the modern medical system, is of paramount importance for the timely and accurate prevention and treatment of diseases. In recent years, BDL has demonstrated its potential advantages in various medical diagnostic areas, especially when dealing with complex data exhibiting uncertainty.

In the diagnosis of eye diseases, the introduction of BDL offers novel possibilities for the diagnosis of glaucoma, especially when handling multi-modal data. Chai *et al.* developed a BDL model centered on uncertainty information [49]. The research aimed to address challenges in glaucoma diagnosis by combining multi-modal data (including medical indicators, images, and text) and considering uncertainty information, introducing a Bayesian deep multi-source learning (BDMSL) model. This model integrates information from various data sources using multi-source learning and adopts BDL to capture model uncertainty. This means the model can not only diagnose but also provide a measure of uncertainty associated with the diagnosis, enhancing the reliability of diagnostic outcomes. Traditional methods usually only offer definitive diagnostic results. The BDMSL model amalgamates data sources, such as medical indicators, images, and text, to improve the comprehensiveness of the diagnosis. Research findings suggest that the BDMSL model outperforms other methods in glaucoma detection. By considering uncertainty information and integrating multi-modal data, the BDMSL model offers a more reliable and efficient approach for automated glaucoma diagnosis.

In predicting cardiovascular diseases, heartbeat data as a non-invasive means to predict these diseases has gained substantial attention in recent years. BDL offers a novel approach to extract emotional and health information from this data. Harper R and his team devised an end-to-end BDL framework specifically for predicting emotional states from heart rate time series data, typically provided by low-cost heart monitors [50]. Unlike traditional DL models, this framework is designed explicitly for single-modal heart rate data and introduces a Bayesian structure to quantify prediction uncertainty, providing critical confidence measures for decision-making. Moreover, a unique probabilistic procedure in the model takes into account the real-world need to accept or reject model outputs based on prediction uncertainty, offering a more reliable basis for decisions in practical applications. Empirical evidence indicates a peak classification accuracy of 90%. This high accuracy, combined with its ability to handle uncertainty, makes this model particularly suitable for sectors with stringent requirements for non-invasive data collection and prediction certainty, such as healthcare.

In skin cancer classification and treatment, early detection and categorization of skin cancer are crucial for the successful treatment of the disease. With advancements in medical imaging technologies, there's a demand for more sophisticated analytical tools to process this image data. BDL offers new methods for the classification and diagnosis of skin cancer images and seeks to address the uncertainty problems inherent in traditional methods. Abdar et al. utilized BDL based on ternary decision-making to quantify the uncertainty in skin cancer classification and carried out skin cancer image classification [51]. The study employed a BDL approach to quantify the classification uncertainty of DL models. Specifically, they introduced three uncertainty quantification methods: MC Dropout, EEMC and DE. Furthermore, a novel hybrid dynamic BDL model was proposed, based on ternary decision-making theory (TWD), to further reduce residual uncertainty. Compared to conventional DL methods, the BDL approach introduces uncertainty quantification of classification results, effectively overcoming the overconfidence issue in traditional methods which might lead to erroneous decisions. Notably, the hybrid dynamic BDL model permits the flexible use of different quantification strategies and network structures during the classification stage to cater to various data and requirements. Experimental results demonstrate the model ensures cautious classification decisions on the skin cancer dataset and exhibits outstanding performance in accuracy and F1 score, affirming its utility and efficiency in medical image analysis.

13.4 Challenges faced by Bayesian deep learning in the application of medical big data

BDL, by integrating the advantages of Bayesian inference and the powerful representational capacity of DL, offers promising directions for numerous applications, especially in the realm of medical big data. However, in practical implementations, this approach also confronts various challenges.

13.4.1 Computational complexity and resource demands

One major concern is computational complexity. Bayesian methods necessitate the estimation of posterior distributions for models. This often involves intricate mathematical procedures, such as MCMC sampling or variational inference, which can be particularly time-consuming with large datasets or intricate model architectures [52]. To exacerbate matters, DL models typically have millions to billions of parameters, drastically intensifying the computational demands of Bayesian methods. Compared to conventional DL methods, BDL requires significantly more storage resources [53]. This is not merely for storing model parameters but also for preserving information about the uncertainty related to these parameters. Such requirements, especially when dealing with vast datasets like medical imaging data, might surpass the computational capacities of many labs or hospitals. Although BDL offers uncertainty estimates for model predictions, it doesn't necessarily mean it always delivers superior predictions. In certain circumstances, incorporating Bayesian techniques might slightly degrade the model's performance, particularly when the available data is limited or the model itself is exceedingly complex.

13.4.2 Modeling and interpretation of model uncertainty

Starting with modeling strategies, we are essentially exploring how to fuse Bayesian methods with DL and how to choose appropriate prior distributions for model parameters [54]. Given the unique nature of medical data, this integration is crucial for the model's efficacy. First, model designs must be tailored to specific medical issues and data types. For example, 3D medical images might be suitable for 3D CNNs, while time series data like electrocardiograms might require RNNs or long short-term memory networks. Second, the selection of prior distributions is pivotal within the Bayesian framework, as it reflects beliefs about parameters before observing any data. Although broad non-informative priors are common, the unique context of medical data occasionally permits the use of more informative priors. Additionally, given the scarcity and high-dimensionality of medical data, variational Bayesian methods have emerged as a preferable choice. They can effectively approximate posterior distributions, enhance computational efficiency, and modulate model complexity to prevent overfitting. Lastly, to bolster model robustness, ensemble techniques, such as utilizing Dropout as a Bayesian approximation, present a method to simulate uncertainty within models.

In terms of interpreting results, a distinctive aspect of BDL is that it provides a measure of uncertainty for model predictions [54–56]. This measure is paramount in medical applications, assisting clinicians in conducting more in-depth examinations or consultations when predictions are uncertain. Decisions in the medical domain typically demand clarity and precision, so information on model uncertainty might lead to decision hesitancy or inappropriate medical choices. While

Bayesian approaches offer a means to quantify uncertainty, this also introduces challenges in interpretation. How the model's uncertainty information is interpreted and applied remains an outstanding issue.

Ensuring the efficacy and robustness of BDL models is vitally important in medical big data [55]. Given the scarcity, imbalance, and high dimensionality of medical big data, evaluations become even more challenging. Conventional evaluation metrics might not be suitable for these models, prompting the need for new evaluation metrics to ensure prediction accuracy and the appropriateness of probability distributions. In medical big data applications, not only should the accuracy of BDL model predictions be considered, but also their provided uncertainty estimates. Conventional evaluation techniques might fall short of fully appraising such models, especially in cases of sparse or imbalanced data. Given the high stakes in the medical field, model evaluations must also ensure their real-world safety and reliability. These novel challenges necessitate a rethinking of evaluation strategies to ensure models are both robust and safe in medical decision-making.

13.4.3 Challenges and prospects

The application of BDL in big data-assisted healthcare is gradually revealing its latent value. With the continuous growth of medical big data, this technology is ushering in transformative changes in medical practice and research. Not only does it demonstrate outstanding capabilities in modeling complex data, but it also imparts more certainty to medical decision-making. The essence of Bayesian methods lies in estimating uncertainty, which is crucial for diagnostic or therapeutic recommendations in the medical domain. Despite these advantages, many challenges still loom over the application of BDL in healthcare.

First, data bias remains a predominant issue. Many studies cannot share their data and code due to confidentiality constraints, making method verification and result reproduction difficult. Second, due to the diversity and heterogeneity of medical data, model generalization emerges as a significant challenge. This means a model might perform exceptionally on one dataset but fail on another. Data privacy is also a core concern, especially considering the sensitive personal health information embedded in the data. While data sharing can propel research forward, it also escalates the risks of privacy breaches. Lastly, despite the impressive performance of DL models in medical applications, their "black box" nature is frequently criticized.

Currently, BDL offers immense potential in big data-assisted healthcare. In the future, we anticipate that with enhanced computational capabilities, BDL models will become increasingly complex, better capturing the subtle structures and patterns in data. First, elevated model complexity brings about more precise data modeling capabilities for medical applications. As computational prowess grows, complex models can discern subtle data structures and patterns, thus offering more accurate diagnostic recommendations to clinicians. Second, the cornerstone of Bayesian methods is the estimation of uncertainty. In the medical domain, evaluating the uncertainty of a diagnosis or therapeutic recommendation is vitally important. Integrating with other techniques opens up novel application domains for BDL, not only enhancing model performance but also broadening its applicability in healthcare. Finally, improving interpretability and transparency remains a pressing issue for DL applications in healthcare. Even though these models excel in diagnosis and prediction, their "black box" nature often raises eyebrows. Providing a model that clinicians and patients can understand and trust becomes crucial. By enhancing model interpretability, we can gain a deeper understanding of how decisions are made, thereby offering a more solid foundation for medical decisions.

References

[1] Suganyadevi, S., V. Seethalakshmi, and K. Balasamy, A review on deep learning in medical image analysis. *International Journal of Multimedia Information Retrieval*, 2022. 11(1): p. 19–38.

[2] Chen, X., Wang, X., Zhang, K., *et al.*, Recent advances and clinical applications of deep learning in medical image analysis. *Medical Image Analysis*, 2022. 79: p. 102444.

[3] Yu, Y., Li, M., Liu, L., *et al.*, Clinical big data and deep learning: Applications, challenges, and future outlooks. *Big Data Mining and Analytics*, 2019. 2(4): p. 288–305.

[4] Liu, S., *et al.*, Deep learning in medical ultrasound analysis: A review. *Engineering*, 2019. 5(2): p. 261–275.

[5] Tran, D., Hoffman, M. D., Moore, D., *et al.*, Simple, distributed, and accelerated probabilistic programming. *Advances in Neural Information Processing Systems*, 2018. 31: p. 7609–7620.

[6] Lundervold, A.S. and A. Lundervold, An overview of deep learning in medical imaging focusing on MRI. *Zeitschrift für Medizinische Physik*, 2019. 29(2): p. 102–127.

[7] Roberts, D.A., S. Yaida, and B. Hanin, *The Principles of Deep Learning Theory*. 2022: Cambridge University Press Cambridge, MA, USA.

[8] Bórquez, S., Pezoa, R., Salinas, L., and Torres, C. E., Uncertainty estimation in the classification of histopathological images with HER2 overexpression using Monte Carlo Dropout. *Biomedical Signal Processing and Control*, 2023. 85: p. 104864.

[9] Sedai, S., Antony, B., Mahapatra, D., and Garnavi, R., Joint segmentation and uncertainty visualization of retinal layers in optical coherence tomography images using Bayesian deep learning. *In Computational Pathology and Ophthalmic Medical Image Analysis: First International Workshop, COMPAY 2018, and 5th International Workshop, OMIA 2018, Held in Conjunction with MICCAI 2018*, Granada, Spain, September 16–20, 2018, Proceedings 5. 2018. Springer.

[10] Jospin, L.V., Laga, H., Boussaid, F., Buntine, W., and Bennamoun, M., Hands-on Bayesian neural networks—A tutorial for deep learning users. *IEEE Computational Intelligence Magazine*, 2022. 17(2): p. 29–48.

[11] Kwon, Y., Won, J. H., Kim, B. J., and Paik, M. C., Uncertainty quantification using Bayesian neural networks in classification: Application to biomedical image segmentation. *Computational Statistics & Data Analysis*, 2020. 142: p. 106816.

[12] Yang, X., *et al.*, A large language model for electronic health records. *NPJ Digital Medicine*, 2022. 5(1): p. 194.

[13] Cerchione, R., Centobelli, P., Riccio, E., Abbate, S., and Oropallo, E., Blockchain's coming to hospital to digitalize healthcare services: Designing a distributed electronic health record ecosystem. *Technovation*, 2023. 120: p. 102480.

[14] Li, I., Pan, J, Goldwasser, J, *et al.*, Neural natural language processing for unstructured data in electronic health records: A review. *Computer Science Review*, 2022. 46: p. 100511.

[15] Vuong, Q.-H., Le, T. T., La, V. P., and Nguyen, M. H., The psychological mechanism of internet information processing for post-treatment evaluation. *Heliyon*, 2022. 8(5): e09351.

[16] Ji, Y., Bai, H., Ge, C., *et al.*, AMOS: A large-scale abdominal multi-organ benchmark for versatile medical image segmentation. *Advances in Neural Information Processing Systems*, 2022. 35: p. 36722–36732.

[17] Sreedevi, A., *et al.*, Application of cognitive computing in healthcare, cybersecurity, big data and IoT: A literature review. *Information Processing & Management*, 2022. 59(2): p. 102888.

[18] Banabilah, S., *et al.*, Federated learning review: Fundamentals, enabling technologies, and future applications. *Information Processing & Management*, 2022. 59(6): p. 103061.

[19] Abdar, M., *et al.*, A review of uncertainty quantification in deep learning: Techniques, applications and challenges. *Information Fusion*, 2021. 76: p. 243–297.

[20] Gawlikowski, J., Tassi, C. R. N., Ali, M., *et al.*, A survey of uncertainty in deep neural networks. *Artificial Intelligence Review*, 2023:56(Suppl 1): 1513–1589.

[21] Wilson, A.G. and P. Izmailov, Bayesian deep learning and a probabilistic perspective of generalization. *Advances in Neural Information Processing Systems*, 2020. 33: p. 4697–4708.

[22] Peng, W., Z.-S. Ye, and N. Chen, Bayesian deep-learning-based health prognostics toward prognostics uncertainty. *IEEE Transactions on Industrial Electronics*, 2019. 67(3): p. 2283–2293.

[23] Kendall, A. and Y. Gal, What uncertainties do we need in Bayesian deep learning for computer vision? *Advances in Neural Information Processing Systems*, 2017. 30: 5580–5590.

[24] Abdullah, A.A., M.M. Hassan, and Y.T. Mustafa, A review on Bayesian deep learning in healthcare: Applications and challenges. *IEEE Access*, 2022. 10: p. 36538–36562.

[25] Ashukha, A., Lyzhov, A., Molchanov, D., *et al.*, Pitfalls of in-domain uncertainty estimation and ensembling in deep learning. International

Conference on Learning Representations. 2020. Available from: https://openreview.net/forum?id=BJxI5gHKDr

[26] Zhang, D., T. Liu, and J. Kang, Density regression and uncertainty quantification with Bayesian deep noise neural networks. *Stat*, 2023. 12(1): p. e604.

[27] García-Franco, J.D., Díez, F.J., Carrasco, M.Á., Probabilistic graphical model for the evaluation of the emotional and dramatic personality disorders [J]. *Frontiers in Psychology*, 2022, 13: 996609.

[28] Zou, K., Chen, Z., Yuan, X., et al., A review of uncertainty estimation and its application in medical imaging. *arXiv* preprint arXiv:2302.08119, 2023: 100003.

[29] Mena, J., O. Pujol, and J. Vitria, A survey on uncertainty estimation in deep learning classification systems from a Bayesian perspective. *ACM Computing Surveys (CSUR)*, 2021. 54(9): p. 1–35.

[30] Maddox, W.J., Garipov, T, Izmailov, P, et al., A simple baseline for Bayesian uncertainty in deep learning. *Advances in Neural Information Processing Systems*, 2019, 32: 13153–13164.

[31] Ismail, H.R. and M.M. Hassan, Bayesian deep learning methods applied to diabetic retinopathy disease: A review. *Indonesian Journal of Electrical Engineering and Computer Science*, 2023. 30(2): p. 1167–1177.

[32] McDermott, P.L. and C.K. Wikle, Bayesian recurrent neural network models for forecasting and quantifying uncertainty in spatial-temporal data. *Entropy*, 2019. 21(2): p. 184.

[33] Wang, H. and D.-Y. Yeung, A survey on Bayesian deep learning. *ACM Computing Surveys (CSUR)*, 2020. 53(5): p. 1–37.

[34] Tran, B.-H., Rossi, S., Milios, D., et al., All you need is a good functional prior for Bayesian deep learning. *The Journal of Machine Learning Research*, 2022. 23(1): p. 3210–3265.

[35] Shridhar, K., F. Laumann, and M. Liwicki, A comprehensive guide to Bayesian convolutional neural network with variational inference. *arXiv* preprint arXiv:1901.02731, 2019.

[36] Kapoor, S., Maddox, W. J., Izmailov, P., et al., On uncertainty, tempering, and data augmentation in Bayesian classification. *Advances in Neural Information Processing Systems*, 2022. 35: p. 18211–18225.

[37] Hüllermeier, E. and W. Waegeman, Aleatoric and epistemic uncertainty in machine learning: An introduction to concepts and methods. *Machine Learning*, 2021. 110: p. 457–506.

[38] Goan, E. and C. Fookes, Bayesian neural networks: An introduction and survey. *Case Studies in Applied Bayesian Data Science: CIRM Jean-Morlet Chair, Fall 2018*, 2020: 2259: 45.

[39] Balandat, M., Karrer, B, Jiang, D, et al., BoTorch: A framework for efficient Monte-Carlo Bayesian optimization. *Advances in Neural Information Processing Systems*, 2020. 33: p. 21524–21538.

[40] Tran, D., Dusenberry, M., Van Der Wilk, M., and Hafner, D., Bayesian layers : A module for neural network uncertainty. *Advances in Neural Information Processing Systems*, 2019. 32: 14660–14672.

[41] Dürr, O., B. Sick, and E. Murina, *Probabilistic Deep Learning: With Python, Keras and Tensorflow Probability*. 2020: Shelter Island, NY: Manning Publications.
[42] Bingham, E., Chen, J. P., Jankowiak, M., et al., Pyro: Deep universal probabilistic programming. *The Journal of Machine Learning Research*, 2019. 20 (1): p. 973–978.
[43] Blundell, C., Cornebise, J., Kavukcuoglu, K, et al. Weight uncertainty in neural network. in *International Conference on Machine Learning*. 2015. PMLR.
[44] Daxberger, E., et al., Laplace redux-effortless Bayesian deep learning. *Advances in Neural Information Processing Systems*, 2021. 34: p. 20089–20103.
[45] Yu, J., D. Wang, and M. Zheng, Uncertainty quantification: Can we trust artificial intelligence in drug discovery? *Iscience*, 2022, 25(8).
[46] Lee, H.H. and H. Kim, Bayesian deep learning-based 1H-MRS of the brain: Metabolite quantification with uncertainty estimation using Monte Carlo dropout. *Magnetic Resonance in Medicine*, 2022. 88(1): p. 38–52.
[47] Abdar, M., Salari, S., Qahremani, S., et al., UncertaintyFuseNet: robust uncertainty-aware hierarchical feature fusion model with ensemble Monte Carlo dropout for COVID-19 detection. *Information Fusion*, 2023, 90: 364–381.
[48] Khawaled, S. and M. Freiman, NPBDREG: Uncertainty assessment in diffeomorphic brain MRI registration using a non-parametric Bayesian deep-learning based approach. *Computerized Medical Imaging and Graphics*, 2022. 99: p. 102087.
[49] Chai, Y., Bian, Y., Liu, H., et al., Glaucoma diagnosis in the Chinese context: An uncertainty information-centric Bayesian deep learning model. *Information Processing & Management*, 2021. 58(2): p. 102454.
[50] Harper, R. and J. Southern, A Bayesian deep learning framework for end-to-end prediction of emotion from heartbeat. *IEEE Transactions on Affective Computing*, 2020. 13(2): p. 985–991.
[51] Abdar, M., Samami, M., Mahmoodabad, S.D., et al., Uncertainty quantification in skin cancer classification using three-way decision-based Bayesian deep learning. *Computers in Biology and Medicine*, 2021. 135: p. 104418.
[52] Tran, T., Do, T.T., Reid, I., et al. Bayesian generative active deep learning. in *International Conference on Machine Learning*. 2019. PMLR.
[53] Hernández, S. and J.L. López, Uncertainty quantification for plant disease detection using Bayesian deep learning. *Applied Soft Computing*, 2020. 96: p. 106597.
[54] Mena, J., Pujol, O., Vitrià, J. et al., A survey on uncertainty estimation in deep learning classification systems from a bayesian perspective. *ACM Computing Surveys (CSUR)*, 2021, 54(9): 1–35.
[55] Dera, D., Bouaynaya, N.C., Rasool, G., et al., Premium-CNN: Propagating uncertainty towards robust convolutional neural networks. *IEEE Transactions on Signal Processing*, 2021. 69: p. 4669–4684.
[56] Li, Y., Rao, S., Hassaine, A., et al. Deep Bayesian Gaussian processes for uncertainty estimation in electronic health records. *Scientific reports*, 2021, 11(1): 20685.

Chapter 14
Causal inference in healthcare: effective evaluation of clinical programs and other applications

Zhen Hu[1], Jing Fan[2], Deyu Sun[3], Haipeng Liu[4] and Vikram Bandugula[5]

14.1 Introduction

14.1.1 Motivation and objectives

The pursuit of causal understanding in healthcare is a centuries-old endeavor, essential for professionals and researchers dedicated to determining the effects of interventions on patient health. This pursuit has progressed with the development of methodologies in causal inference, pivotal for steering clinical practices and health policy decisions. The evolution of this field is notably shaped by two dominant methodologies: clinical trials and observational studies.

Clinical trials: Rooted in history with James Lind's seminal scurvy trial, clinical trials have become fundamental in establishing the efficacy and safety of medical interventions. These controlled, randomized experiments are crucial in determining the causal impact of interventions, thus setting the benchmark for causality in healthcare.

Observational studies: Observational studies, in contrast, assess interventions' effects in naturalistic settings, drawing on data sources like electronic health records and administrative databases. While invaluable for exploring outcomes not readily tested in trials, these studies grapple with confounding and selection biases, presenting challenges in confirming causality.

These biases—confounding, where third variables influence both exposure and outcome, and selection bias, where the study population does not represent the broader group—are significant hurdles in observational research. As the healthcare

---

[1]Institute for Health Informatics, University of Minnesota, USA
[2]Carelon, Atlanta, GA, USA
[3]David Geffen School of Medicine, University of California Los Angeles, USA
[4]Centre for Intelligent Healthcare, Coventry University, UK
[5]Carelon, Chicago, IL, USA

landscape becomes increasingly complex with a surge in real-world data and personalized medicine, the demand for rigorous causal inference methods intensifies.

This chapter's main aim is to demystify causal inference methods for observational healthcare studies, offering insights into the methodologies that have been widely applied. This discussion intends to furnish readers with the necessary knowledge and tools to critically evaluate and utilize these methods within their healthcare domains.

14.1.2 Fundamental causal inference frameworks

The potential outcome framework, also recognized as the Rubin Causal Model, is the backbone of modern causal inference in healthcare research. It utilizes the notion of potential outcomes—what would happen with and without treatment—introducing the "fundamental problem of causal inference": for any individual, we can observe only one potential outcome, either with or without treatment. While we cannot directly measure individual causal effects, we can estimate the average treatment effect (ATE) and the average treatment effect of the treated (ATT) by comparing observed outcomes, which helps control for confounding in observational studies.

Aside from this widely adopted framework, other approaches like directed acyclic graphs (DAGs) and structural equation modeling (SEM) provide further analytical depth. DAGs visually outline causal pathways and confounders, while SEM dissects complex variable relationships through equations. This chapter will concentrate on the potential outcome framework and explore the most prominent methods derived from it.

As a guide into the world of causal inference, we will delve into methods such as propensity score matching (PSM), difference-in-differences (DiD), instrumental variables (IV), and regression discontinuity design (RDD), illuminating their technicalities and real-world applications in healthcare. Finally, we will address the challenges and prospects in this dynamic field.

14.2 Methodology

14.2.1 Propensity score matching

PSM is a statistical technique widely accepted and used in observational studies to estimate the effect of a treatment, intervention, or exposure when random assignment is not feasible. PSM aims to reduce bias due to confounding variables that could affect the assignment to treatment and control groups. It involves the following steps:

Propensity score estimation: The first step in PSM is to estimate the propensity score for each individual in the study. The propensity score is a fundamental component in PSM because it balances the covariates across treatment and control groups, reducing selection bias. By simulating randomization, it ensures that the groups are comparable based on observed characteristics. Logistic regression or any other binary classifiers models the probability of treatment assignment as a function of covariates, and it's essential because it aims to account for all the observed factors that might influence the selection into the treatment group. This way, the effect of the treatment is isolated from those confounding covariates, allowing for a more accurate estimation of the treatment's causal effect. The propensity score is a balancing score, meaning that the distribution of observed baseline covariates will be similar between treated and untreated subjects with the same score, which is why it's crucial for reducing confounding in observational studies where random assignment is not possible.

Matching: Once the propensity scores are estimated, individuals in the treatment group are matched with individuals in the control group who have similar propensity scores. The goal is to create a matched sample where the distribution of the covariates is similar between the treatment and control groups, mimicking the conditions of a randomized experiment. Various matching algorithms can be used. For example, nearest neighbor matching matches a treated unit to a control unit with the closest propensity score within a specified caliper. Caliper matching matches within a specified propensity score range, often a fraction of the standard deviation of the score. Kernel matching employs weights control units to create a synthetic match that approximates the propensity score of a treated unit.

Assessing balance: After matching, it's crucial to assess the balance of covariates between the treatment and control groups. Balance diagnostics are used to ensure that the matching process has successfully created comparable groups. A widely used metric is standardized mean differences as in equation (14.1), where $\overline{X_t}$ and $\overline{X_c}$ are the treatment and control group means, and s_t^2 and s_c^2 are the variances of the treated and control group means. A small SMD indicates good balance, typically considered as less than 0.1 or 0.2, suggesting that the means of covariates are similar between the groups after matching.

$$\text{SMD} = \frac{\overline{X_t} - \overline{X_c}}{\sqrt{\frac{s_t^2 + s_c^2}{2}}} \tag{14.1}$$

Graphical methods can also be beneficial. For instance, we can examine the propensity score distributions of the treated and control groups before and after matching. As depicted in Figure 14.1, the disparate distributions in the two groups before matching suggest significant differences, whereas similar distributions after matching indicate a favorable similarity between the two matched groups.

Estimating treatment effects: With a well-matched sample, the treatment effect can be estimated by comparing outcomes between the treatment and control groups. This can be done using various statistical methods, such as paired t-tests could be used for continuous outcomes or McNemar's test could for binary outcomes. A paired t-test then compares each treated subject to their specific matched control and accounts for the pairing in the analysis. McNemar's test can be used to assess whether there is a significant change in outcomes within the pairs. It is particularly useful when the outcome is dichotomous, such as the presence or absence of a condition, and takes into account the matched pair design by focusing on the

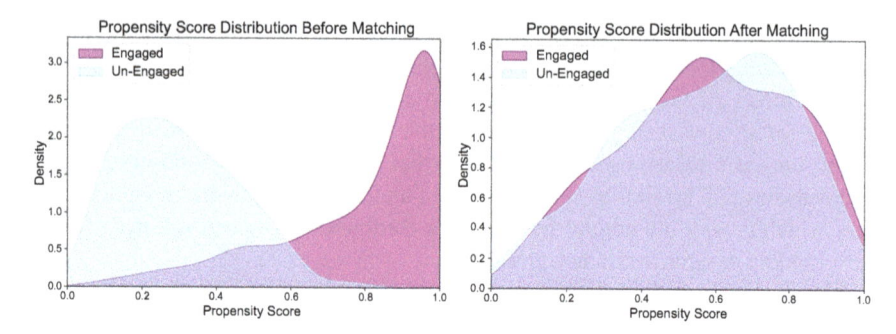

Figure 14.1 Distribution of propensity scores before and after matching for engaged and unengaged groups

discordant pairs. To directly estimate the ATE on the treated (ATT), we can use equation (14.2). N_T is the number of treated participants, Y_i is the outcome for the treated participant i, and $Y_{i(j)}$ is the outcome for the matched control participant j.

$$ATT = \frac{1}{N_T} \sum_{i \in T} \left(Y_i - Y_{i(j)} \right) \tag{14.2}$$

Sensitivity analysis: Finally, conducting sensitivity analyses is important to assess the robustness of the findings to potential unmeasured confounding. This involves testing how sensitive the results are to changes in the matching process or the inclusion of different covariates.

PSM is particularly useful in healthcare research where randomized controlled trials are not always ethical or feasible. It allows researchers to approximate the conditions of a randomized trial, thereby providing more credible estimates of treatment effects. However, PSM has its limitations, including reliance on observed covariates (ignoring unmeasured confounding), potential loss of sample size due to unmatched units, and the subjectivity in choosing a matching algorithm and covariates.

Advancements in machine learning (ML) are increasingly employed to improve PSM, especially in handling high-dimensional data. ML algorithms can discern complex patterns and interactions among covariates, potentially offering a more nuanced propensity score estimation than traditional logistic regression. This approach can enhance the quality of matches and reduce bias further, leading to more accurate causal effect estimations.

In summary, PSM is a powerful tool in causal inference for observational studies, enabling researchers to estimate treatment effects more reliably by creating comparable groups based on observed characteristics. Its application in healthcare research can provide valuable insights into the effectiveness of treatments, interventions, and health policies.

14.2.2 Difference-in-difference

DiD is a robust quasi-experimental approach that allows researchers to infer causal relationships from observational data. By leveraging "natural experiments", DiD contrasts changes in outcomes over time between a group affected by a treatment (the treatment group) and a group that is not (the control group).

Conceptual framework: Central to DiD is the parallel trends assumption. This assumes that, in the absence of the treatment, the outcome trajectories for the treatment and control groups would have been the same over time. Understanding this assumption is crucial, and we illustrate its importance with an example. Consider two hospitals, one which adopts a new health protocol while the other continues with standard care. If, before the adoption of the new protocol, both hospitals had similar trends in patient recovery rates, then any post-adoption divergence in these trends can be attributed to the protocol itself, provided there are no other confounding changes.

Methodology: DiD relies on a regression framework articulated in equation (14.3), which is designed to model the outcome variable Y_{it} as a function of treatment status, time, and the interaction of the two, alongside other control covariates:

$$Y_{it} = \alpha + \beta_1 Treated_i + \beta_2 Post_t + \delta(Treated_i \times Post_t) + X'_{it}\gamma + \varepsilon_{it} \quad (14.3)$$

Here:

- Y_{it} is the outcome for entity i at time t
- $Treated_i$ is an indicator that equals 1 if the entity is in the treatment group.
- $Post_t$ is an indicator for the post-treatment time period.
- $Treated_i \times Post_t$ is the interaction term where δ measures the DiD estimate—the ATT.
- $X'_{it}\gamma$ represents other covariates.
- ε_{it} is the error term.

In this model, the term δ captures the DiD estimate, providing the treatment effect we aim to measure. The illustration in Figure 14.2 brings this to life by showing the expected and observed outcomes for the treatment and control groups.

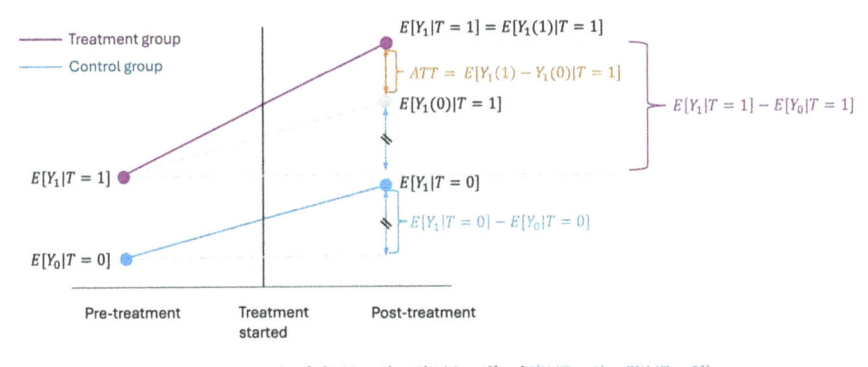

Figure 14.2 Estimation of causal effect: average treatment effect on the treated (ATT)

The vertical distance between the post-treatment outcome for the control group ($E[Y|T=0]$) and the treatment group ($E[Y|T=1]$) demonstrates the ATT.

To interpret Figure 14.2, observe that prior to treatment, the outcomes for both groups follow their own paths, depicted by the dashed lines. Once the treatment begins, we see a divergence in the treatment group's path. This divergence, captured by δ in our formula, signifies the treatment's effect over and above any trend observed in the control group. Here are more detailed steps visualizes the calculation of ATT:

- Calculation of the expected outcome for the treatment group if the treatment had not taken place, represented as $E[Y_0|T=1]$.
- Observation of the actual outcome for the treatment group after the treatment, $E[Y_1|T=1]$.
- Calculation of the expected outcome for the control group, both before and after the treatment started, as $E[Y_0|T=1]$ and $E[Y_1|T=1]$, respectively. The control group serves as a counterfactual to estimate what the outcome for the treatment group would have been in the absence of the treatment.

The ATT is then the difference between the treatment effect ($E[Y_1|T=1] - E[Y_0|T=1]$) and the control group's change over the same period ($E[Y_1|T=0] - E[Y_0|T=0]$), which is mathematically represented as

$$(E[Y_1|T=1] - E[Y_0|T=1]) - (E[Y_1|T=0] - E[Y_0|T=0]).$$

This method assumes that the difference between the treatment and control groups remains constant over time in the absence of the treatment, a condition known as the parallel trends assumption. If this assumption holds, any changes in the treatment group's outcomes can be causally attributed to the treatment. By utilizing the changes in outcomes within the treatment group and comparing them to the changes within the control group, DiD isolates and identifies the causal effect of the treatment.

Empirical application: To clarify the methodology, let's walk through a hypothetical case. Suppose a new drug policy aimed at improving prescription adherence is introduced in a set of clinics. Researchers could measure adherence rates before and after the policy's implementation, comparing changes in the clinics subject to the new policy against those that did not change their policies. The DiD estimator would then isolate the impact of the new drug policy from other changes over time.

Challenges and mitigation strategies: DiD's validity rests on the parallel trends assumption, which, if violated, can lead to biased estimates. A practical strategy to test for this assumption is to examine pre-treatment trends in the outcome variable. Should these trends diverge between the groups, researchers might add control variables to the model, alter the model's specification, or use advanced techniques like synthetic control to mitigate potential biases.

Extensions and variations: DiD's flexibility makes it amenable to various extensions. For example, in situations with multiple post-treatment periods or treatments, researchers might consider variations like the triple-differences estimator. This approach adds another layer of comparison, such as different cohorts within the treatment group, providing a more granular understanding of the treatment effect.

In summary, the DiD method offers a powerful approach to causal inference in scenarios where randomized controlled trials are infeasible. It hinges on a robust theoretical framework and has proven valuable in health policy evaluation, healthcare delivery research, and more. With careful application, it allows researchers to uncover causal effects that can inform policy and practice, enhancing the welfare of patients and the efficiency of healthcare systems.

14.2.3 Instrumental variables

IV is a way to estimate causal relationships when the ideal conditions for controlled experiments are unavailable. IV is particularly valuable when the assignment of treatments in a study is related to factors that also affect outcomes—a scenario that introduces endogeneity.

14.2.3.1 Understanding endogeneity

Regression analysis is a powerful tool for investigating the relationships between dependent and independent variables. However, standard regression models are susceptible to endogeneity, a condition where explanatory variables are correlated with the error term. This correlation can compromise the model's integrity, leading to biased estimates. Consider (14.4), where T_i denotes the outcome for the ith observation, T_i is the treatment (an explanatory variable), and ε_i represents the error term for each observation. The ideal assumptions for ε_i would be $E(\varepsilon_i) = 0$, and $cov(T_i, \varepsilon_i) = 0$. However, in observational studies, the latter often does not hold. For instance, in evaluating the effectiveness of a weight-loss program, patients undergoing treatment might also engage in healthier lifestyles. Consequently, ε_i encompassing all other patient-level information, is not independent of the treatment T_i, leading to endogeneity. Endogeneity significantly threatens the validity of our inferences, introducing bias into our treatment effect estimates.

$$Y_i = \alpha + \beta T_i + \varepsilon_i \tag{14.4}$$

14.2.3.2 IV approach

The crux of the IV method is to find an instrument—a factor that influences the likelihood of treatment but is not related to the factors causing endogeneity. For example, the distance from a patient's home to a clinic might affect whether they receive a treatment without influencing the health outcomes directly, making it a potential instrument. In other words, a valid instrument satisfies two critical assumptions: it must influence the treatment decision ($E(\varepsilon_i) = 0$) and be uncorrelated with the error term ($cov(T_i, \varepsilon_i) = 0$), establishing its relevance and exogeneity.

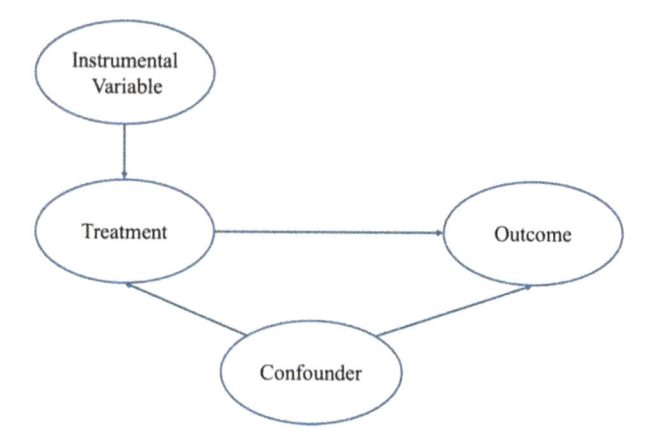

Figure 14.3 Visualizing IV with the directed acyclic graph

We can explore the IV idea through the lens of DAGs. Figure 14.3 unfolds this complexity into an illustrative diagram, accentuating the nuanced relationships pivotal to IV's methodology. Here, the instrument, identifiable by its causal arrow towards the treatment, underscores its instrumental role in influencing treatment assignment without directly affecting the outcome. This configuration emphasizes the instrument's unique position: it is sufficiently correlated with the treatment (relevance) yet remains insulated from the outcome, except through its influence on treatment (exogeneity).

14.2.3.3 IV estimation process

The IV estimation process traditionally follows two stages, as shown in equation (14.5). In the initial stage, the treatment variable is regressed against the instrument to predict treatment values. Subsequently, these predicted values are employed to gauge the treatment's effect on the outcome. The two-stage least squares (2SLS) estimator exemplifies this approach:

$$\begin{aligned} \text{1st Stage}: T_i &= \pi_0 + \pi_1 Z_i + \pi_2 W_i + u_i \\ \text{2nd Stage}: Y_i &= \alpha + \beta T_i + \gamma W_i + \varepsilon_i \end{aligned} \quad (14.5)$$

where T_i is the treatment, Z_i is the instrument, and Y_i is the outcome. u_i contains all other factors affecting T_i that are not included in the model. For a good instrument, u_i should not be correlated with Z_i. W_i includes other control variables such as patient age, gender, etc., that are presumed to affect the outcome directly. This 2SLS approach effectively removes the endogeneity from T_i, assuming the instrument Z_i is valid. The validity hinges on the instrument being correlated with T_i (relevance) and uncorrelated with the error term ε_i (exogeneity).

14.2.3.4 Limitations and considerations

Finding a valid instrument is challenging and critical for the IV approach. Weak instruments may lead to imprecise and biased estimates of β. The exclusion restriction, which assumes that the instrument affects the outcome solely through the treatment, can be particularly difficult to satisfy and test.

14.2.3.5 Conclusion

IV offer a powerful tool for estimating causal effects, particularly in observational healthcare studies where randomization is unfeasible. By carefully selecting instruments and adhering to the IV methodology, researchers can derive more credible estimates of causal effects, contributing to the development of evidence-based healthcare policies and practices.

14.2.4 Regression discontinuity design

The RDD stands as a rigorous methodological approach within observational studies, distinguished by its ability to infer causal effects where treatment assignment is determined by a cutoff point on a continuous variable. This design bifurcates into two distinct models: sharp and fuzzy RDD, each tailored to specific scenarios of treatment assignment compliance.

Sharp RDD: Sharp RDD is characterized by an absolute adherence to a pre-defined cutoff in the assignment variable. For individuals on either side of this threshold, the assignment to treatment or control groups is unequivocal. The essence of sharp RDD is captured by evaluating the immediate differences in outcomes at the threshold c (as shown in the left picture of Figure 14.4), formally denoted as $\tau_{sharp} = \lim_{x \downarrow c} E[Y|X=x] - \lim_{x \uparrow c} E[Y|X=x]$. This design hinges on the premise that the cutoff point creates a quasi-random division, akin to a randomized trial, thus allowing for a robust estimation of the treatment effect for individuals at the threshold.

Fuzzy RDD: Contrastingly, fuzzy RDD accounts for instances where the treatment assignment does not strictly follow the cutoff criterion, leading to a discontinuous jump in the probability of receiving the treatment rather than an absolute division. This scenario necessitates employing the cutoff as an IV to estimate the treatment effect, which is formally expressed as $\tau_{fuzzy} = \frac{\lim_{x \downarrow c} E[Y|X=c] - \lim_{x \uparrow c} E[Y|X=c]}{\lim_{x \downarrow c} E[D|X=c] - \lim_{x \uparrow c} E[D|X=c]}$, where D denotes actual treatment receipt.

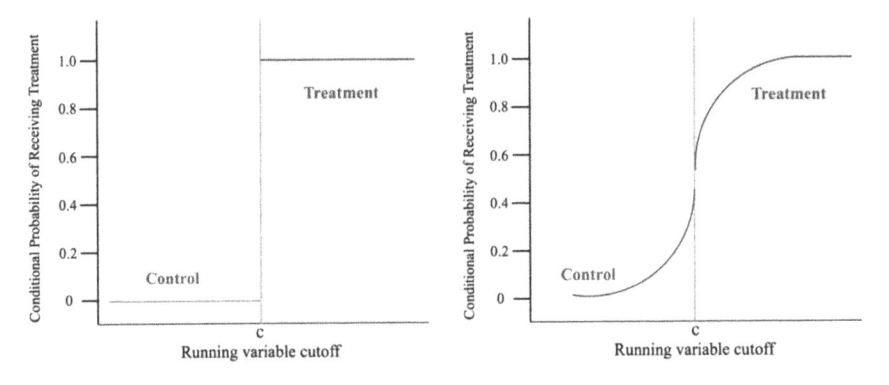

Figure 14.4 The mechanism of treatment assignment in sharp and fuzzy RDD

14.2.4.1 Addressing bandwidth

Both sharp and fuzzy RDD demand meticulous bandwidth consideration around the cutoff, with the chosen bandwidth profoundly influencing the estimation's bias and variance balance. As demonstrated in Figure 14.5, bandwidth selection crucially impacts the causal effect estimation's smoothness and precision. A narrow bandwidth, while potentially enhancing precision by focusing on data closely surrounding the cutoff, risks introducing bias if the running variable and outcome relationship near the cutoff is incorrectly specified. Conversely, a broader bandwidth, though possibly reducing this bias by including a wider range of observations, might dilute the causal effect by incorporating less comparable observations across the cutoff.

Figure 14.5 vividly illustrates these considerations, highlighting how varying bandwidth choices affect the estimated treatment effect and the effect in control group (i.e., without treatment) between the running variable and eventually the estimated treatment effect. This visual guide aids in comprehending the trade-offs involved in bandwidth selection and underscores the importance of this decision in RDD analysis.

Optimal bandwidth determination requires a balanced approach, often involving sensitivity analysis, theoretical insights, and advanced bandwidth selection methods. These strategies aim to minimize both bias and variance, ensuring a reliable estimation of the causal effect.

Applications and implications: RDD, encompassing both sharp and fuzzy variants, finds valuable applications across healthcare research, education policy, and economics. It offers a robust alternative for causal inference when randomized trials are not feasible, enabling strong causal claims from observational data by leveraging cutoff-based treatment assignment.

To conclude, RDD, in its sharp and fuzzy forms, provides researchers with a rigorous framework for causal inference when randomized controlled trials are not

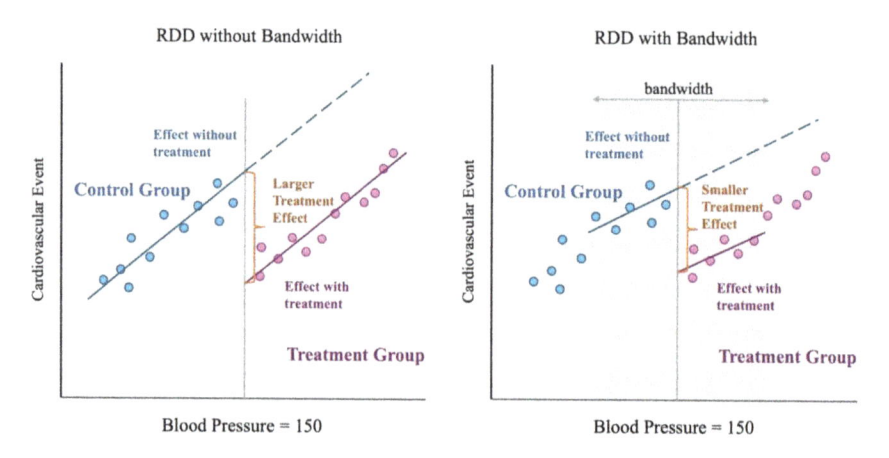

Figure 14.5 Influence of bandwidth on treatment effect estimation

feasible. Understanding the distinction between sharp and fuzzy RDD and appropriately applying the corresponding analysis is crucial for obtaining valid causal estimates in observational studies. The method's strength lies in its straightforward conceptual framework and its flexibility, which allows for adaptation to various practical scenarios also in other areas, such as in policy evaluation and social research.

14.3 Case studies: practical applications of causal inference in healthcare

14.3.1 Use case 1: robotic vs open pancreatoduodenectomy on incidence of pancreatic fistula using PSM method

The rise of robotic pancreatoduodenectomy (RPD) in surgical practice prompts a need for comprehensive assessment of its comparative efficacy, particularly in relation to traditional open pancreatoduodenectomy (OPD) and the occurrence of clinically relevant pancreatic fistula (CR-POPF). While minimally invasive approaches offer advantages such as smaller incisions and quicker recovery, concerns persist regarding their applicability to pancreatoduodenectomy due to factors like oncological effectiveness, cost, training, and technical complexities. Robotic surgery, with its enhanced visualization and dexterity, holds promise in addressing some of these concerns, potentially improving the reconstruction phase. However, CR-POPF remains a significant postoperative complication, impacting patient recovery and mortality rates. Previous studies, often limited in size and scope, have failed to definitively establish differences in CR-POPF incidence between RPD and OPD, thus necessitating further investigation.

Method: In this investigation, a multi-institutional analysis was conducted utilizing PSM to compare outcomes between RPD and OPD procedures among 2,846 patients spanning 17 high-volume institutions. Two PSM matching experiments were conducted:

- Experiment 1: Propensity scores were adjusted to account for seven variables, which included the texture of the pancreatic gland, duct diameter, intraoperative blood loss, pathologic findings indicating high-risk disease, intraoperative drain placement, octreotide prophylaxis, and the placement of a transanastomotic stent. Following this adjustment, patients undergoing OPD and RPD were matched 1:1 based on these propensity scores using exact matching, with a caliper size set at 0.2 times the standard deviation of the log-transformed propensity score. To evaluate the balance of covariates before and after matching, standardized differences were calculated, with minimal absolute values (<0.1) indicating that the treatment groups were well balanced.
- Experiment 2: The propensity scores were calculated by only associated variables with RPD based on a test before the matching, such as pancreatic gland texture, pancreatic duct diameter, and transanastomotic stent placement. The following matching and covariate balance assessment were the same as procedures used in Experiment 1.

Table 14.1 CR-POPF and other postoperative outcomes after matching in Experiment 1

Variable, No. (%)	Difference between OPD and RPD (%)	p-Value
Patients		
CR-POPF (main outcome)	4.6	0.23
FRS risk zone		
Negligible, FRS 0	−4.2	>0.99
Low, FRS 0–2	6.7	0.50
Moderate, FRS 3–6	8.2	0.14
High, FRS 7–10	−7.2	>0.99
Grade B POPF	2.6	0.52
Grade C POPF	2.0	0.25
Complications		
Any, Accordion severity grading system grade ≥ 1	−7.3	0.21
Mild/moderate, Accordion score 1–2	−7.9	0.24
Severe, Accordion severity grading system grade ≥ 3	0.7	>0.99
Readmission, 30-d	−0.7	>0.99
Duration of hospital stay, d		
Mean (SD)	3.7	0.22
Mortality, 90-d	−2.0	0.38

Results: As depicted in Table 14.1, the analysis of the matched cohort in Experiment 1 indicated that RPD was linked to a 4.6% lower risk of CR-POPF, although this difference was not statistically significant. Postoperative outcomes between the matched cohorts of RPD and OPD were also compared. The OPD group did not show significantly better outcomes than the RPD group in terms of any complication occurrence (difference = −7.3; p = 0.21), mild to moderate complications (difference = −7.9; p = 0.24), severe complications (0.7; p > 0.99), readmissions (difference = −0.7; p > 0.99), and mortality (difference = −2.0; p = 0.38).

Similarly, the results from Experiment 1 showed no significant differences between the RPD and OPD cohorts in the rates of CR-POPF (7.0% vs 12.3%; p = 0.10), grade B POPF (7.0% vs 9.9%; p = 0.33), or grade C POPF (0% vs 2.3%; p = 0.12). Additionally, the RPD cohort demonstrated noninferior outcomes compared to the OPD cohort regarding any complication occurrence (Accordion grade ≥ 1: 74.3% vs 68.4%; p = 0.23), mild to moderate complications (Accordion grade 1–2: 49.7% vs 43.3%; p = 0.23), severe complications (Accordion grade ≥ 3: 24.6% vs 25.1%; P = 0.90), readmissions (21.6% vs 17.9%; p = 0.38), and mortality (2.9% vs 3.5%; p = 0.76).

Discussion: This study is reported as the first PSM-based analysis comparing RPD with OPD, demonstrating noninferiority of RPD in terms of pancreatic fistula development and other major postoperative outcomes. It addresses the pivotal issue of CR-POPF, which is a major contributor to morbidity and mortality following pancreatoduodenectomy. The rigorous matching process helped to control for biases, approximating the conditions of a randomized clinical trial. Despite previous studies reporting equivalency or noninferiority in CR-POPF outcomes and other postoperative complications between RPD and OPD, this study's findings are particularly robust due to the large and well-matched cohort, providing more reliable evidence that RPD is a viable alternative to OPD with potential advantages in the surgical management of pancreatic conditions.

14.3.2 Use case 2: Medicaid expansion and variability in mortality in the United States

This study addresses the critical public health question of how Medicaid expansion, a key component of the Affordable Care Act (ACA) in the United States, impacts mortality among adults. Prior research has shown mixed results, with some studies suggesting Medicaid expansion leads to significant health benefits, including reductions in mortality rates, while others find minimal or no impact. This study seeks to contribute to the ongoing debate by providing a comprehensive analysis of the relationship between Medicaid expansion and all-cause mortality among U.S. adults aged 25–64, a demographic that stands to benefit significantly from expanded healthcare access.

Methods: The study employs an observational cohort derived from national death certificate data spanning from 2010 to 2018. This timeframe allows for a comparison of mortality rates before and after Medicaid expansion, which began in most participating states in 2014. The analysis focuses on all-cause mortality among adults aged 25–64, excluding causes of death not directly related to healthcare access (e.g., accidents, injuries). The study uses a DiD approach to compare mortality trends in states that expanded Medicaid under the ACA to those that did not, adjusting for a range of demographic, economic, and healthcare system factors that could influence mortality rates independently of Medicaid expansion.

Results: The results in Figure 14.6 indicate a statistically significant association between Medicaid expansion and reduced all-cause mortality among adults

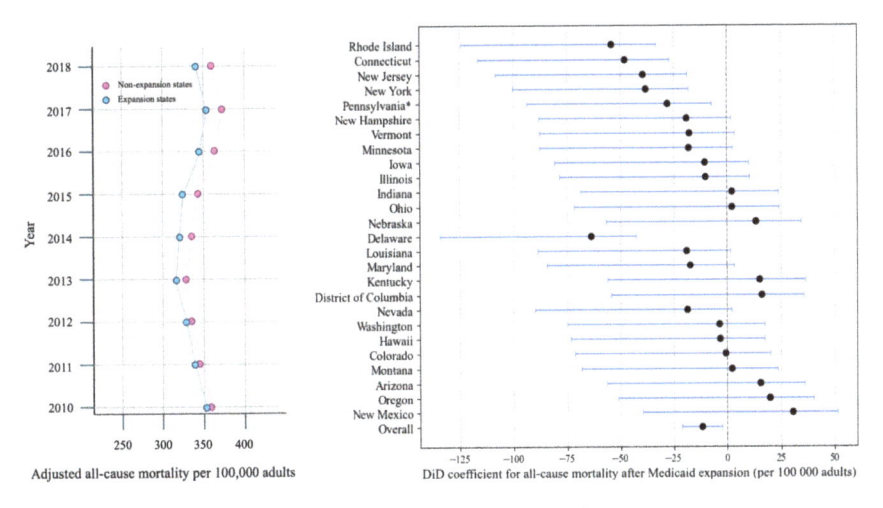

Figure 14.6 Impact of Medicaid expansion on mortality rates: a comparative analysis of time trends and state-by-state effects

aged 25–64. States that expanded Medicaid saw a more significant decline in mortality rates compared to non-expansion states, after controlling for other factors. The study highlights variations in the impact of Medicaid expansion across states, suggesting that local implementation details, population demographics, and baseline healthcare access levels may influence the magnitude of mortality reductions. The analysis also points to larger mortality reductions among specific subpopulations, such as low-income adults and certain racial and ethnic minority groups, who are disproportionately represented among the uninsured in non-expansion states.

Discussion: The findings of this study contribute to the growing body of evidence suggesting that Medicaid expansion under the ACA is associated with positive health outcomes, including reduced mortality rates among adults. The observed state-level variations in the impact of Medicaid expansion underscore the importance of considering local context in healthcare policy implementation and evaluation. The study's results support the argument for further expansion of Medicaid in states that have yet to adopt the ACA's expansion provisions, highlighting the potential for significant public health benefits.

By demonstrating a link between Medicaid expansion and reduced mortality, this research adds to the understanding of the ACA's impact on public health and informs ongoing policy debates about the future of Medicaid and healthcare access in the United States. The study calls for continued research to explore the mechanisms through which Medicaid expansion leads to improved health outcomes and to identify strategies for maximizing the public health benefits of expanded healthcare coverage.

In conclusion, the project offers compelling evidence that Medicaid expansion is an effective tool for reducing mortality among adults, particularly in underserved populations. It underscores the role of healthcare access in determining health outcomes and provides a strong argument for policies aimed at expanding coverage to improve public health.

14.3.3 Use case 3: explore the causal effect of intravenous radiocontrast for kidney function

There has been the concern regarding the potential nephrotoxic effects of intravenous radiocontrast used in diagnostic imaging, which is feared to cause kidney injury known as contrast-induced nephropathy (CIN). Despite recent studies suggesting no significant link between radiocontrast exposure and adverse kidney outcomes, the debate persists due to potential biases in observational research. This study aims to provide a more definitive answer using a fuzzy RDD to minimize confounding factors and offer stronger causal inference regarding the effects of radiocontrast on kidney function.

Method: This study employed a quasi-experimental RDD approach, targeting patients who underwent D-dimer testing in emergency departments, primarily to rule out pulmonary embolism. The D-dimer cutoff level for deciding on subsequent diagnostic imaging with computed tomographic pulmonary angiography (CTPA) served as the basis for this natural experiment. This setup allowed for the comparison of patients just above and below the threshold, making them similar except for their exposure to radiocontrast. Thus, the D-dimer value was utilized as the running variable in this scenario. The study population consisted of individuals aged 18 and older who had a D-dimer test during an emergency department visit in Alberta, Canada, between April 1, 2013 and June 30, 2018. Those with a history of kidney replacement therapy were excluded. The main outcome was long-term kidney function, assessed by the estimated glomerular filtration rate (eGFR) up to six months after the visit. Variables considered to evaluate the causal effect of radiocontrast near the D-dimer cutoff included age, baseline eGFR, sex, diabetes, hypertension, cancer, coronary artery disease, ED triage score, and Charlson comorbidity index.

The study used a fuzzy RDD to estimate the effect of CTPA exposure on long-term eGFR, with the D-dimer as the running variable. This type of IV analysis adjusts for imperfect compliance with the treatment threshold, providing the complier average causal effect (CACE), which represents the effect of the intervention on those whose treatment assignment is determined by the cutoff. Both intention-to-treat (ITT) effects and rescaled CACE attributable to CTPA were reported for each outcome. The primary outcome was the difference in long-term eGFR, while binary secondary outcomes were reported as risk differences (RD). Relationships between the running variable and both exposure and outcome were assessed using local linear regression, fitting separate regression lines above and below the threshold. This method minimized bias by focusing on a defined bandwidth around the cutoff, selected using a data-driven approach to balance the bias-variance trade-off. An asymmetric bandwidth was applied to account for the expected asymmetric distribution of the D-dimer running variable. Additionally, bias-adjusted robust confidence intervals were estimated to address potential misspecifications of the regression function and additional variance.

Sensitivity analyses examined the impact of bandwidth size and symmetry, along with global analyses using polynomials of varying degrees. Subgroup analyses were conducted to explore treatment effects across different risk groups. Additionally, an analysis incorporating all eGFR measurements between 7 days and 6 months post-index ED visit was performed to improve precision in effect estimation. All analyses were limited to complete cases, and potential selection bias due to missing data was evaluated.

Results: As depicted in Figure 14.7, local linear and global polynomial approach plots were generated separately. The purple circles represent the mean values for individual patients, while the dashed lines indicate the D-dimer cutoff, and the shaded area shows the local linear regression bandwidth. The analysis revealed that intravenous contrast exposure was associated with a non-significant 0.4 mL/min/1.73 m^2 reduction in eGFR up to 6 months later, suggesting no clinically meaningful impact on long-term kidney function. Secondary outcomes, including the receipt of kidney replacement therapy, acute kidney injury, and all-cause mortality at 6 months, also showed no significant associations with contrast exposure.

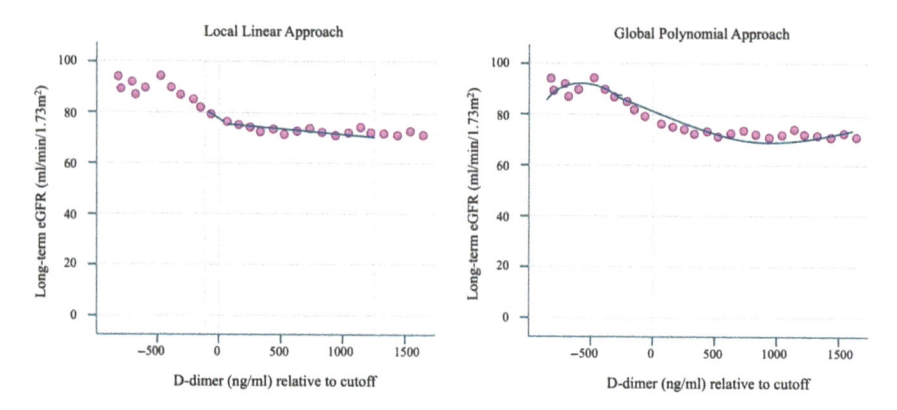

Figure 14.7 Long-term eGFR value around the D-dimer cutoff

Discussion: The findings challenge the prevalent clinical concern over CIN, suggesting that modern contrast agents and doses may not be harmful to kidney function. This study provides stronger evidence against the nephrotoxicity of intravenous radiocontrast, potentially altering clinical practices and reducing hesitancy in utilizing diagnostic imaging for patients at risk of kidney impairment. However, the results' generalizability may be limited to the specific cutoff and population studied, and further research may be needed to explore the effects in different settings or among high-risk subgroups.

14.3.4 Use case 4: use IV analysis to compare effectiveness of stents in the extremely elderly

Evaluating the effectiveness of novel therapies for the extremely elderly, particularly for percutaneous coronary intervention (PCI), poses significant challenges due to the common exclusion of this age group from randomized clinical trials. This gap in research leaves the impact of new technologies like drug-eluting stents (DES) and bare metal stents (BMS) on the elderly largely uncharted. The study leverages IV methods to mitigate confounding inherent in observational studies, aiming to elucidate the efficacy of stents in patients aged 85 and older.

Method: The study encompassed all patients aged 85 or above undergoing PCI with stenting in nonfederal Massachusetts hospitals between 2003 and 2009, totaling 2,690 subjects. Using quarterly DES use rates as the IV, the researchers employed a 2SLS analysis to estimate risk-adjusted outcome differences between DES and BMS. This approach adjusted for patient and procedural characteristics to assess all-cause mortality, target vessel revascularization (TVR), and bleeding requiring hospitalization at 30 days and 1 year.

For the IV analysis, the researchers identified quarterly rates of DES use among patients aged 85 or older as the instrument. This measure, varying between 0% and 100% per quarter, was correlated with the likelihood of receiving a DES but hypothesized to be independent of patient outcomes, aside from through the stent type used. A two-stage least squares (2SLS) regression analysis was employed.

In the first stage of 2SLS, the researchers constructed a linear regression model using the IV to predict the treatment type (DES or BMS). In the second stage, they used the predicted probabilities from the first stage as an explanatory variable in a regression model to estimate the outcome differences attributable to the treatment type. This two-stage method helps address the endogeneity of treatment decisions—a common issue where treatment choice is correlated with unobserved patient characteristics.

The researchers further ensured that the IV analysis was robust by evaluating the instrument against several key assumptions. The strength of the IV was assessed using the Cragg–Donald Wald F statistic, where values above 10 indicate a strong instrument. They confirmed that the IV strongly predicted the exposure of interest and did not directly affect the outcome, thereby satisfying the necessary conditions for a valid instrument.

Additionally, they examined the balance of measured patient characteristics across different levels of DES use to indirectly assess the assumption that the IV should not be related to outcomes through channels other than the treatment. This step aimed to demonstrate that the instrument effectively randomized patients similarly across varying DES use rates.

The study analyzed both unadjusted and risk-adjusted outcomes using the IV, considering a comprehensive list of patient and procedural covariates. These covariates, including sociodemographic characteristics and medical history, were integrated into both stages of the 2SLS analysis to ensure that the adjusted results accounted for potential confounders.

Results: The primary results are represented in Table 14.2. Unadjusted one-year mortality rates suggested an implausibly higher survival rate for DES compared with BMS for all three outcomes, which contradicted randomized trial findings. However, IV analysis showed no significant differences in one-year mortality (p-value = 0.76) or bleeding rates (p-value = 0.33) between DES and BMS, while indicating a significant reduction in TVR for DES (risk difference = 2.0 with the p-value < 0.001). The variability in DES usage underscored the instrument's potential for comparative effectiveness research in typically underrepresented groups.

Discussion: In this study, IV analysis showcased its potential in assessing treatment effects where randomization is absent. However, this method assumes the instrument impacts the outcome solely through treatment, an assumption that, while plausible, remains untestable and requires careful consideration. Notably, this analysis aligns with prior work suggesting the comparability of IV results to randomized trials in lower-risk cohorts, providing a crucial bridge where randomized evidence is scarce. These findings thus reinforce the importance of rigorous selection of IVs in observational studies. Forthcoming research should pursue the identification of strong instruments and expand upon the generalizability of this approach, furthering its application in evaluating medical technologies across diverse patient demographics.

Table 14.2 Risk differences between DES and BMS based on three analysis

	Unadjusted outcomes		Unadjusted IV outcomes		Adjusted IV outcomes	
1-year Outcome	DES ($n = 1507$)	BMS ($n = 1183$)	Risk difference	Risk difference	Robust SE	Risk difference	Robust SE
Mortality (%)	14.5	23.0	−8.5 (p-value < 0.001)	−2.7 (p-value = 0.35)	2.8	−0.8 (p-value = 0.76)	2.8
Bleeding (%)	10.3	12.4	−2.1 (p-value = 0.08)	1.0 (p-value = 0.68)	2.4	2.3 (p-value = 0.33)	2.4
TVR (%)	4.3	9.3	−5.0 (p-value < 0.001)	−7.3 (p-value < 0.001)	1.9	−8.3 (p-value<0.001)	2.0

14.4 Challenges, future directions, and conclusion

14.4.1 Challenges in modern causal inference

The advancement of causal inference in healthcare has been accompanied by an expanding landscape of challenges. Observational studies, despite their potential, grapple with confounding variables that blur the lines between correlation and causation. This problem is exacerbated as the amount of available healthcare data balloons with the inclusion of diverse patient populations and the rise of personalized medicine. Another considerable challenge is endogeneity in regression analysis where variables of interest may be correlated with unobserved factors, leading to biased estimates that can misguide healthcare decisions.

14.4.2 Emerging approaches in causal inference

As causal inference marches into the future, it beckons the integration of innovative analytical techniques and interdisciplinary collaboration. The field stands at the cusp of a transformative shift with the burgeoning use of ML algorithms to enhance traditional statistical methods. For example, ensemble methods are being harnessed to improve the robustness of PSM, while IV analyses are growing more nuanced with the identification of novel instruments through data mining techniques.

Another forward-looking direction is the adoption of big data analytics, which promises to refine causal estimates by utilizing a vast spectrum of data sources, ranging from genomic databases to patient-generated health data. Such approaches aim to tailor healthcare interventions at an individual level, embracing the era of personalized medicine.

14.4.3 Concluding reflections

In reflection, the journey of causal inference in healthcare is marked by both its storied past and its progressive trajectory. The methods discussed in this chapter—PSM, DiD, IV, and RDD—have laid a robust foundation for discerning causality in the complex realm of healthcare. As we steer towards the future, these methodologies must adapt to the evolving data landscapes and integrate with cutting-edge computational tools. The union of traditional statistical rigor and computational innovation will be pivotal in developing the next generation of causal inference methods that can meet the demands of modern healthcare research.

14.4.4 Vision for the future

Looking ahead, the prospect of causal inference is intricately tied to advancements in computational capabilities and the democratization of healthcare data. The development of transparent, interpretable, and generalizable causal inference models will be essential to address the pressing needs of healthcare policy and practice.

Additionally, as the methodologies of causal inference become more sophisticated, there will be an increasing need for educational initiatives to equip the next generation of healthcare professionals with the necessary skills to apply these techniques effectively.

To conclude, the chapter posits causal inference as a critical component of evidence-based healthcare, one that has significant implications for patient outcomes and healthcare policy. The discussed methodologies illuminate a path forward, offering robust solutions to long-standing challenges in healthcare research. The future holds the promise of refined, data-driven healthcare interventions that can significantly enhance patient care and promote public health.

Through persistent effort, critical evaluation, and innovative thinking, the field of causal inference can continue to evolve, offering insightful contributions to the complex questions at the heart of healthcare. It remains our collective responsibility to harness these tools thoughtfully, ensuring that healthcare decisions are grounded in the most reliable evidence available.

References

[1] Greenland S, Pearl J, and Robins JM, Causal diagrams for epidemiological research. *Epidemiology*. 1999;10(1):37–48.
[2] Rosenbaum PR, and Rubin DB. The central role of the propensity score in observational studies for causal effects. *Biometrika*. 1983;70(1):41–55.
[3] Card D, and Krueger AB. Minimum wages and employment: a case study of the fast-food industry in New Jersey and Pennsylvania. *The American Economic Review*. 1994;84(4):772–793.
[4] Angrist JD, and Imbens GW. Identification and estimation of local average treatment effects. *Econometrica*. 1996;62(2):467–475.
[5] Lee DS Randomized experiments from non-random selection in U.S. House elections. *Journal of Econometrics*. 2008;142(2):675–697.
[6] Austin PC. An introduction to propensity score methods for reducing the effects of confounding in observational studies. *Multivariate Behavioral Research*. 2011;46(3):399–424.
[7] Imbens GW, and Wooldridge JM. Recent developments in the econometrics of program evaluation. *Journal of Economic Literature*. 2009;47(1):5–86.
[8] Lee DS, and Lemieux T. Regression discontinuity designs in economics. *Journal of Economic Literature*. 2010;48(2):281–355.
[9] Oldenburg, CE, Moscoe, E, and Bärnighausen, T. Regression discontinuity for causal effect estimation in epidemiology. *Current Epidemiology Reports*. 2016;3:233–241.
[10] Abadie A. Semiparametric difference-in-differences estimators. *Review of Economic Studies*. 2005;72(1):1–19.
[11] Hernán MA, and Robins JM. *Causal Inference: What If*. Boca Raton, FL: Chapman & Hall/CRC Press. 2020.
[12] Morgan SL, and Winship C. *Counterfactuals and Causal Inference*. Cambridge: Cambridge University Press. 2015.

[13] Stuart EA. Matching methods for causal inference: a review and a look forward. *Statistical Science*. 2010;25(1):1–21.
[14] Dunning T. *Natural Experiments in the Social Sciences: A Design-Based Approach*. Cambridge: Cambridge University Press. 2012.
[15] Heckman JJ, and Vytlacil EJ. Econometric evaluation of social programs, part I: causal models, structural models and econometric policy evaluation. *Handbook of Econometrics*. 2007;6:4779–4874.
[16] Imai K, and Van Dyk DA. Causal inference with general treatment regimes: generalizing the propensity score. *Journal of the American Statistical Association*. 2004;99(467):854–866.
[17] Robins JM, and Greenland S. Identifiability and exchangeability for direct and indirect effects. *Epidemiology*. 1992;3(2):143–155.
[18] Shadish WR, Cook TD, and Campbell DT. *Experimental and Quasi-Experimental Designs for Generalized Causal Inference*. Boston, MA: Houghton Mifflin. 2002.
[19] Imbens GW. Nonparametric estimation of average treatment effects under exogeneity: a review. *Review of Economics and Statistics*. 2004;86(1):4–29.
[20] Pearl J. *Causality: Models, Reasoning, and Inference*. Cambridge: Cambridge University Press. 2000.
[21] Hill JL. Bayesian nonparametric modeling for causal inference. *Journal of Computational and Graphical Statistics*. 2011;20(1):217–240.
[22] Efron B, and Tibshirani RJ. *An Introduction to the Bootstrap*. Boca Raton, FL: Chapman & Hall/CRC Press. 1993.
[23] Hernán MA, Brumback B, and Robins JM. Marginal structural models to estimate the causal effect of zidovudine on the survival of HIV-positive men. *Epidemiology*. 2000;11(5):561–570.
[24] Ho DE, Imai K, King G, and Stuart EA. Matching as nonparametric preprocessing for reducing model dependence in parametric causal inference. *Political Analysis*. 2007;15(3):199–236.
[25] Ravallion M. Evaluating anti-poverty programs. *Handbook of Development Economics*. 2008;4:3787–3846.
[26] Rosenbaum PR. *Observational Studies*. Berlin: Springer. 2002.
[27] Sun D, Simon GJ, Skube S, Blaes AH, Melton GB, and Zhang R. Causal phenotyping for susceptibility to cardiotoxicity from antineoplastic breast cancer medications. *AMIA Annual Symposium Proceedings*. 2018; 2017:1655–1664.
[28] Tsiatis AA. *Semiparametric Theory and Missing Data*. Berlin: Springer. 2006.
[29] Bang H, and Robins JM. Doubly robust estimation in missing data and causal inference models. *Biometrics*. 2005;61(4):962–973.
[30] Vansteelandt S, Bekaert M, and Claeskens G. On model selection and model misspecification in causal inference. *Statistical Methods in Medical Research*. 2012;21(1):7–30.
[31] Robins JM and Hernán MA. Estimation of the causal effects of time-varying exposures. *Longitudinal Data Analysis*. 2009:553–599.

[32] King G, and Zeng L. The dangers of extreme counterfactuals. *Political Analysis*. 2006;14(2):131–159.

[33] McMillan MT, Zureikat AH, Hogg ME, *et al.* A propensity score-matched analysis of robotic vs open pancreatoduodenectomy on incidence of pancreatic fistula. *JAMA Surgery*. 2017;152(4):327–335. doi:10.1001/jamasurg.2016.4755.

[34] Lee BP, Dodge JL, and Terrault NA. Medicaid expansion and variability in mortality in the USA: a national, observational cohort study. *Lancet Public Health*. 2022;7(1):e48–e55. doi:10.1016/S2468-2667(21)00252-8.

[35] Goulden R, Rowe BH, Abrahamowicz M, Strumpf E, and Tamblyn R. Association of intravenous radiocontrast with kidney function: a regression discontinuity analysis. *JAMA Internal Medicine*. 2021;181(6):767–774. doi:10.1001/jamainternmed.2021.0916.

[36] Yeh RW, Vasaiwala S, Forman DE, *et al.* Instrumental variable analysis to compare effectiveness of stents in the extremely elderly. *Circulation Cardiovascular Quality and Outcomes*. 2014;7(1):118–124. doi:10.1161/CIRCOUTCOMES.113.000476.

Chapter 15
Clinical risk modeling using medical big data: a machine learning approach

Zhen Hu[1], Jing Fan[2], Deyu Sun[3], Haipeng Liu[4] and Vikram Bandugula[5]

15.1 Introduction

Healthcare is an ever-evolving field, and these days precision and personalized medicine have become the cornerstones of providing the best possible patient care. Clinical risk modeling, which makes use of sophisticated machine learning (ML) techniques, fueled by medical big data, represents a transformative approach to achieving these objectives. This chapter will begin to introduce the world of clinical risk modeling, and its potential for impacting healthcare.

15.1.1 The crucial role of clinical risk modeling

Clinical risk modeling is the art and science of quantifying the likelihood of adverse events or disease progression for individual patients or populations. Taking a personalized approach, clinicians can estimate, predict and subsequently target clinical risks for people with specific conditions. Traditionally, clinical decisions were often population-based—based on broad recommendations and general guidelines. Before evidence-based medicine was prominent, clinicians often relied on nothing more than their subjective biases. Building on this, decision-analytic guidelines and population-based statistics have helped to personalize care to some extent, contouring clinical practice.

By harnessing the power of medical big data and ML, healthcare providers can now tailor their strategies to each patient's unique characteristics, history, and risk factors. Whether it's predicting the likelihood of a cardiovascular event, identifying patients at high risk of developing diabetes, or anticipating complications during

---

[1]Institute for Health Informatics, University of Minnesota, USA
[2]Carelon, Atlanta, GA, USA
[3]David Geffen School of Medicine, University of California Los Angeles, USA
[4]Centre for Intelligent Healthcare, Coventry University, UK
[5]Carelon, Chicago, IL, USA

surgery, clinical risk models offer the promise of more precise and proactive healthcare interventions.

15.1.2 The data-driven revolution

The driving force behind this transformation is the unprecedented availability of medical big data. Electronic health records (EHRs), medical imaging, genetic information, wearable devices, and a multitude of other data sources contribute to this vast and dynamic ecosystem. These rich datasets provide a comprehensive view of a patient's health journey, from their medical history and diagnostic tests to their lifestyle and genetic makeup.

Traditionally, medical data were often siloed in disparate systems, making it challenging to derive meaningful insights. However, with the advent of interoperability standards and data-sharing initiatives, the integration of diverse data sources has become increasingly feasible. ML algorithms thrive in this data-rich environment, extracting patterns, trends, and hidden correlations that were previously elusive.

At the heart of clinical risk modeling lies the utilization of advanced ML algorithms. These algorithms, ranging from classical regression techniques to cutting-edge deep learning approaches, serve as the analytical engine that processes the deluge of medical data. They have the remarkable capacity to discern complex relationships within the data and learn from it, enabling the development of predictive models that are both accurate and adaptable.

15.1.3 The promise of personalized medicine

The marriage of medical big data and ML offers the promise of personalized medicine—a paradigm shift in healthcare. Imagine a patient visiting their healthcare provider, not as a statistic within a population, but as a unique individual with a health profile crafted from a multitude of data points. Clinical risk models empower healthcare professionals to tailor treatments and interventions to address the specific risks and needs of each patient.

For instance, a cardiologist can use a predictive model to assess a patient's risk of heart disease, factoring in their age, gender, genetic predispositions, lifestyle choices, and historical health data. Armed with this personalized risk assessment, the cardiologist can recommend a tailored prevention plan that may include lifestyle modifications, medications, or specific diagnostic tests. This proactive approach has the potential to significantly improve patient outcomes while reducing healthcare costs.

This chapter aims to be your guide into this exciting world of clinical risk modeling using medical big data and ML. We will begin by delving deeper into the ML algorithms that underpin these models, understanding their technical aspects and practical applications through real-world case studies. We will explore the integration of multimodal medical data to enhance the reliability of risk assessments and discuss the challenges, opportunities, and future directions in this rapidly evolving field.

15.2 Machine learning for clinical risk modeling

In the realm of healthcare, where patient outcomes are of paramount importance, the ability to accurately predict and manage clinical risks is a game-changer. ML, a subset of artificial intelligence (AI), has emerged as a powerful tool in this pursuit. In this session, we will introduce a few traditional ML methods and more advanced methods like neural network as well, and its pivotal role in clinical risk modeling.

15.2.1 Traditional machine learning algorithms

ML is a branch of AI that focuses on the development of algorithms and models that enable computers to learn from and make predictions or decisions based on data. Unlike traditional programming, where explicit instructions are provided to achieve a specific task, ML algorithms learn patterns and relationships from data.

15.2.1.1 Regression techniques

Linear regression is one of the foundational techniques in ML. It is used to model the relationship between a dependent variable (in this case, clinical risk) and one or more independent variables (risk factors). Linear regression assumes a linear relationship between the variables and aims to find the best-fit line that minimizes the difference between predicted and actual values.

For clinical risk modeling, linear regression can be applied to predict risk scores based on various patient characteristics. It provides a straightforward way to quantify risk and establish associations between risk factors and outcomes.

While linear regression is a valuable tool for modeling relationships between continuous variables, logistic regression is particularly well suited for binary classification tasks common in clinical risk modeling. In healthcare, many risk assessments involve predicting binary outcomes, such as the presence or absence of a specific medical condition. Logistic regression extends the principles of linear regression to the realm of classification by employing a logistic (or sigmoid) function to transform the linear combination of predictors into a probability score between 0 and 1.

By analyzing patient demographics, medical history, and other relevant variables, logistic regression models can calculate the probability of an event occurring, which can then be used to classify patients into risk categories. These models are interpretable, making them valuable not only for predictive accuracy but also for understanding the contributions of various risk factors to the outcome. Logistic regression provides healthcare professionals with a transparent and easily interpretable tool for assessing clinical risks and making informed decisions regarding patient care and interventions.

15.2.1.2 Decision trees

Decision trees are another class of algorithms frequently used in healthcare risk modeling. A decision tree is a hierarchical structure comprising nodes and branches. Each node represents a condition or a feature, while branches emanating from

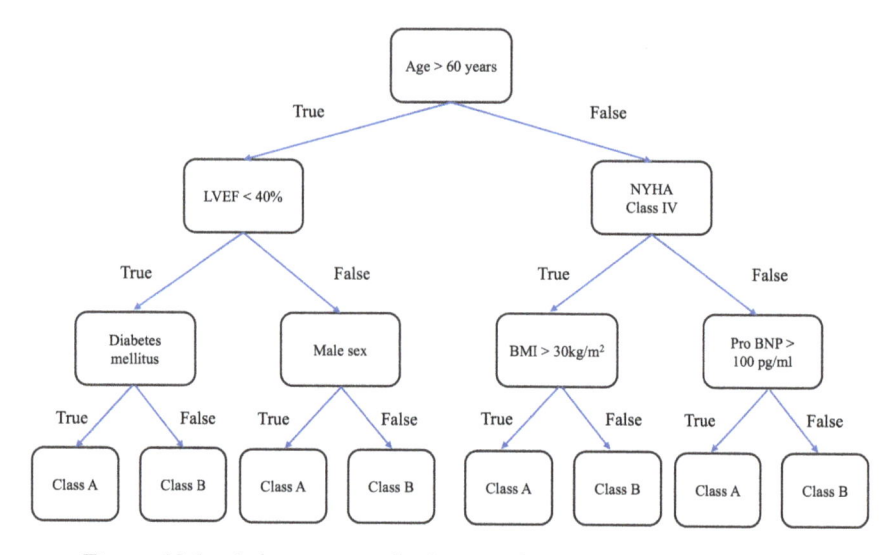

Figure 15.1 A decision tree built to predict mortality in heart failure

nodes represent possible outcomes or decisions. The top node, known as the root, represents the initial condition. As one moves down the tree, decisions are made at each node based on specific criteria. The final nodes, called leaves, correspond to the ultimate outcomes or predictions.

Decision trees are particularly useful for scenarios where decisions need to be made based on a series of conditions. Decision trees are hierarchical structures consisting of nodes (representing conditions) and branches (representing possible outcomes). In clinical risk modeling, decision trees can be employed to create rules or decision pathways for assessing risk. These trees can capture complex relationships between risk factors and outcomes, making them valuable tools for modeling healthcare scenarios.

Figure 15.1 illustrates a decision tree based on predictors of mortality in heart failure patients. The predictors include age, gender, BMI, body mass index, BNP, beta natriuretic peptide, LVEF, etc.

15.2.1.3 Support vector machine

Support vector machine (SVM) is a powerful and versatile ML algorithm used for both classification and regression. At its core, SVM seeks to find the best separating boundary, or 'hyperplane', between data points of different classes. In a two-dimensional space, this hyperplane can be thought of as a line dividing a plane in such a way that data points of separate categories are on different sides of the line. For a case where the data is not linearly separable, SVM employs a technique known as the kernel trick. This trick transforms the data into a higher-dimensional space where a hyperplane can be used to separate the classes. Figure 15.2 represents an example where the dataset, not separable in 2D, can be separated in 3D after applying the kernel trick. The beauty of the kernel trick is that it can handle

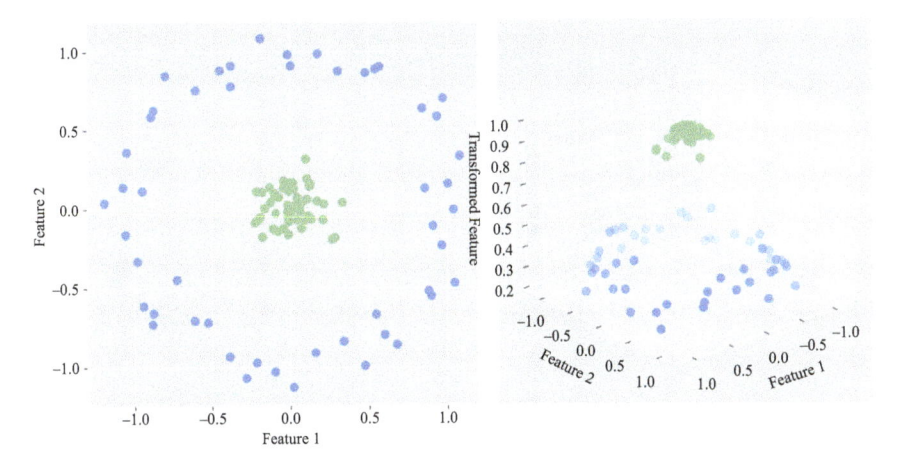

Figure 15.2   Labeled data in two dimension and three dimension

the computation of high-dimensional space without actually transforming the data, thus allowing SVM to efficiently handle complex, nonlinear relationships between data points.

In clinical risk modeling, SVM can be particularly useful when dealing with complex datasets where the relationship between input features (like patient characteristics) and the target variable (like disease presence) is not easily defined by a straight line or simple curve. SVM models can efficiently classify patients into high and low-risk categories, even when the boundaries between these categories are not immediately apparent.

SVMs are also appreciated for their robustness, especially in situations where the data has a lot of dimensions (features), which is common in medical datasets that can include a wide range of variables from patient demographics to genetic information. This makes SVM a valuable tool for developing predictive models that can assist healthcare professionals in making diagnostic and treatment decisions.

15.2.1.4   Random forests

Random forests are an ensemble learning method that builds multiple decision trees and combines their predictions to improve accuracy and reduce overfitting. Each tree is grown using a random subset of the data (bootstrap samples) and a random subset of the available features. This randomness introduces diversity among the individual trees. Predictions are made by aggregating the results from all the trees, typically through a majority vote (for classification tasks) or averaging (for regression tasks, as shown in Figure 15.3).

In healthcare, datasets often consist of numerous variables, including patient demographics, medical history, genetic information, environmental factors, and more. Random forests excel in handling high-dimensional data, making them suitable for risk assessments that involve a wide range of patient attributes and

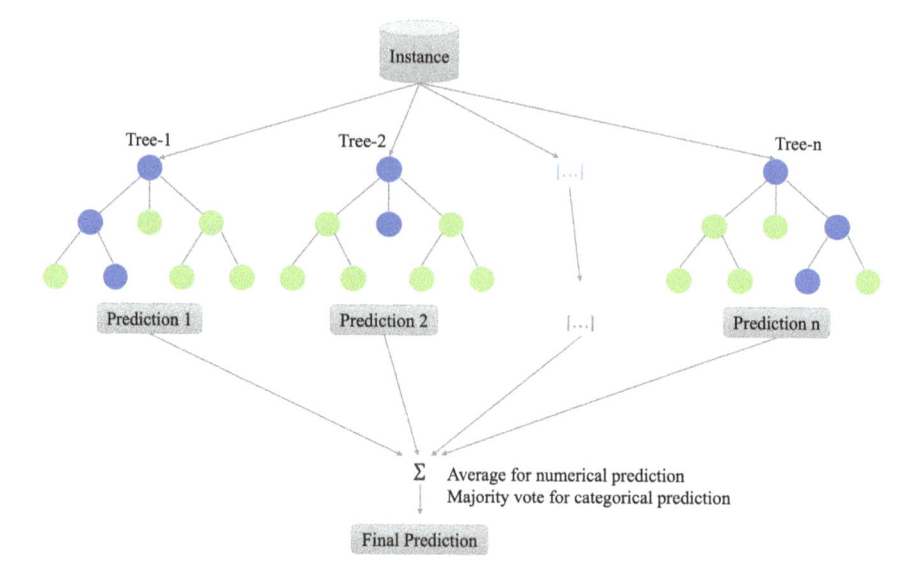

Figure 15.3   A basic structure of random forests for regression tasks

potential risk factors. The algorithm automatically selects relevant features, reducing the risk of overfitting and improving generalization. In addition, clinical risk modeling frequently involves complex and nonlinear relationships between risk factors and outcomes. Random forests are well suited to capture these intricate associations, thanks to their ability to create decision boundaries that adapt to the data's complexity. This flexibility ensures that risk assessments are not limited to linear relationships and can account for the multifaceted nature of healthcare data.

15.2.2   Deep learning approaches
15.2.2.1   Neural networks
Deep learning, a subset of ML, has gained immense popularity in recent years, owing to its exceptional performance in tasks involving complex and unstructured data. At the core of deep learning lies neural networks, computational models inspired by the human brain's structure and functioning.

Neural networks consist of layers of interconnected neurons, each layer serving a specific purpose in information processing. As an example shown in Figure 15.4, these layers include:

Input layer: This layer receives the raw data, which can include patient demographics, medical images, genetic information, and environmental variables. Each input feature corresponds to a neuron in the input layer.
Hidden layers: One or more hidden layers process the input data through a series of weighted connections and nonlinear activation functions. These hidden layers learn complex representations and relationships within the data.

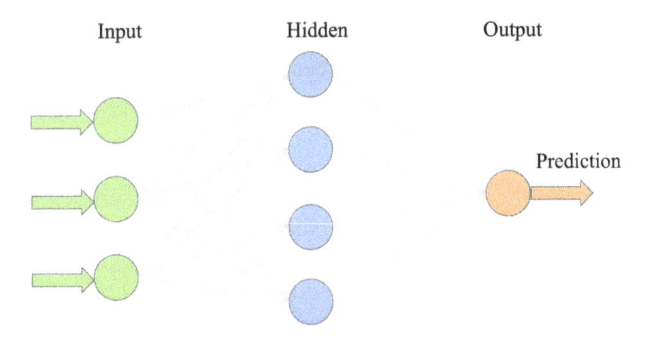

Figure 15.4 An example of a basic neural network

Output layer: The output layer produces the final predictions or classifications. Depending on the clinical risk modeling task, this layer may have one neuron for binary classification (e.g., presence or absence of a medical condition) or multiple neurons for multiclass classification (e.g., risk categories).

Neural networks learn from data through a process called training. During training, the network adjusts the weights of its connections to minimize the difference between predicted and actual outcomes. This process involves:

Forward propagation: The network makes predictions by passing input data through the layers, applying weights, and activation functions to produce output values.

Loss calculation: A loss function measures the difference between predicted and actual outcomes. Common loss functions include mean squared error (for regression tasks) and cross-entropy (for classification tasks).

Backpropagation: The network computes gradients of the loss with respect to its parameters (weights and biases) and updates them using optimization techniques like gradient descent. This iterative process improves the network's performance over time.

15.2.2.2 Convolutional neural networks and recurrent neural networks

Convolutional neural networks (CNNs) and recurrent neural networks (RNNs) have revolutionized the field of deep learning. CNNs, designed for image analysis, are characterized by their hierarchical feature learning. They employ convolutional layers that automatically detect patterns and features in visual data. These layers are followed by pooling operations to reduce spatial dimensions, resulting in a hierarchical representation of visual features. This hierarchical approach enables CNNs to capture intricate details within images, making them well suited for tasks like object detection and image classification.

However, RNNs specialize in processing sequential data by utilizing recurrent connections. They maintain a hidden state that captures information from previous time steps, allowing them to model temporal dependencies. This recurrent architecture makes RNNs suitable for tasks that involve sequences, such as natural language processing, time-series analysis, and sequential data generation. Long short-term memory (LSTM) and gated recurrent unit (GRU) variants of RNNs address the vanishing gradient problem, improving their ability to capture long-range dependencies.

In healthcare, CNNs have seamlessly integrated into the diagnostic process. Medical images, including X-rays, MRIs, and CT scans, are prime candidates for CNN analysis. These networks can autonomously identify abnormalities, tumors, and anomalies within images. For instance, CNNs have been instrumental in early cancer detection, assisting radiologists in making quicker and more accurate diagnoses. Additionally, they facilitate the interpretation of complex medical imagery, leading to improved patient outcomes.

RNNs, with their temporal modeling capabilities, have ushered in a new era of patient care. They are invaluable for analyzing time-series data such as patient records and physiological signals. RNNs predict disease progression, personalize treatment plans, and provide real-time monitoring, enhancing chronic disease management. Moreover, they excel in predictive analytics, enabling healthcare professionals to anticipate patient needs and optimize resource allocation.

15.2.3 The relevance of machine learning in clinical risk modeling

The application of ML techniques in clinical risk modeling offers several distinct advantages:

15.2.3.1 Data-driven insights
ML models can extract valuable insights and patterns from large and complex healthcare datasets. They have the ability to identify subtle relationships and dependencies among various risk factors, allowing for a more comprehensive understanding of clinical risks.

15.2.3.2 Personalization of risk assessment
ML models enable the personalization of risk assessments. Instead of applying generic risk scores to all patients, these models can tailor risk predictions based on individual patient characteristics. This personalization improves the precision of risk assessments and allows for more targeted interventions.

15.2.3.3 Adaptability and scalability
ML models are adaptable and scalable. They can accommodate changes in data and continuously update risk assessments as new information becomes available. This adaptability is particularly useful in dynamic healthcare environments.

15.2.4 Conclusion

ML has brought forth a new era in healthcare risk assessment, enabling data-driven insights, personalization of risk assessments, and adaptability to changing conditions. As we move forward in this chapter, we will delve deeper into the technical aspects of model development, using case studies to illustrate the practical application of these algorithms in real-world healthcare scenarios. In the following sessions, we will explore how these models can be integrated into healthcare workflows and discuss the challenges, opportunities, and future directions in this evolving field.

15.3 Model development and case studies

In this session, we will introduce the general model development process and explore real-world case studies. By examining these use cases, we aim to illustrate how ML can translate into practical solutions, benefiting both healthcare professionals and patients.

15.3.1 Model development process

Before delving into the case studies, it's essential to understand the general process of developing clinical risk models using ML:

Data collection and preparation: The foundation of any successful clinical risk model lies in robust data collection and preparation. This initial phase involves aggregating relevant medical data from diverse sources, such as EHRs, laboratory results, medical imaging, wearable devices, and patient-reported outcomes. Ensuring data quality, accuracy, and consistency is paramount during this stage. Additionally, handling imbalanced datasets, where one class significantly outweighs the other, requires special attention to avoid biased predictions. Techniques such as resampling (oversampling or under-sampling) and algorithms like Synthetic Minority Over-sampling Technique (SMOTE) can help address class imbalance and improve model performance. Data cleaning, normalization, and handling missing values remain essential tasks to create a reliable dataset.

Feature selection and engineering: Identifying and harnessing the most informative features or variables is central to risk assessment. This phase entails not only selecting the relevant attributes but also engineering them to enhance their predictive power. Feature engineering techniques may involve creating new variables, aggregating data over time, or applying mathematical transformations. Additionally, handling missing data is a crucial aspect of feature engineering, where techniques such as imputation or deletion of missing values are employed. It's in this stage that the data scientist or researcher adds domain knowledge to extract meaningful insights from the data.

Model selection: Choosing the right ML algorithms is a pivotal decision that hinges on the specific nature of the clinical problem at hand. Factors like interpretability, scalability, and model performance come into play. Decision trees, random forests, logistic regression, and neural networks are among the myriad of algorithms available. Selecting the most suitable algorithm is often a balance between model complexity and the interpretability needs of healthcare stakeholders.

Training and evaluation: Training ML models using historical data is the next crucial step. During this phase, a portion of the dataset is allocated for validation and testing. Model performance is assessed using relevant evaluation metrics, including accuracy, sensitivity, specificity, and the area under the receiver operating characteristic curve (AUC-ROC). Rigorous evaluation ensures that the model can make reliable predictions on unseen patient data.

Table 15.1 represents the confusion matrix for a binary classification problem. It includes the following components:

- True positives (TP): The number of cases predicted as 'Yes' for the binary target variable, and they actually have that value.
- False negatives (FN): The number of cases with an actual value of 'Yes' for the target variable, but they were predicted as 'No.'
- False positives (FP): The number of cases with an actual value of 'No,' but they were predicted as 'Yes.'
- True negatives (TN): The number of cases with an actual value of 'No,' and they were correctly predicted as such.

In Table 15.2, we provide definitions for common model performance evaluation metrics used in binary classification. These metrics are explicitly based on

Table 15.1 A typical confusion matrix for binary classification problem

Actual class	Predicted class	
	Yes (1)	**No (0)**
Yes (1)	True positive (TP)	False negative (FN)
No (0)	False positive (FP)	True negative (TN)

Table 15.2 A list of commonly used model performance evaluation metrics

Evaluation metrics	Also known as	Formula
Sensitivity	True positive rate (TPR); hit rate; recall	TP/(TP + FN)
Specificity	True negative rate (TNR)	TN/(TN + FP)
Positive predictivity	Positive predictive value (PPV); precision	TP/(TP + FP)
Negative predictivity	Negative predictive value	TN/(TN + FN)
False negative rate	Miss rate	FN/(TP + FN)
False positive rate	False-out	FP/(FP + TN)
False discovery rate	NA	FP/(TP + FP)
False omission rate	NA	FN/(FN + TN)
Percent correctly classified	Accuracy	(TP + TN)/(TP + TN + FP + FN)

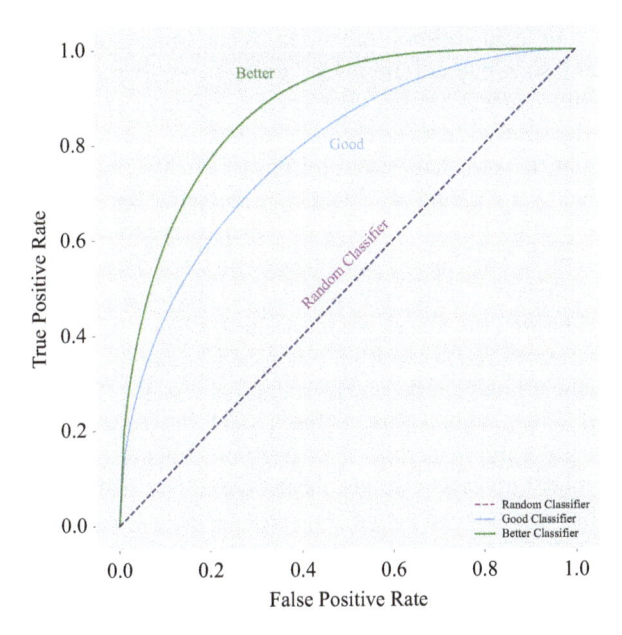

Figure 15.5 Analysis of receiver operating characteristic curves for different classifiers

the cell counts presented in Table 15.1. One notable metric not directly derived from the confusion matrix is the area under the curve (AUC) and receiver operating characteristic (ROC) curve. The ROC curve illustrates the relationship between the true positive rate (sensitivity) and the false positive rate (1−specificity) at various thresholds used for binary classification. As shown in Figure 15.5, an AUC value near 0.5 suggests a poor-fitting classification model, while values closer to 1 indicate more accurate models. The AUC statistic quantifies the probability that the model will rank a randomly selected 'Yes' case higher than a randomly chosen 'No' case.

For regression tasks, model evaluation involves metrics tailored to continuous output predictions. Common regression evaluation metrics include:

- **Mean absolute error (MAE)**: This metric calculates the average of the absolute differences between predictions and the actual values. It provides a straightforward measure of prediction accuracy.
- **Mean squared error (MSE)**: Squaring the differences between predictions and actual values before averaging them, MSE penalizes larger errors more heavily than MAE.
- **Root mean squared error (RMSE)**: RMSE is the square root of the MSE, offering an interpretable metric in the same units as the target variable.
- **R-squared (R2)**: Also known as the coefficient of determination, R2 represents the proportion of the variance in the dependent variable that is predictable from the independent variables. It ranges from 0 to 1, with higher values indicating a better fit of the model to the data.

Validation and calibration: Validation is an important step that extends beyond the initial testing phase. It involves rigorously verifying the performance of the model on an independent dataset, thereby demonstrating its generalizability and reliability in real-world scenarios. Through validation, we assess how well the model performs on unseen data, ensuring that it doesn't merely memorize the training data but can accurately predict outcomes for new observations. Additionally, calibration of the model is essential to ensure its predictions align with actual outcomes. This calibration process involves fine-tuning the model's predicted probabilities to accurately reflect the likelihood of specific events occurring. By calibrating the model, we ensure that when it assigns a risk score or probability estimate, it does so with precision and reliability, thus enhancing its usability and trustworthiness in decision-making processes.

Deployment: The culmination of the model development process is its deployment into real clinical workflows or decision support systems. This crucial step makes the model accessible to healthcare providers, enabling them to make informed decisions and take proactive measures for patient care. Implementation considerations, including integration with existing systems, security, and user-friendly interfaces, play a pivotal role in the successful deployment of clinical risk models.

15.3.2 Model performance monitoring and potential Re-fit

The development of clinical risk models doesn't conclude with their deployment; it's an ongoing process that requires continuous monitoring and, in some cases, refinement. This phase is critical for ensuring that the models maintain their predictive accuracy and effectiveness over time. Below are key components of model performance monitoring and potential re-fit:

Performance metrics tracking: After deployment, it's imperative to continuously track the performance of the clinical risk model using real-world patient data. This involves calculating the same evaluation metrics as during the initial evaluation phase, such as accuracy, sensitivity, specificity, and AUC-ROC. Monitoring these metrics over time can reveal if the model's performance is degrading or if it remains consistent.

Concept drift detection: One challenge in healthcare is the concept drift phenomenon, where the statistical properties of the input data change over time. This can result from evolving medical practices, changes in patient demographics, or updates to EHR systems. Detecting concept drift is crucial because it may necessitate model re-fitting or adaptation to new data distributions.

Regular model updating: As new data becomes available and the model is in use, it may be necessary to periodically re-train the model with the most recent data to ensure it continues to capture underlying patterns and relationships. This process can help mitigate the impact of concept drift and maintain the model's accuracy.

Retraining strategies: When deciding on retraining strategies, consider the balance between retaining historical knowledge and adapting to new information. Techniques such as online learning, transfer learning, and incremental learning

can be valuable in updating models efficiently without discarding previously learned insights.
Ethical and regulatory considerations: It's essential to monitor not only the technical performance of the model but also its ethical and regulatory compliance. Ensure that the model continues to align with privacy regulations and ethical guidelines, especially as new data sources or patient populations are incorporated.
Stakeholder communication: Effective communication with healthcare stakeholders, including clinicians and decision-makers, is essential throughout the model's lifecycle. Keep stakeholders informed about any changes or updates to the model and solicit their feedback to ensure that it remains aligned with clinical goals and requirements.
Decision on re-fitting: Based on the performance metrics, concept drift detection, and retraining strategies, make informed decisions on whether to re-fit the model. Re-fitting may involve updating the algorithm, revisiting feature selection, or adjusting model parameters to adapt to changing conditions.

By incorporating these elements into the model performance monitoring and potential re-fit phase, healthcare organizations can ensure the continued effectiveness and relevance of their clinical risk models in improving patient care and outcomes.

15.3.3 Case studies: practical applications of machine learning in clinical risk modeling

15.3.3.1 Use case 1: predicting chronic diseases using logistic regression versus machine learning models

In recent years, there's been a marked shift towards exploring the potential of ML within healthcare, spurring discussions about the comparative strengths of traditional statistical models versus cutting-edge ML approaches. This shift is especially pronounced when predicting the onset of chronic diseases. Drawing from a comprehensive study involving a cohort of Asian adults from the Singapore Epidemiology of Eye Disease, the comparative predictive power of various algorithms against standard logistic regression was assessed. The focus was on forecasting major chronic ailments like cardiovascular diseases, chronic kidney disease, diabetes, and hypertension.

Objective: The study aimed to assess the performance of ML algorithms in predicting the risk of prevalent chronic diseases and juxtapose them with logistic regression utilizing uncomplicated clinical predictors.

Study design: A population-based cohort study was conducted among Asian adults, encompassing 6,762 participants. The diseases under scrutiny included cardiovascular diseases (CVD), chronic kidney disease (CKD), diabetes (DM), and hypertension (HTN). Five distinct ML models were tested, namely single-hidden-layer neural network (NN), SVM, random forest (RR), gradient boosting machine (GBM), and k-nearest neighbor (KNN). These were juxtaposed with the conventional logistic regression (LR) approach. Together six modeling algorithms were explored.

Methods: The Singapore Epidemiology of Eye Disease cohort study provided the data, focusing on Asian ethnicities ranging from ages 40 to 80. Outcomes considered were CVD, CKD, DM, and HTN. For each outcome, predictors were selected based on clinical expertise and literature. Figure 15.6 showcases the modeling strategy and development process, including preprocessing, considering six different models, a specific resampling strategy, and assessing predictive performance. Interaction and nonlinearity among predictors were gauged using gradient boosting machines. The issue of class imbalance, especially when the disease incidence was below 10%, was addressed using SMOTE.

Findings: As shown in Figure 15.7, interestingly, the results revealed that the traditional logistic regression outperformed most models in predicting CVD and DM. For CVD and HTN, while the neural network and SVM showed marginally enhanced performance, the difference was statistically non-significant when juxtaposed with logistic regression. Across the board, logistic regression, combined with gradient boosting machine and neural network, emerged as the top-performing models.

Conclusion: In epidemiological contexts with moderate sample sizes, limited incident events, and uncomplicated clinical predictors, logistic regression exhibited comparable performance to ML models for chronic disease risk prediction. When equipped with a limited predictor set, traditional regression models remain paramount in disease risk prediction. For seasoned data scientists, this study serves as a pertinent reminder. Despite the allure and potential of advanced ML techniques,

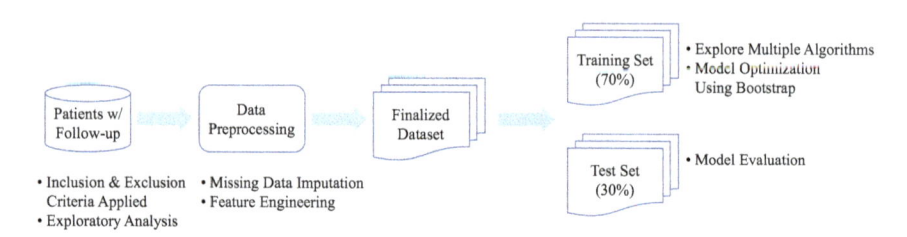

Figure 15.6 The pipeline for the model development and evaluation process

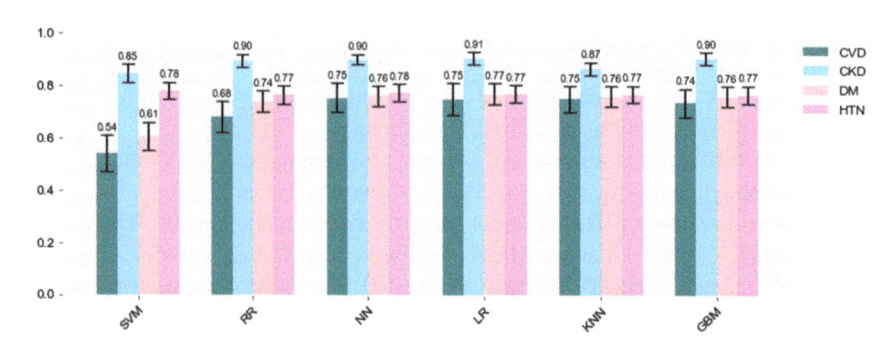

Figure 15.7 Model performance in AUC across different diseases

logistic regression remains a potent tool, especially when dealing with datasets characterized by moderate sample sizes, fewer events, and a set of straightforward clinical predictors. ML models might reveal their true strength in situations where the data exhibits complex nonlinear relationships and high levels of interaction. However, data experts should exercise discernment and caution, weighing the computational and interpretability benefits of traditional models against the sophistication of ML algorithms. The overarching takeaway is the importance of matching the choice of model to the unique intricacies of the dataset, the goals of the research, and the specific clinical or real-world context in which it operates.

15.3.3.2 Use case 2: predicting Alzheimer's disease progression with multi-modal deep learning

Alzheimer's disease (AD), a progressive neurodegenerative condition, presents significant challenges for timely detection and treatment. A pivotal stage, mild cognitive impairment (MCI), lies between cognitively normal older adults and AD. Successfully predicting the conversion from MCI to AD can have significant implications for early interventions.

The use of multi-modal data, including EHRs, biomarkers, and imaging data, is revolutionizing disease prediction with ML. These diverse data sources provide a holistic view of a patient's health, enabling more accurate predictions, early intervention, and personalized treatment strategies. By integrating these modalities, researchers move beyond isolated variables and unlock the power to transform healthcare delivery.

Methodology and data: Researchers leveraged the Alzheimer's Disease Neuroimaging Initiative cohort (ADNI) to design an integrative framework for prediction. This framework hinges on multiple data sources, mainly including four categories of dataset:

- Demographic information (including age, sex, education, and APOE ε4 status).
- Neuroimaging data from MRI scans, emphasizing features like hippocampal volume and entorhinal cortical thickness.
- Cognitive performance scores covering executive functioning and memory.
- CSF biomarkers linked to AD, like amyloid-β 1–42 peptide, total tau, and tau phosphorylated at threonine 181.

As represented in Figure 15.8, a multi-modal deep learning method, specifically a variant called GRU, was at the heart of this framework. GRUs excel at analyzing sequential data, and in this study, they processed the above four data types. Multiple GRUs were employed, in the first training process, one for each data modality, converting both time series (cognitive performance and CSF data) or non-time series data (i.e., demographics and MRI imaging data) into fixed-size feature vectors. Afterward, in the second training process, the outputs of those GRUs generated in the previous step were concatenated, forming an integrated input that was then fed into a final prediction layer based on L1-regularized logistic regression.

To assess the performance of the proposed multi-modal deep learning method using three different schemes: baseline, single modal, and proposed. In the baseline

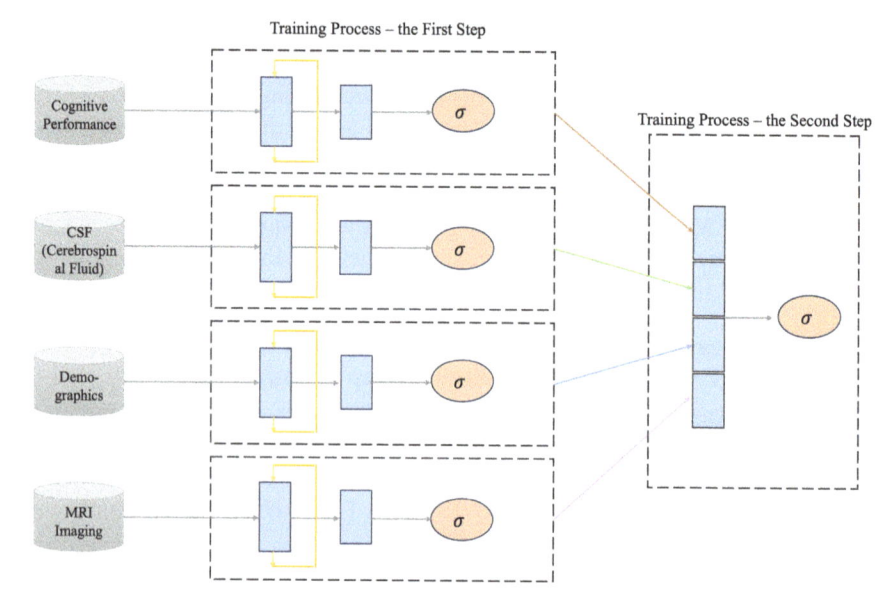

Figure 15.8 Overview of the proposed multi-modal deep learning method

scheme, four modalities of data at the initial visit were integrated. The single modal scheme utilized only longitudinal cognitive performance data. Lastly, the proposed scheme combined four modalities of longitudinal data for training the classifier. The study involved training models on subjects within the cognitively normal (CN) and AD groups, as well as those with MCI converting (MCI-C) and MCI not converting (MCI-NC) to AD.

Results: As shown in Figure 15.9, compared with model using baseline or three signal modal data separately, the proposed prediction model using multi-modal data exhibited significant higher accuracy, sensitivity, and specificity to predict cross all four events from 6 to 24 months. Notably, the proposed model achieved higher sensitivity, though it was observed to have a slightly lower specificity.

Discussion: The proposed multi-modal deep learning approach demonstrated the advantages of integrating various data modalities for the timely prediction of MCI to AD conversion. The capacity to incorporate variable-length longitudinal data, even without preliminary preprocessing, was a standout feature of this method. Moreover, the inclusion of non-overlapping samples enhanced the model's training set, a crucial advantage in scenarios of data scarcity. However, the model was not without its limitations. One primary concern was the potential filtering out of critical features during the initial GRU-based feature extraction, especially those discernable only when data modalities were combined. To address this, the researchers aim to modify the model structure to allow GRUs to extract integrative features, ensuring a more holistic representation.

In conclusion, this innovative deep learning approach, by leveraging diverse data modalities, offers significant promise for early AD detection. It heralds a

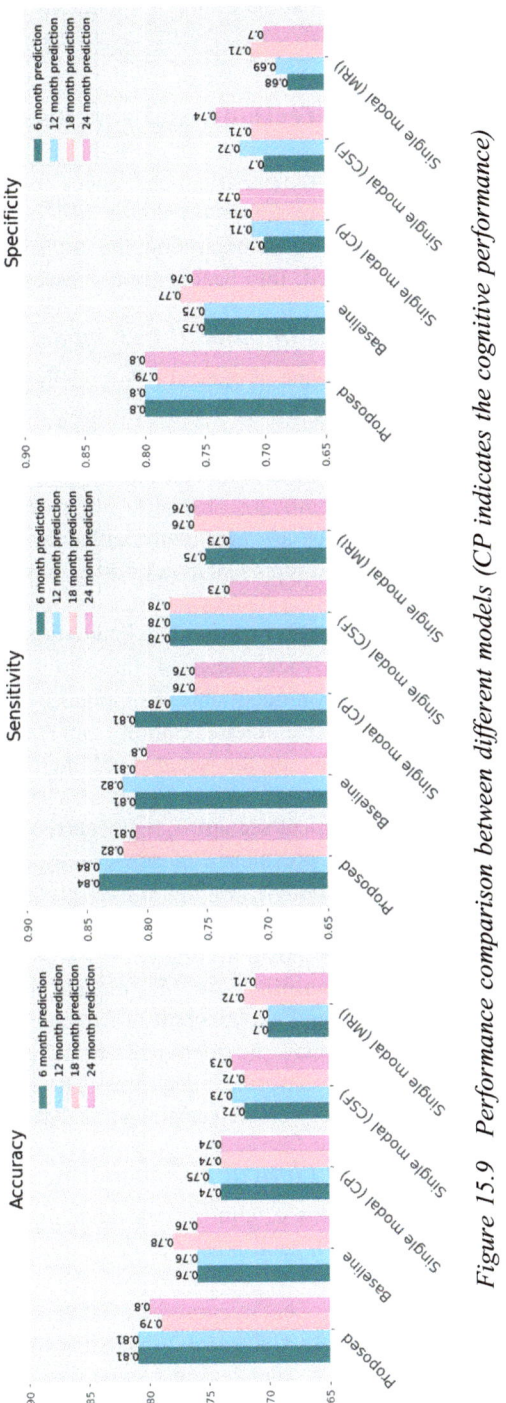

Figure 15.9 Performance comparison between different models (CP indicates the cognitive performance)

future where high-risk individuals can be promptly identified for potential clinical trials or targeted interventions.

15.4 Challenges, future directions, and conclusion

In this final session, we delve into the persistent challenges encountered in clinical risk modeling, explore the exciting future directions that hold the potential to reshape the field, and conclude by summarizing the transformative impact of integrating medical big data and ML into healthcare risk assessment.

15.4.1 Persistent challenges in clinical risk modeling

As we navigate the complex landscape of clinical risk modeling, several challenges remain constant, requiring ongoing attention and innovative solutions.

Data quality and accessibility: High-quality data serves as the bedrock of effective risk modeling. However, issues related to data quality, completeness, and accessibility continue to pose significant obstacles. Variability in data sources, missing values, and inconsistencies are prevalent challenges. Ensuring that data collected is accurate, complete, and representative of diverse patient populations is imperative.

Data privacy and ethical considerations: The integration of sensitive patient data necessitates stringent data privacy measures. Protecting patient privacy and ensuring ethical use of data are non-negotiable. Compliance with regulatory frameworks, such as HIPAA (Health Insurance Portability and Accountability Act), is essential. Maintaining patient trust in the security of their health information remains an ongoing challenge.

Data imbalance: In many clinical scenarios, the occurrence of adverse events is relatively rare compared to the prevalence of non-events. This data imbalance can skew the performance of risk models, leading to over-prediction of rare events. Techniques for handling imbalanced data, such as resampling methods and cost-sensitive learning, are essential for model accuracy.

Interpretability and explainability: As ML models become increasingly sophisticated, the interpretability and explainability of model predictions become challenging. Clinicians and healthcare providers need to understand and trust the outputs of these models to make informed decisions. Developing methods for making complex models more interpretable remains an active area of research.

15.4.2 Future directions in clinical risk modeling

While challenges persist, the horizon of clinical risk modeling is illuminated by a host of promising future directions, each poised to drive innovation in healthcare risk assessment.

Advanced data integration: The integration of diverse data sources will continue to advance. Beyond EHRs and genetic data, real-time wearable device data, omics data (e.g., proteomics, metabolomics), and social determinants of health will be incorporated into risk assessments. This comprehensive data integration will enable a more holistic view of patient health and enhance the precision of risk predictions.

AI and predictive analytics: AI and predictive analytics will play an increasingly central role in clinical risk modeling. ML algorithms will become more sophisticated, capable of processing vast datasets and identifying intricate patterns. AI-driven decision support systems will become commonplace in clinical practice, aiding healthcare providers in making data-informed decisions.

Patient-centered care: The paradigm of patient-centered care will gain further traction. Patients will not only receive risk assessments but will actively participate in their healthcare decision-making. Empowered with personalized risk assessments, patients will collaborate with healthcare providers to choose interventions and treatments aligned with their individual preferences and values.

Preventive and proactive healthcare: Proactive healthcare, driven by risk assessments, will take center stage. The identification of individuals at high risk for adverse events will enable timely and targeted interventions. Preventive measures, early detection, and proactive interventions will reduce the burden of chronic diseases and complications, ultimately improving patient outcomes and reducing healthcare costs.

Large language model (LLM): LLMs are revolutionizing clinical risk modeling through their advanced natural language processing capabilities. By analyzing extensive healthcare datasets including medical literature, patient records, and clinical trial data, LLMs excel in identifying complex correlations and predicting patient outcomes with remarkable precision. Leveraging their ability to extract insights from unstructured clinical notes, LLMs augment traditional risk factors with nuanced contextual information, enriching the depth of risk assessments. As LLM technology continues to evolve, its seamless integration into clinical risk modeling promises to significantly enhance patient outcomes and drive forward precision medicine initiatives.

As we gaze into the future, we recognize that the field of clinical risk modeling is poised for further transformation. Addressing persistent data challenges, ensuring data privacy, and advancing data integration will be central to this evolution. By placing patient-centered care at the forefront and embracing proactive healthcare, the future of healthcare risk assessment promises to benefit both individual patients and healthcare systems worldwide.

In conclusion, clinical risk modeling, driven by medical big data and ML, is reshaping the landscape of healthcare. It has ushered in an era of precision medicine, proactive healthcare, and patient empowerment. As we navigate the challenges and seize the opportunities on this journey, we stand on the cusp of a healthcare revolution that has the potential to improve patient outcomes, reduce healthcare costs, and enhance the overall quality of healthcare delivery.

References

[1] Ribeiro MT, Singh S, and Guestrin C. 'Why should I trust you?' Explaining the predictions of any classifier. In: *Proceedings of the 22nd ACM SIGKDD*

International Conference on Knowledge Discovery and Data Mining. 2016. pp. 1135–1144.
[2] Shortliffe EH, Sepúlveda MJ, Healthcare IOF. Clinical decision support in the era of artificial intelligence. *JAMA*. 2018;320(21):2199–2200.
[3] Darcy AM, Louie AK, and Roberts LW. Machine learning and the profession of medicine. *JAMA*. 2016;315(6):551–552.
[4] Rajkomar A, Dean J, and Kohane I. Machine learning in medicine. *N Engl J Med*. 2019;380(14):1347–1358.
[5] Chen JH, and Asch SM. Machine learning and prediction in medicine. Machine learning and prediction in medicine—beyond the peak of inflated expectations. *N Engl J Med*. 2017;376(26):2507–2509.
[6] Esteva A, Kuprel B, Novoa RA, *et al*. Dermatologist-level classification of skin cancer with deep neural networks. *Nature*. 2017;542(7639):115–118.
[7] Beam AL, and Kohane IS. Big data and machine learning in health care. *JAMA*. 2018;319(13):1317–1318.
[8] Goldstein BA, Navar AM, Pencina MJ, and Ioannidis JP. Opportunities and challenges in developing risk prediction models with electronic health records data: a systematic review. *JAMA Cardiol*. 2017;2(11):1205–1210.
[9] Chen M, Hao Y, Hwang K, and Wang L. Disease prediction by machine learning over big data from healthcare communities. *IEEE Access*. 2015; 5:8869–8879.
[10] Hu Z, Melton GB, Arsoniadis EG, Wang Y, Kwaan MR, and Simon GJ. Strategies for handling missing clinical data for automated surgical site infection detection from the electronic health record. *J Biomed Inform*. 2017; 68:112–120. doi:10.1016/j.jbi.2017.03.009.
[11] Anyanwu EC, Chua RFM, Besser SA, Sun D, Liao JK, and Tabit CE. SALAD-BAAR: a numerical risk score for hospital admission or emergency department presentation in ambulatory patients with cardiovascular disease. *Clin Cardiol*. 2021;44(2):193–199. doi:10.1002/clc.23525.
[12] Hu Z, Simon GJ, Arsoniadis EG, Wang Y, Kwaan MR, and Melton GB. Automated detection of postoperative surgical site infections using supervised methods with electronic health record data. *Stud Health Technol Inform*. 2015;216:706–710.
[13] Chen JH, and Asch SM. Machine learning and prediction in medicine. Machine learning and prediction in medicine—beyond the peak of inflated expectations. *N Engl J Med*. 2017;376(26):2507–2509.
[14] Obermeyer Z, and Emanuel EJ. Predicting the future—big data, machine learning, and clinical medicine. *N Engl J Med*. 2016;375(13):1216–1219.
[15] Beam AL, and Kohane IS. Big data and machine learning in health care. *JAMA*. 2018;319(13):1317–1318.
[16] Esteva A, Kuprel B, Novoa RA, *et al*. Dermatologist-level classification of skin cancer with deep neural networks. *Nature*. 2017;542(7639):115–118.
[17] Goldstein BA, Navar AM, Pencina MJ, and Ioannidis JP. Opportunities and challenges in developing risk prediction models with electronic health records data: a systematic review. *JAMA Cardiol*. 2017;2(11):1205–1210.

[18] Chen M, Hao Y, Hwang K, and Wang L. Disease prediction by machine learning over big data from healthcare communities. *IEEE Access*. 2015; 5:8869–8879.
[19] Ngiam KY, Khor IW, Jin L, and Sweeney TE. Adversarial machine learning in healthcare: a survey. *ACM Comput Surv (CSUR)*. 2019;52(3):1–36.
[20] Miotto R, Wang F, Wang S, Jiang X, and Dudley JT. Deep learning for healthcare: review, opportunities, and challenges. *Brief Bioinform*. 2017;19(6): 1236–1246.
[21] Caruana R, Lou Y, Gehrke J, Koch P, Sturm M, and Elhadad N. Intelligible models for healthcare: predicting pneumonia risk and hospital 30-day readmission. In: *Proceedings of the 21st ACM SIGKDD International Conference on Knowledge Discovery and Data Mining*. 2015. pp. 1721–1730.
[22] Rajkomar A, Oren E, Chen K, *et al.* Scalable and accurate deep learning with electronic health records. *NPJ Digit Med*. 2018;1(1):1–10.
[23] Char DS, Shah NH, and Magnus D. Implementing machine learning in health care—addressing ethical challenges. *N Engl J Med*. 2018;378(11):981–983.
[24] Ting DS, Cheung CY, Lim G, *et al.* Development and validation of a deep learning system for diabetic retinopathy and related eye diseases using retinal images from multiethnic populations with diabetes. *JAMA*. 2017;318 (22):2211–2223.
[25] Rajpurkar P, Irvin J, Zhu K, Yang B, Mehta H, Duan T, *et al.* CheXNet: Radiologist-Level Pneumonia Detection on Chest X-Rays with Deep Learning. arXiv: 1711.05225. 2017 Dec.
[26] Choi E, Bahadori MT, Schuetz A, Stewart WF, and Sun J. Doctor AI: predicting clinical events via recurrent neural networks. *J Healthc Inform Res*. 2016;2(4):327–349.
[27] Esteva A, Robicquet A, Ramsundar B, *et al.* A guide to deep learning in healthcare. *Nat Med*. 2019;25(1):24–29.
[28] Shameer K, Johnson KW, Yahi A, *et al.* Predictive modeling of hospital readmission rates using electronic medical record-wide machine learning: a case-study using Mount Sinai Heart Failure Cohort. *NPJ Digit Med*. 2018;1(1): 1–10.
[29] Wiens J, Guttag J, and Horvitz E. Patient risk stratification with time-varying parameters: a multitask learning approach. *J Mach Learn Res*. 2017;18 (1):3065–3091.
[30] Sevenster M, Sun D, Oliveira L, Lee ME, Spencer KT, and Blair JAE. Development and evaluation of a system that executes an interventional cardiology risk model based on patient phenotypes automatically extracted from the EMR. In: *2020 IEEE International Conference on Healthcare Informatics (ICHI)*. Oldenburg, Germany; 2020. pp. 1–8. doi:10.1109/ ICHI48887.2020.9374317.
[31] Hu Z, Melton GB, Moeller ND, *et al.* Accelerating chart review using automated methods on electronic health record data for postoperative complications. *AMIA Annu Symp Proc*. 2016;2017:1822–1831.

[32] Skube SJ, Hu Z, Simon GJ, *et al.* Accelerating surgical site infection abstraction with a semi-automated machine-learning approach. *Ann Surg.* 2022;276(1):180–185. doi:10.1097/SLA.0000000000004354.

[33] Nusinovici S, Tham YC, Chak Yan MY, *et al.* Logistic regression was as good as machine learning for predicting major chronic diseases. *J Clin Epidemiol.* 2020;122:56–69. https://doi.org/10.1016/j.jclinepi.2020.03.002.

[34] Lee G, Nho K, Kang B, Sohn KA, and Kim D. Alzheimer's disease neuroimaging initiative (ADNI). Predicting Alzheimer's disease progression using multi-modal deep learning approach. *Sci Rep.* 2019;9(1):1952. https://doi.org/10.1038/s41598-018-37769-z.

[35] Kianian R, Sun D, Crowell EL, and Tsui E. The use of large language models to generate education materials about uveitis. *Ophthalmol Retina.* 2024;8(2):195–201. doi:10.1016/j.oret.2023.09.008.

Chapter 16
Unlock potential of artificial intelligence and blockchain integration for preserving privacy and medical data: high-fidelity data sharing and healthcare analytics lensing legal aspects

Bhupinder Singh[1] and Christian Kaunert[2]

The personal health data sharing is made possible by mobile and wearable technology. It has a tremendous and growing value for healthcare, helping both providers of care and medical research. The enhancement of engagement and collaboration within the healthcare business depends on the secure and convenient sharing of personal health data. This chapter proposes an innovative user-centric health data sharing solution using a decentralized and permissioned blockchain to protect privacy using channel formation scheme and enhance identity management using the membership service. It is supported by the blockchain in response to the potential privacy issues and vulnerabilities existing in current personal health data storage and sharing systems as well as the concept of self-sovereign data ownership. Secure data sharing and collaboration in healthcare analytics are essential components to harness the power of data for informed decision-making and improved patient outcomes while maintaining patient privacy and data security. Achieving this delicate balance requires a combination of technological solutions, legal frameworks, and best practices to ensure that sensitive healthcare data is shared and analyzed in a secure and ethical manner. For the purpose of exchanging health information with healthcare professionals and health insurance providers, a mobile application is used to gather data from medical equipment, wearable personal gadgets, manual input, and other sources. Each record has a proof of integrity and validation that can be permanently retrieved from a cloud database and is anchored to the blockchain network in order to protect the integrity of health data. In addition, to handle massive data sets of personal health data collected and uploaded via the mobile platform, we utilize a tree-based data processing and batching mechanism for scalability and performance concerns.

[1]Sharda School of Law, Sharda University Greater Noida, India
[2]International Security, Dublin City University, Ireland

16.1 Introduction

The artificial intelligence (AI) and blockchain technologies holds immense promise for revolutionizing the preservation of privacy and security in the realm of medical data. As healthcare systems increasingly digitize patient information, concerns over data breaches, unauthorized access, and compromised patient confidentiality have become paramount. AI, with its capabilities in data analysis, pattern recognition, and predictive modeling, can enable robust encryption, anonymization, and access controls to safeguard sensitive medical information. When seamlessly integrated with blockchain, a decentralized and immutable ledger, AI can facilitate high-fidelity data sharing while ensuring that only authorized entities possess access to specific patient records. Blockchain's inherent transparency and tamper-resistant nature establish trust among stakeholders, mitigating the risks of data manipulation or unauthorized changes.

In the face of a rapidly digitizing healthcare landscape, concerns surrounding data breaches, unauthorized access, and the integrity of sensitive medical records have become paramount. AI, with its prowess in data analysis, pattern recognition, and predictive modeling, offers a formidable solution by enabling sophisticated encryption, anonymization, and stringent access controls. When coupled with the inherent attributes of blockchain – decentralization, immutability, and transparency – AI's capabilities are amplified, enabling high-fidelity data sharing while mitigating risks associated with data manipulation, unauthorized alteration, and breaches of patient confidentiality.

The fusion of AI and blockchain holds particular promise in reshaping healthcare analytics. By harnessing AI's computational might on blockchain-secured datasets, healthcare professionals can extract deeper insights, drive evidence-based decision-making, and facilitate personalized treatment strategies, all while maintaining the sanctity of individual patient information. The integration fosters a collaborative environment where multidisciplinary teams can seamlessly access and analyze comprehensive patient records, breaking down silos, expediting diagnoses, and fostering innovative research.

However, this transformative potential is accompanied by intricate legal and ethical considerations that demand careful scrutiny. The healthcare industry is governed by an intricate web of regulations and standards, such as the Health Insurance Portability and Accountability Act (HIPAA) and the General Data Protection Regulation (GDPR), designed to safeguard patient privacy and data security. The convergence of AI and blockchain introduces novel challenges in navigating consent mechanisms, data ownership, and liability attribution, necessitating a nuanced approach that harmonizes technological innovation with established legal frameworks.

The ethical dimensions of AI and blockchain integration require thoughtful exploration. Balancing the pursuit of technological advancement with the rights and autonomy of patients is a critical imperative. Transparent communication, informed consent, and the establishment of robust governance mechanisms are vital to engendering trust among patients and stakeholders alike.

The AI and blockchain for preserving privacy and enhancing medical data sharing through a high-fidelity lens is a transformative step towards a more secure, interconnected, and efficient healthcare ecosystem. By leveraging the complementary strengths of AI and blockchain, healthcare stakeholders can unlock unprecedented potential while upholding legal and ethical principles. This paradigm shift underscores the need for ongoing collaboration among technologists, legal experts, healthcare practitioners, and policymakers to harness the full spectrum of benefits offered by this convergence, while diligently addressing its multifaceted challenges.

This convergence addresses the challenges of interoperability, data silos, and fragmented healthcare information, thereby enhancing patient-centric care coordination and research endeavors. By employing AI-driven analytics on blockchain-enabled datasets, healthcare professionals can extract meaningful insights while maintaining individual privacy. However, this fusion of AI and blockchain also necessitates a comprehensive examination of legal and ethical considerations, including compliance with healthcare regulations like the HIPAA and GDPR. Striking a delicate balance between technological innovation and patient privacy rights remains pivotal, emphasizing the urgency for interdisciplinary collaboration among technologists, legal experts, and healthcare practitioners to navigate the evolving landscape of preserving privacy and securing medical data through AI and blockchain integration.

16.1.1 Importance of preserving privacy and ensuring data security in medical settings

Preserving privacy and ensuring data security in medical settings are of paramount importance for a multitude of reasons that encompass both individual well-being and the overall integrity of healthcare systems. The significance of these principles extends to patients, healthcare providers, researchers, and the broader society. Several key reasons underscore the critical nature of privacy preservation and data security in medical contexts:

Patient trust and confidence: Patient trust forms the cornerstone of effective healthcare delivery. When individuals seek medical attention, they entrust healthcare providers with their most sensitive and personal information. Ensuring the confidentiality of medical data not only respects patients' privacy rights but also instills confidence in the healthcare system. A breach of this trust can have far-reaching consequences, eroding patient-provider relationships and dissuading individuals from seeking timely medical care.

Sensitive nature of health information: Medical data often includes highly personal and sensitive details about an individual's health conditions, treatments, medications, and genetic information. Unauthorized access, misuse, or exposure of this information can lead to stigmatization, discrimination, or even identity theft. Protecting the confidentiality of such data is essential to preserving patients' dignity and preventing potential harm.

Legal and regulatory compliance: Healthcare is subject to a complex web of regulations and laws designed to safeguard patient privacy and data security.

Non-compliance can result in severe legal consequences, including fines and legal liabilities. Regulatory frameworks such as the HIPAA in the United States and the GDPR in the European Union explicitly emphasize the need to protect patient data.

Medical identity theft and fraud prevention: Medical data breaches can expose patients to the risk of identity theft and medical fraud. Stolen medical information can be used to obtain unauthorized medical services, prescription drugs, or insurance claims, leading to financial losses and compromised patient safety.

Healthcare decision-making: Accurate and comprehensive medical data is vital for making informed healthcare decisions. When healthcare professionals have access to complete and secure patient records, they can provide more accurate diagnoses, develop personalized treatment plans, and avoid potentially harmful drug interactions.

Research and public health: Medical data is crucial for advancing medical research, epidemiological studies, and public health initiatives. Ensuring data security and privacy encourages patients to participate in research studies, which ultimately contributes to the advancement of medical knowledge and the development of innovative treatments.

Data interoperability and continuity of care: In a digital healthcare ecosystem, patient data needs to be shared across different healthcare providers and institutions to ensure seamless care coordination. Ensuring privacy and security in data sharing supports effective communication between healthcare entities and enhances the continuity of care for patients.

Ethical considerations: Respecting patient privacy is not only a legal obligation but also an ethical imperative. Upholding privacy rights demonstrates a commitment to treating patients with dignity, respect, and autonomy.

So, preserving privacy and ensuring data security in medical settings are fundamental components of ethical healthcare practice. These principles not only safeguard individual patients' rights but also contribute to building a trustworthy and resilient healthcare system that can effectively deliver quality care, facilitate medical research, and promote the well-being of both patients and the broader community.

16.1.1.1 Legal challenges associated with healthcare data sharing and analytics

The landscape of healthcare data sharing and analytics is marked by a myriad of complex legal challenges that intersect with the evolving nature of technology, patient privacy, and regulatory frameworks. As healthcare systems increasingly adopt digital solutions for data sharing and analysis, a delicate balance must be struck between harnessing the potential of innovative technologies and navigating the intricate legal considerations that accompany the exchange and utilization of sensitive medical information.

One of the foremost legal challenges pertains to regulatory compliance, with healthcare data being subject to a mosaic of national and international regulations aimed at safeguarding patient privacy and data security. In the United States, the HIPAA imposes stringent requirements on the protection of individually identifiable health information, mandating strict controls over data disclosure and access. Similarly, the European Union's GDPR establishes stringent standards for the processing of personal data, including health-related information, necessitating explicit patient consent, data minimization, and the provision of clear information to data subjects. Navigating these regulatory landscapes necessitates robust governance mechanisms, robust consent management, and a comprehensive understanding of the legal implications that accompany data sharing and analytics in healthcare contexts.

The interoperability of healthcare systems and the exchange of patient data between disparate entities introduce challenges related to data ownership, liability, and accountability. Determining who owns the data, who is responsible for its accuracy, and how liability is apportioned in cases of data misuse or breaches requires careful legal delineation. Additionally, the granularity of data sharing and access controls raises questions about the legal definition of "authorized" parties and the mechanisms for ensuring that data is accessed only by legitimate entities.

Intellectual property rights also come to the forefront when healthcare data is shared and analyzed. Novel insights derived from data analytics may hold significant commercial value, leading to disputes over ownership of analytical models, algorithms, and predictive tools. Addressing these intellectual property concerns is essential to fostering a fair and transparent ecosystem where innovation can thrive while protecting the rights of data contributors.

These legal challenges extend beyond domestic borders as healthcare data sharing often involves international collaboration. Differences in legal frameworks, data protection standards, and jurisdictional complexities can impede seamless cross-border data exchange. The need to reconcile these disparities requires international cooperation and the establishment of clear protocols for handling data across jurisdictions. It associated with healthcare data sharing and analytics are multifaceted and multifarious. Navigating these challenges necessitates a comprehensive understanding of local and international regulations, robust consent management, sophisticated data governance mechanisms, and ethical considerations. Successfully addressing these legal hurdles is paramount to unlocking the full potential of healthcare data sharing and analytics, fostering innovation, improving patient outcomes, and advancing medical research, all while upholding the highest standards of patient privacy and data security.

16.2 AI and blockchain integration

The integration of AI and blockchain technologies represents a convergence of two groundbreaking paradigms that holds the potential to reshape industries, economies, and societies on a global scale. At the forefront of technological innovation, AI brings to the table a plethora of capabilities ranging from advanced data analytics and natural language processing to machine learning and cognitive reasoning. These capabilities empower systems to discern patterns, make informed decisions, and emulate human-like cognitive functions. On the other hand, blockchain, with its decentralized and tamper-resistant ledger, offers a transformative solution for establishing trust, security, and transparency in a wide array of applications.

The high standards set by the integration of AI and blockchain are multifaceted and extend across various domains. In data-driven industries such as finance, healthcare, and supply chain management, this fusion has the potential to revolutionize processes by providing unparalleled security, traceability, and efficiency. In financial transactions, for instance, blockchain's cryptographic validation coupled with AI's fraud detection capabilities can elevate security to unprecedented levels, enabling secure and real-time cross-border transactions while mitigating risks of cyber threats. Similarly, in healthcare, the integration can facilitate secure sharing of patient records, ensuring data privacy while allowing healthcare providers to access critical information for accurate diagnoses and personalized treatment strategies.

It holds immense promise in bolstering the concept of the Internet of Things (IoT), where a network of interconnected devices communicates and collaborates seamlessly. AI's data analysis can extract meaningful insights from the vast amounts of data generated by IoT devices, while blockchain's decentralized nature ensures the reliability and integrity of the shared data. This synergy can enhance everything from smart cities and intelligent transportation systems to precision agriculture and environmental monitoring.

The establishment of high standards for AI and blockchain integration is intrinsically tied to ethical considerations as well. As these technologies become increasingly intertwined with daily life, it becomes imperative to address issues of transparency, accountability, and bias. Striking a balance between innovation and responsibility requires a concerted effort to develop AI models that are fair, explainable, and unbiased. Blockchain's transparency can also be harnessed to ensure ethical sourcing, authentication of goods, and prevention of counterfeit products in supply chains, contributing to sustainable and responsible business practices.

While the potential of AI and blockchain integration is undeniable, the journey towards realizing this potential is not without challenges. Technical hurdles, interoperability issues, regulatory landscapes, and the need for scalable solutions are among the complexities that must be navigated. However, as industries and innovators collaboratively raise the standards for AI and blockchain integration, the resulting synergy promises to transcend boundaries, ignite innovation, and usher in a new era of trust, security, and efficiency in the digital age. This integration signifies not only technological progress but a profound paradigm shift that demands a commitment to excellence, collaboration, and ethical stewardship to harness its full transformative power [1].

16.2.1 Integration of AI and blockchain technologies addressing privacy and data security concerns

The assimilation of AI and blockchain technologies emerges as a groundbreaking solution that directly addresses the paramount concerns surrounding privacy and data security in our increasingly digitized world. As information becomes the lifeblood of modern economies and societies, the safeguarding of sensitive data has become a critical imperative. AI, with its remarkable capabilities in data analysis, prediction, and decision-making, holds the key to unlocking invaluable insights from vast datasets. However, this potential has been accompanied by apprehensions about data breaches, unauthorized access, and the erosion of individual privacy.

Blockchain, characterized by its decentralized and immutable ledger, offers an elegant response to these concerns. By establishing a secure and transparent network, blockchain ensures that data records are tamper-resistant and can only be altered with consensus from network participants. This inherent trust and data integrity resonate powerfully in the context of data security and privacy. When AI and blockchain converge, a new paradigm emerges where privacy is not sacrificed for innovation. Instead, AI algorithms can operate on encrypted and anonymized data stored on the blockchain, effectively mitigating the risk of data leaks while still delivering meaningful outcomes.

This integration also empowers individuals with a newfound sense of control over their personal information. In a world where data is often amassed by various entities without explicit consent, blockchain's self-sovereign identity systems grant individuals the authority to grant or deny access to their data. AI algorithms can access only the data that users permit, effectively putting individuals in the driver's seat of their data-sharing preferences. This shift from data control by corporations to data control by individuals not only safeguards privacy but also engenders trust and transparency in a data-driven ecosystem.

The fusion of AI and blockchain introduces a novel dimension to consent mechanisms. Smart contracts, which are self-executing agreements triggered by predefined conditions, can be employed to govern data access and utilization. These contracts ensure that data is accessed only for specific purposes and timeframes, fostering a dynamic and granular approach to data sharing. This not only streamlines compliance with regulations like the GDPR but also upholds ethical principles by empowering users with informed and context-specific consent.

But AI and blockchain is not devoid of challenges. Striking the right balance between data privacy and the utility of AI requires careful calibration. Ensuring that encryption techniques do not compromise the efficacy of AI algorithms is a technical hurdle that necessitates continuous research and development. Scalability concerns and energy efficiency within blockchain networks also require innovative solutions to create a seamless and sustainable ecosystem.

The integration of AI and blockchain technologies marks a pivotal juncture where privacy and data security concerns are not merely addressed but elevated to the forefront of innovation. By forging a symbiotic relationship between AI's analytical prowess and blockchain's trust-enhancing attributes, this integration empowers individuals, safeguards sensitive information, and paves the way for ethical data utilization. As the landscape continues to evolve, it is essential for stakeholders, technologists, and policymakers to collaboratively advance this integration, ensuring that the potential for data-driven insights is realized without compromising the fundamental rights and values of individuals in the digital age.

16.2.2 Data provenance, encryption, and access control mechanisms

Encryption, data provenance, and access control mechanisms are the cornerstones of securing sensitive information and fostering responsible utilization of data in the realm of AI. In an era where data fuels the capabilities of AI algorithms, these techniques play an indispensable role in ensuring privacy, traceability, and authorized usage [2].

Encryption, a fundamental technique in data security, serves as a shield against unauthorized access and data breaches. By transforming raw data into an unreadable format using complex algorithms, encryption renders information indecipherable to anyone without the appropriate decryption key. In the context of AI, encryption preserves the confidentiality of sensitive datasets while enabling AI algorithms to operate on the encrypted data. Homomorphic encryption, a cutting-edge approach, even allows computations to be performed on encrypted data without the need for decryption, striking a delicate balance between data privacy and AI functionality. This technique not only safeguards data during transmission and storage but also empowers data owners to maintain control over who can access and utilize their information, a paramount consideration in the age of data-driven innovation.

Data provenance, or the ability to trace the origin and history of data, is essential for establishing the authenticity and reliability of AI-driven insights. In an era of complex data supply chains and collaborative research, understanding the lineage of data sources is crucial for ensuring the accuracy and credibility of AI models. Blockchain technology offers an elegant solution by recording data transactions in an immutable and transparent ledger. By anchoring data provenance in a blockchain, AI practitioners and stakeholders gain an auditable trail of every data point's journey, from acquisition to utilization. This not only enhances data quality and accountability but also facilitates compliance with regulations and ethical standards, enabling confident decision-making based on a clear understanding of data lineage.

Access control mechanisms, another pivotal aspect, empower data owners to define who can access, modify, or utilize their information. In the context of AI, where multiple parties may contribute to, train, or use models, access control ensures that only authorized individuals or entities can interact with specific datasets or algorithms. Role-based access control, attribute-based access control, and tokenization are some techniques that grant precise control over data access. Integrating blockchain technology with access control mechanisms further reinforces security by decentralizing authorization, reducing single points of failure, and preventing unauthorized alterations. Through these measures, data owners can confidently participate in collaborative AI initiatives, secure in the knowledge that their sensitive information is accessed and utilized within the bounds they define.

As AI continues to revolutionize industries and domains, these techniques ensure that the potential for transformative insights is harnessed without compromising data privacy, traceability, or authorized usage. By integrating these measures into AI workflows, stakeholders demonstrate a commitment to ethical data stewardship and contribute to a future where AI-driven innovation coexists harmoniously with the protection of individual rights and data integrity [3].

16.3 Preserving privacy through high-fidelity data sharing

Preserving privacy through high-fidelity data sharing stands as an intricate endeavor that seeks to reconcile the seemingly contradictory goals of enhanced information exchange and safeguarding individual confidentiality. In an era marked by unprecedented data proliferation and connectivity, the concept of high-fidelity data sharing emerges as a compelling response to the demand for comprehensive insights, collaborative research, and informed decision-making. At its core, high-fidelity data sharing involves the seamless exchange of detailed and accurate information among authorized stakeholders while rigorously upholding privacy principles.

Central to this concept is the notion of data minimization, where only the most pertinent and relevant information is shared, thereby reducing the risk of exposing sensitive details. High-fidelity data sharing aims to strike a delicate balance between data richness and data privacy, ensuring that insights are both meaningful and actionable without compromising the anonymity and security of individuals whose information is being shared. By adhering to stringent data anonymization techniques, such as differential privacy or k-anonymity, organizations can remove identifying attributes from datasets while retaining the integrity of aggregated trends and patterns. This approach empowers stakeholders to draw valuable conclusions without infringing upon the personal information of data subjects.

Emerging technologies, such as homomorphic encryption, further amplify the potential for high-fidelity data sharing. Homomorphic encryption allows computations to be performed directly on encrypted data, eliminating the need for decryption prior to analysis. This technique augments privacy by ensuring that even during data processing, sensitive information remains obfuscated. Integrating homomorphic encryption into high-fidelity data sharing workflows empowers stakeholders to collaborate and gain insights from shared data without ever having direct access to the original unencrypted information, thus upholding the principle of data privacy throughout the analysis process [4].

The high-fidelity data sharing hinges on the establishment of robust access control mechanisms that govern who can access, manipulate, and contribute to shared datasets. By adopting role-based access controls, fine-grained permissions, and secure authentication protocols, organizations can meticulously manage data access based on user roles, responsibilities, and necessity. This approach ensures that data is made available only to individuals with legitimate reasons to access it, reducing the potential for unauthorized use or inadvertent exposure.

As high-fidelity data sharing becomes increasingly intertwined with cutting-edge fields such as healthcare analytics, smart cities, and personalized services, the imperative to preserve privacy becomes even more pronounced. In healthcare, for instance, the ability to share patient records and medical data while safeguarding individual privacy is paramount. By implementing privacy-preserving techniques within high-fidelity data sharing frameworks, healthcare professionals can collectively leverage a wealth of information to enhance diagnostics, treatment plans, and medical research while upholding the ethical and legal obligations to protect patient privacy.

This concept of preserving privacy through high-fidelity data sharing signifies a strategic shift towards a future where rich and meaningful insights can be extracted from shared data without compromising the rights and dignity of individuals. By embracing data minimization, advanced encryption, and rigorous access controls, stakeholders foster an environment of responsible collaboration and innovation, where the collective benefits of high-fidelity data sharing are realized while the sanctity of privacy remains paramount. This paradigm, marked by harmonious coexistence between data-driven progress and ethical considerations, is integral to the sustainable advancement of modern societies [5].

16.4 Healthcare analytics and insights

Healthcare analytics and insights represent a transformative approach to understanding, optimizing, and enhancing healthcare systems, patient care, and medical research through the power of data-driven analysis. In an era where healthcare generates vast volumes of data, ranging from patient records and clinical notes to medical images and genomic information, the application of advanced analytics techniques holds immense potential for improving outcomes, reducing costs, and revolutionizing medical practices [6].

At its core, healthcare analytics involves the systematic exploration and interpretation of healthcare data to extract meaningful patterns, trends, and correlations. By leveraging techniques from statistics, machine learning, AI, and data mining, healthcare professionals and researchers can gain actionable insights that have far-reaching implications across the entire healthcare spectrum. These insights can inform clinical decision-making, guide public health policies, support medical research, and facilitate the development of innovative treatment approaches. The healthcare analytics encompasses various dimensions such as mentioned below.

Clinical decision support: By analyzing patient data and historical records, healthcare analytics tools can aid clinicians in making more informed and accurate decisions about diagnosis, treatment, and care plans. Predictive analytics can help identify patients at risk of specific conditions, enabling proactive interventions to prevent adverse outcomes.

Population health management: Healthcare analytics allows health organizations to understand and manage the health of populations more effectively. It enables the identification of trends, risk factors, and disease prevalence, thereby supporting the design of targeted interventions and preventive strategies.

Operational efficiency: Analytics can optimize hospital operations, resource allocation, and patient flow. By analyzing patient wait times, resource utilization,

Unlock potential of AI and blockchain integration   345

and workflow patterns, healthcare providers can streamline processes, reduce bottlenecks, and enhance patient satisfaction.

Drug discovery and development: Analytics can expedite drug discovery and development by analyzing large datasets to identify potential drug candidates, predict drug interactions, and optimize clinical trial designs.

Personalized medicine: Healthcare analytics plays a crucial role in the emergence of personalized medicine, tailoring treatments and interventions to individual patient characteristics. This involves analyzing genetic information, medical histories, and other data to optimize treatment plans and predict patient responses.

Real-time monitoring and surveillance: Healthcare analytics enables real-time monitoring of patient vitals, disease outbreaks, and other critical health indicators. Timely data analysis helps healthcare professionals respond promptly to emerging health threats and manage patient conditions effectively.

Research and epidemiology: By analyzing aggregated data from various sources, healthcare analytics contributes to epidemiological studies, enabling researchers to identify disease trends, assess public health risks, and inform policies for disease prevention and control.

As the healthcare landscape continues to evolve, healthcare analytics and insights hold the potential to drive evidence-based decision-making, enhance patient outcomes, and shape the future of medical practices. However, the adoption of healthcare analytics also comes with ethical and privacy considerations, highlighting the importance of robust data governance, security measures, and compliance with regulations to ensure responsible and beneficial utilization of healthcare data [7].

16.4.1 AI-driven analytics leveraging blockchain-enabled data to derive meaningful insights

The convergence of AI and blockchain technologies heralds a new era in data-driven analytics, where the fusion of AI's cognitive capabilities and blockchain's immutable ledger gives rise to a paradigm of unprecedented trust, security, and meaningful insights. AI-driven analytics, powered by advanced machine learning algorithms and predictive modeling, has transformed industries by extracting actionable insights from vast datasets. This integration with blockchain technology further elevates the potential of analytics by ensuring the integrity, transparency, and privacy of the underlying data, thereby enhancing the reliability and credibility of the insights derived [8].

At the heart of this integration is the principle of data immutability offered by blockchain. Data recorded on a blockchain ledger is tamper-proof, unalterable, and transparently traceable to its origin. By anchoring data sources on a blockchain, AI-driven analytics can tap into a repository of trusted and verified data. This safeguards against data manipulation, unauthorized alterations, and fraudulent activities, ensuring that the insights generated by AI are built upon a foundation of accurate and reliable information. The decentralized nature of blockchain technology eliminates the need for intermediaries and central authorities, reducing the risks associated with single points of failure and unauthorized access. This attribute aligns seamlessly with the autonomous nature of AI algorithms, fostering a synergistic environment where data analytics can occur securely and efficiently without compromising the privacy of sensitive information.

Blockchain's cryptographic techniques also play a pivotal role in data privacy. In scenarios where organizations are hesitant to share sensitive data for fear of compromising confidentiality, blockchain's encryption capabilities offer a solution. Through encryption, data can be securely stored and shared on the blockchain, ensuring that only authorized parties with the decryption keys can access the original information. This enables collaborative analytics among multiple stakeholders, such as researchers, without exposing raw data and compromising privacy [9].

This integration finds compelling applications in domains such as healthcare, supply chain management, finance, and more. In healthcare, for instance, AI-driven analytics can leverage blockchain-enabled medical records to derive insights for personalized treatments, disease prediction, and drug development, while maintaining patient privacy and data security. In supply chain management, the fusion can enhance traceability and transparency, enabling real-time tracking of goods and verifying the authenticity of products. In finance, AI-powered analytics can leverage blockchain-enabled transaction histories to detect anomalies, prevent fraud, and optimize investment strategies.

But the journey toward realizing the full potential of AI-driven analytics leveraging blockchain-enabled data is not without its challenges. Ensuring scalability, interoperability, and standardization across blockchain networks and AI algorithms remains a complex endeavor. Regulatory considerations and ethical implications, particularly concerning data privacy and ownership, demand careful navigation. By combining AI's analytical prowess with blockchain's foundational attributes of immutability, transparency, and encryption, organizations and industries can harness the true power of data-driven decision-making while preserving data integrity and individual privacy. As this synergy continues to evolve, it reinforces the imperative for collaborative efforts among technologists, researchers, policymakers, and industry leaders to forge a future where the potential of AI analytics is fully realized within a framework of responsible innovation and ethical considerations [10].

16.4.1.1 Potential for improved clinical decision-making, predictive modeling, and public health research

This research holds boundless potential to revolutionize healthcare practices and outcomes on a global scale. In the realm of clinical decision-making, AI-driven algorithms have the capacity to analyze vast and intricate patient datasets, aiding healthcare professionals in diagnosing complex conditions, devising tailored treatment plans, and optimizing patient care trajectories. By assimilating a multitude of patient attributes and historical data, AI can provide clinicians with evidence-based insights that transcend human capabilities, enabling more accurate prognoses and personalized interventions.

The predictive modeling emerges as a game-changing tool, leveraging AI's prowess to anticipate disease trends, patient outcomes, and treatment responses. Through the amalgamation of diverse datasets encompassing genetics, lifestyle, environmental factors, and medical histories, AI-powered predictive models can forecast disease outbreaks, identify high-risk patient populations, and guide preventative strategies. This anticipatory approach empowers healthcare systems to allocate resources more efficiently, enhance early intervention efforts, and mitigate the burden of chronic diseases. The AI-driven analytics hold the promise of unlocking hidden patterns within massive datasets, allowing researchers to gain deeper insights into disease etiology, transmission dynamics, and intervention efficacy. AI's ability to analyze vast genomic, epidemiological, and socioeconomic information fosters a more comprehensive understanding of health trends and disparities. Furthermore, the integration of AI with blockchain technology ensures data integrity, tamper-proof records, and secure sharing, facilitating collaborative research across institutions and jurisdictions while safeguarding patient privacy [11].

But collectively, the potential for improved clinical decision-making, predictive modeling, and public health research through AI-driven analytics is transformative. However, realizing this potential requires a multifaceted approach that encompasses not only technological advancement but also ethical considerations, regulatory compliance, and multidisciplinary collaboration. As we navigate the path toward a data-driven healthcare future, it is imperative to ensure that these advancements are harnessed responsibly and inclusively, with a relentless commitment to the well-being of individuals and the broader public health [12].

AI-powered healthcare analytics, with their remarkable ability to sift through vast and complex datasets, have ushered in a new era of transformative potential for improving patient outcomes across the healthcare spectrum. The integration of AI into healthcare analytics has elevated the precision, speed, and depth with which medical information is analyzed, leading to more accurate diagnoses, personalized treatment strategies, and proactive interventions. At the heart of this impact is AI's capacity to discern patterns, correlations, and anomalies within medical data that might elude human observation, thus enabling healthcare providers to make more informed and data-driven decisions. One of the profound contributions of AI-powered healthcare analytics lies in early disease detection and prevention. By leveraging historical patient data and medical literature, AI algorithms can identify subtle indicators and risk factors associated with specific diseases. This empowers clinicians to predict the onset of conditions such as diabetes, cardiovascular diseases, or even certain types of cancers with greater accuracy. Timely intervention becomes possible, enabling healthcare professionals to implement preventative measures and personalized interventions that potentially mitigate disease progression and improve patient outcomes [13].

In addition, AI's impact on treatment optimization is striking. Healthcare analytics powered by AI can analyze a patient's genetic makeup, medical history, and responses to various treatments, assisting clinicians in tailoring therapies that are not only more effective but also free from adverse side effects. AI-driven insights enable a level of personalization that was previously unattainable, offering patients treatments that align with their unique physiological characteristics and increasing the likelihood of successful outcome. This analytics transforms patient care pathways. Through predictive modeling, AI algorithms can forecast patient trajectories, resource requirements, and potential complications. This empowers healthcare providers to allocate resources efficiently, streamline workflows, and improve patient flow within hospitals and clinics. By optimizing resource utilization and reducing delays, AI-powered analytics contribute to shorter hospital stays, decreased readmission rates, and improved patient experiences.

While the potential of AI-powered healthcare analytics is vast, it is crucial to acknowledge the challenges that accompany this transformative shift. Ethical considerations, data privacy, regulatory compliance, and the need for transparent and explainable AI models are all essential facets that demand careful attention. Nonetheless, as the synergy between AI and healthcare analytics continues to evolve, the collective impact on patient outcomes is undeniable. The ability to harness data-driven insights, optimize treatments, and drive proactive interventions through AI empowers healthcare professionals to deliver a new standard of care, where the promise of improved patient outcomes is no longer a distant aspiration, but a tangible reality shaping the future of healthcare [14].

16.5 Legal and ethical considerations

The convergence of high-fidelity data sharing and healthcare analytics brings forth a host of profound legal and ethical considerations that underscore the delicate balance between advancing medical knowledge and safeguarding individual rights and privacy. At the heart of these considerations is the imperative to adhere to a robust framework of laws and regulations governing healthcare data.

Ethical considerations play an equally pivotal role, as the fusion of high-fidelity data sharing and healthcare analytics involves the utilization of personal health information for research, diagnostics, and treatment optimization. Respecting patient autonomy and privacy rights is of utmost importance, necessitating transparent informed consent processes that empower individuals to make informed decisions about how their data will be used. Moreover, the concept of data minimization comes into play, advocating for the sharing of only the necessary data elements to achieve research or clinical goals, thereby reducing the potential exposure of sensitive information.

Transparency and explainability in healthcare analytics are ethical imperatives that promote accountability and trust. As AI algorithms become integral to healthcare decision-making, it is crucial for healthcare practitioners and researchers to comprehend how these algorithms arrive at their conclusions. Ethical considerations dictate the need for interpretable AI models that can provide clear explanations for their recommendations, ensuring that healthcare professionals can confidently make decisions based on data-driven insights [15].

Data ownership and stewardship are also central ethical tenets. Establishing clear guidelines for ownership, access, and control of shared healthcare data is essential to prevent misunderstandings and disputes among stakeholders. Patients should retain ownership of their health data and have the agency to decide how and when it is shared, while healthcare institutions and researchers must uphold their fiduciary responsibility to handle this data with the utmost care and respect for patient interests.

A critical ethical dimension in high-fidelity data sharing and healthcare analytics pertains to equity and fairness. It is imperative to ensure that the benefits derived from data-driven insights are equitably distributed across diverse populations and socioeconomic strata. Addressing bias in datasets and AI algorithms becomes pivotal to prevent perpetuating disparities in healthcare outcomes. The striking a harmonious balance between advancing medical knowledge and upholding ethical principles requires collaborative efforts from healthcare practitioners, legal experts, policymakers, and technologists, fostering an environment where innovation coexists seamlessly with patient welfare and respect for individual rights [16].

16.5.1 Legal challenges associated with healthcare data sharing such as compliance, data ownership, and liability

The global landscape of healthcare data sharing is rife with intricate legal challenges that span across jurisdictions, encompassing a complex interplay of regulations, data protection laws, and cross-border considerations. One of the foremost challenges is ensuring compliance with a multitude of divergent legal frameworks governing data sharing and patient privacy across different countries. A myriad of other national laws globally necessitate distinct standards for data protection, consent management, and security measures. Navigating this intricate patchwork of regulations becomes a formidable task for healthcare entities engaged in cross-border data sharing, as they must ensure alignment with the legal requirements of all relevant jurisdictions to avoid potential legal liabilities and breaches.

The issue of data ownership takes on an added layer of complexity in the global context of healthcare data sharing. With data often traversing international boundaries, questions surrounding who owns the shared data and has control over its usage become convoluted. Differing interpretations of data ownership laws across countries can lead to disputes and uncertainties, inhibiting the seamless exchange of medical information crucial for patient care and research collaboration. Resolving this challenge requires clear contractual agreements and standardized legal mechanisms that delineate ownership rights and usage permissions in a manner that transcends national borders [17].

Liability is yet another intricate legal facet that becomes amplified in the global arena of healthcare data sharing. As data-driven decision-making becomes increasingly integrated into medical practices worldwide, issues of liability for errors, omissions, or misinterpretations of shared healthcare data can arise. The complexities intensify when shared data originates from different legal jurisdictions, each with its own standards of liability and responsibility. Determining who bears accountability when a medical decision based on shared data leads to an adverse outcome requires a harmonized legal approach that spans borders and provides clear guidelines for attribution of liability.

The extraterritorial reach of data protection laws, exemplified by the GDPR's applicability to entities outside the European Union that process data of EU residents, underscores the global implications of healthcare data sharing legal challenges. This necessitates a comprehensive understanding of the legal obligations and potential consequences that extend beyond a specific country's boundaries [18].

16.5.1.1 Ethical considerations related to consent, transparency, and patient autonomy

The ethical considerations take on paramount significance, particularly in the domains of consent, transparency, and patient autonomy. The infusion of AI into various facets of healthcare, from diagnostics and treatment recommendations to personalized interventions, brings forth a complex interplay between technological advancement and the fundamental principles of patient rights and well-being.

The concept of consent emerges as a cornerstone of AI ethics, especially as AI systems increasingly rely on vast datasets for training and fine-tuning. Informed consent becomes a crucial mechanism to ensure that individuals understand and agree to the utilization of their data for AI-driven purposes. This ethical imperative mandates that patients are provided with comprehensive and comprehensible information about how their data will be used, who will have access to it, and for what specific purposes. Transparent and unambiguous consent processes are essential to respect patient autonomy, fostering a sense of empowerment over data-sharing decisions and engendering trust between patients and healthcare providers [19].

Transparency, closely interwoven with consent, is another ethical dimension that demands meticulous attention. Ethical considerations in AI necessitate the development of interpretable and explainable AI models that provide clear insights into the decision-making process. Transparency is pivotal not only for patient trust but also for healthcare professionals who must understand the rationale behind AI-generated recommendations to make informed clinical judgments. Transparent AI systems also facilitate accountability and enable the identification and rectification of biases or errors that may arise within the algorithms.

The patient autonomy, a foundational principle in healthcare ethics, takes on new dimensions in the context of AI. As AI systems become integral to medical decision-making, preserving patient autonomy requires striking a delicate balance between AI assistance and human agency. While AI can augment clinical insights and facilitate informed decisions, it is imperative to ensure that AI does not usurp or undermine the individual's ability to participate in medical choices. Ethical considerations underscore the need for healthcare practitioners to engage patients in shared decision-making processes, enabling them to understand the implications of AI-generated recommendations and make choices that align with their values and preferences. As AI technologies continue to evolve, ongoing vigilance and adaptation of ethical standards are essential to ensure that the promise of AI is harnessed for the betterment of patient care while safeguarding the values of consent, transparency, and patient autonomy that lie at the heart of ethical healthcare practices [20].

The incorporation of AI and blockchain technologies with existing healthcare regulations and frameworks necessitates a multi-pronged approach that harmonizes technological innovation with legal, ethical, and patient-centric considerations. First, establishing cross-disciplinary collaboration among healthcare practitioners, legal experts, technologists, and policymakers is paramount. This collaborative effort can lead to the identification of regulatory gaps, the formulation of new guidelines, and the adaptation of existing regulations to accommodate the unique challenges and opportunities posed by the convergence of AI and blockchain in healthcare.

Second, the development of standardized protocols and interoperability frameworks becomes pivotal. Creating protocols that ensure seamless data exchange and interoperability between AI algorithms and blockchain networks is essential to maintain data integrity, privacy, and security while complying with regulatory mandates. These protocols should encompass data encryption, identity management, and access controls, all of which are central to existing healthcare regulations [21].

Third, adopting transparent and explainable AI models is integral to aligning AI and blockchain integration with healthcare regulations. Providing insights into how AI algorithms arrive at their conclusions enhances accountability, facilitates regulatory audits, and engenders trust among patients, practitioners, and regulatory bodies. Blockchain's transparency and tamper-proof nature complement this endeavor by enabling auditable records of data transactions and algorithmic processes, thereby ensuring compliance with data governance and transparency requirements. The informed consent mechanisms should be extended to encompass AI and blockchain integration. Patients and data owners must be educated about how their data will be used, the benefits of AI-driven insights, and the security measures in place to protect their information. Implementing dynamic and granular consent mechanisms through blockchain-based smart contracts empowers individuals to exercise control over their data sharing preferences in accordance with regulatory mandates.

Lastly, proactive engagement with regulatory authorities is crucial for fostering an environment of mutual understanding and collaboration. By actively involving regulatory bodies in discussions about the potential applications and implications of AI and blockchain in healthcare, stakeholders can work together to address regulatory concerns, establish testing frameworks, and facilitate the piloting of innovative solutions within the bounds of existing regulations [22].

16.6 Future directions and challenges

The intersection of AI and blockchain technologies holds immense untapped potential for further research and development within the healthcare domain, offering a plethora of exciting avenues that can revolutionize patient care, data security, and medical research. One promising area is the enhancement of interoperability and data sharing among disparate healthcare systems. The integration of AI-driven data processing with blockchain's secure and decentralized ledger can enable seamless exchange of patient information across healthcare providers, facilitating holistic care coordination and reducing redundant procedures. Further research could delve into developing standardized protocols and data formats that leverage AI algorithms to ensure data accuracy, while blockchain ensures the integrity, provenance, and secure sharing of this information among authorized stakeholders [23].

Another promising direction is the advancement of personalized medicine through AI–blockchain integration. Tailoring medical treatments and interventions to individual patient profiles requires an intricate amalgamation of genetic, clinical, and lifestyle data. AI's data analysis capabilities can be harnessed to extract meaningful insights from this diverse data landscape, while blockchain ensures the secure storage and traceability of patients' personalized treatment plans. Research in this area can explore the creation of decentralized, patient-controlled health records, powered by AI, that enable patients to contribute and curate their medical data while maintaining control over who accesses and utilizes it [24].

The convergence of AI and blockchain can also catalyze breakthroughs in clinical trials and drug development. By combining AI's predictive modeling and data analysis capabilities with blockchain's tamper-proof data storage, researchers can streamline and enhance the entire drug discovery process. Smart contracts on a blockchain can automate consent management, data sharing, and compensation for clinical trial participants, while AI algorithms can analyze complex biological data to identify potential drug candidates and predict their efficacy. This area of research could explore novel ways to accelerate drug development, optimize trial designs, and increase transparency in the pharmaceutical industry [25].

The research in this area can include into creating robust decentralized healthcare platforms that leverage AI to offer real-time medical insights and therapeutic recommendations, all while maintaining the security and privacy of patient data through blockchain-enabled encryption and access controls. The ethical implications and societal impacts of AI–blockchain integration in healthcare are critical areas for further exploration. Research can delve into creating frameworks that address potential biases in AI algorithms and ensure equitable access to AI-driven healthcare innovations. Additionally, the ethical considerations surrounding patient consent, data ownership, and the long-term effects of AI–blockchain integration on healthcare ecosystems warrant thorough examination to ensure that technological advancements align with patient rights and societal values.

The potential for research and development in AI–blockchain integration for healthcare is vast and transformative. As these technologies continue to evolve, interdisciplinary collaborations between technologists, healthcare practitioners, legal experts, and policymakers will be crucial to unlock the full potential of this convergence, creating a future where patient-centric care, data security, and medical innovation are seamlessly interwoven [26].

16.6.1 Discuss ongoing challenges such as scalability, interoperability, and standardization

The integration of AI and blockchain technologies for preserving privacy and managing medical data, while promising significant benefits, is not without its share of ongoing challenges. Scalability, interoperability, and standardization stand out as critical hurdles that must be addressed to fully realize the potential of this integration in the healthcare domain.

Scalability is a central concern, as both AI and blockchain applications generate and process massive amounts of data. AI algorithms require substantial computational resources, and the ever-increasing volume of medical data poses a challenge in terms of processing speed and efficiency. Integrating AI into blockchain networks can exacerbate these scalability issues, potentially leading to bottlenecks and hindering real-time data analysis. Research and development efforts are required to optimize the performance of AI algorithms within blockchain frameworks, ensuring that the integration can seamlessly handle the high data throughput demands of healthcare applications [27].

Interoperability is another complex challenge in the AI–blockchain integration landscape. Healthcare systems rely on diverse data sources, electronic health record formats, and information sharing protocols. Integrating AI with blockchain requires creating seamless data pathways that traverse different healthcare systems, platforms, and technologies. Achieving interoperability necessitates standardized data formats, communication protocols, and interfaces that facilitate the frictionless exchange of information between AI-driven analytics and blockchain networks. Collaborative efforts are essential to develop interoperability frameworks that accommodate the complex data needs of healthcare while preserving the security and privacy features of blockchain [28].

Standardization is an imperative challenge that impacts the harmonious integration of AI and blockchain for preserving privacy and medical data. The absence of unified standards across different AI algorithms and blockchain platforms can lead to compatibility issues, hinder data sharing, and complicate compliance with healthcare regulations. Establishing common frameworks, data models, and coding practices for AI-driven analytics and blockchain implementations is essential to ensure a cohesive ecosystem that supports interoperability and consistent data handling practices. Research endeavors should focus on developing standardized approaches that encompass data encryption, identity management, consent mechanisms, and audit trails within the context of AI–blockchain integration. As solutions to these challenges emerge, the full potential of AI–blockchain integration in healthcare can be harnessed to drive innovation, protect patient privacy, and advance the quality of medical care and research [29].

16.7 Conclusion

The synergistic integration of AI and blockchain technologies presents a transformative pathway towards unlocking the potential for preserving privacy and managing medical data in the realm of high-fidelity data sharing and healthcare analytics. Through a lens focused on legal aspects, this convergence offers a compelling framework to address the intricate challenges of data security, patient privacy, and regulatory compliance within the healthcare ecosystem.

AI's data analysis capabilities, coupled with blockchain's immutability and transparency, lay the foundation for a secure and accountable environment where patient data can be harnessed for meaningful insights while safeguarding individual rights. This integration, however, is not without its complexities. The landscape of healthcare regulations and data protection laws necessitates meticulous adherence to ethical principles, informed consent mechanisms, and robust security protocols. As such, navigating the legal considerations is paramount to ensure responsible innovation that upholds patient trust, confidentiality, and the integrity of medical information.

By embracing a patient-centric approach, stakeholders can leverage AI-driven analytics to deliver personalized medical interventions and enhance clinical decision-making, all while ensuring that data sharing adheres to legal frameworks and preserves patient autonomy. The blockchain's decentralized architecture empowers patients with greater control over their health data, enabling transparent consent management and granular data sharing preferences.

Nonetheless, the realization of this potential demands ongoing collaboration among healthcare practitioners, legal experts, policymakers, and technology developers. It requires the formulation of standardized protocols, interoperability frameworks, and transparent AI models that uphold data privacy, accuracy, and security in alignment with existing healthcare regulations. Ethical considerations, such as data ownership, transparency, and equitable access, should remain at the forefront of AI–blockchain integration strategies.

In essence, the integration of AI and blockchain for high-fidelity data sharing and healthcare analytics, when approached with a keen awareness of legal considerations, paves the way for a future where cutting-edge technological innovation converges harmoniously with patient welfare and ethical imperatives. By navigating the legal landscape with diligence and foresight, we can unlock the full potential of this integration to revolutionize healthcare, preserving privacy while forging new frontiers in medical research, diagnosis, and treatment.

References

[1] Siddiqui, Z. A., and Haroon, M. (2022). Application of artificial intelligence and machine learning in blockchain technology. In *Artificial Intelligence and Machine Learning for EDGE Computing* (pp. 169–185). New York: Academic Press.

[2] Shahzad, F., Javed, A. R., Zikria, Y. B., Rehman, S., and Jalil, Z. (2021). Future smart cities: requirements, emerging technologies, applications, challenges, and future aspects. *TechRxiv* 1, 14.

[3] Alzubi, O. A., Alzubi, J. A., Shankar, K., and Gupta, D. (2021). Blockchain and artificial intelligence enabled privacy-preserving medical data transmission in internet of things. *Transactions on Emerging Telecommunications Technologies, 32*(12), e4360.

[4] Dhar Dwivedi, A., Singh, R., Kaushik, K., Rao Mukkamala, R., and Alnumay, W. S. (2021). Blockchain and artificial intelligence for 5G-enabled internet of things: challenges, opportunities, and solutions. *Transactions on Emerging Telecommunications Technologies*, 1, e4329.

[5] Deebak, B. D., and Fadi, A. T. (2021). Privacy-preserving in smart contracts using blockchain and artificial intelligence for cyber risk measurements. *Journal of Information Security and Applications, 58*, 102749.

[6] Tagde, P., Tagde, S., Bhattacharya, T., et al. (2021). Blockchain and artificial intelligence technology in e-Health. *Environmental Science and Pollution Research, 28*, 52810–52831.

[7] Bosri, R., Rahman, M. S., Bhuiyan, M. Z. A., and Al Omar, A. (2020). Integrating blockchain with artificial intelligence for privacy-preserving recommender systems. *IEEE Transactions on Network Science and Engineering, 8*(2), 1009–1018.

[8] Anoop, V. S., and Asharaf, S. (2022). Integrating artificial intelligence and blockchain for enabling a trusted ecosystem for healthcare sector. In *Intelligent Healthcare: Infrastructure, Algorithms and Management* (pp. 281–295). Singapore: Springer Nature Singapore.

[9] Jebamikyous, H., Li, M., Suhas, Y., and Kashef, R. (2023). Leveraging machine learning and blockchain in e-commerce and beyond: benefits, models, and application. *Discover Artificial Intelligence, 3*(1), 3.

[10] Taherdoost, H. (2022). Blockchain technology and artificial intelligence together: a critical review on applications. *Applied Sciences, 12*(24), 12948.

[11] Kumar, R., Kumar, J., Khan, A. A., et al. (2022). Blockchain and homomorphic encryption based privacy-preserving model aggregation for medical images. *Computerized Medical Imaging and Graphics, 102*, 102139.

[12] Kuo, T. T., and Ohno-Machado, L. (2018). Modelchain: decentralized privacy-preserving healthcare predictive modeling framework on private blockchain networks. *arXiv preprint arXiv:1802*, 01746.

[13] Hussien, H. M., Yasin, S. M., Udzir, N. I., Ninggal, M. I. H., and Salman, S. (2021). Blockchain technology in the healthcare industry: trends and opportunities. *Journal of Industrial Information Integration*, *22*, 100217.

[14] Singh, B. (2019). Affordability of medicines, public health and TRIPS regime: a comparative analysis. *Indian Journal of Health and Medical Law*, *2*(1), 1–7.

[15] Singh, B. (2023). Revolution in informatics medical education and research for health financing and health insurance: trends in advancement of health technology safety and legal provisions concerning medical malpractices. *Journal of Informatics Education and Research*, *3*(2), 45.

[16] Singh, B. (2021). Demystifying data justice: legal responses and India's privacy and security standards: challenges in cloud computing. *SPAST Abstracts*, *1*(1), 5.

[17] Mohanta, B. K., Jena, D., Satapathy, U., and Patnaik, S. (2020). Survey on IoT security: challenges and solution using machine learning, artificial intelligence and blockchain technology. *Internet of Things*, *11*, 100227.

[18] Koppu, S., Somayaji, S. R. K., Meenakshisundaram, I., Wang, W., and Su, C. (2022). Fusion of blockchain, IoT and artificial intelligence-A survey. *IEICE Transactions on Information and Systems*, *105*(2), 300–308.

[19] Maher, M., Kaziunas, E., Ackerman, M., et al. (2016). User-centered design groups to engage patients and caregivers with a personalized health information technology tool. *Biology of Blood and Marrow Transplantation*, *22*(2), 349–358.

[20] Isett, K. R., Burnam, M. A., Coleman-Beattie, B., et al. (2007). The state policy context of implementation issues for evidence-based practices in mental health. *Psychiatric Services*, *58*(7), 914–921.

[21] Risendal, B., Dwyer, A., Seidel, R., et al. (2014). Adaptation of the chronic disease self-management program for cancer survivors: feasibility, acceptability, and lessons for implementation. *Journal of Cancer Education*, *29*, 762–771.

[22] Goniewicz, K., Misztal-Okońska, P., Pawłowski, W., et al. (2020). Evacuation from healthcare facilities in Poland: legal preparedness and preparation. *International Journal of Environmental Research and Public Health*, *17*(5), 1779.

[23] Leser, P. E. (2017). *Probabilistic Prognostics and Health Management for Fatigue-Critical Components Using High-Fidelity Models*. Raleigh, NC: North Carolina State University.

[24] Hopper, K. B., and Johns, C. L. (2012). Educational technology in the medical industry. In *Wireless Technologies: Concepts, Methodologies, Tools and Applications* (pp. 1306–1322). Hershey, PA: IGI Global.

[25] Spiess, J. (2022). Machine learning explainability and fairness: insights from consumer lending. *FinRegLab Whitepaper*.

[26] Khomami, M. B., Teede, H. J., Enticott, J., O'Reilly, S., Bailey, C., and Harrison, C. L. (2022). Implementation of antenatal lifestyle interventions

into routine care: secondary analysis of a systematic review. *JAMA Network Open, 5*(10), 67–69.
[27] Barron, J., Randall, V. F., Villareal, C., Ramirez, V., and Vojta, L. (2021). Medical student experiences in operation bushmaster 2019: "I now see myself as equal parts physician and leader". *Military Medicine, 186*(11–12), e1066–e1070.
[28] Chen, Z., Sheng, H., Xia, Y., Wang, W., and He, J. (2021). A comprehensive review on blade tip timing-based health monitoring: status and future. *Mechanical Systems and Signal Processing, 149*, 107330.
[29] Ennab, M., and Mcheick, H. (2022). Designing an interpretability-based model to explain the artificial intelligence algorithms in healthcare. *Diagnostics, 12*(7), 1557.

Chapter 17
The nuances of legal deviations in modern computing: A relook into the privacy and data protection laws in India and beyond

Shambhu Prasad Chakrabarty[1], Niladri Mondal[2] and Shrabana Chattopadhyay[1]

Modern computing, like the Industrial Revolution, has transformed the world we live in. Irrespective of its unrivalled potential, some necessary evils can inherently be found in it, as is the case with any other technology. This chapter engages with some of those deviations in general and infringement to privacy rights, data protection and security issues embedded with the technology in particular. A brief discussion of overlapping legal situations across jurisdictions on data protection has also been highlighted with special reference to India. This chapter delves into the basic understanding of these concepts with relevant case studies emerging out of them. It highlights the laws and directives that are required to be complied with, especially by the developers and those engaged in modern computing to avoid legal impediments to their creativity and commercial endeavours at a later stage.

17.1 Introduction

Information technology (IT) has transformed the way world is functioning today in comparison to the way things used to work even twenty years ago. Various complicated aspects can now be mitigated at a much faster and effective way with the use of technology ensuring a quality output. The strength of technology has overwhelmed almost all facets of life and this has made technology acceptable in all societies, irrespective of cultural, economic or political stratification. With increase in demand of the growing market, technology became affordable in all jurisdictions. The use of technology is integrated in almost all profession with law being the slowest entry to this list. The dependency on modern computing can be noticed to solve complicated crimes in countries advanced in technology. Countries in the Global South have also stepped up in that direction in recent decades. As IT

[1]Department of Law, University of Engineering and Management, India
[2]Chotonagpur Law College, Ranchi, India

advances at a lightning speed, other aspects became readily dependent on it. However, the development of law in the sector got hindered by the mismatched pacing of the technology-making entities and law-making entities [1]. Hence, laws are mostly playing the catch up game with technology [1]. The pace factor is becoming a significant challenge for innovation in IT in India along with its applicability [1].

This chapter focuses on the interaction of law and technology. It explores the evolving data protection laws which modern computing must align with. It empowers the developers to prepare themselves for a smoother transition and aligned with the laws concerning data protection.

The chapter adopts a doctrinal method of research where multiple aspects of the method has been delved with. A critical assessment of the existing laws of the country has been explored to make a strategic set of findings to make technology more viable for developing economies in general and India in particular.

17.2 What is privacy

One of the major concern of the law with growing technological intervention is the question of privacy of data that the technology facilitates to generate, store and share across communities. To know what privacy means from the legal parlance, the words of Judge Cooley is interesting. According to him, privacy is a 'right to be let alone' which is an inherent to any human being [2]. John Gilmer Speed stated, 'as the man comes into the world alone, goes out of it alone, and is alone accountable for his life, so may he be presumed to have by the law of his nature full right to live alone when, to what extent, and as long as he pleases' [3]. All these facets have entered the legislative texts of various jurisdictions with the latest being in the DPDP Act 2023 passed by the Indian Parliament recognising them as rights inherent in legal system. The idea of privacy as a right, however has its roots in the Constitution of India.

17.2.1 Privacy: a Fundamental Right in India

The Constitution of India was criticised as a framework, where various aspects of different constitutions of the world were collated to fit in the Indian setup. It took more than two years[*] for the Constituent Assembly to develop our Constitution. Part III was borrowed from the Bill of Rights of the US Constitution to form the Fundamental Rights [4]. Strong influence can also be noticed from the Universal Declaration of Human Rights, 1948 [5]. Once infringed, the Fundamental Rights are justiciable and enforceable in a court of law [5]. Amongst the various rights conferred by the Constitution, Articles 14, 19 and 21 play a significant role in protecting the rights of the people. Article 21 [6] upholds the right to life, and with time, over 30 rights have been considered to be within the domain of the 'right to life'. The latest is the right to privacy. In the case of J. Puttaswamy, the apex court of the country declared privacy as a fundamental right to human existence. Life

---

[*]The first session was held on 11th December, 1946 and it was adopted on 26th November, 1949.

does not merely mean animal existence; it includes the right to live with human dignity. The Supreme Court, in the Olga Tellis [7] case, stated,

> life in its wholesome meaning, under a beneficial interpretation, should include all those aspects of life that are essential to make a person's life more meaningful and worth living [7].

17.2.2 Privacy is intrinsic to right to life

In its most fundamental essence, privacy bestows upon each individual the realm to exist autonomously, encased within an inviolable nucleus. However, an individual's autonomy is intricately interwoven with their engagements within the societal fabric. These interactions frequently give rise to queries concerning personal autonomy and unrestricted decision-making. Entities, both governmental and nongovernmental, extensively oversee facets of public existence that bear an impact on an individual's liberties. The preservation of constitutional freedoms remains an ongoing pursuit, demanding the resolution of prevailing concerns and the adept management of emergent trials while operating within the framework of constitutional interpretation. This framework delineates an individual's stance in relation to personal freedoms within the context of society.

New challenges emerge in the persistent dialogue encompassing privacy in an increasingly interconnected global society rooted in information. As we navigate an era dominated by IT, which exerts its sway over nearly every facet of our lives, the judiciary shoulders the responsibility of ascribing constitutional significance to personal liberty in this interwoven sphere. While re-evaluating whether our constitution inherently upholds privacy as a foundational principle, the judiciary must evince cognizance of the prerequisites, possibilities and hazards presented to liberty in an era characterised by digital progress. Over time, judicial interpretations have adapted to fresh challenges posed by technological advancement, surveillance methodologies and evolving societal norms. This adaptation ensures the preservation of individual privacy in an increasingly interconnected world.

A chronology of key judicial precedents of the Supreme Court of India cannot be avoided to reflect a strong understanding of the evolution of 'Right to Privacy'. Some of them are as follows:

17.2.2.1 1950–1980: Early Recognition and Establishment

In the case of 'M P Sharma vs. Satish Chandra' in 1954, 'the Supreme Court of India determined that Article 20(3) of the Constitution does not encompass a right to privacy' [8]. Another significant case, 'Kharak Singh v. State of Uttar Pradesh' (1962), acknowledged, 'the right to privacy as an intrinsic facet of the right to life and personal liberty stated in Article 21 of the Constitution' [9]. The Supreme Court asserted that the term 'life' in Article 21 goes beyond mere 'animal existence', and 'personal liberty' guards against intrusion into a person's home and personal security. This case also aptly emphasised that the concept of 'personal liberty' is informed by an individual's dignity. In 'Govind v. State of Madhya

Pradesh' (1975) [10], the court ruled that the right to privacy is not absolute and must be weighed against substantial public interest. It stressed that legal principles must justify any encroachments on privacy.

17.2.2.2 1981–2000: Expanding dimensions

The 1980s witnessed a synergy of right to privacy with other rights. In 'Olga Tellis v. Bombay Municipal Corporation' case of 1985 the 'SC recognizing the right to shelter as an integral part of the right to privacy and personal liberty' [7]. Again in 'R. Rajagopal v. State of Tamil Nadu' (1994) [11], the court upheld the right to privacy in conjunction with personal autonomy, ensuring an individual's privacy in cases involving defamation and press freedom. The 'People's Union for Civil Liberties (PUCL) v. Union of India' [12] case in 1997 highlighted the necessity for well-defined protocols for wiretapping and intercepting communications to protect an individual's privacy rights.

17.2.2.3 2001–2023: Technological advancements and global impact

The cases post 2000 saw a new trend in privacy jurisprudence. 'Justice K.S. Puttaswamy (Retd.) v. Union of India' [13] of 2017 made a historic change in the Indian landscape. The SC established privacy as an inherent Fundamental Right within the ambit of Article 21, which pertains to the right to life and personal liberty. It underscored that privacy is not solely a common law principle but also a constitutional entitlement. In a separate ruling of the same court (Aadhaar Case) in 2018, the constitutionality of the Aadhaar project while imposing specific limitations to safeguard the right to privacy. It decreed that Aadhaar could be employed for government welfare programs, provided privacy is adequately preserved [13]. The 'Navtej Singh Johar v. Union of India' [14] case in 2018 primarily addressed the decriminalisation of homosexuality; however, the court also acknowledged the relevance of privacy in matters pertaining to personal and intimate relationships. The 'K.S. Puttaswamy (Privacy) v. Union of India' case in 2021 [13] further broadened the scope of privacy by acknowledging the significance of informational privacy, data protection and surveillance oversight. These measures aimed to strike a balance between individual rights and state interests.

The progressive judicial interpretations and these seminal decisions of the Indian Supreme Court have consistently moulded and delineated the dimensions of the right to privacy, ensuring its enduring and evolving status within the constitutional jurisprudence.

17.2.3 Is privacy and data protection similar

Privacy is the genus, whereas data protection is a specie. Article 12 of the UDHR declares privacy as an independent right. The provision states,

> No one shall be subjected to arbitrary interference with his privacy, family, home or correspondence, nor to attacks upon his honour and reputation. Everyone has the right to the protection of the law against such interference or attacks [15].

Depending on the context, privacy may mean the right to freedom of thought in conscience; the right to be left alone; the right to control one's own body; the right to protect one's reputation; the right to family life; the right to sexuality of one's definition.

As already discussed, it is also a fundamental right and encompasses an inclusive interpretation. However, it is not an absolute right and may be restricted in national security or public safety cases.

Data protection is a specie of right to privacy. Privacy broadly circulates around an individual's human dignity and autonomy, whereas data protection is specific. It encompasses how third parties handle information about us, including how such data is collected, processed, shared, stored and used.

The affordability of technology has paved the platform for creating an enormous amount of data prompting legal intervention at national, regional and global levels. In India, legislation has been passed to protect data from being used otherwise.

17.3 Data protection

Deckle McLean identified "four basic types of privacy' viz., access control; room to grow, safety-valve; and 'respect for the individual' [3] which is required to be addressed in the new millennium amidst the growth of IoT on one hand and the responsibility to attain the UNSDGs on the other.

In the contemporary era of digital technology, the preservation of data assumes paramount importance due to its role in safeguarding sensitive information such as personal identity, financial transactions and health-related data. This protection is essential in order to prevent any type of misuse, exploitation, or unauthorised access to such valuable information. The utilisation of this technology fosters the establishment of trust, enables the facilitation of secure online transactions and contributes to the spread of the digital economy. The absence of effective implementation of comprehensive policies may lead to significant repercussions.

There is no universal or global data protection law. This void has instituted innumerable disputes ending up in court across jurisdictions. India, the EU, China and the US have different data protection initiatives like many other countries, due to their political, legal and cultural contexts. To comprehensibly assess the effects on privacy in general and data security in particular, one must try to understand the similarities and dissimilarities in data protection laws in these jurisdictions. Table 17.1 identifies the various legislations prevalent in various countries to manage and regulate data.

17.4 Data protection laws in India

India offers very little protection in practice for breach of data rights through legislations, either supreme and subordinate till the enactment of the Digital Personal Data Protection Act, 2023 (DPDP Act).

Table 17.1 Indicating privacy and data protection laws in selected countries [16]

Country	Laws	Features
US	The Privacy Act, 1974	Establish a regulatory framework with regard to information of individuals held by federal agencies.
US	HIPPA	Right to privacy for every individual from 12 years to 18 years. 'Individuals violating the confidentiality provisions are subjected to a civil penalty' [17].
UK	DPA	Individuals are provided with ways to control information. Prohibition of data transfer to other jurisdictions excluding the EEA.
EU	General Data Protection Regulation (GDPR)	Protects the people's 'right to privacy including the processing of personal data' [18].
Russia	'Russian Federal Law on Data Protection'	Creates an obligation over the data operators regarding the 'protection of personal data against unlawful or accidental access' [19].
India	IT Act DPDP Act, 2023 to India	Reasonable data protection practices including civil and penal provisions in case of violation [20].
Canada	PIPEDA	'Individuals have the right to know the reasons for the collection of data. Organisations dealing with data are required to protect such information' [21].
Brazil	Constitution	'The intimacy, private life, honour, image of the people including assured rights to indigenization by material or moral damage resulting from its violation' [22].
Morocco	The 09-08 Act	'Protects the one's privacy through the establishment of the CNDP authority by limiting the use of personal and sensitive data using the data controllers in any data processing operation' [23].
Angola	'Data Protection Law no. 22/11 of 17 June'	'Concerning the sensitive data processing, collecting and processing is only allowed where there is a legal authorisation from APD' [24].
Bangladesh	Digital Security Act, 2018	Section 26 guarantees the need for explicit consent of individuals for collecting, selling, storing or preserving personal information.
Pakistan	No specific law (Personal Data Protection Bill is there)	Certain requirements and restrictions in 'processing of personal data' have been proposed in the Bill.
Nepal	No specific law	Section 28(2) of 'The Right to Information Act, 2007' has tried to address this legal vacuum.
Kenya	Data Protection Act, 2019	Comprehensive laws to protect the personal information of individuals.
Australia	The Privacy Act 1988	It promotes and protects the privacy rights of individuals and regulates state agencies and some other organisations.

The protection has their roots in Article 21 of the Constitution providing citizens the right to personal liberty, including that of privacy and data protection.

Electronic data is protected by Section 66E of the Information Technology Act, 2000 ('IT Act'), which punishes infringement to the right to privacy. Database copyright, which protects labour and investment in data compilation, verification, presentation and use, is protected by the Copyright Act, 1957 ('Copyright Act') and the IT Act. Penalties for violating these enactments include civil (compensation) and criminal (deterrence) preventing data disclosure.

Despite the presence of a comprehensive and robust legal framework in India, the country lacks clear and effective legislation pertaining to data protection.

The evolution of the internet has given rise to a distinct array of intricate legal challenges. Subsequent outsourcing of data driven work, further complicated the situation. In order to counter the situation, the IT Act came up in the year 2000 to encompass laws to safeguard data and prosecute cybercrimes by amending some other prominent legislations including the Indian Penal Code and the Indian Evidence Act. In other cases, the judiciary provides a limited number of protective measures.

i. The Indian Penal Code, 1860 [25] which has two important provisions in Section 406 addressing unlawful breaches of reliability, and Section 420, addressing cheating and dishonestly influencing transfer of property.
ii. The Indian Contract Act, 1872 [26] governs *inter alia* commercial contracts in India. A breach of contract happens where a person fails to carry out its duties under an agreement.

17.5 Enforcement mechanisms and penalties

Information Technology Act provides a robust deterrence to acts violating *inter alia*, data privacy. The penalty for damage to computer, Computer Systems is punitive and deterrent in nature. Downloading data without permission is penalised by INR 10 million under IT Act Section 43 [27]. Introducing a computer-borne contamination or malware into a machine, system, or network carries the same punishment. In accordance with Section 65 of the Act, anybody who intentionally or knowingly hides, annihilates or changes computer source code for a computing device, computer systems, or network of computers that must be kept or maintained faces a period of 3 years in imprisonment, monetary penalty of a maximum of INR 200,000, or both [27].

Section 66 [27] of the IT Act defined 'hacking' and imposes penalties. However, the IT Amendment Act, 2008 has rendered 'hacking' obsolete. The amended Section 66 punishes dishonest or fraudulent actors in Section 43. The sentence may include three years in prison, a five lakh rupee fine, or both [27].

17.5.1 Penalty for privacy and confidentiality breach

The IT Act's Section 72 [27] penalises privacy violations as well. In accordance to the Section, people who obtain unauthorised entry to digitally stored publications, records, messages, data, paperwork, or other records without the relevant person's consent and provide such information to another person may be punished. The sentence may be two years in prison, INR 100,000 in fine, or both [27].

17.6 A very promising move: Information Security Technology Development Council

The establishment of the Information Security Technology Development Council (ISTDC) has been lately undertaken by India can be very effective amidst the chaos of data privacy and emerging disputes. The primary aim of this program is to enhance, synchronise and foster technological progress, as well as to address national-level occurrences, threats and attacks pertaining to information security. The establishment of ISTDC serves the purpose of fulfilling the following functions:

The purpose of this evaluation is to assess the cyber security project proposals that have been submitted and provide suggestions for their continued processing by the Department of Information Technology (DIT). The process of evaluating ongoing projects is conducted through the utilisation of monitoring committees. These committees are responsible for reviewing the projects and providing recommendations for potential modifications in various aspects such as scope, funding, length, new inputs, termination and transfer of technology, among others. Suggesting subsequent measures for concluded projects, such as technology transfer and the commencement of the subsequent phase, among others. Establishing project review and steering committees for initiatives that have been authorised and financially supported by the DIT.

17.7 The computer emergency response team[†]

Another strategic step to counter issues inter alia, data protection is the development of an emergency response team. The Computer Emergency Response Team (CERT-In) was founded by the DIT with the objective of becoming an integral member of the global CERT community. The establishment of CERT was initiated with the aim of safeguarding India's IT assets from the detrimental effects of viruses and various other security threats. It carries out the subsequent operations:

I. The entity in question functions as a pivotal hub, effectively addressing computer security problems and serving as a dependable and reputable 24-hour point of contact for urgent matters.

   The primary objective of this initiative is to distribute optimal methodologies and strategies to system administrators and service providers.

II. The aim of this initiative is to elevate the degree of consciousness and understanding of privacy and computer security issues within the cyber user community in India.

[†]In the Information Technology Amendment Act of 2008, CERT-In has been designated to serve as the national agency to function in the area of cyber security.

III. The organisation proficiently conveys relevant security concerns to the community by distributing notifications, susceptibility written notes, and incident notes.
  IV. It serves as a focal point for enterprises to engage in collaborative efforts aimed at tackling computer security concerns. The organisation establishes linkages with analogous organisations on a global level.
  V. The company actively participates in research and development initiatives in collaboration with reputable research and educational institutes, with a specific emphasis on the security of existing systems and new cyber security issues.

17.8 The Digital Personal Data Protection Act, 2023

In 2017, Justice B N Srikrishna Committee[‡] was set up to draft a framework which shall be comprehensive on data protection. The primary objective of the Act is to develop strategic regulating provisions concerning collecting, processing, storing and transferring personal data being held by others in possession of such data. In 2023, the Government of India placed the Bill in Parliament and came into effect on 11th August, 2023.

The Act proposes the establishment of an authority to look over issues and disputes pertaining to data protection called the Data Protection Authority (DPA) [28]. DPA is also authorised under the proposed law to impose penalties and recommend punishments in case of non-compliance.

Apart from categorising sensitive personal data amidst personal data, it defines the two distinctively, while the former includes financial, health, religious, political and sexual orientations. The Act also ensures consent while collecting data and restricts unnecessary data collection.

17.8.1 Limitations of Data Protection Act

Even when the DPA is a positive step in protecting data, it may been criticised for certain shortcomings. Some of them are discussed below:

17.8.1.1 Parens patriae

The state can act as the parent of the nation. Hence, for national security, safety, or integrity, data can be accessed by the government without the concerned individual's consent. Critics, especially libertarians, dislike this paternal approach. Other critics identify that 'one cannot approbate and reprobate at the same time'. The law ensures consent in sharing of data on the one hand and takes away this precondition on another.

17.8.1.2 Trans-boundary data sharing

There are innumerable reasons for data sharing across borders. Irrespective of the clarity in understanding this policy to be adhered to regarding data transfer, there still needs to be more transparency in this mechanism.

[‡]In July 2017, the ministry of electronics and information technology (MeitY) appointed a ten-member Srikrishna Committee, under the chairmanship of Justice BN Srikrishna, to submit a detailed report on privacy and draft the Personal Data Protection Bill. The committee submitted its draft in 2018.

17.8.1.3 *Ubi jus ibi remedium*
The law protects the rights of people, and when one's right is violated, the law provides a remedy for the loss. However, the Act falls short of this basic principle of law. The Act fails to provide any damages for violating data protection rights conferred by this proposed law. We fail to see any provision in the Act providing for compensation for data breaches.

17.8.1.4 Events have seriously overtaken the substance of DPB
Technological advancements in the area of artificial intelligence, social media platforms, online profiling and big data analytics have brought significant economic and institutional changes within the country and across. Unfortunately, these aspects have not been considered significantly and pose a risk to privacy right.

17.9 Globalisation, international law and technology

International law gained significant importance in the post WW-2. The changing dynamics of international relations paved the way law will function globally. Globalisation and industrialisation attracted strategic development in the functioning of international law. It was the digital revolution which challenged the developing international law rules and regulations and shaped it in the form we can see it today. Global IT companies have the greatest share in the world economy today and can be seen in constant interaction with the host countries where the technology has gained significant popularity. However, the fatal flaws that can be seen diluting the efforts is the way technology has evolved sans adequate knowledge of law amongst the developers. This limitation has unfolded complicated and puzzling techno-legal issues. A few of them will be highlighted later in this part of the chapter.

A brief understanding of international law can make things easier to understand the challenges of implementing international law in local jurisdictions. International law is a universe of authoritative norms and procedures which are linked with international institutions that are in some measure controlling across jurisdictional boundaries [29]. It is considered to be a legitimate and important influence in the development of the idea of universal human rights [29].

Majority of technological development can be noticed in the US where the laws of Privacy and Data Protection is different from the EU and India which host the majority of the user base of those technologies. A significant challenge is that the developers are not aware of the law, making their efforts futile due to the non-acceptability of the technology due to legal and ethical limitations, which needs early intervention.

17.10 Data protection law and the position in EU and US

17.10.1 EU data protection law
The technological advancement inspired the European nations 'to address the issue of protection of data privacy as a collective' [30]. The member nations of the European

Council, with a view of protecting fundamental rights, especially the right to privacy and a significant rise in automated personal data processing ('data protection'), came up with the 'Convention for Protection of Individuals concerning Automatic Processing of Personal Data, 1981' also known as 'Convention 108' [31].

17.10.1.1 EU General Data Protection Regulation

The EU General Data Protection Regulation continues to be in effect, but, further legislation pertaining to data privacy has been recently enacted inside the European Union, most notably the Digital Services Act and Digital Markets Act. In addition, it is important to note that there exist other suggestions that warrant attention in the year 2023. This document provides a brief overview of the General Data Protection Regulation (GDPR) [32] and presents a compilation of further ideas that need attention in order to ensure that one remains well-informed about data privacy developments in the year 2023. The GDPR is widely regarded as the most significant legislation pertaining to data protection that has been implemented thus far. The legislation in question pertains to the regulation of data collecting, utilisation, transfer and safeguarding procedures concerning individuals residing inside any of the 28 constituent nations of the European Union. The legal framework extends its jurisdiction to encompass all European Union residents, irrespective of the geographical location of the business responsible for gathering their personal data. Organisations who fail to adhere to the GDPR may face significant penalties, which can amount to a maximum of €20 million or 4% of their entire global revenue [32].

17.10.2 US data protection laws

In contrast to Europe, the US has no single data privacy framework or directive. Instead, US data protection law is a patchwork of federal and state laws and regulations that control data treatment across industries and corporate operations. The development and implementation of federal data protection regulations in the US are predominantly influenced by the specific industry and type of data involved. Given the growing emphasis on data privacy and consumer protection in recent times, it is probable that regulatory bodies will adopt a more rigorous approach in enforcing data protection legislation in the foreseeable future.

17.10.2.1 US state level legislations

The US possesses a multitude of state-level legislation pertaining to data privacy and data security across several sectors (Table 17.2). The task of supervising data privacy regulations concerning the acquisition, retention, protection, elimination and exploitation of personal information acquired from individuals is entrusted to state attorneys general. This oversight particularly focuses on matters such as data breach notifications and the security measures in place for protecting Social Security numbers. Certain regulations are specifically designated for government agencies, while others are exclusively applicable to private entities. Additionally, there exist laws which are relevant to the two kinds of entities.

Table 17.2 Various federal and state laws of US pertaining to data privacy

List of US data protection laws

Federal laws

Serial no.	Name	Objective
1	Health Insurance Portability and Accountability Act (HIPAA)	This Act establishes regulations pertaining to the safeguarding of patient health information. The HIPAA Privacy Rule establishes comprehensive requirements at a national level to ensure the protection of patient medical records and other personal health information, with a particular focus on maintaining confidentiality and security.
2	Gramm-Leach-Bliley Act (GLBA)	Financial institutions are obligated to maintain the confidentiality and safeguard the personal financial information of their customers, as mandated by the Gramm-Leach-Bliley Act (GLBA) of 1999, which largely pertains to their operations. The legislation mandates that financial institutions are obligated to provide privacy notifications to their consumers and have robust security protocols to safeguard sensitive financial information.
3	Children's Online Privacy Protection Act	This Act relates to websites and online services that specifically cater to individuals under the age of 13, with the primary objective of safeguarding children's privacy in the online realm. The legislation imposes restrictions on data retention and distribution, and requires operators to obtain parental consent before to collecting personal information of minors.
4	Family Educational Rights and Privacy Act	The Act governs educational institutions receiving federal funding and safeguards the confidentiality of student educational information. In accordance with legal provisions, parents and eligible students, defined as individuals who have reached the age of 18 or are currently enrolled in post-secondary education, possess the prerogative to determine the disclosure of their educational data.
4	Fair Credit Reporting Act	This Act governs the procedures and practices employed by consumer reporting agencies in the collection, dissemination and utilisation of consumer credit information. The provision grants clients specific entitlements, including the capacity to check their credit reports, contest inaccurate information and impose limitations on the accessibility of their credit data.

State laws

1	California Privacy Rights Act (CPRA)	The CPRA is a piece of legislation that encompasses multiple sectors and establishes significant meanings and extensive distinct customer rights. It also levies major obligations on companies/individuals who gather personal information from or about residents of California. The responsibilities encompass notifying individuals about the collection of data, specifying the methods employed for data collection, providing them with the option to decline participation in data collection, granting them the ability to view, rectify and erase said information, and imposing limitations on the transfer of personal data by enterprises to other entities.
2	Virginia's Consumer Data Protection Act	The law exhibits certain resemblances to the regulations of the European Union General Data Protection Regulation (GDPR) and the California Privacy Rights Act (CPRA). This criterion is applicable to companies engaged in commercial activities within the state of Virginia or those who offer goods and services specifically intended for citizens of Virginia upon fulfilment of certain conditions.
3	Colorado Privacy Act	The Colorado Privacy Act bestows upon individuals residing in Colorado certain entitlements pertaining to personal data, while also imposing responsibilities onto entities that manage and process this data. The Act pertains to enterprises that gather personal information from a minimum of 100,000 inhabitants of Colorado, or those that collect data from at least 25,000 Colorado residents and generate revenue through the sale of this data.
4	Utah Consumer Privacy Act	The legal provisions are applicable to both data controllers and processors who generate an annual income over $25 million and meet either of the following criteria: • Exercise control over or engage in the processing of personal data for more than 100,000 consumers on an annual basis, or the entity in question must obtain more than 50% of its total revenue from the sale of personal data and must also have control over or engage in the processing of personal data belonging to a minimum of 25,000 consumers. The law does not apply to government entities, third parties acting on their behalf, tribes, higher education institutions, not-for-profit corporations, business associates, or protected health information under HIPAA and related regulations.
5	New York SHIELD Act	The legislation serves to modify the current data breach reporting statute in New York and imposes additional data security obligations on entities that gather data pertaining to citizens of New York. As of March 2020, the legislation is completely enforced.

17.11 US and EU: conflicts of data protection laws

While comparing US and EU data protection laws, innumerable instances of discord between laws between jurisdictions can be noticed. Instead of a harmonious co-existence, overlap and variances have plagued the two systems. For instance, if any authority in the US requests personal data from a company based in the EU, it would invariably put the company in a dilemma. Complying with such a request will infringe the EU laws on data privacy, and non-compliance with the request will trigger questions and the veracity of the subject whose data was requested. In most probability, an adverse consequence will ensue. A few instances will clear the issue even further.

17.11.1 Direct access

Another country should not access the data in possession of a country. A deviation thereof hits hard on the sovereignty of the host country granting access. In case when this cannot be avoided, a prior agreement between the countries concerned can reasonably settle the issue. Direct access to data pertaining to the PNR of passengers travelling from the EU to the US has been done to further the agreement between the two between 2004 and 2012. 'In 2001 [33], the Aviation and Transportation Security Act moved the authority to perform a pre-screening process of passengers to the Department of Homeland Security (DHS)'. As the Aviation and Transportation Security Act expanded in 2004 by including Intelligence Reform and Terrorism Prevention Act [34], an 'agreement with the EU became necessary due to the requirement that the European Commission (EC) assess the data protection laws of a non- EU country before a transfer of EU personal data can take place' [34]. Once the EC is satisfied with the data provided by the other country, the issue is resolved, else an agreement can only be a viable solution. The issue of direct data access to another country (in this case, a region of 28 member states) involves considerable sovereignty issues. A request for such data, or a warrant for data, involves the challenge of a large amount of unspecified data.

17.11.2 Warrants

The probable cause for issuance of warrant for collecting personal data in criminal investigation is a *sine que non* of the Fourth Amendment[§]. Even when warrant is a process slower in comparison to subpoena, it provides a stronger protection to the person concerned.

> In the context of private companies supplying data to law enforcement, the 1986 Stored Communications Act (SCA) [35] allows the government to obtain a warrant requiring an electronic communication service provider to produce data such as customer information, emails, and other materials provided that probable cause is shown [36].

[§]Applicable US legislation is 18 USC Chapter 109 and Rule 41 of the Federal Rules of Criminal Procedure.

SCA warrants in comparison to warrants are different and are closer to subpoenas and are hence 'hybrids'. 'The latter means that the warrant is obtained upon showing probable cause, but it 'is executed like a subpoena' since it is served on the provider and does not involve government agents entering the premises' of the provider '*to search its servers and seize the e-mail account in question*' [37]. The matter poses the questions regarding the extraterritoriality of such hybrid warrants.

A similar situation arose in a recent Microsoft case. When the company was slapped with SCA warrant, demanding data on an email account the server of which is located in Ireland, the court stated overruling the defence of MS that, 'even when applied to information that is stored in servers abroad, an SCA Warrant does not violate the presumption against extraterritorial application of American law' [37]. On an appeal by MS, the appellate court (the Second Circuit court) favoured the claim of the company and limited the role of SCA warrants.

Data protection requires a holistic approach to system design that incorporates a combination of legal, administrative and technical safeguards.

17.12 Case study 1: Can the government access data, unhindered?

The state's claim to access any data of anyone by overriding any law whatsoever has been criticised globally and resisted in some cases.

One of the prominent case studies in this regard is the dispute between Apple and the FBI, when an iPhone of one of the shooters that killed 14 innocent people in San Bernardino, California, could not be decrypted (Figure 17.1). When Apple decided not to assist the law enforcement agency, the FBI obtained a court order compelling Apple to help the FBI unlock the phone [39]. In reply, Apple declared to challenge the court in an open letter [38], which sparked the debate between national security and user privacy. Issues involving people's constitutional rights to

Figure 17.1   Apple v FBI [43]

privacy and data privacy are confronted with national security. The issue of patriotism was prioritised by many. In contrast, many others believed this to be a slippery slope where the government claims unfettered power and authority to break into people's personal information.

The debate was heading to the US Supreme Court. However, the matter was settled without the court's intervention as the FBI successfully broke open the iPhone encryption with the help of an undisclosed Israeli agency.

Even when the court's role was cut short, the debate about the government's autocratic intervention over the data of a private individual continued. Very soon, it came to the knowledge that this is not the only case where Government agencies have approached the court for directions against Apple or Google. The American Civil Liberties Union published 63 similar cases [39] under the All Writs Act [40] asking Apple or Google to help unlock smartphones or tablets to gain access to encrypted data involving drug abuse, im-personification, counterfeiting and other similar cases.

17.13 Conclusion

The intersection of law and technology may have matured amidst some deviations in countries of the global north but not in the global south. The countries using technology without adequate legal protection fall easy prey to the developed economies. Thus, to improve the quality of life by limiting the risk of damage, adequate laws are the need of the hour. Some basic legal principles are discussed in this chapter, along with selective legislative provisions that can guide those engaged with the IT industry in India.

Ignorentia juris non-excusat principal may be a significant problem for those engaged in developing and promoting business of the developing jurisdictions violating lex loci. Professionals involved and engaged in computer programming must be well conversant with the laws of the land and beyond, especially where their work are projected to be used. Absence thereof, may risk such creation being prejudiced and interfered by law. One such example being non copyrightable AI generated work. The limitation if cured could bring great commercial value to generative AI works. AI which has evolved and improved over more than five decades missed the legal formalities making amazing work generated without commercial viability. Kris Kashtanova who was granted copyright for 'Zarya of the Dawn' last year in September 2022 was considered to be the first AI generated copyrighted work and the news rocked the digital world by storm. However, a little more than a month later, the US Copyright office required her 'to show that there was substantial human involvement in the process of creation of this graphic novel' [41]. The office later cancelled the registration process on the ground that 'the information in [her] application was incorrect or, at a minimum, substantively incomplete' [42].

In the aspect of data-intensive computer systems, where algorithm rules predominate, data processing has crossed all forms of data protection norms and encroached upon people's fundamental rights. Under the failing traditional data protection models, which fall short of the broader social and ethical questions, a human-centric system can be more relevant and a better alternative to the demand for justice.

References

[1] Greenstein, S. Preserving the rule of law in the era of artificial intelligence (AI). *Artif Intell Law* 30, 291–323 (2022). https://doi.org/10.1007/s10506-021-09294-4.
[2] Commentary of The Charter of Fundamental Rights of The European Union, 'Article 6. Right to liberty and security', p. 67, Available at: http://ec.europa.eu/justice/fundamental-rights/files/networkcommentaryfinal_en.pdf.
[3] McLean, D. *Privacy and Its Invasion*, Westport CT: Praeger (1995), pp. 47–60.
[4] United States Bill of Rights, ratified on December 15, 1791.
[5] Universal Declaration of Human Rights, 1948.
[6] Article21, Constitution of India, 1950, Available at: https://www.constitutionofindia.net/articles/article-21-protection-of-life-and-personal-liberty/.
[7] Olga Tellis v. Bombay Municipal Corporation, AIR 1986 SC 180.
[8] M P Sharma vs. Satish Chandra, AIR 1954 SC 300.
[9] Kharak Singh v. State of Uttar Pradesh, AIR 1963 SC 1295.
[10] Govind v. State of Madhya Pradesh, AIR 1975 SC 1378.
[11] R. Rajagopal v. State of Tamil Nadu, AIR 1995 SC 264.
[12] People's Union for Civil Liberties (PUCL) v. Union of India, AIR 1997 SC 568.
[13] Justice K.S. Puttaswamy (Retd.) v. Union of India, MANU/SC/1044/2017.
[14] Navtej Singh Johar v. Union of India, MANU/SC/0947/2018.
[15] Article 12, Universal Declaration of Human Rights, 1946, https://www.un.org/en/about-us/universal-declaration-of-human-rights#:~:text=Article%2012,against%20such%20interference%20or%20attacks.
[16] Chakrabarty, Shambhu Prasad, Jayanta Ghosh, and Souvik Mukherjee. 'Privacy issues of smart cities: legal outlook'. In *Data-Driven Mining, Learning and Analytics for Secured Smart Cities: Trends and Advances*, Cham: Springer International Publishing, (2021), pp. 295–311.
[17] Health Insurance Portability and Accountability Act, Pub. L. 104–191, published on 21 August, 1996.
[18] General Data Protection Regulation, L119, 4 May 2016, p. 1–88, published on 27 April 2016.
[19] The Russian Federal Law on Personal Data (No. 152-FZ), implemented on July 27, 2006.
[20] Abouelmehdi, K., Beni-Hessane, A. and Khaloufi, H. 'Big healthcare data: preserving security and privacy'. *J Big Data*' 5, 1 (2018). https://doi.org/10.1186/s40537-017-0110-7.

[21] Data Protection overview (Morocco)-Florence Chafiol-Chaumont and Anne-Laure Falkman. 2013.
[22] Solove, D.J. and Schwartz, P. *Information Privacy Law*. New York: Wolters Kluwer Law & Business, 2014.
[23] Speed, J.G. 'The right of privacy'. *The North American Review*, 163(476), pp. 64–74 (1896).
[24] Data Protection Law no. 22/11 of 17 June, 2011.
[25] The Indian Penal Code, 1860, Act No. 45 of 1860, https://lddashboard.legislative.gov.in/actsofparliamentfromtheyear/indian-penal-code.
[26] The Indian Contract Act, 1872, Act No. 9 of 1872, https://lddashboard.legislative.gov.in/actsofparliamentfromtheyear/indian-contract-act-1872.
[27] Information Technology Act, 2000, Act No. 21 of 2000, https://lddashboard.legislative.gov.in/actsofparliamentfromtheyear/information-technology-act-2000.
[28] The Digital Personal Data Protection Act, 2023 (No. 22 of 2023) https://prsindia.org/files/bills_acts/bills_parliament/2023/Digital_Personal_Data_Protection_Act,_2023.pdf.
[29] Anaya, S. J. *Indigenous Peoples in International Law*. USA: Oxford University Press, (2004).
[30] Data Protection Directive, Regulation (EC) No. 1882/2003, came into force on 13 December 1995.
[31] Convention for Protection of Individuals concerning Automatic Processing of Personal Data, 1981, European Treaty Series - No. 108.
[32] General Data Protection Regulation, EC Directive 95/46/EC L119, 4 May 2016, p. 1–88, published on 27 April 2016.
[33] Aviation and Transportation Security Act, Public Law no. 107-71, November 19, 2001.
[34] See Section 7210, Exchange of Terrorist Information and Increased Pre-inspection at Foreign Airports, Intelligence Reform and Terrorism Prevention Act of 2004, Public Law no. 108-458, December 17, 2004.
[35] Required disclosure of customer communications or records, 18 US Code (USC) § 2703, https://www.law.cornell.edu/uscode/text/18/2703.
[36] Recent cases, 'In re warrant to search a certain email account controlled & maintained by Microsoft Corp., 15 F. Supp. 3d 466 (US District Court New York, 2014)', *Harvard Law Review*, 128, 1019 (2015).
[37] In re Warrant to Search a Certain Email Account Controlled & Maintained by Microsoft Corp., 15 F. Supp. 3d 466 (United States District Court, SDNY, 2014), 25.4.2014, 12, https://casetext.com/case/in-re-of-184.
[38] In the Matter of the Search of An Apple iPhone Seized During the Execution of a Search Warrant on a Black Lexus IS300, California License Plate 35KGD203, February 16, 2016. https://epic.org/documents/apple-v-fbi-2.
[39] Matt Drange, Here Are 63 Other Cases Where The Government Asked For Help To Unlock A Smartphone, Forbes, Mar 30, 2016, 06:00 am EDT https://www.forbes.com/sites/mattdrange/2016/03/30/.
[40] The All Writs Act, 28 U.S.C. § 1651.

[41] Franklin Graves, Copyright Office Pilot Public Records System Mistakenly Reflects Cancellation of Registration for AI Graphic Novel, IP WATCHDOG (Jan. 24, 2023), https://ipwatchdog.com/2023/01/24/copyright-office-publishes-retracts-official-cancellation-registration-ai-graphic-novel/id=155686/[https://perma.cc/3QMV-NY5C].

[42] Letter from Van Lindberg, Taylor English Duma, LLP, to Robert J. Kasunic, U.S. Copyright Office (Nov. 21, 2022), https://drive.google.com/file/d/1Idhn8eb9t883mm_U4CxAQQ_aANTI7UTX/view [https://perma.cc/RD4U-YXUV].

[43] Inside the FBI's encryption battle with Apple [https://www.theguardian.com/technology/2016/feb/17/inside-the-fbis-encryption-battle-with-apple,] *The Guardian* (Feb.18, 2016).

Chapter 18
Charting the course: Secure big-data analytics and 5G in healthcare's transformative journey

Vivek Kumar Prasad[1], Pronaya Bhattacharya[2],
D. Jude Hemanth[3], Pushan Kumar Dutta[2], Atul Kathait[4]
and Daniela Dănciulescu[5]

As we conclude this comprehensive exploration of secure big data analytics and 5G technologies in healthcare, we find ourselves at the cusp of a transformative era in medicine. Throughout this book, we have delved deep into the intricate tapestry of technologies, methodologies, and paradigms that are reshaping the healthcare landscape. From advanced medical imaging techniques to robust security frameworks, from AI-driven diagnostics to blockchain-enhanced data integrity, we have witnessed the immense potential that lies at the intersection of big data, 5G connectivity, and healthcare innovation. "Secure Big-Data Analytics for Modern Healthcare in 5G and Beyond" is a comprehensive guide to the cutting-edge intersection of big data, 5G technology, and healthcare innovation. This book explores how these transformative technologies are revolutionizing patient care, from personalized medicine to remote diagnostics. Written by leading experts, it offers invaluable insights into the challenges and opportunities of implementing secure, data-driven healthcare solutions. Essential reading for healthcare professionals, technologists, and policymakers shaping the future of medicine. The purpose of writing this book is to provide a comprehensive, up-to-date resource that bridges the gap between rapidly evolving technologies and their practical applications in healthcare. There is a pressing need for a new resource in this area due to the rapid pace of technological advancements and the unique challenges faced by the healthcare sector in adopting these innovations securely and ethically.

The journey we've undertaken has revealed a future where healthcare is not just reactive, but proactive and predictive. We've seen how the integration of these

[1]CSE Department, Nirma University, India
[2]School of Engineering Campus, Amity University Kolkata, India
[3]Electronics and Communications, Karunya Institute of Technology & Sciences, India
[4]IQAC, Amity University, India
[5]Departamentul De Informaticӑ, Universitatea Din Craiova, Romania

technologies can streamline clinical workflows, enhance operational efficiencies, and most importantly, improve patient outcomes. The promise of personalized medicine, powered by genetic profiling and AI-driven analytics, stands ready to revolutionize treatment protocols. Telemedicine and remote patient monitoring, bolstered by 5G's low-latency capabilities, are poised to bridge geographical gaps in healthcare access. Yet, as we stand on this threshold of innovation, we are also acutely aware of the challenges that lie ahead – the imperative to protect patient privacy, ensure data security, and navigate complex ethical and regulatory landscapes. These challenges, while significant, are not insurmountable, and addressing them is crucial to realizing the full potential of these groundbreaking advancements.

1. Data as the new lifeblood: We've seen how big-data analytics is becoming the lifeblood of modern healthcare, enabling us to shift from reactive to proactive care models.
2. The 5G promise: Together, we've unraveled the potential of 5G networks, witnessing how they're breaking down barriers to care delivery and enabling unprecedented connectivity in healthcare.
3. Security in the digital age: We've grappled with the critical importance of robust security measures, recognizing that trust is paramount as we digitize sensitive health information.
4. AI's rising influence: Our journey has revealed the growing influence of AI and machine learning, tools that are reshaping diagnostics, treatment, and healthcare administration.
5. The interoperability quest: We've acknowledged the ongoing challenges and efforts in achieving true interoperability, a key to unlocking the full potential of healthcare data.
6. Ethical crossroads: Throughout our exploration, we've confronted the ethical dilemmas posed by these technologies, wrestling with questions of privacy, consent, and equitable access.
7. Regulatory pathways: We've navigated the complex regulatory landscape, understanding how it's evolving to balance innovation with patient protection.
8. The personalized medicine revolution: Our investigation has shown how the convergence of genomics and analytics is ushering in an era of truly personalized healthcare.
9. The connected health ecosystem: We've mapped out the emerging internet of medical things, envisioning a future of continuous health monitoring and early intervention.
10. Workforce evolution: Together, we've recognized the changing face of healthcare professions, where data literacy is becoming as crucial as clinical skills.
11. The empowered patient: We've observed the shift toward patient empowerment, as individuals gain unprecedented access to their health data and AI-powered tools.

Charting the course 381

12. Global health perspectives: Our exploration has highlighted the potential of these technologies to address global health disparities and improve outcomes worldwide.

The journey toward revolutionizing healthcare through big data analytics and 5G technologies is ongoing, and this book provides a solid foundation for future research and development. It is now up to the research community to build upon these insights, push the boundaries of what's possible, and translate these advancements into tangible improvements in healthcare delivery and patient outcomes worldwide.

Moreover, this book has shed light on the transformative potential of 5G and beyond technologies in enabling real-time data transmission, remote monitoring, and seamless communication within healthcare ecosystems. The discussions have encompassed authentication, access control, and performance considerations, underscoring the importance of robust security measures in 5G-assisted healthcare environments.

Emerging technologies such as AI, deep learning, and blockchain have also taken center stage, offering novel approaches to challenges such as captioning healthcare imaging data, mental health dialogue systems, Bayesian learning in medical big data, and preserving privacy through distributed ledger technologies. The exploration of these cutting-edge solutions has highlighted the boundless possibilities that arise when innovation meets healthcare needs.

Throughout the chapters, real-world case studies, lessons learned, and best practices have been shared, providing valuable insights and practical guidance for healthcare professionals, researchers, and technology developers alike. The book has also delved into the legal and regulatory aspects of health data protection, offering a comprehensive understanding of the compliance landscape and its nuances across different regions.

Looking ahead, the healthcare sector must embrace a culture of continuous learning, adaptation, and innovation. By fostering interdisciplinary collaboration, nurturing talent, and actively engaging with stakeholders across the healthcare ecosystem, we can pave the way for a future where secure big data analytics and emerging technologies shape a healthcare landscape that prioritizes patient well-being, empowers healthcare professionals, and drives groundbreaking advancements in the field.

As we conclude this comprehensive exploration of secure big-data analytics and 5G technologies in healthcare, it's clear that we stand at the cusp of a revolutionary transformation in medical practices and patient care. The techniques and approaches discussed throughout this book offer a wealth of opportunities for the research community to advance healthcare delivery, improve patient outcomes, and address long-standing challenges in the field.

Key takeaways for the research community:

1. Advanced medical imaging:
   The big data-driven medical image processing technologies presented in Chapter 2 open new avenues for researchers to develop more accurate

diagnostic tools. By leveraging these advanced techniques, the research community can work toward creating AI-assisted imaging systems that enhance early detection of diseases and improve treatment planning.
2. Security and privacy frameworks:
The security challenges and privacy-preserving techniques discussed in Chapters 4–7 provide a foundation for researchers to develop robust security protocols and privacy-enhancing technologies. This knowledge is crucial for creating trustworthy systems that encourage data sharing while protecting sensitive patient information.
3. 5G integration in healthcare:
The potential of 5G technology, explored in various chapters, offers researchers a new frontier in telemedicine, remote patient monitoring, and real-time health data analysis. The research community can leverage this information to design and test innovative healthcare applications that take full advantage of 5G's capabilities.
4. AI and machine learning applications:
The discussions on AI, particularly in mental health (Chapter 12) and clinical risk modeling (Chapter 15), provide researchers with insights into developing AI-driven solutions for various healthcare challenges. These chapters serve as a springboard for further research into AI's role in personalized medicine and predictive healthcare.
5. Blockchain and AI integration:
The exploration of blockchain and AI integration for data privacy in Chapter 16 offers researchers a novel approach to tackle data security issues. This can inspire new studies on decentralized healthcare data management systems that ensure both data integrity and patient privacy.
6. Legal and ethical considerations:
The chapters dealing with legal aspects (Chapters 17 and 18) highlight the importance of aligning technological advancements with regulatory frameworks. Researchers can use this information to ensure their innovations comply with legal standards and address ethical concerns in healthcare data management.
7. Specific application areas:
Chapters like 19, which focuses on AI-powered pneumonia detection, demonstrate how big data and AI can be applied to specific medical challenges. This serves as a model for researchers to develop similar applications in other areas of diagnostics and treatment.
8. Interoperability and data sharing:
The emphasis on trustworthy data sharing and collaborative insights (Chapter 8) encourages researchers to work on interoperability solutions and standardization efforts, crucial for the seamless exchange of healthcare data across different systems and institutions.
9. Causal inference in healthcare:
The focus on causal inference methodologies in Chapter 14 provides researchers with tools to improve the evaluation of clinical programs and

interventions, potentially leading to more effective evidence-based practices in healthcare.
10. Emerging technologies:
The book's coverage of emerging technologies like Bayesian deep learning (Chapter 13) and advanced authentication schemes (Chapter 10) offers researchers new tools and methodologies to explore in their quest for innovative healthcare solutions.

In conclusion, this book serves as a comprehensive resource for the research community, offering insights into the latest advancements in big data analytics and 5G technologies in healthcare. By building upon the techniques, concepts, and case studies presented here, researchers can drive forward the next generation of healthcare innovations. The potential for improving patient care, enhancing diagnostic accuracy, streamlining healthcare operations, and addressing global health challenges is immense.

As we move forward, it is crucial for the research community to collaborate across disciplines, considering not only the technological aspects but also the ethical, legal, and societal implications of these advancements. By doing so, we can ensure that the future of healthcare is not only technologically advanced but also equitable, secure, and patient-centered.

Thank you for joining us on this enlightening journey. The future of healthcare is in our hands – let's shape it wisely and compassionately.

In conclusion, the integration of secure big data analytics and 5G and beyond technologies into modern healthcare represents a transformative opportunity to redefine the boundaries of what is possible in the realm of patient care. By capitalizing on these advancements, we can pave the way for a future where healthcare is more efficient, personalized, and accessible, ultimately improving the well-being of individuals and communities worldwide.

Index

access controls 154
  mechanisms 342
  principles 153
  protocols 208
  strategies 212–13
accessibility 2
accountability 77, 155–6
adaptability 320
adaptation 156
Advanced Encryption Standard (AES) 151
adversarial attacks 277
adversarial training 81
Affordable Care Act (ACA) 303
AI-driven analytics 380
AI-driven threat detection 225
Aleatory uncertainty 277
AlexNet 22
AlphaGo 256
Alzheimer's disease (AD) 22, 250, 327
Alzheimer's Disease Neuroimaging Initiative cohort (ADNI) 327
anomaly detection 61, 82, 181–3
anonymization 51, 141, 159
anonymized information exchange 162
Apache Ambari 37
Apache NiFi 38
AppDynamics 38
Application Programming Interfaces (APIs) 187
area under the curve (AUC) 323

artificial intelligence (AI) 92, 130, 177, 249, 315, 331, 336
  and blockchain integration 339
    addressing privacy and data security concerns 340–1
    data provenance, encryption, and access control mechanisms 342–3
    future directions and challenges 352–4
    healthcare analytics and insights 344
      AI-driven analytics leveraging blockchain-enabled data to derive meaningful insights 345–8
    importance of preserving privacy and ensuring data security in medical settings 337–9
    legal and ethical considerations 348–51
    preserving privacy through high-fidelity data sharing 343–4
artificially intelligent agents (AIAs) 249
  to adopt simulation as tool for understanding others' mental illnesses 253–61
  artificial agents going to replace human doctors 261–5
  subtle nuances of language 251–3
associative arrays 234
asymmetric encryption 151–2

Atomicity, Consistency, Isolation, and Durability (ACID) 237
attribute-based access control (ABAC) 208, 212, 342
attribute-centric sparse indexing scheme 241–4
augmented reality (AR) 3
authentication mechanisms 153–4
autoencoders 181
average treatment effect (ATE) 292

bare metal stents (BMS) 306
BaseX 230, 237–8
Bayesian approximation 285
Bayesian convolutional neural network (BCNN) 282
Bayesian deep learning (BDL) 269
  application of deep learning in medical big data 270
    medical image analysis 270–1
    other medical information processing 271–2
    processing of clinical electronic health records 271
  challenges faced by Bayesian deep learning in application of medical big data 284
  challenges and prospects 286–7
  computational complexity and resource demands 285
  modeling and interpretation of model uncertainty 285–6
  common algorithms in 280–1
  comparison of 274–5
  concept of 273–4
  frameworks 277
    BoTorch 278
    Edward 278–9
    Pyro 280
    TensorFlow probability 279–80
  limitations of deep learning 272–3
  in medical big data 281
    clinical diagnostic assistance 283–4
    medical image analysis 282
    research in life sciences 282–3
  principles of 275–7
  probabilistic graphical model 276
Bayesian deep multi-source learning (BDMSL) model 283
Bayesian inference 269, 274
Bayesian learning 381
Bayes theorem 276
belief network 274
big data 13–16, 92, 256, 379
  balance between openness and safety 99
  common form of 93–4
  data sharing 94–6
  in healthcare 137–8
  limitations and future directions 103
  loopholes and challenges in secure data sharing 96–8
  privacy-preserving methods in healthcare system using 140–1
  secure environment for data sharing 99–103
  security life cycle in 138–40
  specific data types and vulnerable groups 98
  technology 12
  work in healthcare domain 92–3
big data analytics 2, 31, 70, 111, 170
  adversarial attacks in machine learning models 80–2
  analytical case study 58–9
  breach of data and unauthorized access 72–4
  case studies highlighting security breaches and their impact 53

Index   387

Equifax data breach 53
target data breach 54
challenges encountered and overcoming strategies 127–8
challenges in big data analytics monitoring 39
challenges related to data quality and consistency in 42–3
consequences of high latency in monitoring 49–50
data quality monitoring crucial for accurate analytics 43–4
e-commerce platform scalability challenge 41–2
implications of poor data quality and consistency 45–6
importance of low latency in monitoring and decision-making 48–9
latency challenges 46–8
monitoring systems handling the vast amounts of data generated 40–1
scalability challenges in 39–40
social media analytics scalability challenge 42
challenges in healthcare data security 122
Internet of Medical Things 123
regulatory compliance and ethical considerations 124
vulnerabilities introduced by extensive data aggregation 123–4
complexity challenges 54
challenges of integrating diverse technologies and systems for monitoring 55–6
financial services firm 57–8
multinational e-commerce platform 56–7

conformity with data protection laws 79–80
data encryption 77–9
exemplary implementations of healthcare data security measures 126–7
future prospects and emerging technologies 130
anticipated developments in 130
integration of artificial intelligence for advanced threat detection 130–1
privacy-preserving technologies and trends 131–2
in healthcare 120
leveraging vast datasets for evidence-based decision-making 122
role and impact of 121–2
implementation of tailored monitoring solutions to address challenges 61–2
importance of monitoring in 33–4
insider threats 74
function of technology in insider threat mitigation 76–7
making security awareness and accountability culture priority 76
monitoring and auditing to reduce insider threats 75–6
types of 75
key needs and reasons for effective monitoring 34–5
need for secure monitoring processes to protect sensitive data 52–3
paradigms for modern healthcare 5
potential directions for healthcare data encryption 82–4
privacy-preserving techniques for 7

real-world applications of 5G and big data security protocols in healthcare 128–30
recommendations for improving monitoring strategies 62–3
security and privacy challenges 50
  anonymization and de-identification 51
  data access control 50–1
  data compliance 51
  data encryption 51
  data provenance 51
  data sensitivity 50
  insider threats 52
  monitoring at scale 51
setup 59–61
significance of 32
strategies for comprehensive healthcare data security 125–6
understanding big data analytics monitoring 35
  importance of real-time monitoring and analysis in handling large volumes of data 36–7
  key components of monitoring in 35–6
  overview of tools and technologies used for monitoring 37–9
biometric advancements 224
biometric authentication 126, 153
bitcoin 100
black boxes 182
BLiTZ 280
blockchain technology 100, 125, 136, 146, 159, 214, 341
  for data integrity 129
BoTorch 278
B-trees 233

California Consumer Privacy Act (CCPA) 71, 79
cardiovascular diseases (CVD) 325
care.data 98
causal inference methods
  challenges in modern causal inference 309
  concluding reflections 309
  difference-in-difference 294–7
  emerging approaches in 309
  fundamental causal inference frameworks 292
  instrumental variable 297–9
  motivation and objectives 291–2
  practical applications of causal inference in healthcare 301
  exploring causal effect of intravenous radiocontrast for kidney function 304–6
  Medicaid expansion and variability in mortality in United States 303–4
  robotic vs open pancreatoduodenectomy on incidence of pancreatic fistula using PSM method 301–3
  use IV analysis to compare effectiveness of stents in extremely elderly 306–8
  propensity score matching 292–4
  regression discontinuity design 299–301
  vision for the future 309–10
central processing unit (CPU) 189
ChatGPT 251
China Resident Health and Nutrition Survey (CHNS) 94
chronic kidney disease (CKD) 325
city of Barcelona, Spain 165
clinical decision-making 156–7

clinical decision support 344
clinical decision support systems (CDSS) 5
clinically relevant pancreatic fistula (CR-POPF) 301
clinical risk modeling 313
  crucial role of 313–14
  data-driven revolution 314
  future directions in 330–1
  machine learning for 315
    deep learning approaches 318–20
    relevance of machine learning in 320
    traditional machine learning algorithms 315–18
  model development process 321–4
  model performance monitoring and potential Re-fit 324–5
  persistent challenges in 330
  personalized medicine 314
  practical applications of machine learning in 325
    predicting Alzheimer's disease progression with multi-modal deep learning 327–30
    predicting chronic diseases using logistic regression *versus* machine learning models 325–7
clinical trials 291
cloud computing 94, 170, 175
cloud providers 203
Cloud Radio Access Networks (C-RANs) 216
coefficient of determination 323
cognitively normal (CN) 328
column databases 234
commodity hardware 232
compliance frameworks 72
complier average causal effect (CACE) 305

computational complexity 272
computed tomographic pulmonary angiography (CTPA) 304
computed tomography (CT) 12, 270
computer-aided diagnosis (CADx) 270
computer emergency response team (CERT-In) 366
concept drift detection 324
conceptual framework 295
consent mechanisms 155
continuous authentication 224
contrast-induced nephropathy (CIN) 304
Convention 108, 369
convolutional neural networks (CNNs) 12, 18, 181, 270, 319–20
Couchbase 230, 240
CouchDB 230, 239–40
COVID-19 117
Create_ActiveIndex 243
Cross Entropy 19
custom scripting 38–9
cutting-edge technology 173
cyberattacks 6, 70, 113
cybercriminals 52
cybersecurity 52
cyber threats 115, 123–4, 150
CycleGAN 20

data access controls 50–1, 155
data-at-rest encryption 152
data breaches 70, 79, 150
data classification 153, 155
data compliance 51
data dependency 272
data-driven decision-making 84, 136, 172
data-driven healthcare transformation 141

data-driven insights 320
data encryption 51, 76, 77–9, 82
Data Encryption Standard (DES) 151
data encryption techniques 125
data enhancement 17–18
data entry errors 157
data fragmentation 70
data fusion algorithms 92
data governance 155
data integration issues 157–8
data integrity 77
data interoperability 123, 338
data lakes 123–4
data lineage 77
data loss prevention (DLP) 75
data mining 70
data preprocessing 14
data privacy 149
  compliance with regulations 150
Data Protection Authority (DPA) 367
Data Protection Officers (DPOs) 80
data provenance 51, 342
data quality monitoring crucial for accurate analytics 43
  ensuring data accuracy 43–4
  ensuring data completeness 44
  ensuring data consistency 44
  ensuring data integrity and reliability 44
data quality variability 158
data replication 233
data security 95, 153, 155, 158
data sensitivity 50
data sharing 94–6, 159
  for conservation 163
  secure environment for 99–103
data variety 47
D-dimer test 305

deception aim 81
decision-making process 182
decision trees 315–16
deep Bayesian networks 276
deep convolutional neural networks (DCNN) 22
deep learning (DL) 23, 260, 269, 381
  algorithms 174, 179
  approaches 318
  convolutional neural networks and recurrent neural networks 319–20
  neural networks 318–19
DeepMind 256
deep neural networks (DNN) 271
Defensive distillation 81
de-identification techniques 51, 141
dense connections 19
Department of Information Technology (DIT) 366
Dice loss 19
dice similarity coefficient (DSC) 17
difference-in-differences (DiD) 292
  challenges and mitigation strategies 296
  conceptual framework 295
  empirical application 296
  extensions and variations 296–7
  methodology 295–6
differential privacy 138, 141, 213
diffusion tensor imaging (DTI) 270
digital age 160, 380
digital pathology (DP) 12
Digital Personal Data Protection Act 2023 (DPDP Act) 363, 367
  events have seriously overtaken the substance of DPB 368
  Parens patriae 367
  trans-boundary data sharing 367

Ubi jus ibi remedium 368
digital signatures 152, 202
digital transformation 150
direct access 372
directed acyclic graphical model 274
directed acyclic graphs (DAGs) 292
Distributed Denial of Service (DDoS) attacks 180–1
document-centric big data
  active indexing approach 241
    attribute-centric sparse indexing scheme 241–4
  elucidate on abstraction of data for storage and retrieval 236
    JSON database 238–40
    XML database 237–8
  fundamentals of JSNON and XML 235–6
Document Object Model (DOM) 238
Document-Oriented Databases (DODBMSes) 234, 237
drug development 345
drug discovery 345
drug-eluting stents (DES) 306
Dynatrace 38

eavesdropping 73
e-commerce 41–2
Ed-Fi Alliance 164
edge computing 83, 117, 132
  for data processing 129
  integration 224
Edward 278–9
electrocardiograms (ECG) 216, 272
electroencephalograms (EEG) 272
electronic health records (EHRs) 2, 3, 92, 151, 157–8, 162, 177, 270, 314
electronic medical records (EMRs) 94

ELK Stack (Elasticsearch, Logstash, Kibana) 38
Elliptic Curve Cryptography (ECC) 151
Embedded method 15
emergency medical service (EMS) 217
encryption algorithms 99, 151, 342
Endpoint Detection and Response (EDR) 76
end-to-end encryption (E2EE) 152, 208
Ensemble Monte Carlo Dropout (EMCD) technique 282
epistemic information security (EIS) 97
estimated glomerular filtration rate (eGFR) 305
EU data protection law 368–9
European Union (EU) 79
evaluation metrics 16
evidence-based medicine (EBM) 91
eXist-db 230, 238
eXtensible Markup Language (XML) 230, 235–6
  BaseX 237–8
  eXist-db 238
  Sedna 238
extraction, transformation, and loading (ETL) processes 62

facial recognition 126, 211, 224
feature extraction 14–15
feature selection 14–15
federated identity management 224–5
federated learning 132, 136, 146, 213
fifth-generation (5G) wireless network 207
5G healthcare systems 207
  authentication and access control schemes in 208
  authentication mechanisms in 211

access control strategies 212–13
privacy-preserving techniques 213–14
regulatory compliance and standards 214–15
case study 215
  optimal resource algorithm for maximum clinical data transmission 220
  optimal resource algorithm for maximum video data transmission 218–19
  performance analysis 220–2
  proposed methodology for 4K-video transmission from ambulance 217–18
  proposed methodology for clinical data transmission with ultrahigh reliable and low latency 219–20
  results and analysis 222–3
challenges in 225–6
future trends 224
  AI-driven threat detection 225
  biometric advancements 224
  continuous authentication 224
  edge computing integration 224
  federated identity management 224–5
  privacy-preserving authentication 225
  quantum-safe authentication 225
  user-centric access control 225
  zero trust architecture adoption 224
in healthcare 209–10
security challenges in 210–11
5G technology 111, 170, 379
  addressing public health challenges through population health management 6–10
  anticipated developments in 130

applications and use cases 4
architecture of proposed solution 184
  host platform 187
  TPM interface 187–90
  virtual machine manager 187
  virtual machines/cloud instances 187
background and significance 112–13
big data analytics paradigms for modern healthcare 5
connection with cloud 175
contribution 173–5
emerging technologies in healthcare 4
enhancing clinical decisions with support systems 5
flowchart and algorithm 190–6
in healthcare 117
  applications in 118–19
  challenges and opportunities 119–20
  overview of 118
key characteristics of 4
methodology 178
  anomaly detection 181–3
  comparison between threat detection and anomaly detection 183–4
  threat detection 179–81
motivation 172–3
performance evaluation 196
  mathematical equations 202–3
  parameters used and their values 196–7
  performance metrics 198
  result analysis 198
  result obtained and its comparison with existing techniques 198–201
  test beds 197–8

Index 393

predictive analytics 5
revolutionizing patient care with real-time analytics 5
root of trust 176–8
security and privacy considerations 4
tailoring treatments through precision medicine 5
transformative changes vs. data security challenges 114–16
5Vs 93
filter method 15
financial services firm 57–8
Financial Services Information Sharing and Analysis Center (FS-ISAC) 161–2
fog computing 117
forward error correction (FEC) techniques 217
4G LTE networks 169
fully convolutional network (FCN) 18
functional MRI (fMRI) 270
functional split (FS) 222

gated recurrent unit (GRU) 320, 327
Gaussian process (GP) modeling 278
general advantage estimation (GAE) 24
General Data Protection Regulation (GDPR) 71, 79, 102, 136, 146, 150, 214, 336
generative adversarial network (GAN) 17
Genetic Information Nondiscrimination Act (GINA) 102
genomic sequencing 2, 270
gigabits per second (Gbps) 223
GoogLeNet 18, 22
GPyTorch 278
gradient boosting machine (GBM) 325

Grafana 37
graph convolutional networks (GCN) 24
graphical methods 293
graph information 234
graph modeling methods 24

Hadoop 55
hash of the string 100
healthcare 313
 big data security life cycle in 138
  data collection phase 139–40
  data modeling phase 140
  data transformation phase 140
  knowledge creation phase 140
 sector 113, 170
 telemedicine platform 49–50
healthcare analytics 91, 145, 344–8
 access controls and authentication mechanisms for collaborative analytics 152
 access control principles 153
 authentication mechanisms 153–4
 significance of access controls and authentication in 153
 best practices for establishing secure healthcare analytics collaborations 165–6
 data integrity in 156
  challenges to 157–8
  collaboration and data sharing 159
  critical role of 156–7
  solutions and strategies for ensuring data integrity 158–9
 ensuring patient confidentiality through encryption techniques 150
 best practices for implementing encryption in 152

imperative of patient
  confidentiality 150
methods of encryption in
  healthcare 151–2
understanding encryption in
  healthcare 151
exploring blockchain technology for
  trustworthy healthcare
  collaboration 159
blockchain benefits in healthcare
  collaboration 160
blockchain technology overview
  160
imperative of trustworthy
  healthcare collaboration 159
importance of secure data sharing in
  146
collaborative imperative 147
data-driven healthcare revolution
  146–7
policy frameworks for ethical and
  secure data sharing 154
balancing ethical considerations
  and innovation 155
collaboration and stakeholder
  engagement 156
continuous evaluation and
  adaptation 156
elements of effective policy
  frameworks 155
imperative of ethical and secure
  data sharing 154–5
transparency and accountability
  155–6
secure data sharing in 147
  challenges in 148
  fundamentals of data privacy and
  security measures 149
  role of technology in 149
secure data sharing success stories
  160

data sharing for environmental
  conservation 163–4
genomic data sharing for medical
  research 161
healthcare interoperability and
  patient data sharing 162–3
in public health 164
secure cross-industry data sharing
  161–2
in smart cities 165
understanding data privacy 149–50
Health Insurance Portability and
  Accountability Act (HIPAA)
  102, 135, 136, 146, 150, 157–8,
  214, 330, 336
Health Level Seven International
  (HL7) standards 215
high-frequency trading (HFT) 49
homomorphic encryption 135, 140,
  170, 213
horizontal scalability 232
Husserl's reasoning 253

Identity and Access Management
  (IAM) 213
IEEE Xplore 95
image acquisition 14
image alignment 20–1
image classification 21–2
image fusion 271
image matching 271
ImageNet 20
image segmentation methods 18
  for supervised learning 18–19
  for weakly supervised learning
  19–20
independent component analysis
  (ICA) 15
indexing scheme 230
Indian Contract Act 365

Indian Evidence Act 365
Indian Penal Code 365
Information Security Technology Development Council (ISTDC) 366
information technology (IT) 359
Information Technology Act 2000 ('IT Act') 365
infrastructural information security (IIS) 97
insider threats 52
instrumental variables (IV) 292
  IV approach 297–8
  IV estimation process 298
  limitations and considerations 298–9
  understanding endogeneity 297
intellectual property 339
intention-to-treat (ITT) effects 305
interactive segmentation 20
International Organization for Standardization (ISO) 215
Internet of Medical Things (IoMT) 2, 112, 123, 177, 210, 213
Internet of Things (IoT) 94, 117, 340
internet protocol (IP) 94
interoperability 208
interpretability 25, 182, 272
intrusion detection systems (IDS) 125
intrusion prevention systems (IPS) 125
ISO/IEC 27001 215
ISO/IEC 27799 215

Java Message Service (JMS) 238
JavaScript 236
JavaScript Object Notation (JSON) 229, 230, 235, 238
JDBMS 238

k-anonymity algorithms 100
kernel trick 316

key management systems (KMS) 151
key performance indicators (KPIs) 62
keystroke dynamics 224
k-nearest neighbor (KNN) 325
Kyoto Encyclopedia of Genes and Genomes (KEGG) 94

large language model (LLM) 251, 331
latency challenges 46
  data quality and noise 47
  data variety 47
  data velocity and volume 46
  resource management 47–8
  and responsiveness 46
  scalability 47
latent Dirichlet allocation (LDA) 276
Learning with Errors (LWE) issue 82
leaves 316
lineage tracing 78
linear discriminant analysis (LDA) 15
linear regression 315
local optima 272–3
logistic regression (LR) approach 315, 325
long short-term memory (LSTM) 271, 320

machine learning (ML) 23, 70, 159, 250, 294
  algorithms 121, 125, 130
  models 84
Macro Base Station (MBS) 216
magnetic resonance imaging (MRI) 12, 270
Mandatory Access Control (MAC) 212
mathematical equations 202–3
Matplotlib 192
Maximum Dependency Dimensionality Reduction Method (MDDM) 23

Mayo Clinic 126, 132
  adaptability and continuous improvement 127
  advanced threat detection 126
  balancing accessibility and security 127
  biometric authentication 126
  blockchain for data integrity 127
  comprehensive encryption 126
  integration of technologies 127
McEliece cryptosystem 83
McNemar's test 293
mean absolute error (MAE) 323
mean squared error (MSE) 323
medical and environmental data mashup infrastructure (MEDMI) 99
medical data 338
medical database 93–4
medical diagnosis 283
medical image analysis 270–1
medical image processing technology 11
  with big data 13–16
  commonly used evaluation indexes for 16
  development of 11–12
  importance of big data in 12–13
  key technologies and progress 17
    data enhancement 17–18
    image alignment 20–1
    image classification 21–2
    image segmentation 18–20
  problems and challenges 22
    complex high-dimensional image features 23
    difficulty in extracting data labels 23
    improvements in graph modeling algorithms 24
    shortcomings of multimodal image processing 23–4
medical imaging 23, 118–19, 170
Mendelian randomization inferring causality 93
mental illness 253, 265
Merkle tree structure 100
metagenomics 94
meta-learning 26
method of difference 258
Michelson's experiments 259
mild cognitive impairment (MCI) 327
MobileNet-V1 22
Model-Agnostic Meta-Learning (MAML) 26
model development process 321
  data collection and preparation 321
  deployment 324
  feature selection and engineering 321
  model selection 321
  training and evaluation 322–3
  validation and calibration 324
modern computing 359
  computer emergency response team 366–7
  conflicts of data protection laws 372
    direct access 372
    Warrants 372–3
  data protection 363
  data protection law and the position in EU and US 368
    EU data protection law 368–9
    US data protection laws 369–71
  data protection laws in India 363–5
  Digital Personal Data Protection Act 2023 367
    events have seriously overtaken the substance of DPB 368

Parens patriae 367
  trans-boundary data sharing 367
  Ubi jus ibi remedium 368
  enforcement mechanisms and penalties 365
  penalty for privacy and confidentiality breach 365–6
  globalisation, international law and technology 368
  government access data 373–4
  Information Security Technology Development Council 366
privacy 360
  1950–80: early recognition and establishment 361–2
  1981–2000: expanding dimensions 362
  2001–23: technological advancements and global impact 362
  and data protection 362–3
  fundamental right in India 360–1
MongoDB 230, 238–9
Monte Carlo methods 278
multidimensional scaling (MDS) 15
multi-factor authentication (MFA) 73, 153
multifactor authentication (MFA) 207
multinational e-commerce platform 56–7

Nagios 38
National Health and Nutrition Examination Survey (NHANES) program 92
National Health Services (NHS) 98
National Institutes of Health (US) 98
National Notifiable Diseases Surveillance System (NNDSS) 164
natural language processing (NLP) 250, 270, 339

Netflix 58–9
neural networks 318
  backpropagation 319
  forward propagation 319
  hidden layers 318
  input layer 318
  loss calculation 319
  output layer 319
New Relic 38
non-compliance 338
NoSQL 94

object-relational mapping (ORM) 232
observational studies 291–2
omics data 94
one-time passwords (OTP) 153
open pancreatoduodenectomy (OPD) 301
operational efficiency 344–5
overfitting 272–3

parallel trends assumption 296
Parkinson's disease 274
patient-centered care 331
patient-centric approach 163
patient-centric healthcare 2
patient confidentiality 150
People's Union for Civil Liberties (PUCL) 362
percutaneous coronary intervention (PCI) 306
performance analysis 220–2
performance evaluation 196
  mathematical equations 202–3
  parameters used and their values 196–7
  performance metrics 198
  result analysis 198

result obtained and its comparison with existing techniques 198–201
test beds 197–8
performance metrics 62, 198
tracking 324
personal health data sharing 335
Personal Health Trains (PHTs) 100
personalization 2
  of risk assessment 320
personalized medicine 113, 314, 345, 380
personally identifiable information (PII) 50, 162
P-Net 20
population health management 344
positron emission tomography (PET) 12, 270
PostgreSQL 237
predictive analytics 70, 331
predictive analytics (PA) 250
primary indexing 239
principal components analysis (PCA) 15
privacy-preserving authentication 225
privacy-preserving techniques 130, 135, 213–14
privacy protection 155
privileged access management (PAM) solutions 75
proactive healthcare 331
probabilistic graphical models (PGM) 274, 276
Prometheus 37
propensity score matching (PSM) 292
  assessing balance 293
  estimating treatment effects 293–4
  matching 293
  propensity score estimation 292–3
  sensitivity analysis 294

proteomics data 272
public health 164, 338
public-key encryption 151–2
Pyro programs 280
Python 280

quality assurance 77
Quality of Service (QoS) 216
quantum computing 82, 132
quantum-resistant encryption techniques 82
quantum-safe authentication 225
quantum-safe encryption 132
quasi-Monte Carlo acquisition functions 278

random forest (RF) 317–18, 325
real-time data transmission 115
real-time monitoring 33, 37, 118–19, 345
real-time security measures 123
receiver operating characteristic (ROC) curve 323
recurrent neural networks (RNNs) 24, 181–2, 270, 319–20
regression analysis 297
regression discontinuity design (RDD) 292
  addressing bandwidth 300–1
  fuzzy RDD 299
  sharp RDD 299
regular model updating 324
regulatory compliance 157
relational database management systems (RDBMS) 94, 231
remote patient monitoring 380
Remote Radio Heads (RRHs) 216, 222
resilience building 162
Resource Blocks (RBs) 222
resource management 47–8

Index   399

return on investment (ROI) segmentation 270
risk assessments 125
risk-control measures 99
risk differences (RD) 305
Rivest-Shamir-Adleman (RSA) 151
R-Net 20
robotic pancreatoduodenectomy (RPD) 301
role-based access control (RBAC) 73, 153, 165, 212, 342
root 316
root mean squared error (RMSE) 323
root of trust (RoT) 176–8, 203
  hardware root of trust 185
  software root of trust 185
R-squared (R2) 323
Rubin Causal Model 292

safe enclaves 186
scalability 39, 47, 61, 320
schizophrenia 249–50
secondary indexing 239
second canon 258
secure anonymized information linkage (SAIL) 102
secure big-data analytics 379
  5G integration in healthcare 382
  advanced medical imaging 381–2
  AI and machine learning applications 382
  blockchain and AI integration 382
  causal inference in healthcare 382–3
  emerging technologies 383
  interoperability and data sharing 382
  legal and ethical considerations 382
  security and privacy frameworks 382
  specific application areas 382
secure hash algorithms 100, 202–3

secure multi-party computation (SMPC) 138
secure sockets layer (SSL) 152
security 2
security breaches 34
security information and event management (SIEM) 36
Sedna 230, 238
single nucleotide polymorphisms (SNPs) 98
singular value decomposition (SVD) 15
SLICING 5G Network technique 223
smart cities 165
smart contracts 341
social media analytics 42
social psychologists 258
Software-Defined Networking (SDN) 216
Spark 55
split-query processing paradigm 232
Splunk 38
stakeholder communication 325
state-of-the-art techniques 92
statistical linkage key (SLK) 100
stigma-free platform 251
structural equation modeling (SEM) 292
supervised deep learning techniques 20
supervised learning 18–19
support vector machine (SVM) 181, 316–17
symmetric encryption 151
Synthetic Minority Over-sampling Technique (SMOTE) 321

tailored monitoring solutions 61
target vessel revascularization (TVR) 306
telemedicine 2, 118–19, 380

TensorFlow probability (TFP) 279–80
ternary decision-making theory (TWD) 284
test beds 197–8
threat detection 179–81, 183
token-based authentication 154
traditional machine learning algorithms 315
　decision trees 315–16
　Random forests 317–18
　regression techniques 315
　support vector machine 316–17
training 319
trans-boundary data sharing 367
transfer learning 20, 22, 25
transparency 155–6, 272, 348
transport layer security (TLS) 152
Trusted Execution Environments (TEEs) 208
Trusted Platform Modules (TPMs) 176, 187, 189
trusted research environments (TREs) 100
two-factor authentication (2FA) 209
two-stage least squares (2SLS)
　estimator 298
　regression analysis 307

ultra-reliable and low-latency communications (uRLLC) 216
uncertainty 273
uncertainty quantification (UQ) 273
U-Net 18, 25
University Medical Center (UMC) 127–8

unsupervised learning 21, 25
US data protection laws 369–71
User and Entity Behavior Analytics (UEBA) 76
user-centric access control 225

VGG16 18
virtualization based security (VBS) 184
Virtual Machine Manager (VMM) 184, 187
virtual machines (VMs) 187, 216
virtual reality (VR) 3
vulnerability assessments 125

Warrants 372–3
wearable devices 2
wireless communication technology 169, 208
Wrapper method 15

XDBMS 234
X rays 270
XYZ Healthcare 59
　analytics tools 60
　context 59–60
　data integration 60
　data sources 60
　security and compliance 61
　use cases 60

Zabbix 38
zero trust architecture adoption 224
zero-trust security models 83–4
ZhuSuan 280